RUSSIA, POLAND AND THE WEST

"Mickiewicz improvising in the salon of Princess Zinaida Volkonsky", by G. G. Myasoedov

RUSSIA, POLAND
AND
THE WEST

Essays in Literary and Cultural History

WACŁAW LEDNICKI

ROY PUBLISHERS · NEW YORK

124807

Library of Congress Catalog Number 54-6541

DK
67
L4

Printed in Great Britain

La vertu assignee aux affaires du monde, est vne vertu à plusieurs plis, encoigneures, & couddes, pour s'appliquer & ioindre à l'humaine foiblesse: meslee & artificielle; non droitte, nette, constante, ny purement innocente. Les annales reprochent iusques à cette heure à quelqu'vn de nos Roys, de s'estre trop simplement laissé aller aux consciencieuses persuasions de son confesseur. Les affaires d'estat ont des preceptes plus hardis.

exeat aula,
Qui vult esse pius.

MONTAIGNE, *Essais*, Livre III, Chapitre IX.

ACKNOWLEDGMENT

I am deeply grateful to my students: Mrs. Olive (Terry) Tomlinson, Mrs. Mary (Furman) Arnold, Mr. George Kreshka, and particularly to Mr. John Mersereau, Junr., and to my friend and colleague, Professor Francis J. Whitfield, who assisted me in the editing of the manuscript.

I am greatly indebted to Dr. Alfred Berlstein of the New York Public Library for his kind help in providing me with necessary materials.

CONTENTS

	PREFACE	*Page* 13
I	RUSSIA AND THE WEST	
	(Chaadaev, Mickiewicz, Pushkin, Lermontov and Custine)	21
II	PUSHKIN, TYUTCHEV, MICKIEWICZ AND THE DECEMBRISTS	
	Legend and Facts	105
III	EUROPE IN DOSTOEVSKY'S IDEOLOGICAL NOVEL	
	Part I	133
	Appendix	150
	Part II	159
IV	DOSTOEVSKY—THE MAN FROM UNDERGROUND	180
V	DOSTOEVSKY AND BELINSKY	249
VI	DOSTOEVSKY AND POLAND	
	1. Dostoevsky and the Poles in Siberia	262
	2. Dostoevsky and Spasowicz	291
	3. Dostoevsky and Mickiewicz	
	(*a*) Petersburg	295
	(*b*) Jankiel's "Polonaise of the Third of May" and Lyamshin's "Franco-Prussian War"	303
	(*c*) The Feldjäger	308
	(*d*) "Pro and Contra" and *Forefathers' Eve, Part III*	310
VII	BLOK'S "POLISH POEM"	349
VIII	CONCLUSION	400
	INDEX	411

LIST OF ILLUSTRATIONS

"Mickiewicz improvising in the salon of
Princess Zinaida Volkonsky" *Frontispiece*

Chaadaev	FACING PAGE 32
Lermontov in the late thirties	64
Pushkin in 1827	72
Prince P. A. Vyazemsky in 1853	88
Dostoevsky in Semipalatinsk (1858)	160
Turgenev in 1859	208
Belinsky in the thirties	256
Słowacki in the late thirties	260
"Two Worlds"	272
Mickiewicz	304
"A Reading of *Pan Tadeusz* in the Mines" (1835)	336
Blok, *c.* 1807	352
Krasiński in 1850	384
Tolstoy in 1908	400

PREFACE

One of the greatest problems in Russian history is Russia's relations with the West. For several centuries Russian and Western statesmen have been preoccupied with this problem, and for more than a century the historical significance of these relations has attracted the attention of Russian and Western thinkers. And there is certainly no greater world problem at the present time than the dilemma of Russia and the West. The present book in its entirety deals with this fateful historical question within the frames of Russian and European thought of the pre-revolutionary era.

Besides considering the general question of Russia and the West, I have dealt with the problem of Russian-Polish relations, studied here as a component part of the general problem and as an illustration of it.

After thirty years of work devoted to studies of Russian-Polish relations in literary, cultural and political fields, I have come to the conclusion that the "Russian-Polish Thebaid" is, for the scholar, one of the richest episodes in European history. The Russian-Polish conflict is a focus in which is concentrated the essence of Eastern and Western historical trends. Around this conflict are crystallized the chief Eastern and Western principles and conceptions of individual and collective life. For centuries Russia and Poland opposed to each other the elemental trends of their historical development. This ancient conflict continually mobilized the basic forces of their respective civilizations. Geographically and historically, during the thousand years of her existence, Poland has been an outpost of the West, to which she was allied by her own free will as well as by circumstances. Her geographical situation, her political development and activities, her cultural traditions made of her a missionary of the West; she was preserving and spreading the ideas of Western civilization. For these reasons, after centuries of fighting for this civilization, although having been so often betrayed by Europe, Poland's ties with the West resulted in a particularly deep and indestructible attachment to Europe, to her ideals, concepts and beliefs. In a sense, therefore, Poland has always been more Western in her feelings than the most thoroughly Western nations. This tense Europeanism is generally characteristic for every Polish intellectual. Joseph Conrad is an excellent example of the phenomenon: he is much more devoted to the West than any purely English writer could be.

Comparative studies on Russia and Poland are useful for the understanding of some of the basic trends in western-European history. These trends, carrying with them Western ideology as a superior inspiration for the actual life of a nation, have often reverberated with a particular power in Poland; the European myth has left deep traces in the Polish soul. It is thus often easier for a scholar to discern the very essence of these traditions using just this area for research.

The Muscovite Czardom, and later the Russian Empire, acted in much the same way in its fight for expansion toward the West. In its long struggle Russia utilized all the weapons of her own Eastern ideology; Eastern Europe became a battlefield on which two different, opposed, and even conflicting civilizations met. So again, for the sake of purely Russian studies, this juxtaposition, this comparative method, becomes especially efficient and fruitful. One may perceive in this way many important traits in Russian ideology which otherwise would remain hidden. Studies devoted to Poland may be considered an extremely important instrument for a more precise understanding of Russia: their function should be to create a more adequate perspective for studies of Russia.

The problem of Russia and the West is not a simple one, for, besides the Russian westward expansion, there remains to be considered the historical phenomenon of the westernization of Russian culture. Herein lies the tragic essence of Russian history. Geographically pushing toward the West, Europeanized Russia at the same time was building a moral barrier between herself and western Europe. Many Russians were aware of this tragedy and many gave eloquent expression to their deep concern. There were some others who tried to repress their conscience, to reject their doubts; they became involved in the triumphant conceptions of Russian imperialism and quite a few assumed the rôle of its apostles and preachers.

But the other side of the picture is not less deceiving. Poland, as I have mentioned, for centuries considered herself the *antemurale Christianitatis*, and this idea of Poland's historical rôle was probably true up to the nineteenth century, but toward the end of that century there occurred the invasion of Russian spiritual culture in Europe. This invasion was prepared by many factors, the detailed analysis of which is not within the scope of this work. It suffices to mention that western-European thought, already weary and shaken, was ready to welcome this new art, "complex and barbarian—and so intensely human that all other models seemed to be colourless and superficial".[1] Schopenhauer, with his philosophy of irrationalism and intuition (which led finally to Bergson), Wagner's music, Nietzsche's morality of the Superman, contemporary trends in French literature toward "decadence" and *fin de siècle,* opened the way for the "Russian suggestive emphasis on the despotic power of irrational factors in human life with the new mystic conception of humanity, of suffering and of pity which was emerging from the novels of Tolstoy and Dostoevsky".[2] The favourable acceptance of the Russian outlook was prepared by Mérimée's interest in Russian literature, by Turgenev's long stay in France and his personal relations with the French and Anglo-Saxon literary world, by the studies of Melchior de Vogüé, Dupuy, Leger, Phelps, by such historians as Leroy-Beaulieu and Rambaud, and by Carlyle and Henry James.

Against the background of the growing prestige of Russian art and culture—ballet, novel, ikon, music—and of France's conception of the military power of the czars as a barrier against the Mongol threat on one side and against the Germans on the other, Poland's insistence on her devotion to western-European culture and on her historical merits connected with the defense of that culture acquired all the features of unrequited love. The situation in England and in America was no better. The Russian threat in the Far and Near East induced these two countries to be as liberal as France to the western-European Russian expansion. All the political developments since the end of the last century, culminating in the present situation, tend to make one skeptical of the moral prestige of the Western world. Besides, the very conception of Western culture and of its superiority is historically and geographically relativistic. And so historical contradictions are often tragic, not in themselves, but in our evaluation of their results. The fatal necessity which determines tragic contradictions is independent of moral and ethical evaluations. I believe that Max Scheler was right when he stressed the fact that "tragic fault is a fault for which it is impossible for anyone to be accused and of which there can be no judge". The great Polish poet Stanisław Wyspiański, endowed with a particularly deep comprehension of the essence of tragedy, shows how the punishing God in His anger smashes at once the sinner and the prophet. Historical tragedy occurs in a world in which "the sun shines equally on the evil and on the good".

[1] R. Lalou, *Histoire de la Littérature Française Contemporaine* (Paris, 1941), p. 110.
[2] *Ibid.* See also W. Lednicki, *Poland and the World* (New York, 1943), p. 78, and Henri Massis, *Jugements* (Paris: Plon, 1923).

Paradoxically, although the main energies ruling historical processes are human, history strikes us as being indifferent and inhuman. But man cannot liberate himself from an ethical evaluation of history and thus historical events acquire moral significance. This is the source of the so-called "tragic sorrow" with which the spectator views a tragic play. In other words, I believe that the modern "scientific" approach to history, whether Marxist dialectic or any other positivistic doctrine, cannot eliminate an ideological judging of history. The teachings of the Polish writers of the sixteenth century, of the Polish Romantic poets—Mickiewicz, Krasiński, Słowacki—of the French and English moralists of the seventeenth and eighteenth centuries, and of the Russian thinkers, Soloviev and Tolstoy, aiming at the Christianization of politics, were not a "bourgeois prejudice" but an expression of a moral feeling natural to the human soul. As a matter of fact, these teachings were not at all different in essence from those of Aristotle. He proclaimed the identity of ethics in private and in public life.

We may discuss the delimitations between the moral rights of subjugated nations and the law of the natural growth of a victorious nation building an empire, we may bring all kinds of justifications for or criticisms against the empire in defense of the subjugated nations—cultural advancement, economic necessity, organizational superiority, political decay—and still the voice of "immanent morality" cannot be suppressed, that voice that continues to tell us that every nation, great or small, has a spiritual personality which demands respect. Although we know that when modern statesmen were dividing the world into spheres of influence they were evidently guided by every kind of consideration other than moral and ethical ones, we observed their deeds with "tragic sorrow".

Despite all these considerations, comparable to the Polish saying, "like a drunkard clinging to a [wobbly] fence", I with my generation still cling to the myth of the superiority of western-European culture and still hope for a Christianization of politics.

One of the most important factors in any "scientific" approach to reality is the choice of one's point of view, for this is what creates hierarchy and perspective. Humanities do not know as strict sanctions as do sciences, but just because of this the feeling of responsibility in a humanist scholar must be even stronger than in a scientist, for the humanist's work is essentially speculative. Still, then, what is the source of that feeling of responsibility? The earnest belief in truth, in a subjective truth, as the surest way to reach objective truth, may be the answer. The denial of the validity of ideological judgments in modern humanities is the denial to the modern humanist of any chance of ultimately reaching objective truth. He is also thus deprived of the prime requisite of dignity for a humanistic scholar.

It is the acceptance of conflicts between the moral sense of the scholar and historical reality which creates his dignity and helps determine the moral progress of humanity. Even one of the greatest skeptics, Montaigne, stressed the existence of immanent morality: "We take no heed to be good men according to God's laws. We cannot be so according to our laws. Human wisdom never yet came up to the duties she has prescribed for herself, and if she did come up to them, she would prescribe others beyond them, to which she would ever aim and aspire; so hostile to consistency is our human condition! Man has ordained that he shall necessarily be at fault."[1] This is one of the most precise and realistic affirmations of the immanence of morality in the human being. I believe that this attitude is characteristic of our times. Not only have we become accustomed particularly to praise goodness as a free gift of art, but we often expect of art an intentional and directed good. This is a reaction of our times against the "decadent" slogans of art for art's sake. Ironically, nowadays Tolstoy's treatise on art is not at all novel. Montaigne also said: "I love and honour learning as much as those who possess it; and, if rightly used, it is the noblest and most powerful human acquisition. But in those (and there is an endless number of their kind) who make it the ground of their worth and excellence, who appeal from their understanding to their memory, *sub aliena umbra latentes* (Seneca: 'cowering under the shelter of others'), who are powerless without their book, I hate it, if I may venture to say so, a little more than I do stupidity."[2] What kind of knowledge does Montaigne hate? Indifferent knowledge, that which is not attached to life, that which lacks the moral evaluations of life. The French saying *"fais ce que dois, advienne que pourra"* might be changed to: "say what you must, let come what may", and be a motto for the scholar.

* * * * *

The first essay in this book deals with the great discussion on Russia and the West which was started in the first part of the nineteenth century by one of the most representative and brilliant Russian Westerners, almost unknown to the English-speaking reader, Peter Chaadaev; he, together with Pushkin, Lermontov and others, represents the Russian side in my study, while Mickiewicz and Custine represent the European. This first essay is devoted to the philosophy of Russian history and the historical break between Russia and the West. It also

[1] *The Essays of Montaigne*, translated by E. J. Trechmann (Cambridge: Oxford University Press, 1927), Vol. II, p. 460.
[2] *Ibid.*, pp. 389–90.

contains a Russian-Polish episode, in which Pushkin plays the chief rôle. The second essay tells the story of the Decembrists and of the spiritual reactions toward their Revolution among Russians, Poles and the French; it serves to illustrate the moral degradation of a society under autocratic rule.

A large part of the book deals with Dostoevsky. The first essay, "Europe in Dostoevsky's Ideological Novel", is concerned with Dostoevsky's attitude toward Europe as expressed in his novels, his *Diary of a Writer*, and his private correspondence. The second essay, which is dedicated to his *Notes from Underground*, deals with the theme of the psychological and ideological speculation of Dostoevsky on the theme of the usurper and develops the theme of the contrast between Russian and European mores and traditions. The concept of honour and human dignity has been especially envisaged. A literary genealogy of the *Notes* is also presented. The sketch on Dostoevsky and Belinsky tries to prove a possible dependence of the "Legend of the Grand Inquisitor" on Belinsky and casts a light on Dostoevsky's methods of ideological attack.

The second set of Dostoevsky studies brings to the fore Dostoevsky's attitudes toward Poland, as expressed in his novels, short stories, letters and in his *Diary of a Writer*. The memoirs of a Polish political exile who met Dostoevsky in Siberia reveal new traits of character in the Russian author and provide some interesting details connected with *The House of the Dead*. A possible indebtedness of the Russian author to Mickiewicz is also suggested. These studies not only exemplify the place which the Polish question acquired in Dostoevsky's works, but again they shed indirect light on Dostoevsky's personality and his literary technique. Thus they are another proof of the "creative powers" of the Russian-Polish problem. Finally, the last study presents quite a unique phenomenon in Russian literature—a deeply pro-Polish poem of the greatest modern Russian poet, Alexander Blok. This study analyses the literary connections between Blok and the Polish Romantic poets, Mickiewicz, Słowacki and Krasiński, showing Blok's domination of his nationalism by feelings of a "superior Europeanism".

I encountered a number of difficulties while writing these studies. All the subjects treated here are quite clear to me against the background of several books which I have published in Polish and French. In these books I treated the most important episodes in the history of Russian-Polish relations: Pushkin and his anti-Polish and anti-European odes, Pushkin and Mickiewicz, Pushkin's *Bronze Horseman* and its relationship with Mickiewicz's *Digression*, Tolstoy and Poland, and topics dealing with several other Russian and Polish writers. Thus the studies collected in the present book are an addition to my previous publications, which unfortunately have not appeared in English. I have tried to explain here to my English reader the essentials which he most probably needs in order to understand the special significance of some statements by the authors whom I discuss. Another difficulty is connected with the fact that many of these authors, with the sole exception of Dostoevsky, are not sufficiently known to the English reader to allow me simple allusions to their works and texts. This at times necessitates extensive quotations, which I could either have omitted or reduced had I been writing for the Russian, Polish, or even French or German, reader.

In almost every study of this book Mickiewicz plays an important rôle. As it would be impossible to explain to the English reader on every occasion the significance of various works of the great Polish poet, I should like to mention here four sources of reference: Juljan Krzyżanowski's *Polish Romantic Literature* (George Allen and Unwin, Ltd., London, 1930); *Poems by Adam Mickiewicz*, translated by various hands and edited by George Rapall Noyes (Polish Institute of Arts and Sciences in America, New York, 1944); a symposium, *Adam Mickiewicz*, edited by Manfred Kridl (Columbia University Press, New York, 1951); and finally, my own book, *Life and Culture of Poland* (Roy Publishers, New York, 1944), of which the fifth chapter gives a general outline of Mickiewicz's life and literary activities. Lastly, I should like to provide the reader with the following aid: of Mickiewicz's works I am mostly concerned with *Forefathers' Eve, Part III*. This work consists of a Preface, a *Prologue*, a Dramatic Section (Act I), which includes the "Improvisation" (Scene 2), the *Digression* (containing several long poems: *The Road to Russia, The Suburbs of the Capital, Saint Petersburg, The Monument of Peter the Great, The Review of the Army*, and *Oleszkiewicz*. The *Digression* is followed by a dedicational poem, "To My Russian Friends". The other works of Mickiewicz which from time to time are discussed in this book do not require any special explanatory comments here.

*   *   *   *   *

In my footnotes, while transcribing Russian names and words, I have strictly followed the principle of transliteration as the only consistent one. In the text itself, taking into consideration that the average reader is unaccustomed to the technique of transliteration, I have accepted popular transcription, while still trying to remain as close as possible to the system of transliteration, avoiding phonetic transcription and aiming at general simplification.

Berkeley, California,
December 1953.

I

Russia and the West

(CHAADAEV, MICKIEWICZ, PUSHKIN, LERMONTOV AND CUSTINE)

WHEN, after the triumph of the French Revolution of February, 1848, Michelet and Quinet resumed their chairs at the Collège de France, from which they had been expelled by order of the king, they organized a solemn ceremony in honour of the occasion. For this event, which took place on 6 March, they had to borrow from the Sorbonne its greatest hall, the largest in Paris.

"We had three chairs placed on the podium," wrote Michelet, "one of which was intended for Mickiewicz, unfortunately absent."[1] Michelet gave a moving speech at the ceremony, in which he said:

> "It is the mission of France to give peace to the world, the only durable peace, which is that of freedom. The price of this is not important. We owe everything to that one thing, yes, everything, our own blood included."[2]

After this preamble Michelet continued his speech, in which he stressed the significance of the Revolution of 1848, and he emphasized the new rôle of France in the establishment of world unity, "a free unity, a sacred unity, a unity of the soul and of the heart". And then he turned to Mickiewicz's chair and said:

> "What sign of this unity do we see from the fact that this chair remains empty? It is that of Poland, that of our great and dear Mickiewicz, the national poet of fifty million people, whose voice symbolized a world alliance, a federation of the East and the West, which, from the Collège de France, extended to Asia. This chair is that of Poland. But what is Poland?—the most general representative of universal suffering. In her I see the suffering people. It is

---

[1] L. Mickiewicz, *Adam Mickiewicz, sa vie et son oeuvre* (Paris: Nouvelle Librairie Parisienne, 1888), p. 226.
[2] *Loc. cit.*

Ireland and the famine. It is Germany and censorship, that tyranny of thought over the most thoughtful of all nations. It is Italy, Gentlemen, at this moment hanging between life and death, like the soul in Michelangelo's *Last Judgment*. Death and barbarity are pulling it down, but France is drawing it upwards. She is saved by this day ... and let no man touch her. Yes, Gentlemen, I see all the banners of Europe floating over this empty seat. I see here ten nations in tears, nations which are rising from their graves. ... Their soul and breath are here."[1]

The Mickiewicz of whom Michelet spoke in such laudatory tones was a man who had acquired at this time a great prestige and authority indeed in the whole of Europe. He was known not only as the author of *Pan Tadeusz*, the greatest European epic of the nineteenth century and the only modern work comparable to that of Homer, but he was also the author of the *Books of the Polish Nation and the Polish Pilgrimage*, the famous romantic drama *Forefathers' Eve*, and the refined *Crimean Sonnets*. He was also famed as an erudite and eloquent professor of Slavic literatures, having presented a course on this subject at the Collège de France from 1840–1844. But the most striking fact in the biography of the poet is that he, like Tolstoy, sacrificed his art for goals he considered to be superior. He abandoned his poetry and devoted himself entirely to the cause of universal freedom, in which he perceived the only guarantee for the freedom of his own country.

At the time Michelet paid his tribute and homage to Mickiewicz, the poet, like another, Byron, was involved in a fight for the cause of the independence of subjugated nations: he was engaged in the organizational activities of his Polish legion, the aim of which was to fight in Italy against Austria for the emancipation of Italy and the liberation of the Slavic nations. This was, certainly, the apogee of Mickiewicz's fame in Europe.

The conditions of Mickiewicz's life were very different twenty-four years earlier when he, as a young beginning poet, a former student of the University of Wilno, and a modest teacher of a high school in Kovno, was leaving Wilno for St. Petersburg in the fall of 1824. He had been arrested and imprisoned by the Russian authorities in Wilno for his activities in student secret societies called the *Philomaths* and *Philarets*, societies which devoted themselves to studies in literature and ethics, and which also directed their efforts to the enlightenment of Polish society, the preservation of the national spirit among the Poles, and the elevation of the moral and cultural level of the Polish people. These activities, which were not quite of a detached nature, but

[1] L. Mickiewicz, *op. cit.*, pp. 226–7.

certainly not revolutionary in their external manifestations, had been discovered by the Russian authorities and severely judged. The guilty, and Mickiewicz among them, after imprisonment had been exiled either to central Russia or to the western confines of Siberia.

The young Polish poet, who was now travelling in a kibitka from Wilno to Petersburg at the end of October, 1824, was, as astonishing as it might seem, almost enjoying the trip. A deep, passionate, but unfortunate love for a girl, who was denied him because of aristocratic prejudices and married to another, had exhausted him. His life in the dull town of Kovno had tired the young man, who was aware, as were his intimate friends, of the rich intellectual, spiritual, and moral forces with which he had been endowed by Nature. He was looking for wider horizons. The imprisonment had been an additional moral torment, and so, despite the drastic conditions of the journey to Petersburg, he was leaving Wilno with a feeling of relief.

By the time he arrived in Petersburg he was becoming less a prisoner and more and more a tourist, who opened his avid and curious eyes and analysed and evaluated with amazing rapidity the things he saw and the men he met. Mickiewicz possessed a rare gift of observation which later found such brilliant expression in his poetic masterpieces. The realistic details with which his works are filled indicate that Mickiewicz had, as have all great poets, an exceptional memory. He did not forget the vast and gloomy northern plains—so empty—through which he passed before his arrival at the imposing and powerful capital of the Russian Empire. Nor did he forget the impression which Petersburg made on him. Before his arrival there, Mickiewicz had known only three cities: Nowogródek, a small town where he spent his childhood; Wilno, where he studied at the University; and Kovno, where he taught. Among these, Wilno was certainly the most beautiful, with its impressive baroque churches and its picturesque location on the banks of the charming Wilja.

But how magnificent and unusual the vast urban landscapes of the city of the Russian emperors, the city of a triumphant imperialism, must have appeared to the young Polish provincial whose visual imagination had been filled until then only with cosy and attractive pictures of rural life. He later treated with satirical bitterness the artificial and arbitrary mixture of various European styles characterizing Petersburg. He emphasized in his poems that this capital, by its very origin and existence, violated the historical and national Russian traditions. However, at his first approach, Mickiewicz could not have been but deeply impressed by the parade of monumental palaces, by the caravans of colonnades, by the wide avenues, by the Dutch canals traversing the city which were spanned by Venetian bridges, by the formidable granite banks which sought, as it were, to imprison the powerful and menacing Neva.

Mickiewicz arrived in Petersburg at a time when the city was suffering from a terrible catastrophe caused by the famous flood of 6 and 7 November of 1824. This flood acquired prophetic meaning in the poet's imagination: the apocalyptic vision of Petersburg which emerges from his poems results from the reminiscences of the November calamity. Mickiewicz was deeply affected by the capital of the Czars, which became for him a symbol of the invincible power of the oppressors of Poland, and he sought forces which would be able to destroy this enemy. But these ideas and conceptions, as I have mentioned, belong to a slightly later period of his life.

As well as we know the *dramatis personæ* of Mickiewicz's first Petersburg episode, there is one fact which has been obscure but which, nevertheless, is very significant: the extremely rapid establishment by Mickiewicz of intimate relations with those who, one year later, became the Decembrists—the insurrectionists of 14 December, 1825. These people belonged to the social and intellectual élite of Petersburg; in addition they were bound by membership in secret political societies whose plans were as far-reaching as they were fatally dangerous to the members in the event of failure. We still do not know who could have introduced Mickiewicz into these circles. Possibly, the Polish painter and mystic, Oleszkiewicz, a Mason, played a rôle in this.

What is amazing is the very fact of Mickiewicz's immediate intimacy with the Decembrists. These men never had taken Pushkin into their confidence, yet they now admitted a foreigner, a young Polish poet, to their secret assemblies. How much Mickiewicz learned about the Decembrists and their purposes is evident from his Parisian lectures, in which he gave strikingly detailed information about them. When Mickiewicz left Petersburg for Odessa at the end of January, 1825, he carried a warm letter of recommendation to a Russian poet, V. Tumansky, written by the two most representative Decembrists and well-known poets, A. Bestuzhev and K. Ryleev. And this immediate acceptance into the highest social and intellectual circles of Petersburg was only the first triumph of Mickiewicz's moral authority and personal charm. The same thing happened in Odessa in Polish aristocratic circles and finally in Moscow, where he was transferred in December, 1825.

He spent several months there in complete seclusion, seeing only his Polish companions in exile, but as soon as the Russians discovered him he again immediately became an object of universal interest and admiration. I have described in my *Life and Culture of Poland*[1] Mickie-

[1] Ch. V.

wicz's extraordinary success in Russian society. Even Pushkin's popularity did not overshadow that of Mickiewicz. There is no doubt that his phenomenal gift of improvisation, which often brought his Russian audiences to a state of delirium, created a special aura around him. Reminiscences of these improvisations performed in salons of Russian aristocrats before crowds of distinguished poets and men of letters were so consistently enthusiastic that from them developed a kind of indestructible legend. The well-known Russian painter, Myasoedov, the founder of the "Peredvizhniki" (a famous school of Russian realistic painting), composed a large and beautiful canvas depicting Mickiewicz improvising in the salon of Princess Zinaida Volkonsky and surrounded by a group of his famous Russian friends.

There are innumerable and touching testimonies to the enduring respect the Russians had for him, which even the catastrophe of 1830–1831 (the Polish Insurrection) and the anti-Russian poems which Mickiewicz later published abroad did not destroy. Mickiewicz became acquainted with almost every prominent Russian writer and poet. His friendship with Pushkin became another legend constantly utilized by those among the Russians and Poles who were seeking peaceful Russian-Polish relations.

The successes of Mickiewicz in Moscow and Petersburg did not at all interrupt his creative activities nor change the character of his meditations on the historical Russian-Polish conflict and its general significance. On the contrary, in Moscow he wrote his *Konrad Wallenrod*, a poem in the form of a Byronic tale dealing with medieval conflicts between the Lithuanians and the Teutonic Knights; in this work he indirectly expressed the tragic essence of the "Russian-Polish Thebaid". There in Russia he not only conceived but started to write his famous *Digression*, which later, in its finished form, became one of the most fascinating interpretations in European literature of Russia's historical development. Mickiewicz did not wish to remain in Russia. After many efforts and with the help of his Russian friends he finally obtained the authorization of the government to go abroad.

The Polish Insurrection of 1830–1831 left deep traces in Mickiewicz's poetry as well as in that of Pushkin. The latter, seized by nationalistic and imperialistic passions, wrote and published his famous anti-Polish and anti-European odes immediately after the defeat of the Polish uprising. Mickiewicz spent the first year following the Polish defeat in a mood of internal agitation. The crisis through which he passed found its expression in *Forefathers' Eve, Part III*, with its *Digression* and a dedicational poem in which he praised the Russian Decembrists and indignantly alluded to Pushkin's political servility. Pushkin, as if feeling his guilt and being still faithful to his great Polish friend, a few years later wrote, as I mentioned above, his *Bronze Horseman* as an answer to Mickiewicz's interpretation of Russia, an answer in which he tried to justify national as well as individual sacrifices for the sake of the greatness of the Russian Empire. Moreover, the depth of Pushkin's attachment to Mickiewicz is shown by Pushkin's beautiful poem about Mickiewicz, addressed to him, which he wrote in 1834. Significantly enough, this was the only poem which Pushkin wrote in that year.

And so, after the catastrophe of the Decembrist Revolution of 1825, after the suppression of the Polish Insurrection of 1830–1831, and after the publication of Mickiewicz's poems in Paris, there occurred a very important event in the development of Russian historical and philosophical ideas: the publication of Chaadaev's fatally pro-Western *Philosophical Letter*. This *Letter* became a catalyzer of Russian thought in the formation of major political and social movements. It became a foundation for the doctrine of the Russian Westerners in the second part of the nineteenth century and a provocative and stimulating agent for the Russian Slavophils and Panslavists. This event was perhaps no less important to Chaadaev himself, as it deeply affected his personal life. For him, indeed, the event was a tragic one.

*   *   *   *   *

Peter Chaadaev was born in 1793 and grew up in the family of his uncle, Prince D. M. Shcherbatov, where Chaadaev and his brother, together with Shcherbatov's son Ivan, received a Western education. In 1808 or 1809 he entered the University of Moscow, where he became acquainted with Nicholas Turgenev, Yakushkin, Obleukhov, Griboedov and other men who were to be influential in Russia's literary, political and cultural development. At the University he studied political economy, history, philosophy, fine arts, archeology, Greek, Latin, and Russian literature under Christian Schloezer, J. G. Buhle, M. T. Kachenovsky, R. F. Timkovsky, and A. F. Merzlyakov. It should be stressed that Buhle introduced Chaadaev to Kant, Fichte, and Schelling; the philosophy of the latter deeply influenced Chaadaev's later doctrines. Worthy of mention also is the fact that both Schloezer and Kachenovsky represented the so-called Russian historical skepticism. In 1812 Chaadaev entered the army as an officer in the Semenovsky regiment and finally became an adjutant in the guards. In this capacity he enjoyed outstanding successes both in the army and in Petersburg society. His friendship with Pushkin dates from this period. We know that this brilliant young man was known not only as a dandy, a kind of Russian *arbiter elegantiarum*, but also as a private philosopher and scholar who was plunged in reading and who frequented libraries and bookshops. His successful rise was interrupted by a trip to Troppau at the end of 1820, when he brought an important but unpleasant message to Alexander I concerning a revolt in the Semenovsky regiment of imperial guards. This event led to Chaadaev's retirement from the army under rather unfavourable circumstances and caused vicious rumours and comments, and Chaadaev became a victim even of calumny. There is no doubt that Chaadaev was at this time in close relations and friendship with the circles of Russian nobility from which emerged the 1825 Decembrist Insurrection and with European, Polish, and Russian Masonic groups. He was a member of the Russian Masonic order from 1816 to, probably, 1821 and had been accepted into a Polish Masonic lodge in Cracow in 1814,[1] in which he received the first two Masonic degrees. For two years he tried vainly to occupy himself in Moscow, but in 1823 he travelled abroad, where he met Schlegel, Schelling, and Lamennais, all of whom regarded him highly. (This was not his first trip abroad; he had travelled through Europe with the Russian army during the Napoleonic war of 1812 and was in Paris in 1814 with the allied armies.) He returned to Moscow in 1826 and spent the next five years reading and writing in complete seclusion. It is during this period that he wrote his famous *Philosophical Letters*, the writing of which was motivated by the philosophical and religious inquiries of an acquaintance and neighbour of his, Ekaterina Panov. Only one of these letters was published during Chaadaev's lifetime. Its publication in 1836 in Nadezhdin's review *The Telescope* was called by Alexander Herzen "a shot sounding in the dark night". Chaadaev's *Letter* was the most provocative criticism of Russia and her historical development. It was an expression of the despair of a Russian deeply attached to the West and the unity of its religious and cultural tradition, of a Russian who dared publicly to deplore the chasm between Russia and this historical unity and who showed an obvious leaning toward Catholicism and an antipathy to the Russian clergy. Russia appeared in his *Letter* as an outcast of civilization. Chaadaev's views could not be favorably greeted by Nicholas I and his Government, and as a consequence *The Telescope* was banned, its editor, Nadezhdin, was sent to Siberia and Chaadaev himself was officially declared insane. He spent the next twenty years almost exclusively in Moscow, where he died in 1856. Among the main teachers who influenced his doctrine should be mentioned Chateaubriand, Bonald, Lamennais, Guizot, Descartes, Kant, Schelling, D'Eckstein, Spinoza, Hegel, and Schlegel. Elsewhere I have advanced the supposition that Chaadaev could have discussed his views with Mickiewicz.

[1] Cf. *Literaturnoe Nasledstvo* (Moscow, 1935), Vols. 19–21, p. 24.

Chaadaev's works have interested scholars from the time of the publication of the first *Letter* up to the present. Besides the previously cited French publications we shall have to mention a Russian scholar, M. O. Gershenzon, who took exception to the traditional attitude of Herzen toward the works of Chaadaev.[1] Gershenzon's interpretation of Chaadaev showed the latter as a "Decembrist turned mystic". He tried to deduce the content of several of the *Philosophical Letters* which had not up to his time been brought to light and his deductions are heavily weighted with mystical-religious considerations.

More recently, in 1935, there appeared still another evaluation of Chaadaev and his works, based on the appearance in print of five *Philosophical Letters* which had not before been published.[2] V. Asmus and D. Shakhovskoy point out that essentially Herzen's conception was more accurate and true to the content of the *Letters* as a whole and that Gershenzon felt obliged to give his interpretation because of the reactionary period in which he published his material. To this I would add that Gershenzon's political inclinations were of a rather reactionary orthodox character. Indeed, it has been shown that Gershenzon himself was susceptible to the influence of Chaadaev's oecumenical religious ideas, along with the Russian philosopher Vladimir Soloviev.

Worthy of attention is the fact that Chaadaev's views greatly influenced Custine's critique of Russia. Custine's book, *Russia in 1839*, has recently been published in America in a completely new English translation.[3] Chaadaev's *Letters* should be translated into English because of their brilliant style and the enthusiastic devotion to Western civilization reflected in them. In my own study I am not so interested in the man and his writings as in the striking similarities of his views and those of Mickiewicz concerning the interpretation of Russian historical development.

However, one should also keep in mind the weakness of Chaadaev's moral character; he was a brilliant mind and an eloquent writer, but a man lacking moral firmness. We have a great variety of characteristics and evaluations of Chaadaev, not only among the modern

---

[1] Cf. M. Geršenzon, *P. Ja. Čaadaev, Žizn' i myšlenie* (St. Petersburg: Tip. M. M. Stasjuleviča, 1908) and *Sočinenija i pis'ma P. Ja. Čaadaeva*, pod red. M. Geršenzona (Moscow, 1913–1914).

[2] Cf. "Neizdannye *Filosofičeskie Pis'ma* P. Ja. Čaadaeva", with introductory articles by V. Asmus and D. Šakhovskoj in *Literaturnoe Nasledstvo* (Moscow, 1935), Vols. 22–4, pp. 1–78, and P. Ja. Čaadaeva, "Neopublikovannaja Stat'ja", published with an introduction and commentaries by D. Šakhovskoj in *Zven'ja* (Moscow-Leningrad: Academia, 1934), Vols. 3–4, pp. 365–90. This publication contains some additional valuable bibliographical information.

[3] Cf. *Journey for our Time*; the journals of the Marquis de Custine, edited and translated by Phyllis Penn Rohler. (New York, Pellegrini & Cudahy, 1951.)

students of his writings but also among Chaadaev's contemporaries. This creates the main difficulty as concerns a definite interpretation of the man and of the thinker. The catastrophe of the first *Philosophical Letter* obliged Chaadaev to modulate, to correct and to deny his views. But even before this, during the French, Belgian and Polish revolutions of 1830–1831, Chaadaev could not find a consistent solution for his philosophy of history and his practical political views. His behaviour toward the Russian authorities was uncertain and timid, to say the least. Herein lies the greatest difficulty in solving the problem of Pushkin's "mysterious Polonophil", which is the main object of the second part of my study. Chaadaev's well-known letter to Pushkin in 1831 with its bewildering postscript will probably remain forever an enigma of either a weak heart or an inconsistent mind—probably of the former—as Chaadaev's thoughts on Russia and her relations with Europe remained the same until the end of his life. A revealing confirmation of this statement might be found in Chaadaev's article "*L'Univers* January 15th, 1854", discovered by D. Shakhovskoy. This article, written two years before Chaadaev's death, is important not only as it confirms the historical views Chaadaev expressed in his *Philosophical Letters*,[1] but it is significant as it shows to what stratagems and tricks he was obliged to resort under the unbearable moral conditions of his life in Moscow after the catastrophe of 1836. As usual, he wrote his article in French. Whether he had hopes of being able to publish this article we don't know. The date (15 January, 1854) is, however, important, as it was on the eve of the Crimean War, which started on 14 March, 1854. The title itself is a misleading one—maybe purposely so. It could have given the impression to any indiscreet investigator of a copy of an article from the well-known French Catholic review of those times, *L'Univers*. The article is not only written in French but gives the impression of having been written by a French author who knew Russia well and who was writing in France to his French compatriots about Russia at a moment of international crisis. However, the flame of the real author's intellectual excitement burned so hot while he touched problems and subjects which were so vital to him that he inadvertently dropped his French mask and started to write as a Russian. I should like to present to the reader the most striking passages of this article in order better to acquaint him with Chaadaev before I start my analysis of the similarities of Chaadaev's and Mickiewicz's views. This is the first one:

---

[1] D. Shakhovskoy showed the identity of the ideas Chaadaev expressed in this article with those of his former writings. See Shakhovskoy's introductory comments to Chaadaev's article in *Zven'ja*, as above, Vols. 3–4, p. 371.

"I, of course, know very well that there are not a few Russians—there are such people even in Paris itself—who assert that Russia underwent the reform of Peter the Great against her own will, but these maladroit patriots, ascribing to the energy of one man, as if he were the greatest of mortals, such an upheaval, which by their own admissions transformed their country from head to foot, certainly in no way exculpate their own people by this, but, on the contrary, insult them cruelly. And the majority of Russians, not carried away by the retrospective Utopias of the new national school, don't look at this matter in this way at all. Indeed, what kind of an opinion must one have about people who, from the first, would be deprived of all the fruits of their history through the capricious whim of one of their sovereigns; then, when Providence itself, it seemed, endeavoured to facilitate their return to the sacred traditions of their forebears, having given them four consecutive women rulers—and what women, O God! the dregs of their sex—and what is still more important, a whole century of praetorian revolutions—would continue indifferently to be ground by the millstones between which they found themselves as if despite their own will. And these real Russians of the new school, so jealous of Russia's fame, have just such an opinion of their own people. Happily for the honour of mankind nothing of the sort happened. Peter the Great affixed his signature to that upheaval, the beginning of which we discern on the first pages of Russian history. He reformed that which existed merely by name, he did away only with that which simply could not be retained, he created only that which through itself was in the process of creation, he completed only that which his predecessors had already endeavoured to complete. Such, in our opinion, is the only intelligent way to understand his significant reform and the reception which it met among the people. But if one remembers that the whole history of these people consisted without exception of one series of abdications in favor of their rulers, that they began their historical course by delivering themselves into the power of a handful of Scandinavian adventurers, whom they had summoned themselves, that they subsequently went off to foreign peoples in search of a religion for themselves, that they later borrowed from the savage conquerors of their country the latter's most shameful habits, and, finally, that they ceaselessly subjected themselves to various foreign influences—if one remembers all this, then the great act of subjugation which united them to our civilization and introduced them into the circle of our political system becomes even more natural, and there will no longer be room for astonishment that the primordial possessors of this civilization and this political system are so little occupied with the study of the social essence of the Russian people."

The second passage is not less important and eloquent:

"One must not forget that in comparison with Russia everything in Europe is filled to the brim with the spirit of freedom: sovereigns, governments, and peoples. How can one expect after this that this Europe would be penetrated with a sincere sympathy for Russia? Here is just the natural conflict of light with darkness! And in our own times the agitation of the nations against Russia is still growing, because Russia, not satisfied that as a government she is entering the body of the European system, seeks in this family of civilized peoples to be ranked as the nation with a civilization superior to the others', pointing out her preservation of calm during the recently experienced European disturbance. And notice, it is not the government alone which asserts these pretenses but the whole country. Instead of docile and subordinate pupils, which we [here Chaadaev forgets his disguise and begins to write as a Russian] still were not so long ago, we have suddenly become the teachers of those who yesterday we admitted were our teachers. This is the essence of the whole Eastern question reduced to its most simple expression. An opportunity presented itself—and Europe seized upon it in order to put us in our place, and that's the whole of it.

Speaking about Russia it is always imagined that one is speaking about a certain government like others; indeed, this is absolutely not so. Russia is a whole special world, submissive to the will, the arbitrariness, the whim of one man—whether he bears the name of Peter or Ivan doesn't matter; in all cases this is the same—the personification of despotism. In opposition to all the laws of human co-existence Russia moves only in the direction of her own individual enslavement and the enslavement of all neighbouring peoples. And, therefore, it would be useful not only in the interests of other peoples but even in her own interests to force her to change to new paths."

D. Shakhovskoy is right when he compares this article to Chaadaev's letter of 1854 "to an unknown woman". These are the most significant passages:

"No, a thousand times no. It was not in this way that we loved our country when we were young. We desired her well-being, we desired good institutions for her, and at times we even went so far as to wish her to have more freedom, if this were feasible. We knew that she was great and powerful, with a great future before her, but we didn't think that she was the most powerful country in the world or the most fortunate. We were far from imagining that Russia represented God knows what kind of abstract principle containing the definitive solution of the social problem; that she by herself constituted a world apart, a direct and legitimate heir of the glorious Eastern empire as well as of its titles and virtues; that her special mission would be to absorb within her pale all the Slavic peoples and to effect by these means the regeneration of mankind. In particular we didn't think that Europe was at the point of slipping back into barbarism and that we were called upon to save civilization with a few scraps of this same civilization, which formerly had served to drag us out of our ancient torpor. We treated Europe with civility, even with respect, because we knew that she had taught us many things, and among them our own history. When by chance we happened to triumph over her, as did Peter the Great, we said, 'We are indebted to you for this, gentlemen.' And this is how, one fine day, we arrived in Paris, and you know what a reception they gave us, having forgotten for a moment that we still had not poured anything into the common treasury of nations, not even a poor, petty solar system, as have our subjects, the Poles, not even a miserable algebra, as have the infidel Arabs, against whose absurd and barbaric religion we are fighting today. We were well treated, because we had the manners of well-educated people, because we were polite and modest, as was appropriate for newcomers who had no other claim to consideration than their good builds."[1]

How merciless, ironic, and, in essence, contemptuous are these statements of Chaadaev.

As I mentioned, I quoted Chaadaev's article (and his letter "to an unknown woman") so extensively for the purpose of a preliminary general characterization of their author. These texts do not play any rôle in my comparative study of Chaadaev's *Philosophical Letters* and Mickiewicz's *Digression*, but there is no doubt that one may find many concordant statements in Mickiewicz's lectures on Slavic literatures at the Collège de France (from 1840–1844) as well as in the articles which the great Polish poet published in France. This is another proof of the analogy of Chaadaev's and Mickiewicz's interpretations of the historical development of Russia, and of their approaches to the problem of Russia's relations with Western Europe.

[1] For the passages from Chaadaev's article see *Zven'ja*, as above, pp. 376–7, 379–80, and for his letter see *ibid.*, pp. 368–9, and P. Ja. Čaadaev, *Sočinenija i pis'ma*, as above, Vol. I, p. 308 (French text) and Vol. II, pp. 280–1 (Russian translation).

Chaadaev
Engraving by X. Steifensand

It would be, perhaps, worth while to remind the reader that very soon after Chaadaev wrote his article,[1] Mickiewicz went to Constantinople to take part in the organization of Polish legions which were being formed to fight on the side of the Allies. The poet's vast ideas of a common fight of all enslaved nations for freedom was close to realization. In these Polish legions Poles, Rumanians, Cossacks, Bulgarians, Turks, and Frenchmen fraternized. The poet had intended to add to these divisions and regiments a Jewish legion. His activities were interrupted on 24 November, 1855, when he was stricken with cholera, which was then prevalent in Constantinople, and two days later he died.

* * * * *

"... As regards the importance of nations in mankind, it is determined exclusively by their spiritual power, and the attention which they focus on themselves derives from their moral influence in the world and not from the noise which they make...."
(From "The Unpublished Philosophical Letters of P. Ya. Chaadaev", *Literaturnoe Nasledstvo* (Moscow: 1935), Vols. 22–24, p. 23.)

No written record has survived of any meeting between Mickiewicz and Chaadaev, but there is one place where we know that they did meet and where they are still together—in Myasoedov's famous painting, mentioned above: "Pushkin and his Friends Listen to Mickiewicz's Declamation in the Salon of Princess Zinaida Volkonsky". Myasoedov surrounded Mickiewicz with his "Muscovite friends" who used to visit the Princess. In the painting are Princess Volkonsky, Pushkin, Prince P. A. Vyazemsky and his wife, S. A. Sobolevsky, M. P. Pogodin, D. V. Venevitinov, S. P. Shevyrev, and A. S. Khomyakov. Among them, too, is Chaadaev. The painter caught him in a characteristic pose: separated a little from the rest of the group, the Muscovite

---

[1] Besides the Russian and Polish works there are several important publications in French, German, and English, which deal directly or indirectly with the subject: Cf. *Oeuvres choisies de Pierre Tchaadaief*, publiées, pour la première fois par le P. Gagarin de la compagnie de Jésus (Paris: Librairie A. Franck, 1862); Charles Quénet, *Tchaadaev et Les Lettres Philosophiques* (Paris: Librairie Ancienne Honoré Champion, 1931). Cf. also A. von Schelting, *Russland und Europa* (Bern: A. Francke ag. Verlag, 1948); the excellent book of the great Polish historian, Jan Kucharzewski, *The Origins of Modern Russia* (New York: The Polish Institute of Arts and Sciences in America, 1948); and finally T. G. Masaryk, *The Spirit of Russia* (London: G. Allen & Unwin Ltd.; New York: The Macmillan Co., 1919).

"Brutus" leans against a pillar in the "Greek room" of the Muscovite "Corinna"; his arms crossed, he stands almost opposite Mickiewicz, who is improvising. Chaadaev is listening attentively, as is everyone else in the picture. ". . . He spoke of future times, when nations, having forgotten their disputes, will be united in one great family. Greedily we listened to the poet. . . ." Thus did Pushkin immortalize Mickiewicz's Moscow improvisations, in the single poem written by him in 1834.

I do not know whether Myasoedov had any documentary proof that Chaadaev and Mickiewicz knew each other or that Chaadaev attended Mickiewicz's improvisations. I rather doubt it, because if such were the case, we should also have those proofs. However, we know that in 1826, after his return from abroad, Chaadaev went to the country first. Then he came to Moscow, but he saw almost no one, and only in the summer of 1831 did he leave his seclusion and start to frequent the English Club and to visit his friends.[1] But Mickiewicz had by this time departed from Moscow.

Still, the author of the *Philosophical Letters* had allowed himself exceptions earlier. We know, for instance, that he attended Pushkin's first reading of *Boris Godunov*, which took place at Sobolevsky's on 10 September, 1826,[2] but Mickiewicz was not present. At the end of September or the beginning of October of the same year Chaadaev left for the country and returned to Moscow only in 1828, still in a state of depression.[3]

These facts and dates do not encourage belief that Mickiewicz met Chaadaev personally. And yet it is difficult to imagine that Mickiewicz would not have made efforts to meet the Muscovite "Pericles". Chaadaev was too outstanding a personality, too well known, too popular in Moscow, even before the publication in *The Telescope* of his first *Philosophical Letter*. On the other hand, Chaadaev, too, should have been attracted by Mickiewicz, who, at that time, became a sensation in the literary and social circles of Moscow. Is it possible that Pushkin, Sobolevsky, or Prince Vyazemsky would not have introduced them to each other?[4] And yet, concrete facts are lacking. Chaadaev does not mention Mickiewicz; Mickiewicz makes no reference to Chaadaev.

As we know, Pushkin carried on a poetical argument with the

---

[1] *Literaturnoe Nasledstvo* (Moscow: Izdatel'stvo Akademii Nauk S.S.S.R., 1935), Vols. 22-4, pp. 13-14.

[2] Puškin, *Pis'ma*, edited by B. L. Modzalevskij (Moscow-Leningrad: Gos. Izdat., 1928), Vol. II, p. 188. See also *Puškin i ego sovremenniki* (Petersburg: Tipografija Imperatorskoj Akademii Nauk, 1903-30), Vols. 31-2, p. 40.

[3] Quénet, Charles, *Tchaadaev et les Lettres Philosophiques*, etc. (Paris: "Champion", 1931), p. 95.

[4] We know, for instance, that Pushkin told Pogodin in December, 1828, of Chaadaev's acquaintanceship with Schelling, and this caused Pogodin to begin a correspondence with Chaadaev. See, *Puškin i ego sovremenniki*, Vols. 19-20, pp. 92-3.

Digression of the *Forefathers' Eve, Part III* on the one hand, and, on the other, with the *Philosophical Letters*. He did not notice, however, the resemblance between these two texts. And no one since Pushkin has noticed this similarity. One comparison would suffice. First, Mickiewicz:

> I meet the men who dwell within this land,
> Broad-chested, great of strength, a stalwart band;
> And, like the trees and creatures of the North,
> They pulse with life and health that knows no pain;
> But every face is like their home, a plain,
> A waste on which no inward light shines forth.
> Their hearts, like underground volcanoes, throw
> Upon the cheeks no flame of fierce desire.
> Their moving lips reflect no ardent glow;
> No wrinkled brows fade with the dying fire
> Seen on men's foreheads in more favored lands,
> O'er which have passed, through many weary years,
> Such strong traditions, sorrows, hopes and fears
> That in each face a nation's history stands.
> And here the eyes of men are large and clear,
> Like their unstoried towns; no storm-tossed heart
> Makes anguished glances from their pupils dart
> Or hopeless sorrow in their depths appear:
> Viewed from afar they seem austere and great;
> But near at hand, empty and desolate.[1]

Now, Chaadaev:

"There is, I think, even in our glance something, I do not know what, but something strangely vague, cold, uncertain, resembling a little the physiognomy of peoples placed at the very bottom of the social ladder. How many times in a foreign country, especially in the South, where physiognomies are so animated and eloquent, have I not been struck, on comparing the faces of my compatriots with those of the natives, by the mute air of our features."[2]

These parallelisms consist not only of resemblances in images, examples, comparisons, and characteristics. The affinity lies deeper:

---

[1] G. R. Noyes, *Poems by Adam Mickiewicz* (New York: The Polish Institute of Arts and Sciences in America, 1944), p. 339.

[2] *Sočinenija i pis'ma P. Ja. Čaadaeva*, Vol I, pp. 82–93. This same thought will be repeated by Marquis de Custine in his book *La Russie en 1839*: "... This race is almost without physiognomy. The middle of the face is flattened to a degree that renders it deformed. The men, though ugly and dirty, are said to be strong, which, however, does not prevent their being poor." (Refer to the English translation, entitled *Russia* (London, 1844), Vol. I, p. 119.)

their philosophy of history is identical, the basis of their religious outlook is analogous, the principle of evaluation of Russian history is the same.

Yet, there remains the fact that Mickiewicz did not have the *Philosophical Letters* in his hands when he wrote the *Digression*, and he probably did not even know of them, or he would certainly have at least mentioned Chaadaev in his Parisian lectures. And as far as Chaadaev is concerned, he could have read Mickiewicz only after 1833, having eventually been introduced to Mickiewicz's poems by Pushkin, who, as we know, received the Parisian edition of Mickiewicz from Sobolevsky in the fall of 1833. However, at this time the *Philosophical Letters* had long before been written.[1]

Chaadaev completed his work in 1831, although the first *Letter* was published only in 1836. It was then that the thunderbolt of the Czar's anger fell upon him, and the hurricane of sensation started. Nevertheless, many of Chaadaev's friends were previously cognizant of his treatise (which had been in manuscript form from 1829) either directly or from talks with the author.[2] We know from Herzen how strong an impression this "shot in the dark" had created—"the whole of thinking Russia was shaken".[3] But the effect was negative: Chaadaev was considered to be an enemy of his country, a writer who hated Russia.

I still cannot avoid the temptation to admit the possibility that Mickiewicz and Chaadaev met. They could have discussed their ideas, and we must not forget that we are now almost sure that Mickiewicz started to write his *Digression* while still in Russia. It seems, therefore, that the similarity of their views was not quite accidental. There are, indeed, too many coincidences other than their general approach to Russian and European history. These constitute striking resemblances of a formal and thematic nature. For instance, we find in the *Digression*:

> No cities and no mountains meet the eye;
> No works of man or nature tower on high:
> The plain lies bleak and barren to the sight
> As if it had been fashioned yesternight.[4]

---

[1] Quénet, *op. cit.* Also, *Literaturnoe Nasledstvo*, as above.
[2] Puškin, *Pis'ma*, Vol. II, pp. 443–4.
[3] A. I. Gercen, *Byloe i dumy*, Part IV, ch. XXX.
[4] Noyes, *op. cit.*, p. 337. Similarly in Custine: ". . . Nothing can be more melancholy than the aspect of nature in the approach to St. Petersburg. As you advance up the Gulf, the flat marshes of Ingria terminate in a little wavering line drawn between the sky and the sea; this line is Russia. It presents the appearance of a wet lowland, with here and there a few birch trees thinly scattered. The landscape is void of objects and colours, has no bounds, and yet no sublimity. It has just light enough to be visible. . . . I have never seen, in the approaches to any other great city, a landscape so melancholy as the banks of the Neva." (Custine, *op. cit.*, Vol I, p. 117.) Compare, too, with J. A. F. P. Ancelot, *Six mois en Russie* (Paris, 1827).

Obviously, it is a symbolic picture—the poet emphasizes the historical emptiness of Russia. The lines

> So hordes of people crossed it, band on band,
> Leaving no traces of their mode of life . . .[1]

accentuate even more strongly the proper significance of the picture. Further, the lines

> This level plain lies open, waste and white,
> A wide-spread page prepared for God to write . . .[2]

are almost entirely clear: until now history has not written anything on this page. It might be that it *will* write, but *what* will it write? And the answer:

> Will he [God] trace here his message from above;
> And, using for his letters holy men,
> Will he sketch here his writ of faith again,
> That all the human race is ruled by love
> And offerings remain the world's best prize?
> Or will that fiend who still the Lord defies
> Appear and carve with his oft-sharpened sword
> That prisons should forbid mankind to rise,
> And scourges are humanity's reward?[3]

I should like to add here the following passage, also from the *Digression*:

> These mighty trees have here and there been cut,
> Stripped bare and laid together, side by side,
> To make strange forms, a roof and wall, a hut:
> Such are the dwellings where the people hide . . .[4]

in which Mickiewicz emphasizes the instability and lack of firm foundations for Russia's civilization, its temporal aspect, suggesting by this the nomadic characters of that civilization.[5] There is no doubt that Mickiewicz's picture of the bleak Russian landscape derives from the poet's personal observations. Mickiewicz travelled in a kibitka from Wilno to Petersburg, then from Petersburg to Odessa, and from Odessa to

---
[1] *Ibid.*
[2] *Ibid.*, p. 338.
[3] Noyes, *op. cit.*, p. 338.
[4] *Ibid.*
[5] Compare again with Ancelot, *op. cit.*

Moscow. Of course, everyone knows of the existence of beautiful, old Russian towns and cities, such as Novgorod and Yaroslav, not to mention the famous Russian monasteries, but Mickiewicz's poetic stylization of the Russian landscape was determined by his interpretation of Russian history and especially of the autocratic reforms of Peter the Great, which smashed the Russian national past—this is a common theme in Mickiewicz's works. Significantly enough, Mickiewicz's moral reaction to the Russian landscape was not too alien to Russians themselves. This is confirmed by the fact that Chatsky, the protagonist in Griboedov's famous comedy, *Wit Works Woe*, in one of his vexed monologues gives a similar picture; the wording is almost the same. Chatsky's remarks convey the "exasperating dullness" of the Russian countryside:

> While on your cart with listless mind
> Over the endless plain still onward idly carried,
>   Before you, always undefined,
> There's something bright and blue and varied.
> An hour, two hours, all day, still on. A dash to spare,
> And there's the stage and bed. And all around you blinking
> That great smooth stretch of plain, so silent and so bare!
> Confound! It can't be borne; the more one goes on thinking——[1]

Mickiewicz knew Griboedov. I have elsewhere established the fact that they met several times, and of course there is no doubt that Mickiewicz was acquainted with Griboedov's comedy, which was being circulated in manuscript copies among Mickiewicz's Russian friends.[2] I should like to add, too, that the recent studies of Russian scholars on Griboedov disclosed many surprising details connected with the story of Griboedov's relations with Chaadaev.[3] Even at the time when Griboedov wrote his comedy, people were inclined to see in Chatsky a kind of literary portrayal of Chaadaev. For a long time, despite his Westernizing education, his broad political views in his rôle as a distinguished statesman and his literary orientation, Griboedov was erroneously considered a "Slavophil" because of Chatsky's philippics against Gallomania. The recent revelations, to which I have alluded above, destroy entirely this presumption and cast a new light on the whole comedy and on Chatsky. Need I remind the reader of the fact that Chatsky after his disillusionment in Moscow abandons Russia for Europe? (This, by the way, is a fact which deeply irritated Dostoevsky.)

---

[1] G. R. Noyes, *Masterpieces of the Russian Drama*, Wit Works Woe, Act IV, Scene 3, p. 140.
[2] W. Lednicki, *Przyjaciele Moskale* (Cracow, 1935), pp. 55–8.
[3] *Literaturnoe Nasledstvo*, Vols. 47–8, on Griboedov.

Now let us return to Mickiewicz. To the poet, who in his poem, "To Lelewel", denoted the Poles as inhabitants of Europe and who, later in his *Books of the Polish Nation*, came back to the same theme, to the theme of the unity of the western-European nations—

"And all the nations that believed, whether they were Germans, or Italians, or French, or Poles, looked upon themselves as one nation, and this nation was called Christendom. And all the kings of the different nations looked upon themselves as brothers, and marched under the one sign of the cross...."[1]

—this concept of European unity was not at all accidental. It derived from the ideology of the Enlightenment.[2] The historiosophic attack against Russia was a natural expression of faith, a faith that was founded in him, first of all, by Lelewel's lectures which he attended in Wilno; then, by the mystic, Oleszkiewicz, whom he met in Petersburg and whom he described in his *Digression*; later, by Rome; by the *Imitation* of Thomas à Kempis; and, finally, by Lamennais.

These are only a few of the main ideas to be found in the *Digression*. One should not forget the description of Petersburg as an artificial, imposed, anti-historical, inorganic, cosmopolitan city based on the sufferings and martyrdom of enslaved nations; the poetical analysis of the artificial Europeanization of Russia; the suggestion of the ephemeral quality of this phantom city, so wonderfully depicted by the poet, a theme which later tempted so many Russian writers and poets; the violent and pathetic attacks upon Russian militarism; the profound pity for Russian serfdom; and, lastly, the apocalyptic vision of final judgment and punishment, when the sins and abuses of the modern Babylon would be weighed.

Prophecy and satire, lyricism and realistic painting, political perspicacity, a deep knowledge of Russian history and psychology, vast landscapes of Russian deserts and marble palaces in Petersburg, of the white snow on the earth and of the phantasmagorical, transparent, frosty Petersburg sky—this is what creates the particular character of this poetical pamphlet. It is a kind of journalism in poetry, a kind of poetical report à la Byron, Alfred de Vigny, Heine. Of course the poet was limited by poetry: he could not develop his ideas and conceptions too consistently, too "scientifically". And this is precisely what we find in Chaadaev.

In Chaadaev's opinion, God gave to man essential ideas which

[1] Noyes, *op. cit.*, p. 372.
[2] I. Chrzanowski, *Archivum Komisji badania historii filozofii w Polsce* (Kraków, 1917), Vol. I, p. 170. Also S. Pigoń, *A. Mickiewicz—Księgi Narodu i Pielgrzymstwa Polskiego*, Bibljoteka Narodowa No. 17 (Kraków, 1924), pp. 23-4.

became *des idées traditives*. God directs individuals as He governs the evolution of humanity. The Christian religion is His instrument. The individual aspect of Christianity is to be found in the virtue of every Christian, the social aspect—in the action of the Christian in society. It is Catholicism which is the center of Christianity, as it is the agent of the triple social, universal and unitarian principle. It finds its own center in the Pope.

What is the task of the historian? To discover the divine idea of which history is the expression. The idea seen in God is rule by Providence; seen in history, it is infinite, spiritual progress by the action of Christianity. A fact is great only when it is philosophically great: that is, when it is not in contradiction with the idea. A man is great when he is an agent for an idea. History should abandon the field of criticism and enter the field of philosophy. An historian is not a seeker nor a gatherer of facts: he must search for the permanent results and eternal effects of historical phenomena. The idea is the definite criterion; it suffices in itself. It is not a construction of the human mind. The historian does not establish it, he discovers and recognizes it. Therefore, it cannot be affected by any new fact, and on it depend the truth and value of all facts.

Chaadaev saw two adversaries to this ideology: in the first place, the philosophers of the eighteenth century, who believed that history depends only upon accidental causes and effects, and, thus, is purely human, and that progress is made by man and is indefinite; in the second place, the Protestants, with their attack on Catholicism, the essential organ of the Christian religion. They had broken unity and reintroduced pagan division into Christianity.

Russia remained outside of Catholicism and unity, because she had obtained Christianity in the form of the Byzantine schism, and that is why she remained outside of history. She is without a past, not only in the sense that until now everything in her is dull and sombre, but because everything in her is unproductive. She has not created any national tradition for herself, and she has not given humanity anything which would serve general progress. She might save herself only if she amalgamated herself with western and Catholic Europe.

This is a general résumé of Chaadaev's doctrine which anyone may find in the excellent book by Quénet.[1] Quénet, however, based his book mostly on those *Letters* and texts of Chaadaev which were published in the Gershenzon edition of 1913. Gershenzon himself has written about Chaadaev, but as he belonged to a group of Russian writers who dissociated themselves from any revolutionary ideas, he gave a rather one-sided picture of him.

[1] Quénet, *op. cit.*, pp. 132–3.

In 1935 Prince D. I. Shakhovskoy and W. Asmus, as I mentioned, published some unknown *Letters* of Chaadaev in the *Literaturnoe Nasledstvo*,[1] and these texts reveal a new aspect of the man.

Certainly Chaadaev was primarily a religious thinker, but his attitude toward Russia was not only critical, but even revolutionary. Of extreme importance, for instance, is his opinion of serfdom to be found in one of those recently published *Letters*. He considered serfdom to be a paralysis of the will. He thought serfdom should awaken doubts of Orthodoxy. Antiquity could not imagine a world without slaves; the abolition of serfdom was an achievement of Christianity; serfs were liberated *pro redemptione animae*. Why did Christianity not act in the same way in Russia? On the contrary, enslavement came after Christianization: that is, in the period of Godunov and Shuysky.

"Let the Orthodox," says Chaadaev, "explain this phenomenon. Let them only tell why they did not protest against the violence of one part of the nation against the other. Please notice how little they know us in spite of all our external power. In these very days the thunder of our guns has roared simultaneously in the Bosporus and the Euphrates. And yet the historians, who nowadays prove that the abolition of serfdom is an achievement of Christianity, do not even suspect that there is a Christian nation of forty millions which continues to live in chains. As regards the importance of nations in mankind, it is determined exclusively by their spiritual power, and the attention which they focus on themselves derives from their moral influence in the world and not from the noise which they make."[2]

I believe the conformity of Mickiewicz's and Chaadaev's views is already obvious to the reader. Let us, however, approach Chaadaev a little more closely and select some of his most eloquent and fascinating texts.

In his first letter from the cycle *Letters of a Philosophy of History* (1829–1831) Chaadaev begins almost exactly like Mickiewicz with the affirmation of the "superior principle of unity" which governs the world through the Church.[3] He then emphasizes the separation of Russia from this united world.

"We never marched with other peoples; we do not belong to any of the great families of mankind; we are of neither the West nor

[1] *Literaturnoe Nasledstvo*, Vols. 22–4.
[2] *Op. cit.*, pp. 22–3.
[3] *Sočinenija i pis'ma P. Ja. Čaadaeva*, Vol. I, p. 75.

the East; we have not the tradition of one nor the other. Placed as if outside of time, the universal education of mankind passed us by."[1]

How can one avoid quoting Dostoevsky at this point? Dostoevsky was opposed to all of Chaadaev's views, yet Chaadaev intrigued him. We know that when he was preparing his materials for his novels *Atheism* and *The Story of a Great Sinner*, which finally emerged as *The Possessed* and the *Brothers Karamazov*, his mind was absorbed by Chaadaev. No wonder, therefore, that we find familiar tones in his writings.

"We understood," wrote Dostoevsky, "that we might also be Europeans, not only with the help of French clothes and powdered hair. We understood this, and yet we did not know what to do. Slowly we started to understand that in general we had nothing to do! No independent activity remained for us, and so from despair we plunged into auto-analysis and self-observation. It was no longer the cold, superficial skepticism of Kantemir or Fonvizin. The skepticism of Onegin from the beginning contained something tragic, sometimes tainted with mischievous irony. It was in Onegin that the Russian for the first time realized with bitterness, or at least started to feel, that there was nothing for him to do in the world. He is a European: what will he bring to Europe, and does Europe need him? He is a Russian: what will he do for Russia, and besides, does he understand Russia? The type of Onegin had to originate in our so-called 'upper society', which separates itself to the greatest possible degree from the soil, and in which external civilization has reached its highest development.

This is a very true historical trait in Pushkin. In this society we needlessly spoke all languages as we had nothing better to do. We travelled in Europe, longed for Russia, and at the same time realized that we were not entirely similar to the French, Germans nor English, that those have work and we have none, that they are at home and we are nowhere."[2]

Let us return now to Chaadaev, our Russian "poet" of the West:

". . . There is a time for all peoples of violent agitation, of passionate anxiety, of activity without reasoned motives. . . . This

[1] *Sočinenija i pis'ma P. Ja. Čaadaeva*, Vol. I, p. 77.
[2] F. M. Dostoevskij, *Sobranie Sočinenij* (Moscow-Leningrad: Gos. Izd., 1930), Vol. XIII, pp. 101–102.

is the age of great emotions, of great enterprises, of great passions of the peoples.... All societies passed through these periods. They furnished them with the most lively reminiscences, with myths and poetry, with all their strongest and most fertile ideas: these are the necessary bases of societies. Otherwise they would not have anything in their memory to which to attach themselves, to love; they would hold only to the dust of their soil. This interesting epoch in the history of peoples is the adolescence of nations, this is the moment when their faculties develop with the greatest power, and the moment of which the memory creates the happiness and lessons of the mature age. But we have nothing like that. First, brutal barbarism, afterwards, rude superstition, then, foreign, ferocious, debasing domination, the spirit of which was later inherited by the national power. This was the sorrowful history of our youth. Nothing similar with us to the age of exuberant activity, of exalted play of the moral forces of other peoples. The epoch of our social life which corresponds to this moment was filled with a dull and sombre existence, without vigour, without energy, animated only by crime and softened only by servitude."[1]

Mickiewicz complained in the same tones:

> Poor nation, I deplore thy tragedy!
> Thy heroism is naught but slavery.[2]

Continuing in Chaadaev:

"No charming recollections, no gracious images in our memory, no powerful instructions in our national tradition. Cast a glance over the centuries we have traversed, over the land which we cover, and you will not find a single attractive reminiscence, a single venerable monument which would revive past ages with power, which would retrace them vividly and picturesquely. We live only in the most narrow present, without past and without future, in the midst of an insipid calm...."[3]

The reader may recall the words of Mickiewicz in which he makes a comparison between the faces of south Europeans and the flat faces of the Russians, as well as his observation that every European face is a monument to Europe's historical past.

On the other hand, in Chaadaev:

---
[1] *Sočinenija i pis'ma P. Ja. Čaadaeva*, Vol. I, pp. 78–9.
[2] Noyes, *op. cit.*, p. 362.
[3] *Sočinenija i pis'ma P. Ja. Čaadaeva*, loc. cit.

"... Look around. Does not everyone have a foot in the air? It seems that everyone is travelling. No determined sphere of existence for anyone, no good habits for anything, no rule for anything, not even a domestic hearth; nothing which attaches, nothing which lasts, nothing which remains; everything vanishes, everything crumbles without leaving traces without or within us. We even seem to camp in our houses; we seem to be strangers in our families; we seem to be nomads in our cities, even more so than those who pasture on our steppes, because they are more attached to their deserts than we to our town....

... Isolated by a strange destiny from the universal movement of humanity, we lack that universal movement. We have acquired naught of the traditional ideas (*idées traditives*) of the human race. And it is on these ideas that the life of a nation rests; it is from these ideas that a nation's future springs and its moral development proceeds...."

In another passage he says:

"... One could not understand anything in Christianity, if one did not realize that there is in it a purely historical aspect which is such an essential part of the dogma, which encloses in some way the entire philosophy of Christianity, as it reveals what it has done for men and what it must do for them in the future. This is how the Christian religion appears not only as a moral system, conceived in the perishable forms of the human mind, but as an eternal, divine power, universally acting in the world of the intellect and the visible action of which must be a perpetual instruction for us. This is the real sense of the dogma, symbolically expressed by faith in one universal church.... All European nations grasped one another by the hand when they advanced through the centuries. Whatever they do today in order to diverge in their own particular direction, they always find themselves again on the same road. To comprehend the familial development of these nations, one need not study history. Read only Tasso and look at all of them prostrated at the foot of the walls of Jerusalem. Remember that during fifteen centuries they had only one idiom with which to speak to God, only one moral authority, only one conviction. Realize that during fifteen centuries, every year, on the same day and at the same hour, in the same words, all of them simultaneously raised their voices toward the Supreme Being to celebrate His glory in the greatest of His benefactions...."[1]

[1] *Sočinenija Čaadaeva*, Vol. I, pp. 78 ff.

Then comes the concept of European unity. Again there is a strong resemblance to Mickiewicz. I have already cited this passage from the *Books of the Polish Nation*:

> "And all the nations that believed, whether they were Germans, or Italians, or French, or Poles, looked upon themselves as one nation, and this nation was called Christendom. And the kings of the different nations looked upon themselves as brothers, and marched under the one sign of the cross."[1]

Similarly in Chaadaev:

> ". . . The peoples of Europe have a common physiognomy, a family resemblance. In spite of the general division of these peoples into Latin, Teutonic, Southern and Northern branches, there is a common tie which unites them in one bundle, a tie visible for anyone who has approved their general history. You know that it was not long ago that the whole of Europe was called Christendom, and this word had its place in public law. Besides this general character, each of these peoples has a particular character, but this is merely its history and tradition. This composes the inherited patrimony of ideas of a people. . . . Do you want to know what these ideas are? They are the concepts of duty, justice, law and order. They derive from the very events which have constituted society; they are integral elements of the social life of these countries. . . ."[2]

And, finally, we come to the most striking resemblances. In Mickiewicz we read:

> So hordes of people crossed it, band on band,
> Leaving no traces of their mode of life.
> Yet on the Alpine mountains far away
> They left their mark in that long-distant day;
> And farther still, upon Rome's monuments
> One reads of those bold robbers coming hence.[3]

In the same vein in Chaadaev:

> ". . . If the barbarian hordes which convulsed the world had not crossed the country which we inhabit before they precipitated themselves on the West, we scarcely would have furnished a chapter for universal history. In order to attract attention we had to expand from the Bering Straits to the Oder. . . .

[1] Noyes, *op. cit.*, pp. 372–3.
[2] *Sočinenija Čaadaeva*, Vol. I., p. 81.
[3] Noyes, *op. cit.*, p. 337.

Lastly, we have lived and we live only to serve as some lesson to distant posterity which will comprehend it; today, whatever may be said, we are absent from the intellectual order. I do not tire of admiring the vacuum and astonishing solitude of our social existence...."[1]

I may now take the liberty of quoting again the following passage from Mickiewicz:

> This level plain lies open, waste and white,
> A wide-spread page prepared for God to write.—
> Will he trace here his message from above;
> And, using for his letters holy men,
> Will he sketch here his writ of faith again,
> That all the human race is ruled by love
> And offerings remain the world's best prize?
> Or will that fiend who still the Lord defies
> Appear and carve with his oft-sharpened sword
> That prisons should forbid mankind to rise,
> And scourges are humanity's reward?[2]

Compare Chaadaev:

"... We are one of those nations which does not seem to be an integral part of the human race, but which exists only to give some great lesson to the world. The instruction which we are destined to give will certainly not be lost; but who knows the day when we will find ourselves amidst humanity and how much misery we shall experience before the fulfilment of our destiny?"[3]

There is another passage in the *Philosophical Letters* which calls to mind the Messianic and apocalyptic motifs in the *Forefathers' Eve*. In the poem *Oleszkiewicz* (part of the *Digression*) Mickiewicz prophesied the punishment which would befall Petersburg, the modern Babylon:

> ... Those who survive this night
> Will see great marvels of Jehovah's might:
> This is his second test, beware the next!
> The Lord will shake the fair Assyrian throne;
> The Lord will shake the walls of Babylon.
> Lord, ere the third test come, let me be gone![4]

[1] *Sočinenija Čaadaeva*, Vol. I, pp. 84–5.
[2] Noyes, *op. cit.*, p. 338.
[3] *Sočinenija Čaadaeva*, Vol. I, p. 81.
[4] Noyes, *op. cit.*, p. 364.

Involuntarily Chaadaev once again comes to mind, although his text contains some significant reservations:

". . . And, probably, in some particular visions of the future by which privileged minds have been favoured . . . one will find that these prophecies are not concerned with any determined epoch; but, rather, these are instructions which concern indiscriminately all times, and, moreover, one has in some way to glance around oneself in order to see perpetual fulfilment of these prophecies in successive phases of the life of human society as daily and luminous manifestations of the eternal law of the moral world, so that the fact of the prophecy will be as perceptible as the very fact of the events which transport us."[1]

To this passage Chaadaev added a significant note:

"One will not find, for instance, as used to occur formerly, a great Babylon in any empire of the earth; but one will feel, living amidst the din of its collapse, that is to say, one will know that the sublime historian of future ages who has told us of this terrifying ruin was not thinking about any particular empire but about the collapse of material society in general, such as it exists . . ."[2]

This development is certainly similar to the ideas contained in Mickiewicz's *Books of the Polish Nation and of the Polish Pilgrimage*, in which he expressed his belief in the abolition of the European society based on injustice and enslavement among nations and predicted the future of Europe's history as an epoch of general liberty and an era of God's kingdom on earth, introducing the new period of Christian civilization.

These similarities are certainly not accidental. Of course, the similarity in the ultimate conclusions of Mickiewicz's and Chaadaev's philosophy of history could have resulted from similar premises of their thought and from similar sources of their historical and philosophical studies. However, there still remains the strong conjecture that they discussed these items, the more so that the theme of the collapse of the materialistic European civilization, developed in Mickiewicz's *Books*, was the main subject of *A History of the Future*, a work which he meditated in Petersburg and which he discussed with many friends.[3]

It is possible that Oleszkiewicz played a great rôle in this connection. This mystic, Mason and Martinist lived in Petersburg from

---

[1] *Sočinenija Čaadaeva*, Vol. I, p. 103.
[2] *Ibid.*, p. 104.
[3] J. Kallenbach, *Adam Mickiewicz* (Cracow, 1926), Vol. I, p. 414.

1810, and, therefore, could easily have met Chaadaev. Chaadaev was in Petersburg in June, 1821, and he probably belonged to the Masons up to that time. We know that in 1816 he was a member of the Lodge of United Friends, a lodge to which individuals of the Russian and Polish aristocracy belonged. It is known that Oleszkiewicz was a high dignitary in Polish Masonry and that he participated in the work of several Polish and Polish-Lithuanian lodges in Petersburg. We have reason to presume that Chaadaev met Oleszkiewicz in these circles. Undoubtedly he also met Count Joseph de Maistre, whom we may call to mind appropriately here. It is true that *Les soirées de St. Pétersbourg* appeared only in 1837, but the doctrine and views of de Maistre expressed in *The Evenings* had been elaborated and even formulated much earlier in his preceding works. As I mentioned above, we also learn from Chaadaev's own statement that when in Cracow, in 1814, he was "accepted into a Masonic lodge", the name of which was forgotten, but in which "the two first degrees had been conferred upon him".[1]

However, even more important than all these meetings was the general intellectual and spiritual atmosphere of the Russian élite of those times, to which Chaadaev belonged and to which Mickiewicz also had access. Indeed, the most significant fact was just this general atmosphere. In a certain sense Schelling confirms this in a letter to Chaadaev, written in 1833:

> "At the moment when we are finishing a work which was begun in silence long ago and the result of which is a new intellectual world previously inaccessible to philosophy, it is pleasant to learn that others are with us on the same road, that they hear us, that they understand beforehand, and that it was not the poor and feeble spirit of the individual, but the general spirit of the time that inspired us and sought to reveal itself in and through us."[2]

Chaadaev built and based his doctrine and views on Russia and her historical development on Chateaubriand, Ballanche, Lamennais, Guizot, J. de Maistre, Bonald, Plato, Spinoza, Descartes, Kant, Bacon, Schelling, etc.[3] Mickiewicz also read and studied quite a few of these philosophers. In other words, the thoughts of these two men revolved around the same subject and followed almost the same path. Besides, one should remember, too, that the criticism of Russia and her history

---

[1] D. I. Šakhovskoj, "P. Ja. Čaadaev na puti v Rossiju v 1826 godu", *Literaturnoe Nasledstvo* (Moscow, 1935), Vols. 19–21, p. 24.
[2] *Sočinenija Čaadaeva*, Vol. I, p. 382.
[3] Quénet, *loc. cit.*

which Chaadaev presented was especially damning, because of the exceptional literary talent with which the *Letters* were written. As a matter of fact, not a few of Chaadaev's opinions conformed, for example, to the so-called school of skeptics (Kachenovsky), to some of the views of Prince Vyazemsky, and even to some of Pushkin's opinions. How close, indeed, some Russians were to the views of Mickiewicz and Chaadaev, as far as their judgments about Russia were concerned, may be seen from the following statement of S. Glinka: "There is nothing in Russia, there is not even any Russia. . . . In Russia everything is phantom." A hundred years later the great Alexander Blok said exactly the same thing: "For me, Russia will always have only a sentimental value. In truth, she does not exist, she never did exist, and she will never exist."[1] And how often the same theme of Russia the phantom appears not only in Blok's letters but in his poems.

In 1837—that is, after Mickiewicz's *Digression*, at a time when Chaadaev might already have known of it, at least from Pushkin—Chaadaev wrote in his *Apology of a Madman*:

"Peter the Great found at home only a blank page and with his powerful hand he traced these words, 'Europe and the West', and since that time we have belonged to Europe and to the West. One should not make a mistake: no matter how great was the genius of this man and how enormous the energy of his will, his work was possible only amidst a nation whose antecedents did not imperiously command the course which it was to follow, whose traditions had not the power to create for it a future, and whose remembrances could have been effaced with impunity by an audacious legislator. If we were so docile to the voice of a prince who invited us to a new life, it was because there was nothing in our past existence to justify any resistance. The deepest trait of our historical physiognomy is the absence of spontaneity in our social development. Examine attentively and you will see that every fact important in our history is an imposed fact, every new idea is almost always an imported idea. . . . Fashioned, moulded, and created by our sovereigns and by our climate, we became a great nation only by submission. Glance through our annals from beginning to end and you will find on every page the profound action of the political power, the unceasing influence of the soil, and almost never the public will. All the same, it is just to say that the Russian people proved its high wisdom in relinquishing its power into the hands of its masters and in giving way to the nature of its country, thereby

[1] See for Glinka, Quénet, *op. cit.*, p. 185; for Blok, N. Berberova, *Alexandre Blok et son temps* (Paris: Editions du Chêne, 1947), p. 109.

recognizing the superior law of its destiny. . . . A rapid glance directed upon our history from the vantage point where we now stand will, I hope, show this law in its full clarity. . . . There is one fact which utterly dominates our course through the centuries, which runs through the whole of our history and embraces its whole philosophy, which appears in all epochs of our social life and determines its character, which is at the same time the essential element of our political greatness and the true cause of our intellectual impotence: this fact is the geographical one."[1]

The Leibniz-Mickiewicz blank page[2] was revived here, as well as the "heroism of serfdom", the warnings and deep observations of Pushkin contained in his famous letter to Chaadaev of 19 October, 1836, in which Pushkin came forth with a fervent defense of the "historicalness" of Russia and also referred to the universal prestige of Russia at that time. In a rough draft of this letter he also made another important reservation:

"What should have been said and what you have said is that our present society is as contemptible as stupid; that this absence of public opinion, this indifference to everything that is duty, justice, law, truth, to everything that is not necessity, this cynical contempt for human thought and dignity—all this is, indeed, a desolation. You did well to have said it aloud. . . . You should have added (not as a concession, but as a truth) that the government is the only European in Russia, and, brutal as it is, it only rests with it to be a hundred times more so. No one would pay any attention to it."[3]

* * * * *

We know that Pushkin's *Bronze Horseman* was a poetical answer to Mickiewicz's *Digression*.[4] Indeed, it would be impossible to understand completely this dualistic poem with its apology for Russian imperialism and its refutation of the same for the sake of the rights of the human personality, its glorification of Petersburg and the revelation of the city's tragic essence, without taking into consideration Mickiewicz's *Digression*. These profound ties between Mickiewicz and Pushkin are, unfortunately, insufficiently known in the Anglo-Saxon world, just as, in general, there is little knowledge of Russian-Polish relations.

[1] Quénet, *op. cit.*, pp. 223–4, 234.
[2] *Tabula rasa*. Cf. *Oeuvres de Leibniz* (Paris, 1875), Vol. VII, pp. 423, 490.
[3] Puškin, *Sočinenija, Perepiska*, pod red. Saitova, Vol. III, pp. 387–9.
[4] *Jeździec Miedziany*, etc., przekład J. Tuwima, studjum W. Lednickiego (Warsaw: Bibljoteka Polska, 1931).

It appears that the enlightening views of Mickiewicz reached not only some of his devoted Russian friends, but also some Westerners. I have in mind a person I should like to bring to the fore and not quite parenthetically this time. This writer has, fortunately, been translated into English. I am thinking of the Marquis de Custine and his famous book *La Russie en 1839*, entitled in the English edition *Russia*.

Dostoevsky once said, when mocking foreign stupidities about Russia, that every Frenchman publishing a book on Russia goes to Russia after having written the book in order to justify its publication. This joke contains some elements of seriousness. Indeed, when expecting to write on some subject or about a country, one must have some general preconceived ideas and information. This was certainly true of Custine. He met Mickiewicz in Paris before his trip to Russia and he had read his poems.

The theme of tyranny, despotism, oppression and regimentation, characterizing Petersburg, has been effectively developed by Custine in the style of Mickiewicz. For example, in Mickiewicz's *The Road to Russia* we find:

> Who travels on these roads? Here swiftly ride
> Snow-powdered troops of Russian cavalry,
> And there are seen dark ranks of infantry,
> With wagons, guns, kibitkas at their side.
> By edict of the czar this regiment
> Comes from the east to fight a northern foe;
> That from the north to Caucasus is sent:
> Whither they march, or why, they do not know—
> And no one asks. Here a Mongolian
> Is seen, with slanting eyes and puffy face;
> And there a homesick Lithuanian,
> With pallid brow and slow, uncertain pace.
> Some men have bows, some English muskets hold;
> The Kalmucks carry bowstrings stiff with cold.
> Their officers?—A German in a coach,
> Humming his Schiller's sentimental lays,
> Whacks on the back the men as they approach;
> A Frenchman, whistling his brisk Marseillaise—
> A strayed philosopher—seeks a career,
> And asks the Kalmuck chief, who stands near by,
> How they may get supplies most cheaply here.
> What if from famine half that rabble die?
> Then they can plunder half the treasury;
> And if the deed is hidden carefully,
> The minister will grant them an advance,
> The czar a medal for their skilled finance.

> Now a kibitka suddenly flies by:
> The ambulances, guns, and guards who ride,
> Rush madly from the road as it comes nigh;
> Even the leaders' wagons draw aside.
> Still on and on it flies: the gendarme whacks
> The driver with his fist; the driver thwacks
> The soldiers with his whip; the throng gives way;
> The wheels crush anyone who dares to stay.
> Whither?—Who rides within?—No one will ask.[1]

Similarly in Custine:

"The movements of the men whom I met were stiff and constrained; every gesture expressed a will which was not their own.... Military discipline reigns throughout Russia.... Love and liberty for the heart, brilliancy and variety of colour for the eye, are here unknown.... Fancy can almost descry the shadow of death hovering over this portion of the globe. Now appears a cavalry officer passing at full gallop to bear *an order* to some commanding officer; now a chasseur, carrying *an order* to some provincial governor perhaps at the other extremity of the empire, whither he proceeds in a kibitka.... Next are seen foot soldiers returning from exercise to their quarters, to *receive orders* from their captain.... This automaton population resembles one side of a chess-board, where a single individual causes the movements of all the pieces, but where the adversary is invisible.... Tyranny is the imaginary ailment of the people; the tyrant disguised as a doctor has persuaded them that health is not the natural condition for the civilized man, and that the greater the danger, the more violent must be the cure; it is thus that he maintains the ailment under the pretext of the cure...."[2]

"When Peter the Great established what is here called the *chin*, that is to say, when he applied the military system to the general administration of the empire, he changed his nation into a regiment of mutes, of which he declared himself and successors the hereditary colonels."[3]

Custine repeats almost the same in the chapter entitled "Résumé du voyage":

---

[1] Noyes, *op. cit.*, p. 340.
[2] Custine, *Russia*, Vol. I, pp. 145–6. As the English version is incomplete, the quotation is translated in part by me. When I was writing this study the new English edition had not yet appeared.
[3] Custine, *op. cit.*, p. 147.

"In Russia, all that strikes the eye, everything that passes around, bears the impress of a regularity that is startling; and the first thought that enters the mind of the traveller, when he contemplates this symmetrical system, is that a uniformity so complete, a regularity so contrary to the natural inclinations of men, cannot have been established, and cannot be maintained except by violence. . . . In Russia, the government interferes with everything and vivifies nothing. In that immense empire, the people, if not tranquil, are mute;" [compare with "the people is silent" in Pushkin's *Boris Godunov*], "death hovers over all heads. . . ."[1]

Custine's chess-game corresponds to Mickiewicz's card-game in "The Review of the Army" in the *Digression*:

> As an old gamester still with loving care
> Stacks, shuffles, deals to an imagined foe:
> Although he is deserted and ignored,
> He watches and enjoys how each card falls.
> But e'en the czar himself at last was bored,
> Turned sharp and hid among his generals.[2]

Compare, too, with the same metaphor utilized in the poem *St. Petersburg*:

> Officials, ladies, marshals make their way;
> First, second, fourth, in even sets they pass,
> Like cards thrown from a gamester's hand in play,
> Kings, queens, and knaves, the mighty ruling class!
> Court cards and common cards, both black and red,
> Fall to this side and that.[3]

It would be worth while, in addition, to compare the following passages. In *The Suburbs of the Capital* of Mickiewicz we find:

> Now all is silent here.—The city calls
> The czar in winter, and the courtly flies
> Follow the scent of carrion to their prize.
> Only the winds dance now within these halls,
> Unto the city with its court and czar
> Speeds the kibitka.[4]

[1] *Op. cit.*, Vol. III, pp. 304–5.
[2] Noyes, *op. cit.*, p. 359.
[3] Page 346.
[4] Page 342.

On the same theme Custine writes:

> "It is impossible to describe the dullness of St. Petersburg during the absence of the Emperor. At no time does the city exhibit what may be called gaiety; but without the court, it is a desert. The reader is aware that it is constantly menaced with destruction by the sea. This morning, while traversing its solitary quays and empty streets, I said to myself, 'Surely the city must be about to be inundated; the inhabitants have fled, and the water will soon recover possession of the marsh; this time nature has recognized the efforts of art.' Nothing of the kind: Petersburg is lifeless only because the Emperor is at Peterhof: that is all."[1]

Of striking similarity are the remarks of Mickiewicz and Custine concerning the architecture of Petersburg. The beginning of the poem *St. Petersburg* contains, one might say, a general exposition of this theme:

> In ancient times of Italy and Greece,
> Beneath a temple men sought calm and peace,
> 'Mid holy trees, a wood nymph's spring below;
> Or on the heights took refuge from a foe:
> And thus was builded Athens, Sparta, Rome.
> In Gothic days, beneath a baron's tower,
> Where it might be protected by his power,
> The humble peasant built his cottage home.
> And where some navigable stream flowed by,
> Towns, small at first, with ages towered high.
> These cities were by reverence inspired,
> Or for defense or trading were desired.
> How did the Russian capital begin?[2]

And here is Custine:

> "Elsewhere, great cities were raised in memory of the past: or they originated by themselves, with the aid of circumstances and of history, at least with the help of human calculations; St. Petersburg, in all its magnificence and immensity, is a trophy raised by the Russians to the greatness of the future...."[3]

The idea of Petersburg's ephemeral and fantastic quality is given again, the style and conception being typical of Mickiewicz. For example, in *The Suburbs of the Capital*:

[1] Custine, *op. cit.*, Vol. II, p. 138.
[2] Noyes, *op. cit.*, p. 343.
[3] Custine, *op. cit.*, Vol. I, p. 157.

... Snow is on the ground,
The clocks have thundered twelve from near and far,
And now the winter sun is westward bound.
The spacious heavens their vaulted depths unfold,
Cloudless and silent, empty, pure, and cold;
Quite colorless, a pale, transparent sky,
As lifeless as a frozen traveler's eye.
Above that city which we now draw near
Rise fairy castles gleaming in the sun;
Pillars and walls and balconies appear
Like hanging gardens reared in Babylon.
From out two hundred thousand chimney throats
Upward the smoke in straight, dense columns floats;
These like Carrara marble gleam and shine,
Those glow like rubies with a rosy light.
Aloft the summits perish and unite,
And into balcony and arch entwine,
While roofs and walls of pearl ascend the skies,
Like those illusive cities that arise
From out the Great Sea's waters, calm and clear,
Or in the Libyan desert haze appear:
These from afar the weary travelers see—
They ever seem at hand and ever flee.[1]

Similarly in Custine:

"The slow melting of the tints of twilight, which appeared to perpetuate the day in struggling against an ever-increasing gloom, communicated to all nature a mysterious movement; the low lands of the city, with their structures little raised above the banks of the Neva, seemed to oscillate betwixt the sky and the water, which gave the impression of their being about to vanish in the void. ... That little spot of earth which seemed to detach itself from the water and to tremble upon it like the froth of an inundation, those small, dark, irregular points scarcely observable between the white of the sky and the white of the river, could they form the capital of a vast empire? —or rather, was it not all an optical illusion, a phantasmagoria? ... The whole scene was beautiful;—scarcely any movement, but a solemn calm, a vague inspiration. All the sounds and bustle of ordinary life were interrupted; man had disappeared, the earth remained in the possession of the supernatural powers. There are in these remains of day, these unequal and dying lights of a boreal night, mysteries which I know not how to define, but which explain to me the mythology of the North. ... The spectre of a sleeping city

[1] Noyes, *op. cit.*, pp. 342–3.

reminds me of that ballad of Coleridge, in which the English mariner beholds the phantom of a vessel gliding across the sea. These nocturnal illusions are to the inhabitants of the polar regions what the Fata Morgana, in broad day, is to the men of the South: the colours, the lines, and the hour are different; the illusion is the same."[1]

From the foregoing we see that Custine refers to Coleridge and not to the beautiful picture drawn by Mickiewicz. I should like to advance the supposition that it was perhaps Coleridge who suggested to Mickiewicz, too, the idea of the Fata Morgana, although we do not find anything definite in this respect in the footnote which Mickiewicz added to the passage quoted above from *The Suburbs*:

"In northern cities on cold days, the smoke rises skyward in fantastic forms, making a spectacle similar to the *mirage* that leads astray sailors on the sea and travelers on the Arabian sands. The *mirage* counterfeits now a city, now a village, now a lake or oasis: all objects can be seen very distinctly, but it is impossible to approach them; they always remain at the same distance from the traveler—and at last they vanish."[2]

A penetrating and thorough observer of Russia, such as Custine was, could not have missed Chaadaev in Moscow, or at least could not have failed to become acquainted with his *Philosophical Letters* and his *Apology of a Madman*. In his book Custine relates the story of Chaadaev and reviews the contents of his works. The memoirists of those times affirm that Custine visited Chaadaev in Moscow, but he denies this. Perhaps out of prudence? Perhaps he did not desire to expose Chaadaev to danger. The fact that he described Chaadaev's tragedy with great indignation supports this.[3]

There exists particularly one passage in Custine's book which seems to prove his dependence on Chaadaev. While drawing a general characterization of the Russian moral type, Custine says:

"Notwithstanding the contrasts which I here point out, all resemble each other in one respect—all have levity of character. Among these men of the moment, the projects of the evening are

---

[1] Custine, *op. cit.*, Vol. II, pp. 205–7.
[2] Noyes, *op. cit.*, p. 469. Compare, also, Coleridge's *The Rime of the Ancient Mariner*.
[3] Custine, *op. cit.*, Vol. III, pp. 349–52. See, too, M. Lemke, *Nikolaevskie Žandarmy*, p. 453.

constantly lost in the forgetfulness of the morrow. It may be said that with them the heart is the empire of chance; nothing can stand against their propensity to embrace and to abandon. They live and die without perceiving the serious side of existence. Neither good nor evil seems in their eyes to possess any reality: they can cry, but they cannot be unhappy. . . . Their prompt and contemptuous glance surveys, without admiring, the monuments raised by human intelligence during centuries. They fancy they can place themselves above everything, because they despise everything. Their very praises are insults: they eulogize like people who envy; they prostrate themselves, but always unwillingly, before the objects they believe to be the idols of fashion. But at the first breath of wind, the cloud succeeds the picture, and soon the cloud vanishes in turn. Dust, smoke, and chaotic nothingness are all that can issue from such inconsistent heads. No plant takes root in a soil thus profoundly agitated. Everything is swept away; everything becomes levelled; all is wrapt in vapour. But from this fluid element nothing is finally expelled."[1] And, turning to Chaadaev: "Our memories do not go back further than yesterday; we are, so to speak, strangers to ourselves, we march so singularly through time that the more we advance, the more the yesterdays escape from us forever. . . . New ideas sweep out the old, because they do not originate in the latter, but fall upon us, from where I know not. . . . We grow up, but we do not mature; we advance, but obliquely, that is, in a line leading to no goal. . . . There is something worse than frivolity in our best heads."

Continuing his reasonings, Chaadaev insists on the fact that Russia lacks any tradition, that the feeling of permanent duration is unknown to the Russians, that they have no feeling of solidarity with any other community, that their life is one without any experience or provision, without ideas attached to the past or the future.

"There is nothing general in our heads. Everything is individual, everything is volatile and incomplete. . . .

Certain foreigners praised us for possessing a sort of careless temerity which is to be observed especially in the lower classes of the nation. They were unaware that the same principle which renders us so audacious is sometimes the cause of our being incapable of deep thinking or of perseverance; they did not understand that the thing which makes us so indifferent to the hazards of life at the same time makes us indifferent to every good, to every evil, to every

[1] Custine, *op. cit.*, pp. 73–4.

truth, to every lie, thus depriving us of all the powerful energies which urge men to follow the road of improvement; they did not see that, with us, we must painfully admit, even the superior classes are not exempt from the vices which elsewhere belong only to the lowest classes...."[1]

We see that three men, a Pole, a Frenchman, and a Russian, are agreed in their pessimism. However, Custine was aware of the opinions of the Russian and the Pole, so that he simply developed what he had learned from them. What are we to say about the Russian and the Pole? One has to remember, of course, that at the time when Chaadaev and Mickiewicz made their pessimistic evaluation of the historical fate of the Russian nation, Russia was just laying the foundations for her later great cultural achievements in every field. These achievements were the result of the co-operation with the West by the Russian cultivated classes.

Both Chaadaev and Mickiewicz were right as far as the past of Russia was concerned. The silent Russian genius was forced to wait until the magic wand of Europe touched its heart and the howling of Avvakum (we must not forget that Avvakum was a contemporary of Pascal) became the fascinating symphony of Tolstoy and Dostoevsky.

But the class which was responsible for these great cultural achievements has disappeared, and here again the prophecy of Mickiewicz comes to mind. The reader will remember the end of his wonderful poem, *The Monument of Peter the Great*, in which he describes Falconet's "Bronze Horseman":

> His charger's reins Czar Peter has released;
> He has been flying down the road, perchance,
> And here the precipice checks his advance.
> With hoofs aloft now stands the maddened beast,
> Champing its bit unchecked, with slackened rein:
> You guess that it will fall and be destroyed.
> Thus it has galloped long, with tossing mane,
> Like a cascade, leaping into the void,
> That, fettered by the frost, hangs dizzily.
> But soon will shine the sun of liberty,
> And from the west a wind will warm this land.—
> Will the cascade of tyranny then stand?

and the following lines in *The Road to Russia*:

[1] *Sočinenija Čaadaeva, op. cit.*, Vol. I, pp. 80–3.

> But when the sun of liberty shall rise,
> What kind of insect then will greet the light?
> Will a bright butterfly soar from the earth,
> Or a dull moth, of dark, uncleanly birth?[1]

* * * * *

In the meantime, at a point following Mickiewicz's *Digression* and Chaadaev's *Philosophical Letters*, but preceding Custine's *Russia*—in 1838—M. Yu. Lermontov wrote his poem "Meditation", which was published in 1839. Among all of the great Russian literary figures, Lermontov, second only to Pushkin in fame, was one of the most attractive and, at the same time, tragic personalities on the Russian scene. During his short life he was continually in conflict with Russian society and autocracy. He was a man of great moral dignity and courage, endowed with a truly brilliant mind. Lermontov was a romantic poet, perhaps the only typical romantic in Russian poetry. In his romanticism one may find all of the characteristic literary traits of the school, especially a consistently maintained ideology founded on the western-European romantic concept of the prestige of the individual and of the poet. Lermontov's death was a result of the constant challenge hurled at Fate by this deep pessimist, who felt lost in the darkness of post-Decembrist Russia. Nicholas I's attitude toward the poet was no less vehement than his attitude toward Chaadaev. It suffices to say that when the Emperor read the military report of Lermontov's death he wrote on it simply: "A dog's death for a dog."

Throughout the nineteenth century, and even later, "Meditation" continued to be the sensation of Russian poetry. It was usually compared with the *Iambes* of Auguste Barbier, which the Russian poet loved passionately, especially the fragment "Bianca" which is part of the poem *Il Pianto*, written in 1833.

It might be possible to find in Lermontov's "Meditation" some reminiscences from Barbier. I believe, however, that the dependence on Chaadaev is much more obvious and interesting.

The Russian critics, without exception, beginning with Belinsky and ending with Mikhaylovsky and Veselovsky, made one mistake: they understood only literally the overture of the poem "With sorrow am I looking at our generation", and they argued with the poet on the subject of so sombre an evaluation of the brilliant generation of the 'thirties and 'forties to which the poet himself belonged. I believe that they misunderstood the significance of this line: perhaps the poet, in order to dupe the censor, wrote about "our generation" having in mind Russia in general. This becomes particularly clear against the back-

---

[1] Noyes, *op. cit.*, pp. 350 and 339.

ground of Chaadaev's *Philosophical Letter* and Mickiewicz's *Digression*. The poem speaks for itself:

> With sorrow I look at our generation.
> Its future is either empty or dark;
> Meanwhile, under the weight of knowledge and doubt,
> In inactivity it will grow old.
> We are rich, even from the cradle,
> In the mistakes of our fathers and in their tardy understanding;
> And life tires us, as a straight and aimless road,
> As a banquet at a fête which is not ours.
> Toward good and evil shamefully indifferent,
> At the beginning of the course we fade away without fight.
> Before danger we are ignominious poltroons,
> And toward power—despised slaves.
> Thus, the lean fruit, ripe before its time,
> Does not give pleasure to our taste and eyes,
> It hangs among the flowers as an orphaned newcomer,
> And the hour of their beauty is the hour of its falling!
> Our intellect is consumed by a sterile science,
> We hide from friends and neighbours
> The best hopes and noble voice
> Behind passions ridiculed by incredulity.
> Scarcely did we touch the cup of pleasure,
> But our young forces were not preserved:
> From every joy, afraid of saturation,
> We have forever extracted the best juices.
> The dreams of poetry, art's masterpieces
> Do not awaken in our minds sweet enthusiasm;
> With avidity we store in our breast the remnant of feeling—
> This useless treasure buried by our avarice.
> We love and hate by accident,
> We do not sacrifice anything to hatred or to love,
> And in the soul there reigns a mysterious coldness,
> When fire burns within our blood.
> And dull for us are our ancestors' joys,
> Their honest and childish debaucheries;
> And to the grave we hurry without happiness and glory,
> Looking backwards with irony and laughter.
> As a crowd, morose and quickly forgotten,
> We shall pass through the world without trace,
> Leaving to the ages no fertile thought,
> Nor any work by a genius begun.
> Our ashes will be insulted by a descendant,
> With the severity of a judge and citizen,
> In contemptuous verse, and with a bitter,
> Mocking smile, a wastrel father by his betrayed son.

Mikhaylovsky, the famous Russian critic of the second part of the nineteenth century, tried to defend the poet's attack against "enlightenment", and affirmed that the Russian critics confused the proper meaning of this poem with their own speculations:

"One has to know how to read. Lermontov clearly showed the issue of dissension between reason and emotion which has to be found in the third human spiritual element—in the will, which, uniting reason and emotion, positively demands action and fight."[1]

Alexey Veselovsky launched an argument against this defense:

"It is a severe and near-sighted sentence; the faded generation, which dried its brain and supposedly lost its forces beneath the burden of knowledge and doubt, was the generation which produced the literature and social movement of the 'forties. To this generation there belonged the circle of Belinsky and his friends, whom the poet did not know, although he was their schoolmate; to this generation there belonged Herzen's group and the young Granovsky."[2]

Of course, this pathetic indignation might be justified if one saw in this poem a judgment of this very generation. It might even be pointed out that Pushkin himself belonged to this generation. But no, the pessimism of this poem goes farther and reaches deeper. It is a judgment of Russia, of the historical Russian moral type. It is a judgment which conforms entirely with Chaadaev's, Mickiewicz's and Custine's writings. Hence, a further conclusion: the proper and essential significance of this poem is not to be found in the evaluation of a certain definite period of Russian history; the poet, with the help of a few sentences in the beginning and at the end of the poem, concealed a more general content which tends to offer a universal conception of the Russian historical, cultural type.

As I have previously mentioned, Lermontov's "Meditation" appeared in 1839 in the first issue of *Notes of the Fatherland*. In July, 1839, Custine arrived in Russia.[3] Although he did not devote much space to Russian literature in his study *Russia*, he did mention Pushkin. He even compared him to Mickiewicz, recognizing the latter as "more Slavic".[4] But what is more important in this case is that he not only

---

[1] N. K. Mikhajlovskij, "Geroj bezvremen'ja". See *Sočinenija N. K. Mikhajlovskago* (St. Petersburg, 1897), Vol. V, pp. 320–1.
[2] A. N. Veselovskij, *Zapadnoe vlijanie v novoj russkoj literature*, Moscow, p. 185.
[3] Custine, *op. cit.*, Vol. I.
[4] *Ibid.*, Vol. II, p. 87.

knew Pushkin (whom he read in French translations) but he knew Lermontov's poem on the death of Pushkin, at least by hearsay. "I have read the verses..." says Custine's informant, from whom Custine cites the detailed story of the painful fate of Lermontov, which was the consequence of his risky publication.[1] Besides, he finds this poem remarkable.[2] Custine does not mention "Meditation", but it would be rather difficult to imagine that he did not hear about this poem which appeared just before his arrival in Russia and which created such a sensation following immediately upon the tempest caused by Chaadaev. Lermontov was too well known in Moscow and Petersburg salons, and the content of his poem was too close to the views held by Custine himself to have passed unnoticed. The fame and popularity of Lermontov was definitely established in 1837, and the poet owed this precisely to his poem "On the Death of the Poet".[3]

I cannot insist that Custine was repeating from the "Meditation". I simply believe that this meditative, reflective poem by Lermontov further confirmed and strengthened Custine's own opinions about the Russian character and perhaps even suggested some ideas to him. Here are a few examples of these correspondences:

"... Nowhere have the mental maladies engendered in the soul by ennui—that passion of men who have no passions—appeared to men so serious or so frequent as among the higher classes in Russia: it may be said that society has here commenced by its abuses.... They never labour to produce results useful to others, but always to obtain some recompense for themselves. Creative genius has been denied them; the enthusiasm which produces the sublime is to them unknown.... Time and the world, engagements and affairs, are forgotten; the duties of society are abolished; one single interest remains—the interest of the moment.... In matters of the affections, the Russians are the gentlest wild beasts that are to be seen on earth; and their well-concealed claws unfortunately divest them of none of their charms.... Civilization, which elsewhere elevates the mind, here perverts it. It would have been better for the Russians had they remained savages:—to polish slaves is to betray society."[4]

Lermontov stressed the strange apathy regarding hatred and love in the Russians, the astonishing coldness in the soul, "when fire burns

[1] *Ibid.*, pp. 85–6.
[2] *Loc. cit.*
[3] C. Zgorzelski, "Lermontow Puszkinowi", in *Puszkin, 1837–1937*, published by The Polish Society for Studies of Eastern Europe and the Near East (Cracow, 1939), Vol. I, p. 213.
[4] Custine, *op. cit.*, Vol. III, pp. 64, 67, 70, 72, 78.

within our blood". Custine seizes on this theme in his reference to the ferocious cruelty of the Russian peasant:

"Murder is designed and executed in an orderly manner; no rage, no emotion, no words: a calm is preserved, more terrible than the delirium of hate. They struggle with, overthrow, trample, and destroy each other with the steady regularity of machines turning upon their pivots. This physical impassibility in the midst of the most violent scenes, this monstrous audacity in the conception, and calmness in the execution, this silent passion and speechless fanaticism is, if one might so express it, the innocence of crime. A certain order, contrary to nature, presides in this strange country over the most monstrous excesses...."[1]

Lermontov's "Meditation" was not written extemporaneously, without preparation or poetical antecedents. V. M. Fisher's outstanding study devoted to Lermontov's *ars poetica* points out how frequently poetical auto-reminiscences occur in Lermontov. They are no less frequent than in Pushkin, in whom they were pointed out by Khodasevich in his brilliant study entitled *Pushkin's Poetical Household*. Indeed, Lermontov's poetry offers us very interesting material for observation. The ramifications of auto-reminiscences, the transfer of poetical formulations from one piece to another, the thematic and phraseological filiations, all these appear very frequently. And this holds true for "Meditation".

I once listed all the poet's poems which may be connected with "Meditation". My purpose was to show that the views which Lermontov expressed in his "Meditation" were not at all casual or accidental.[2]

Nine years earlier, in 1830, appeared the truly prophetic poem "Prediction", in Lermontov's youthful years. It is related at least by the pessimistic view expressed on Russia and her future.

---

[1] *Ibid.*, Vol. II, p. 93.
[2] For the general problem of auto-reminiscences occurring in Lermontov's poetry, see V. M. Fisher, "Poetika Lermontova", in *Venok M. Ju. Lermontovu* (Moscow-Petrograd: 1914), pp. 196–237. My own list of poems connected with the "Meditation" is as follows: "Pover' ničtožestvo est' blago v zdešnem svete" (1829), "Gljažu na buduščnost' s bojazn'ju" (1837), "On byl rožděn dlja sčast'ja, dlja molitv" (1832). In these works one notices a phraseology similar to that of the "Meditation", as well as an identically reflective, philosophic and lyric atmosphere. The same may be said about the poems "K drugu, Epilog k D-vu" (1829), "Monolog" (1829), "Nastanet den'—i mirom osužděnnyj" (1830), "Dlja čego ja ne rodilsja ètoj sineju volnoj" (1832), poems in which there resounds a sharp invective against the North and Petersburg, all the more characteristic because occasional.

> A year will come, a black year for Russia,
> When the crown of czars will fall,
> The mob will forget its former love for them,
> And the food for many will be death and blood;
> When children and innocent women shall go
> Unprotected by the dethroned law;
> When the plague, rising from foul, dead bodies,
> Shall spread among the mournful villages,
> With its handkerchief waving forth
> The people from their huts;
> And hunger shall torture this poor land:
> And crimson shall colour the river's waves. . . .
> On that day a powerful man will appear,
> And you will know and understand
> Why he holds a steel blade in hand.
> Woe unto you! Your groan
> Will only make him laugh;
> And everything will be black and terrible in him,
> Like his cloak and his high forehead.

This youthful poem simply shows a certain predisposition of Lermontov to treat historiosophic themes in an apocalyptic style which was probably derived from Byron's "prophecies". What is important here above all is the pessimism of the poet as far as Russia is concerned. We see that this pessimism endured: "Meditation" is the most eloquent proof of this.

It is admissible, perhaps, to advance the supposition that while writing his "Meditation", Lermontov knew not only the content of Chaadaev's *Letters*, with which "Meditation" has obvious relationship, but also Mickiewiez's *Digression*, and that the ideological refutation of Russia contained in the *Digression* left traces in "Meditation". This is not quite an arbitrary conjecture. Lermontov knew Mickiewicz. He translated him and appropriated some of Mickiewicz's metaphors and images. Spasowicz, with his customary perspicacity and his wonderful gift of observation, ferreted out numerous evidences of the influence of Mickiewicz on Lermontov.[1]

Besides, we do not find any anti-Polish tendencies in Lermontov's poetry. On the contrary, there appear in the novel *Princess Ligovskaya* two incidental characters with historical Polish names: Krasiński and Branicki, the first of whom is drawn with great sympathy. These "Polonica" are not accidental at all: Lermontov was tied by a sincere friendship to the two brothers Aleksander and Ksawery Branicki.[2]

---

[1] W. Spasowicz, "Bajronizm Lermontowa" (1888), *Pisma* (Petersburg, 1892), pp. 298–300.

[2] *Polski Słownik Biograficzny*, Polska Akademia Umiejętności, Vol. II, pp. 397, 408–9.

Lermontov in the late thirties
Portrait by I. Astafyev (1883)

Aleksander, who lived in Petersburg, where he owned a house on the Nevsky Prospect,[1] played, incidentally, a casual rôle in the duel which Lermontov fought with Baron Ernest de Barante, son of the French ambassador in Petersburg at that time. The rôle of Aleksander Branicki in this episode was, as I have pointed out, only a casual one—the deposition given by him in this connection[2] proves this clearly—but the episode itself indicates that Lermontov and Aleksander were close friends.

Of greater interest, it seems, was the friendship between the poet and Ksawery Branicki, primarily because Ksawery had closer ties with the poet. He was not an average man. His rôle in the Polish Emigration, his relations with Mickiewicz, Herzen and others, prove this, not to mention his French publications which appeared at the end of his life in Paris. Unfortunately, we do not know very much about his friendship with Lermontov. In fact, we know only as much as he himself disclosed in the preface to his book *Les Nationalités slaves*, and there he did not tell very much. What he said about Lermontov was connected with the information (unfortunately, also quite summary) which he gave in the same preface about the "circle of the sixteen" to which both belonged in Petersburg. There is little known about this extremely interesting organization, the quality of its members suggesting its level. It consisted of persons belonging to the intellectual élite of the "golden youth" of Petersburg of those times. Not very much has as yet been published about this secret organization,[3] but let us see what Branicki has to say about it. His book *Les Nationalités slaves* was written in the form of letters addressed to Father I. S. Gagarin, S.J. The famous Jesuit, Prince I. S. Gagarin, was a friend of Ksawery Branicki. In the *lettre préliminaire*, written as a preface to the book, Branicki wrote:

> "In the year of our Lord 1839, there was in St. Petersburg a society of young men who were called, because of their number, 'The Sixteen'. Their comradeship was formed either on university benches or in the battalions of the Caucasian army. Every night after the theatre or a ball, they would meet at one or another's place. There, after a frugal supper, smoking their cigars, they commented on the events of the day, talked about everything, discussed every-

---

[1] P. S. Ščegolev, *Kniga o Lermontove* ("Priboj", 1929), Vol. II, pp. 47–8.
[2] Ščegolev, *op. cit.*, pp. 51–2.
Dr. M. Grydzewski considers that A. Branicki's rôle in this episode was not casual as, besides having been Lermontov's second, Branicki arranged Barante's encounter with Lermontov in the guard-room. (Cf. "Silva Rerum", *Wiadomości*, London, 5 August, 1951, p. 4.)
[3] E. G. Gerštein, "Lermontov i kružok šestnadcati", in *Žizn' i tvorčestvo M. Ju. Lermontova*, pod red. N. L. Brodskogo i dr. (Moscow, 1941), Vol. I, pp. 77–125. This article contains the main bibliographical sources connected with this subject.

thing with perfect freedom of speech—as though the Third Section of the Imperial Chancellery did not exist at all, so sure were they of each one's discretion. We belonged to the sincere and gay association of The Sixteen: you, my Reverend Father, who in those times were an embassy secretary, and myself, who wore the uniform of the Imperial Guard. How few of those friends, so full of life in those days, so exuberant in their youth, remain today on this earth, where a long and happy existence seemed vouchsafed them. Lermontov, exiled to the Caucasus for having written an admirable poem on Pushkin's death, fell in 1841 in a duel like the great poet of whom he sang...."

Continuing further, Branicki mentions Prince A. Dolgoruky, Gervais, Frédricks, "Mongo" Stolypin, Prince S. Dolgoruky ("le beau"), Count Shuvalov, and, lastly, Minister Valuev.[1]

[1] Xavier Branicki, *Les Nationalités slaves* (Paris, 1879), pp. 1–3. Apropos, I should like to mention that Branicki's book is very interesting, written in a lively manner and contains many anecdotic details which the author knew through his wide connections. He did not break with the Russians after his emigration from Russia, continuing to visit Bakunin in London, maintaining constant contact with Herzen, whom he helped at a certain period (at the court of Napoleon III) to obtain authorization for a sojourn in Paris. He gave rather detailed information about his Russian relations in the last chapters of his book, in which he dealt with Russian history. Herzen often mentions him in *Byloe i dumy*. See more about Ksawery Branicki in the *Polski Słownik Biograficzny* (Polska Akad. Um.), Vol. II, pp. 48–9, as well as in the commentary of L. B. Kamenev contained in the "Academia" edition of *Byloe i dumy*, Vol. III, p. 354. This commentary, however, makes some inexact statements. For instance, Kamenev, when referring to Shchegolev (*Kniga o Lermontove*), confuses Ksawery Branicki with his brother, Aleksander. The latter, as we know, took part in Lermontov's duel with de Barante, and not Ksawery, as Kamenev affirms. (See *Polski Słownik Biograficzny, ibid.*, p. 397). In addition, Kamenev states that it was Ksawery who appeared in Lermontov's *Princess Ligovskaya*. We do not know this—the rôle of the hero bearing the name of Branicki is so episodic and his characterization so superficial that it would be difficult to decide which of the two Branicki brothers Lermontov had in mind. (Compare the beginning and the end of Chapter VI.) In favour of Ksawery is the fact that the Branicki of the novel is an officer of the artillery, whereas Aleksander never served in the Russian army. (See *Kniga o Lermontove*, p. 52.) Ksawery, on the contrary, served in exactly the same regiment of the hussars of the guard in which Lermontov was stationed before his exile to the Caucasus. I shall add, finally, that in the second volume of Professor B. M. Eichenbaum's edition of Lermontov's works one may find a reproduction of an excellent pencil sketch of Ksawery Branicki made by a famous amateur painter of those times, Prince G. Gagarin. (See Lermontov, M. Ju., *Polnoe sobranie sočinenij*, "Academia", 1936, Vol. II, pp. 196–7.) I should also like to add that Ksawery Branicki has given incorrect information about the time and circumstances of the last exile of Lermontov to the Caucasus. As is generally known, after his duel with de Barante, in 1840, Lermontov was transferred from the guard to one of the line regiments in the Caucasus (the real cause of this exile was the fact that at a masquerade in Petersburg he offended one of the daughters of Nicholas I, having returned to Petersburg in 1838 from his first exile, which was caused by his poem about Pushkin written in 1837). With regard to Ksawery Branicki, there are additional details to be found in the article of E. G. Gershtein referred to previously.

I believe that it was Ksawery Branicki who was Lermontov's informant, and a very intelligent one, in Polish affairs, and that through him the poet could have been acquainted with Mickiewicz's *Digression*. This is, of course, only a supposition, but it seems to me to be an admissible one. In any case, Lermontov undoubtedly knew the content of Chaadaev's *Philosophical Letters*, and it is probable, I repeat, that Mickiewicz's satires were also known to him.

As far as Custine's interpretation of the Russian character is concerned, which I showed could have been suggested to him by Chaadaev, Lermontov, and also Mickiewicz, one must not forget Pushkin's *Eugene Onegin*, in which the poet stressed the "early coolness" of his hero, his cynicism, his sentimental instability, his servile obedience to the most futile conventions which stilled the voice of his conscience. In vain did Dostoevsky try to justify Onegin's strange and morally exotic behaviour with the help of speculations on the theme of the Russian pilgrim. Let us, rather, listen to Pushkin himself. As complacent and pardoning as the poet seems to be, as delicate as is his brush in this charming water colour, this novel in verse, the poet remains true to his extraordinary knowledge of life and man. He does not impose his own judgment of his hero, but he as if whispers it through the doubts of Tatyana:

> So Tanya bit by bit is learning
> The truth, and, God be praised, can see
> At last for whom her heart is yearning
> By Fate's imperious decree.
> A danger to all lovely ladies,
> Is he from Heaven or from Hades?
> This strange and sorry character,
> Angel or fiend, as you prefer,
> What is he? A mere imitation,
> A Muscovite in Harold's cloak,
> A wretched ghost, a foreign joke
> But with a new interpretation,
> A lexicon of snobbery
> And fashion, or a parody?
>
> Has she the answer to the riddle
> And has she found *the word*?[1]

* * * * *

[1] *Works of Alexander Pushkin*, edited by A. Yarmolinsky (New York: Random House, 1936), p. 259.

Now we have to face a purely Russian-Polish historical episode, an important and a puzzling one. I have in mind a mysterious poem drafted by Pushkin—an enigma which still remains unsolved. I am somewhat embarrassed as I, too, cannot put forward any definite solution. I can only suggest two possible answers. In the forthcoming discussion we shall meet again with some of our friends.

Probably very soon after 1831, following the collapse of the Polish Insurrection, or perhaps a little later, Pushkin drafted a poem which he never completed. In this sketch, which is rather an outline, one finds only a few complete sentences. Yet the poem is clearly significant, although wrapped in mystery.

This fragment is a "dramatic portrait" of a Russian who remained a steadfast friend of Poland from the very beginning to the end of the Insurrection of 1830–1831. Polish triumphs were his triumphs. The Polish defeat was his defeat. In his usual manner, the poet framed the story of the feelings of this mysterious Russian Polonophil in compact, synthetic and eloquent formulations. What remains as an enigma is whom Pushkin had in mind. Let us turn to this brief outline:

> By education you enlightened your mind,
> You saw the face of truth
> And the sacred mysteries of the world,
> And tenderly you loved the foreign people,
> And wisely hated your own nation.
> When the silent Warsaw arose
> And was delirious from revolt,
> And a mortal struggle started
> With the shout, 'Poland is not yet lost.'
> When our blood, like a river, flowed,
> When the French babbler howled in the Chair,
> You drank to the health of Lelewel,
> You glorified Lelewel,
> You rubbed your hands at our defeats,
> With cunning laughter you listened to the news
> When [our army] galloped in retreat
> And the standards of our honour perished.
> But when the Warsaw revolt was broken,
> You collapsed, and woefully did you weep,
> Like the Jew over Jerusalem.[1]

These are only fragments, yet how loudly they speak, how full they are of emotion and tension. As a matter of fact, this outline contains more pathos than the odes, "To the Calumniators of Russia" and "The Anniversary of Borodino". Why did not Pushkin finish this work; it

[1] *Puškin*, S. A. Vengerov's edition, Vol. III, pp. 508–9.

would have been a wonderful counter-part to the poem "Before the sacred tomb . . ." which opens Pushkin's anti-Polish trilogy. In that poem the poet expressed his deep anxiety regarding the result of the war against Poland and the fate of the Russian state: the poet waved the standards of 1812, as if desirous of calming his own national agony with the rustling of these glorious banners of the past. The fragment gives the picture of a man spiritually bound to the enemy, and how strong these bonds are! After the defeat of the enemy, he sobbed "like a Jew over Jerusalem". Who could have felt, who could have thought in such a manner in those crucial historical days? Who could so dramatically and even tragically have lived through that crisis? Whence came this strange and unexpected moral solidarity of a Muscovite with the Warsaw revolt? To a certain degree the beginning of the fragment explains this phenomenon: "By education you enlightened your mind, —you saw the face of truth—And the sacred mysteries of the world,— And tenderly you loved the foreign people,—And wisely hated your own nation." This is rather an exhaustive explanation of the attitude of our mysterious Russian toward Poland, which becomes more or less comprehensible against the background of this information. This fragment represents a "little tragedy". It deals with the conflict in the life of an individual, inwardly torn by two contradictory sentiments; it is a conflict between the individual and the collectivity, between the individual and the majority of the nation to which he belongs. In this sketch every word is important, weighty, loaded with great significance. The poet speaks about "hatred in wisdom". What does it mean? Such hatred might originate only from an ardent love. Such criticism of one's people might arise only from passionate patriotism. An ardent and deep attachment to the essential spirit of one's nation and to its historical tradition—both, of course, always being regarded subjectively—might, under certain conditions, change into a diametrically opposite feeling—hatred. But hatred of what and of whom?—either of the present national mass, or of the so-called official representatives responsible for the fate of the nation. It might occur when, in the conception of such a patriotic individual, either the masses or those official representatives sully the true spirit of the nation and violate national traditions.

It is obvious that Pushkin did not have a vulgar traitor, a spy, or a betrayer, in mind. However, in this case there appears also another element, to a certain degree a specifically Russian element: the pathetic feeling of belonging to Europe, to its universalistic civilization. In some individuals this feeling might have become stronger than the national one. And naturally, I do not have in mind such an assertion as that of Ivanushka in Fonvizin's *Brigadier*: "My body was born in Russia, but my spirit belongs to the French crown." I am thinking about a really great inner dissension in a certain type of Russian Westerner. The problem here is complicated. Peter the Great is responsible for this. The feeling of belonging to European civilization is followed by another: the feeling of freedom from the national past, from a rejected past. This is a special comment on the Russian universalistic Messianism of the nineteenth century. Dostoevsky gives the best expression of this in Versilov's talk with the Raw Youth:

" 'I emigrated,' he went on, 'and I regretted nothing I had left behind. I had served Russia to the utmost of my abilities as long as I was there. When I went away I served her far more than if I had remained only a Russian just as the Frenchman at that time was only a Frenchman, and a German only a German. In Europe they don't understand that yet. Europe has created a noble type of Frenchman, of Englishman, and of German, but of the man of the future she scarcely knows at present. And, I fancy, so far she does not want to know. And that one can well imagine; they are not free and we are free. I, with my Russian melancholy, was the only one free in Europe. Take note, my dear, of a strange fact. Every Frenchman can serve not only his France, but humanity, only on condition that he remains French to the utmost possible degree, and it's the same for the Englishman and the German. Only to the Russian, even in our day, has been vouchsafed the capacity to become most of all Russian only when he is most European, and this is true even in our day; that is, long before the millennium has been reached. That is the most essential difference between us Russians and all the rest, and in that respect the position in Russia is as nowhere else. I am in France a Frenchman, with a German I am a German, with the ancient Greeks, I am a Greek, and by that very fact I am most typically a Russian. By that very fact I am a true Russian, and am most truly serving Russia, for I am bringing out her leading idea. I am a pioneer of that idea.

'I was an emigrant then, but had I forsaken Russia? No, I was still serving her. What though I did nothing in Europe, what if I only went there as a wanderer (indeed, I know that was so), it was enough that I went there with my thought and my consciousness. I carried thither my Russian melancholy. Oh, it was not only the bloodshed in those days that appalled me, and it was not the Tuileries, but all that was bound to follow it. They are doomed to strife for a long time yet, because they are still too German and too French, and have not yet finished struggling in those national characters. And I regret the destruction that must come before they have finished. To the Russian, Europe is as precious as Russia, every stone in her is cherished and dear. No one could love Russia more than I do, but I never reproached myself that Venice, Rome, Paris, the treasures of their arts and sciences, their whole history, are dearer to me than Russia.' "[1]

Yet this is still not enough for Dostoevsky, for here is his amazing conclusion:

" 'Oh, those old stones of foreign lands, those wonders of God's ancient world, those fragments of holy marvels, are dear to the Russian, and are even dearer to us than to the inhabitants of those lands themselves! They now have other thoughts and other feelings, and they have ceased to treasure the old stones.... There the conservative struggles only for existence, and the vitriol-thrower is only fighting for a crust of bread. Only Russia lives not for herself, but for an idea, and you must admit, my dear, the remarkable fact that for almost the last hundred years Russia has lived absolutely not for herself, but only for the other states of Europe! And what of them? Oh, they are doomed to pass through fearful agonies before they attain the Kingdom of God.' "[2]

Let us return, however, to Pushkin's fragment. There we have someone who wisely hated his own nation. It took Pushkin to reveal such a powerful and significant fact. This feeling was not alien to Pushkin himself. He knew it, as did later Potugin, Turgenev's hero in *Smoke*, who had the following to say about Russia: "I love and I hate her at the same time." Dostoevsky knew it too, for he ordered Versilov "to love Russia and for this reason to reject her". In addition, such motifs of negation, refutation, and passionate criticism of one's country appeared quite frequently in Poland. It will suffice to mention Słowacki, Wyspiański, Kasprowicz and Żeromski.

In the particular case of the fragment, Pushkin was concerned with some definite person, with someone who, at an historical moment, broke off morally with his nation. This is a grave affair. Theoretically it is possible in every country, but, naturally, only complete disinterestedness may accompany such a gesture—this is the condition *sine qua*

---

[1] F. Dostoevsky, *A Raw Youth*, translated by Constance Garnett, Part III, ch. 7. Compare also the following statement of Belinsky: "We are people without a fatherland—no, even worse than without a fatherland. We are people whose fatherland is a phantom, and is it a wonder that we ourselves are phantoms, that our friendships, our loves, our efforts, our activities—are all phantoms." (Letter to V. P. Botkin of 8 September, 1841.) See V. G. Belinskij, *Izbrannye sočinenija* (Moscow: Ogiz, 1947), p. 645.

[2] *Ibid*. Compare Ivan Karamazov's reasonings on the same subject.

non—or there would be no tragedy. The plot of this "little tragedy" is as follows: a highly cultivated person, greatly concerned with the cultural and moral fate of his nation and closely bound to Western civilization, suddenly finds himself in the midst of great historical events —Russia's "mortal fight" against the West. By its senseless injustice and the wrongs it inflicts on its own and foreign peoples, by its utilitarianism and chauvinism, the majority of his nation succeeds in provoking such an aversion and irritability in this man who feels so differently from the society, to which he no longer morally belongs and which he can no longer bear, that he begins to seek an escape. And in this way every process of "internal emigration" starts. The external emigration follows, if and whenever it is feasible. There were and there remain many such interior émigrés, naturally recruited from the cultural élite in every country. In our times they are almost everywhere. In the epoch of Nicholas I there were quite a few of them in Russia. Yet in the above instance Pushkin grasped a rather rare phenomenon, rare in the sense that the hatred for Russia was wed to an enthusiasm for Poland, that the emotional crisis took place during a war.

I have already indicated that these feelings were not quite foreign to Pushkin himself. However, with one reservation—this feeling automatically vanished at the moment that the poet came into contact with non-Russians. Then the surge of tribal pride overwhelmed him entirely. He once wrote to Vyazemsky: "I despise my country from its head to its toes, but I am angry when a foreigner shares my feeling."[1]

Thus, we are now face to face with the question: Whom had Pushkin in mind when he wrote his poem? Who was that unusual Russian, who in 1830–1831, in Russia, drank to the health of Lelewel?

Prince Vyazemsky might be considered. We know how sharply he reacted to the anti-Polish poems of Pushkin and Zhukovsky. We know how worried and how indignant he was about both poets.[2]

It would also be possible to consider Alexander Turgenev.[3] I shall show below Vyazemsky's and Turgenev's eloquent criticism of Pushkin's and Zhukovsky's anti-Polish poems. Of the two, Vyazemsky was the stronger in his condemnation.

Another supposition was advanced, a long time ago, that the mysterious "Polonophil" in Pushkin's fragment was none other than Chaadaev. Bartenev[4] presented such an opinion. This is a very tempting point of view, particularly in the light of the phrases: "And tenderly you loved the foreign people, and wisely hated your own

---

[1] W. Lednicki, *Aleksander Puszkin*, p. 99.
[2] *Ibid.*, pp. 139–45.
[3] *Loc. cit.*
[4] *Puškin*, Vengerov's edition, Vol. VI, p. 468.

Pushkin in 1827
Engraving by N. Utkin after portrait by O. Kiprensky

nation", as well as the words, "You saw the face of truth and the sacred mysteries of the world", which induce us to share Bartenev's views.

Chaadaev, immediately after the publication of the *Philosophical Letter* in *The Telescope* in 1836 (it is to be noted that we do not know when Pushkin wrote his fragment: it could just as well have been written at the end of 1831 as in 1836), was considered an enemy of his nation. Such was the prevailing opinion in the wide spheres of society and in governmental circles.

"Never," says Chaadaev's biographer, N. I. Zhikharev, "since reading and writing began in Russia, never since our own printed texts and enlightenment appeared in Russia, had any literary or scientific event, the death of Pushkin not excepted, produced such a tremendous effect and had such wide repercussions; never had the news of such an event spread with such speed and so much noise. For almost a whole month there was not a single house in Moscow in which they did not talk about 'Chaadaev's article' and 'Chaadaev's story': even people who were never busy with any literary affairs; complete ignoramuses; ladies of society whose intellectual level was not so very different from that of their cooks and protégées; all kinds of petty clerks and small officials, plunged in bribery and fraud; dull, unpolished, half-insane, hypocritical bigots, fanatics, devotees, who became wild and grey in drunkenness, debauchery and prejudice; young 'saviours of the country', and old patriots—all these people united in one howling of curses and contempt for a man who dared to offend Russia."[1]

The main accusation against Chaadaev was that he "hated Russia". The head of the police, General Benckendorff, when editing the order of Nicholas I, in a letter about this affair to the Governor-General of Moscow, Prince D. V. Golitsyn, expressed the general view: "This article, known to Your Excellency, of course, provoked stupefaction among the inhabitants of Moscow. This article spoke about Russia, about the Russian nation, about its concepts, fate and history with such contempt that it is difficult to realize how a Russian could lower himself to such a degree as to write something like this."[2] In his pertinent book Lemke quotes many more official and private opinions

---

[1] M. Žikharev, "P. Ja. Čaadaev—Iz vospominanij sovremennika", in *Vestnik Evropy*, 1871, Vol. V, pp. 31–2. See also the account of the same events in Custine, *op. cit.*, Vol. III, pp. 349–52.
[2] M. Lemke, *Nikolaevskie žandarmy i literatura 1826–1855 gg.*, izd. S. V. Bunina, 1908, pp. 413–14.

of this same kind. A colourful account of the Chaadaev story is also contained in Kucharzewski's book.[1]

Now to return to Chaadaev as the possible "Polonophil" appearing incognito in the fragment—one would be permitted, on the basis of the above facts, to come to the conclusion that we are right to support this hypothesis. There are, however, some other texts, facts and arguments which I have not yet mentioned.

Let us begin with the texts, which might justify connecting the first phrases of Pushkin's fragment with Chaadaev. I am interested, first of all, in the "tender love for foreign people" and the "wise hatred for one's own", that is, in the peculiar national feelings in Chaadaev which were in conflict with the feelings of the collectivity. Even before the storm, in 1835, Chaadaev wrote to A. I. Turgenev:

"At the present moment a peculiar operation is taking place in our spirits. A kind of nationality is being worked out which, as it cannot be based on anything—since there is absolutely no material to utilize—, would naturally be, should it succeed in being fabricated, a completely artificial creation. Tell me, please, is it not a pity to see us retreat into ourselves and return to the love of our village steeples, at a moment when all people fraternize, when all local or geographical units efface themselves?"[2]

Again in 1835, writing to the same Turgenev, he expresses some ideas which, by the way, Dostoevsky repeated, if not adopted:

"Why couldn't I say that Russia is too powerful to be occupied with the politics of nations; that her business in the world is the politics of mankind; that the emperor Alexander understood this very well, and this was his greatest glory; that Providence made us too great to be selfish; that it placed us outside the interests of nationalities, and placed upon us the charge of the interests of humanity; that all our ideas in life, in science, in art, should start from there and there return; that there is our future, there is our progress; that we are an immense spontaneity, without intimate ties with the past of the world, without any definite relationship with its present, that it is our real logical task; that if we disregard these cases, all our subsequent progress will be forever nothing but an anomaly, an anachronism, and an absurdity."[3]

[1] Kucharzewski, J., *Od białego caratu do czerwonego*, Vol. I, pp. 169–85. See also the English edition under the title, *The Origin of Modern Russia* (New York: The Polish Institute of Arts and Sciences in America, 1948).
[2] *Sočinenija Čaadaeva*, Vol. I, p. 181.
[3] *Ibid.*, p. 185. See also pp. 181–2, 187, 188, 191.

And on still another occasion in 1835, again to Turgenev, writing about a play of Kukolnik, Chaadaev stressed the fact that the public did not applaud the historical character in the play who represented European trends in Russia, but rather a barbarian, a savage, with whom, by the way, the author overshadowed his first hero. Chaadaev felt indignant about "that ferocious energy against everything that comes from the West, against every kind of civilization . . . and this is what the pit applauds."[1] He called this "an apotheosis of barbarism".

Although his *Apology of a Madman*, written in 1837, was a defense against accusations of a lack of patriotism and "a contempt for the national past", he still tried to preserve and explain the essence of his point of view:

> "There are different ways of loving one's country: the Eskimo, for instance, who loves his native snow, which makes him near-sighted, his smoky igloo where he crouches half his days, the rancid fat of his reindeer which surrounds him with a nauseous atmosphere, certainly doesn't love his country in the same way that an English citizen loves his, being proud of its institutions, of the lofty civilization of his glorious island; and no doubt it would be a sad thing for us to see that we were still cherishing the localities where we were born as the Eskimos do. The love of one's country is a beautiful thing, but there exists something better—the love of truth. Love of the fatherland makes heroes; love of truth makes sages, the benefactors of humanity." [Here we have a purely Tolstoyan text— I have in mind *Christianity and Patriotism*.] "It is love of the fatherland," Chaadaev continues, "that divides people, that feeds national hatreds, and that sometimes covers the earth with mourning; it is love of truth that spreads enlightenment, that creates the joys of the spirit, that brings man closer to divinity. It is not through the fatherland but through truth that one reaches heaven. . . . More than any one of you, believe me, I cherish my country, I am ambitious for its glory, I know how to appreciate the eminent qualities of my nation; but it is also true that the patriotic feeling which animates me is not made in exactly the same fashion as that which animates those whose shouts have upset my quiet existence and who have again launched on the ocean of human misery my boat beached at the foot of the Cross. I did not learn to love my country with closed eyes, with bent head, and with shut mouth. I think that one cannot be useful to one's country unless one is able to see clearly;

[1] *Ibid.*, pp. 180–1.

I believe that the time of blind love is past, that today, above everything, one owes truth to one's country."[1]

There is a possibility of finding a middle point between the Eskimo and Chaadaev, and this position, common to each of us, found expression in Mickiewicz in the famous beginning of *Pan Tadeusz*, which starts with the words: "Fatherland—you are like health; how much you should be valued, only he can learn who has lost you. . . ." The poet has given, perhaps, the most powerful expression in world literature to the physical, innate, unconscious love for one's native land. The same feelings find voice in the old man, J. du Bellay, in his sonnets dedicated to his native Liré.

Lermontov's charming poem "Fatherland", written in 1841, re-echoes, it is possible, the very passage quoted from Chaadaev's *Apology*. Lermontov could have known the *Apology*. People talked so much about Chaadaev's story in Moscow and Petersburg, and Chaadaev himself discussed his misadventure with so many friends, that his criticism of unconscious patriotism must have been known to Lermontov, who deliberately came to its defense. This was especially so because Lermontov, as a "descendant of a Scotch bard", always considered himself an exile in Russia and constantly dreamed about "my Scotland". In this case he opposed his unconscious attachment to his native land to his speculative love for the land of his dreams. The poem "Fatherland" reads:

> I love my fatherland, but with a strange love.
> My reason will not vanquish it.
> Neither glory won by blood,
> Nor quietude filled with proud confidence,
> Nor the sacred legends of the dark past
> Will stir pleasant dreams in me.
> But I love,—I know not why—
> The cold silence of her fields,
> The swaying of her dreamy forests,
> The inundations of her rivers which are like seas:
> I like to drive in a waggon following country by-roads
> And, piercing slowly with my glance the shadow of the night.
> To meet here and there, longing for a night's lodgings,
> The shimmering lights of melancholy villages;
> I like the smoke of the dry harvest,
> And a caravan sleeping on the steppes;
> And on a hill amidst the yellow fields a few birch trees.
> With a joy, unknown to many, I see a barn,

[1] *Ibid.*, pp. 219-20, 230.

A hut covered with straw,
And a window with carved shutters;
And on a holy day, on a dewy evening,
I am ready to gaze until midnight
At a dance with stomping and with whistling,
Accompanied by the talk of drunken peasants.

We know that Pushkin was aware of the first *Philosophical Letter* even before its appearance in *The Telescope* and that, having read it in *The Telescope*, he wrote a letter to Chaadaev which was not mailed. Pushkin's letter is a defense of Russia and her history. It is a significant defense. It throws a certain light on Pushkin's poetical fragment with which we are here concerned. Some passages of Pushkin's letter have already been quoted, but here is the most essential part of it:

"There is no doubt that this schism separated us from Europe, and that we did not participate in any of the great events which have moved it; but we have had our own mission. This is Russia, this is its immense extent, which absorbed the conquest of the Mongols. The Tartars did not dare to transgress our Western frontiers and leave us at their backs. They retreated towards their deserts and thereby Christian civilization was saved. For this purpose we had to have an entirely separate existence, which let us remain Christians but left us complete foreigners to the Christian world, so that our martyrdom did not create any distraction for the energetic development of Catholic Europe. You say that the source whither we went to draw our Christianity was impure, that Byzantium was despicable and despised. Well, my friend, and Jesus Christ, was He not Himself a Jew, and was not Jerusalem the byword of nations? Are the Gospels less admirable because of this? We took from the Greeks the Gospels and the traditions, and not the spirit of puerility and controversy. The mores of Byzantium have been those of Kiev. The Russian clergy, until Theofan, was respectable, it never sullied itself with the infamies of the Papacy, and it certainly would never have provoked the Reformation at the very moment humanity most needed unity. I agree that our present clergy is backward. Do you want to know the reason? It is because they are bearded: that is all. They do not belong to good society. And as far as your historical nullity is concerned, I decidedly cannot be of your opinion. The wars of Oleg and Svyatoslav, and even the wars of appanages—is all this not a life of adventurous effervescence and of the harsh and aimless activity which characterizes the youth of all peoples? The Tartar invasion is a sorrowful and grand picture. The awakening of Russia, the development of her power, the march towards unity (Russian unity, of course), the two Ivans, the sublime drama which started at Uglich and ended at the Ipatiev monastery —what? All this not history, but a pale and half-obliterated dream? And Peter the Great, who by himself is an universal history! And Catherine the Second, who placed Russia on the threshold of Europe? And Alexander, who led us to Paris? (My hand on my heart), don't you find anything ... which in all of this would strike the future historian?"[1]

In this letter Pushkin repeated himself. We find almost the same statements in his article "On Russian Literature, together with a Sketch of French Literature" (1834):

"For a long time Russia remained strange to Europe. Having received the light of Christianity from Byzantium, she did not participate in the political upheavals or in the intellectual activity of the Roman Catholic world. The great epoch of the Renaissance had no influence whatsoever upon her; chivalry did not inspire our ancestors with pure enthusiasm; the beneficial shock produced by the Crusades did not affect the lands of the torpid North. ... A high mission was designed for Russia. Her boundless plains absorbed the power of the Mongols and stopped their invasion at the very border of Europe; the barbarians did not dare to leave subjugated Rus behind, and they returned to their eastern steppes. The developing Enlightenment was saved by a tortured and dying Russia ... and not by Poland, as was recently affirmed by European journals,—but Europe was as ignorant as it was ungrateful with regard to Russia.

The clergy, spared by the astonishingly sagacious Tartars, alone, during two centuries, fed the pale embers of the Byzantine culture. In the silence of monasteries the monks wrote their continuous chronicles. Through letters the bishops conversed with princes and boyars, offering consolation to the heart in the dark times of temptation and hopelessness. But the interior life of the

[1] Puškin, *Sočinenija, Perepiska*, pod red. Saitova, Vol. III, pp. 387–9. This was not Pushkin's first letter on the same subject. In 1831, when Pushkin became acquainted with the sixth and seventh of Chaadaev's *Letters* (see Puškin: *Pis'ma*, "Academia", 1935, Vol. III, pp. 332–3), he wrote to Chaadaev his well-known letter of 6 July, in which he discussed Chaadaev's views and said: "You see Christian unity in Catholicism, that is, in the Pope. Is not this unity in the idea of Christ which also appears in Protestantism? The primary idea was monarchic; it became republican. I express myself poorly, but you will understand me ..." (*Ibid.*, p. 33).

subjugated nation did not develop. The Tartars did not resemble the Moors. Having conquered Russia, they brought no gift of algebra or of Aristotle. Our ancient archives and libraries, aside from the chronicles, do not offer any food for the curiosity of investigators. A few tales and songs, constantly renewed by an oral tradition, preserved the half-obliterated national traits, and the *Lay of Igor's Campaign* stands as a solitary monument in the desert of our old literature."[1]

This discussion does not upset my hypothesis; on the contrary, it supports it. The views of Pushkin and Chaadaev were contradictory, but Pushkin could have drawn an "ideological" portrait precisely of Chaadaev using those words which we find in his fragment about the mysterious Polonophil. Up until now everything furthers the advancement of my hypothesis. There remains, however, one point, a very important point, and in this case almost a decisive one. *Chaadaev was never considered a Polonophil.* The case was just the opposite: there is a postscript to his letter of 18 September, 1831, in which he congratulated Pushkin for his anti-Polish odes and even called him a "national poet", "a Russian Dante", on that score!

Prince D. I. Shakhovskoy, who, as I have already indicated, edited the unknown letters of Chaadaev in the *Literaturnoe Nasledstvo* and who may now be considered the best authority on Chaadaev, after Gershenzon, affirms that the November Insurrection was severely criticized by Chaadaev.[2] I do not know anything certain about this, as no text of Chaadaev revealing such an attitude has ever been published. Prince Shakhovskoy mentions *en passant* that a long article by Chaadaev about the "Polish case" was found and that this article had previously been hidden by Chaadaev. It was discovered pasted in one of the volumes of Sismondi's *History of France*.[3] Unfortunately, this article has not been published. However, if this article contained a condemnation of the Polish Insurrection, why did Chaadaev have to hide it so carefully? Of course, it is difficult to discuss texts which one has never seen. Therefore, let us rather tarry with the known texts and with certain facts which have been circulated.

The texts which I have already quoted, especially those concerned with nationalism and patriotism, those which affirm that a nationalistic policy cannot be the policy of Russia, almost *a priori* oblige one to refute the possibility of any condemnation of the Polish Insurrection

---

[1] *Puškin o literature*, pod red. N. V. Bogoslovskogo (Moscow-Leningrad: "Academia", 1934), pp. 331–2.
[2] *Literaturnoe Nasledstvo*, Vols. 22–4, p. 680.
[3] *Ibid*, p. 680.

on Chaadaev's part. Yet there remains the postscript of his letter to Pushkin. Let us take a glance at the letter itself. In it Chaadaev sheds tears over the commotion which the July Revolution provoked in Europe. It seems to me that Prince Shakhovskoy's comments on the opinions of Chaadaev, as expressed in his letter, are quite sound:

> "The July Revolution broke Chaadaev's hopes for a peaceful transformation of mankind and showed him clearly that the struggle for interests in Europe could not be subdued by a simple subordination of world evolution to one idea."[1]

This is quite a pertinent observation. I myself wrote almost the same in 1926, as I see today, having needlessly stressed, however (under Gershenzon's influence), the anti-revolutionary attitude of Chaadaev. Here is what I wrote:

> "The Revolution had no room in the theocratic system of Chaadaev—the unity of the development of Catholic Western civilization recognized by him cracked under the blows of revolutionary hammers. Chaadaev, in his very essence, was an adversary of revolution. The July Revolution had a depressing effect on him, because it revealed those tendencies that, in his opinion, were destroying the Europe which he set up as an example for Russia and for which his historiosophic thought and religious faith were longing."[2]

Today when I read this letter of Chaadaev to Pushkin, I feel some doubts and suspicions. Chaadaev starts with a passage, in which he alludes to "former, better times". Then he touches on the essence of the problem, at the same time warning: "You would like to talk, you said—let us talk then. But be careful, I am not smiling. You, you are nervous... but once more, I say, mind your nerves!"[3] I demonstrated in my book, *Pouchkine et la Pologne*, written twenty years ago, with what excitement Pushkin lived through the days of the Polish Insurrection, so that Chaadaev had every reason to know that Pushkin was in a nervous state of mind. In the same letter, previously quoted, that is, the one written 6 July, 1831, Pushkin wrote about the menacing events of the times.

Let us return to Chaadaev's further reasonings in his letter:

[1] *Literaturnoe Nasledstvo*, Vols. 22–4, p. 77, Note 1.
[2] W. Lednicki, *Aleksander Puszkin*, pp. 149–50.
[3] *سočinenija Čaadaeva*, Vol. I, p. 163.

"This is what I shall tell you. Have you noticed that something extraordinary is going on in the entrails of the moral world? ... Tell me, please, how are you affected by this? As far as I am concerned, it seems to me that this great turning about of things is an entirely poetical theme; you will not be able to remain indifferent to it, all the more so that the selfishness of poetry will find ample fodder in it, or so I believe. This is the way not to be hurt in one's most intimate feelings in the midst of this general bruising of all of the elements of human nature! I recently saw a letter of your friend, that great poet [probably Zhukovsky, who also wrote anti-Polish poems which were published together with those of Pushkin and Khomyakov]; it is playfulness, hilarity, which frightens one. Are you able to tell me how this man, who formerly felt sorrow for everything, does not find today a single, tiny bit of sadness for the ruin of the world?"[1]

To me this is very significant. Farther on he calls upon Pushkin to wrench feelings and thought for poetic expression out of himself. He alludes to the examples of the great poets and prophets—Valmiki, Orpheus, and Byron. This is followed by a long passage devoted more closely to the July Revolution, and here Chaadaev "weeps" over "the destruction of the old society of my society ... of my Europe". But at the same time he expresses his hope, even his certitude (*certitude parfaite*), "that only goodness will emerge from this". He believes in the coming of a better era to which Providence will lead mankind.[2] The letter ends with obvious allusions to the November Insurrection (its liquidation) and to the already expired French appeals for intervention.[3]

"... Do they not speak about a general war? I maintain that this will not occur. No, friend, the ways of blood are no longer the ways of Providence. Men may be beasts, but they will not devour themselves like animals: the last river of blood has flowed, and at this hour, at the moment when I am writing you, its source, thank God, has dried up. ..."[4]

Then follows the last passage in which he deals with the inefficiency of the French calls for war.

The letter has no date. The date of 18 September was put over the postscript, which starts with congratulations on the occasion of the Czar's order to Pushkin to write the history of Peter the Great, about which Chaadaev had already heard. And then, finally, comes the

[1] *Sočinenija Čaadaeva*, Vol. I, p. 163.
[2] *Ibid*, pp. 164–5.
[3] Pp. 165–6.
[4] Page 166.

significant, I confess completely incomprehensible, almost unbelievable passage about Pushkin's anti-Polish poems, a passage completely contradictory to all of Chaadaev's ideology:

> "I have just seen your two pieces of verse. My friend, never have you given me so much pleasure. At last you have become a national poet; at last you have discovered your mission. I cannot express the satisfaction you have made me feel. We shall talk it over again at length. I don't know whether you understand me very well. The piece against the enemies of Russia is especially admirable; it is *I* who tell you this. There are more thoughts in it than have ever been said or born in a century in this country. Yes, my friend, write the history of Peter the Great. Everyone is not of my opinion here, you may easily guess this; but let them talk and let us advance. When one has once discovered . . . a part of the power that pushes us, the second time one will discover all of it . . . be sure. I have the desire to say to myself: at last our Dante has appeared!"[1]

How is one to explain this? Duplicity, of which the Russians are so often suspected? An intellectual dualism à la Dostoevsky *avant la lettre*? A moral ambivalence? This postscript contradicts not only everything in general that Chaadaev wrote and thought; it contradicts the very essence of the letter to which it was added! Do we have here a pathological spiritual breakdown or a disgusting, ugly lie? Something else comes to my mind: fear of censorship [Chaadaev was well aware that private letters were read by the Russian police in those times] and, simultaneously, devilish irony.

First he wrote the letter and, as we have seen, against the background of the moral catastrophes of the times he demanded of Pushkin a song in a great style, in the style of the *Ramayana*, of Orpheus, Byron. . . . He exclaimed over the happiness he felt now that the blood had stopped flowing. . . . The letter was lying on the table waiting to be mailed. And then came the pamphlet with Pushkin's anti-Polish odes and the news that Pushkin had been granted access to the State Archives and was charged with the writing of a history of Peter the Great. So, it was to be a recompense for his anti-Polish act. . . . Having in mind, perhaps, the contents of the letter, which could be dangerously interpreted, Chaadaev added his postscript with all its eulogies. The phrases, "I don't know whether you understand me very well," and "It is *I* who tell you this," are rather significant, for how could Chaadaev acclaim either the content or the tone of Pushkin's odes, which were not only anti-Polish but were essentially anti-European?

[1] *Sočinenija i pis'ma P. Ja. Čaadaeva*, Vol. I, p. 166.

For Chaadaev to call Pushkin "a Russian Dante" on the occasion of Pushkin's unique manifestation of anti-Europeanism seems, indeed, fantastic.

I cannot add anything more to this particular episode, and I confess that the postscript of 18 September, 1831, very strongly undermines my hypothesis about the Polonophil of Pushkin's poem. I do have, however, two more arguments, one textual and the other factual.

The story of Chaadaev worried Pushkin, and although at that very time he was passing through the most dramatic period of his life (his first conflict with Heeckeren and d'Anthès) the poet found time to write to Denis Davydov, asking him for news of Chaadaev. He was anxious about the rôle of the "Catholic maid" (apparently, Chaadaev was called thus among his friends). Davydov answered on 23 November, 1836, and this is what he reported to Pushkin:

> "You ask me about Ch.? As an eyewitness, I cannot say anything about him; I did not visit him formerly, and I do not visit him now. I always considered him a very erudite man and, undoubtedly, a very clever charlatan, who finds himself incessantly in a state of paroxysm of ambition. But he is a man without power of spirit and character, like a blond coquette, and I think that I am not mistaken. S. [Stroganov?][1] told me about his entire talk with him, from beginning to end! Foreseeing the inevitable disaster, he avowed that he wrote this lampoon on the Russian nation after returning from foreign lands in a state of insanity, and that in this condition he made several attempts on his own life; (he told me) that he tried to pass on the whole responsibility for the trouble to the editor [Nadezhdin] and to the censorship; to the first, because he had talked him into permitting the publication of this lampoon, and the second, because it had passed it. It is disgusting, but what is funny is his concern over what his friends and scholars, Ballanche, Lamennais, Guizot and some German boy-metaphysicians, say about the fact that he has been judged insane! But enough about this. If you hadn't asked me I would have remained silent, because I do not like to disillusion; besides, you might ask T. [A. I. Turgenev], who recently went to Petersburg, and perhaps he will tell you about the event not as I have done and will quiet your concern about the Catholic maid. . . ."[2]

The correspondence of Prince Vyazemsky and Turgenev also contains several very interesting references and long passages on this subject.

[1] Count S. G. Stroganov—Moscow curator of public education at that time.
[2] Puškin, *Sočinenija, Perepiska*, Vol. III, pp. 419–20.

From this correspondence we may conclude that the picture given by Davydov was not too tendentious or arbitrary. Although I do not know why, no great consideration has been given to Davydov's letter. It has even been affirmed that Stroganov never repeated to anyone these confessions of Chaadaev.

Here is what Prince Vyazemsky wrote from Petersburg to A. I. Turgenev in Moscow on 28 October, 1836, at the same time that Pushkin was writing to Davydov:

"It is sad, but they are unpardonably guilty themselves. Like lunatics, they live on the moon and do not know how one has to live on the earth. You would not convince anyone here that there were no bad intentions and premeditation in this. When one knows the personalities, then one knows that everything is reduced, on the one side, to immeasurable ambition, to an irritated desire for theatrical effects, and to great confusion, vacillation and fogginess in conception; and, on the other side, to a lazy dullness, lack of intuition, particularly characteristic for our writers and journalists, and, perhaps, to commercial calculation to augment circulation;[1] but here again there is stupidity and lack of knowledge of what *is* and what *is not* allowed. There is, of course, no self-sacrifice, no martyrdom here, not to speak of a free passion, which would have been absurd in this case, as there was nothing to which it could have been applied. How stupid to prophesy the past. Prophets prophesying the future are put in an insane asylum when they prophesy the end of the world, but here we have a prophecy of a by-gone end of the world, of the end of a nation. It is the culmination of insanity! And to think that the nation should be thankful for the fact that one deduces from old accounts not even a false figure, but simply a zero! Had he at least given a false figure, but a zero! Such paradoxes are good by the fireside to animate conversation, but they should not be spread farther, especially in our country, where minds are not prepared and disciplined by an exchange of opposing opinions. It would be impossible even to defeat them, as refutation implies accusation, denunciation. And here the result would be not a discussion on an abstract subject, but a fight with knives in hand for one's blood, for the ashes of our ancestors, for everything which is ours, and for those who are ours. How is it possible to provoke such a struggle and to start such a discussion?"[2]

---

[1] Here he has in mind Nadezhdin, the editor of *The Telescope*.
[2] *Ostaf'evskij arkhiv knjazej Vjazemskikh* (St. Petersburg, 1899), Vol. III, pp. 341-2.

Turgenev hastened to answer immediately. Writing on the first of November, he stated that he shared entirely the opinion of Prince Vyazemsky about the vanity and ambition of Chaadaev and that he had "attacked him so strongly" for this ambition that the latter "had become seriously angered"; he added that "he did not come to see me" for a long time. Turgenev also mentioned that sharp discussions were continuing, but "now he is miserable, he preserves his *sang froid* sufficiently, and he has accepted the decision about his insanity with *a feeling of thankfulness and emotion.* . . ." [*sic!*][1]

Following this, in a letter of 9 November, Turgenev informed Prince Vyazemsky that Chaadaev "has not had his own opinions for a long time, and he has changed them essentially. . . ."[2] Thus, we see that the exaggerated ambition of Chaadaev was stressed by all of them, by Davydov, Prince Vyazemsky, and Turgenev.

The agents of Benckendorff also related the same: "Cheodaev [*sic!*] leads a very modest life, he has no passions, but he is ambitious beyond measure. . . ."[3]

Besides, the friends of Chaadaev noticed this trait of his and his pathetic state of nerves much earlier, in 1831. Therefore, Chaadaev's confession about his "mental disease", maliciously mentioned by Davydov, might not have been too exaggerated and certainly did not entirely disagree with reality. In a letter to Pushkin of 14 July, 1831, Prince Vyazemsky reported that "Chaadaev appears in society, but it constantly seems to me that he is a little bit off. We try to soothe and to take care of him. . . ."[4] In the same letter there is an additional note by Turgenev, who hastens to agree with Pushkin's polemical observations, which were contained in his letter to Chaadaev on 6 July, 1831, and he then continues:

"This speculative work would have been a salvation for his *mental* and physical health, about which I am writing to Zhukovsky, but his disease, that is, his *spleen*, has its roots in his character and in his unrealized ambition, which, by the way, I pardon and understand with my whole heart. Slowly, gradually, I want to remind him that the teaching of Christ embraces the whole of man, even in infinity. . . . Delicately I want to remind him that it is possible and desirable to pay less attention to oneself and to *das liebe ich*, to care less for one's comfort and more for one's fellow men, not to tie five ties each morning, to cherish less the nails,

---

[1] Page 345. In a letter of 24 October, he wrote that "Chaadaev himself writes against himself . . ." (page 336).
[2] Page 354.
[3] Lemke, *op. cit.*, p. 424.
[4] Puškin, *Sočinenija, Perepiska*, Vol. II, p. 271.

teeth and stomach, and to give surplus to those who feed themselves on falling crumbs. Then we shall be less afraid of cholera and hemorrhoids. . . ."[1]

Turgenev writes almost at the same time to Nicholas, his brother, informing him of Chaadaev's "deep melancholy", of the religious thought in which he was absorbed, but also about his thoughts concentrated on himself, his "selfishness" and his "ambition", his "mental disease" and his "physical weakness", his "prematurely senile decrepitude", his "pedantic elegance", his "good appetite" at the English Club, his "constant care for himself and his desire to attract attention to himself. . . ."[2]

Unfortunately, not only selfishness, ambition, and concern for self characterized this man, but also "irresolution", "lack of character and spiritual power", which were mentioned in Davydov's and Prince Vyazemsky's letters. We know that during the investigation, and later, Chaadaev behaved pusillanimously and lied. Here, as in the affair of the Decembrists,[3] one should approach this painful story with some indulgence and generosity. However, with one "lie" of Chaadaev is connected my last and, at the same time, most important argument.

The first inaccuracy in Chaadaev's testimony concerns the publication of his *Philosophical Letter* in Nadezhdin's *Telescope*. He tried to make Nadezhdin responsible for everything.[4]

The second inaccuracy concerns the addressee of the *Philosophical Letters*, Ekaterina Dmitrievna Panov. Lemke reports:

"On the seventeenth of December, 1836, the Moscow Provincial Department checked the state of mind of Ekaterina Dmitrievna Panov, née Ulybyshev, at the request of her husband, who had decided to place his wife in Sabler's Hospital. It appears from the answers she gave to the questions of the office that she was thirty-two years old, that she had married fifteen years previously, that she had no children, that she was residing permanently in Moscow, and sometimes, in the winter, in the country, where she possessed one hundred and fifty souls. To the question whether she was pleased with the place where she was staying, Mrs. Panov answered: 'I am the happiest woman in the world, and I am satisfied with everything!' To the question whether she

[1] Puškin, *op. cit.*, p. 272.
[2] Istrin, V.: "Iz dokumentov arkhiva brat'ev Turgenevykh", *Žurnal Ministerstva Narodnago Prosveščenija*, March 1913, pp. 20–1.
[3] See below, Chapter II.
[4] Lemke, *loc. cit.*

respected the commands of religion and of the civil laws and whether she obeyed them, she gave the answer: 'As far as the civil laws are concerned, I am a republican, and as far as religion is concerned, I am as obedient to spiritual laws as all of you sirs; *when the Polish war was in progress, I prayed to our Lord to send victory to the Poles!*' When she was reprimanded that she would have done better to pray for the Russians, Mrs. Panov replied: '*I prayed to my Lord for the Poles because they fought for freedom. . . .*' "[1]

Mrs. Panov had been an old and good friend of Chaadaev. Her letter to him which has been preserved testifies to this. Besides, it was to her that the *Philosophical Letters* were addressed. However, as soon as Chaadaev heard of the answers his friend had given, he hurried to the chief of the Moscow police, L. M. Tsinsky, and there orally and in writing denied everything Mrs. Panova had said. He referred to his various financial misunderstandings with her; he affirmed that she did not know at all that the *Philosophical Letters* were addressed to her and, finally, that he had never spoken to her on the subject of her republican opinions or about her prayers for the Poles. Chaadaev thought it necessary to present this explanation, because he supposed that among the authorities there might arise the suspicion that Mrs. Panova had evolved her opinions under his influence.[2]

I think that all these facts are extremely interesting. Perhaps, indeed, the mysterious Polonophil of Pushkin was Chaadaev. I must confess that this hypothesis tempts me strongly. One would like to forget the postscript of the letter of 18 September, 1831. And still one has no right not to take it into consideration. There is in this postscript a small observation which, I believe, I have not stressed enough. After his praise of Pushkin's anti-Polish poem, Chaadaev added, as the reader may remember, "Everyone is not of my opinion here, you may easily guess this: but let them talk and let us advance. . . ." I do not think that Chaadaev wrote this for the censorship! We have other evidence that Pushkin's poems aroused adverse comments. Melgunov, Bestuzhev, the brothers Turgenev, and many others were deeply shocked by Pushkin's publication, and they did not hesitate to use the strongest epithets to qualify it. But now I am not concerned with the reactions of the Russian élite to Pushkin's "betrayal of poetry". My purpose is to identify the "mysterious Polonophil", and I am trying to find him in the turmoil of discussions incited by Pushkin's anti-Polish trilogy.

The correspondence of the brothers Turgenev contains some details

[1] Lemke, *op. cit.*, pp. 448–9.
[2] *Ibid.*, 449–50.

which are worthy of attention. On 15 September, 1831, A. I. Turgenev wrote to his brother, Nicholas:

"Zhukovsky and Pushkin (who, as I hear, was made the biographer of Peter I with a salary granted) wrote poems on the conquest of Warsaw. They say that Pushkin's [poems] are beautiful. I already have Zhukovsky's, but have not yet received Pushkin's. They are printing them together."[1]

Later, on 26 September, Turgenev informed his brother about his discussion of these poems with Chaadaev:

"Last week I had dinner [with him] at the English Club. . . . We started to argue heatedly about the value of the poems of Pushkin and others [Zhukovsky and Khomyakov] which were being read the entire week here—'To the Conquest of Warsaw' and 'To the Calumniators of Russia'. We attacked Chaadaev a little for his opinion about [these] poems. . . ."[2]

It also happened that when he was in Munich in 1832 (on 2 October), upon recalling all these affairs and in reply to his brother's comments on Pushkin, A. I. Turgenev wrote:

"Your conclusion about Pushkin is just; there is, indeed, still some barbarity in him, and Vyazemsky harassed him in Moscow for the sake of Poland; but in his verses about you [he has in mind the tenth chapter of *Eugene Onegin* in which Pushkin ironically wrote about the Decembrists and mentioned, among others, N. I. Turgenev] I do not see this; in general, there is very much justice in his opinion about you. He is a barbarian only in his attitude towards Poland. As a poet he thinks that without Russian patriotism, such as he understands it, one cannot be a poet, and for poetry's sake he does not want to abandon barbarity. His poem, 'To the Calumniators of Russia', shows in what way he understands this problem. I noticed only in Vyazemsky a just view on this poem and on this whole world of moral-political (or amoral) problems. I heard their discussions, but I was silent, as Pushkin started to accuse Vyazemsky to justify himself; I suffered for both of them because I love them both. . . ."[3]

[1] Besides the pamphlet, which also contained Pushkin's poems, Zhukovsky published his poem in issue No. 201 of 8 September, 1831, of the *Severnaja Pčela*. See V. Istrin's publication in the *Žurnal Ministerstva Narodnago Prosveščenija*, March 1913, p. 19, for the quoted letters of A. I. Turgenev.

[2] See Istrin, as above, pp. 19–21.

[3] *Ibid.*, p. 19. For more precise and ample information, see my *Pouchkine et la Pologne*, as above, Chapters XIII–XIV.

Prince P. A. Vyazemsky in 1853
Engraving after drawing by F. von Wuzleben

Perhaps, then, Pushkin's poem portrays Prince Vyazemsky? This poem could have reflected the sharp and animated discussions mentioned by Turgenev. Therefore, and for other reasons as well, Vyazemsky deserves some special attention; first because of his intimate friendship with Pushkin and, second, because of his particularly severe judgment about Pushkin's and Zhukovsky's poetic anti-Polish publications. In his *Notebook* he strongly attacked the very idea of publishing poems such as those written by the two poets. He demonstrated that Pushkin's poem containing a series of questions addressed to Europe was, properly speaking, deprived of common sense:

"For what qualities should renascent Europe like us? Our geographical fanfaronades 'from Perm to Tavrida' have irritated me not a little. What advantage is there and why should we boast of the fact that we are so widely spread, that five thousand versts separate one thought from another? . . . It is comical when Pushkin declares 'We shall not set fire to their Warsaw'. Of course we won't, as we would be obliged to rebuild it. All of you are so carried away by your patriotic ecstasy that you don't know where to stop: today Warsaw is for you an enemy city and tomorrow it becomes a Russian colony. . . . The devil only knows what kind of poetry there is in the fact that we have been chased from Warsaw, that we didn't know how to govern it, and that after marches and countermarches, which lasted for several months, we again entered the city. . . . We are surprisingly boastful and, what is regrettable, this bragging smacks of boorishness. No matter how we demonstrate our joy we always resemble flunkeys who sing in the servants' room and congratulate their master on the occasion of his birthday or a new rank, etc. . . . The Polish problem is a disease which showed us the vices of our own organism. It is not enough to cure the disease, it is necessary to extirpate the vices themselves. Of what benefit is it to Russia to be the guardian of Poland? Our situation would be much easier if we would find at a given moment a sincere and frank enemy. . . . I believe that the appointment of a good new governor in Kazan or in Vologda lends itself better to poetry than the conquest of Warsaw. (And, after all, from whom did we seize it? What kind of conquest is this? How absurd is this term—*conquest.*) Compose songs to the government glorifying such deeds if you absolutely must bend your knees and cringe with a lyre in your hands . . ." Earlier, in 1829, Vyazemsky wrote in his notes: "When I lived in Poland I didn't rust in outdated memories about the Poles in the Kremlin and the Russians in Praga [a suburb of

Warsaw—Prince Vyazemsky alludes here to Suvorov's massacre at the time of Kościuszko's insurrection], but, on the contrary, I lived among people of my own kind, with thoughts and heart open to the impressions of the present.' "[1]

Vyazemsky wrote in his *Notebook* that he intended to communicate these observations to Pushkin. He abandoned this project (he was in the country at the time of Pushkin's publication of 1831) because of the censorship, to which private correspondence was then subject, particularly the letters of outstanding personalities like Vyazemsky and Pushkin.

In the further development of these considerations, Vyazemsky comes closer to Pushkin's opinions on the relationship between poetry and current political problems:

> "Why transpose into verse that which is perfectly suitable for a political gazette?"

But, even if Vyazemsky did not write to Pushkin, there is no doubt that he often talked with him about these matters—was he not his most intimate friend?

Vyazemsky's letter, dated 7 October, 1831, which he sent to Pushkin's friend, Madame E. M. Khitrovo, after his arrival in Moscow, proves how deeply he was concerned:

> "In the name of God, if He exists, and in the name of humanity, if humanity exists, propagate feelings of forgiveness, of generosity, of commiseration. . . . Peace to the victims! Let us not imitate the savages who dance and sing around their enemies burning at the stake. Let us become Europeans again in order to expiate poems which are not European. How much pain these poems have caused me! Political power, social order often have sorrowful and bloody obligations to fulfil, but the poet, God be blessed, is not obliged to sing about them. It is not the mission of poetry to mingle with the prose of facts. . . . All of this should remain between us, but I was not able to master myself while talking to you and to restrain my pain and indignation. . . . Now you may say what you wish, but in our days one should not search for generous inspiration in the poetry of bayonets and guns, when they serve only for the triumph of force, regardless of how legitimate it might be. This

---

[1] Cf. Knjaz' P. A. Vjazemskij, *Polnoe sobranie sočinenij* (Petersburg, 1884), Vol. IX, pp. 155ff., and *Ibid.*, Vol. II, pp. 89-90.

poetry is an odious anachronism and degrades the most beautiful talent."[1]

I have mentioned that Prince Vyazemsky had intended to write on this subject to Pushkin himself. A letter which was never sent has, however, been preserved; it contains, in short, everything that Vyazemsky wrote in his *Notebook* and everything he said in his letter to Madame Khitrovo. But Vyazemsky's letter to Pushkin contains something more: its explicit form throws into relief Vyazemsky's fundamental point of view:

"Ask Zhukovsky to send me as soon as possible one of his new fables. What was the idea of writing livery poems [Vyazemsky alludes to rhymesters who wore cloaks and used to go from house to house with rhymed congratulations], and is it not a shame for the author of the odes 'A Bard in the Camp of Russian Warriors' (1812) and 'A Bard in the Kremlin' (1814) to compare the present moment to Borodino? There one of our people was fighting against ten; here, on the contrary, ten are fighting against one. It is very important from the State's point of view, but poetry has absolutely nothing to do with this. One is rather astonished that the whole thing lasted so long, but there is no reason to go into raptures because it was finally settled. A master who has his peasant thrashed because the latter has the idea of claiming his freedom in an insolent way and without any right, such a master commits a good and just action. However, there is no source of inspiration in this for a poet."[2]

One must remember that Pushkin called one of his anti-Polish odes "The Anniversary of Borodino". Therefore, Vyazemsky's shot directed at Zhukovsky was also aimed at Pushkin.

In another letter which Pushkin received immediately after the defeat of the Insurrection, Vyazemsky was no less ironical, although he was more cautious in his wording, certainly having in mind the censorship. While writing about the seventy-first birthday of the poet Dmitriev, he said:

"It is a glorious old age. He likes you very much and greets you. Yesterday morning some livery poet came to him, and, taking a notebook from under his coat, congratulated him. Dmitriev, preoccupied with the thought of his birthday, asked him: 'And how

[1] *Russkij Arkhiv* (Moscow, 1895), Vol. V, pp. 110–13.
[2] Puškin, *Sočinenija, Perepiska*, as above, Vol. II, p. 323.

did you know?' The livery poet, a little bit confused, finally answered: 'I must confess that I read it yesterday in the newspapers.' The thing was that he presented his congratulations on the occasion of the taking of Warsaw and had written an ode in honour of Paskevich."[1]

All of these texts encourage one to consider Prince Vyazemsky a possible addressee of Pushkin's poem to the mysterious Polonophil. However, some reservations are indispensable. Vyazemsky, while staying in Poland and later, frequently criticized in his *Notebook* and in his letters to his friends the abuses characterizing the Russian administration of Poland. He considered the Partitions of Poland an "original sin of Russian policy" and emphasized that it was "impossible to avoid the fatal consequences of this crime". He often praised Polish life, Polish society, and these feelings found their expression in his poetry. But he also confessed that, despite his sympathy for the Poles, he experienced a kind of instinctive enmity towards them. He felt that something in his nature did not agree with the Polish character. And even in the letter and notes in which Vyazemsky expressed his indignation caused by Pushkin's and Zhukovsky's publication, one may see that the way in which he judges Poland betrays his disdain for this country. He was indignant with Pushkin and Zhukovsky because they chose for their poems a subject as little poetic as petty. He treated the Polish cause as a problem of Russian interior policy. He, a great lord, an aristocrat, and European, had pity for the defeated, and he demanded the same pity from Pushkin, being ashamed in the face of Europe of the barbaric attitude of autocratic Russia. He was afraid of the effect which Pushkin's poem, manufactured *ad usum populi*, would produce in the circles of European élite. But as far as Poland is concerned, we can't find in his opinions anything other than pity, or even disdainful pity. He knew Poland and Polish society very well, having spent several years in Warsaw and having travelled in the country; he was even benevolent towards Poland, but he never changed his point of view, which was that of a Russian master of Poland. In his eyes the War of 1831 was nothing but "the rebellion of a peasant who insolently claimed his freedom and his rights". Here is hidden, by the way, the great difference between him and Pushkin. Pushkin treated Poland in his anti-Polish and anti-European poems as an equal of Russia, and he interpreted the War of 1831 as a continuation of the century-old fight between Russia and Poland for leadership of the Slavic world.

Vyazemsky was a humanist and a European humanist, but at the

[1] *Ibid.*, p. 324.

same time he was a man who looked at Poland as one who had been a Russian administrative official there and who judged things from the point of view of the best interests of the Russian State. His idea of Poland was very limited and exactly defined: for him Poland was nothing but the Kingdom constituted by the Congress of Vienna, and hence deprived of Volhynia, Lithuania, and of "Bogdan's heritage". Vyazemsky was a life-long advocate of a liberal Russian Policy in Poland. He was even ready, being conscious of the dangers threatening Russia from the Polish side, to accept the loss of Poland, but he never agreed to treat Poland as an equal and serious rival of Russia. There were two reasons for this: he had an ironic indulgence for Poland and no genuine respect for her; in the period 1830-1831 he was far from having any Slavophil ideas—he wished to see Russia completely separated from the Slavic world, which, in his opinion, would always try to avoid Russia. That is why the question of the rivalry between Poland and Russia in this field was not an actual problem for him. His critique of the poems of Pushkin and Zhukovsky betrays a purely aesthetic point of view: "Chickens would laugh if we were immeasurably astonished that a lion had succeeded in crushing a mouse under his paw"—that was Vyazemsky's formula. I am not sure if, despite its brutality, the shout of the triumphant victors which resounds in Pushkin's odes doesn't cause less offense to "Proud Warsaw" than the aesthetic and humanistic attitude of Prince Vyazemsky, who refused to listen to "the roar of a lion crushing a captive mouse".

Yes, Pushkin's and Vyazemsky's points of view were diametrically opposed. Pushkin lived through the Polish Insurrection in a state of pathetic excitement, even of agony, fed by his tense nationalistic emotion. That is why Vyazemsky's critical and skeptical attitude towards "this world of moral-political problems", to quote Turgenev, must have deeply moved, irritated, and even offended Pushkin.

Later, certainly much later, when Pushkin tried to transfer this whole discussion, this whole "Polonophil" episode, into poetry, he quite naturally coloured it. The poet seized upon the words and phrases of the quarrels and disputes of 1831 which remained in his memory and, thus, prosaic arguments were transformed into eloquent poetic formulae: "tender love for a foreign people", "wise hatred for one's own nation", formulae proclaiming the glory of Lelewel, the glory of the Polish Anthem "Poland is Not Yet Lost", and the lamentations of "a Jew weeping over Jerusalem". Once more the element of poetic transfiguration, of the sublimation of reality, so characteristic for Pushkin, triumphed. But was Prince Vyazemsky the mysterious Polonophil? I still do not dare to say. However, Vyazemsky certainly did not "drink to Lelewel's health"; he wept over Pushkin, but he did not "weep over the fall of Warsaw". It is unlikely that the poem was addressed to him and, therefore, Chaadaev appears the more probable candidate. *Tertium non datur.*

* * * * *

In the light of biographic and historic facts, Chaadaev, the author of the magnificent *Philosophical Letters*, appears unpleasantly overshadowed by Chaadaev, the concrete personality, the actual man. The former finds himself under a distasteful and, perhaps, even ugly cloud. One should not surrender to this impression, however, for more important than the biographic facts are the *Letters* and their rôle in Russian spiritual culture.[1] We must not forget that the distance which separated Chaadaev, the philosopher of history and the interpreter of Russia's historical development, from those who silenced him and who represented the official interpretation of Russia's history, was enormous. Take, for example, the fact that when M. F. Orlov mentioned to Count Benckendorff that Chaadaev "was very severe about the Russian past, but hoped for so much from her future", the chief of gendarmes answered:

"Russia's past is admirable; her present is more than magnificent; and as far as her future is concerned, it is beyond anything the most daring imagination could evoke; this is, my dear man, the point of view from which Russian history should be conceived and written."

"The whole régime spoke through Benckendorff's mouth," justly noted Lemke, who quoted this valuable assertion.[2] There is another example in Gogol, who wrote, we must not forget, in this same spirit, not only in his *Correspondence with Friends*, but also in his *Dead Souls*.

Of course, Chaadaev's patriotism was not of this nature. Nor did he know the "physical" patriotism which Lermontov expressed. The capacity for such emotion was undermined in him by his hyperintellectualism and by a religious obsession, in which the postulate of unity became a kind of monomania. Besides, man may act otherwise than his conscience commands, although he should not, but he

---

[1] See the brilliant monograph of P. Miljukov, *Glavnyja tečenija russkoj istoričeskoj mysli.*

[2] Lemke, *op. cit.*, p. 411.

cannot think otherwise than his very gift of thought permits, though he would frequently like to do so.

Not long before his death Paul Valéry noted, probably not without irony, that intellectual culture does not always imply ethical culture. There are two worlds, two different elements rule over them. In some way the example of Chaadaev confirms this. His philosophy of history was a speculation. His contemporaries did not recognize this quality in it, they felt an offense which, as a matter of fact, did not exist. On the other hand, Chaadaev, the intellectual *par excellence*, in addition a sybarite and dandy, was not a warrior by temperament. In a sense he confessed this himself: "The love of fatherland produces heroes, the love of truth makes sages." He was not a hero—he was a brilliant thinker and perhaps an even more brilliant writer. Bards and prophets are not always heroes. We have to take Chaadaev as he is and even thus to praise him, although his practical faint-heartedness remains in contradiction to his assertions about the decisive importance of moral factors in the life of nations. Or perhaps, on the contrary, the Russia of his philosophical system could not have produced anyone different; there is nothing to be done about it. We may console ourselves with the fact that the confessions and reservations he made to Count Stroganov and to the chief of police, Tsinsky, had no effect upon his *Philosophical Letters*. These *Letters* have reached us in their unsoiled condition, and as such do they act. Moreover, beyond doubt the acting power of this thought was enormous in Russia. We have already seen this in some measure. Nor did his figure—a figure so suggestive albeit too much absorbed by a subtle care for style and an ambition which loved effects—pass without trace. On this score Herzen has truthfully written:

> "The melancholic and original figure of Chaadaev is clearly drawn, like some painful reprimand, against the faded and gloomy background of Muscovite high-life. I liked to look at him and see him amidst the parade of the vain aristocracy, amidst those frivolous senators, grey-haired scamps, and all sorts of mediocrity veiled by honours. As dense as the crowd might be, one's eye found him immediately. The years did not deform his elegant figure. He used to dress very carefully, his pale, delicate face was completely motionless when he was silent, his 'forehead and bald crown' were as if of wax or marble. His grey-blue eyes were sorrowful, but had kindness in them; his thin lips, on the contrary, smiled ironically. For ten years he stood so, with his crossed arms, somewhere against a pillar, under a tree on a boulevard, in salons, in theatres, at the Club, and, as if an incarnate veto, as if a living protest, he observed

the chain of thoughtless faces circling around him. He was capricious, peculiar, withdrawn from society, and yet he could not detach himself from it. Then he said his word, having quietly hidden it, just as he used to hide passion in his features, under a frosted veil. Then he again became silent, again capricious, again he was engrossed in the life of Moscow society, and again he could not abandon it. The old and the young felt neither comfortable nor free in his presence. God knows why his motionless face and far-distant gaze, his sorrowful, scoffing and bitter indulgence led them into confusion...."[1]

Chaadaev attracted people. It is known how he tempted Dostoevsky. Some of the quoted passages prove this. The great writer even intended to introduce Chaadaev's figure into one of his monumental novels. Tolstoy, too, repeated almost textually what Chaadaev had said in his *Apology* about patriotism as an element of discord and conflict in the life of mankind. But in this last giant various passions co-existed, and elemental nationalism, fed by the "physical patriotism" which Chaadaev lacked, frequently seized him and often overwhelmed his rational Christian criticism of patriotism as such. It seems to me that Turgenev also yielded to this attraction to Chaadaev. The best proof lies in his charming novel, *Smoke*. Everything in it that is Russian appears as a phantasmagory, a will-o'-the-wisp, an unreal dream, simply "smoke". The life of the attractive heroine, Irene, her love for Litvinov, the banality of the "snobbish generals", the extravagances of the "utilitarians", the revolutionary dream of émigré politicians—everything drifts and vanishes like smoke. The sardonic invectives of the writer against "the national style" are coloured with bitterness, with passionate "hatred" sucked from an ardent love for fatherland. Full of sarcasm are his judgments on the barbarity, the "slavish spirit", the servility of Russia. This novel, full of exquisite elegance, is a kind of resumption of the motifs of Chaadaev, Lermontov, and, to some degree, Pushkin, through which the "smoke" and "mirages" of Mickiewicz and Chaadaev mysteriously interweave.

* * * * *

Postscript

In the June issue of the *Slavonic and East European Review* (Vol. XXIX, No. 73, 1951), Professor G. P. Struve published an interesting study

[1] A. I. Gercen, *Byloe i dumy* (Berlin: Slovo, 1921), Vol. II, pp. 292–3.

under the title "Who Was Pushkin's Polonophil?"[1] This article is in part connected with my essay, "Chaadaev, Mickiewicz, Pushkin, Custine, Dostoevsky, Turgenev and the Philosophy of Russian History", which appeared in the two volumes on Pushkin, edited by myself and entitled *Puszkin, 1837-1937* (Cracow, 1937). With few exceptions this printing was destroyed by the Germans. The foregoing chapter is an English development of my Polish study on Chaadaev, in which, as now, I have expressed the opinion that Pushkin's Polonophil might have been either Chaadaev or Prince P. A. Vyazemsky, *tertium non datur*. But Professor Struve has found a third candidate in the person of P. B. Kozlovsky. I must confess that Prince Kozlovsky never occurred to me as one who might have been the addressee of Pushkin's poem. Kozlovsky was known for his infatuation with Europe and his particular attachment to Poland and its western European "knightly" tradition. Professor Struve quotes a passage from Kozlovsky's significant talks with the Marquis de Custine (as reported by Custine in his book). He emphasizes the fact that Kozlovsky influenced Custine's views on Russia and that Kozlovsky's "philosophy" of Russian history had much in common with Chaadaev's. Professor Struve did not mention the perhaps most salient of Kozlovsky's statements quoted by Custine: "Russia, in the present age, is only four hundred years removed from the invasion of barbarian tribes whilst fourteen centuries have elapsed since Western Europe experienced the same crisis. A civilization older by one thousand years of course places an immeasurable distance between the customs of nations." Or another: "The Russian nation was not formed in that brilliant school of good faith by whose instruction chivalrous Europe had so well profited that the word *honour* was, for a long time, synonymous with truth, and the word of *honour* had a sanctity which is still revered even in France where so many things have been forgotten." Then comes the passage about the Polish "knightly" tradition which Professor Struve has quoted and finally the fourth passage: "Nowadays the Poles find themselves face to face with the Russians exactly as the Russians were once face to face with the Mongols under Batu."[2] Certainly these statements are very close to Chaadaev's views. However, I think that Mickiewicz, whom Custine saw before going to Russia and whom he read, was a more important source of introduction to Russia than was Kozlovsky. I have shown how close Custine's opinions on Russia were to Mickiewicz's satires

---

[1] This publication appeared after Professor Struve's Russian book, *Russkij Evropeec* (San Francisco: Izd. "Delo", 1950), in which he deals (in his addenda) with the same problem. I am referring here mostly to his English article as its text is more available to the English-speaking reader.

[2] I quote from the French edition of 1844 *La Russie en 1839*, Vol. I, pp. 116, 117-18.

and to Chaadaev's views. On the other hand, I have also shown the similarity of Mickiewicz's and Chaadaev's opinions on this subject.

Certainly Kozlovsky possessed some of the traits Pushkin described in his poetic fragment. But it seems to me that it is easier to apply the first lines:

> By education you enlightened your mind,
> You saw the face of truth
> And the sacred mysteries of the world,
> And tenderly you loved the foreign people,
> And wisely hated your own nation.

to Chaadaev than to the "tattler" Kozlovsky. As a matter of fact the only justification in even considering Kozlovsky as the original of the portrait in this stanza is the similarity, emphasized by Professor Struve, between his and Chaadaev's ideas.

The weakness of Professor Struve's hypothesis lies in the factual ties between Kozlovsky and Pushkin's poem. I do not question the dates of the poem, as we have no knowledge of when Pushkin wrote it. In order to be able to connect Pushkin's poem with Kozlovsky, Professor Struve is obliged to place the date of the writing of the poem at the end of 1835 or even in the first half of 1836. In principle, these years are acceptable. I, too, advanced the supposition that Pushkin's fragment may have been written in 1836, after the publication of Chaadaev's *Philosophical Letter*, at the time that Chaadaev had become universally considered an enemy of his country. But there is one consideration, connected with matters of fact, which prevents me from sharing Professor Struve's hypothesis. Professor Struve suggests that the material of the poem, its factual contents, such as the item of the toast in Lelewel's honour, was given to Pushkin by the Polonophil himself. In other words, in 1834 Kozlovsky must have attended the dinner at which Lelewel delivered his speech and later personally discussed his feelings about the Polish Insurrection with Pushkin. And yet Professor Struve confesses: "Whether Kozlovsky ever met Lelewel personally, we do not know." He emphasizes the retrospective nature of Pushkin's poetical draft. I am almost willing to agree that the poem is retrospective: it is the past tense that is used, and the Insurrection has obviously already been defeated, for when the Warsaw revolt was broken, the hero "lowered (his) head and sobbed bitterly, Like the Jew over Jerusalem". Still this is a subtle matter; it depends on one's interpretation, rather, on one's feeling of the poem. To me it does not seem likely that the vivid description of the Polonophil's attitude towards the Polish Insurrection:

> You rubbed your hands at our defeats,
> With cunning laughter you listened to the news
> When [our army] galloped in retreat
> And the standards of our honour perished.
> But when the Warsaw revolt was broken,
> You collapsed, and woefully did you weep,
> Like the Jew about Jerusalem.[1]

could have resulted from only a casual talk between the Polonophil and the poet five years after the event. No, the poem must be concerned with someone Pushkin saw in action during those troubled days.

All the details mentioned above give the impression that Pushkin had personally observed the behaviour of his Polonophil, that he had been close to him at the time of the described action. (We know that Kozlovsky was then in Paris.) It is difficult to imagine that the attitude so concretely portrayed could have been described by the person in question several years later. And the person would not have been likely to give such details about himself.

As I mentioned, Professor Struve confesses that "whether Kozlovsky ever met Lelewel personally, we do not know", and Professor Struve expresses the opinion that

> "such a meeting, either in Paris, where Lelewel went after the collapse of the insurrection, or in Brussels, where he lived after his expulsion from France after 1833, is within the realm of possibility: Kozlovsky frequented the opposition circles in France and they could have easily met there. But it is not necessary to presume such a meeting in order to imagine Kozlovsky drinking a toast to Lelewel in Paris, in the salon of one of the parliamentary 'windbags' (to use Pushkin's expression), or in London or in Brussels."[2]

In his Russian book on Prince Kozlovsky, Professor Struve is even more explicit. After a passage in which he gave the same statement quoted above, he adds: "There is no need to presume, following W. Lednicki, that the addressee of Pushkin's unfinished message provocatively toasted Lelewel in Moscow."[3] I should like to answer this statement with the following quotation from Pushkin's marginal remarks connected with his article on Radishchev, written from December, 1833, to April, 1834: "Nowadays there is no public opinion in Moscow: nowadays to the calamities or the glory of the Fatherland there is no response in this heart of Russia. It was pitiful to listen to

---
[1] I am quoting Professor Struve's translation.
[2] *Slavonic Review*, as above, p. 452.
[3] Struve, *op. cit.*, p. 115.

the comments of the Muscovite society at the time of the last Polish revolt. It was repulsive to see the indifferent reader of the French newspapers smiling at the news of our defeats. . . ."[1] (I may add that, according to the editors of the 1949 edition of Pushkin's works, he wrote the chapter "Moscow" in January, 1835.)[2]

Hard though it is to defend Chaadaev's candidacy, I believe his position is stronger than Kozlovsky's. Professor Struve refers to my statement that the main difficulty with Chaadaev is the fact that he was never known as a Polonophil. Professor Struve also refers to the famous postscript which Chaadaev added to his letter to Pushkin dated 18 September, 1831, in which he congratulated Pushkin on his anti-Polish poems. And Professor Struve considers as weak my suggestion that this postscript was written for the sake of the censor. I myself had some reservations, as the reader could have seen, but the striking ideological contradiction between the letter and its postscript demands some explanation. Professor Struve neglects certain other facts adduced in my study, which show that the problem of Chaadaev's attitude toward Poland was not so simple, so clearly drawn as one might wish. First, as I mentioned, Chaadaev had connections with Polish Masons and in 1814 was accepted into the Masonic Lodge in Cracow, where the first two degrees were conferred upon him.[3] Second is the fact which I have discussed above, as well as in my Polish study[4] used by Professor Struve: Chaadaev's long mysterious memorandum on the Polish problem. Professor Struve has passed over in silence the existence of this memorandum and my comments on it. I may also refer here to Chaadaev's letter "to an unknown woman", quoted in the beginning of my study, in which Chaadaev manifested his respect for Polish civilization and its contributions, such as "a poor, petty solar system".[5] Third, there is the story of Madame Panov. How can we neglect her answer to the government authorities in Moscow and her statement that she prayed for victory for the Poles because they were fighting for freedom?[6] Can we ignore her long and close friendship with Chaadaev and her letters to him testifying to this fact? Besides, it would be difficult to disregard the rather significant detail that it was to her that the *Philosophical Letter* was addressed. Also, there is Chaadaev's visit to L. M. Tsinsky and his oral and written denial of everything

---

[1] Cf. "Putešestvie iz Moskvy v Peterburg" (Otryvki černovoj redakcii) in *A. S. Puškin, Polnoe sobranie sočinenij* (Moscow-Leningrad: Ak. Nauk, 1949), Vol. VII, p. 637.
[2] *Ibid.*, p. 699.
[3] See above, p. 27.
[4] See *Puszkin, 1837–1937*, edited by W. Lednicki (Cracow: Polskie Towarzystwo dla badań Europy Wschodniej i Bliskiego Wschodu, 1939), Vol. I, p. 433.
[5] See above, p. 32.
[6] See above, pp. 86–87.

Madame Panov had said.[1] Chaadaev was a weak character, and this is the main reason for the various complications which must be faced by those who wish to analyze his ideology.

Plausible though Professor Struve's idea is, it does not convince me for the foregoing reasons. I should like to add, however, some facts in favour of his conception—facts which may reconcile the vivid portrayal of the Polonophil with Kozlovsky.

Lelewel's name appeared under Pushkin's pen, not only in the poetical fragment with which we have here been concerned, but also in one of the least attractive of Pushkin's texts. I have analyzed this text in one of the books which Professor Struve mentions in his article (*Aleksander Puszkin*, Cracow, 1926). I have in mind Pushkin's letter to Count Stroganov and a note in Pushkin's diary, in both of which Lelewel plays an important rôle. Professor Struve quotes only one sentence of this letter and only in a footnote. I believe that this item deserves more attention, even for the sake of Professor Struve's hypothesis. Under the date of 23 April, 1834, Pushkin wrote in his *Diary* the following note: "I have just received from Count Stroganov a page of the *Frankfurt Journal*, in which the following article was published." [Pushkin quotes the original French text from *Le Journal de Francfort*, samedi 12 avril, 1834, No. 101.]

> "Saint Petersburg, 27 February. Since the catastrophe of the Warsaw revolt the coryphaei of the Polish emigration have too often demonstrated by their words and writings that, in order to further their designs and exonerate their former conduct, they do not fear falsehood and calumny. Therefore, no one will be astonished by new proofs of their obstinate imprudence."

Pushkin interrupts the quotation with the following parenthetical remark in Russian:

> "The reference is to the ceremonial meeting organized in Brussels by the Polish *émigrés* and to the speeches delivered by Lelewel, Pułaski, Worcell and others. The meeting was organized on the anniversary of the fourteenth of December."

He resumes his French quotation:

> "Having falsified in this way the history of past centuries in order to make it speak in favour of his cause, M. Lelewel also maltreats modern history. In this he is consistent. In his own manner

[1] See above, p. 87.

he relates the progressive development of the revolutionary principle in Russia. He cites one of the best Russian poets of our days in order to reveal by this example the political tendencies of Russian youth. We doubt whether A. Pushkin, in a period when his eminent talent was still in fermentation and had not yet liberated itself from its scum, composed the stanzas quoted by Lelewel. But we may assume with conviction that he would regret the first efforts of his muse all the more for having given an enemy of his country the opportunity of assuming in him some correspondence of ideas and intentions. As far as Pushkin's opinion of the Polish rebellion is concerned, it has been declared in his poem, "To the Calumniators of Russia", which he published at that time. And since M. Lelewel seems to evince some interest in the fate of this poet, confined to the distant borderlands of the empire, our natural humanity prompts us to inform him of the presence of Pushkin in Petersburg and to note that he is often seen at the court, where he is treated with kindness and benevolence by his sovereign. . . ."[1]

Upon receiving this provocative and unpleasant clipping, unpleasant from every point of view, from Count Stroganov, Pushkin had an impulse to react. But he did not react at all in the manner in which civic courage and the feeling of responsibility should have directed him, particularly as he very well knew that the banquet at which Lelewel delivered his speech was connected with the Decembrist Insurrection, with which he had been in solidarity at the time of its

---

[1] Cf. *Dnevnik Puškina (1833–1835)*, pod red. Modzalevskogo (Moscow, 1923), pp. 13–14. As the commentator of the Moscow edition of the *Diary*, Professor M. Speransky states (cf. *Dnevnik A. S. Puškina*, Moscow: Trudy Gos. Rumjanc. Muzeja, 1923, Vol. I, pp. 399–400): "Pushkin precisely enough copied from *Le Journal de Francfort* . . . the beginning and the end of the article, that is the passages which were most concerned with him personally, whereas he omitted the middle, consisting of an historical excursion into the Russian and Polish past, particularly directed against Lelewel and against the Polish emigration in general. The author of the article accuses Lelewel of a tendentious deformation of historical facts, of the desire *assujétir l'histoire à ses idées*, and therefore he constantly elucidates and comments on these facts, considering it necessary to inform European public opinion of the actual state of affairs. After giving in brief the history of the Insurrection of the Fourteenth of December, the anniversary of which was the pretext for the demonstration of the Polish *émigrés*, the author of the article gives a general outline of Russian-Polish relations, on this occasion accusing Poland of aggressive intentions towards the Russian nation and ends with a characterization of the structure of Poland before the partitions." Speransky then quotes the parts of the article omitted by Pushkin and in these sections the author of the article explains that the partitions of Poland brought freedom to the Polish people, who for centuries had been under the tyrannical yoke of the Polish nobility. In addition, Speransky suggests that the author was a certain Bekhteev, who obviously wrote under the dictation of the Russian government. (For details see Speransky's edition of Pushkin's *Diary* and my *Aleksander Puszkin*, pp. 184–5.)

explosion. It is possible to object that an outburst of sympathy from Pushkin would have been foolhardy, as even without any other compromising actions this article could have caused him much trouble. In addition, this incident occurred in 1834, when Pushkin had changed his opinions and now sincerely condemned the Decembrist Insurrection. However, he could simply have corrected some inaccuracies in reporting Lelewel's speech (I do not know whether it was known to Pushkin, as from the text cited by him from the *Frankfurt Journal* it is difficult to conclude to what extent the article exhausted Lelewel's speech) or he could have remained silent about the whole affair. Actually, this is what Pushkin finally did. His first impulse was to write and answer, and this spontaneous gesture is extremely characteristic.

Several days after the receipt of the clipping he wrote to Count Stroganov: "Monsieur le Comte, I am sadly expiating the chimeras of my youth. Lelewel's embrace appears harsher to me than exile to Siberia. I thank you, however, for kindly sending me the article in question. It will serve me as a sermon...."[1]

Pushkin was not quite correctly informed about the essentials of the Polish manifestation in Brussels. Lelewel delivered his speech on 25 January, 1834. It was published under the following title: "Speech delivered in Brussels on 25 January, 1834, on the anniversary of the overthrow of Nicholas from the Polish throne and also in memory of the Russian Revolution of 1825 and the executed Russian patriots."[2] In this speech Lelewel erroneously attributed to Pushkin the authorship of several "tales". One of these was a well-known Russian product of French origin—the result of an adaptation of Ségur's fables.[3] Pushkin was not aware of all these details; his information was fragmentary and based only on the clipping mentioned previously.

We have seen what his spontaneous reaction was. Actually there was no need to write in such violent terms, as he knew Stroganov well and was even related to him. Still he considered Lelewel's "embrace harsher than exile to Siberia". He certainly did not suppose that he was seriously threatened by Siberia. But the praise of a Polish enemy appeared so offensive to him that he thought of the Decembrists, chained to their wheelbarrows in the Nerchinsk mines, and considered their fate more supportable than his own. I think it would be difficult to justify Pushkin's attitude in this case, although some Polish scholars have been obliged to do so under their present conditions of work in

[1] Cf. A. Puškin, *Sočinenija, Perepiska*, Vol. III, p. 96.
[2] Cf. *Polska i rzeczy jej, rozpatrywane przez Joachima Lelewela* (Poznań, 1864), Vol. XX, p. 188. These details have been disclosed by N. Lerner (see *Istoričeskij vestnik*, 1904, Vol. VIII, pp. 621–3) and by B. L. Modzalevsky (see *Dnevnik Puškina*, pp. 152–3).
[3] See *Dnevnik Puškina*, pp. 152–3; also *Puškin i ego sovremenniki*, Vol. V, pp. 110–15.

Poland. In my opinion this is indeed one of the least attractive pages in Pushkin's biography.

This story might be used for the support of Professor Struve's hypothesis, as it shows the vehement, even ferocious feelings of Pushkin towards Lelewel. If Professor Struve is right, then one may easily imagine how Pushkin reacted to Kozlovsky's revelations about his participation in the Brussels dinner. This might explain and justify the emotional tension of his poetical fragment. But we do not know that Kozlovsky took part in the Polish manifestation of 1834—this is only a conjecture on Professor Struve's part. In the light of Pushkin's remarks in his article on Radishchev, however, it seems much more acceptable to believe that Pushkin's poem deals with a Russian who manifested his pro-Polish feelings in Moscow during the Polish Insurrection of 1830–31.

II

Pushkin, Tyutchev, Mickiewicz and the Decembrists

LEGEND AND FACTS

> "... Peuple silencieux, souverain gigantesque!
> Lutteurs de fer toujours muets et combattants!
> Pierre avait commencé ce duel romanesque:
> Le verrons-nous fini? Est-il de notre temps?
> Le dompteur est debout nuit et jour et surveille
> Le dompté qui se tait jusqu'à ce qu'il s'éveille,
> Se regardant l'un l'autre ainsi que deux Titans...."[1]
> (A. de Vigny: *Wanda*, (xvi), 5 November, 1847.)

THIS is only a discussion, a purely speculative work, for comparativism proves little and seldom leads to any concrete results. In this case, at any rate, there will be no results and no conclusions. I shall pose questions and these questions will remain unanswered, for the charm of comparativism lies precisely in its character of literary speculation.

The theme of freedom is frequently touched upon by Mickiewicz in the *Digression* of *The Forefathers' Eve, Part III*, but in the form of a question. In *The Road to Russia* he writes:

> Each body is a web, a coarse-spun roll,
> In which there sleeps a caterpillar's soul,
> Ere it transforms its tiny breast for flight
> And weaves and tints its wings to fairy guise.
> But when the sun of liberty shall rise,
> What kind of insect then will greet the light?
> Will a bright butterfly soar from the earth,
> Or a dull moth of dark, uncleanly birth?[2]

---

[1] "... Silent People, gigantic sovereign!/Fighters of iron always mute and struggling!/Peter began this romantic duel:/Shall we see it brought to an end? Does it belong to our time?/The tamer is up night and day and surveys,/The tamed one who is silent till his awakening,/And each observes the other like two Titans...."

[2] Cf. Noyes, *Poems by Adam Mickiewicz*, p. 339.

The following passage contains the same idea, also expressed in the form of a question:

>This level plain lies open, waste and white,
>A wide-spread page prepared for God to write.—
>Will he trace here his message from above;
>And, using for his letters holy men,
>Will he sketch here his writ of faith again,
>That all the human race is ruled by love
>And offerings remain the world's best prize?
>Or will that fiend who still the Lord defies
>Appear and carve with his oft-sharpened sword
>That prison should forbid mankind to rise,
>And scourges are humanity's reward?[1]

The poet is even more pessimistic in *Saint Petersburg* as he accentuates his skepticism:

>A few lads wandered in that crowded place,
>Unlike the others both in garb and face.
>They scarcely glanced at all the passers-by,
>But viewed the city with astonished eye.
>Upon the summits, walls, foundation rocks,
>Upon the gratings and the granite blocks,
>They fixed their gaze as though to ascertain
>Whether each brick were solid as it lay.
>Hopeless, they dropped their arms, as if to say,
>'To overturn them man will strive in vain.'[2]

And further:

>He stood, hands raised to heaven, long in thought,
>His gentle face with hopeless pity fraught,
>He gazed as might an angel, tenderly,
>When, sent to purgatory from above,
>He sees whole nations writhe in agony,
>And suffers with them through his perfect love,
>Foreseeing how far-off is their release
>To lasting freedom, heavenly bliss, and peace.
>He leaned against the coping, weeping low;
>Hot tears ran down and perished in the snow:
>Each tear will be remembered by the Lord,
>And each will gain a vast and sweet reward.[3]

---

[1] *Ibid.*, p. 338.
[2] *Ibid.*, p. 347.
[3] *Ibid.*, pp. 347–8.

The poem *Oleszkiewicz* has as the main motif this prophecy:

> The Lord will shake the fair Assyrian throne;—
> The Lord will shake the walls of Babylon . . .[1]

This poem contains in a sense the last answer to the posed questions. This answer establishes the hope, and even more, the apocalyptic certainty that the era of slavery must come to an end. The forecast of this inevitable end stems from the approaching storm on the Neva and the flood which is brought in its wake. In this rhythm of a particular "progress" the poet presents his eschatology of Petersburg and of Russian slavery. The coming catastrophe contains an apocalyptic meaning, it announces freedom!

All these variations on the theme of freedom and slavery are Polish "variations", pronouncements of the author himself, of a group of Polish "lads . . . unlike the others in both garb and face", and finally, of Oleszkiewicz. In the same way this pronouncement appears—with some difference, as we may have noticed—in *The Road to Russia, Saint Petersburg* and *Oleszkiewicz*. The variation contained in *The Road to Russia* giving voice to the opinion of the author, skeptical and doubting as it were, is repeated in almost identical form in the poem *The Monument of Peter the Great*, in which the monument is a symbol of autocracy. In this instance, however, one should note that Mickiewicz employed a stratagem: he expressed his views through the mouth of the "Russian bard"; this is the end of the monologue in which the "Russian bard" depicts the Czar and his horse:

> Thus it has galloped long, with tossing mane,
> Like a cascade, leaping into the void,
> That, fettered by the frost, hangs dizzily.
> But soon will shine the sun of liberty,
> And from the west a wind will warm this land.—
> Will the cascade of tyranny then stand?[2]

As we know, the whole *Digression* was written after the Decembrist Insurrection. It is significant that in the poem "To My Russian Friends" Mickiewicz alludes precisely to the Decembrists, returning to the theme of freedom and slavery and extending quite personally to his "Russian friends" the message of freedom. To a certain extent this detail fixes the interior chronology as well as the *realia* of the *Digression*: everything mentioned in the *Digression* obviously deals with the times preceding the Decembrist Revolution—(the flood in *Oleszkiewicz* also confirms this). And what is more important, the

[1] *Ibid.*, p. 364.
[2] Cf. Noyes, *op. cit.*, p. 350.

composition of the poem, the words put in the mouth of Pushkin (the "Russian bard") acquire a concrete, historically real meaning. Indeed, Pushkin must have said something of that sort to Mickiewicz. Therefore, the skepticism contained in the quoted passage derives from Pushkin. But in this case the actual chronology was upset by the poet. As we know, Mickiewicz became acquainted with Pushkin in Moscow after the Decembrist Revolt and even after the coronation of Nicholas I, whereas the talk to which Mickiewicz alludes in his poem, if in general it occurred at the foot of the monument of Peter the Great and if it dealt with this particular theme, could have taken place only later, perhaps in 1828.[1]

Both Mickiewicz and Pushkin had genuine sympathy for the Decembrists, although they rather critically judged certain aspects of their activities preceding the outbreak of the Rebellion. In any case, the harsh fate which overtook all of them and the painful lot in Siberia of those who escaped execution awakened in Pushkin and Mickiewicz a deep, heartfelt poetic compassion. Neither of them belonged to the Decembrist conspiracy, but both knew very well their milieu, for they attended the meetings of the Decembrists. The sympathies of the two poets towards the Decembrists are evident in Pushkin's poem addressed to the Volkonskys, in his allusions to the Decembrists in *Eugene Onegin* and in Mickiewicz's poem "To My Russian Friends". Mickiewicz's course on Slavic literatures proves his intimate knowledge of the environment of the Decembrists. To what degree Pushkin knew the Decembrists is attested to by innumerable biographical facts. Of particular importance in this respect also is the so-called tenth chapter of *Eugene Onegin*, in which we find critical remarks of the poet about the Decembrists. These remarks are to a certain degree of the same nature as the critical opinions of Mickiewicz in his *Slavic Literature*.[2] Neither the criticism of Pushkin nor of Mickiewicz ever acquires the character of distinct moral condemnation of the Decembrist Revolution. The only exception to this, in a way, is Pushkin's memorandum *On Public Education* (1826). One has to remember, however, that Pushkin wrote his memorandum for Nicholas I and therefore was forced to proceed from an official interpretation and appraisal of this Revolution. In any case, Pushkin in his poetic writings never resorted to pathetic accusations and indignation. Besides, none of the more or less important Russian poets ever wrote in such a tone about the Decembrists. On the contrary, Russian (and not only Russian) poetry created a poetic legend out of

---

[1] Cf. W. Lednicki, *Przyjaciele Moskale* (Cracow, 1935), pp. 170-1, and also my essay on *The Bronze Horseman*, in the edition of the Instytut Wydawniczy "Bibljoteka Polska", (Warsaw, 1932), p. 66.

[2] Cf. Lecture XXVIII in 1840.

the upheaval surrounding the insurrectionists, a legend with an aureole of martyrdom and heroism. In our times the Decembrists have been subjected to a review trial which has thrown new light on the entire episode. The publication by the Soviet Central Archive of the files of the Decembrist trials and the works of the Soviet historian Pokrovsky and some others contributed to the revision. Modern Russian historiography opposes the opinions concerning the Decembrist Revolution held by Russian historians of the second part of the nineteenth century and the beginning of the twentieth who represented the ideology of Russian liberalism. This school, in the opinion of contemporary historians, deformed the historic reality and created two "golden legends", one about the Decembrists as inflexible knights of freedom, the other about the deep and general mourning which supposedly embraced the whole of Russian society, which, according to the authors of this legend, was solidly in agreement with the Decembrist Revolution after the execution of five Decembrists and after the exile to Siberia of all others who had escaped the death sentence of Nicholas' trial.

Foreigners who visited Russia in those times similarly characterized the mood of Russian society and the Decembrist movement. Below, in another connection, I shall quote the remarks of J. A. Ancelot (a French poet and playwright) about the attitude of Russian society towards the tragedy of the Decembrists, but this is what the French observer says about the Revolution itself:

> ". . . It was apparently in the name of freedom that all these powerful lords armed. But did they not desire this freedom only for themselves? They attempted to tear away from the yoke of the monarch's power—but what was the part of the people in this entirely aristocratic conspiracy? Does the sceptre weigh on them? No, because the peasants of the crown are free. Are we to believe that these proud descendants of the boyars enfranchised from the fetters which chained them to the throne of Peter the First have suddenly found similar human beings among those slaves whose lives had been bequeathed to them by their ancestors and whom they sell like cattle? The people did not believe it, and their immobility during the bloody scenes which took place before their eyes proves how little they were interested in this question. No doubt, among these aristocratic conspirators, there were several young men nurtured on generous ideas, who listened only to an exalted imagination and who dreamed about a new destiny for the people whom they believed they served and who did not understand them."[1]

[1] Cf. J. A. F. P. Ancelot, *op. cit.*, pp. 171–2.

Today the whole affair has a different aspect, which, in a way, confirms Ancelot's view. Contemporary historiography (the influence of Russian Marxism of course could not have been avoided) sees in the Decembrist Insurrection of 1825 purely a *class* revolution, unsuccessful in its very inception; besides, this revolution destroyed itself from the moral point of view as soon as its leaders became afraid that they were threatened by the "companionship" of the masses. They held aloof from this stratum and from that moment found themselves, so to speak, back again within the framework of their own class and their own social structure. They found themselves in the rôle of common political criminals and insurrectionist officers face to face with an aristocratic monarchy which was their own. They themselves could not help seeing in their own revolution *rebus sic stantibus* elements of betrayal and disloyalty. Their social backgrounds led them to this view. This is the leitmotif of their repentance during the trial. They possessed no objective arguments in their own defense. On the other hand, the whole of Russian society, with very few exceptions, turned away from them and manifested its legitimist stand and loyal attachment to the throne. Such was the reaction of the nobility toward the Revolution: Russian society hastened to exhibit its complete solidarity with Nicholas I and to condemn the Revolutionary Movement. This is the spirit in which the contemporaries of the Decembrists wrote of this group, authors of memoirs, poets, journalists, private observers, in their letters. In such a spirit also Pushkin wrote his famous memorandum *On Public Education*, in which he faithfully reflected the moods of the ruling class.[1] This very attitude of the gentry on one hand, and, on the other, the indifference of the masses towards "Decembrism" and the fear of the Decembrists of a popular revolution explain in the opinion of some modern Russian historians the almost general repentance of the Decembrists during their trial.

"It became clear," writes N. Piksanov in an interesting study about the reaction of the nobility toward the Decembrist Insurrection, "that without the masses the upheaval was impossible, but at the same time they expressed no desire to involve the masses. It became clear that Russian society was not behind the Decembrists —that is, that they had no strong social group which could sympathize with the revolution and support it. Very soon the Decembrists realized with stunning clearness that their reformism had outgrown

[1] In this respect the correspondence of the Bolotovs is interesting: Cf. "Iz perepiski Bolotovykh o Dekabristakh i A. S. Puškine"—publikacija N. A. Šimanova, in *Literaturnyj Arkhiv* Akademii Nauk SSSR, Inst. Lit. (Puškinskij Dom) I, pod red. S. D. Balukhatogo, N. K. Piksanova i O. V. Cekhnovicera, Moscow-Leningrad, 1939, pp. 273–89.

the needs of the only social group which could have supported them and with which group they themselves were tied by bonds of close social relationship—the nobility. At the same time there emerged a sharp feeling of social proximity towards the vindictive and victorious power, a power which was the vanguard of the ruling class."[1]

In other words, the Decembrists at the moment of defeat faced the necessity of recognizing themselves as common traitors and rebels. They underwent a radical, moral and ideological breakdown, which was followed by a complete psychological collapse. This is the essence of Piksanov's interesting documented study. There is no exaggeration in his conclusions, no schematism, no simplification of the problem.

"One cannot say that they all failed to maintain a heroic countenance. Traits of firm convictions, courage, devotion to the cause and to their comrades appear from time to time in the enormous files of the investigating commission. . . . But when one consults the six volumes published by the Central Archives it is impossible not to be struck by something else: faint-heartedness, readiness to recant ideas and actions. People who as free men had cultivated their military and personal honour as noblemen, always ready to defend it against the duelist's pistol, men who had been face to face with death in battle . . . debased themselves in the fortress before authority. They begged forgiveness, denounced one another, repented their sins. At the very first question, as if by agreement, they began to enumerate the rolls of secret organizations, to describe meetings and characterize the misdeeds of particular persons. They mentioned not only the active but also the proposed members, quoting speeches they had heard through second and third persons. Kakhovsky, a man close to Ryleev, attributed to his friend the intention to destroy the dynasty. When he was confronted with Ryleev, the latter denied this and Kakhovsky insisted on his grave testimony. In his turn Ryleev described Kakhovsky as an ardent terrorist and regicide. . . ."[2]

I will not continue Piksanov's dark enumeration.

Indeed, history shows similar trials, the Inquisition, the terrible trial of the Knights Templars in the fourteenth century and even the perhaps more terrible Bolshevik trials which have taken place in

[1] Cf. N. Piksanov: "Dvorjanskaja reakcija na dekabrism (1825–1827)" in *Zven'ja*, Academia, Moscow-Leningrad, 1933, Vol. II, p. 191.
[2] Page 187.

our own time; all these trials reveal one infinitely sad truth: the complete moral helplessness of the accused (in certain political conditions) who for months and years awaits a prisoner's death. One of the most courageous of the Templars, the knight Aimery de Villiers-le-Duc, a man of fifty, who for twenty-eight years had been a member of the Order, for several years bravely defended himself against ignominious and false accusations hurled against the Order. Suddenly on 13 May, 1310, when he had heard the points of accusation before the inquisitorial commission, he interrupted the debate,

> "pale and as if terrified, he protested, affirming that if he was lying he would be immediately ready to be sent to eternal damnation and to forfeit his life to sudden death; at the same time he beat his breast, stretched his arms to the altar and kneeled. 'I confessed to several accusations because of the tortures inflicted on me by the royal knights G. de Marcilli and Hugues de la Celle, but all this is a falsification. Yesterday when I saw fifty-four brothers of mine driven in vans to be burned at the stake because they had refused to confess our alleged sins, I thought that I would not be able to overcome my fear of fire. I should now be able to confess everything, I feel this; I would confess that I killed the Lord if this were demanded of me . . .' and he began to beseech the commission and the notaries not to repeat to his guards what he had just said out of fear of the stake which had been the fate of those fifty-four."[1]

The most terrible physical tortures were used in this trial. In the Bolshevik trials moral tortures were applied—threats, blackmail, the play of the so-called "two deaths" alternative, etc. In the trial of the Decembrists this torture was not undertaken. But a talk with the Emperor was in a sense a kind of torture. However, I am not defending

---

[1] Cf. Ch. V. Langlois, "Le procès des Templiers", etc., *Revue des Deux Mondes*, 1891, Vol. 103, p. 411. Cf. also the book of M. Zdziechowski, *W obliczu końca* (In the Face of the End), the essay "O okrucieństwie" ("About Cruelty"), in which there are quoted numerous examples of similar confessions. This is what Herzen says about torture in Russia: "Peter III abolished the torture chamber and the Secret Chancery. Catherine II abolished torture, and Alexander I *once more* abolished it. Answers given 'under the pressure of fear' are not considered legally valid. An official who tortures an accused person is subjected himself to trial and severe punishment. And still in the whole of Russia, from the Bering Straits to Taurogen, people are tortured; where it is dangerous to torture by beating, they torture with intolerable heat, thirst, and salty food. In Moscow the police put an accused man barefoot on an iron floor at ten degrees of frost (nine degrees Fahrenheit); he fell ill and died in a hospital which was under the control of Prince Meshchersky who related this story with indignation. The authorities know all this, the governors screen it, the *ruling* Senate connives at this, the ministers are silent, the Emperor and the Synod, the landlords and policemen—all agree with Seliphan: 'Why not thrash the peasant? Sometimes it is necessary to thrash him.' " Cf. A. I. Gercen, *Byloe i dumy* (Leningrad: Ogiz, 1946), pp. 102–3.

the Decembrists as such—I am simply trying not to overlook some human qualities. The trials mentioned here—is it necessary to point out the fearfully inhuman proceedings of the German Gestapo and the Russian GPU?—made clear the fact that there exist no limits to that to which the victims can be brought by a "vindictive and victorious" political power uncontrolled by the people. In this sense the moral helplessness of the victim in certain political conditions can also be limitless. Besides, there are periods during which the whole nation is so fatigued and weakened that even the most common and vulgar men are able to remain in power. These men arm themselves so well with the prestige of the state that the smallest criticism of their actions in private, social and state life, actions which might be base and even criminal, threatens with imprisonment or worse everyone who dares such criticism. A nation which tolerates such a state of affairs renounces its rights to convictions and actions. Such tolerance is not far removed from cowardly repentance. The attitude of the Decembrists with regard to the court of Nicholas I was deeply sad, but it was an individually human attitude, which fact one must remember. The dialectics of historical materialism does not suffice, although it explains quite a few things: Piksanov's study is a brilliant proof of this. And yet Ryleev's letter to his wife, written from the prison on the eve of his death, will remain forever a deeply moving document of human misfortune and not just a document of the political defeat of the nobility. Besides, those Decembrists in Siberia who escaped death led a noble life full of dignity and sometimes heroism. Some of them remained to the end faithful to the tradition of freedom and revolution. Not a crumb of this tradition or of their aristocratic social altruism had been lost in the Siberian mines, not a whit of their old habits of politico-philanthropic thoughts. And what of their wives!

> Non, non, il n'est pas vrai que le Peuple en tout âge
> Lui seul ait travaillé, lui seul ait combattu,
> Que l'immolation, la force et le courage
> N'habitent pas un coeur de velour revêtu.
> Plus belle était la vie et plus grande est sa perte,
> Plus pur est le calice où l'hostie est offerte.
> —Sacrifice, ô toi seul peut-être es la vertu!...[1]

On the other hand, it is true that Russian society as a whole, led by fear and opportunism, turned away from the Decembrists and

[1] "No, no, it is not true that the People in all ages,/Were the only ones to work, the only ones to fight,/That sacrifice, strength and courage/Do not dwell in a heart clothed in velvet./The more beautiful the life, the greater is its loss,/The purer is the chalice in which the Host is offered./—Sacrifice, o, thou alone perhaps art virtue!" A. de Vigny: *Wanda*, XIV.

hastened to manifest its solidarity with the victorious Nicholas; and the loyal manifestations of these "faithful subjects" were indeed repulsive and base enough. Piksanov quotes numerous examples of such an attitude on the part of Russian society. This is Russian testimony. We also have other, foreign, testimony, predominantly Polish. This is what Count Gustaw Olizar writes:

> "So ended this terrible political tragedy. Many families in the capital and the country were in deep mourning. The Russian women in general played a beautiful rôle as wives, faithful despite the greatest sacrifices. Ladies of the greatest families, such as the wife of Prince Sergey Trubetskoy [née Countess Laval], the wife of Nikita Muraviev [née Countess Chernyshev], Maria Raevsky [the wife of Prince Sergey Volkonsky], who abandoned her son, her only love—all of them dragged themselves to Nerchinsk despite the pleas of their families and the threats of the allegedly benevolent government. All of them knew that they would have to share their husbands' fate, which meant labour at the wheelbarrow in the rough garb of enslavement! Providence provided a Polish commandant of the camp, Leparski, a good and kind man who eased and assuaged their many unpleasant conditions. In face of the wonderful devotion of the women, how repulsive was the sight of the men's meanness. Quite a few brothers and other relatives of the victims deported to external exile exhibited their faithfulness to the Czar, seeing honour in any embroidery added to their livery of service, and unfortunately I knew a father who had lost three sons in this affair. . . . He was an enlightened and intelligent man who wrote in honour of the deceased a fable about three laurels planted by him, which the storm had broken. As a senator from Moscow he travelled for a long time in Italy at Nicholas' expense. To what depths of moral decline are people brought by the golden enslavement of autocracy! Let us hope that these remarks at least will be of some use to you, in the third generation—to you, enemies on earth but brothers in the spirit of superior Christian tenets."[1]

This beautiful passage is entirely in the spirit of Mickiewicz's "To My Russian Friends":

> Now to the world I pour this poisoned chalice
> A bitter tale sucked forth from burning veins;
> My country's blood and tears compound its malice;
> Let it corrode—not you, friends, but your chains!

[1] Cf. *Pamiętniki 1798–1865 Gustawa Olizara* (Lwów, 1892), pp. 261–2.

> If one of you cry out, his plaint unsteady
> The barking of a dog shall seem to me,
> Chained up so long that he at last is ready
> To bite the hand that gives him liberty.[1]

It brings to mind the pitiful lines about the Princess Trubetskoy in Słowacki's *Anhelli*:

> "Come, and we will show you the damp pit where that martyr dwelleth with her husband.
> She was a great lady and a princess and now she is a handmaiden of a beggar.
> And unworthy of her pity is he whom she loves; for, kneeling before the Emperor, he pleaded for his life, and they gave it to him, despising him."
> So saying, they came up close to a wall, and through the grating they beheld that wedded pair.
> The woman was kneeling before the man and in a basin of water was washing his feet; for he had returned from his work as a laborer.
> And the water in the basin was reddened from his blood, and the woman did not shudder at the man and the blood, and she was young and beautiful like the angels of heaven.
> That man and that woman were of the Czar's people.[2]

Had Gustaw Olizar known A. de Vigny's *Wanda*, he would have quoted this charming poem, at least its sixth and seventh stanzas:

> ... La fatigue a courbé sa poitrine écrasée;
> Le froid gonfle ses pieds dans des chemins mauvais;
> La neige tombe en lots sur sa tête rasée,
> Il brise les glaçons sur le bord des marais.
> Lui de qui les aïeux s'élisaient pour l'Empire,
> Répond: 'Serge,' au camp même où tous leur disaient: 'Sire.'
> Comment puis-je, à Moscou, dormir dans mon palais?
>
> 'Prenez donc, ô mes soeurs, ces signes de mollesse.
> J'irai dans les caveaux, dans l'air empoisonneur,
> Conservant seulement, de toute ma richesse,
> L'aiguille et le marteau pour luxe et pour honneur:
> Et puisqu'il est écrit que la race des Slaves

---

[1] Cf. Noyes, *Poems by Mickiewicz*, p. 368.

[2] Juljusz Słowacki, *Anhelli*, translated from the Polish by Dorthea Prall Radin. Edited with an introduction by G. R. Noyes (London: George Allen & Unwin Ltd., 1930), p. 55.

Doit porter et le joug et le nom des esclaves,
Je descendrai vivante au tombeau du mineur' ... [1]

Even more sharply than the Pole Olizar, a Frenchman—Ancelot—writes the following:

". . . We all thought that this bloody catastrophe which had preceded by so few days the coronation ceremony would sadden the festivities that were supposed to follow it; because there are hardly any families in Russia which would not have victims to weep over: what was my surprise, my friend, when I saw the relatives, the brothers, the sisters, the mothers of the condemned take active part in these brilliant balls, these magnificent repasts, these sumptuous parties! In the case of some of these noblemen an ambitious egoism and the habit of slavery have stifled the sweetest feelings of nature; some others, continually on their knees before power, were undoubtedly afraid that their grief would be accused of sedition, and their servile fear was a calumny against the sovereign. If in a despotic state one can explain this forgetting of the most natural feelings by that weakness of humanity which imposes on a man who has arrived at the age of ambition the needs for honour and wealth, what would one say of a woman, of a mother in the last phase of life, who, bent by the years towards the tomb which claims her, comes every day covered with diamonds to take part in the boisterous expressions of public gaiety while her son approaches painful exile or perhaps death? Well, my friend, this painful spectacle has offended our eyes all through the festivities, the description of which I have presented to you! Let us add, though, the fact that some women have not at all followed this example . . ."
(Then follows a description of the deeds of the Decembrists' wives.)[2]

And still one should not generalize. Ancelot arrived in Russia almost simultaneously with an extraordinary embassy which France had sent for the Russian coronation, and, although he stresses the fact that he did not belong to the embassy and did not play an official

---

[1] ". . . Fatigue has bent his crushed bosom;/The cold swells his feet in the bad roads;/The snow falls in lumps on his shaven head,/He breaks the ice floes at the edge of marshes./He, whose ancestors formed the Empire,/Answers: 'Serge,' in the very camp where everyone called them: 'Sir'./ How can I sleep in my Moscow palace? 'Take then, O my sisters, these signs of weakness./I will go into the caves, into poisonous air,/Conserving only from all my riches/The needle and hammer for luxury and honour:/And because it is written that the race of the Slavs/Has to carry both the name and burden of slaves,/I will descend alive into the tomb of the miner' . . ."

[2] J. A. Ancelot, *Six mois en Russie en 1826* (Paris, 1827), pp. 411–13.

rôle, still he mixed in official circles and together with the embassy staff he took part in the ceremonies and festivities of the coronation. Naturally he met there people of a particular type. I do not deny that this type represented the majority of the Russian gentry of that time. We know from Mickiewicz that the moods depicted by Ancelot were not general.

Mickiewicz in his necrology dedicated to Pushkin writes explicitly:

> "... I am deeply convinced that the enormous sums which the Russian cabinet spends to acquire obliging defenders outside the borders of the state would not suffice to pay any Russian writer for a single newspaper article, for the smallest praise or even for a polite word. What I am saying here is so true that during the coronation of Czar Nicholas it was impossible to find a single poet willing to sing the praises of this ceremony, which could have passed unnoticed if it had not been for a foreign bard from Paris who put at the feet of His Imperial Majesty the Czar of All the Russias an ardently legitimistic dithyramb."[1]

Accident had it that this "foreign bard" was Ancelot. Besides this, Mickiewicz mentions him earlier—with similar irritation in his letter to Madame B. Zaleska (27 September–9 October, 1826):

> "I do not dare to describe to you the ceremony, the banquets, spectacles, illuminations, because I have not so much confidence in my pen; I direct your curiosity to the newspapers, which will describe everything more precisely and in a more straight-forward way. We also have a beautiful work of a certain author in which are collected all these historically important events; I preferred to look on as a spectator and (as you may easily imagine) I rejoiced with the others. ..."[2]

The poet probably had the same "author" in mind when he wrote in his *The Review of the Army* (this passage was omitted by Mickiewicz from the text published by him):

> I leave this song to you, Frenchmen,
> You travelled as far as the city of Moscow,
> You came to the rubble created by your hands,
> Marching over the fresh corpses of your nation
> To sing the praises of the Czars

---

[1] Cf. *Adama Mickiewicza Dzieła Wszystkie* (Warsaw, 1936), Vol. VII, p. 56
[2] Vol. XIII, p. 275.

To praise the wisdom and kindness of the government
Which has not yet been praised by any of the Muscovites!
You born poets of banquets, anointments,
Massacres, partitions, enslavements, conquests,
You do not know any national prejudices:
You should be the bards of military reviews![1]

It is obvious that Mickiewicz's allusion to Ancelot in his letter to Madame B. Zaleska was not connected with Ancelot's book on Russia, as this book appeared in Paris in 1827. On the other hand, it is probable that while writing the passage quoted above from his *Digression*, Mickiewicz knew this book. The only possible conjecture involves an admission that Mickiewicz knew Ancelot's poem written on the occasion of the coronation, as I shall try to show below.

Ancelot's sojourn in Russia interested the Russian literary circles. He was received (before the coronation) in those circles with much to-do, caused mainly by a notice published in Bułharyn's *Northern Bee* (15 May, 1826, No. 58, p. 1)[2] on the occasion of Ancelot's arrival in Petersburg. This notice, couched in a tone of enthusiastic courtesy undoubtedly had the effect of allowing Ancelot to form quickly and easily deeper contacts with Russian literature. Very soon a dinner was arranged in his honour, with speeches and toasts ("some thirty writers and men-of-letters of both nations" were present) to the health of the Emperor, to the Imperial family, and to the successes of French literature. There followed Ancelot's reading of several fragments of his comedy *Incognito*, the text of which he gave at that very time to the troupe in Petersburg.[3] This dinner was described in No. 66 of the same *Northern Bee (Severnaya Pchela)* in an article which considerably worried and irritated Pushkin, who at that time was in seclusion in Mikhaylovskoe. This is what he wrote to Prince Vyazemsky on 27 May, 1826, in reference to the dinner:

"I have read in the papers that Lancelot" [Pushkin's name for Ancelot] "is in Petersburg.... I have also read that thirty men-of-letters gave him a dinner—who are these immortals? I have started to count them on my fingers, but even ten fingers are too many. When you come to Petersburg seize this Lancelot (I don't remember a single verse he has written) and do not let him go the rounds of the ale houses and taverns of our men-of-letters. In our relations with foreigners we have neither pride nor shame.... Of course I despise

---

[1] Cf. A. Mickiewicz: *Dziady, cz. III*, Wyd. "Bibljoteki Narodowej" (opr. Prof. J. Kallenbacha), Kraków, 1924, p. 248.
[2] Cf. Puškin, *Pis'ma*, pod red. B. L. Modzalevskogo, Vol. II, pp. 159–61.
[3] *Loc. cit.*

my fatherland quite thoroughly—but it vexes me when a foreigner shares this feeling with me. You, who are not tied up here—how can you remain in Russia? If the Czar gives me my freedom I shall not remain a month. We are living in sad times, but when I imagine London, the railroads, the steamships, English journals or Paris theatres and brothels—my deserted Mikhaylovskoe makes me so sad I could lose my mind."[1]

After Ancelot's return to France, he published his book *Six mois en Russie* (Paris 1827). In it, besides general information about Russia, he wrote about Russian literature (he even printed some translations from Pushkin, Zhukovsky, Boratynsky and Ryleev). He described the Petersburg literary dinner, the Decembrist insurrection and finally the coronation ceremonies in Moscow. His book was not well accepted in Russia, and some Russians (abroad and in Russia)—P. Sviniin, Count Yakov Tolstoy, Pushkin, Prince Vyazemsky—protested against it. This exasperation could easily have been foreseen, as the Russians, perhaps even more than the Poles, are sensitive to foreign criticism—Pushkin in his letter gave eloquent proof of this. Prince P. A. Vyazemsky in 1827 published in the *Moscow Telegraph* an extensive polemical review of this book which was later reprinted in the complete edition of his works.[2] This review appeared under the general title "Letters from Paris", and, as I have said, reappeared in the first volume of Vyazemsky's works, with an appendix in which he said the following: "He [Ancelot] arrived in Russia following the embassy of the Prince de Ragouse and in acknowledgment of his sojourn here left his 'Ode on the Occasion of the Coronation'."[3]

It is obvious that Mickiewicz alludes to this ode in his letter to Madame Zaleska, in the extracted passage from *The Review of the Army*, and of course in his article on Pushkin Mickiewicz clearly points out the song in praise of the imperial crown and the "bard" who "put at the feet of His Imperial majesty the Czar of all the Russias an ardently legitimistic dithyramb". It might be that by the word "work" Mickiewicz meant Ancelot's ode.

And yet Mickiewicz was in error when he so optimistically described the attitude and the mood of the Russian "men-of-letters". At the dinner described in the *Northern Bee* and by Ancelot, "toasts were drunk to the health of the Emperor Nicholas I".[4] This took place in May, 1826. In

[1] Cf. Puškin, *op. cit.*, pp. 12–13.
[2] Cf. *Polnoe Sobranie Sočinenij Knjazja P. A. Vjazemskago* (St. Petersburg, 1878), Vol. I, p. 232.
[3] *Ibid.*
[4] Cf. Ancelot, *op. cit.*, p. 47.

1827, this mood was even more in the spirit of "most ardent legitimism". The following is the report of von Fock (Director of Nicholas' Office of Secret Police and the right hand of Benckendorff) about a literary evening at O. M. Somov's on 31 August, 1827:

> "The spirit of the local men-of-letters appeared in its best form at an evening given by Somov August 31, 1827, on the occasion of a house-warming. There were not many people there, but there were represented all who, so to speak, direct the trends of opinion among the men-of-letters: journalists, editors of almanacs and several of the better poets. Among them was also the censor Serbinovich. Complete frankness presided in this gathering; they spoke about the literary life of former times, they recalled the men-of-letters who had lost their lives through being unreasonable, they told literary anecdotes, spoke about censorship and so forth. After the meal, over a glass of wine, the guests became very jolly, sang couplets, read some poems of Pushkin which the Czar had allowed to be printed. Baron Delvig had set to music the stanzas of Pushkin in which the Czar is compared to Peter. They began to speak about the Czar's dislike for abuse and corruption, about the frankness of his character, about his desire to form new laws for Russia; and finally the men-of-letters became excited to the extent that, as though on impulse, they jumped up from their chairs with a glass of champagne and drank a toast to the health of the Czar. One of them quite delicately proposed a toast to Pushkin's censor in order that mention of the Czar's name should not seem open flattery,—they all tossed off their champagne, steeping the stanzas of Pushkin in wine (!) 'If the fool Ryleev were alive and had some sense,' said one of the party, 'I swear that he would get to like the Czar and write verses in his honour'. 'Good chap, God grant him health,—the dashing fellow'—this is what was repeated on all sides. It is quite remarkable that now during private parties the Czar is remembered spontaneously as though on inspiration."[1]

At a dinner which took place in October or November of the same year this tone was manifested even more eloquently. Again we quote von Fock:

> "The poet Pushkin is getting along extremely well politically. He sincerely loves the Czar and even says that he owes his life to him, for he was so bored with life in exile and the constant chains that he wanted to die. Not long ago there was a literary dinner at which

[1] Piksanov, *op. cit.*, pp. 179–80.

champagne and Tokay wine awakened sincerity in everyone. They joked a great deal and laughed, surprisingly enough, for they were now openly and sincerely praising the Czar, whereas formerly they had made jokes about him. Pushkin said: 'I should have the name or patronym Nicholas, for without him I would not be alive. He gave me life and, what is much greater, freedom: Vivat!' "[1]

Finally, as we learn from Piksanov, on 6 December, 1827, there was held a well-attended literary party at N. I. Grech's, which is thoroughly described by von Fock:

"On St. Nicholas' day, the journalist Nicholas Grech gave a dinner for those celebrating his name day and also on the occasion of his having finished his *Grammar*. There were sixty-two guests, all men-of-letters, poets, scholars and particular lovers of literature. There had never before been quite such a gathering in which so many learned people, having come together and warmed themselves with wine, did not speak of the Czar ambiguously and criticize his measures. Now, on the contrary, all that one heard were anecdotes about the just rule of the Czar, praises of his new edicts and expressions of warm desire that the Czar should choose noble aides in his work. As far as the ministers were concerned *on ne se gênait pas*, and just as before—everyone told amusing anecdotes about abuses, always adding: 'Under this Czar all these will end. All our hope is in him, he knows all, sees all, is interested in everything; under him the innocent are not oppressed, he does not execute prisoners without trial; under his rule there is no idle slander, he hates only bribe-takers and scoundrels, but no one would dare to touch the harmless and the meek while he is Czar!' Before the end of the dinner one of the guests sang couplets written by A. E. Izmaylov (whom we know) in honour of Grech and his *Grammar* . . ."

The fourth couplet ends with the following lines: "And so, after prayer,/First—to the health of the Czar!"

"It is difficult to describe the joy these couplets evoked. But most pleasant of all was the fact that the couplets to the Czar were repeated in a loud voice by all the guests over and over with rapture. Many began to copy these couplets after dinner. Pushkin was delighted and continuously sang them to himself. He copied them and later took them to Madame Karamzin [the widow of the

[1] *Ibid.*

historiographer N. M. Karamzin]. Nechaev sent them to Moscow. Everyone is amazed by the present state of affairs: previously there was no mention of the Czars during such gatherings—if they did speak of him it was done ambiguously. Now they are singing couplets and delightedly repeating them."[1]

This is not the end of it. We must remember that Pushkin himself wrote his "Stanzas" to the Czar and, besides him, Prince P. S. Shalikov wrote his "Blessing of Hearts", a dithyramb in which he, even before Pushkin, compared Nicholas to Peter the Great. Prince Shalikov offered his poem to the Czar in May, 1826, that is, even before the coronation.[2] There were other people who also wrote tributes and they were even lesser figures than Shalikov.[3] All this contradicts whatever Mickiewicz said on the subject. Of course Mickiewicz could have neglected Prince Shalikov. We know from his letter to Odyniec, March, 1827, how casually he regarded Prince Shalikov and his *Ladies' Review*; of course he could also have ignored Viskovatov.[4] At the Grech dinner were assembled people belonging to a special literary group, but—I repeat it again—we should not forget that Pushkin himself wrote his famous "Stanzas" in the same dithyrambic tone about Nicholas I. The difference then was merely in talent. And Piksanov is quite correct in saying that when we put Pushkin's "Stanzas" against the background of this panegyric chorus "Pushkin's voice loses its particular timbre and mixes with the general rumbling."[5]

Mickiewicz tried to defend Pushkin in his article about the poet and in his lectures at the Collège de France.[6] He was probably right in stating that Pushkin was sincere in his enthusiasm and that he was not guided by pure ambition and opportunism. But undoubtedly Bułharyn and Sękowski were also present at Grech's dinner. Therefore Mickiewicz had quite sufficient sources for precise information about the moods which prevailed in the Russian literary world of that time. What, then, could have brought Mickiewicz to write in such a categorical fashion about the intransigent spirit of opposition among the Russian men-of-letters and poets after the execution of the Decembrists and during the time of the coronation? I believe that Mickiewicz's friendship with Prince Vyazemsky played an important rôle here: Prince Vyazemsky most certainly formed Mickiewicz's views in this case. I mention

[1] Cf. Piksanov, *op. cit., loc. cit.*
[2] Page 183.
[3] Page 184.
[4] *Ibid.*
[5] Page 185.
[6] Cf. Lecture XXVIII in 1842.

Prince Vyazemsky because his opinions in that period of his liberalism were absolutely unyielding. This "would-be Decembrist" was much more determined in his views than all the Decembrists taken together. The following is what he wrote in March, 1826, and to whom!—to Zhukovsky!

"You misunderstood the end of my letter. Why should the recent events change my views? Truth, or what is considered the truth, cannot be forced aside by incidental circumstances or accidental applications, by partial contradictions. . . . Why are you astonished that, despite senseless attempts of many and even criminal attempts of some, I do not desert opinions in which it seems to me that the truth was and is and always will be . . . For instance I know for certain that Muraviev Apostol did not hand over the town Vasilkov to looting and fire as is stated in the report of Roth. The town and its inhabitants remained untouched. What reason is there for this voluntary calumny? And after all this you are astonished that I sympathize with the victims and that I am even repelled by the thought of being a collaborator of their hangmen? How is it possible for us to avoid the shocks and explosions of rage when we are held in such oppression . . . I willingly believe that the worst crimes, the most unwise designs must be born in the minds of people who are painfully and violently held down. Is not our situation one of violence? Have we not been forced down and broken? Open wide, though not limitless fields for the activity of the brain—and then it will have no reason to throw itself into conspiracy in order to restore its free blood circulation, without which it is subject to convulsions. . . . I am preaching here quite disinterestedly because I am sure that my words are ineffective as far as you are concerned. But I feel more relieved having expressed what was burning in my heart" . . .[1]

We also know about the circle of the *lyubomudry*—the *arkhivnye yunoshi*[2]—the closest Russian friends of Mickiewicz in Moscow. This circle included Venevitinov, Prince Vladimir F. Odoevsky, Kireevsky, Rozhalin, Titov, Shevyrev and Koshelev. This group, despite its absolutely non-political character and only distant ties with the Decembrists, was in moral solidarity with them:

[1] *Ibid.*
[2] "Youths from the archives"—distinguished young men of the Moscow nobility who served in the archives of the Russian Foreign Office which at that time were located in Moscow. Among these young Russian intellectuals were many well-known poets, writers, influenced mostly by the German idealistic philosophy and romantic poetry. They appear under the appellation "youths of the archives" in *Eugene Onegin*. Cf. Chapter VII, Stanza 49.

"We youths were rather in a state of excitement than suffering and almost desired to be arrested in order to acquire fame and the martyr's crown. These events brought us remarkably closer to each other and, perhaps, strengthened the ties of friendship which bound Venevitinov, Odoevsky, Kireevsky, Rozhalin, Shevyrev and myself,"

writes E. A. Koshelev.[1]

Although these moods were probably only romantic dreams and, as we know, the circle of the *lyubomudry* never showed any real readiness for, or interest in, any political demonstration, the atmosphere could have impressed Mickiewicz. One may believe that it was in the atmosphere of this circle and through the talks of its members that Mickiewicz formed the opinions expressed in his necrology on Pushkin.

M. Aronson's study "*Konrad Wallenrod* and *Poltava*" puts a clear light on this question. Aronson shows that it was precisely in Moscow in general and in the circle of the *lyubomudry* in particular that liberal and opposition moods were long preserved, even revolutionary views characterized by an ideological solidarity with the Decembrists. Sobolevsky, Shevyrev and even to a certain degree Pogodin had similar attitudes. These attitudes were accompanied by hopes in the possible willingness of Nicholas I to initiate reforms.[2] All these men, as we know, were Mickiewicz's closest friends. As a matter of fact, Pushkin inwardly thought and felt in the same way. Who knows, perhaps von Fock coloured his reports—perhaps in this way he tried to smuggle in some elements of criticism which were in his opinion justified. We know in addition that his attitude towards Pushkin and Mickiewicz was friendly, a fact that is indirectly proved by von Fock's *Sekretnaya Gazeta* (Secret Report) in the case of Mickiewicz and Malewski. Above all, the rôle which Pushkin could have played in this affair is in the effectiveness of his intervention with respect to von Fock. One is tempted to suppose that von Fock intentionally spared Pushkin and Mickiewicz.[3] Perhaps von Fock's informants while writing their reports also tendentiously exaggerated their emphasis on the loyal atmosphere in the circle of the Russian men-of-letters.

It is also possible to advance here another supposition: Mickiewicz might have read Ancelot's book, but he could not have found anything in it to awaken any unfriendly feelings on his part toward Ancelot.

[1] Piksanov, *op. cit.*, p. 146.
[2] Cf. M. Aronson, "*Konrad Wallenrod i Poltava*", in *Puškin Vremennik* (Moscow—Leningrad, 1936), Vol. II, pp. 43–56.
[3] Cf. W. Lednicki, *Aleksander Puszkin* (Kraków, 1926), pp. 218–25 ("Pushkin—Mickiewicz's Protector").

Ancelot gave a description of Petersburg which remains entirely in Mickiewicz's style:

> "My first glances demanded a people for this artificial capital of Russia; but they met only princes, palaces and barracks ... Indeed the natives are, so to speak, lost among the crowd of Livonians, Lithuanians, Estonians, Finns and foreigners of all types...."

Along with the barracks character and cosmopolitanism of Petersburg he emphasizes the fantastic magnificence of the Russian capital which had, as it were, emerged from the mud and the marshes, exactly the picture found in Mickiewicz's description of the city.[1] Ancelot describes the "road to Petersburg" in only a slightly different manner from Mickiewicz:

> "This city is not dominated by hills which would permit its sudden discovery, and the miserable wooden huts scattered along the road do not suggest the approach to a great city. One suspects it only at the moment when one sees the elegant and frail country houses which luxury has sown around it...." But on the other hand: "One is quickly tired with astonishment and admiration because one feels at every step that there is no place here for happiness, no place for freedom..."

This is again a completely Mickiewiczian assertion although made independently of Mickiewicz. Custine, Ancelot and Mickiewicz looked at Petersburg with their Western eyes, and this is why they discovered in the Russian capital the same traits. About Russia, in general, Ancelot says the following, again like Mickiewicz: "... the whole nobility is transformed into an innumerable regiment and the empire is a vast barracks..." Petersburg is for him "a gigantic creation of a strong will, a real prodigy of obedience..." The monumentality of Petersburg is unstable, "made of paper" and "... the buildings have a certain air of fragility which makes them similar to cardboard; and a foreigner could feel that he is in a city which has been placed here today, to be transferred tomorrow to another place." Only some few palaces and the granite quays of the city would prevent this. A superficial Europeanization of Russia—this is the result of Peter's reforms:

> "Armed with an unshakeable will, the absolute sovereign of a nation which knows one duty, obedience, he undertook to force it to cross with one jump the enormous space separating it from the

[1] Cf. Mickiewicz's *Digression*, Noyes, *op. cit.*, p. 337.

rest of Europe; the élan was given and the Russian nation leapt over centuries...."

Indeed it seems that Mickiewicz read this book before writing his *Digression*. The characterization of Russian revolutionary moods which filled Pushkin's "Ode to the Dagger" also suggests the comparison with Mickiewicz's remarks on the subject:

> "The republican fanaticism which breathes in this poem, the wild energy of emotions which inspired it announce what the ideas are that are sown in the minds of a large class of young Muscovites by the education given to them and by the communications which became more frequent between them and the various nations of Europe...."[1]

Here we have again ideas which could have been remembered by Mickiewicz when he wrote his *Monument of Peter the Great*. It is worth while to observe that Pushkin in his *Memorandum on Public Education* developed views also very close to Ancelot's observations. Ancelot based all his hopes on Nicholas:

> "By bringing youthful and prudent modification into the government let the wisdom of the monarch calm this exaltation which might one day push an entire generation toward crime. These ideas have not yet infiltrated to the people; but they have invaded the views of all educated young Russians whose studies have brought them into contact with new mores and modern institutions. And one should not believe that this new education will not make them less dangerous by enlightening them. Similar to their buildings of brick, from which the smallest accident might take away the white polished stucco cover, the Russians quickly allow their Tartar-like characteristics to be discovered under this shining cover with which a precocious civilization has clothed them."[2]

It would be sufficient to look into Pushkin's *Memorandum* to be convinced that the plan of "state education" which he develops in it is in complete conformity with Ancelot's opinion. It is possible to admit that Pushkin and Mickiewicz could have become acquainted with Ancelot during the coronation ceremonies in Moscow and that Ancelot could have expressed some of the views which appeared in his "Epistles" on Russia to his Petersburg and Moscow acquaintances. But enough about Ancelot.

[1] Cf. Ancelot, *op. cit.*, pp. 39, 42, 43, 89, 221, 224, 229, 232, and 307-8.
[2] Page 308.

Pushkin severely rebuked the Decembrist movement, but he also rebuked the causes that lead to revolution. Of course Pushkin advanced his "totalitarianism" unexpectedly far for those times. Therefore it would not be easy to find a justification for such a violent change of attitude as that which occurred in Pushkin. Opportunistic considerations certainly played a rôle here. I think that Mickiewicz was the one who gave the final, the best and the most delicate report of this affair, although he touched on it only indirectly in his *Necrology on Pushkin*[1] and in his Paris lectures.[2] Mickiewicz tries to be as tolerant and friendly as possible towards Pushkin. He emphasizes the effect of the famous talk between Pushkin and Nicholas I during the latter's stay in Moscow for the coronation. He stresses how charming the Emperor was during this talk, and he quotes Pushkin's sincere enthusiasm and faith in the young monarch. He underlines the exceptional character of this talk. He says that "during all of Russia's history this is the first time that the Czar deigned to talk with a man who lacked any rank giving him the right to such an honour"; that "the Czar almost tried to excuse his ascension to the throne"; that "he encouraged the poet in further literary work", and that "Pushkin was deeply moved"; that "he confessed to his foreign friends what he could not confess to Russians"; that "he was unable to feel any hatred toward the Czar".[3] However, he also said that "the painful end of the conspiracy nevertheless had a negative influence on Pushkin's mind; it robbed him of courage and political enthusiasm. From this time he begins to decline, as one may see in his poems. He did not admit to himself as yet that he had been ruined, but in trusted groups he mocked his former friends, or at least their ideas".[4] Mickiewicz eloquently described the split which took place between Pushkin and Russian society, the accusations of the latter expressing its mistrust and disillusionment in a man who had been considered the ideological leader of Russia. He also mentioned the bitterness which these accusations created in Pushkin's mind.

All this entirely confirms what I have said above, that it would seem to be impossible to find in Russian poetry a directly hostile ethical condemnation of the Decembrist Revolution. Even the tenth chapter of *Eugene Onegin*, although it contains political and historical criticism of the Decembrists, although it is written in an ironic tone, is still not an insulting and morally degrading refutation of the insurrection. Besides, the poet does not spare himself in these stanzas, he binds himself with the Decembrists and admits the fact that he had recited

---

[1] *Adama Mickiewicza Dzieła Wszystkie*, Vol. VII, pp. 57–8.
[2] Cf. Lecture XXVIII in 1842.
[3] Cf. *Necrology* and the lecture.
[4] Cf. Lecture III in 1842.

his own "Noëls" at their secret meetings. But there is an exception. In 1826 or 1827 there was written a poem which is a *curiosum* in Russian literature. It was the work of a young poet, Tyutchev, who later became one of Russia's greatest.

L. Grossman in his fine essay on Tyutchev dedicated the following remarks to this poem:

> "He is opposed to the Decembrists. And this time his indignation swells with a creative anger. When he learns that in Yaroslav mud was thrown at the Decembrists marching to Siberia, he joins this explosion of dark popular hatred and also adds a faggot to this stake of Hus. He does not pardon these 'victims of reckless thought' their mad courage; he justifies the people who slander their names, and he threatens them with eternal oblivion in posterity. This is the only condemnation of the Decembrist martyrs from the heights of Russian poetry, and it is the only dark spot on the pure cloth of Tyutchev's muse."[1]

I do not quite agree with Grossman's statement. First, I do not consider at all "the cloth of Tyutchev's muse" so pure and I believe that there are many other spots of the same kind on it. But Tyutchev's poem "To the Decembrists" is not so simple. The ambivalent nature of this "Russian prophet of world revolution" and "apostle of Russian imperialistic monarchy and triumphant orthodoxy", who always appears in his political poems with a sword in one hand and a cross in the other, found an equivocal and ambiguous expression in this early poem. But let us first look at the poem.

To the Decembrists

Autocracy has perverted you,
And its sword has routed you,
And the law, in the spirit of uncorruptible impartiality,
Has confirmed this verdict.

The people, foreign to treachery,
Slander your names,
And your memory for posterity
Is buried in the earth like a corpse.

O, victims of reckless thought!
You hoped perhaps
That your poor blood would suffice
To melt the eternal pole.

[1] Cf. L. Grossman, *Ot Puškina do Bloka*, etc. (Moskow, 1926), p. 103. Cf. also the remarks of Piksanov, *op. cit.*, p. 158.

Scarcely smoking, your blood sparkled
On the ageless pile of ice:
The iron winter breathed,
And not a trace remained.[1]

Some time ago I yielded to the temptation of defending this poem, as I seemed to find in it a hidden meaning behind the official condemnation, so to speak, of the Decembrists which emerges from its façade.[2] This was my reasoning: first of all the first line is ambiguous—"Autocracy has perverted you". It is ambiguous in connection with the other parts of the poem, for taken by itself its sense is absolutely clear. It does not express any condemnation of the Decembrists. The next line, "And its sword has routed you", simply asserts a fact. The last two lines of the first stanza are particularly ambiguous—"And the law, in the spirit of uncorruptible impartiality,/Has confirmed this verdict". These two lines, inasmuch as they were ambiguous, could not give the censor any opportunity for reservations. But still "the spirit of uncorruptible impartiality" might sound ironical. The second stanza again simply asserts facts and it might be that it does not express anything else. For this reason it is perhaps far from any "creative anger". The most striking and interesting are the two last stanzas. The poet risked a very drastic confession. He says that it was madness to admit the possibility of melting the "eternal pole" with the "poor blood"; that this "smoking blood" only "sparkled on the ageless pile of ice" and one breath of the "iron winter" sufficed to destroy the slightest trace of it. Again I thought that this did not represent the poet "swelling with creative anger". On the contrary, the sense of these last two stanzas appears to be

[1] Vas razvratilo samovlast'e
I meč' jego vas porazil,
I v nepodkupnom bezpristrast'e
Sej prigovor zakon skrepil.

Narod, čuždajas' verolomstva
Ponosit vaši imena,
I vaša pamjat' dlja potomstva,
Kak trup v zemli, skhoronena.

O, žertvy mysli bezrassudnoj!
Vy upovali, možet byt',
Čto stanet vašej krovi skudnoj,
Čtob večnyj poljus rastopit'.

Edva dymjas', ona sverknula
Na vekovoj gromade l'dov:
Zima železnaja dokhnula,
I ne ostalos' i sledov.

[2] Cf. *Puszkin 1837–1937* (Kraków: Prace Polskiego Towarzystwa dla badań Europy Wschodniej i Bliskiego Wschodu, 1939), Vol. I, pp. 311–12.

not at all clear. My opinions have been wholeheartedly supported by two distinguished Russian scholars who reviewed my book.[1]

As I stressed above, the poem is ambiguous and equivocal, and for this reason it is difficult to present a final verdict. Perhaps I was right in stating that this poem contains simply statements of fact and that if it contains any philosophy, any historical evaluation, this would be a skeptical one. This skepticism, by the way, represents a very close parallelism with Pushkin's view of the Decembrists. Tyutchev shows their weakness, the invincible power of autocracy and the isolation of the Decembrists, their separation from the people. All this is true. But now my feelings are different; there remains one thing: "c'est le ton qui fait la musique". Tyutchev's wording, his vocabulary is significant enough. Epithets and definitions like "people foreign to treachery", "buried corpse", and especially "poor blood" are not in the least ambiguous. On the other hand, the lines "Autocracy has perverted you" and "the spirit of uncorruptible impartiality" under the blows of expressions such as "treachery", "corpses" and "poor blood" lose the equivocation and irony which one may discover in them when one detaches them from the rest of the poem. I should also add that the case of the lines "And your memory for posterity/Is buried in the earth like a corpse" is again not quite simple. We know a variant of these lines: "And your memory for posterity/Is given to the earth alive" (I pamyat' vasha dlya potomstva/zemli, zhivaya, predana).[2] This shows that the poet was not quite sure of his way. The "living memory" is a tribute to the Decembrists. But the poet renounced this homage—one would be inclined to believe that the phantom of cowardice was following him. And when one takes into consideration the general character of Tyutchev's political poetry one might find it difficult, to say the least, not to sense that the poem really echoes the official condemnation and contempt for the Decembrists. This is precisely what is so uninviting in this poem—its poetic impurity. I do not feel any "creative anger" in it —what I do feel is the poet's daring but cautious, intentional ambiguity, the speech of a false prophet, of someone who plays not only with words but with ethics, the performance of an intellectual deceiver.

Besides the problem of the ideological interpretation of this poem there remains a purely literary question. I call the attention of the reader to the last two stanzas of the poem. Involuntarily there appears before one's eyes the image which Mickiewicz brought out at the end

---

[1] Cf. P. Bicilli, "Puškin i Rossija v pol'skom literaturovedenii" in *Russkie Zapiski*, XX–XXI, Paris 1939, p. 175. Cf. also R. Jakobson: "Polish Scholarship and Pushkin" in *The American Slavic and East European Review*, 1946, Vol. V, Parts 12–13, p. 88.

[2] Cf. F. I. Tjutčev, *Polnoe sobranie stikhotvorenij*, pod red. V. Gippiusa i K. Pigareva (Leningrad, 1939), p. 261.

of his poem *The Monument of Peter the Great*: "Thus it has galloped long, with tossing mane, etc."[1] Is not this image a reversed picture of Tyutchev's image? These are opposed, contrary elements; but the idea, the conception of the image is almost the same. Mickiewicz composed an image which became a kind of answer to the end of Tyutchev's poem. The similarity, or rather the kinship between these two images is clear to me. Is it accidental? Probably it is. But it also could have been otherwise. Tyutchev wrote his poem in Munich in 1826 or 1827; the recent editions publish it with the date 1826 followed by a question mark; the poem did not appear in print until 1881. Who knows, however, whether Tyutchev had not sent his poem to Petersburg to his friends? Who knows whether Mickiewicz did not become acquainted with this poem abroad? His "Muscovite friends" could have shown it to him; there is nothing improbable in such a supposition. In that case Tyutchev's poem could have been remembered by Mickiewicz and could have suggested to him the spectacular image which appears in *The Monument of Peter the Great*, an image which is an excellent pendant to the finale of Tyutchev's poem about the Decembrists.[2]

I had no intention of bringing my speculations to any conclusions. But now, as I summarize in my mind the story of the Decembrists and the foreign and Russian reactions to these historical facts, I once more think about the terrible influence which any uncontrolled, despotic political power fatally exercises on the human personality. The greatest disaster which inevitably follows a long period of autocratic rule is the loss of moral character and personal dignity in the heart of the subjugated human being. The Westerners who observed Russian society of those times, Ancelot, Custine, Vigny, Olizar and Mickiewicz, were unanimous in their judgment. This judgment was filled with pity and its pathetic essence is still true for today. Was not Mickiewicz right when he alluded in his poem "To My Russian Friends" to the dog "chained up so long that he at last is ready to bite the hand that gives him liberty"?[3]

[1] Cf. above, p. 107.
[2] It is interesting to note, at any rate, that during his stay in Russia in the spring and summer of 1825 Tyutchev betrayed obvious liberal tendencies. Pogodin, who met him at that time, noted in his diary: "I talked with Tyutchev about foreign literature, politics and about the character of life there. He tosses sharp words about although one may see that he did not work there too seriously. He smells of the court. He throws about many witticisms. In Russia—offices and barracks. Everything is centered about whip and rank." Cf. F. I. Tjutčev, *Polnoe sobranie stikhotvorenij*, red. i kommentarii G. Čulkova Vst. st. D.D. Blagogo (Moscow-Leningrad: Academia, 1933), Vol. I, pp. 307–8. For more detailed information see *Puszkin, 1837–1237* (Cracow, 1939), Vol. I, p. 313, a footnote in which there are references to the works of D. Strémeoukhoff and R. Blüth. Independently of each other, Blüth and I were attracted by the striking parallelism in the images of Mickiewicz and Tyutchev.
[3] Cf. above, p. 115.

This is how Herzen characterized the moral degradation of Russian high society which followed the catastrophe of 14 December, 1825:

> "The mood of society changed before one's very eyes. The rapid moral decline served as sad proof of the limited development of the feeling of personal dignity among the Russian aristocrats. No one (except the women) dared to manifest sympathy or to say a warm word about the relatives and friends with whom on the eve of their arrest he had been shaking hands. On the contrary, there appeared wild fanatics of slavery: some were naturally base and others were even worse, as they debased themselves disinterestedly."[1]

---

[1] A. I. Gercen, *op. cit.*, pp. 30–1.

III

Europe in Dostoevsky's Ideological Novel

I

I SHALL not try to give here any new definition of the genre of Dostoevsky's novel, nor shall I start any detailed analysis of the complex nature of Dostoevsky's art. The works of modern scholars and critics such as V. Ivanov, B. Engelhardt, L. Grossman, M. Bakhtin, and K. Mochulsky, among others, have revealed this complexity and established several essential features of Dostoevsky's novelistic technique, without mentioning Dostoevsky himself and his own comments concerning the basic character of his art. Since the appearance of these works we have at our disposal a great variety of definitions: "the novel-tragedy", "the ideological novel", "the polyphonic novel", "the novel of incident—with the idea as its main hero", "the sensational novel", "the detective novel", and, finally, Dostoevsky's formulae: "the historian of the accidental tribe" and "fantastic realism".

There is no doubt that the extraordinary amassing of action which destroys the empiric notion of time, to a degree not encountered in any other novels, and which necessitates a concentration of space, brings Dostoevsky's novel very close to the three unities of the classical tragedy. Dostoevsky's novels, so often voluminous, present stories which generally last only a few days, and their action is frequently located not only in one town but in many cases in one house, with some nonessential exceptions. For this reason Dostoevsky's works have been, without any great difficulty, so often adapted to the stage. Significantly enough, Dostoevsky's first teachers were Schiller, Racine, Corneille, Molière, and Shakespeare. From this point of view Dostoevsky's "fantastic realism" is based on dramatic conventions.

Among the definitions which I have mentioned above there are two which are important for the purpose of the studies which I am presenting here: "the ideological novel" and "the polyphonic novel". Both B. Engelhardt and M. Bakhtin justly emphasized the fact that for a long time Russian literary critique remained not above but beneath the novels of Dostoevsky, and, being dominated by Dostoevsky's heroes and their ideas, was lost in the labyrinth of contradictions in which these heroes were themselves involved. The definition of "polyphonic novel" became very helpful. Indeed, Dostoevsky's admirable ability to create various independent characters, who have egos which are as if completely autonomous, produces the impression of a polyphony, in which every voice has its intrinsic value, one would say even—an uncontrolled power. The hero for Dostoevsky, following Bakhtin, is a point of view for the observation of the world and of human life, something more than a means of lyrical expression. Taken from this angle, the "dialogical" novel of Dostoevsky is in opposition to Tolstoy's "monological" novel. Dostoevsky's novel is one about ideas and about their fate in the life of Russian society. Dostoevsky's heroes are seized by ideas and carried away by them. Engelhardt gives many illustrations of this.

The circumstance that Dostoevsky was, in his own opinion, the "historian of the accidental tribe" has a special significance. The term "accidental tribe" refers to the Russian intelligentsia, which was formed from various representatives of the historical classes of Russian society. This "accidental tribe" consisted of people who were free from the social and cultural traditions essential to the historical classes of their origin, or even opposed to these traditions. Hence, they were defenseless in the face of ideas and could be more easily enslaved by them than, for instance, the heroes of Goncharov, Turgenev, and Tolstoy especially, who were deeply rooted in the historical past of Russia. Dostoevsky himself emphasized the fact that Tolstoy was the historian of the Russian gentry, who had the last word to say about this class. True, the term "accidental tribe" acquired in the mind of Dostoevsky a wider meaning. Dostoevsky considered the Europeanization of the Russian élite a fateful accident in the historical development of Russian society. But this, for the time being, is a parenthetical remark. What is important is the fact that by utilizing representatives taken from this new "tribe" or class, Dostoevsky could illustrate with particular force the power of ideas over human beings. From the polyphonic structure of his novels emerges a relativistic vision of the world. One may say that here the monistic conception of the world has been fractured; one world has been replaced by a plurality of worlds which are functions of the various individual conceptions of Dostoevsky's heroes. Dostoevsky is interested not in the position of the hero in the world but in the idea of the hero about the world and about himself. These explanations of Dostoevsky's "ideological novel" would seem to eliminate any ideological responsibility of the author: Dostoevsky supposedly is only an observer, an historian, and a reporter.

The question of the independence of the heroes from the author has been often discussed and even on the level of purely aesthetic evaluations.

A great Polish novelist, Stefan Żeromski, who was, by the way, someone deeply influenced by Dostoevsky, was often accused of an aesthetically questionable tendency to give his heroes his own thoughts, emotions, and even erudition. Being thus realistically unmotivated, the verisimilitude of his characters was destroyed. Needless to say, we have many examples of the same vice not only in the early novels of Dostoevsky (in *The Insulted and Injured* Natasha discusses with Prince Valkovsky like a well-trained "ancient sophist", as Dobrolyubov ironically observed) but also in his great novels. It suffices to mention Raskolnikov, Myshkin, Shatov, and all of the Karamazovs. Dostoevsky often manifests the intentional disregard of the "fantastic realist" for any sociological consistence: particularly illustrative is the abuse of French. How many of his heroes from obviously low social strata and conditions of life unexpectedly speak perfect French, how many of them startle us with their unexpected knowledge: Marya Alexandrovna Moskalev in *Uncle's Dream* with her Lauzun or Shakespeare, Lebedyev in *The Idiot* with his du Barry, Nastasya Filippovna and General Ivolgin with their *Indépendence Belge*, and even Myshkin with his speculations on the theme of Catholicism, Mrs. Marmeladov with her German citations from Heine, and Dmitry Karamazov with his long quotations (in Russian) from Schiller.

With regard to *The Insulted and Injured* Dostoevsky himself felt obliged to admit that "in my novel are exhibited many dolls and not people, that in it are walking books, and not persons who have acquired an artistic form",[1] and by this he confesses a lack of artistic maturity. It would be difficult to presume that an artistic unconsciousness produced the same phenomena in Dostoevsky's novels belonging to the period of his greatest literary achievements. I simply think that Dostoevsky intentionally disregarded these "details" of novelistic technique and, being carried away by his "ideological" frenzy, had one thing in mind: "to express himself entirely even at the cost of art", as he stated in his letters.

François Mauriac, in his study on the novel, emphasized not only the independence of the heroes from the author but even a reality of existence which is superior to the reality of living beings of blood, bones, and flesh, for it is not a metaphysical belief that secures immortality for their souls as is the case with any one of us—their imperishability is an empiric fact. As an example, Mauriac notes the heroes of *War and Peace*, who are eternally healthy and alive: one generation after the other takes to its pale these eternally young people. Besides, we know that in some cases the hero acquires as it were a life of his own. The fate of Prince Bolkonsky in *War and Peace* serves as a good example of this. Tolstoy

[1] G. Čulkov, *Kak rabotal Dostoevskij* (Moscow: Sovetskij pisatel', 1939), p. 88.

once revealed that he had created this character because he needed, for the purposes of his novel, a young aristocratic snob from Petersburg, and his first intention was to kill him in the battle of Austerlitz. But Prince Andrew asserted himself so strongly in the novel that Tolstoy simply wounded him lightly at this battle, and Prince Bolkonsky continued to live for several years a life full of dramatic experiences, until the battle of Borodino, in which he was mortally wounded. It is obvious that the coexistence of heroes forms them and very often develops new traits in them which result not from the first conception of the author but from the environment in which they are placed. The comparative study of an author's notes and variants with the final text of his novel, especially in the case of Dostoevsky, as well as in that of Tolstoy, is very illustrative.

Long ago the brilliant critic Pisarev wrote the following in his excellent article on *War and Peace*:

"But precisely because the author expended a great deal of time, work, and devotion on the study and depiction of the epoch and its representatives, precisely because of this the figures created by him live their own life, which is independent of the author's intention, enter themselves into direct relations with the readers, speak for themselves, and invincibly lead the reader to thoughts and conclusions which the author did not have in view and of which, perhaps, he would not even approve."[1]

But my main problem here is the rôle of the hero as an exponent of the views of the author, the problem of the ideological identity of the hero's views and the author's views. We may, of course, omit the protagonists. It would not be advisable to make a search for them in Dostoevsky's novels. The great artist, despite the temptation he so often confessed to give a direct expression to the ideas and emotions which obsessed him, certainly preferred to act by means of implications. He was aware of the essentially symbolic character of his art. Therefore, even if only for purely artistic motives, he used his skill to conceal himself sufficiently well. Sometimes even the title of his novel was itself, in a way, enigmatic, examples being *Notes from Underground* and *Crime and Punishment*. Long ago (see L. Shestov) the assertions of the underground man were identified, and since Merezhkovsky's work on Tolstoy and Dostoevsky the doubtfulness of the didactic significance of the title *Crime and Punishment* has been established. The other difficulty

---

[1] Cf. D. I. Pisarev, "Staroe barstvo", in *L. N. Tolstoj v russkoj kritike* (Moscow: Gos. Izdat., 1952), p. 208.

is connected with psychology, especially in the light of modern science, which leads to relativistic conclusions. Who could deny Dostoevsky's great achievements and merits in this field? From the purely psychological point of view they are unquestionable. But the religious and moralistic author, as Dostoevsky essentially considered himself, naturally can expect to be approached from the religious and moral angle. Almost in every one of his characters he emphasized duality, the simultaneous coexistence of sinful desires and holy aspirations. Stavrogin, Versilov, and Dmitry Karamazov are particularly good examples of this. Here again arises the problem of dualism: psychology and morality. And then we are still faced with the problem of the author's responsibility; in other words, the ideological problem. The choice itself of characters, the whole gallery of types, and the moral situations remain a responsibility of the author.

In Dostoevsky's world sin is an attribute of holiness: God and sin are indispensable to each other. There is no sin without God, and there is no real knowledge of God without sin in this world. This last point is particularly significant. Anatole France once said that the greatest saints were often the greatest sinners. But even the skeptical France did not mean by this a simultaneous existence of evil and good in the human soul. Father Zossima is the only saint in Dostoevsky's works endowed with the principle of a consistent spiritual evolution and moral progress, with the Heraclitean principle of movement: all his other heroes, despite their stormy tempers, are imprisoned in a congealing spiritual immobility which originates from the nightmare of the simultaneous coexistence of evil and good in their souls. This coexistence is a result of their essential inability to make a choice. But Zossima is simply an ikon which Dostoevsky has put in the corner of his "house of the dead" in order to save this "house" in the eyes of public opinion.

One must not forget that the famous apostle of Russian reaction, the philosopher of Orthodox intolerance, the "Ober-prokuror" of the Holy Synod, Pobedonostsev, the Russian "Grand Inquisitor", who was an intimate friend of Dostoevsky, particularly at the time when the latter was writing his *Brothers Karamazov*, guided the author and discussed with him the most important political and religious problems included in the novel. In his letter to Ivan Aksakov, Pobedonostsev openly said: "He conceived his Zossima following my instructions."[1] When "Pro and Contra" appeared, Pobedonostsev asked the "most imperative question": "Will there be an objection?" After finishing his "Russian Hermit" (Zossima), at which Dostoevsky worked terribly hard, he

---

[1] Cf. L. Grossman, "Dostoevskij i pravitel'stvennye krugi 70-x godov", in *Literaturnoe Nasledstvo* (Moscow, 1934), Vol. XV, p. 89.

wrote to Pobedonostsev, on 24 August, 1879: "I fear and tremble, will it be satisfactory?"[1]

Dostoevsky's dialectical adroitness is well known. He is a master of ambivalence:

> "It would be better if I myself believed at least some of what I have just written. I swear to you, gentlemen, there is not one thing, not one word of what I have written that I really believe. That is, I believe it, perhaps, but at the same time I feel and suspect that I am lying like a cobbler.
>
> 'Isn't that shameful, isn't that humiliating?' you will say, perhaps, wagging your heads contemptuously. 'You thirst for life and try to settle the problems of life by a logical tangle. And how persistent, how insolent are your sallies, and at the same time what a scare you are in! You talk nonsense and are pleased with it; you say impudent things and are in continual alarm and apologizing for them. You declare that you are afraid of nothing and at the same time try to ingratiate yourself in our good opinion . . .' "[2]

How would one, then, be able to judge and to know whether one has the truth or a lie before him? The hero of the *Notes* in his talks with the prostitute displays the poetry of his love for children, for their rosy cheeks, for their angelic smiles, and then the same man monstrously offends this girl after having seduced the best of her soul by his philanthropic sentimentality. One might ask, "Perhaps you are lying?" Svidrigaylov declares his fondness for children—"I am always fond of children, very fond of them"—and then he commits the crime of raping a child. Where is the truth, attached to his word or to his deed? Ivan Karamazov tells long stories about the unjustifiable suffering of innocent children, stories which brought even Alesha to a revolt, and then Ivan himself was the inspirer of his father's murder. Does not the formula which Dostoevsky applied to Fedor Pavlovich Karamazov, "he was evil and sentimental", embrace, in addition to old Karamazov, the hero of the *Notes*, Svidrigaylov, and Ivan Karamazov? But again, where is the truth?

We may now ask another question, one which was raised many times before, among others by Strakhov, Freud, Zweig, and Gide: is the crime of Svidrigaylov and Stavrogin—the rape of a child—only their own crime; are these episodes merely pure fiction serving the

[1] Cf. *F. M. Dostoevskij—Materialy i issledovanija* pod red. A. Dolinina (Leningrad, 1935), p. 66.
[2] *Notes from Underground* in *White Nights and Other Stories by Fyodor Dostoevsky*, translated by Constance Garnett (New York: The MacMillan Co., 1918), pp. 78–9. (Corrected translation.)

superior needs of Dostoevsky, the profound and penetrating investigator of the human soul, or do we see in this the author's own confession?

The question as to whether we have the right to charge Dostoevsky with Stavrogin's and Svidrigaylov's crimes will remain unsolved. The autobiographical elements appearing here and there in Dostoevsky's novels are of course of a different order than those constituting Tolstoy's autobiographical monologue. However, some of them contain autobiographical episodes. *The Gambler,* for example, has a double biographical background: Dostoevsky's passion for gambling and Dostoevsky's passion for Apolinaria Suslov. The literary connections with *Manon Lescaut* do not alter the fact of the biographical foundation of this novel. In *The Gambler* we have the episode of the gambler's scandalous behaviour in the Vatican Legation in Paris. The gambler, irritated by having to wait for his visa, which had to be signed by the prelate, started to cause a commotion. When he learned that the Monseigneur was "taking coffee with the Cardinal", he shouted: " 'Let me tell you, I am ready to spit in your Monseigneur's coffee.' " He added that he was a "heretic and a barbarian", "*que je suis hérétique et barbare*", and that he "cared nothing for all these Archbishops, Cardinals, Monseigneurs and all of them".[1] By the way, Baron Wrangel tells exactly the same story about Dostoevsky himself: "Finding himself in Paris Dostoevsky thought to spend some time in Rome. For this it was necessary that he receive a visa of the papal nuncio at the French court. Dostoevsky went to him once—he was not home; a second time—again he was not home. He came a third time; there appeared a young abbé who asked him to take his seat and wait, inasmuch as the Monseigneur was at his meal and was about to have a cup of coffee. Dostoevsky became enraged, sprang from his chair and shouted: '*Dites à votre Monseigneur, que je crache dans son café,—qu'il me signe immédiatement mon passeport,—ou je me précipiterai chez lui avec scandale.*' " In this case, fortunately, we have the testimony of Wrangel's *Memoirs*.[2] The average reader would naturally ascribe the scandal at the Vatican Legation to the violent and explosive character of Dostoevsky's hero. In my study on Dostoevsky and Poland I shall utilize some other memoirs which, again, will be of great importance for my purpose. When we read the story of the Poles in *The House of the Dead* we have no doubts about Dostoevsky's fairness and truthfulness. But, in the light of the memoirs of one of these Polish prison mates we come to the conclusion that Dostoevsky's fairness and truthfulness are very questionable.

[1] Cf. *The Gambler, op. cit.,* ch. 1.
[2] Baron A. E. Wrangel, *Vospominanija o F. M. Dostoevskom v Sibiri, 1854–56 gg,* (St. Petersburg, 1912), p. 217.

It is, then, possible to trace an intimate relationship which existed between biography and fiction, but it is also possible to reveal the author's deviations from the actual truth, and these deviations are often motivated not by purely aesthetic considerations.

But all these arguments are still only preparatory ones. I should like to stress the rôle of the prestige with which Dostoevsky, as any other author, endows some of his heroes. Such particular moral prestige is given by the author to Myshkin, to Shatov, to Alesha Karamazov, and, in a way, to Versilov and to several secondary characters. Involuntarily we listen to them with special attention, the more so as all of them discuss very important problems and ideas. Here again comparative studies are not only of great but of decisive help.

We have three big volumes of articles written and published by Dostoevsky between 1845 and 1881 in various reviews and also his private letters. In both, in his articles and letters, we frequently find absolutely identical opinions and formulations to those expressed by some of the heroes of his novels. More than often Dostoevsky transfers, even without embellishments, whole passages from his articles and letters to his novels. This problem of identity of the ideas of the author with those of his heroes is important for me inasmuch as in my studies I am primarily interested in Dostoevsky as an ideological writer, and I believe that this approach is a legitimate one: in his *Diary of a Writer*, as well as in his letters, Dostoevsky constantly emphasizes, and often with great violence, the *ideological* character of his novels. The examples of the similarities of views expressed by his heroes with the views which he expressed in his articles and letters are innumerable. I will illustrate this only by a few quotations. Let us take Myshkin's comments on Catholicism:

> "An unchristian religion in the first place!" Myshkin began, in extreme agitation and with excessive abruptness. "And in the second place Roman Catholicism is even more than atheism itself, in my opinion! Yes, that's my opinion! Atheism only preaches a negation, but Catholicism goes further: it preaches a distorted Christ, a Christ calumniated and defamed by themselves, the opposite of Christ! It preaches the Antichrist, I declare it does, I assure you it does! This is the conviction I have long held, and it has distressed me, myself . . . Roman Catholicism cannot hold its position without universal political supremacy, and cries: '*Non possumus!*' To my thinking Roman Catholicism is not even a religion, but simply the continuation of the Western Roman Empire, and everything in it is subordinated to that idea, faith to begin with. The Pope seized the earth, an earthly throne, and grasped the

sword; everything has gone on in the same way since, only they have added to the sword lying, fraud, deceit, fanaticism, superstition, villainy. They have trifled with the most holy, truthful, sincere, fervent feelings of the people; they have bartered it all, all for money, for base earthly power. And isn't that the teaching of Antichrist? How could atheism fail to come from them? Atheism has sprung from Roman Catholicism itself. It originated with them themselves. Can they have believed themselves? It has been strengthened by revulsion from them; it is begotten by their lying and their spiritual impotence! Atheism! Among us it is only the exceptional classes who don't believe, those who, as Yevgeny Pavlovich splendidly expressed it the other day, have lost their roots. But over there, in Europe, a terrible mass of the people themselves are beginning to lose their faith—at first from darkness and lying, and now from fanaticism and hatred of the Church and Christianity.

Oh, no, no! It's not only a theological question, I assure you it's not! It concerns us much more closely than you think. That's our whole mistake, that we can't see that this is not exclusively a theological question! Why, socialism too springs from Catholicism and the Catholic idea! Like its brother atheism, it comes from despair in opposition to Catholicism on the moral side, to replace the lost moral power of religion, to quench the spiritual thirst of parched humanity, and to save them not by Christ but also by violence. That, too, is freedom through violence, that, too, is union through sword and blood. 'Don't dare to believe in God, don't dare to have property and individuality, *fraternitié ou la mort*, two millions of heads!' By their works ye shall know them—as it is said. And don't imagine that all this is so harmless and without danger for us. Oh, we need to make resistance at once, at once! Our Christ whom we have kept and they have never known must shine forth and vanquish the West. Not letting ourselves be slavishly caught by the wiles of the Jesuits, but carrying our Russian civilization to them, we ought to stand before them and not let it be said among us, as it was just now, that their preaching is skilful."[1]

In his *Diary of a Writer* (March, 1876), in the chapter entitled "Dead Force and Future Forces", Dostoevsky writes that Catholicism "has been plotting only with those possessing mundane power and has been relying on them to the last moment".

"Roman Catholicism . . . did not hesitate to sell Christ in exchange for mundane power. Having proclaimed the dogma that

[1] Cf. *The Idiot*, translated by Constance Garnett (London-Toronto: William Heinemann Ltd., 1948), pp. 532-4.

'Christianity cannot survive on earth without the earthly power of the Pope', it thereby proclaimed a new Christ, not like the former one, but one who has been seduced by the third temptation of the devil—the temptation of the kingdoms of the world: 'all these things will I give thee if thou wilt fall down and worship me!'[1]

In days past the main force of faith consisted of humility, but now humility must come to an end, and the Pope has the authority to abrogate it, since he possesses the full power. Yes, you are all brethren, and Christ Himself has ordained that all be brethren; if, however, your elder brothers refuse to accept you as brethren, arm yourselves with sticks and enter their houses and compel them to become your brethren by force. Christ has long waited for your corrupt elder brothers to repent, and now He grants you His own permission to proclaim: *'Fraternité ou la mort.'* ('Be my brother or else death to you!') Should your brother refuse to share with you his property, half and half, take it all away from him, since Christ has long waited for his repentance, but now the time for wrath and vengeance has come."[2]

Dostoevsky himself states that his article repeats almost textually Myshkin's words: "On one occasion I have already discussed all these things, but merely in passing, in a novel. Let people excuse my self-reliance, but I am convinced that, in this or that form, all this will come to pass in western Europe, i.e., that Catholicism will thrust itself into democracy, into the people, and will forsake the earthly kings, because they, on their part, forsook it."[3]

In his article "Three Ideas", in the *Diary of a Writer* (January, 1877), he repeats almost exactly the same thoughts:

"... France which has evolved from the ideas of 1789 her own peculiar French socialism, i.e., the pacification and organization of human society without and beyond Christ, as Catholicism has sought but failed to organize society in the name of Christ; that same France with her revolutionists of the Convention, with her atheists, with her socialists and with her present-day communards, —is, continues to be, in the highest degree, full and altogether a Catholic nation, completely contaminated with the spirit and letter of Catholicism, which by the mouths of her most arrant atheists is proclaiming: *Liberté, Egalité, Fraternité—ou la mort*, i.e., exactly as this would be proclaimed by the Pope himself were he compelled

---
[1] *Diary of a Writer*, p. 255.
[2] Page 257.
[3] Page 258.

to formulate the Catholic *liberté, égalité, fraternité* in his style, in his spirit, in the genuine style and spirit of a medieval Pope."[1]

In my study on Chaadaev I quoted *in extenso* Versilov's long harangue on Russian universalism and his assertion that "for more than a century Russia decidedly has been living not for herself but for Europe". In Dostoevsky's famous speech on Pushkin we find all Versilov's universalistic slogans and the same formula—that to be a real Russian means "to become a brother of all men, *a universal man*", and Dostoevsky emphasizes once more the altruistic character of Russian policies: ". . . for what else has Russia been doing in her policies, during these two centuries, than serving Europe much more than herself".[2] The only difference is that this time the author has extended the services of Russia dedicated to Europe from one to two centuries. It is possible to present many more illustrations of the same sort. I should like, however, to emphasize another characteristic trait of Dostoevsky's ideological novel. One is struck by the constant reappearance of the same ideas, themes, statements, and situations in his novels. This phenomenon is, of course, neither uncommon nor accidental. As any other writer, Dostoevsky had some *idées maîtresses* which ran through his works and which determined the situations and formed the characters. Some might be surprised, even, that an artist of Dostoevsky's calibre did not try to be more inventive. However, this belongs to the sphere of aesthetic speculations, especially as despite this repetitiousness each of Dostoevsky's dramatic episodes still fascinates the reader. But, as I have stressed, my purposes are different, and I find in the very fact of this ideological obsession another argument for my thesis of Dostoevsky's personal rôle in the world of ideas expressed by his heroes. I will again bring to the fore only a few examples, collected at random from Dostoevsky's works, illustrating this recurrence of motifs and episodes. This obliges one to accept the term "polyphony" with some reservations. No doubt Dostoevsky's polyphony is not a cacophony; some principles of order and hierarchy are obviously discernible. Dostoevsky harmonized the rôle of ideas with his novelistic situations. So, for example, when we listen to the vehement assertions of the hero from underground about selfishness as the essential principle in the attitude of the individual towards collectivity, and about his disregard for the interests of mankind, our impressions are determined not only by the tone of his speech but also by the very personality of Dostoevsky's hero, and they are different from those which we receive from, for instance, Versilov's and Ivan Karamazov's quiet, candid,

[1] Page 563.
[2] Page 979.

authoritative statements about "the physical impossibility of love for one's fellow man". We learn that "one may yet love one's fellow man abstractedly, and even sometimes from a distance, but almost never from near at hand".[1]

No less significant is the comparison of Prince Valkovsky, Svidrigaylov, Stavrogin, and Dmitry Karamazov. Valkovsky's avowals give us the feeling of exaggerated parody, those of Svidrigaylov instil horror in us, whereas the same items acquire a kind of prestige when they are attached to the figure of Stavrogin and a sort of attractiveness, even, when they appear in "the confession of an ardent heart".

I should like to end my examples with one more quotation, which, in a way, summarizes several items which I have discussed here. I found this other illustration for my theses of Dostoevsky's ambivalence in the horrifying dialogue of Alesha Karamazov, the "young prophet", the favourite disciple of Zossima, with the "charming, capricious" girl, Liza Khoklyakova. Both the avowals of Liza and Alesha's answers are significant:

> "Do you know, Alesha, I sometimes think about committing a terrible amount of evil, and all kinds of vileness. And I shall secretly do it for a long time. And suddenly everyone will find out. And they will all surround me and point their fingers at me, and I will look at all of them. This is very pleasant. Why is it so pleasant, Alesha?"

And this is Alesha's answer:

> "Just so, the need to squash something good, or, as you said, to set fire to it. This also happens . . ."
> *Liza*: "Listen. Now they are trying your brother for killing his father. And everyone likes the fact that he killed his father."
> *Alesha*: "They like the fact that he killed his father?"
> *Liza*: "They do like it. All of them like it! Everyone says that this is terrible, but inwardly they like it terribly. I am the first to like it."
> " 'In your words, about them all, there is a certain amount of truth,' quietly murmured Alesha."

And in the same dialogue Alesha "pensively murmurs:" "There are moments when people love crime." Later Liza says:

> "I have a certain book. I read in it about a certain trial somewhere and that a Jew [Dostoevsky uses the derogatory Russian

[1] *The Brothers Karamazov*, "Pro and Contra".

word 'zhid'] first cut off all the little fingers from the little hands of a four year old boy and then crucified him on a wall, he hammered in nails and crucified him. And later at the trial he said that the boy died quickly, in four hours. How quickly! He said: 'He moaned, he kept on moaning.' And the Jew stood there and feasted his eyes. This is nice."
Alesha: "Nice?"
Liza: "Nice. I sometimes think that I myself crucified him. He is hanging and moaning, and I am sitting in front of him and eating pineapple compote. I like pineapple compote very much ..."[1]

And later Liza tells Alesha that she confessed *everything* to Ivan.

But, as I have mentioned, sometimes we meet an absolute similarity not only in themes but even in the wording. Versilov brings the item of turning stones into bread which reappears in "The Legend of the Grand Inquisitor". The same Versilov sees the decay of Europe, hears "the sound of funeral bells" over Europe, mentions the "dear stones" and monuments of the European past; in the eyes of Ivan Karamazov "Europe is a cherished cemetery and nothing else," and he doesn't forget the "dear stones". The Raw Youth says: "It has always been a mystery to me and thousands of times have I been astonished by the capacity of man (and it seems this is a capacity primarily of a Russian man) to cherish in his soul the highest ideal together with the lowest baseness, and all this in complete sincerity." Is it necessary to remind the reader of the fact that this statement is fully developed in the character of Dmitry Karamazov, with his "ideals of a Madonna and his ideals of Sodom"? Versilov confesses that "I can feel in the most comfortable way two contradictory feelings at one and the same time—and this, of course, not by my own will." Stavrogin's confessions and his last letter to Dasha are too well-known to be cited here. It would be superfluous to stress the fact that in Dostoevsky's articles on Catholicism as well as in Myshkin's tirades, some of which I have quoted above, we find items from which Dostoevsky created his "Legend of the Grand Inquisitor". Even Shatov, in his talks with Stavrogin, develops exactly the same idea and uses the same phraseology:

"... You believed that Roman Catholicism was not Christianity; you asserted that Rome proclaimed Christ subject to the third temptation of the devil. Announcing to all the world that Christ without an earthly kingdom cannot hold his ground upon earth, Catholicism by so doing proclaimed Antichrist and ruined the whole

[1] *The Brothers Karamazov*, Book XI, ch. 3.

Western world. You pointed out that if France is in agonies now it's simply the fault of Catholicism, for she has rejected the iniquitous God of Rome and has not found a new one."[1]

I hope that all the above quotations justify my basic point of view: that one has the right to search in the "ideological novel" for ideas of the author which he expressed in them or by them. And many interpreters of Dostoevsky's ideology have done just this. In this respect my attempts do not differ from theirs. By this last statement I simply want to conclude my previous argumentation, the aim of which was to establish the right of an ideological interpretation of Dostoevsky's novels. But now, I approach the second essential point of my development: I should like to find the real essence of Dostoevsky's ideology. Dostoevsky's perpetual affirmation of Christian ideals, his incessant apology of the Russian Church, his discussions on religious themes, his efforts to present truly Christian characters (it suffices to mention Makar in *The Raw Youth*, the *anima naturaliter Christiana* in *The Idiot*, Zossima and Alesha in *The Brothers Karamazov*, as well as Sonya Marmeladov, the "holy prostitute", in whom, by the way, we may find the only Christian chapel in *Crime and Punishment*) created, with the help of innumerable pious interpreters, a myth of his religiosity. Dostoevsky has often been considered a deep and sincere Christian thinker. It is precisely on this point that I disagree most with these interpretations.

The fundamental difficulty still remains: the ambivalence of Dostoevsky. Dostoevsky's apologists, as for instance Berdyaev, first of all try to diminish the value of the *Diary of a Writer*. They recur to an apodictic statement that the *Diary* contains "very banal, conservative, political opinions", and that "it does not conform to the spiritual depth of Dostoevsky's novels". The novels are more ambivalent, and, of course, they conceal the views of the author which he openly expressed in his *Diary*. Berdyaev, for instance, tries to explain that the only solution of the problem of universal harmony which is acceptable to Dostoevsky is the harmony granted by God's kingdom. And then he says: "Ivan Karamazov's dialectic is complex, and it isn't always easy to grasp on which side is Dostoevsky himself. I think that he is half on Ivan Karamazov's side."[2]

[1] *The Possessed*, Part II, ch. 6.
[2] N. Berdjaev, *Russkaja ideja* (Paris: Y.M.C.A. Press, 1946), p. 126. In order to support my view, may I quote V. A. Desnitsky's preface to the Soviet edition of Dostoevsky's *Diary of a Writer*. In his polemics with V. F. Pereverzev's book, *Tvorchestvo Dostoevskogo*, Desnitsky states: "Let us study in Dostoevsky only 'the living characters, the living souls', having a 'universal objective value', and not his 'thoughts', remembering *'that trifle that Dostoevsky was never a thinker'*. (!? The italics are mine. V.D.)

"The attitude of Dostoevsky towards evil was deeply antinomian. The complexity of this attitude causes many people to doubt whether this attitude was a Christian one . . . Dostoevsky wanted to know evil, and in this he was a gnostic. Evil is evil. The nature of evil is interior, metaphysical and not exterior, social. Man as a free being is responsible for evil. Evil must be unmasked in its nothingness and must be consumed. And Dostoevsky ardently unmasks and burns evil. This is one side of his attitude toward evil. But evil is also the road of man, his tragic road, the fate of the free man, an experience which might also enrich man and bring him to a superior love. In Dostoevsky appears this other aspect of his attitude towards evil—the immanent perception of evil. In this way free men and not slaves experience evil."

However, even Berdjaev has to admit that

"this truth is a dangerous one. It exists for the genuinely free and the spiritually mature. It must be concealed from the immature. And this is why Dostoevsky might seem to be a dangerous writer. One must read him in the atmosphere of spiritual emancipation."[1]

In his book *The Russian Idea*, which appeared more than twenty years after his book on Dostoevsky, Berdjaev seems to be more cautious, and his formulation of this theme shows an effort to reveal a Christian essence supposedly existing in Dostoevsky's conception of evil:

"On his road man might be enriched by the experience of evil. But one has to understand this correctly. He is enriched not by evil itself but by the spiritual force which is awakened in order to overcome evil."[2]

I am not convinced by this sophistry. I do not see in the heroes of Dostoevsky attitudes which would make one accept this interpretation.

Let us agree that Dostoevsky was a bad thinker (but still a thinker!), that his philosophical, religious, and other views are 'rubbish' in our opinion. But we have absolutely no grounds to affirm that this 'rubbish', that these journalistic writings of Dostoevsky did not exert any influence, didn't leave any trace on his 'living characters', unless we return to the archaic notions of the special substance of the creative soul of the poet. We can scarcely imagine a poet's creative process in such a way that his world outlook . . . would in no way manifest an influence on the form of 'life' in his works." Cf. F. M. Dostoevskij, *Dnevnik Pisatelja za 1873 i 1876 gody* (Moscow-Leningrad: Gos. Izdat., 1929), p. vii.
[1] N. Berdjaev, *Mirosozercanie Dostoevskago* (Prague: Y.M.C.A. Press, 1923), p. 92.
[2] *Russkaja Ideja*, p. 127.

Another example of similar irresponsible formulations may be found in Mochulsky's recent monograph, which, in many respects, is a very useful study: Mochulsky establishes a Dantean trilogy: *The Possessed*—Inferno, *A Raw Youth*—Purgatory, *The Brothers Karamazov*—Paradise. What can one say to this?

Dostoevsky was not only a brilliant dialectician but at times one is tempted to compare him to a prestidigitator. The hero of the *Notes from Underground* is ready to kick world harmony, "the happy ant hill", to the winds if this universal happiness would be an obstacle to his having a cup of tea at the moment when he wants it. Ivan Karamazov does not accept universal harmony because "it isn't worth one single tear of a tortured, little child". A cup of tea becomes a child's tear. Versilov, in his dreams about the earthly paradise, in which Dostoevsky developed the theme of his "Legend of the Grand Inquisitor", presents the picture of a happy, but lonely, mankind which arranged its happiness without Christ. And then suddenly he recurs to Heine's poem, "Christ on the Baltic Sea":

"I could not get along without Him. Finally, I could not but visualize Him among the orphaned people. He was coming to them, His hands were extended toward them, and He was speaking: 'How could you forget me?' And here the veil as if fell from the eyes of all of them and a great, exalted hymn as if resounded of the new and the last Resurrection."

The same Versilov breaks his wife's ikon into *exactly two equal pieces*. The break is a symbolic one. It symbolizes the duality of Versilov. Let us not forget that Fedor Pavlovich Karamazov spits on his wife's ikon.

But the incense which was burned in our century by the metaphysicians of various confessions, schools, and orders at the altar of Dostoevsky's religion has created a shroud which now conceals from the layman the "mystery" of this "religion".[1]

[1] An example of this modern deification may be quoted from Boris Brasol's preface to his recent edition of *The Diary of a Writer*: "Whom did Russia bury with so great a reverence? Was it only one of her famous men of letters? Indeed not: in that coffin lay a noble and lofty *man*, a prudent teacher, an inspired prophet whose thoughts, like mountain peaks, were always pointed toward heaven, and who had measured the depths of man's quivering heart with all its struggles, sins and tempests; its riddles, pains and sorrows; its unseen tears and burning passions. For he did teach men to live and love and suffer. And to the meekest he would offer his brotherly compassion—to all who labor and are heavy laden. He would come to them as an equal, laying before them the wisdom of his soul, his tender understanding of all that, in modern man, is human and even inhuman. He would counsel the doubting and soothe the wounds of those afflicted with distress. And many a hope would thus be restored, many a soul resurrected by the grand visions and magic of his genius." Cf. *Diary of a Writer*, p. viii.

The speculations on the "mystery" of Dostoevsky's "religion" produced a situation which in itself is not uncommon but is uncomfortable for those who do not belong to the "initiated", as we have seen. Although many of Dostoevsky's contemporaries, like Turgenev, Strakhov, Mikhaylovsky, and many modern writers, like Merezhkovsky, Shestov, Veresaev, have questioned the sincerity of Dostoevsky's religiosity, it is not so easy to raise the same question in our day. Any sober, rational, and unbigoted approach to Dostoevsky is easily accused of iconoclasm and qualified as "unscientific oversimplification". Being fully aware of the dangers I am facing, I nevertheless dare to confess that my personal studies dedicated to the great novelist have brought me to the conclusion that the essence of Dostoevsky's ideological novel is a political one and that his "theologia est ancilla rei politicae". I will try to illustrate this statement by a study of Dostoevsky's attitude towards Europe and, in particular, towards Poland. The exploration of this complex problem focuses a brighter light on the essence of Dostoevsky's Christianity.

Before beginning my argumentation, I should like to support my general views on Dostoevsky the artist and Dostoevsky the moralist by quoting Freud's opinions, with which I fully agree:

> "The creative artist is the least doubtful; Dostoevsky's place is not far behind Shakespeare. *The Brothers Karamazov* is the most magnificent novel ever written; the episode of the Grand Inquisitor, one of the peaks in the literature of the world, can hardly be over-praised. Unfortunately, before the problem of the creative artist, analysis must lay down its arms.
>
> The moralist in Dostoevsky is the most readily assailable. If we try to rank him high as a moralist on the plea that only a man who has gone through the depths of sin can reach the highest heights of morality, we are neglecting one consideration. A moral man is one who reacts to the temptation he feels in his heart without yielding to it. The man who alternately sins, and in his remorse makes high moral demands, lays himself open to the reproach that he has made things too easy for himself. He has not achieved the most important thing in morality, renunciation, for the moral conduct of life is a practical human interest. He reminds one of the barbarians of the great migrations, who murder and do penance therefor, where penitence becomes a technique to enable murder to be done. Ivan the Terrible behaved in exactly this way—in fact, this compromise with morality is a characteristic Russian trait. Nor was the ultimate result of Dostoevsky's moral struggles anything very glorious. After the most violent battles to reconcile the impulsive claims of the

individual with the demands of the community, he ended up, retrograde fashion, with submission both to the temporal and spiritual authorities, with veneration for the Czar and the God of the Christians, and a narrow Russian nationalism, a position which lesser minds have reached with less effort. This is the weak point of the great personality. Dostoevsky threw away the chance of becoming a teacher and liberator of humanity; instead, he appointed himself its jailor. The future of civilization will have little to thank him for. It is probable that he was condemned to such frustration by his neurosis. The greatness of his intellect and the strength of his love for humanity should have opened to him another, apostolic, way of life."[1]

Later I will have some comments to add about the "God of the Christians": as the reader will see, for the "God of the Christians" an impostor has been substituted.

Appendix

Dostoevsky's Obsessing Theme

Although this theme, the rape of a child, is not a novelty and has been discussed in various psychological and biographical studies dedicated to Dostoevsky, I should like to devote some attention to it in connection with my general problem of "Dichtung und Wahrheit".

Dostoevsky's friend, Baron A. E. Wrangel, tells in his *Memoirs* dealing with Dostoevsky in Siberia the following episode: In Semipalatinsk Dostoevsky met a Polish girl, the daughter of a certain O., who, after the death of his wife, married his cook. The girl found herself in strained circumstances. Madame M. D. Isaev (the one who later became Dostoevsky's first wife) took an interest in this girl and asked Dostoevsky to take care of her. When Wrangel and Dostoevsky were spending the vacation in the summer house which Wrangel had rented near Semipalatinsk, Dostoevsky gained O.'s permission to allow the girl to take lessons from him in Wrangel's house. She was seventeen years old, very attractive and provocative. Wrangel left on a trip of two thousand versts. Having noticed the interest which the girl showed in Dostoevsky, Wrangel hoped that she might distract him from his passion for Madame Isaev. Wrangel says that when he returned he

---

[1] "Freud on Dostoevsky" in *F. M. Dostoevsky—Stavrogin's Confession* (New York: Lear Publishers, 1947), pp. 87–8.

realized that events had proceeded in an entirely different direction. He found out that Marina had gone through a terrible tragedy. An eighteen-year-old boy called Vanka had seduced the girl and abandoned her. His coachman, an old filthy Kirghiz, whose task it was to bring the girl to the rendezvous with Vanka, had blackmailed her. During one of the trips he threatened to reveal her love story to her parents and obliged the girl to give herself to him. He continued to persecute her later. Wrangel found her in a terrible physical and moral state. He interfered, using his power as a prosecutor, and expelled the Kirghiz from Semipalatinsk. Wrangel maintains that Dostoevsky did not know about the whole story and that the girl confessed her tragedy to both of them after Wrangel's return. However, Wrangel stresses the fact that later on Dostoevsky's wife was very jealous of the girl and the latter became an object of quarrels between the writer and his wife.[1] One may find some distant echoes of Marina's tragedy in the story of Zina and Vasya in *Uncle's Dream*. Of course I have no right to suspect Dostoevsky himself as far as this story is concerned, and I do not suspect him. Wrangel's report is so evasive that only another Dostoevsky could build an insinuative story from this incomplete material. However, the theme of an abused child is precisely the theme to which I alluded above; it is one which obsessed Dostoevsky: it suffices to mention Svidrigaylov, Stavrogin, Fedor Pavlovich Karamazov, and it appears even in Kirillov's talks. We know that the writer's own possible experiences in this direction became an object of discussion and polemics in which Turgenev, Strakhov, and even Dostoevsky's second wife took part. Here we enter into the sphere of the guilt complex. I hasten to say that as far as Wrangel's episode is concerned, Dostoevsky could have simply utilized some of its details in the stories of Svidrigaylov, Stavrogin and others.

The famous *Confession* of Stavrogin should not be neglected in this regard. It is important because of, first of all, the significance which Stavrogin has for Dostoevsky. We know that Dostoevsky affirmed his love for Stavrogin and said: "I took him from my heart." We also know from Shatov (in *The Possessed*) about Stavrogin's views concerning Christ and the truth. Shatov reminds Stavrogin: "But didn't you tell me that if it were mathematically proved to you that the truth excludes Christ, you'd prefer to stick to Christ rather than to the truth?"[2]

This is exactly what Dostoevsky wrote to Madame N. D. Fon-Vizin from Omsk in February, 1854: "If someone would prove to me that

[1] Cf. Wrangel, *op. cit.*, pp. 47, 82-4, 215.
[2] Cf. Dostoevsky, *The Possessed*, translated by Constance Garnett (New York, 1936), p. 253.

Christ is outside the truth, ... then I would prefer to remain with Christ, rather than truth."[1]

Certainly this is clear proof of how dear Stavrogin was to Dostoevsky. The author endowed him with his most intimate and grave thoughts.

The *Confession* is important also from the point of view of its style. Grossman makes a penetrating examination of Stavrogin's writing. He emphasizes Dostoevsky's efforts to give to Stavrogin's *Confession* all possible features of an unliterary text in order to create the impression of an unpolished, human document. Grossman stresses Stavrogin's literary ineptness, the poverty of his primitive phraseology, the ugliness of his syntax, and his awkward, official style. By this Dostoevsky endowed Stavrogin's *Confession* with the power of actual truth. The monstrous crime, in this way, acquired all the features of reality.

On the other hand, Grossman remarks that Stavrogin's testimony is still "maintained in the traditional style of a classical confession", and he gives several examples, among them, of course, Rousseau's *Confessions*.[2] I should like to add a comparative analysis of Stavrogin's *Confession* with some other texts of Dostoevsky. For the moment I will utilize *The Idiot*, in particular those passages in which Myshkin relates Dostoevsky's own experiences at the time the author was waiting to be executed after the trial of the Petrashevtsy. This sentence of execution was commuted at the last moment to one of hard labour.

Stavrogin's *Confession* contains a meticulous preciseness concerning time—the days and even the minutes are counted out (Stavrogin "looked at his watch and noted the time with perfect accuracy"). The scenery is also carefully described—a van noisily entering the courtyard; Stavrogin notes the windows, the light, a "leaf of geranium", "a tiny reddish spider", "a buzzing fly". He minutely describes how he abused the child and later how he awaited her suicide with watch in hand.

Exactly in the same style, with the same meticulous counting of minutes, Myshkin tells his story. Similar tiny details are mentioned: the light, the scenery, the long white gown, white caps, bright sunshine, the nearby church with its gilded roof.

I am aware of the fact that I am acting here as a prosecutor who compares the handwriting on various documents which might serve to prove the guilt of a suspected criminal. However, I must stress again that Stavrogin's "style" is significant to me. Why? I simply think that the minute details, their extraordinary preciseness, cannot be explained

---

[1] Dostoevskij, *Pis'ma*, Vol. I, p. 142.
[2] Cf. L. Grossman, *Tvorčestvo Dostoevskogo* (Moscow: "Sovremennye problemy," 1928).

only by an artistic imagination. But here I have performed my rôle of prosecutor, and I leave the verdict to the jury.

Stavrogin's abused girl was called Matresha. "Her mother," says Stavrogin, "loved her, but often beat her and, as is the custom of this people, shouted at her horribly."

This is what Wrangel says about Marina:

"Once, when I went with Dostoevsky to the Isaevs, I saw at their house a tattered, dirty girl about sixteen years old, a pretty blonde. They explained to me that she was the eldest daughter of a Pole, O. . . ., who had been transferred to Siberia for service on account of some misdeed. Now he was a treasurer of a battalion. He had an unpleasant personality and was constantly drunk; he was a widower with three daughters of whom Marina was the eldest. After the death of his wife he soon married his cook, who heartlessly persecuted the poor girl. She performed the duties of a workwoman and servant. She washed the floors and the laundry, and as far as her mental development was concerned, she was completely neglected."[1]

Here again we may find some similarities. But still I cannot insist that Stavrogin's Matresha was Dostoevsky's Marina. I should even add that in Stavrogin's description of the abuse of his girl Matresha one may find some motives and tones reminiscent of *The Christmas Tree and the Wedding*, a story written in 1848, before Siberia.

Svidrigaylov's stories, which he tells to Raskolnikov, as well as his dreams, are connected with the same theme. Whereas in Stavrogin's *Confession* the crime was depicted abruptly in the style of a factual report, Svidrigaylov's avowals and dreams reveal the emotions involved in this sexual perversion. They also contain some details of the Siberian episode. I will not quote all of these passages *in extenso* but only some fragments:

". . . they've taken from school their youngest daughter, a girl who'll be sixteen in another month, so that then she can be married. She was for me . . . I don't know how you feel about female faces, but to my mind these sixteen years, these childish eyes, shyness and tears of bashfulness are better than beauty; and she is a perfect little picture, too. Fair hair in little curls, like a lamb's, full little rosy lips, tiny feet, a charmer! . . . When I go now I take her on my knee at once and keep her there . . . Well, she flushes like a sunset and I kiss her every minute. Her mamma of course impresses on her that this

[1] Cf. Wrangel, *op. cit.*, p. 47.

is her husband and that this must be so. It's simply delicious! The present betrothed condition is perhaps better than marriage. Here you have what is called *la nature et la verité*, ha-ha! I've talked to her twice, she is far from a fool. Sometimes she steals a look at me that positively scorches me. Her face is like Raphael's Madonna. You know, the Sistine Madonna's face has something fantastic in it, the face of mournful religious ecstasy. Haven't you noticed it? Well, she's something in that line. The day after we'd been betrothed, I bought her presents to the value of fifteen hundred roubles—a set of diamonds, and another of pearls, and a silver dressing-case as large as this, with all sorts of things in it, so that even my Madonna's face glowed. I sat her on my knee yesterday, and I suppose rather too unceremoniously—she flushed crimson and the tears started, but she didn't want to show it. We were left alone, she suddenly flung herself on my neck (for the first time of her own accord), put her little arms round me, kissed me, and vowed that she would be an obedient, faithful, and good wife, would make me happy, would devote all her life, every minute of her life, would sacrifice everything, everything, and that all she asks in return is my *respect*, and that she wants 'nothing, nothing more from me, no presents'. You'll admit that to hear such a confession, alone, from an angel of sixteen in a muslin frock, with little curls, with a flush of maiden shyness in her cheeks and tears of enthusiasm in her eyes is rather fascinating! Isn't it fascinating? It's worth paying for, isn't it? Well . . . listen, we'll go see my betrothed, only not just now."

No less eloquent is the episode with the dancing girl, related to Raskolnikov in the same talk. Particularly terrible are both of Svidrigaylov's dreams:

"The coffin was covered with white silk and edged with a thick white frill; wreaths of flowers surrounded it on all sides. Among the flowers lay a girl in a white muslin dress, with her arms crossed and pressed on her bosom as though carved out of marble. But her loose fair hair was wet; there was a wreath of roses on her head. . . . Svidrigaylov knew that girl; there was no holy image, no burning candle beside the coffin; no sound of prayer: the girl had drowned herself. She was only fourteen, but her heart was broken. And she had destroyed herself, crushed by an insult that had appalled and amazed the childish soul. . . ."

"He bent down with the candle and saw a little girl, not more than five years old, shivering and crying, with her clothes as wet as a soaking house-flannel. . . . The child's face was pale and tired, she was numb with cold. 'How can she have come here? She must have hidden here and not slept all night.' He began questioning her. The child, suddenly becoming animated, chattered away in her baby language, something about 'mammy' and that 'mammy would beat her', and about some cup that she had 'bwoken' . . . He took her in his arms, went back to his room, sat her on the bed, and began undressing her . . . When he had undressed her, he put her on the bed, covered her up and wrapped her in the blanket from her head downwards. She fell asleep at once. . . . The child was sleeping soundly, she had got warm under the blanket, and her pale cheeks were flushed. . . . Her crimson lips were hot and glowing; but what was this? He suddenly fancied that her long black eyelashes were quivering, as though the lids were opening, and a sly crafty eye peeped out with an unchildlike wink, as though the little girl were not asleep, but pretending. Yes, it was so. Her lips parted in a smile. the corners of her mouth quivered, as though she were trying to control them. But now she quite gave up all effort, now it was a grin, a broad grin; there was something shameless, provocative in that quite unchildish face; it was depravity, it was the face of a harlot, the shameless face of a French harlot. Now both eyes opened wide; they turned a glowing, shameless glance upon him; they laughed, invited him . . . There was something infinitely hideous and shocking in that laugh, in those eyes, in such nastiness in the face of the child. 'What, at five years old?' Svidrigaylov muttered in genuine horror. 'What does it mean?' And now she turned to him, her little face all aglow, holding out her arms . . . 'Accursed child!' Svidrigaylov cried, raising his hand to strike her, but at that moment he woke up."

Madame Sophia Kovalevsky tells in her memoirs that in 1866 Dostoevsky once related to her family a scene from a novel which he had conceived in his youth. However, Dostoevsky himself wrote to Strakhov that the idea for this novel came to him in 1865. This novel was to be about a middle-aged landlord, well educated, who in his youth led a dissipated life but later married and acquired a general respect. He was quite happy and felt pure and deserving of respect. But suddenly, amidst these pleasant dreams and meditations, he felt a pain, as if caused by a vague remembrance. After lengthy efforts of his memory he realized just what was this painful memory. "He remembered how, once, after a night of revelry, carried away by his drunken comrades, he raped a small girl, ten years old." Madame Kovalevsky recalls that her mother interrupted the narration by a cry of horror.[1]

[1] Cf. K. Močul'skij, *Dostoevskij* (Paris: Y.M.C.A. Press, 1947), p. 316.

Equally interesting is the story which Myshkin relates about his stay in Switzerland, his friendship with children, and his platonic relations with Marie—Marie, whom Myshkin once kissed—Marie, who was "scrubbing floors, washing, sweeping out yards, and minding cattle", whom "a French commercial traveller seduced" and who "made her way home begging, all mud-stained and in rags, with her shoes coming to pieces". Like Stavrogin's Matresha, she sings and she kisses Myshkin's hands. It might be that this is another variant of the same obsessing theme. Indeed, we have here a *sonata quasi una fantasia*.

It is still plausible to me that Stavrogin's *Confession* was, in a sense, Dostoevsky's confession. If my supposition is true, it indicates a psychological need on the part of Dostoevsky. Not in vain does he put in Stavrogin's mouth at the end of his interview with Tikhon the angry shout: "You cursed psychologist!" Tikhon perfectly understands Stavrogin and expresses his opinion that Stavrogin would be ready to commit still another crime "in order to avoid the publication of these pages"—the pages of Stavrogin's *Confession*.

I believe that, as a reflected psychological need, this was at least a half-avowal: *Dixi et animam salvavi*.

In order to support my argument I may cite another quotation, this time from *Notes from Underground*. This is what Dostoevsky's hero says at the end of the first part:

"Every man has reminiscences which he would not tell to every one, but only to his friends. He has other matters in his mind which he would not reveal even to his friends, but only to himself, and that in secret. But there are other things which a man is afraid to tell even to himself, and every decent man has a number of such things stored away in his mind. The more decent he is, the greater the number of such things in his mind. Anyway, I have only lately determined to remember some of my early adventures. Till now I have always avoided them, even with a certain uneasiness. Now, when I am not only recalling them, but have actually decided to write an account of them, I want to try the experiment whether one can, even with oneself, be perfectly open and not take fright at the whole truth. I will observe, in parenthesis, that Heine says that a true autobiography is almost an impossibility, and that man is bound to lie about himself. He considers that Rousseau certainly told lies about himself in his confessions, and even intentionally lied, out of vanity. I am convinced that Heine is right. . . . Besides, I shall perhaps obtain actual relief from writing. Today, for instance, I am particularly oppressed by one memory of a distant past. It came back vividly to my mind a few days ago, and has remained haunting me like an annoying tune that one cannot get rid of. And yet I must get rid of it somehow. I have hundreds of such reminiscences; but at times some one stands out from the hundred and oppresses me. For some reason I believe that if I write it down I should get rid of it. Why not try?"

An oral legend affirms that Dostoevsky once visited Turgenev and confessed to him his most ugly act. "Why did you tell me this?" asked Turgenev. "In order to show you how I disrespect you."[1]

André Gide, while referring to Dostoevsky's avowal to Turgenev, emphasizes that "the need for confession became urgent, but confession not merely to a priest".[2] Gide thinks that the circumstance that Dostoevsky's relations with Turgenev were uncommonly bad at that time granted to Dostoevsky the opportunity of suffering acutely. In other words, this was the most severe punishment that Dostoevsky could impose upon himself. I do not agree with Gide, however. It seems to me that a confession to a highly respected friend would have been a far more difficult task.

My speculations on this theme of the rape of a child might be supported by the discussion, mentioned above, between N. Strakhov and Dostoevsky's second wife. Mrs. A. G. Dostoevsky quotes in her *Memoirs* a well-known letter written by N. Strakhov to Tolstoy in which Strakhov confesses that when he was writing his biography of Dostoevsky he was "constantly in a state of conflict", that he "fought against rising feelings of disgust" and tried to overcome in himself this "ugly feeling". He further states that he could "consider Dostoevsky neither a good nor a happy man. . . ."

> "He was evil, envious, dissolute, and spent his whole life in waves of emotion which made him pitiful and which would also have made him comical if he had not been so evil and intelligent. He, like Rousseau, considered himself the best of men and the most happy. In connection with the Biography I recalled all these traits. In Switzerland in my presence he was so rude to a servant that the latter took offense and spoke up to him, 'I too am a man.' I remember that this answer was striking to me as it was spoken to a preacher of humanitarianism, and that it reechoed conceptions of the free Switzerland about the rights of man. He was constantly causing such scenes because he could not control his fury. I often

---

[1] For details see Ju. Nikol'skij, *Turgenev i Dostoevskij* (Sophia: Rossijsko-bolgarskoe knigoizdatel'stvo, 1921), p. 30.

[2] Cf. André Gide, *Dostoevsky* (London: Knopf, 1926), p. 86.

remained silent during his excesses, in which he indulged very much in the manner of a fish-wife, unexpectedly and covertly; and from time to time I also had the opportunity to offend him. But of course as far as offenses are concerned, he generally had the more advantageous position in respect to others; and worst of all is the fact that he enjoyed all this, that to the very end he never repented all his filthiness. He was attracted by filth and boasted about it. Viskovatov told me how he once boasted that in a bathhouse he had . . . with a little girl whom a governess had brought to him. Notice here that with his animal sensuality he had no taste at all, no feeling for feminine beauty and charm. One may see this in his novels. The characters who resemble him most are the hero from *The Underground*, Svidrigaylov from *Crime and Punishment*, Stavrogin from *The Possessed*. Katkov even refused to print one scene which contains Stavrogin's abuse of a little girl; Dostoevsky read this scene to many people."[1]

Mrs. Dostoevsky did not leave this challenge unanswered; she devoted several pages in her *Memoirs* to her arguments with Strakhov. In her answer she confirms the fact that Katkov indeed had been unwilling to publish *Stavrogin's Confession*, that her husband was very unhappy because of this refusal and read this particular chapter to Pobedonostsev, Maykov, and Strakhov, not so much for praise as for their judgment. When his friends found it too realistic, he began to consider some other variants. "Among them was a scene in the bathhouse (an actual happening, about which someone told my husband)." Then she explains that Dostoevsky did mention a governess but that he excluded her on the grounds that it might be interpreted as a slur on feminism. However, the best part of Mrs. Dostoevsky's argumentation is the following: She expresses her indignation against Strakhov for daring to ascribe this episode to Dostoevsky himself, and she states that Strakhov "forgot that such a refined perversion involves great expense and is affordable only to very rich people, and my husband was in financial difficulties all his life."[2]

But this is for me the most important statement that Strakhov made on the subject:

> "With such a nature, he [Dostoevsky] was very much inclined towards sweet sentimentality and high humanitarian dreams; these dreams illustrate his tendency, his literary muse and his path. As a

[1] Cf. *Vospominanija A. G. Dostoevskoj*, pod red. L. P. Grossman (Moscow-Leningrad: Gos. Izdat., 1925), pp. 285–6.
[2] A. G. Dostoevskaja, *op. cit.*, p. 290 and p. 286.

matter of fact, all his novels represent *self-justification*. They prove that in one person there may co-exist nobility and all manner of villainy."

II

Of all the Russian writers, with perhaps the exception of Pushkin, Dostoevsky is the one who is most indebted to Europe and who, with perhaps the exception of Turgenev and Tyutchev, spent the most time there. Dostoevsky formed his novelistic art in the school of the great western-European literatures, particularly French, English, and German. In his early youth he was absorbed in the enthusiastic reading of Molière, Corneille, Racine, Schiller, Dickens, George Sand, Balzac, and Shakespeare. His first literary step was a translation of *Eugénie Grandet*. We know of his infatuation for Victor Hugo, Alexander Dumas, Eugène Sue, Frédéric Soulié, Paul de Kock. From these writers he elaborated the technique of his sensational and detective novel.

In his youth he was a pupil of western-European idealistic, political, and social conceptions. At the time of his activities in the circle of the Petrashevtsy he was attracted by Fourier, Considérant, Stirner, and Marx, without mentioning Voltaire, Rousseau, and Lamennais. No doubt his first short stories, written before his Siberian exile, amply reflected the philanthropic, altruistic trends of western-European humanitarianism of those times. One may also note that Dostoevsky's novels which were written after his Siberian period, especially the greatest masterpieces of his art, contain almost as much about Europe as about Russia—if not more. His "Russian boys" are constantly occupied with the "Russian God", but even more with the "Catholic God". They are concerned with European capitalism, socialism, rationalism, atheism, inquisition, revolutionism, and European politics, and this is so in spite of the fact that in his novels we find ourselves most often in Russia: in Russian taverns, in Russian apartment houses, or on the streets of Petersburg or in some Russian provincial town. But in the author who was so deeply indebted to Balzac, Dickens, Hugo, Schiller, Stendhal, the great French poets and writers of the seventeenth and eighteenth centuries, and to Shakespeare, who found his "wealth" in them—this debt did not arouse any real feeling of gratitude for the European source of his inspiration. He very often declaims his enthusiastic love for Europe, but does not hide the fact that this love is addressed only to "the holy stones" of the "European cemetery". Although Dostoevsky's novels are filled with western-European names and with allusions to various European historical events, seldom can we find in them any element of genuine sympathy for the European civilization that had formed his art and thought. Dostoevsky infrequently speaks about European monuments of art in his novels and letters; he prefers anecdotes or political items. The European types that appear in his novels and journalistic sketches, the descriptions of European people which we find in his private letters—all give the most negative impression. His Frenchmen, Italians, Poles, and Germans are extremely repulsive, as are his pictures of Europe, taken either from the gambling casinos, London streets, Parisian hotels or restaurants. Dostoevsky's only positive foreigner is Mr. Astley in *The Gambler*.

The statements which we find about Germans, Frenchmen, Poles and Jews in his letters, his wife's reports about his attitude towards the Europeans whom he observed while abroad, show that Dostoevsky felt nothing but disgust and hatred for Europe. These particular texts prove Dostoevsky's personal, one would even say physical, aversion: almost every contact with a European, whoever it might be—a railway conductor, a waiter, the proprietor of an hotel, an accidental companion in a train compartment—simply irritated him. He constantly uses abusive, injurious invectives such as "scoundrels", "base people", "dull, repulsive Germans", "vile French", etc. No less negative is his theoretical approach to western European civilization and to its effects on the development of Russian society. This derogatory attitude towards Europe found its printed expression after Dostoevsky's Siberian period, but before his first trip to Europe. Indeed, his works of the pre-Siberian period do not express any anti-European sentiments.

The Siberian period, as we know, was one of crisis. While in prison and afterwards, during his years of exile, Dostoevsky gradually rejected all his former progressive and idealistic opinions and conceptions. It would be difficult to deny the rôle of opportunism in the ideological crisis, although one should, of course, also take into consideration some psychological factors: after all, the horrible punishment Dostoevsky received had been caused by his Europeanism. However, we know that Dostoevsky lowered himself, to say the least, in his efforts to convince the Russian authorities that he was filled with repentance and remorse, that he justified to himself the punishment, that he accepted this punishment and considered that he deserved it. We may, then, easily assume that his criticism of the Europeanization of Russia, his anti-Polish manifestations, his Slavophile declarations, his anti-Semitism—all these were also connected with his desire to gain the confidence of the Government. The expressions of loyalty to the Government which

Dostoevsky in Semipalatinsk (1858)

he displayed in Siberia contained, however, some particularly interesting and significant elements. I have in mind his patriotic odes written at the very end of the Crimean War in which he emphasized the idea of Russia's conquest of Constantinople. In these odes he combined the cross and the sword, he announced the renaissance of the ancient East with the help of Russia. We may, therefore, consider Siberia the cradle of Dostoevsky's Russian Messianic imperialism. His letters from Siberia, even his private letters, emphasized the same ideas and sentiments. We know that in his discussions with the Poles in Siberia Dostoevsky approved the partitions of Poland, that he considered all Russian territorial annexations, not only in Poland but in the Caucasus and the Baltic provinces, legitimate and natural, as well as historically justified.

When one examines Dostovesky's short stories and novels belonging to the second and great period of his life, one may find in them several great conflicts with Europe. The first skirmishes appear in *Uncle's Dream*, in which he mocks the superficial Europeanization of Russian society. This mockery might be considered a preamble, not only to his attack on Europe but on the Europeanization of Russia. Here, by the way, I should introduce a parenthetical remark: Dostoevsky in some strange and very apodictic way combined his anti-Western attitude with the glorification of Peter the Great, as the reader shall see. In *The House of the Dead* he manifests his opposition to Polish individualism and social exclusiveness. But the first real battle takes place in his *Winter Notes on Summer Impressions* (1863), which was connected with his first trip abroad in 1862; this report slanders Europe from beginning to end. It is also worth while mentioning the story of Dostoevsky's review, *Vremya*, which had been suspended in connection with Strakhov's famous article on the Polish question. Dostoevsky described the whole affair in his letter to Turgenev on 17 June, 1863, in which he stressed the fact that his review had been essentially anti-Polish and anti-Western. The next battlefield is *Crime and Punishment*. In this novel Dostoevsky attacks European individualism and the Napoleonic idea and shows the fatal effects of these conceptions on the Russian soul. True enough, this reduction of the ideological content of *Crime and Punishment* might be accepted with some reservations, as we know how deeply Dostoevsky admired the "determined man" whom he met among the criminals and murderers in his Siberian prison camp. One should also remember that Dostoevsky often applies European labels to his own ideas. However, officially, so to speak, Raskolnikov is one of the Russian little Napoleons. If in *Crime and Punishment* Dostoevsky shows the crisis of the Russian conscience of the nineteenth century in the soul of one Russian man who was, in his conception, an absolute Petersburg type, in *The Idiot* all

L

the characters are seized by a crisis and belong to a perishing world. In this novel Dostoevsky gives a catastrophic picture of Russian society imprisoned by western-European capitalistic ideas and forms of life. *The Raw Youth* presents a vision of Russian "chaos", a picture of the life of nationally uprooted Russian intellectuals. *The Possessed* illustrates the rôle of the disaggregating western-European revolutionary ideas in Russian society. Finally, his last battle takes place in *The Brothers Karamazov*, in which novel Dostoevsky fights against Catholicism; that is, against Catholicism in Dostoevsky's own stylization.

Of course, all these novels have a much vaster content. However, as my theme is Europe, I shall analyse Dostoevsky's texts belonging to his novels, his correspondence, and to his *Diary of a Writer* from this point of view. In his first letter from Paris of 26 June–8 July, 1862, to N. N. Strakhov, Dostoevsky writes:

"Paris is absolutely the dullest city, and if there were not in it some really remarkable things one might die of boredom. The French are indeed such a people as to make one sick to his stomach. You mentioned the self-satisfied, insolent, vile faces raging at our spas, but I swear that what you have here is as good. Our people are simply carnivorous scoundrels and, in the majority, conscious ones, but here everyone is sure that this is as it should be. The Frenchman is quiet, honest, polite, but false, and money means everything to him. He has no ideals at all. Do not ask here for convictions or even reflection. The level of general education is low to the last degree."

He emphasizes that in half an hour one could notice and understand all this! He states, further, that it is not worth while to go to Paris for only three days, but if one were to go there for two weeks as a tourist one would be bored.[1] He develops some of these items in his *Winter Notes on Summer Impressions*: for instance, in Chapters 6 and 7, in which he describes the French bourgeoisie, and Chapter 8, "Bribri and Mabiche", in which he continues to insult France in the same way. There appear pictures of the innumerable dull French couples on the streets, of the well-reared children, whom Dostoevsky mocks, as well as the "solemn, dignified appearance" of all these "Gustaves", "all these distinguished gentlemen who despite their noble manners are ready to sell their own fathers for twenty-five cents". "A salesman will sell you a shawl worth fifteen hundred francs for twelve thousand." "This is his duty, this is his virtue; but he will not pardon a thief if this thief steals for his hungry children." Every Gustave is prepared to sell his mistress's letters for ten thousand francs and to denounce her to her

[1] F. M. Dostoevskij, *Pis'ma* (Moscow: Gos. Izdat., 1928), Vol. I, pp. 310–11.

husband. Dostoevsky remarks, however, that he perhaps exaggerates, but "maybe", he says, "these remarks are based on some facts". "Do you know," asks Dostoevsky, "that one may even be a scoundrel without losing the feeling of honour? But here there are many honest people who nevertheless have completely lost this sense of honour and therefore act basely, not knowing what they are doing for the sake of virtue." In other words, the French bourgeoisie is the embodiment of distinguished baseness, stupidity, avarice, false eloquence, and arrogant hypocrisy. It represents a self-satisfied, self-confident, vulgar mediocrity.

His first trip, from which *Winter Notes on Summer Impressions* originated, did not provide him with better impressions of Germany. He ran away from Berlin because that city was for him "like Petersburg!" In Dresden he came to the conclusion that nothing could be more disgusting than the Dresden type of woman. In Cologne he did not admire the cathedral; he found in it only "laces, laces, and laces", and heard in Cologne only shouts of "Eau de Cologne ou la vie!" In Switzerland he saw "wild mores, low spiritual development, drunkenness, thievery, petty swindling, terrible mediocrity in everything, and paupery". He even abuses the climate and calls Geneva "damned filthy". Those who have read his *Winter Notes on Summer Impressions* know the disastrous picture he gives of London. I should like to stress one detail—Dostoevsky opposed bourgeois Paris, which he treated as a culmination of bourgeois philistine mediocrity, to London, the culmination of capitalistic exploitation. His picture of London assumes the shape of an apocalyptic vision. It is a kingdom of Baal, of a demon who devours human victims and a nation with the qualities of a herd. This chapter on London (Chapter 5) contains some particularly interesting details. Dostoevsky describes London prostitution, mothers bringing their pubescent daughters to Haymarket for this trade, a six year old girl, sick and in rags, to whom he gave half a shilling and who, frightened, ran away from him . . . "In general, frivolous matters," says Dostoevsky. And then he launches an attack against Catholic missionaries and priests, who seek to penetrate everywhere and

> "to feed, to clothe, to hospitalize, to treat the ill, who buy medicine, who become friends of the house, and finally convert everybody to Catholicism. Sometimes, however, after being cured, people chase the priests away with obloquy and blows. The priest is indefatigable and goes to other people . . ."

"The Anglican priest does not go the poor. The poor are not even admitted to the church, because they have no money to pay for their seats." "The proud and rich Anglican priests and bishops," "those dull professors of religion," "become fat in the perfect tranquillity of their consciences," officiate "without any masks, at least rationally and without deceit." However, they have one hobby, proselyting. "They would go to the depths of Africa in order to convert one savage, but they forget a million savages in London because the latter have no money to pay them." By the way, this passage might be an answer to Pushkin's remarks in his *Journey to Erzerum* in which, speaking of the Circassians' hatred for Russia, Pushkin suggests, as the one method capable of assuaging it, the propagation of the gospel among them. The great Russian poet complains about the idleness of the Orthodox Church, which doesn't follow the example of "the ancient apostles and the modern Roman Catholic missionaries", who spread the Christian word with "devotion and humility" "throughout the wilderness of Africa, Asia, and America" to the savages.

The *Winter Notes* is an interesting document because it is related to Dostoevsky's first personal acquaintance with Europe and because it shows his emotional and even physical reaction to Europe.

Now let us analyze Dostoevsky's ideological criticism of Europe and his Russian Messianism. To the "bestialized, soiled, vile, base" Europe he contrasts his "Holy" Russia and develops his doctrine of Russia's historical mission.

In his letter to A. N. Maykov from Geneva, 18 February–1 March, 1868, Dostoevsky touched on the problem of Russian and European courts:

"The moral character of our court and especially of our jury is infinitely higher than that of the European court: crimes are looked upon in a Christian manner. The Russian traitors abroad even agree with this. But one thing is as if not quite settled: it seems to me that in this humanity with respect to the criminal there is still much that is bookish, liberal, and not independent. This is often the case. By the way, in judging this from a distance it is possible that I am awfully mistaken. But, in any case, our essence in this regard is immeasurably higher than the European one. In general, all the moral concepts and goals of the Russians are higher than those of the European world. We have more of a direct and noble belief in good as a Christian value than the European belief, for which 'good' means comfort.

A great restoration through Russian thought is being prepared for the entire world (closely connected with orthodoxy, you are right), and this will come to pass in some generation—this is my passionate belief—But in order for this to come into being it is necessary that the *political justice* and preeminence of the Great

Russian peoples over all the Slavic world be established definitely and indisputably. (And our little liberals are preaching the break-up of Russia into confederate states! Oh, the bunglers!)"[1]

However, even more outstanding is his letter to Maykov from Geneva of 20 March–2 April, 1868, in which we find a marriage of love and hatred: Dostoevsky affirms love as the essence of the Russian historico-political development and, at the same time, appeals to the necessity for armaments. In this letter he contrasts love as the principle of the Russian nation to conquest as the principle of western-European historical development. And at the end of these historical reflections he suddenly arrives at the surprising acceptance of the all-Slavic importance and significance of Peter the Great.

"My friend, you are decidedly of exactly the same opinion as I, and in essence you expressed the same thing which I uttered aloud three years ago when I was still publishing my review, and they did not understand me. What I said was this: our constitution is a reciprocal love of the Monarch for the nation and of the nation for the Monarch. Yes, love and conquest is the great idea of our state (which was revealed, it seems, by the first Slavophils) upon which much is founded. We will convey this idea to Europe, which still will not understand anything in it. Alas, our unfortunate, uprooted class of 'wise men' necessarily came to the same result. They will die anyhow without your being able to change them. (Look at Turgenev!) But the younger generation—that is where we should devote our attention. (A classical education could help a great deal. What is this lyceum of Katkov? Here abroad I had become a decided monarchist for Russia. In our land if anyone did something it was certainly the monarch, and not only for the simple reason that he is the Czar, loved by the people of Russia, but because he is personally a Czar. In our country every Czar has received and still receives the love of the people, and they believe only in him. For the people this is a holy mystery, priesthood, and anointment.) The Westerners do not understand anything of this, and they, praising themselves with their foundation on facts, have overlooked the chief and greatest facts of our history. I like your idea of the all-Slavic significance of Peter. This is the first time in my life that I have heard this idea and it is perfectly true."

And then comes his statement about the urgent necessity of having strategic railroads and new guns.[2] Dostoevsky gives full development

[1] *Ibid.*, Vol. II, p. 81.
[2] *Ibid.*, Vol. II, pp. 100–1.

to these items in his article "The Utopian Conception of History" (*Diary of a Writer*, June, 1876). In this article he explains how ancient Russia first "passively" preserved "her treasure", "her orthodoxy", for "herself". "With Peter's reform there ensued an unparalleled broadening of the view," "an expansion of the view". Dostoevsky then infers "the active application of our treasure—of orthodoxy" "to the universal service of mankind to which orthodoxy is designated and which, in fact, constitutes its essence". "Thus, through Peter's reform our former idea—the Russian Moscow idea—was broadened," etc. He emphasizes, again dogmatically, without any effort to prove his point, the historical truth of his assertions that Peter's reform was unique, that a reform like that had never happened anywhere, and that its essence "is our brotherly love of other peoples".[1] In his "swan-song", his speech on Pushkin in 1880, Dostoevsky fully develops his conception of the real significance of Peter's reform. In connection with the theme of the broadening of "Russian views", Dostoevsky presents his idea about Constantinople: "Yes, the Golden Horn and Constantinople—they will be ours, but not for the purpose of seizure, not for the sake of violence." He then alludes to the legend of the "testament of Peter the Great", and explains that even if the idea of the seizure of Constantinople had come to Peter's mind instead of the foundation of Petersburg, he would then have abandoned this idea, even if he had been powerful enough "to crush the Sultan", as this would perhaps have brought "ruin to Russia".[2] Constantinople is a permanent refrain in Dostoevsky's "political ballads".

We have here, however, only a preamble to even more eloquent confessions. Perhaps the most important of all his letters is the one to Maykov from Florence of 15–27 May, 1869. Maykov had sent Dostoevsky outlines of historical *byliny*. After having read these outlines Dostoevsky presented his friend with his own idea of a historical epic. Dostoevsky here reveals his imperialistic tendencies in their full light. First he suggests that the goal of these historical *byliny* should be the engraving into the imagination of the Russian people the most essential facts and ideas of Russian historical development. He suggests that they be written in a simple and naïve style and that love for Russia should "gush out as from a hot spring". Dostoevsky starts his own outline with the fall of Constantinople, and he emphasizes that this great historical episode had emerged in his mind "automatically", "without any intention", "directly", "involuntarily", "as a *bylina* from *Russian history*". There follows the description of the conquest of Constantinople by Mohammed II and the massacre of Saint Sophia. After these

[1] *Ibid.*, Vol. I, p. 360 ff.
[2] *Loc. cit.*

events Dostoevsky proposes a poetic description of the last of the Paleologs arriving with her "two-headed eagle instead of a dowry", "of a Russian wedding". Then our poet writes of the Russian Grand Duke Ivan III in his wooden hut instead of a palace. To this hut is transferred

> ". . . the great idea of the all-orthodox significance of Russia, and the first stone is laid of her future leadership in the East; the circle of the Russian future is widened, the idea is founded not only of a great state but of an entirely new world for whom she is fated to renew Christianity by the all-Slav Orthodox ideas and to bring to mankind a new thought. All this will come about when the West decays and it will decay when the Pope definitely deforms Christ and through this distortion engenders atheism among soiled Western humanity."[1]

In his letter to Maykov from Dresden, 9–21 October, 1870, he describes the main idea of his novel *The Possessed* and also preaches the necessity for Russia to take the offensive:

> "The whole significance of Russia is contained in Orthodoxy, in the light from the East, which will flow to blind mankind in the West, which has lost Christ. All the misery of Europe, all, all, without any exception, came from the fact that with the Roman church they lost Christ and then decided that they could get along even without Christ. Well now, can you imagine, my dear friend, that even in such superior Russian people as, for example, the author of *Russia and Europe* (Danilevsky) I have not encountered this idea about Russia, that is, about her exclusively orthodox mission for mankind, and if this is the case—it is certainly early to ask independence of us."[2]

Dostoevsky here follows the line of Moscow Messianism of the fifteenth century and the so-called theory of "Moscow the Third Rome". All the most important elements of it are present: the idea of Moscow as the heir of Byzantium, the prophecy of the decay of Rome, the all-Orthodox mission of Moscow, the fight of the Ivans for the orthodox provinces which belong to the Polish–Ruthenian–Lithuanian Commonwealth, and, finally, the vision of not only an all-Orthodox and all-Slav, but an all-World mission for Moscow. All these statements are dogmatic, and in his *Diary of a Writer* Dostoevsky writes following

[1] *Ibid.*, Vol. II, pp. 190–2.
[2] *Op. cit.*, Vol. II, pp. 291–3.

the same pattern, making assertions which he imposes on his readers with no proof whatsoever, and even often emphasizing the fact that proof cannot be provided and that it is needless. Perhaps the most illustrative example of this style of thinking and writing is his famous "Vlas", which appeared in 1873 in his *Diary of a Writer*. First Dostoevsky tells the story of a Russian peasant whose ambition it was to outdo everyone in some "temerarious deed". The peasant went to communion, but he did not swallow the host. Later he put it on a road and was about to shoot it. He aimed at the Eucharist, but at that very moment " 'there appeared before me a cross, and on the cross—our Savior. I fell down with the gun and became unconscious!' "[1] Dostoevsky dedicated several long pages to speculations on the theme of these repenting and non-repenting Russians who will provide the new solution to insoluble difficulties, on the theme of the "oblivion of every measure in everything", the urge for the "extreme", "for the fainting sensation of approaching an abyss", on the themes of the search for suffering, impulses of negation and self destruction, etc. In order to support these speculations Dostoevsky even compares a Russian drunkard to a German one and states that the "German drunkard is unmistakably more stupid and ridiculous than the Russian". But let us abandon these rather comical anecdotes. Dostoevsky's story displays the "philosophy of the tortuous delight connected with the realization of incredible challenges". Dostoevsky himself is puzzled by the truth of Russian life revealed to him through his knowledge of it. And still he insists in this very story that there are no other people on earth who have such a genuine knowledge of Christ as the Russian people have.

"It is said that the Russian people know the Gospel poorly, that they are ignorant of the fundamental principles of faith. Of course, this is true, but they do know Christ and they have been carrying Him in their hearts from time immemorial. Of this there can be no doubt. How is the true conception of Christ possible without religious teaching? This is a different question. But the heart-knowledge of Christ, a true conception of Him, does fully exist. It is being passed from generation to generation, and it has merged with the heart of the people. Perhaps, Christ is the only love of the Russian people, and they love His image in their own way, to the limit of sufferance. And, more than on anything else, the people pride themselves on the name 'orthodox', that is, as confessing Christ more genuinely than all others. I repeat, much may be known unconsciously."[2]

[1] *Diary of a Writer*, Vol. I, p. 34.
[2] Pages 38–9.

In 1881 Dostoevsky develops with the same apodictic force the theme of Russia's exclusive knowledge of Christ and of the specific character of Russian socialism, "the ultimate aim of which is the establishment of an oecumenical Church on earth insofar as the earth is capable of embracing it". He stresses that the Russians would not accept communism in its mechanical form—"they believe that they shall be finally saved. *through the universal communion in the name of Christ.*"[1]

The Russian people, Dostoevsky says in the same article,

"have only God and the Czar; these two forces, these two great hopes are the people's only support. . . . The overwhelming mass of the Russian people is Orthodox; it lives by the idea of Orthodoxy in all its completeness despite the fact that rationally and scientifically they do not comprehend this idea. *Essentially*, save for this 'idea' there dwells no other in our people; everything is derived from it."[2]

Dostoevsky did not forget, however, his second idea—the idea of the Czar.

"Our people . . . are true, loyal children of the Czar, and he is their father. Is the saying 'the Czar is their father' a mere phrase, an empty sound in Russia? He who so believes understands nothing about Russia!"

He emphasizes that this "childlike affection" for the Czar is the basic foundation of Russian life.

"The Czar to the people is not an extrinsic force such as that of some conqueror (as were, for instance, the dynasties of the former kings of France), but a national, all-unifying force, which the people themselves desired, which they nurtured in their hearts, which they came to love . . . to the people the Czar is the incarnation of themselves, their whole ideology, their hopes and beliefs."

Dostoevsky considers this "a profound and most original idea". He affirms that

"there is in Russia no creative, protective and leading force other than this live organic bond of the people with their Czar from which everything is derived".[3]

[1] *Op. cit.*, Vol. II, p. 1029.
[2] *Ibid.*, Vol. II, p. 1028.
[3] Pages 1032–3.

The Russian writer is certain that

> "civil liberty may be established in Russia on an integral scale, more complete than anywhere in the world, whether in Europe or even in North America, and precisely on the same adamant foundation. It will be based not upon a written sheet of paper, but upon the children's affection of the people for the Czar, as their father, since children may be permitted many a thing which is inconceivable in the case of contractual nations...."[1]

Obviously Dostoevsky here follows closely the Russian Slavophils.[2]

Dostoevsky often contradicts himself. For instance, in his articles "My Paradox" and "Deduction from the Paradox" (June, 1876) he asserts that European culture in many of its manifestations has always, ever since Peter, been hateful and has always been felt alien to the Russian soul, and he simply declares that this was an unconscious and instinctive protest. He even says that "a Russian who has become a genuine European cannot help but become at the same time a national enemy of Russia...," "that under no circumstance can a Russian be converted into a real European as long as he remains the least bit Russian".[3] How can one reconcile these assertions with the emphatic declarations of Russia's love for Europe which we find in Dostoevsky's speech on Pushkin in which he stresses that "the Russian's destiny is incontestably all-European and universal", that

> "to become a genuine and all-round Russian means perhaps... to become brother of all men, *a universal man* if you please... To a genuine Russian, Europe and the destiny of the great Aryan race are as dear as Russia herself..."[4]

Must I remind the reader of Versilov's similar declarations?

As I mentioned, Dostoevsky's main ideas about Europe, Russia, Orthodoxy, Catholicism, Russian Christianity, and European Socialism expressed in his private correspondence and in *The Diary of a Writer* were almost textually repeated in the speeches of his favorite heroes, such as the Idiot, Shatov, Versilov, and Ivan Karamazov. I have quoted above Myshkin's tirades against Catholicism. Now I should like to attract the reader's attention to the item of Russian Messianism. Myshkin develops his conception of a national god which later becomes

---

[1] *Ibid.*, p. 1033.
[2] See W. Lednicki, "Panslavism" in *European Ideologies* (New York: Philosophical Library, 1948), pp. 807–912.
[3] *Diary of a Writer*, pp. 350–7.
[4] *Ibid.*, p. 979.

in *The Possessed* Shatov's profession of faith. Dostoevsky is forced to admit, and this is also what the Idiot emphasizes, the existence of Russian atheists and even of Russian Jesuits. His explanation of this "terrible fact" is that of "spiritual agony", "spiritual thirst", "a craving for something higher, for a firmer footing, for a fatherland in which they have ceased to believe because they have never even known it!" The only real belief is the belief in a national God. In *The Idiot* we read that "the man who has renounced his fatherland has renounced his God". The only remedy against this disease is to show to that soiled Russian "the whole of humanity, rising again, and renewed by Russian thought alone, perhaps by the Russian God and Christ", and then one will see

> "into what a mighty and truthful, what a wise and gentle giant he will grow before the eyes of the astounded world, astounded and dismayed because it expects of us nothing but the sword, only the sword and violence, because, judging us by themselves, the other peoples cannot picture us free from barbarism".[1]

As the reader knows, these philippics were interrupted by an incident: the Idiot, following the example of Stendhal's Julien Sorel, broke a Chinese vase. But in *The Possessed* there was no vase to break and Shatov had time enough to explain to Stavrogin the latter's own former ideas. These pages in *The Possessed* are indeed striking. In them we read that

> "God is a synthetic personality of the whole nation taken from its beginning to its end. There has never existed among all or many nations one common God, but each one has had its own. It's a sign of the decay of nations when they begin to have Gods in common. When Gods begin to be common to several nations, the Gods are dying and the faith in them, together with the nations themselves. The stronger a people the more individual their God. There has never been a nation without a religion, that is, without an idea of good and evil. Every people has its own conception of good and evil, and its own good and evil. When the same conceptions of good and evil become prevalent in several nations, then these nations are dying, and then the very distinction between good and evil is beginning to disappear...."

And here we find a marvelous *pendant* to Myshkin's pacifism, which, by the way, contradicted Dostoevsky's assertions in the letter to

[1] Cf. *The Idiot* (Constance Garnett translation) (London-Toronto, 1948), pp. 532-5.

Maykov mentioned above. This time Dostoevsky becomes even more outspoken:

> "Every people is only a people so long as it has its own God and excludes all other Gods on earth irreconcilably; so long as it believes that by its God it will conquer and drive out of the world all other Gods. Such, from the beginning of time, has been the belief of all great nations, all, anyway, who have been specially remarkable, all who have been leaders of humanity. There is no going against facts . . ."

Dostoevsky, in listing various deifications of national ideas, mentions the Jews, the Greeks, Romans, French, and follows with a statement that every great nation believes that the truth is only in it and exclusively in it, and that as soon as it loses this belief it becomes mere "ethnographic material". Dostoevsky's idea and hope, as we know, was that not only the Poles but the whole of Europe would become pure "ethnographic material" under the rule of the Russian nation. Here he does not hide his view at all:

> " 'The only God-bearing nation,' continued Shatov, 'is the Russian nation.' " And then follows the most astounding confession: " 'I believe in Russia . . . I believe in her orthodoxy . . . I believe in the body of Christ . . . I believe that the new advent will take place in Russia . . . I believe . . .' Shatov muttered frantically. 'And in God? In God?' asked Stavrogin. Shatov answered, 'I . . . I will believe in God.' "[1]

How strange against this background are some of Dostoevsky's assertions expressed in his articles, in his famous Pushkin speech, and those which he puts into the mouths of his heroes, such as Ivan Karamazov or Versilov in *The Raw Youth*, by which assertions he emphasizes the attachment of Russia to Europe and the particularly wide and deep comprehension which Russians have for Europe. Dostoevsky claims, as the reader may remember, that "to be a real Russian means being a real European", and that some of his heroes felt when abroad that they were the only Europeans among Europeans, that the French were French, the English, English, the Germans, German, but only the Russians, besides being Russian, were also Europeans! Whom should we believe? Shatov and Stavrogin with their particular Russian God, or Versilov with his cosmopolitanism and universalism? Must I recall Dostoevsky's strange speculations about the

---

[1] Cf. *The Possessed* (Constance Garnett translation) (New York, 1936), pp. 254–6.

"Russian seekers" Aleko and Onegin, whom he glorifies in his Pushkin speech? His assertions that Onegin killed his friend and Aleko his wife possibly due to their longing for universalistic ideals are hardly convincing. I should like to remark that, in a sense, he put them on the same level as those Russian atheists and Russian Jesuits mentioned by Myshkin, who fell into the abysses of European thought because they were trying to reach a lost fatherland. He hated Europe and expressed the belief that only Russian thought was able to embrace universalistic human goals. By these trends of his beliefs he certainly approached the Slavophils and later the Russian *narodniki*, as well as the Panslavists. And in his political articles he very often waved the banners of Slavic brotherhood, of a Panslavic union under Russian leadership.[1]

L. Grossman, in his essay "Dostoevsky and Europe", has brilliantly studied and presented Dostoevsky's general philosophy of history. This, however, was not a very difficult thing to do as one may find a well-developed outline of Dostoevsky's *res politica* in the *Diary of a Writer* and particularly in his articles of May–June, 1877, September, 1877, November, 1877, and in his articles of 1881. Dostoevsky's philosophy implies the following: ancient Rome was the first to originate the idea of the universal unity of man and to realize this idea in the form of a universal empire. "However, this formula fell before Christianity—the form but not the idea." This idea was that of "European mankind". This idea is at the bottom of European civilization.

> "For it alone mankind lives." "Only the idea of the universal Roman empire succumbed, and it was replaced by a new ideal, also universal, of a communion in Christ. This new ideal bifurcated into the Eastern ideal of the purely spiritual communion of men and the Western European, Roman Catholic, Papal ideal diametrically opposed to the Eastern one."

The Eastern Slavic idea of union based on the Gospel was facing the Roman Catholic idea of a universal monarchy with the Pope at its head. The Papacy yielded to the third temptation of the Devil; it "sold Christ for earthly domination".

> "The fullest incarnation of the Catholic idea, of the organization of human society without and beyond Christ, is to be found in France: French socialism is the development of the Catholic idea and it means the next deformation of Christian ideals."[2] "French socialism is nothing else but the *compulsory* union of mankind, an

---
[1] Cf. W. Lednicki, "Panslavism", cited above.
[2] *Diary of a Writer*, p. 523.

idea which dates back to ancient Rome and which was fully conserved in Catholicism. Thus, the idea of the liberation of the human spirit from Catholicism became vested there precisely in the narrowest Catholic form, borrowed from the very heart of its spirit, from its letter, from its materialism, from its despotism, from its morality."[1]

In this period the definite victory of materialism over spiritualism was achieved. To this extreme formulation of Western conceptions was opposed the German idea, which, from the times of Arminius to Bismarck, was a protest against Rome. In its essence it was a purely negative idea. "This is the German who blindly believes that in him alone and not in the Catholic civilization resides the rejuvenation of mankind." Dostoevsky emphasizes the purely negative character of the German protest:

"Through the nineteen centuries of her existence, Germany herself, who has been doing nothing but protesting, has not uttered her own *new word* but has been living all along by negation and protest against her enemy."

Further, Dostoevsky predicts that although Luther's Protestantism is a fact, yet since it exists by "merely denying faith", it will "unfailingly" disappear as soon as Catholicism disappears.[2]

These are the two conflicting ideas; their goal is world domination, but they both face ultimate failure.

"Meanwhile in the East there really begins to kindle and shine with unprecedented and never heard of light the third world idea —the Slavic idea—an idea which is coming into being,—perhaps the third future possibility of the solution of European and human destinies."[3]

Dostoevsky asks, "What is this idea?" "What does the Slavs' communion bring with it?" and he candidly answers: "All this is still too indeterminate, but that something new must be introduced and uttered,—this virtually no one doubts." Nevertheless, dogmatic as usual, he asserts:

"Here we had something universal and final, which, though by no means solving all human destinies, brings with it the beginning

[1] *Ibid.*, p. 563.
[2] *Ibid.*, p. 564.
[3] *Ibid.*, p. 565.

of the end of the whole former history of European mankind, the beginning of the solution of its further destinies, which are in the hands of God and about which man can guess nothing although he may forebode them."

He is certain that these events cannot be arrested, that "ideas of this magnitude cannot be subjected to petty, Judaized, third-rate considerations". The guarantee of the materialization is to be found in "two dreadful powers" which are at the disposal of Russia, "worth all others in the world—the unity, the spiritual indivisibility of the millions of our people, and their closest communion with the monarch".[1]

The final phase of this world struggle will take on an apocalyptical character. The Pope will lose all his allies in the persons of emperors and kings and will throw himself into the arms of the proletariat, trying to become a socialistic vicar of Saint Peter. "On foot and bare footed, the Pope will go to all the beggars, and he will tell them that everything the socialists teach and strive for is contained in the gospel . . ." Dostoevsky repeats again, "Roman Catholicism doesn't mean Christ (this is all too clear)."[2]

There was one man in whom Dostoevsky put his hopes, Prince Bismarck. The figure of the German Chancellor deeply attracted Dostoevsky, and his name constantly appears in the *Diary of a Writer*. Dostoevsky emphasized that Prince Bismarck hates socialism not less than Popery, that he foresees the union of the Pope and socialism,

"because he alone, among all diplomats, was so quick sighted as to prefigure the viability of the Roman idea and that energy with which it is determined to defend itself regardless, by any means. It is inspired with the devilish desire to live, and it is difficult to kill it —it is a snake! This is what Prince Bismarck alone—the principal enemy of Papacy and the Roman idea—realizes to the fullest extent."[3]

In this way does Dostoevsky foresee the ultimate battle.

But the last word will be said by the united East, although Dostoevsky mentioned here and there the fact that Prince Bismarck was in general not too favorable to the "Slavic idea". However, he expressed in his articles of 1877 a firm assurance that the German Chancellor will knock at the door of Russia.

[1] *Ibid.*, p. 566.
[2] *Ibid.*, p. 738.
[3] *Ibid.*

"*At all events* one thing seems clear to me, that Germany *needs us*, even more than we think, and she needs us not for a momentary political alliance but *forever*."

This time Dostoevsky accepts the "German idea" as not a purely "negative one":

"The idea of reunited Germany is a broad and stately one; it goes back into the depth of ages. What has Germany to divide with us?—Her object is all Western mankind. She has selected for herself the European Western world where she seeks to inculcate her principles in lieu of the Roman and Romanic tenants, and henceforth to become its leader, leaving the East to Russia. Thus, two great peoples are destined to transform the face of this world."[1]

In another article, prior to this one, Dostoevsky stated: "*The dependency upon an alliance with Russia, especially after the Franco-Prussian war, seems to be Germany's fatal destiny.*"[2] This alliance opens the road to the realization of Russia's worldly mission: "the two-headed monster" of Catholicism and socialism will be destroyed and then the domination of the Germans in the West and the domination of Russia in the East will be established. Dostoevsky hoped that the creator of the formula of "union in blood and iron" would split Europe with his powerful sword and that "after rivers of blood and hundreds of millions of heads" the world would accept the new word of the Slavic gospel. And this was to be what Dostoevsky called "the free Panslavic union of Europe".

L. Grossman is right when he says that the Franco-Prussian War became a source of inspiration for Dostoevsky's conceptions. "Just like the most aggressive German professor, he calls for a march against France" and "wants to enlighten Europe by the light of the Gospel, by Bismarck's formulae, and by the direct help of the German armies".[3] France will be broken by "blood and iron", "Czargrad" will be in the hands of Russia, England and France will be defeated by the Russian–German armies, and so the triumph of Russian Christianity will be achieved. The last formulation of the idea of the universal Russian mission is to be found in Dostoevsky's famous speech on Pushkin:

"Oh, the peoples of Europe have no idea how dear they are to us! And later—in this I believe—we, well, not we but the future

[1] Page 912.
[2] Page 743.
[3] L. Grossman, *Tvorčestvo Dostoevskogo* (Moscow, 1928), p. 207.

Russians, to the last man, will comprehend that to become a genuine Russian means to seek finally to reconcile all European controversies, to show the solution of European anguish in our all-humanitarian and all-unifying Russian soul, to embrace in it with brotherly love all our brethren, and finally, perhaps, to utter the ultimate word of great, universal harmony, of the brotherly accord of all nations abiding by the law of Christ's Gospel!"[1]

In other words, Dostoevsky follows the reasonings of his Raskolnikov: "*Vive la guerre éternelle*—till the new Jerusalem."

However, all these texts do not cover the whole scope of Dostoevsky's "foreign policy". In the very last period of his life, in his articles of January, 1881, the month of his death, Dostoevsky turned his eyes towards Asia:

> "Skobelev's victory resounded all over Asia to her remotest corners: 'Another fierce and proud orthodox people bowed before the White Czar!' And let this rumor echo and re-echo. Let the conviction of the invincibility of the White Czar and of his sword grow and spread among the millions of those peoples,—to the very borders of India and in India herself . . . the peoples may have their khans and emirs; in their imagination. England, whose strength they admire, may stand as a menace, but the name of the White Czar must soar above those of the khans and emirs, above the name of the Caliph himself. Such is the conviction that must prevail in Asia!"

A little further Dostoevsky stresses:

> "This is necessary because Russia is not only in Europe but also in Asia; because the Russian is not only a European but also an Asiatic. Moreover, Asia, perhaps, holds out greater promises to us than Europe. In our future destinies Asia is perhaps our main outlet."[2]

In Dostoevsky's very last article we read:

> "In Europe we were hangers-on and slaves, whereas we shall go to Asia as masters. In Europe we were Asiatics, whereas in Asia we, too, are Europeans. Our civilizing mission in Asia will bribe our spirit and drive us thither. It is only necessary that the movement

[1] *Diary of a Writer*, Vol. II, pp. 979–80.
[2] Page 1044.

should start. Build only two railroads: begin with the one to Siberia, and then—to Central Asia,—and at once you will see the consequences."[1]

And this is Dostoevsky's last message:

"Wherever a 'Uruss' settles in Asia, the land will forthwith become Russian land. A new Russia will arise which in due time will regenerate and resurrect the old one and will show the latter the road which she has to follow. . . . Let it be only slightly fathomed (but fathomed) that Asia is our future outlet, that our riches are there, that there is our ocean; that when in Europe, because of the overcrowded conditions alone, inevitable and humiliating communism is established, communism which Europe herself will loathe; when whole throngs will crowd around one hearth, and gradually individual economies will be ruined, while families will forsake their homes and will start living in collective communes; when children (three quarters of them foundlings) will be brought up in foundling institutions,—then we shall still have wide expanses, meadows and forests, and our children will grow up in their parents' homes, not in stone barracks—amidst gardens and sowed fields, beholding above them clear, blue skies."

Dostoevsky's prophecies undoubtedly found some confirmation in the development of the political events of our times. His apocalyptical vision of the death of European civilization was not a unique one. He certainly foresaw the dangers threatening this civilization, dangers which were hidden in the capitalistic organization of European society, in pragmatism, in utilitarian rationalism, empiricism, and materialism, which characterized modern European thought. His perspicacious analysis of the psychology of the modern man, his portrayal of the superman, which preceded Nietzsche and predicted the modern dictatorship, made of him a kind of Delphic oracle. On many occasions his interpretation of "Russian chaos" and of the destructive elements which lay hidden at the bottom of the "chaos" were, perhaps, not entirely unjustified, so that his diagnosis may still be convincing. True, one may have some doubts as to whether his idea that this Russian chaos and its destructive elements were of European origin was correct. It would not be easy, either, to share his belief that from this chaos will originate a blessing beneficial to the world. He was not quite right either when he depicted the future communist barracks of Europe and the "flowering paradise" of Russia. So, if we may recognize

[1] *Ibid.*, p. 1048.

with some reservations Dostoevsky-the-diagnostician, one may doubt whether Dostoevsky-the-physician deserves the same recognition; it would be rather difficult to accept the medicine which he prescribed and which was to cure the world of its disease. And besides, there remains another point which is connected with his Christianity. How can we reconcile his violent hatred of so many nations and confessions, his animosity for so many people with his preaching of love and compassion? How can one explain his cruel contempt for so many suffering nations and people against the background of his affirmations that precisely the Russian people are those who possess the secret of real Christian pity? How can one solve the problem of Dostoevsky's supposed universality? Dostoevsky's texts show that when the writer searched for a universal God he found him only in his Russian Orthodox God. He even proclaimed a war of gods and hoped for the defeat of all of them by the Russian God. Yes, it would be difficult to accept this as a satisfactory remedy for the conflict and contradictions characterizing our world. The advent of Dostoevsky's triumphant Russian Christ would be possible as the *finale* of a complete disaster of the western-European world. Needless to say, this is how Dostoevsky himself understood Russia's world mission.

Let me answer with his own words:

> "Too high a price is asked for harmony; it's beyond our means to pay so much to enter on it. And I hasten to give back my entrance ticket, and if I am an honest man, I am bound to give it back as soon as possible. And that I am doing."[1]

---

[1] Dostoevsky, *The Brothers Karamazov*, Book V, ch. 4.

IV

Dostoevsky—The Man From Underground

> "The ancestor of these evil people in our literature was Sylvio in the story *The Shot*, taken by the simple and beautiful Pushkin from Byron."
>
> (Dostoevsky, *Diary of a Writer*, 1876, "February", Chapter I.)

DOSTOEVSKY'S *Notes from Underground* has long been considered the key work in his literary evolution. Indeed, even the very time of its appearance—between the *House of the Dead* and *Crime and Punishment*—makes it significant. From a certain point of view the *Notes* represents a kind of philosophical development of the conclusions to which Dostoevsky was brought by his stay in the convict prison and which he formulated in *The House of the Dead*. On the other hand, the *Notes* is in many respects a sort of preface to *Crime and Punishment*, and some of its trends reach into *The Possessed*, *A Raw Youth* and *The Brothers Karamazov*. But one must not forget that in the *Notes* we also find speculations connected with items, themes, and ideas which absorbed Dostoevsky before his Siberian period.

The House of the Dead, insofar as it expresses the pathetic change which occurred in Dostoevsky's ideology, may be pictured as a stone under which Dostoevsky tried to bury his past. And, just as in his terrible story, *Bobok*, the corpses start to talk in their graves and arrive at a decision to denude and unmask themselves, so in the *Notes* Dostoevsky denudes and unmasks, with unrestrained cruelty, his former idealism, and all his former idealistic infatuations like morbid ghosts reappear from under the stone with which he tried to crush them in *The House of the Dead*.

However, it is not only former philosophical conceptions that reappear here. Some previous literary themes are reborn as well. These bring us to his first works, which, as we know, are closely connected with Gogol and with Pushkin. And these themes are especially important for the purpose of the present study.

* * * * *

The Romantic Duel

I shall not enter into all details of the immense suggestivity of Pushkin and of its deep traces in Dostoevsky's works. Merezhkovsky and Bem have given convincing proofs of this fact.[1] I would like only to pause over one small episode in the *Notes* which, in my opinion, deserves some special attention. From the purely formal point of view, I cannot claim any original discovery, as Dostoevsky himself points to Pushkin in the *Notes*. It seems to me, nevertheless, that his open allusion to Pushkin's *Shot* is rather a strategic diversion than anything else. It seems to me that the episode is attached to much more important items, which Dostoevsky developed behind the small Pushkin label that we find in his book.

Perhaps the reader remembers the painful story in the *Notes* of the dinner at the Hôtel de Paris and what happens later. In a state of fury and with a desire for immediate revenge the disgusting hero of the *Notes* runs to the brothel. His thoughts become more and more disordered, and finally he conceives a deliberate offense which is to compromise his rival entirely and after which he himself will be sent to Siberia.

> "In fifteen years when they let me out of prison I will trudge off to him, a beggar, in rags. I shall find him in some provincial town. He will be married and happy, he will have a grown-up daughter . . . I shall say to him: 'Look, monster, at my hollow cheeks and my rags! I've lost everything—my career, my happiness, art, science, *the woman I loved*, and all through you. Here are pistols. I have come to discharge my pistol . . . and I . . . forgive you.' Then I shall fire into the air, and he will hear nothing more of me. . . ."[2]

This was not the first time that Dostoevsky had followed Pushkin so closely. In his *St. Petersburg Dreams in Verse and Prose*, when writing about Soloviev, "a colossal personality", he talked with such excitement about *his* Covetous Knight that he suddenly had to interrupt his paraphrase and simply confess that he was "stealing from Pushkin".[3] The same thing occurred in this case. "I was actually," continues the hero from underground, "on the point of tears, though I knew perfectly well at that moment that all this was out of Pushkin's *Sylvio* and

---

[1] Cf. D. Merežkovskij, *Tolstoj i Dostoevskij* (St. Petersburg, 1912); and A. L. Bem, *O Dostoevskom* (Prague, 1929), Vol. III.

[2] *Notes from Underground*, translated by Constance Garnett, Part II, ch. 5.

[3] Dostoevskij, *Dnevnik pisatelja* (Moscow-Leningrad: Gos. Izdat., 1930), Vol. XIII, p. 161.

Lermontov's *Masquerade*."[1] There is obviously nothing more to say here about Pushkin's *Shot*. Dostoevsky himself has made his confession.

It does seem to me, however, that there is another short story which acted as a bridge between *The Shot* and the *Notes*, particularly with regard to the item of the romantic duel and revenge, but also in certain other respects. This story is Turgenev's *Diary of a Superfluous Man*, which appeared in 1850. We may assume that Dostoevsky had read the story before he wrote the *Notes* in 1864.[2] The obvious connections between this story and Dostoevsky's *Notes* confirm our assumption.

The *Diary* is quite an unusual story for Turgenev. After it appeared the term "superfluous man" became a fixed expression, applied to figures like Onegin, Rudin, and even Chatsky and Pechorin—in other words, to figures representing primarily a social and historical phenomenon, rather than an individual psychological problem. Paradoxical as it may seem, Turgenev's Chulkaturin is a closer relative of the hero from underground than of any of those mentioned. I shall come a little later to the analysis of the striking resemblances between Chulkaturin and the underground man, as well as to the obvious similarity of the entire tone and psychological atmosphere of these two works. For the moment I am interested in Dostoevsky's conception of the romantic duel and of revenge, which remained unrealized in the *Notes*, but to which Dostoevsky returned much later in *The Possessed* and *The Brothers Karamazov*. In my opinion, although Dostoevsky acknowledged his debt to Pushkin, he might also be presented with a bill on behalf of Turgenev.

I have just mentioned the dreams *à la Sylvio* of the underground hero. Here is a passage in Turgenev's *Diary of a Superfluous Man*, the whole tone and implications of which parallel the *Notes*:

". . . I swore to myself, wrapping my cloak about me like a Spaniard, to rush out from some dark corner and stab my lucky rival, and with brutal glee I imagined Liza's despair. . . . But, in the first place, such corners were few in the town of O——; and, secondly,—the wooden fence, the street lamp, the police-man in the distance. . . . No! in such corners it was somehow far more suitable to sell buns and oranges than to shed human blood."[3]

---

[1] *Notes, loc. cit.*
[2] Dostoevsky, F., *Diary of a Writer*. In an entry for November, 1877 (chapter I, Part 2), Dostoevsky wrote: "I remember that having left the prison in Siberia in 1854, I started to reread all the literature which had been written in my absence (*The Notes of a Hunter* . . . and the first short stories of Turgenev). I read them then in one sitting, at one swoop, and got a delightful impression."
[3] *The Novels of Ivan Turgenev*, translated by Constance Garnett (New York: Macmillan Co., 1899), Vol. XIII, p. 50.

Let us recall the two extravagant duels of Sylvio and the young Count in *The Shot*. In the first one Sylvio simply withheld his shot in order to find a more satisfactory opportunity to avenge himself. In the second he was satisfied by a purely moral triumph. In fact, his cruel plan turned into an adventure which was no longer a duel and which suggested only the possibility of a romantic, generous pardoning of his enemy.

It was Turgenev who gave a developed story of such a duel, in which he reversed the rôles and gave the privilege of manifesting generosity to a character, who, in his story, represents a psychological descendant of Pushkin's young Count and is opposed to Chulkaturin, who here represents Sylvio to a certain degree and is a predecessor of Dostoevsky's hero.

The Shot contains a variant of the juxtaposition of two contrasting characters frequently found in Pushkin's works. There are several pairs that illustrate this: Boris Godunov and Dimitri the Impostor, Salieri and Mozart, the Covetous Knight and his son. Sylvio summarizes the psychological situation that cannot but end in the clash of these personalities:

"I was calmly, or rather boisterously enjoying my reputation, when a young man belonging to a wealthy and distinguished family —I will not mention his name—joined our regiment. Never in my life have I met with such a fortunate fellow! Imagine to yourself youth, wit, beauty, unbounded gaiety, the most reckless bravery, a famous name, untold wealth—imagine all these, and you can form some idea of the effect that he would be sure to produce among us. My supremacy was shaken. Dazzled by my reputation, he began to seek my friendship, but I received him coldly, and without the least regret he held aloof from me. I developed a hatred for him. His success in the regiment and in the society of ladies brought me to the verge of despair. I began to seek a quarrel with him; to my epigrams he replied with epigrams which always seemed to me more spontaneous and more cutting than mine, and which were decidedly more amusing, for he joked while I fumed. At last, at a ball given by a Polish landed proprietor, seeing him the object of the attention of all the ladies, and especially of the mistress of the house, with whom I was upon very good terms, I whispered some grossly insulting remark in his ear. He flamed up and gave me a slap in the face. We grasped our swords; the ladies fainted; we were separated; and that same night we set out to fight."[1]

---
[1] *The Poems, Prose and Plays of Alexander Pushkin* (edited by Avrahm Yarmolinsky) (New York: Random House, 1936), pp. 478–9.

Pushkin is always very concise in his descriptions. Perhaps this is why each of his conceptions has such enormous suggestive power. If one were to fill those delicate outlines with a less symbolic and more concrete, realistic, psychological content, one would come forth with the situations described by Turgenev and later by Dostoevsky. Without as yet entering into all the details which became the bricks of Turgenev's bridge between *The Shot* and *Notes from Underground*, I would now like to cite the essential elements connected with the story of the Superfluous Man and the Prince which indicate that *The Shot* was, indeed, the foundation for Turgenev's story. Take the very first meeting of these two characters:

"One day—it was in the morning about twelve o'clock—I had hardly entered Mr. Ozhogin's hall, when I heard an unfamiliar, mellow voice in the drawing room, the door opened, and a tall and slim man of five-and-twenty appeared in the doorway, escorted by the master of the house. He rapidly put on a military overcoat which lay on the slab, and took cordial leave of Kirilla Matveyich. As he brushed past me, he carelessly touched his foraging cap, and vanished with a clink of his spurs."[1]

A little later the hero observes that the arrival of Prince N. did not make "any special impression" on him at the time. However, he stresses the feelings of hostility and envy

"of a shy and obscure person from Moscow toward a brilliant officer from Petersburg. 'The Prince,' I mused, 'is an upstart from the capital; he'll look down upon us. . . .' I had not seen him for more than an instant, but I had had time to perceive that he was good-looking, clever, and at his ease."

Even more revealing are the lines in the diary for the next day in which the Superfluous Man describes his second meeting with the Prince:

"When, next day, after long hesitation and with a low sinking at my heart I went to Ozhogin's familiar drawing-room, I was no longer the same man as they had known during the last three weeks. . . . After the first courtesies, Ozhogin introduced me to the prince, who was very affable in his behavior to me. He was as a rule very affable with everyone; and in spite of the immeasurable distance between him and our obscure circle, he was clever enough to

[1] Turgenev, *op. cit.*, p. 38.

avoid being a source of constraint to any one, and even to make a show of being on our level, and only living at Petersburg, as it were, by accident. ... My continual forced smile and painful vigilance, my idiotic silence, my miserable and ineffectual desire to get away—all that was doubtless something truly remarkable in its own way. It was not one wild beast alone gnawing at my vitals; jealousy, envy, the sense of my own insignificance, and helpless hatred were torturing me. I could not but admit that the prince really was a very agreeable young man. ... I devoured him with my eyes; I really believe I forgot to blink as usual, as I stared at him. ... He must have felt me a great bore. ... From sympathy for me and also from a profound sense of my absolute harmlessness, he treated me with extraordinary gentleness. You can fancy how this wounded me!"[1]

The Superfluous Man further describes the victory of the Prince:

"The prince was not only handsome and clever: he played the piano, sang, sketched fairly well, and was a good hand at telling stories. His anecdotes drawn from the highest circles of Petersburg society always made a great impression on his audience, all the more so from the fact that he seemed to attach no importance to them. ... The consequence of this, if you like, simple accomplishment of the prince was that in the course of his not very protracted stay in the town of O—— he completely fascinated all the neighborhood. ..."[2]

The story of the ball and of the provocation of the duel in the *Diary* is equally close to Pushkin's *Shot*, although the Prince's attitude is more reserved and sophisticated than that of his prototype. We must not forget that both characters in the *Diary* have been developed and modernized by Turgenev. The power of Pushkin's suggestivity is particularly evident in the episode of the duel. Here almost every detail of the scenery and the attitudes of the participants is similar to those in Pushkin, with some small deviations, however, connected with the psychological elaboration of the theme. Let us start with Pushkin:

"The dawn was just breaking. I was standing at the appointed place with my three seconds. With inexplicable impatience I awaited my opponent. The spring sun rose, and it was already

[1] Turgenev, *op. cit.*, pp. 42, 45–6.
[2] Turgenev, *op. cit.*, pp. 52–3.

growing hot. I saw him coming in the distance. He was walking on foot, accompanied by one second. We advanced to meet him. He approached, holding his cap filled with black cherries. The seconds measured twelve paces for us. I had to fire first, but my agitation was so great, that I could not depend upon the steadiness of my hand; and in order to give myself time to become calm, I ceded to him the first shot. My adversary would not agree to this. It was decided that we should cast lots. The first number fell to him, the constant favorite of fortune. He took aim, and his bullet went through my cap. It was now my turn. His life at last was in my hands; I looked at him eagerly, endeavoring to detect if only the faintest shadow of uneasiness. But he stood in front of my pistol, picking out the ripest cherries from his cap and spitting out the stones, which flew almost as far as my feet. His indifference annoyed me beyond measure. 'What is the use,' thought I, 'of depriving him of life, when he attaches no value whatever to it?' A malicious thought flashed through my mind. I lowered my pistol."[1]

Let us now turn to Turgenev's scene of the duel:

"We arrived first; but the prince and Bezmenkov did not keep us long waiting. The prince was, without exaggeration, as fresh as a rose; his brown eyes looked out with excessive cordiality from under the peak of his cap. He was smoking a cigar, and on seeing Koloberdyaev shook his hand in a friendly way. Even to me he bowed very genially. I was conscious, on the contrary, of being very pale, and my hands, to my terrible vexation, were slightly trembling . . . my throat was parched . . . I had never fought a duel before. 'O God!' I thought, 'if only that ironical gentleman doesn't take my agitation for timidity!' I was inwardly cursing my nerves; but glancing, at last, straight in the prince's face, and catching on his lips an almost imperceptible smile, I suddenly felt furious again, and was at once at my ease. Meanwhile, our seconds were fixing the barrier, measuring out the paces, loading the pistols. Koloberdyaev did most; Bezmenkov rather watched him. It was a magnificent day—as fine as the day of that ever-memorable walk. The thick blue of the sky peeped, as then, through the golden green of the leaves. Their lisping seemed to mock me. The prince went on smoking his cigar, leaning with his shoulder against the trunk of a young lime-tree. . . ."[2]

[1] Pushkin (Yarmolinsky's ed.), pp. 479–80.
[2] Turgenev, *op. cit.*, pp. 70–1.

In this instance it was the Prince who received the bullet in his cap and was lightly wounded. And immediately after, "without even giving himself the satisfaction of tormenting" his rival, "replied with a smile, 'The duel is at an end,' and fired into air." The Superfluous Man is in a rage, crushed by the magnanimity of the Prince. He is "shattered—morally shattered". His "vanity suffered indescribably", especially from the consciousness of his imbecility: " 'I have given myself the last decisive blow by my own act,' I kept repeating as I strode up and down my room. 'The prince, wounded by me, and forgiving me!' "

The item of the romantic, generous duel was not abandoned, even after Turgenev. Precisely the same situation appears in *The Possessed*. Of course, Dostoevsky introduced some new details of his own, but he remained within Pushkin's and Turgenev's outline. The reader will recall that Gaganov, who was "morbidly suspicious and always ready to be deeply offended", felt insulted by the fact that Stavrogin and Kirillov arrived at the duel on horseback rather than in a carriage, and this has some reference to the situation in *Eugene Onegin*, where Lensky was insulted because Onegin brought his servant, Guillot, as a second. There are also details in *The Possessed* that are reminiscent of the duel scene in Turgenev's *Diary* which has been described above. For example, "he (Gaganov) got out of his char-a-banc, yellow with anger, and felt that his hands were trembling. . . . He made no response at all to Nikolay Vsevolodovich's bow, and turned away." The description of the duel itself follows almost exactly Turgenev's pattern: the enraged Gaganov fires first, Stavrogin is slightly scratched and fires without aiming. This is followed by the furious revolt of Gaganov against Stavrogin's obvious determination not to aim at him. Finally, at the third attempt, Gaganov's bullet pierces Stavrogin's hat, and Stavrogin deliberately fires in the opposite direction.

Beyond a doubt, similar echoes of the romantic duel are to be found in the episode of Zossima's duel, described in *The Brothers Karamazov* (Part VI, entitled "The Russian Monk"):

"So we reached the place and found them there, awaiting us. We were placed twelve paces apart; he had the first shot. I stood gaily, looking him full in the face; I did not twitch an eyelash, I looked lovingly at him for I knew what I would do. His shot just grazed my cheek and ear. 'Thank God,' I cried, 'no man has been killed,' and I seized my pistol, turned back and flung it far away into the wood. 'That's the place for you,' I cried. I turned to my adversary. 'Forgive me, young fool that I am, sir,' I said, 'for my unprovoked insult to you and for forcing you to fire at me. I am ten times worse than you and more, maybe. Tell that to the person whom you hold dearest in the world.' 'Upon my word,' cried my adversary, annoyed, 'if you did not want to fight, why did not you let me alone?' 'Yesterday I was a fool, today I know better,' I answered him gaily. . . . I ought to have owned my fault as soon as I got here, before he had fired a shot, before leading him into a great and deadly sin; but we have made our life so grotesque, that to act in that way would have been almost impossible, for only after I have faced his shot at the distance of twelve paces could my words have any significance for him, and if I had spoken before, he would have said 'he is a coward, the sight of the pistols had frightened him, no use to listen to him.' 'Gentlemen,' I cried suddenly, speaking straight from my heart, 'look around you at the gifts of God, the clear sky, the pure air, the tender grass, the birds; nature is beautiful and sinless, and we, only we, are sinful and foolish, and we don't understand that life is heaven, for we have only to understand that and it will at once be fulfilled in all its beauty, we shall embrace each other and weep.' "

There exists, undoubtedly, a direct tie between Zossima's duel and the dreams of the hero from underground about a duel to be followed by a generous reconciliation. In Zossima's duel, however, the reconciliation is evidently a kind of sublimation, a Christian repentance, a humbleness and self-humiliation, all of which is combined with sentimental motifs to be seen in the opposition of a peaceful and benevolent nature to a belligerent and destructive man. Incidentally, these motifs were all practically clichés. They constantly appear in Russian literature. It will suffice to mention Karamzin, Lermontov and Tolstoy's *Caucasian Tales*.

French "point d'honneur" and Russian formlessness

The novel *A Raw Youth* contains several statements of Dostoevsky concerning the Russian "chaos" and "formlessness" characterizing the "accidental tribe". The "historian" of this "tribe" opposes himself to Tolstoy, who "gave the last word about the Russian gentry, which represented the educational period of our history". "Comeliness", "beautiful, finished forms", "finished customs of honour and duty", these are the essential traits brought to the fore by the "historiographer of our nobility". This is what we read in the epilogue of *A Raw Youth*, in Dostoevsky's letters about Tolstoy, in Versilov's talks with the Raw Youth, and in the author's notes and drafts for this novel. Mochulsky believes that Versilov's "exaggerated enthusiasm" for "the comeliness of forms characterizing the Russian gentry", as represented by Tolstoy, "unmasks the artificiality and instability" of this order. Dostoevsky was the "first to guess" that the "beautiful order" of the forms of life established by the Russian nobility was only a "semblance". "He guessed that behind the harmonious mirage chaos stormed." Dostoevsky's paradoxical idea was to "display formlessness in an artistic form, to enclose the picture of chaos in the frames of art".[1] Indeed, Dostoevsky's purpose was not only a paradoxical but a dangerous one: "There are things which are not even sinful and not quite criminal, but the revelation of them would frighten even an honest and firm man," we read in *A Raw Youth*.[2] The novel itself naturally gives innumerable illustrations of this Russian "formlessness". But if the revelation of the Russian "chaos" was the main idea which guided Dostoevsky in *A Raw Youth*, the *Notes from Underground* is a work which is preparatory for the full development of this theme.

Thus, in the *Notes from Underground* one may find several manifestations of this essentially rebellious, revolutionary attitude of Dostoevsky's heroes toward the established order, in the most general sense of the word. In these manifestations we may discover traits connected not only with the social and psychological déclassé, but with the Russian revolt against European "formalism", against the century-old forms of European civilization and European social tradition. Let us take an example first not from the *Notes from Underground* but from *The Gambler*, as this example is particularly illustrative. The reader may remember the meeting between the gambler and Baron and Baroness Burmerhelm. This is how the gambler himself describes it:

> " 'When I was in Berlin the sound was for ever in my ears of that *ja wohl*, continually repeated at every word and disgustingly drawled out by them. When I met them in the avenue that *ja wohl* suddenly came to my mind, I don't know why, and—well, it had an irritating effect on me. . . . Besides, the Baroness, who has met me three times, has the habit of walking straight at me as though I were a worm who might be trampled underfoot. You must admit that I, too, may have my proper pride.' "[3]

This act of the gambler, although still connected with the item of absurd self-assertion, of someone who suffers from an inferiority complex, nevertheless hides revolutionary tendencies: it aims at the destruction of established conventions and reveals the elemental fight of

---
[1] Močul'skij, *op. cit.*, pp. 405–13.
[2] *A Raw Youth*, Part III, chapter 4, Section 1.
[3] Cf. *The Gambler*, chapter 6.

the Russian against the principle of European life based on hierarchy, law, and order, a fact which many Russian philosophers have emphasized. This is essentially anarchism. No less eloquent is the story of the same gambler with the Catholic prelate in the Vatican Legation in Paris, which I related in my previous study.[1]

On the same page the gambler tells still another story:

" 'Why, am I to model myself upon our Russians here? They sit, not daring to open their lips, and almost ready to deny they are Russians. In Paris, anyway in my hotel, they began to treat me much more attentively when I told everyone about my passage-at-arms with the abbé. The fat Polish *pan*, the person most antagonistic to me at *table d'hôte*, sank into the background. The Frenchmen did not even resent it when I told them that I had, two years previously, seen a man at whom, in 1812, a French *chasseur* had shot simply in order to discharge his gun. The man was at that time a child of ten, and his family had not succeeded in leaving Moscow.'

'That's impossible,' the Frenchman boiled up; 'a French soldier would not fire at a child!'

'Yet it happened,' I answered. 'I was told it by a most respectable captain on the retired list, and I saw the scar on his cheek from the bullet myself.' "[2]

I strongly suspect that this time the gambler's story was not so true to reality, and I believe that the detail about the "chasseur" was taken from Pushkin's *Journey to Erzerum*, in which Pushkin mentions the Circassian who killed a Russian soldier merely because his gun had been charged too long.[3] But this is only a parenthetical remark; let us not wander from our theme. This theme of opposition against conventions and established forms of social behaviour is connected with Dostoevsky's reasonings on still another subject, that one of honour, moral dignity, and their defense. This is what we read in the *Notes from Underground*:

"I did not slink away through cowardice, but through an unbounded vanity. I was afraid not of his six foot, not of getting a sound thrashing and being thrown out of the window; I should have had physical courage enough, I assure you; but I had not the moral courage. What I was afraid of was that everyone present, from the insolent marker down to the lowest little stinking, pimply clerk in a greasy collar, would jeer at me and fail to understand

[1] Cf. "Europe in Dostoevsky's Ideological Novel".
[2] Cf. *The Gambler*, chapter 1.
[3] Cf. Pushkin's *Journey to Erzerum*, chapter 1.

when I began to protest and to address them in literary language. For of the point of honor—not of honor, but of the point of honor (*point d'honneur*)—one cannot speak among us except in literary language. You can't allude to the 'point of honor' in ordinary language."[1]

No less significant is the following passage from *The Gambler*:

"You simply take for granted that I don't know how to behave with dignity; that is, that perhaps I am a man of moral dignity but that I don't know how to behave with dignity. You understand that perhaps that may be so. Yes, all Russians are like that; and do you know why? Because Russians are too richly endowed and many-sided to be able readily to evolve a code of manners. It is a question of good form. For the most part we Russians are so richly endowed that we need genius to evolve our code of manners. And genius is most often absent, for, indeed, it is a rarity at all times. It's only among the French, and perhaps some other Europeans, that the code of manners is so well defined that one may have an air of the utmost dignity and yet be a man of no moral dignity whatever. That's why good form means so much with them. A Frenchman will put up with an insult, a real, moral insult, without blinking, but he wouldn't endure a flip on the nose for anything, because that is a breach of the received code, sanctified for ages. That's why our Russian young ladies have such a weakness for Frenchmen, that their manners are so good. Though, to my thinking they have no manners at all . . ."[2]

Dostoevsky here repeats what he said in his *Winter Notes on Summer Impressions*, in which he ferociously attacked the French "bourgeois" "who would be ready to sell his own father for twenty-five centimes":

"Do you know what? One may be even a scoundrel and not lose the feeling of honor; and here [in France] there are many honest people, but they nevertheless have completely lost their sense of honor. . . ."[3]

Dostoevsky's idea is that the Russians have no code of honour, but they have a feeling of honour; whereas the French have their code but

[1] Cf. *Notes from Underground*, Part II, chapter 1.
[2] Cf. *The Gambler*, chapter 5.
[3] Cf. *Winter Notes on Summer Impressions*, chapter 7. Cf. also Dostoevsky's letter to A. N. Maykov, 16–28 August, 1876, in which Dostoevsky refers to his famous talk with Turgenev about *Smoke*; he again insists that despite their civilization the German masses are "much worse and more dishonest than our masses and, of course, much more stupid". (Cf. Dostoevskij, *Pis'ma*, Vol. II.)

no honour. Similar, as we have seen, are the reasonings of the hero from *Underground* and of the gambler, both eccentric men, to say the least. But, speaking for himself, Dostoevsky wrote much later in *The Diary of a Writer* (1877):

> "In olden times we had no concept of European honour. Our boyars used to curse and even to fight openly among themselves, and a slap across the face was not considered a great and definitive offense to honour. But, on the other hand, they had their own notion of honour, although not in a European form, still no less sacred and serious than that. For the sake of this honour a boyar would on occasion neglect his wealth, his position at the court and even the Czar's favour. However, along with the change in dress and with the introduction of the European sword, the new European concept of honour arose, though in the course of two long centuries it never took root seriously, so that the old was forgotten and scorned and the new was accepted mistrustfully and skeptically. The people accepted it, so to say, mechanically, forgetting in their spirit what honour means. They lost the heart-felt need of it. And this is so, it is terrible to confess, with very few exceptions."[1]

Dostoevsky's remarks, I believe, are correct in their essence. He gives a true picture of the Russian notion of honour. In this regard, Pushkin's story *Dubrovsky* deserves some mention. This story has always struck me as being Polish in atmosphere. The conflict between Dubrovsky the father and Troekurov is essentially Polish, based as it is on a strong feeling of personal dignity and honour of the rights of a nobleman, modest as he may be, but equal to the magnate. These attitudes are illustrated by the well-known Polish proverb: "The squire in his cottage is equal to a *wojewoda*." My impression about *Dubrovsky* was not purely accidental. It is known that the plot of the story was suggested to Pushkin by P. V. Nashchokin, who told the poet of a similar incident which occurred in White Ruthenia between a poor Polish squire, Ostrowski, and his wealthy neighbour, who took over his estate by force. It is also known that the first title of Pushkin's "novel" was intended to be *Ostrovsky*. (The name Dubrovsky might be considered a Russianized form of the Polish historical name, Dąbrowski.)

At any rate, Dostoevsky was particularly interested in the problem of honour, and he stressed in *The Possessed* the difference between Russia

---

[1] Cf. Dostoevskij, *Dnevnik pisatelja za 1877, 1878 i 1881 gg.* (Moscow-Leningrad: Gos. Izdat., 1929), p. 133. Compare to this Versilov's remarks on the Russian nobility in which Dostoevsky, by the way, repeats Pushkin's statements dealing with the essential differences which characterize the Russian and the western-European nobilities. See *A Raw Youth*, Part II, chapter 2, Section 2.

and the West in this respect. In characterizing Gaganov he mentions: "He loved castles, chivalry; all the theatrical part of it. He was ready to cry with shame that in the days of the Moscow Czars the sovereign had the right to inflict corporal punishment on the Russian boyars, and blushed at the contrast."[1] Karmazinov also has something to say on this problem:

> " 'So far as I see and am able to judge, the whole essence of the Russian revolutionary idea lies in the negation of honor. I like its being so boldly and fearlessly expressed. No, in Europe they wouldn't understand it yet, but that's just what we shall clutch at. For a Russian a sense of honor is only a superfluous burden, and it always has been a burden through all its history. The open "right to dishonor" will attract him more than anything.' "[2]

It is quite legitimate, as I have shown, to identify Dostoevsky's views with those of the underground man and the gambler. The situation changes somewhat with Karmazinov. In him, as the reader may know, Dostoevsky parodied Turgenev. Therefore, Karmazinov's grumblings about Russian lack of understanding for the European notion of honour are a mocking of Turgenev's Westernism. But Dostoevsky's ambivalence is well known, and Karmazinov's opinions are still not quite foreign to Dostoevsky's views on this subject.[3]

---

[1] Cf. *The Possessed*, Garnett translation, New York, 1913, p. 266.

[2] Cf. *The Possessed*, p. 347.

[3] I recently discovered a passage in Herzen's *Diaries* which Dostoevsky might have used, had he known it, as support for his reasonings. Herzen, in his *Diary* of 1843 (22 September), stresses the chaos in the field of contemporary ideas, the co-existence of old and new conceptions and opinions, often conflicting. Then he goes on to say the following: "Who would dare to speak against the duel, against the scrupulous nobiliary honour and *point d'honneur*, despite the fact that the absurdity of the duel is obvious. Man can touch God or universal problems, but he does not dare to touch particular, private problems. Honour, honour—and never to consider what exactly is honourable and what is offensive, what kind of satisfaction is achieved and in what way improvement is accomplished. The duel is capital punishment joined with an element of danger for the executioner; the duel is a savage act of bloody revenge, to which not only separate individuals but even societies have no right. The feudal ages proved the entire accidental character of the meaning of honour, but at those times the individual was obliged to demand an infinite amount of recognition, otherwise there would not have developed the conception of human dignity. And in the present times!..." (Cf. *Sočinenija A. I. Gercena*, Vol. I, pp. 137–8.)

In the *Journal des Goncourt* we find the following statement of Turgenev himself, as reported by Edmond de Goncourt: "We are thieves in Russia, and in spite of this a man might commit twenty thefts, but if he admits his guilt, if it is proven that he was in hunger and need, he is acquitted.... Yes, you are men of law, of honour, and we, as *autocratized* as we are, we are men——" and here Goncourt suggested to Turgenev the word for which he was searching—"of humanity". "Yes, it is this," he continues, "we are less conventional men; we are men of humanity." (Cf. *Journal des Goncourt* (Paris, 1891), Vol. V, p. 266.)

All this reasoning leads me to pose a problem of more general interest. One may be amazed by the frequency of the duel episode in Russian literature, in the literature of a country, which, as Dostoevsky justly pointed out, has not the historical tradition of the duel, inasmuch as the institution of knighthood and the concept of chivalry never existed in her historical development. The modern European duel has acquired the character of a purely formal and abstract solution for every conflict involving honour. Any empiric approach, any effort to rationalize the duel would be in vain under these circumstances. In its very essence, as I have already stressed, the duel is abstract and formal, and all European codes of honour tend to accentuate the formalistic details of its procedure. It is not a rational act of justice with punishment or exculpation. It cannot and does not replace the court. It is an anti-Christian, but at the same time a "divine" judgment, an abstract cleansing of personal honour. Whether the offended is killed and the offender, the guilty one, triumphs is of no importance, as the duel does not aim at punishment, but at the rehabilitation of honour, and this is realized through the very fact of the encounter. Honour is superior to death and dearer than life.

As I have mentioned, we may find in Russian literature a long sequence of duels. The first and most spectacular is the duel between Onegin and Lensky. Then we have several duels in Pushkin's short stories and in *The Captain's Daughter*, the duel of Pechorin and Grushnitsky in Lermontov's novel *A Hero of Our Times*, the duel in Turgenev's *The Bully, Three Portraits, Two Friends, Torrents of Spring* (with obvious allusions to the duel in *Eugene Onegin*), *The Diary of a Superfluous Man* and *Fathers and Sons*; there is the duel of Dolokhov and Pierre in *War and Peace*—obviously filled with reminiscences of Pushkin's duel—and there are the duels in Dostoevsky's novels and the ones mentioned in this study. Finally we may cite Chekhov's *Duel*, Kuprin's *Duel* and Artsybashev's *Sanin*, which contains a story of an attempted duel. The characteristic trait of all these duels is precisely an abuse of the form, very often not even an unconscious abuse but a provocative violation. This is quite characteristic of Onegin's duel. The nonchalant Onegin brings as a second his valet, "Monsieur Guillot". Pushkin feels at least obliged to make some ironic comments on this occasion:

> " 'But where is,'—muttered with astonishment
> Zaretsky,—'Where is your second?'
> In duels he was a classicist and a pedant.
> Being devoted to method
> He wouldn't allow a man

> To be stretched out just in any way
> But according to the strict rules of the art,
> Following traditions of olden days,
> (For which we should give him credit)."[1]

The main elements of the classic duel are strict discretion and rigorous observation of the dueling code and ritual; these essential elements are at the same time the most efficient factors of the abstract solution which the duel grants to every conflict. All these principles are constantly violated in Russian literary episodes, and the rigid relations between the adversaries which the duel imposes are unknown to the Russian duellists. They talk together, they even insult one another, and the seconds behave like boors. Besides, the Russian duel takes on rather the character of a challenge to fate than a chivalrous cleansing of honour. One may even come to the conclusion that what we find in Russian literature is all a parody of the duel. The story which illustrates this best is Chekhov's *Duel*, which, by the way, re-echoes *A Hero of Our Times*, in that it is an intentional vulgarization and banalization of Lermontov's romantic story. A real parody of a duel is given by Turgenev in his *Three Portraits*, in which the hero, Vasily Ivanovich Luchinov, acts with premeditated cynicism; his enforced and completely unjustified provocation becomes a simple murder. In several details, by the way, this episode contains reminiscences of the duel between Petr Andreich Grinev and Shvabrin. In *Sanin*, Artsybashev's use of a fist instead of a pistol is obviously an answer to Bazarov's inconsistent acceptance of a duel. Bazarov's duel in its turn has some connections with Onegin's episode. Onegin's valet used as a second reappears in the less provocative rôle of an observer in the duel between Kirsanov and Bazarov. Chekhov went even so far as to bring a deacon into his story as an observer. This comedy of errors has its significance. What we see is another example of the Russian "formlessness".

When compared to the treatment of the duel in Russian literature, the encounter of Mr. Winkle and Dr. Slammer in Dickens's *Pickwick Papers* acquires not only a particular charm but also a special significance. Dickens's episode, filled with delightful humour, is intended, it would seem, to mock not so much the duel itself but precisely the conventions attached to duelling. Dickens displayed an excellent knowledge of the codes of honour and illustrates their stipulations with the amusing sequence of situations described in this episode. His heroes demonstrate not an unconscious abuse of form, but, by the author's intention, they carry the observance of form to the limits of absurdity.

[1] *Cf. Eugene Onegin*, chapter VI, Stanza XXVI.

Dickens's rationalistic critique of the duel is neither "offensive, defensive", but—"inoffensive". The Cervantesque, condescending, and knowing smile which illuminates this episode, as well as the whole book, does not offend at all any feeling of human dignity or the ideal of gentlemanly honour.

But why do duels appear so often in Russian novels of the nineteenth century? It might be that the Russians were particularly obsessed by the idea of the duel in connection with the fact that two of their greatest poets were killed in duels. Against the background of my speculations on the theme of the "superior" sense of the duel, Pushkin's death was certainly the more significant. Lermontov, the fatalist, was constantly provoking chance; therefore, his death was in a way a logical conclusion of this fight with destiny. Pushkin's duel was of a completely different nature. I would say that his duel was a European one, a cleansing of his honour for posterity.[1] The best proof of this may be found in Pushkin's discussions with Zhukovsky and other friends who tried to make Pushkin avoid a duel. Zhukovsky at one point said to Pushkin: "Give me the happiness to save you from a mad crime, and your wife from absolute shame. . . ." To a similar statement made by another friend, Pushkin answered: "Oh, what do I care about the opinions of the Countess so-and-so concerning my wife's innocence or guilt! The only opinion which interests me is the opinion of that lower class—which in our times is alone truly Russian—and which could condemn the wife of Pushkin."[2]

I should not like to take the rôle of an apologist for the duel. I am simply trying to explain its "philosophy". I would not hide, however, the opinion that there are cases in human life, especially when the honour of others is involved,—a woman, or an older man who cannot act for himself, or one who is deceased—when the duel often appears to be the only acceptable solution, just because its discretion protects the persons involved against publicity. In the life of every person, in the most honourable and pure life, there are details which cannot be publicized. A film can be exposed only to red light; sunlight covers it with spots. In a way the duel's discretion is the red light of the darkroom.[3]

---

[1] See my article "La souricière de Pouchkine", *Le Flambeau*, Bruxelles, 1937.

[2] Cf. L. Grossman, *Puškin* (Moscow, 1939), pp. 602–3.

[3] In Pushkin's life and work one may find evidence showing that Pushkin had the same feelings on this subject of privacy and discretion, although none of this evidence directly concerns the duel. In *The Captain's Daughter* there is a passage which usually bothers Pushkin's readers because of its psychological improbability. This is how Petr Andreich Grinev describes his attitude at the trial: "I wanted to go on as I had begun and to explain my connection with Maria Ivanovna as candidly as all the rest. But I suddenly felt an overwhelming repulsion. It occurred to me that if I mentioned her, she would be summoned by the Commission; and I was so overcome

Dostoevsky was unable to understand this. His whole nature, filled with destructive anarchism, was perpetually tempted by the delights of revelation: his art is based on unmasking, on scandal, on sensation; Dostoevsky's main ambition, and in this consists his intellectual voluptuousness, is to unveil, his main activity, to break conventions and forms—and all this for the sake of "truth".

May I recall again Dostoevsky's *Bobok*, in which the gay, cynical company of corpses, playing cards in their damp, mud-filled graves in a Petersburg cemetery, decides to "be ashamed of nothing", to live "in a most shameless truth"; "let's uncover ourselves and be nude", they cry.[1] Dostoevsky's living heroes have the same inclinations; they also like this "splendid *petit-jeu*", to quote Ferdyshchenko from *The Idiot*.

"A party of us were together one day [says Ferdyshchenko]—we'd been drinking, it's true—and suddenly someone made the suggestion that each one of us, without leaving the table, should tell something he had done, something that he himself honestly considered the worst of all the evil actions of his life. But it was to be done honestly, that was the point, that it was to be honest, no lying."[2]

Have I to emphasize that Prince Valkovsky's talks with Ivan Petrovich, Stavrogin's confession, the obscene behaviour and banter of Fedor Pavlovich Karamazov, satisfy the same desire of the Russian author, who pretended that by upsetting conventions he was erecting on their ruins a temple to human dignity. But, one may ask, what kind of human dignity did Dostoevsky have in mind?

Quite opposite to this savage cult of truth there stands as a delicate

at the awful thought of connecting her name with the vile slanders of the villains, and of her being confronted with them, that I became confused and hesitated." (Cf. *The Captain's Daughter* in *The Works of Alexander Pushkin*, edited by A. Yarmolinsky (New York, 1936), p. 718. One may indeed doubt whether such subtle feelings are justified in a naïve young boy like Petr Andreich Grinev, but it seems to me that Pushkin here could not resist the temptation to express his own thoughts and feelings. During the time that he was writing *The Captain's Daughter*, Pushkin's troubles began with Nicholas I, with the court, and with his wife's position and behaviour. In his *Diary* (10 May, 1834), Pushkin describes the story of one of his letters to his wife which was opened by the police and presented to the Emperor, who did not like Pushkin's comments about his court appointment. The letter was finally shown to Zhukovsky, who explained the entire matter to the Czar. Pushkin ends his note about this story with the following statement: "But what a deep immorality there exists in the habits of our government! The police open letters of a man to his wife for reading to the Czar (a well-bred and honourable man) and the Czar is not ashamed to admit all this. . . . Say what you will, it is not easy to be an autocrat." (Cf. *A. S. Puškin, Polnoe sobranie sočinenij*, Vol. VIII, p. 50.)

[1] Cf. Dostoevsky, *The Diary of a Writer* (New York, 1949), Vol I, pp. 54-5.
[2] Cf. *The Idiot*, Part I, chapter 13, p. 138, Garnett translation, 1948.

flower of European civilization Pushkin's avowal: "Elevating illusions are dearer to me than myriads of low truths."

To conclude, I should like to stress again that the duel is in its very essence a pure convention, and because of this its very efficiency is possible only in a society whose mores accept this convention.[1] Alfred de Vigny, the poet of the "religion of honour", and at the same time the poet of pity, once said in his *Le Journal d'un poète*:

"The gentleman, or the *gentilhomme*, is the very man of honour who is restrained by conventions within the limits of good behaviour and propriety which religion cannot reach; since there are things which a priest would do but which a man of honour would never do."[2]

The poet also said, "The abolition of the duel brings on assassination."[3]

How essentially Tolstoyan are Nekhlyudov's antinomic thoughts, feelings, and remarks at a conversation about a duel in which an officer was killed defending the honour of his regiment (in *Resurrection*, Book II, Chapter XVII):

"Nekhlyudov listened to the conversation without joining in. Having been an officer himself, he understood, though he did not agree with, young Charsky's arguments, and at the same time he could not help contrasting with the fate of the officer that of a handsome young convict whom he had seen in the prison, condemned to the mines for killing a man in a fight. Both had become murderers through drunkenness. The one, the peasant, having killed a man in a moment of passion, is parted from his wife and family, has chains on his legs, and with shaven head is going to hard labour

---

[1] Pushkin, in a humorous episode in *The Captain's Daughter*, mocks the lack of understanding for the real significance of the duel among those people who approach it strictly from the common-sense point of view. This is the answer which Petr Andreich Grinev receives from the old veteran Ivan Ignatiich, whom the hero wanted as his second in the duel with Shvabrin: " 'You are pleased to say,' he answered, 'that you intend to kill Alexey Ivanych and wish me to witness it? Is that so, may I ask?' 'Quite so.' 'Good heavens, Petr Andreich! What are you thinking about? You have quarrelled with Alexey Ivanych? Whatever does it matter? Bad words are of no consequence. He abuses you—you swear back at him; he hits you in the face—you hit him in the ear, twice, three times—and go your own way; and we shall see to it that you make it up later on. But killing a fellow-creature—is that a right thing to do, let me ask you? And, anyway, if you killed him it wouldn't matter so much; I am not very fond of Alexey Ivanych myself, for the matter of that. But what if he makes a hole in you? What will that be like? Who will be made a fool of then, may I ask?' " (Cf. *The Captain's Daughter*, p. 630.)

[2] Cf. Alfred de Vigny, *Le Journal d'un poète* (1823–41) (Paris: Louis Conard, 1935), Vol. I, p. 307.

[3] *Ibid.*, p. 383.

in Siberia; while the officer sits in a fine room in the guardhouse, eating a good dinner, drinking good wine, and reading books, and will be set free in a day or two to live as before, having become only more interesting by the affair.

Nekhlyudov said what he had been thinking, and at first his aunt, Catherine Ivanovna, seemed to agree with him but at last she became as silent as the rest were, and Nekhlyudov felt that he had committed some kind of impropriety."

*   *   *   *   *

The Avenger

The item of the duel alone does not exhaust the theme of revenge, which Dostoevsky treats in the *Notes* exactly in the manner of *The Shot*. Dostoevsky contributes the description of a man haunted by the thought of vengeance, who mobilizes all his resources to this one purpose.

> "With people who know how to revenge themselves and to stand up for themselves, in general how is it done? Why, when they are possessed, let us suppose, by the feeling of revenge, then for the time there is nothing else but that feeling of revenge, then for the time there is nothing else but that feeling left in their whole being. ... There in its nasty, stinking, underground home our insulted, crushed and ridiculed mouse promptly becomes absorbed in cold, malignant, and above all, everlasting spite. For forty years together it will remember its injury down to the smallest, most ignominious details, and every time will add, of itself, details still more ignominious, spitefully teasing and tormenting itself with its own imagination."[1]

Similarly in Pushkin's story we find that from the moment Sylvio decided to avenge himself, he left the regiment, settled in a remote provincial town, and devoted himself entirely to preparation of his revenge. His life became that of an ascetic, of a monk, of one completely obsessed by a single idea. But note the difference: under Dostoevsky's pen the romantic avenger and mysterious monomaniac, who trained himself every day, in solitude, with pistols and practice shots, who waited for years to realize his dreams, becomes a spiteful mouse confined to its underground home.

The motif of revenge and the story of the romantic duel bring us close to the main psychological and ideological problems treated by

[1] *Notes from Underground*, Part I, chapter 3.

Dostoevsky in the *Notes* on the basis of Pushkin's suggestions. But, as I have already mentioned, between *The Shot* and the *Notes* there exists a bridge in the form of Turgenev's *Diary of a Superfluous Man*. I have given some details to show that the reading of Turgenev's story was not without significance for Dostoevsky. The most convincing proofs, however, of the ties between the *Diary* and the *Notes* are to be found in a comparison of the characterizations of the superfluous man and of the underground man, as well as of the whole atmosphere of both works—an atmosphere which is, one may say, common and ordinary for Dostoevsky but rather strange for Turgenev. This very fact probably attracted Dostoevsky's attention, for, with the exception of *The Bully* (a short story in which Turgenev played with Pushkin's and Lermontov's pairs, that is to say, Onegin and Lensky, Pechorin and Grushnitsky) and *A Hamlet of the Shchigrovsky District*, Turgenev never before nor afterward presented a character similar to the one in the *Diary*. But the traits which Turgenev emphasized in the psychological portrait in the *Diary* reappear in the malevolent and gloomy personality of Dostoevsky's hero.

The first more or less precise development of this character, so unexpected under Turgenev's pen but so familiar to Dostoevsky, appears in the story *A Hamlet of the Shchigrovsky District*. It is a combination of offended, embittered mediocrity and unlimited ambition:

"I am timid, you see, and not timid in virtue of the fact that I am a provincial, without an official rank, a poor man, but in virtue of the fact that I am a frightfully conceited man."

Turgenev's hero is ready to dream about attitudes and gestures in the style of the Gambler or of the hero from the *Notes*:

". . . Sometimes, under the influence of propitious circumstances, accidents, which I am unable, however, either to divine or foresee, my timidity disappears completely. . . . You may set me face to face with the Dalai Lama himself—now,—and I'd ask him for a pinch of snuff."[1]

---

[1] Cf. Turgenev's *Memoirs of a Sportsman*, translated from the Russian by Isabelle F. Hapgood (New York, 1923), Vol. II, p. 163. Turgenev's short story *Petushkov* (1847) should also be taken into consideration. In it appears the theme of the self-assertion of a Gogolian, downtrodden man. The story is obviously connected also with Dostoevsky's *Poor Folk*. On the other hand, the Gogolian couple of valet and master is also present in Turgenev's story. The dialogues between Turgenev's master and valet are morbidly developed by Dostoevsky in his *Notes from Underground*. Therefore, Turgenev's story is a kind of bridge between Gogol and *Poor Folk* on one side and the *Notes from Underground* on the other. I should add parenthetically that *Petushkov* might be placed alongside Tentetnikov's story (in *Dead Souls*) as a probable nucleus for Goncharov's *Oblomov*.

He will complain, just like the hero from underground, that a provincial chief of police would accept only with laughter a comparison between him and a certain Orbasanov.

"I stared for a long time into the mirror at my disconcerted countenance, and, slowly sticking out my tongue, shook my head with a bitter smile. The veil fell from my eyes; I saw clearly, more clearly than I saw my face in the mirror, what an empty, insignificant and useless, unoriginal man I was."

People will address him as "thou". The butlers will overlook him at the table. He will haunt his neighbours and subject himself to all sorts of petty humiliation; they will not allow him to mingle in the general conversation; he will beg the attention of some insignificant man in a corner of the room. In other words, he behaves exactly like Dostoevsky's hero from the *Notes from Underground*.

But certainly the fullest presentation of this type was given by Turgenev in *The Diary of a Superfluous Man*, whose hero is even closer to Dostoevsky's hero.

To begin with, both are sick and both take advantage of this to write their sombre memoirs. In addition, at times nature plays the same rôle in both works: dampness, wind, snow, and rain appear in both the *Diary* and the *Notes* as a reason for writing. The Superfluous Man says:

"I am forbidden to go out. What can I write about then? No decent man talks of his maladies; to write a novel is not in my line; reflections on elevated topics are beyond me; descriptions of the life going on around me could not even interest me; while I am weary of doing nothing, and too lazy to read. Ah, I have it, I will write the story of all my life for myself. A first-rate idea! Just before death it is a suitable thing to do, and can be of no harm to any one. I will begin."[1]

And from the Underground Man we hear a similar justification: "But what can a decent man speak of with most pleasure? Answer: of himself. Well, so I will talk about myself."

Turgenev's hero emphasizes again and again that he was brought up "very badly and not happily". He concludes that he is a superfluous man, "an utter superfluous or rather an utterly superfluous bird in this world". In the description of his superfluity one finds a nucleus for the

[1] Turgenev, *op. cit.*, p. 4.

tumultuous implications of the *Notes*, which convey the same impression of the absolute loneliness and complete superfluity of the man from underground who is constantly alone in his "corner". Dostoevsky, with his usual tendency toward extremes, shows why his hero "could not even become an insect".

The Superfluous Man constantly feels that everywhere he is "an unexpected and uninvited guest". "Throughout my whole life," he says, "I was constantly finding my place taken, perhaps because I did not look for my place where I should have." (Who knows but that this assertion is not an echo from Dostoevsky's *Double*: compare the second letter of Mr. Golyadkin to Vakhrameev.)

> "I was apprehensive, reserved, and irritable like all sickly people. Moreover, probably owing to excessive ambition, perhaps as a result of the generally unfortunate cast of my personality, there existed between my thought and feelings and the expression of those feelings and thoughts a sort of inexplicable, irrational, and utterly insuperable barrier; and whenever I made up my mind to overcome this obstacle by force, to break down this barrier, my gestures, the expression of my face, my whole being, took an appearance of painful constraint. I not only seemed, I positively became unnatural and affected. I was conscious of this myself, and hastened to shrink back into myself. Then a terrible commotion was set up within me. I analyzed myself to the last thread, compared myself with others, recalled the slightest glances, smiles, words of the people to whom I had tried to open myself out, put the worst possible interpretation on everything. I laughed venomously at my own pretentions to 'be like everyone else', and suddenly, in the midst of my laughter, collapsed utterly into gloom, sank into absurd dejection, and then began again as before, went round and round, in fact like a squirrel in its wheel. Whole days were spent in this harassing, fruitless exercise."[1]

The Superfluous Man suffers from excessive sensitivity to hurts and wrongs, mostly imagined, to which he is subjected.

> "I do not intend to indulge in minute details, but I cannot pass over in silence one rather serious and significant fact, that is the strange behavior of my friends (I too used to have friends) whenever I met them, or even called on them. They used to seem ill at ease; as they came to meet me, they would give a not quite natural smile, look, not into my eyes nor at my feet, as some people do,

[1] Turgenev, *op. cit.*, pp. 16–17.

but rather at my cheeks, articulate hurriedly, 'Ah, how are you, Chulkaturin!', turn away at once and positively remain stock still for a little while after, as though trying to recollect something. I used to notice all this, as I am not devoid of penetration and the faculty of observation; on the whole, I am not a fool; I sometimes even have ideas come into my head that are amusing, not absolutely commonplace."[1] "I didn't know at all how to behave with women, and in their presence I either scowled and put on a morose air, or grinned in the most idiotic way, and in my embarrassment turned my tongue round and round in my mouth."[2]

The Superfluous Man considers that he has been burdened not only by his clumsy surname, but also by his face with which he is quite dissatisfied. He is beset by feelings of uneasiness in the society of others. This uneasiness paralyzes his movements, though from time to time he is overcome by spasmodic movement. After a "continual forced smile and painful vigilance", "an idiotic silence", and a "miserable and ineffectual desire to get away",

"I seized my opportunity and with a meet but gracious smile, I went up to her ... and suddenly without awaiting her reply, I gave my features an extraordinarily cheerful and free-and-easy expression, with a set grin, passed my hand above my head in the direction of the ceiling (I wanted, I remember, to set my cravat straight), and was even on the point of pirouetting round on one foot, as though to say, 'All is over, I am happy, let's all be happy,'—I did not, however, execute this maneuver, as I was afraid of losing my balance, owing to an unnatural stiffness in my knees. . . ."[3]

Almost all of these morbid psychological traits of Turgenev's hero are present in the man from underground:

"I, for instance, am terribly ambitious, I am mistrustful and sensitive like a hunchback or a dwarf. . . . The worst of it is, look at it which way one will, it still turns out that I was always the most to blame in everything and what is most humiliating of all, to blame for no fault of my own, but so to say, through the laws of nature. In the first place, to blame because I am cleverer than any of these people surrounding me. I have always considered myself cleverer than any of the people surrounding me, and sometimes,

---
[1] *Ibid.*, p. 18.
[2] Turgenev, *op. cit.*, p. 24.
[3] *Ibid.*, pp. 45–7.

would you believe it, have been positively ashamed of it. At any rate, I have all my life, as it were, turned my eyes away and never could look people straight in the face...."[1]

In the second part of the *Notes* there are even more details which expose the dismal existence of the underground man:

"At that time I was only twenty-four. My life was even then gloomy, ill-regulated, and as solitary as that of a savage. I made friends with no one and positively avoided talking, and buried myself more and more in my hole. At work in the office I never looked at anyone, and I was perfectly well aware that my companions looked upon me, not only as a queer fellow, but even looked upon me—I always fancied this—with a sort of loathing. I sometimes wondered why it was that nobody except me fancied that he was looked upon with aversion. . . . I hated my fellow clerks one and all, and I despised them all, yet at the same time I was, as it were, afraid of them. In fact, it happened at times that I thought more highly of them than of myself. . . . I alternated between despising them and thinking them superior to myself. . . . But whether I despised them or thought them superior I dropped my eyes almost every time I met anyone. I even made experiments whether I could face So and So's looking at me, and I was always the first to drop my eyes. . . . I did not, of course, maintain friendly relations with my comrades and soon was at loggerheads with them, and in my youth and inexperience I even gave up bowing to them, as though I had cut off all relations. . . . As a rule, I was always alone."[2]

The unnaturalness and constraint which marked the behavior of the Superfluous Man toward other people created situations, which, from the psychological point of view, are duplicated in the *Notes*. Compare, for example, the following passages. In the *Diary* we read:

"I had absolutely lost all sense of personal dignity and could not tear myself away from the spectacle of my own misery. I remember one day I tried not to go, swore to myself in the morning that I would stay at home, and at eight o'clock in the evening . . . leaped up like a madman, put on my hat, and ran breathless into Kirilla Matveich's drawing-room. My position was excessively

[1] *Notes from Underground*, Part II, chapter 2.
[2] *Notes from Underground*, chapter 1.

absurd. I was obstinately silent; sometimes for whole days together I did not utter a sound. . . ."[1]

And in the *Notes* the underground man exclaims:

" 'What possessed me, what possessed me to force myself upon them?' I wondered, grinding my teeth as I strode along the street. 'For a scoundrel, a pig like that Zverkov! Of course, I had better not go; of course, I must just snap my fingers at them. I am not bound in any way. I'll send Simonov a note by tomorrow's post. . . . ' But what made me furious was that I knew for certain that I should go, that I should make a point of going; and the more tactless, the more unseemly my going would be, the more certainly I would go."[2]

Characteristically enough, anger becomes a constructive factor in the morbid make-up of each of these men. The Superfluous Man observes on several occasions that anger calms him. For instance, in the episode at the ball:

"Finally it infuriated me. I suddenly felt extraordinarily wrathful, and, I remember, was extraordinarily delighted at this new sensation, and even conceived a certain respect for myself."[3]

Again at the scene of the duel, he had been afraid that his agitation might be mistaken for timidity, but when he saw the Prince's smile, he "suddenly felt furious again and was at once at [his] ease". Similarly, the underground man affirms: "Spite, of course, might overcome everything, all my doubts, and so might serve quite successfully in place of a primary cause, precisely because it is not a cause."[4] And though he insists that he does not even have any spite, we know that the whole book presents the unending growth of his fury and anger.

I think that these quotations prove that while he was writing the

---
[1] Turgenev, *op. cit.*, pp. 48–9.
[2] *Notes from Underground*, chapter 3.
[3] Turgenev, *op. cit.*, pp. 57–8.
[4] *Notes from Underground*, chapter 5.

A secondary character in Turgenev's story *A Hamlet of the Shchigrovsky District*, who might be considered as the introductory motif of the psychological theme in this work, says, " 'I am spiteful—what of that! A spiteful man stands in no need of brains, at least. And you wouldn't believe how refreshing it is.' " (Cf. *Memoirs of a Sportsman*, etc., Vol. II, p. 154.) By the way, the perpetually irritable Superfluous Man with his inferiority complex also finds cause for offense in the sound of his own name. Obvious echoes of this motif may be found in Dostoevsky's *A Raw Youth*.

Notes, Dostoevsky remembered Turgenev's story quite well. As I have already mentioned, there is a striking resemblance not only in the main characters, but in the whole tone of narration. Perhaps, even, it is not accidental that the poor prostitute, who becomes the victim of an unspeakable offense on the part of the underground man, bears the name of Liza, the same name as that of the girl in the *Diary*, although the two episodes are actually quite different.

Turgenev's *Diary of a Superfluous Man* certainly did not lead Dostoevsky away from Pushkin's *Shot*. On the contrary, it aided Dostoevsky in the development of the main character in the *Notes* with reference to Pushkin's works. Undoubtedly, the *Notes from Underground* is closely bound with the ideas which particularly absorbed Dostoevsky after his Siberian experience. Indeed, it is the most violent expression of the ideological crisis through which he went during this period of his life. Nevertheless, Pushkin's suggestions, which had certainly impressed themselves upon Dostoevsky before Siberia, remained alive in his mind. There are many examples of how easily Dostoevsky assimilated and absorbed ideas, characters, and situations which he found in the works of other writers. We know how great the influence of Balzac was on him: *Crime and Punishment* derives almost directly from *Le Père Goriot*. Nor is it necessary to dwell on the influences of E. Sue, Soulié, Dickens, V. Hugo, Schiller, and even perhaps Diderot and Prévost. We also know how often Dostoevsky played with ideas from Gogol: it suffices to mention *Poor Folk*, *The Double*, *The Landlady*, *The Faint Heart*, *Stepanchikovo* and *Uncle's Dream*. Besides, this last story has obvious ties with Turgenev's *Provincial Lady*. One might say that in a way it is a replica of Turgenev's vaudeville. Dostoevsky was not afraid of parody; the borrowings from Gogol reveal several examples of this. And in addition to all these borrowings, I believe that my conjectures about a bond between Dostoevsky and Mickiewicz are quite justifiable.[1] However, it was from Pushkin above all that Dostoevsky borrowed most.

In the case of the *Notes from Underground* we face a double borrowing. One part of it is connected with the idea of usurpation, which absorbed Dostoevsky from the very beginning to the very end of his literary career. The other part, although connected with the same idea, represents a kind of parody of *The Shot*. This latter aspect is the less important and simpler one. Let us begin with it.

The parodistic element is contained simply in the obvious degradation of the two characters in Pushkin's story, Sylvio and the

---

[1] W. Lednicki, "Mickiewicz, Dostoevsky, and Blok", in *Slavic Studies*, edited by A. Kaun and E. J. Simmons (New York, 1943), pp. 75–98; and another study in the present volume, "Dostoevsky and Poland".

Count, who appear under different masks in the *Notes*. Sylvio, with his determination, his calculations and rationalistic approach to life, with his *sui generis* asceticism and constant training of will, his carefully and cautiously organized efforts aiming first at the establishment and then at the preservation of his leadership and prestige among the others, degenerates into the man from underground. The young Count, brilliant, nonchalant, self-confident by nature, a lord by birth though perhaps not a leader, aristocratic in his very essence (from a certain point of view Sylvio is endowed with elements of *arrivisme* and plebeian-democratic envy), degenerates into the vulgar, trivial, but also nonchalant and self-confident, and above all self-satisfied Zverkov. (The name probably came from Gogol's *Notes of a Madman*.) I have included here two aspects of these pairs: the psychological and the sociological. I will not concern myself with the latter, although it is possible to find definite and significant manifestations in it. It is obvious that the general attitude of the underground man represents a violent development of the déclassé whom Pushkin merely suggested in Sylvio.

I may add parenthetically that one should also take into consideration Gogol's *Notes of a Madman*,[1] in which the motif of the déclassé in both its aspects, psychological and sociological, plays an important rôle. Particularly illustrative are Poprishchin's remarks about the flunkeys:

"I cannot endure the flunkey set: they are always lolling about in the vestibule and don't as much as trouble themselves to nod. That's nothing: once one of the beasts had the effrontery to offer me his snuff-box without even getting up from his seat. Doesn't the fellow know I am a government clerk, that I am a gentleman by birth!"[2]

Not less to the point are his other outbursts:

"But I spit on him! As though a court councillor were of so much consequence! He hangs a gold chain on his watch and orders boots at thirty roubles—but deuce take him! Am I some plebeian—a tailor or a son of a non-commissioned officer? I am a gentleman."[3]

There are many other small touches in Gogol's short story which Dostoevsky developed in *The Double* and in the *Notes from Underground*.

[1] K. Mochulsky (*Dostoevskij, Žizn' i tvorčestvo* (Paris: Y.M.C.A. Press, 1947), p. 42), mentioned the dependence of *The Double* on Gogol's *Notes of a Madman*.
[2] Cf. *A Madman's Diary* in *The Overcoat and Other Stories*, translated by Constance Garnett (New York, 1923), p. 132.
[3] Cf. *A Madman's Diary*, as above, pp. 133-4.

It is necessary to mention that the tiny sentimental plot in the *Notes of a Madman*, the madman's love for the director's daughter and all the unfortunate adventures this love imposed upon him, became the basic sentimental intrigue in *The Double*. Poprishchin's dream about a general's uniform with epaulettes on both shoulders, about a blue sash across his breast, correspond to the underground man's thoughts about a new overcoat with a beaver collar as weapons in the fight against the officer who became a living symbol of superiority for the madman. And it corresponds in the same sense to Golyadkin's carriage and livery for his valet when Golyadkin starts his offensive toward "winning a place in the world". The motif of "the place in the world" taken by the "Kammerjunkers" which appears in the *Notes of a Madman* is developed in *The Double* and *Notes from Underground*. Poprishchin's constant feelings of personal inferiority, feelings which end with insanity, the essence of which is usurpation, the awareness of his miserable appearance and awkwardness—all this could not but inspire Dostoevsky in the creation of his own morbid characters.

If the general discussion, the reasonings, and the philosophical speculations are Dostoevsky's own, only here and there connected with *The Shot*, with the *Diary of a Superfluous Man*, and with the *Notes of a Madman*, the concrete episodes and adventures which the underground man relates about himself give the impression of parodistic variations on the theme of *The Shot*. Such is, first of all, the story of the underground man and the officer who, in a tavern by a billiard table, "took him by the shoulders and without a word—without a warning or explanation—moved him from where he was standing to another spot and passed by as though he had not noticed him".[1]

The next episode is a further development of the same situation: the underground man fights with the officer for his rights and prestige, this time on a sidewalk. The encounter occurs, after a long period of secret preparation, because the underground man, governed by no "written law", was forced to make way for the officer and step aside, solely because the latter "simply walked over me as though there was nothing but empty space before him". This episode is an eloquent illustration of the wavering feelings of inferiority in the man from underground.[2] When the officer brushes past him, he decides that his

---

[1] *Notes from Underground*, chapter 1.
[2] It may be that a passage of Goncharov's *Frigate Pallada*, which appeared in 1855–1857, lay in Dostoevsky's memory when he composed the episode of the sidewalk encounter between the underground man and the officer. The passage I have in mind is the description of Shanghai, in which there are several examples of the behaviour of the English with respect to the Chinese. "In general," says Goncharov, "the treatment the English accorded the Chinese, as well as other peoples, especially those subjugated to them, is not so much cruel as commanding, rude or coldly

Turgenev in 1859
Lithograph after drawing by P. Borel

external appearance is a handicap and the cause of his constant psychological defeats. Therefore, he should be better dressed. He then embarks on a long period of meditation about a duel and, in general, about how to avenge himself for the billiard-room episode as well. He asks for his salary in advance, buys a pair of black gloves and a decent hat, "a good shirt with white bone studs". He "had to change the collar at any sacrifice and have a beaver one like an officer's". All this is costly, so that he worries, does not sleep for two or three nights, borrows more money, and all the time his heart is "throbbing, throbbing, and throbbing". The ultimate encounter, though its results delight the underground man, is, as a matter of fact, only half satisfactory: it is only with closed eyes that he can throw himself against his enemy, but thereby he displays a desperate courage, like that of Mr. Golyadkin or of Grushnitsky, of which Pechorin scornfully says: "This is not Russian courage."

This episode, however, is only a kind of introduction, the first sounding of the theme, very much as in a sonata. It is noteworthy that the same procedure is followed in *The Shot*, where the quarrel of the new young officer with Sylvio and the hurling of a brass candlestick by the officer at Sylvio occur before the reader knows anything about the Count and his duel with Sylvio. In *The Shot* the young officer is a variant of the Count. In the same way, the underground man's conflict with the officer is a prelude to his encounter with Zverkov. And here the parody follows Pushkin, as well as Turgenev, like an obsessive shadow.

The characterizations of Zverkov given by the underground man do, indeed, repeat the same motifs which are contained in Sylvio's descriptions of the young Count:

> "This Zverkov had been all the time at school with me too. I had begun to hate him particularly in the upper forms. In the lower forms he had simply been a pretty, playful boy whom everybody liked. I had hated him, however, even in the lower forms, just

contemptuous, so that it is painful to look at it. The English do not consider these peoples as human beings, but as some kind of draught beasts which they probably do not beat, and may even curry, that is, feed them well, pay them regularly and generously, but they do not hide their contempt." He continues: "An officer used to come to our hotel; he was not a navy man, but a marine from the *Spartan*, a young man about twenty. He too, it seemed, was not averse to adventure. His name was Stocks. He continually visited the besieged town and the camp. We used to walk together along the streets, and if a Chinese walked ahead of us and, because he did not notice us, would not make way for us for some time, Stocks without ceremony took him by his queue and dragged him aside. The Chinese would at first be dumbfounded and then would look after us with a smile of suppressed indignation." (Gončarov, I. A., *Polnoe sobranie sočinenij*, Glazunov ed. (St. Petersburg, 1896), Vol. VII, pp. 152–3.)

because he was a pretty and playful boy. . . . He was vulgar in the extreme, but at the same time he was a good natured fellow, even in his swaggering. In spite of superficial, fantastic, and sham notions of honor and dignity, all but very few of us positively grovelled before Zverkov, and the more so the more he swaggered. And it was not from any interested motives that they grovelled, but simply because he had been favored by the gifts of nature. Moreover, it was, as it were, an accepted idea among us that Zverkov was a specialist in regard to tact, and the social graces. This last fact particularly infuriated me. I hated the abrupt self-confident tone of his voice, his admiration of his own witticisms, which were often frightfully stupid, though he was bold in his language; I hated his handsome, but stupid face (for which I would, however, have gladly exchanged my intelligent one), and the free-and-easy military manners in fashion in the 'forties'. I hated the way in which he used to talk of his future conquests of women (he did not venture to begin his attack upon women until he had the epaulettes of an officer, and was looking forward to them with impatience), and boasted of the duels he would constantly be fighting. . . .[1]

When Zverkov reveals his future plans, he is "applauded by the servile rabble" and attacked by the underground man, who has to confess in spite of his victory that "the laugh was on his [Zverkov's] side".

"He got the better of me on several occasions afterwards but without malice, jestingly, casually. I remained angrily and contemptuously silent and would not answer him. When we left school he made advances to me. . . ."[2]

Even the most rapid comparison of this text with those which I quoted above from *The Shot* and the *Diary of a Superfluous Man* will immediately reveal the close relationship which exists between these stories. Practically every element, every detail has been reproduced, with some parodistic deformations, of course. In addition, I should like to point out that the parenthetical remarks about epaulettes and women

---

[1] *Notes from Underground,* chapter 3. Zverkov, when talking "of his future relations with the fair sex and growing as sportive as a puppy in the sun, all at once declared that he would not leave a single village girl on his estate unnoticed, that was his 'droit de seigneur', and that if the peasants dared to protest he would have them all flogged and double the task on them, the bearded rascals." (*Ibid.*) This passage is also directly connected with one of the disgusting stories of Prince Valkovsky. Cf. *The Insulted and the Injured* (London, 1915), pp. 240–1.
[2] *Loc. cit.*

is again a secret play, so characteristic for Dostoevsky, on this occasion connected with Lermontov's Grushnitsky. Additional texts describing the actual encounters of the underground man and Zverkov merely develop the same outline and fill it with further concrete, realistic details.

At this point I should like to bring up another story which may have increased the emphasis of Dostoevsky's psychological juxtaposition. I have in mind Tolstoy's *Two Hussars*. Eichenbaum has given a brilliant analysis of the literary genealogy of this story (published in May, 1856) and of the circumstances in which Tolstoy wrote it. I shall concern myself neither with these interesting and important details nor with the polemical intentions against the people of the *Contemporary Review* contained in Tolstoy's juxtaposition of two generations. My purpose is rather to show the Pushkinian character of the story.

Eichenbaum pointed to Gogol and Pushkin in the analysis of the genealogy of this story and stressed the fact that the personality of the father followed Pushkin and Dickens, while the personality of the son—Gogol and Thackeray. Eichenbaum alludes to the following remark from Tolstoy's *Notebook* (26 May, 1856):

"The first condition of an author's popularity, that is, the means of making himself loved, is the love with which he deals with all his characters. Because of this Dickens's characters are friends of the whole world. They serve as a link between the man of America and the man of Petersburg; on the other hand, Thackeray and Gogol are true, malicious, and artistic, but not pleasant."

In connection with this statement, I should like to quote another significant remark from Tolstoy's *Diary* (16 May, 1856), which deals directly with the *Two Hussars*: "I arose late. Fet and Truzson arrived. The latter charmingly said that the second hussar was depicted without love."[1]

However, my purpose is to disclose something additional to Eichenbaum's remarks. Needless to say, Tolstoy's art was based on the principle of juxtaposition, comparison and contrast. From this point of view, *Anna Karenina* is the best example in novel form. Therefore, the fact that in the *Two Hussars*, just as in many other of Tolstoy's novels or stories, the law of contrasting parallelism serves as the basic structural element is not particularly significant. Let us disregard, too, Eichenbaum's discovery of the polemical motives which led Tolstoy to

---

[1] See B. Eichenbaum, *Lev Tolstoj* (Leningrad: "Priboj", 1948), Vol. I, pp. 246–57; also see L. N. Tolstoj, *Polnoe sobranie sočinenij* (Moscow: Gos. Izdat., 1937), Vol. 47, p. 178 and p. 72.

oppose the two generations in this particular case. My main interest is with the pervasive Pushkinian atmosphere, especially in the first part of this diptych. In the first place, I would not agree with Eichenbaum's lineage. I would replace Dubrovsky[1] by Burmin[2] from *The Snowstorm* and the young Count from *The Shot*. The story of Turbin-senior is a development, but not parodistically or ironically, as in the case of Dostoevsky, of Pushkinian characters and episodes. What Pushkin merely suggested in almost abstract symbols, Tolstoy filled in with concrete and realistic content. I believe that everyone will agree that Burmin or the young Count from *The Shot* could have experienced the adventures of Tolstoy's hero. There is in the story not only a sequence of episodes, but also a psychological characterization of the heroes that certainly derives from Pushkin's suggestions. If we take the story of Turbin-senior, we find the same natural, personal prestige, power of commanding, immediate subordination of others, spontaneity of action, nonchalant self-confidence and generosity, disregard of obstacles, reckless courage and love of adventure, and the same successfulness as in Pushkin's heroes. If Pushkin had chosen to describe in detail the arrival of his heroes at the place of action, he could have cited the same details which Tolstoy gives when he introduces Turbin-senior. Turbin's behaviour at the ball is a development of the angry reminiscences of Sylvio about the young Count's conquests at the ball in the house of the Polish landlord. Turbin's success with the attractive widow, whom he wins from under the nose of her young *cicisbeo*, is a kind of variant of the story of Burmin, Maria Gavrilovna and Vladimir. In order to emphasize the elemental powers of his hero, Tolstoy used several additional episodes and details which Pushkin neglected. For example, on several occasions Tolstoy points out the tremendously loud voice of his hero, the frightening strength of his fist, his marvellous dancing ability, his inexhaustible physical energy, his touchiness as regards his gentlemanly honour. For the same reason he includes the episodes with the sharper and the gypsies—to illustrate his determination in action and the general admiration he inspired. In other words, Tolstoy developed the line of his hero's triumphs to a degree which Pushkin would probably have considered superfluous.

To the father Tolstoy opposed the son, whom he endowed with meanness, the spirit of calculation, selfishness, cynicism, and lack of personal dignity. And here again Tolstoy indulges in exaggeration.

---

[1] Eichenbaum, *op. cit.*, p. 252.
[2] In my article, "Tolstoy Through American Eyes" (*The Slavonic and East European Review*, London, April, 1947, Vol. XXV, No. 65, pp. 445–77), and also in my article "Pushkin's Prose" (Part I in Vol. XXVIII, No. 71, April, 1950), I pointed out the similarity of these two names: Burmin-Turbin.

The story ends with the terrible insult delivered to Turbin-junior, an insult which failed to result in any catastrophe. But here we see the triumph of the law of contrast: the reader understands that nothing similar could ever have happened to Turbin-senior. Although some of the traits of the son would not fit into the portraits drawn by Pushkin of those whom he opposed to his "organic lords", the essence of the juxtaposition is the same. The whole of Tolstoy's story follows one motif, which the author puts forth in the middle of the story: "The best results are always obtained involuntarily, and the more one tries, the worse things turn out."

Many of Tolstoy's details and episodes may be connected not only with Pushkin's short stories, but also with Turgenev's *Diary of a Superfluous Man*, from where the figure of the Prince, his easy triumphs, his conflict with the Superfluous Man at the ball reappear in Tolstoy's story. True enough, it is possible to consider all these situations literary clichés. But these clichés both in Tolstoy's version and in Turgenev's story could have, consciously or unconsciously, been used by Dostoevsky while he was busy with his Pushkinian theme, developed in his own way in the *Notes from Underground*.

* * * * *

> All is mine, said the gold;
> All is mine, said the sword.
> I will buy it, said the gold;
> I will take it, said the sword.
> (PUSHKIN: "The Gold and the Sword".)[1]

The Usurper

Let us return to the second of the elements which Dostoevsky borrowed from Pushkin and examine its treatment in the *Notes from Underground*. The *Notes* is written in a style which one may describe as journalistic. Exactly in the manner in which he used to write his *Diary of a Writer*, Dostoevsky introduced some novelistic episodes which illustrate, as required, the ideas developed in this work. But the work in its entirety is filled with reasonings of a theoretical nature. Therefore, it may, at first sight, appear rather difficult to deduce from Pushkin's crystalline and, as a matter of fact, simple, poetic symbols Dostoevsky's morbid and perfidious speculations about the "direct" men of action "who are stupid and are active just because they are stupid and limited"

[1] Pushkin's translation of a French epigram, which appeared in *Moskovskij Vestnik*, 1827, No. 2. Cf. A. S. Puškin, *Polnoe sobranie sočinenij* (Moscow-Leningrad: Academia, 1936), Vol. I, pp. 471 and 752.

and about the intelligent men "who think and consequently do nothing".

Pushkin did not introduce any psychological or philosophical analysis of his characters and situations; he merely presented them. It may even be that Pushkin acted unconsciously, guided by his poetic vision of life and by his intuition. Nevertheless, it appears possible, as I have indicated previously, to distinguish in the mass of his characters a series of pairs with distinct and contrasting personalities and to find in them some special significance. It is much easier to apply to Dostoevsky, or to Tolstoy, than to Pushkin the terms of rationalism and irrationalism. But this does not mean that Dostoevsky found matters for speculation only in his personal psychological adventures. Pushkin's symbol-types may have suggested some ideas to him.

Undoubtedly, the problem of usurpation was one which absorbed Pushkin's attention deeply and for a long time. Permit me to emphasize again that this was also one of the greatest problems in Dostoevsky's works. Pushkin openly treated this problem for the first time in *Boris Godunov*. It has always been my personal belief that *Boris Godunov* was conceived by Pushkin as a kind of cryptic work with political connotations for his contemporaries. I believe, even more, that the subject matter of this tragedy was selected from the end of the sixteenth and the beginning of the seventeenth century because of the poet's thoughts about events at the beginning of the nineteenth century. The story of Boris Godunov could not but appear similar to the story of Alexander I, who succeeded to the throne after his father's forcible deposition (of which Alexander had previous knowledge) and murder. Although Alexander may not have known of preparations for the murder, the moral implications of regicide and patricide remained in the eyes of the nation. As such, his position was worse than Boris's, because in Pushkin's tragedy, in order to open to himself the road to the Russian throne, Boris Godunov had killed Dimitry, another king's son, but not his own father. Throughout, Pushkin was more concerned with usurpation than with the ruthlessness and murder attendant upon it. Preoccupation with this problem was strengthened and deepened in him by the figure of Napoleon, whom Pushkin, in agreement with the general opinion of his times, considered to be a usurper. There was, of course, a difference between Alexander and his great rival, but Pushkin found in the events of his own epoch the same opposition of two types of usurpers which is present in his *Boris Godunov*. Although not surprising, it is still significant that Pushkin often brings Napoleon and Alexander together in various poems. There is one poem, unfortunately unfinished, which is particularly interesting—*Nedvizhny strazh dremal*...—but more of that later.

If these suppositions with regard to Pushkin's considerations in presenting the problem of usurpation are correct, then one may conclude that Karamzin was only a secondary source for Pushkin's *Boris Godunov*. Working in the seclusion of Mikhaylovskoe, in exile, Pushkin was creating an historical tragedy, the implications of which struck at a contemporary tragedy. Everyone knows the deep antipathy, if not hatred, which Pushkin bore for Alexander. I will not enumerate here all the epigrams, allegoric tales, historical remarks (like "Remarks" on the *Annals of Tacitus*), statements in his personal correspondence and entries in his diary (particularly 1834), which reveal his feelings. But I should like to cite one argument which in my opinion is decisive, and which, like a match struck in the darkness, illuminates this whole complex of events. While still in Mikhaylovskoe, before Alexander's death, before the Decembrist Revolt, when *Boris Godunov* had already been completed, Pushkin desperately begged his friends to obtain an authorization from Alexander for him to leave Mikhaylovskoe. In a letter to Prince Vyazemsky (end of October—beginning of November, 1825) he wrote: "Zhukovsky says the Emperor will pardon me for my Tragedy. I doubt it, my dear friend. Although it is written in a good spirit, I couldn't conceal all my ears under the cap of the simpleton [*yurodivy*]; they protrude!"[1] This is my match! For the reference is obviously to the scene in *Boris Godunov* where the Czar appears before the people, among whom is the Simpleton. The following scene takes place:

    The Simpleton: Boris, Boris! The boys are hurting Nick.
    The Czar: Give him alms! What's he crying about?
    The Simpleton: Little children are hurting Nick. . . . Have them killed, as thou hadst the little Czarevitch killed.
    Boyars: Go away, fool! Seize the fool!
    The Czar: Leave him alone. Pray thou for me, poor Nick. (*Exit.*)
    The Simpleton (*calling after him*): No, no! It is impossible to pray for Czar Herod; the Mother of God forbids it![2]

Any comment on this passage appears needless. Pushkin's allusion in his letter is clear enough. I might add only that Pushkin was very anxious to include this scene in the tragedy, and for this purpose asked Zhukovsky to obtain *The Life of the Iron Cap* or the life story of some other simpleton from Karamzin,[3] although Karamzin warned Pushkin

---

[1] A. Puškin, *Pis'ma*, pod red. B. L. Modzalevskogo (Moscow-Leningrad, 1926), Vol. I, pp. 167–8.
[2] Pushkin, Yarmolinsky's ed., p. 395.
[3] Puškin, *Pis'ma*, Vol. I, p. 155.

through Vyazemsky that he would probably not find anything important for his tragedy in this life story. The poet apparently thought otherwise, and, indeed, he received the life of the famous Moscow simpleton, Ioann, from Karamzin.[1] An indirect proof of Pushkin's concern that this item be included in *Boris Godunov* is the fact that he permitted an anachronism, as the Moscow simpleton, whose life story he utilized, died in 1589, that is nine years before Boris's enthronement.

Turning to another aspect of the problem of usurpation in Pushkin's works, it is to be noted that if Shakespeare served as Pushkin's guide in portraying the psychological pattern of political usurpers, then Byron was certainly responsible for fostering Pushkin's admiration for Napoleon and supporting his disdain for Alexander. Although Byron's attitude toward Napoleon was not uniform, it did not undergo any evolutionary change: he capriciously varied his treatment of the Emperor in a number of poems. *Childe Harold's Pilgrimage*, *The Age of Bronze*, *Don Juan*, *Ode* ("We do not curse thee, Waterloo..."), "Must thou go, my glorious chief?...", *On the Star of the Legion of Honour*, *Napoleon's Farewell*, *Additional Stanzas to the Ode to Napoleon Bonaparte*—all of these offer various evaluations of Napoleon. But in one respect they are all in harmony: in each the poet pays his tribute to the undoubted greatness of the man. This does not prevent him from reproaching Napoleon for his tyrannical ambitions, for the suppression of freedom in the world, for the lowering of his own greatness, the greatness of a hero, by donning a royal crown and thereby decreasing his independent and intrinsic magnitude. Nevertheless, to Byron Napoleon remained "a lion", "an eagle", a commander, alone among many, who followed hard upon Caesar's road, a great man who aspired to everything or nothing, a man who had only one weakness—vanity; the greatest, but not the worst, man.

Napoleon's eastern rival, Alexander, was treated unfavourably by Byron. In *The Age of Bronze* he describes him in this way:

> ... Behold the coxcomb czar,
> The autocrat of waltzes and of war!
> As eager for a plaudit as a realm,
> And just as fit for flirting as the helm;
> A Calmuck beauty with a Cossack wit,
> And generous spirit, when 'tis not frost-bit;
> Now half dissolving to a liberal thaw,
> But harden'd back whene'er the morning's raw;
> With no objection to true liberty,
> Except that it would make the nations free.

[1] Cf. *ib.*, p. 163 (letter of 13–15 September, 1825). Compare also with p. 494.

> How well the imperial dandy prates of peace,
> How fain, if Greeks would be his slaves, free Greece!
> How nobly gave he back the Poles their Diet,
> Then told pugnacious Poland to be quiet!
> How kindly would he send the mild Ukraine,
> With all her pleasant pulks, to lecture Spain!
> How royally show off in proud Madrid
> His goodly person, from the South long hid!
> A blessing cheaply purchased, the world knows,
> By having Muscovites for friends or foes.

The advice which Byron extends to Alexander clearly defines his views on Russia:

> Better reclaim thy deserts, turn thy swords
> To ploughshares, shave and wash thy Bashkir hordes,
> Redeem thy realms from slavery and the knout,
> Than follow headlong in the fatal route,
> To infest the clime whose skies and laws are pure
> With thy foul legions. Spain wants no manure;
> Her soil is fertile, but she feeds no foe;
> Her vultures, too, were gorged not long ago;
> And wouldst thou furnish them with fresher prey?
> Alas! thou wilt not conquer, but purvey.
> I am Diogenes, though Russ and Hun
> Stand between mine and many a myriad's sun;
> But were I not Diogenes, I'd wander
> Rather a worm than *such* an Alexander!

The phrase "such an Alexander" is important because of the frequent comparison of Alexander I to Alexander of Macedonia, which in itself represents the usurpation of the prestige of the latter by the former. Equally significant in this poem are the allusions to Napoleon's defeat in Russia. Byron describes the fire of Moscow as a symbol of the fire to come which will destroy all empires and warns of the icy Russian winter which fells "a hero with each flake of snow".

In Pushkin, Alexander I appears in the same Byronic stylization: witness the tenth chapter of *Eugene Onegin*, the epigrams and the tales to which I have previously alluded. We find there mockery connected with the defeat at Austerlitz and the fears of Alexander in 1812, as well as accusations of duplicity and, finally, the ironic question as to whether it was Barclay de Tollay, the Russian winter, or God that brought Alexander to Paris.

As far as our theme of usurpation is concerned, the most impressive and clearly defined opposition of Alexander and Napoleon is contained in the unfinished poem which starts with the line "*Nedvizhny strazh dremal . . .*" Here is Pushkin's description of Napoleon contained in this fragment:

> It was this wonder of a man, a messenger of
> Providence,
> A fateful doer of deeds imposed by an unknown command,
> This horseman, before whom kings bowed down,
> The heir and murderer of rebellious freedom,
> This cold blood-drinker,
> This king who disappeared like a dream, like the
> shadow of the dawn.
> Neither the lazy wrinkles of bloated idleness,
> Nor the heavy gait, nor premature grey hairs,
> Nor the dying flame of frowning eyes—
> Betrayed the exiled hero in him,
> Condemned to the torment of inactivity among the seas,
> By the will of kings.
> No, his wonderful glance, alert, elusive,
> At times lost in the distance, at times irresistible,
> Blazing like a thunderbolt of war;
> In the glory of health, and manfulness and power,
> The threatening Master of the West appeared before the
> Master of the North.

Unfortunately, Pushkin did not complete the poem, and the dialogue between the two Emperors, which would undoubtedly have followed, is missing. However, the state of mind attributed to Alexander in this fragment closely resembles that of Boris Godunov as he awaits the appearance of his rival in the tragedy.

In *Boris Godunov* Pushkin was concerned with two items: the theme of political usurpation and, from this, the theme of psychological usurpation. As a matter of fact, in Pushkin's tragedy there are actually two political usurpers—the historical one, Dimitry the False, and the legal Czar, Boris Godunov. Boris has come to the throne through murder, and Dimitry reaches it by fraud and intrigue. Psychologically, however, it is Boris upon whom Pushkin has loaded the fatal doubts and weaknesses, characterizing a usurper as such. Boris does everything to establish firmly and to legalize his usurped power. His "election" becomes something of a comedy, because he exaggerates his reluctance to accept "the will of the nation". The longer he resists, the more hypocritical the enthusiasm of the people appears. Once elected, Boris tries even harder to capture the goodwill and faithfulness of the people by all kinds of reforms and philanthropic acts, such as building houses and distributing alms and bread in times of national calamity. But all this does not help him. The people remain unconquered, and the usurper falls into gloomy and suspicious solitude. Pushkin goes even farther: he suggests the idea of the fatalism of crime. Once he has committed his murder, the wise, intelligent, and even goodhearted monarch is prepared to use his power for the happiness and welfare of his people (here we have the nucleus for Raskolnikov's speculations). But this appears impossible. Reform and alms are replaced by spying, imprisonments, tortures, and executions. As soon as Dimitry rises on the horizon, Boris considers him an instrument of Providence, the incarnation of divine punishment.

Quite different is the attitude and character of the Pretender. That which made Boris weak, suspicious, gloomy, and pessimistic, caused Dimitry to be strong, self-confident, serene, and optimistic. He, too, considered himself an instrument of Providence, the sword of punishment, the man elected by Fate, and this was the source of his conviction that heaven and earth were with him in his venture. Pushkin emphasizes his lightheartedness, his carelessness and nonchalance. He is friendly with everyone around him. He is spontaneously courageous, knowing no fear; he is sure that the Poles will support him, that the Russian people will welcome him, that Boris will be defeated. In battle he is more absorbed by the battle than by its issue. In the midst of it he deplores the death of his horse.[1] He is not lonely. He has dignity and freedom of spirit enough to share his secret with the one whom he loves. He does not want to share his happiness with the dead Czarevich; he does not want to be loved for his crown. He demands love for himself, for the small, humble, fugitive monk he really is. In other words, to Boris Godunov, who is conscious of his superiority and who believes that this superiority grants him all possible rights over people, to the solitary strategist who is systematically planning his life and gradually organizing his might, there is opposed a natural, spontaneous, optimistic —one might say unconscious—force of an essentially free personality. In Boris Godunov we have a slave to imagined power, whereas in Dimitry we find a master of power. Boris is an *arriviste* who constantly looks for recognition of his prestige; Dimitry is a born leader. Boris is a pretender, Dimitry is a natural nobleman. Dimitry's low social origin appears only as an additional argument in his favour—Pushkin is obviously dealing with a natural, personal prestige as such. Let us

---

[1] These traits in the portrayal of Dimitry and the juxtaposition of the characters of Dimitry and Godunov have often been commented on by the Russian literary critics: Cf. Iskoz as above and M. N. Pokrovsky, "Šekspirizm Puškina" in Vengerov's edition of *Puškin*, Vol. IV; also D. Bernstein, "Boris Godunov" in *Literaturnoe Nasledstvo*, Vols. XVI–XVIII, Moscow, 1934.

remember the Shakespearean advice that Boris gives before his death to his son:

> Be taciturn;
> The royal voice must never lose itself
> Upon the air in vain; it must be like
> A sacred bell that sounds but to announce
> Some great disaster or great festival.

Dimitry would never think of such stage directions because, as in the scene at the fountain, he would always spontaneously find the appropriate royal tone and words.

In using the term "usurper as such" I actually have in mind the present-day term "inferiority complex". In Pushkin's historical tragedy he is concerned with two men who were pretenders or usurpers, first of all because they actually aimed to enjoy someone else's rights. They faced a physical rival, in both cases a legal heir, and therefore both illustrated a concrete usurpation. It seems to me, however, that the study of these two characters and the psychological stylization that Pushkin gave to them led to the analysis of a human character who was absorbed by an imagined rival's threat to his own security. And this imagined rival would be nobody but himself in his sublimated concept of his own personality.[1] Now it is easy for us, especially with the aid of modern psychology, to manipulate the various existing egos: the actual ego, the notion of the ego in the opinion of others, and the ideal ego constantly present in our imagination as the goal to be reached by us. Finally, there is the judging ego, the one that judges the three others.

It seems to me that this was the "great idea" in Dostoevsky's own opinion of his *Double*. This painful and exhausting story relates the struggle of Golyadkin's numerous egos and his final destruction, when he is defeated by himself. Pushkin could not write in this way. I believe that Pushkin was obsessed, in what he wrote after *Boris Godunov*, by the image of the character-pairs illustrating the same two types of the usurper and the non-usurper, simply because there was no other way for him to proceed in his psychological study. He could not present the split personality with Dostoevskian or Freudian technique. This becomes particularly clear in *The Shot*, but I shall return to this story in this particular connection a little later. Let us begin with *Mozart and Salieri*.

[1] In some previous studies I advanced the opinion that Mickiewicz's rich personality and his gift of improvisation deeply impressed Pushkin and may have provided him with elements for his characterization of the free and spontaneous man. (See *Life and Culture of Poland* (New York, 1944), pp. 185–9.)

A. Dolinin has given an excellent analysis of Salieri[1]—of that ascetic servant of fame and power, who "early rejected vain pursuits" and "dedicated himself to music only". He deluded himself with the belief that he was thinking about "music only". His real goal was fame, and to this ambition he sacrificed everything else, "working with effort, tension and constancy". He was full of self-criticism:

> Not seldom, having spent in silent cell
> Two or three days, forgetting sleep and food,
> Tasting the joy and tears of inspiration,
> I threw my labours in the fire and watched
> My thoughts and songs—the children of my brain—
> Flame up, then vanish in a wisp of smoke. . . .

With anxiety he awaited the one who would suddenly overshadow him, and for years he hid the poison with which he would avenge himself against his competitor. He "dissected music like a corpse" and "checked harmony by algebraic rules; and only then, tested and proved in science", he "ventured to indulge creative fancy". This is a confession not only of a musician or composer; this is the confession of a man. The one who was to be his foe, his rival, had to be in flagrant contrast to all these tests and algebraic calculations:

> Oh, ye Heavens!
> Where, where is justice, when the sacred gift,
> When deathless genius comes not to reward
> Perfervid love and utter self-denial,
> And toils and strivings and beseeching prayers,
> But puts her halo round a lack-wit's skull,
> A frivolous idler's brow? . . . O, Mozart, Mozart.

Salieri deeply feels an insult, and his doubts about his own talent bring him to self-hatred and negation of life. The faint hope that he may resolve the contradiction between his real worth and his imagined ideal constantly prevents him from committing suicide. For eighteen years he has carried on his person "Isora's parting gift", and suddenly the choice is made: not himself, but "the unsuspecting foe". Opposed to him is the "frivolous idler", Mozart—"a cherub who brings songs of paradise", an elected one, "a happy idler", "condemning profane utility", a real "priest of beauty" who does not know envy, who is confident like a child, calmly ignoring all warnings of Fate, and who

[1] Cf. the introduction to *Povesti Belkina* in the Vengerov edition of Pushkin's works, Vol. IV.

divides himself between art and the pleasures of life. This was, by the way, the poet's self-portrait.

Mozart does not die without revenge, but even the sentence of punishment that falls from his mouth is an unintentional one. The serene Mozart trusts genius as a divine gift incompatible with crime: "He was a genius like you and me. But villainy and genius are two things that can never go together." This statement once again plunges Salieri into doubt, and the poet abandons him at this point, leaving him to his thoughts on the farewell message of Mozart.

The implications are the same in *Boris Godunov*. Pushkin does not confine himself to a simple study of the psychology of usurpation—he indicates a moral judgment. He condemns usurpation. As a matter of fact, he also condemns aforetime Raskolnikov and all his speculations about great scientific geniuses and legislators, the Keplers, Newtons, Lycurguses, Solons, Mohammed, Napoleons, and about the road from *la guerre éternelle* to "a New Jerusalem" as a sophistry of the Salieri species. However, this is all a small digression.

The main point of interest is still the contrast between acquired power and organic power. Pushkin gave the ultimate illustration of this in *The Covetous Knight*, where acquired power becomes a purely speculative force—the consciousness of the possession of power replaces the actual use of it. In other words, potentiality ends in impotence. This belongs to the sphere of Romantic concepts. For example, Alfred de Vigny, the poet-philosopher, was absorbed with this idea and constantly returned to the statement that imagination kills action. After Bem's studies it will suffice merely to mention to what degree Dostoevsky was impressed with *The Covetous Knight*. Mr. Prokharchin's story, that of Soloviev in *The Diary of a Writer* and *A Raw Youth* are all sufficiently eloquent examples of this regard for Pushkin's "little tragedy". But *The Shot*, to which Dostoevsky discreetly or indiscreetly alludes in his *Notes from Underground*, with its problem of the opposition of two contrasting types, is the main source for Dostoevsky's preoccupation with the same problem. In *The Shot* Sylvio is a usurper who establishes his prestige and leadership by his "extravagant hospitality", by his skill in shooting and by his "habitual sullenness, stern disposition and caustic tongue", but the appearance of the Count becomes such a threat to his position and security that an open conflict is inevitable.

Let us now examine Dostoevsky's *Double* more fully with reference to the problem of usurpation. In it Mr. Golyadkin's dreams of conquest and of a situation for himself in the world are disrupted by his double, who causes his eventual collapse and defeat. It seems to me that the plausible interpretation of this strange story is in considering the second Golyadkin to be nothing but an incarnation of the first Golyadkin's conception of what he should be in order to succeed with those people among whom Fate has placed him. Mr. Golyadkin Number Two acts in the way in which Mr. Golyadkin Number One would like, but is unable, to act. Mr. Golyadkin Number One, who is the real person, is defeated by Mr. Golyadkin Number Two, who replaces him as a seeming reality. In other words, Golyadkin Number Two is an impostor, and Golyadkin Number One treats him as such. The "greatness" of Dostoevsky's idea is revealed through the catastrophe of Mr. Golyadkin, the essence of which is that Golyadkin Number Two ousts him from life: there is no place for the former in the world. Translating this into the terminology of psychiatry we come to the formulation that the actual ego is completely annihilated by the ego existing in the opinion of the outside world.

I should like to interpose the following considerations in order to clarify my point about the difference in the handling of the theme of usurpation in Pushkin and in Dostoevsky's *Double*. Some valuable and pertinent observations have been contributed by the excellent French scholar on Shakespeare, Mézières, in discussing the visions of Richard III on the eve of his last battle. All his former victims arise, cursing and execrating him:

> "The Classic tragedy," says Mézières, "would send a dream to Richard and he would have related it, like Athalie, together with all the anxieties of remembrance. But the English drama speaks to the eyes. Here the dream materializes; instead of listening to a story, one sees on the stage the avenging shades and one hears the words which they pronounce."[1]

What I wish to say is that in a way Dostoevsky followed the example of the French tragedy, whereas Pushkin expressed his idea through the presentation of two separate and contrasting characters in action.

* * * * *

The Determined Man

Dostoevsky never abandoned the double character. There are evidences of him in Stavrogin and in Ivan Karamazov. But in the *Notes from Underground* there is a distinctly Pushkinian apposition of two materialized entities, at least in the episodes dealing with the encounters

[1] A. Mézières, *Shakespeare, ses oeuvres et ses critiques* (Paris, 1882), 3rd edition, p. 261.

of the hero with the officer and with Zverkov. In the *Notes* the successful man has been vulgarized almost to the same degree to which Dostoevsky vulgarized him in the person of Mr. Golyadkin Number Two. There is one book, however, in which this vulgarization does not occur, and that is *The House of the Dead*. The reader will recall Dostoevsky's genuine admiration for the determined men he met among the convicts. Here, for example, is how he speaks of Orlov:

> "a criminal such as there are few, who had murdered old people and children in cold blood": "He was certainly not an ordinary man ... I can confidently say that I have never in my life met a man of such strength, of so iron a will as he.... His was unmistakably the case of a complete triumph over the flesh. It was evident that the man's power of control was unlimited, that he despised every sort of punishment and torture, and was afraid of nothing in the world. We saw in him nothing but unbounded energy, a thirst for action, a thirst for vengeance, an eagerness to attain the object he had set before him. Among other things I was struck by his strange haughtiness. He looked down on everything with incredible disdain, though he made no sort of effort to maintain this lofty attitude—it was somehow natural. ... He was very intelligent, and somehow strangely open, though by no means talkative."[1]

And again, in describing Petrov, another wild character, Dostoevsky reveals his respect for the man:

> "Men like Petrov are only ruled by reason till they have some strong desire. Then there is no obstacle on earth that can hinder them. ... I never noticed in him any great power of reflection or any marked common sense. These people are born with one fixed idea which unconsciously moves them hither and thither; so they shift from one thing to another all their lives, till they find a work after their own hearts. Then they are ready to risk anything. ... I believe M. was right when he said that Petrov was the most determined man in all the prison."[2]

In the amazing conclusion of this book, which describes monsters of cruelty, merciless murderers, unscrupulous fighters for the rights of the strongest, the Christian Dostoevsky utters a fantastic complaint:

---

[1] Dostoevsky, *The House of the Dead*, translated by Constance Garnett (New York: Macmillan Co., 1915), p. 53.
[2] *Ibid.*, pp. 101–3.

"And how much youth lay uselessly buried within those walls, what mighty powers were wasted here in vain! After all, one must tell the whole truth: those men were exceptional men. Perhaps they were the most gifted, the strongest of our people. But their mighty energies were vainly wasted, wasted abnormally, unjustly, hopelessly. And who was to blame, whose fault was it? That's just it, who was to blame?"[1]

As we have seen, in the crowd of criminals Dostoevsky found several whom he admired for their unshakable determination; he appears to worship the men whose dynamic power of will and action knows no obstacles or scruples or even mercy. Yet, even in this instance, there exists in Pushkin a precedent for the extraordinary examples of the human species that are gathered together to form such a "society". The prologue of Pushkin's *Brigand Brothers*, for instance, might serve as the epigraph to *The House of the Dead*:

> What confusion of dress and face,
> Of race, of speech, and of condition!
> From huts, from cells, from prisons
> They have gathered out of greed!
> The only aim for every spirit—
> A life without authority or law.
> Among them the fugitive is seen
> From the banks of the war-like Don,
> And the Jew with his black locks,
> And the wild sons of the steppe,
> The Kalmuck and the ugly Bashkir,
> And the red-haired Finn with his lazy idleness,
> And the gypsy ever-wandering!
> Danger, blood, debauchery, treachery
> Form the bonds of this terrible clan;
> He is theirs who has a soul of stone
> And who has passed all steps of evil-doing;
> Who fells with an indifferent hand
> The widow with her wretched orphan,
> Who laughs at children's moans,
> Who forgives not, neither spares,
> Who takes delight in slaying,
> As youth in meeting with his love.

Dostoevsky might also have been impressed with the allegorical answer given by Pugachev in *The Captain's Daughter*. When Grinev warns Pugachev about the consequences of his dangerous venture, he replies in a presumably Kalmuck tale:

[1] *Ibid.*, p. 282.

"I will tell you a fairy-tale which in my childhood an old Kalmuck woman told me. The eagle asked the raven one day: 'Tell me, raven-bird, why do you live in the world for three hundred years and I only for thirty-three?'—'Because, father-eagle, you drink living blood,' the raven said, 'and I feed on things that are dead.' The eagle thought, 'I will try and feed as he does.' Very well. The eagle and the raven flew along. They saw the carcass of a horse, came down and perched on it. The raven plucked and praised the food. The eagle took a peck or two, then waved his wing and said: 'No, brother raven, rather than feed on carrion flesh for three hundred years, I would have one drink of living blood—and leave the rest to God.' "[1]

And finally, in *Journey to Erzerum*, as the reader remembers, Pushkin mentions still another "determined" man in the Circassian who killed a Russian soldier merely because his gun had been charged too long.[2] But Pushkin differs from Dostoevsky in that he does not confine himself to a simple description of these human beasts. He stresses his own attitude toward them and it is certainly not admiring. The moral implications of *The Brigand Brothers* are clear enough, and when Pushkin mentions the story of the Circassian, he simultaneously exclaims: "What can one do with such people!" and further expounds his views on the necessity of Christian missionaries in the Caucasus. Dostoevsky, on the other hand, cannot hide his rapture over the fearless and merciless "men of action". All this leads to melancholy thoughts, for what is the particular expression of human dignity that one of the greatest Russian writers found to admire? Shestov was right to consider *The House of the Dead* one of the most dangerous and stupefying books, a book which contains a presage of the great moral catastrophe that later occurred in Dostoevsky's thinking and the essence of which is apostasy from all the philanthropic, humanitarian and idealistic conceptions which reigned over the early works of Dostoevsky. Shestov was also right to stress that the *Notes from Underground* is the salient document in this catastrophe.

Because these considerations lead aside from the subject, I shall not dwell upon the figure of Prince Valkovsky, senior, who is a further development of the self-willed type presented in a special sociological stylization. The doubts and uncertainties that troubled Mr. Golyadkin are as foreign to Valkovsky as they were to Orlov and Petrov. However, the next incarnation of the superior, self-willed man, that is Raskolnikov in *Crime and Punishment*, is no longer monolithic. The line

[1] Pushkin, Yarmolinsky's ed, p. 699.
[2] See Pushkin's *Journey to Erzerum*, chapter I.

runs from Valkovsky to Svidrigaylov, who fights like a demon for the soul of Raskolnikov against the protection offered by the angel, Sonya. These two struggling "angels" who constantly hover around Raskolnikov symbolize, just as in Goethe's *Faust*, the split in Raskolnikov's personality.[1] But this ideological allegory, even with all of its metaphysical implications, does not exhaust the psychological problem. For the perspicacious, penetrative reader there exists no doubt that the title of the novel, *Crime and Punishment*, is only a label, because within the framework of the novel Raskolnikov never experiences any real, Christian, ethical remorse. The author persecutes and torments his hero not for the transgression of divine and human laws, but for his ultimate weakness, because the self-confident, superior human personality, conscious of his unquestionable rights, remains only an unattainable ideal for this hero, just as it had been for Golyadkin. Say what one will, he was neither a Napoleon nor an Orlov. And the real secret of his failure was revealed beforehand in the *Notes from Underground*.

The *Notes* make impossible any Christian interpretation of Raskolnikov's drama. As is known, the nucleus of Raskolnikov's crime is contained in Balzac's *Le Père Goriot*. There the problem is presented even more subtly, because the murder is abstract to the highest degree. But this is only one part of Raskolnikov's story. Once he commits the crime, Dostoevsky is no longer concerned with any meditations on the crime itself. It is Raskolnikov's weakness which absorbs Dostoevsky entirely. There is no doubt that psychoanalysis would have revealed in the biographic material of the author and in his personal experiences, especially in the period before his Siberian exile, many defeats and failures that would explain not only Golyadkin's adventures, but even Raskolnikov's collapse. I intend, however, to remain within the sphere of the literary texts.

The *Notes from Underground* explains (as do Pushkin's symbolic pairs) the preoccupation with the problem of the usurper, a matter I would like to underscore once again. And if we are to search for the sources of *Crime and Punishment* in Pushkin, then we find it was Herman of *The Queen of Spades*, a man obsessed and bewitched by one idea, who became, because of his activities and his fate, the prototype for Raskolnikov.[2] But, even in this case, Herman's power exceeded that with which Raskolnikov was endowed.

* * * * *

[1] See Jacques Madaule's extremely interesting book, *Le Christianisme de Dostoïevsky* (Paris: Blond et Gay, 1939).
[2] See A. L. Bem's studies for the further development of this problem.

Rationalism, Irrationalism, and the Imperative of the Heart

At this point it is fitting to examine Dostoevsky's reasonings, as contained in the *Notes*, on the man of action and the man of intellect. Earlier quotations from the *Notes* have shown Dostoevsky's derogatory presentation of the man of action. As I have pointed out, the author vulgarized Pushkin's situations and themes, but even within the framework of this general degradation the man of action, as symbolized by the officer and especially by Zverkov, has been particularly ridiculed. It is true that the hero of the *Notes* cannot count on any sympathy from the reader, but still he is endowed with some superiority, though it passes unrecognized by others. The previous quotations were connected only with several concrete episodes of the frail plot of the book. I treated these as narrative illustrations of Dostoevsky's "theory". If we transfer our attention to the reasonings of the hero, we find that they, too, are full of contempt for the man of action. It would be difficult, naturally, to trace any line of demarcation between Dostoevsky and his hero in this case. It was Shestov who, I think quite successfully, established the coincidence of attitudes in the two. Having created his hero as repulsive as he is, Dostoevsky left for himself the alibi that he was not responsible for his hero's thoughts and feelings. But the invective of the hero of the *Notes* against the man of action may easily be interpreted as the exasperation of weakness and envy on the part of the author. After all, the reactions of Sylvio and Salieri toward their rivals were not much different, but the sober and discreet Pushkin did not arm them with such vehemence of speech. Dostoevsky's hero is no less violent, passionate or hysterical in his reasonings than in his actions, nay, perhaps even more so, as here he is free, and nothing or nobody can stop his wild confession. Probably the most revealing among these unrestrained attacks against the man of action is the very first one, perhaps because it contains an element of surprise: the reader is unprepared for such a sudden offensive, launched as follows:

> "Now, I am living out my life in my corner, taunting myself with the spiteful and useless consolation that an intelligent man cannot become anything seriously, and it is only the fool who becomes anything. Yes, a man in the nineteenth century must and morally ought to be pre-eminently a characterless creature; a man of character, an active man, is pre-eminently a limited creature. That is my conviction of forty years. I am forty years old now, and you know forty years is a whole lifetime; you know it is extreme old age. To live longer than forty years is bad manners, is vulgar, immoral. I will tell you who do: fools and worthless fellows. I tell all old men that to their face, all these venerable old men, all these

silver-haired and reverend seniors! I tell the whole world that to its face. I have a right to say so, for I shall go on living to sixty myself. To seventy! To eighty!... Stay, let me take breath...."[1]

This becomes the leitmotif of the entire story. Almost immediately one hears it again:

"I swear, gentlemen, that to be too conscious is an illness—a real thoroughgoing illness. For man's everyday needs, it would have been quite enough to have the ordinary human consciousness, that is half or a quarter of the amount which falls to the lot of a cultivated man of our unhappy nineteenth century.... It would have been quite enough, for instance, to have the consciousness by which all so-called direct persons and men of action live. I bet you think I am writing all this from affectation, to be witty at the expense of men of action...."[2]

And a further rich development of the theme occurs:

"You know the direct, legitimate fruit of consciousness is inertia, that is conscious sitting-with-the-hands-folded. I have referred to this already. I repeat, I repeat with emphasis: all 'direct' persons and men of action are active just because they are stupid and limited. How explain that? I will tell you: in consequence of their limitation they take immediate and secondary causes for primary ones, and in that way persuade themselves more quickly and easily than other people do that they have found an infallible foundation for their activity, and their minds are at ease and you know that is the chief thing. To begin to act, you know, you must first have your mind completely at ease and no trace of doubt left in it... In consequence again of those accursed laws of consciousness, anger in me is subject to chemical disintegration. You look into it, the object flies off into air, your reasons evaporate, the criminal is not to be found, the wrong becomes not a wrong but a phantom, something like the toothache, for which no one is to blame, and consequently there is only the same outlet left again—that is, to beat the wall as hard as you can. So you give it up with a wave of the hand because you have not found a fundamental cause. And try letting yourself be carried away by your feelings, blindly, without reflection, without a primary cause, repelling consciousness at least for a time; hate or love, if only not to sit with your hands folded. The day after tomorrow, at the latest, you will begin despising yourself for having knowingly deceived yourself. Result:

[1] *Notes*, Part I, chapter 1.
[2] *Notes*, chapter 2.

a soap-bubble and inertia. Oh, gentlemen, do you know, perhaps I consider myself an intelligent man only because all my life I have been able neither to begin nor to finish anything. Granted I am a babbler, a harmless, vexatious babbler, like all of us. But what is to be done if the direct and sole vocation of every intelligent man is babble, that is the intentional pouring of water through a sieve?"[1]

Undoubtedly, Freud or any physician dealing with erotic phenomena would be ready to find in these quotations echoes of the sexual sphere of human activity. But Dostoevsky generalizes, and therefore one may be simply astonished as to why he required such an explosive manner to express his thoughts on the problem of human creativeness and ability for action. For anyone who has ever dwelt on this subject, it is possible to conclude, even without Dostoevsky's help, that every creative act implies some element of naïveté. In order to write a book or paint a picture one must assume the importance of these pronouncements to the world. Creative action is conditioned by a kind of child-like simplicity, of self-confidence and even of self-satisfaction, and of complete freedom. And if we are to consider the sphere of sexual activity, I believe it is needless to stress that, unlike animals, most human beings would find that any intervention, whether of intellect or of invasion of privacy, would result in the inhibition of sexual activity. There exists a variety of speculations on the theme of inspiration and on solitude as a condition for creativeness. The Romantics, in particular, furnished numerous arguments, which they converted into dogmatic assertions, to substantiate this point. It is generally known, too, that any military commander or political leader should possess the ability of prompt judgment and decision. Soldiers have been known to prefer a bad order to no order at all.

This brings up the problem of the will. Naturally, Dostoevsky could not avoid it and, as usual, he treats the question of desire, will and choice in the most drastic way:

"Gentlemen, you must excuse me for being over-philosophical; it's the result of forty years underground! Allow me to indulge my fancy. You see, gentlemen, reason is an excellent thing, there's no disputing that, but reason is nothing but reason and satisfies only the rational side of man's nature, while will is a manifestation of the whole life, that is, of the whole human life including reason and all the impulses. And although our life, in this manifestation of it, is often worthless, yet it is life and not simply extracting square roots. Here I, for instance, quite naturally want to live, in order to

[1] *Ibid.*, chapter 5.

satisfy all my capacities for life, and not simply my capacity for reasoning, that is, not simply one twentieth of my capacity for life. What does reason know? Reason only knows what it has succeeded in learning (some things, perhaps, it will never learn; this is a poor comfort, but why not say so frankly?) and human nature acts as a whole, with everything that is in it, consciously or unconsciously, and, even if it goes wrong, it lives. I suspect, gentlemen, that you are looking at me with compassion; you tell me again that an enlightened and developed man, such, in short, as the future man will be, cannot consciously desire anything disadvantageous to himself and that this can be proved mathematically. I thoroughly agree, it can—by mathematics. But I repeat for the hundredth time, there is one case, one only, when man may consciously, purposely, desire what is injurious to himself, what is stupid, very stupid— simply in order to have the right to desire for himself even what is very stupid and not to be bound by an obligation to desire only what is sensible. Of course, this very stupid thing, this caprice of ours, may be in reality, gentlemen, more advantageous for us than anything else on earth, especially in certain cases. And in particular it may be more advantageous than any advantage even when it does us obvious harm, and contradicts the soundest conclusions of our reason concerning our advantage—for in any circumstances it preserves for us what is most precious and most important—that is, our personality, our individuality. Some, you see, maintain that this really is the most precious thing for mankind; choice can, of course, if it chooses, be in agreement with reason; and especially if this be not abused but kept within bounds. It is profitable and sometimes even praiseworthy. But very often, and even most often, choice is utterly and stubbornly opposed to reason ... and ... and ... do you know that that, too, is profitable, and sometimes even praiseworthy?"[1]

V. Veresaev, in his fascinating book on Tolstoy and Dostoevsky, *The Living Life*, compared Tolstoy and Bergson. Following Veresaev, I should like to support my analysis of Dostoevsky's speculations on the theme of rationalism and irrationalism with the help of Bergson's *Creative Evolution*. In the chapter on intelligence and instinct we find the following statements:

"There are things that intelligence alone is able to see, but which, by itself, it will never find. These things instinct alone could find; but it will never seek them."[2]

[1] *Notes*, chapter 8.
[2] H. Bergson, *Creative Evolution* (New York: Modern Library, 1944), p. 167.

"Of immobility alone does the intellect form a clear idea."[1]

"The intellect is characterized by the unlimited power of decomposing according to any law and of recomposing into any system."[2]

"The intellect is characterized by a natural inability to comprehend life. Instinct, on the contrary, is molded on the very form of life. While intelligence treats everything mechanically, instinct proceeds, so to speak, organically. If the consciousness that slumbers in it should awake, if it were wound up into knowledge instead of being wound off into action, if we could ask and it could reply, it would give up to us the most intimate secrets of life. For it only carries out further the work by which life organizes matter—so that we cannot say, as has often been shown, where organization ends and where instinct begins. When the little chick is breaking its shell with a peck of its beak, it is acting by instinct, and yet it does but carry on the movement which has borne it through embryonic life. Inversely, in the course of embryonic life itself (especially when the embryo lives freely in the form of a larva), many of the acts accomplished must be referred to instinct."[3]

". . . Instinct and intelligence are divergent developments of one and the same principle, which in the one case remains within itself, in the other steps out of itself and becomes absorbed in the utilization of inert matter. This gradual divergence testifies to a radical incompatibility, and points to the fact that it is impossible for intelligence to reabsorb instinct. That which is instinctive in instinct cannot be expressed in terms of intelligence, nor, consequently, can it be analyzed."[4]

"Instinct is sympathy. If this sympathy could extend its object and also reflect upon itself, it would give us the key to vital operations—just as intelligence, developed and disciplined, guides us into matter. For—we cannot too often repeat it—intelligence and instinct are turned in opposite directions, the former toward inert matter, the latter toward life. Intelligence, by means of science, which is its work, will deliver up to us more and more completely the secret of physical operations; of life it brings us, and moreover

---

[1] *Ibid.*, p. 171.
[2] *Ibid.*, p. 173.
[3] *Ibid.*, p. 182.
[4] Bergson, *op. cit.*, pp. 184–5.

only claims to bring us, a translation in terms of inertia. It goes all round life, taking from outside the greatest possible number of views of it, drawing it into itself instead of entering into it. But it is to the very inwardness of life that *intuition* leads us—by intuition I mean instinct that has become disinterested, self-conscious, capable of reflecting upon its object and of enlarging it indefinitely."[1]

"It is of the essence of reasoning to shut us up in the circle of the given. But action breaks the circle. If we had never seen a man swim, we might say that swimming is an impossible thing, inasmuch as, to learn to swim, we must begin by holding ourselves up in the water and, consequently, already know how to swim. Reasoning, in fact, always nails us down to the solid ground. But if, quite simply, I throw myself into the water without fear, I may keep myself up well enough at first by merely struggling, and gradually adapt myself to the new environment: I shall thus have learnt to swim. So, in theory, there is a kind of absurdity in trying to know otherwise than by intelligence; but if the risk be frankly accepted, action will perhaps cut the knot that reasoning has tied and will not unloose."[2]

From these excerpts we see that Bergson sought a solution for the problem of the interaction of desire, will and choice in his conception of intuition and action. All of the quoted assertions point to the close relationship between the philosophic systems of Bergson and Schopenhauer. Similar concepts of the immobilization of life, of the paralysis of movement by the intelligence, became the basis for Schopenhauer's skepticism toward history. And Tolstoy's evaluation of history was no different either. In Tolstoy's case, as Eichenbaum has indicated,[3] it resulted in part from the influences of Tolstoy's friend, Prince Urusov, who searched for a secret formula for universal life and development, in part from Tolstoy's own lengthy observation of the conflict existing between reason and life and from his vain efforts to rationalize the irrational elements of life, and in part, as I believe, from the influence of Schopenhauer's philosophy.

There exists in the philosophy which governed the Romantics, too, the same cult for the secret powers of intuitive knowledge as opposed to reasoning. A typical expression of this philosophy is contained in Mickiewicz's *Ballads*. But of particular relevancy to our discussion is Krasiński's statement in a letter written in 1833:

[1] *Ibid.*, p. 194.
[2] Bergson, *op. cit.*, p. 211.
[3] Cf. G. Eichenbaum, *Lev Tolstoj*, Vol. II.

"A painting, a statue, a word, a sign—it is always the same thing: an instant of life arrested in its passage and immediately struck into immobility and death. Man can express himself only by inanimate things. Each one of these expressions, therefore, is a falsity, as it is charged with representing life while being itself a corpse. . . ."[1]

Mickiewicz's *Ode to Youth*, which certainly had a strong influence on Krasiński, voices this activism and practical voluntarism. But Mickiewicz himself, like his teachers Schiller and, especially, Byron, was ruled by Kant's categorical imperative of the heart, by the "Rousseauistic charter" of sentimental irrationalism, as well as by the beautiful chapter from Helvetius's *Book of the Spirit* concerning the creative power of passions. All of these brought him to his formula of "wisdom through enthusiasm". Romantic irrationalism did not confine itself, as far as Polish poetry is concerned, only to theoretical dialectics of "pure reason". It elaborated its own "practical reason", the "categorical imperative of the heart", the concepts of the universalistic values of individual sacrifice, of pity and humility, thereby defeating its own violent individualism. These ideas lie at the bases of Krasiński's *Undivine Comedy* and *Iridion*, Mickiewicz's *Forefathers' Eve*, and Słowacki's *Anhelli*.[2]

Aside from the Romantics, it is in Tolstoy's "philosophy" and art that we find innumerable illustrations *avant la lettre* of Bergson's philosophy of intuition. I have already mentioned Veresaev's comparison of Tolstoy and Bergson. In addition, both Merezhkovsky and Shestov demonstrated in their books on Tolstoy and Dostoevsky how frequently Tolstoy's instinct of life took the shape of brutal, animal selfishness, and how his reasoned virtue and rationalistic morality and religion were artificial. Paradoxical as it may appear, it is possible to draw a parallel between the quiet words of Marie Rostov in the epilogue of *War and Peace* about "the duties which are closer to us", "the duties indicated to us by God Himself" and the terrible vociferations about the "cup of tea" and "universal harmony" in the *Notes from Underground*. But unrestrained as Tolstoy was in his individualism, he never ceased for a moment in his long and intense life his efforts toward self-perfection and moral improvement. Knowing from personal experience all the temptations which menace the human personality, he described them with cruel veracity. His struggle for goodness and love was all the

---

[1] *Correspondance de Sigismond Krasiński et de Henry Reeve* (Paris: Delagrave, 1902), Vols. I–II.

[2] Cf. the section *Dostoevsky and Poland* in the present volume. In this section I have included a chapter showing the possible relationship between Dostoevsky's "Pro and Contra" of *The Brothers Karamazov* and Mickiewicz's *Forefathers' Eve, Part III*.

more difficult in that his belief in the organic goodness of the human heart and his faith that the raw material of the heart is goodness were constantly shaken by his vision of the destructive powers of passion. What was even more significant in his case was that this Russian aristocrat, filled with the traditions of his caste, received no support from the Church; he fought for morality alone and as if guided by an autonomous morality. In addition, his skepticism concerning human nature was mostly conditioned by sociology: he affirmed "a man of nature" and explained the spoliation of human character by social factors. In justice to Tolstoy, one should remember that his reasoned religion and rationalistic morality were not the only patterns in his efforts to attain goodness. In spite of his personal, overwhelming rationalism, he continuously observed around him and admired the irrational elements of life. He concluded that only the irrational, the spontaneous, the direct, the unconscious are true. That is why it so often happens that his anarchic egoists show a spontaneous generosity, as is illustrated not only in *The Cossacks*, *War and Peace*, and *Anna Karenina*, but also in some of his short stories, particularly *The Two Hussars*, which I have discussed above.

In no place did Dostoevsky more explicitly express his absolute belief in the immanence of evil in human nature—one may even deduce that in his opinion evil is the essence of the human being—and in no place was he more manifestly in contradiction to Tolstoy than in his famous article on *Anna Karenina*, in which he gave a completely erroneous interpretation of Tolstoy's ethics. First he describes the European system for combating evil, in which he sees two possible approaches. One is through obedience to the written code established by the "abnormal" and "absurd" "organization which we call the Great European civilization", by which "evil and good are defined, weighed, measured . . ." "He who fails to abide by it, he who violates it, pays for it with his freedom, his property, his life, pays literally and inhumanly." The second European approach to evil is a revolutionary one, which means that "to overcome crime and human guilt, it is necessary to overcome the abnormality of society and its structure". The destruction of society *in toto* is the second solution which Dostoevsky assigns to European thought.

Turning now to Tolstoy, this is what he says:

"However, in the Russian author's approach to culpability and human delinquency it is clearly revealed that no ant-hill, no triumph of the 'fourth estate', no elimination of poverty, no organization of labor will save mankind from abnormality, and therefore,—from guilt and criminality. This is expressed in an immense psychological analysis of the human soul, with tremendous depth and potency, with a realism of artistic portrayal hitherto unknown in Russia. It is clear and intelligible to the point of obviousness that evil in mankind is concealed deeper than the physician-socialists suppose; that in no organization of society can evil be eliminated; that the human soul will remain identical; that abnormality and sin emanate from the soul itself, and finally, that the laws of the human spirit are so unknown to science, so obscure, so indeterminate and mysterious, that, as yet, there can neither be physicians nor *final* judges, but that there is only He who saith: 'To me belongeth vengeance and recompense.' "[1]

Dostoevsky's conclusion is that the human judge, sinful as he is himself, has no right to judge others, and he "will exclaim with fear and perplexity: 'Nay, it is not always that to me belongeth vengeance and recompense.' "

Tolstoy the advocate of primitive Christianity, Tolstoy the Rousseauist, Tolstoy the worshiper of the spontaneous reactions of the human heart, expressed in his *Anna Karenina* completely opposite views. For Tolstoy evil comes from without, it invades, sometimes in a tragic way, human souls, and his novel shows on almost every page the process of this invasion. Anna is the victim of society, of conventions, and of her lack of courage to fight these conventions and to defend her personality, to give herself to a really true love. On the other hand, the whole novel is certainly a defense of the family, of a pure marriage, and of the domestic hearth. It illustrates the great importance which Tolstoy saw in the relationship between parents and children, it emphasizes Tolstoy's deep conviction—at that time—that a man may have only one wife and a woman only one husband, that a child should have only one father and one mother.

It is known that there were two horrors in Tolstoy's world: death and sensual passion. The demon of *luxuria*—and the terrible devastations which this demon produces in human life—is perhaps the main factor in Tolstoy's tragedies. But these catastrophes are great not only because of the power of this demon, who indeed acquired a kind of metaphysical character in Tolstoy's thoughts and fears, but because of the power of resistance in the moral person. Tragic is the fate only of those who are superior beings: Betsy Tverskaya may live comfortably with her sins, because her way of compromise is tolerated by society, whereas Anna perishes. Veresaev is right when, commenting on Dostoevsky's interpretation of *Anna Karenina*, he says: Tolstoy

[1] *Diary of a Writer*, Vol. II, p. 787.

"definitely refutes 'the conviction of the mysterious and fatal inevitability of evil'. Before 'vengeance' Tolstoy does not bow in 'fear and perplexity', as before a higher mystery about which man does not dare to reason. 'Vengeance' is quite understandable to him, legal, and inevitable: if a man puts a noose about his neck and draws it taut, he will unavoidably die."[1]

*   *   *   *   *

> "Having destroyed all prejudices,
> We consider all people zeros
> And only ourselves the integers.
> We all try to be Napoleons
> And the two-legged millions
> Are only our tools,
> And feelings are for us wild and absurd."
> (Pushkin, *Eugene Onegin*, chapter II, stanza XIV.)

In conclusion, I should like to remind the reader once again that the *Notes from Underground* is an introduction to Dostoevsky's great novels. In the *Notes* Dostoevsky elaborated his philosophy for *Crime and Punishment*. It even appears possible to suggest that two of the characters who appear in the *Notes*—the hero and the prostitute—reappear in *Crime and Punishment* as Raskolnikov and Sonya. Of course the situation is different and Raskolnikov does not subject Sonya to the indignities of his predecessor. I have tried to show that Pushkin's series of heroes, who are like the symbols for two opposite approaches to life, attracted Dostoevsky. His thoughts, constantly revolving around the "direct man" and the "intelligent man", are connected with Pushkin's poetic suggestions. Pushkin's couples serve as an embodiment of his thoughts on the theme of usurpation. The poet obviously shows his preference for the direct man. He does not even undertake to defend the rival of the direct man. One cannot but feel that in Pushkin's case this was a natural predilection, for one feels that the poet had no personal envy of the prestige of the innate lords—he portrayed himself (and perhaps Mickiewicz)[2] in them. In the *Notes*, on the other hand, we meet the rival of the direct man in a state of fury, and Dostoevsky's presentation of the direct man as one who is essentially stupid is significant, especially

---

[1] V. Veresaev, *Živaja Žizn'* (Moscow, 1911), p. 151.
[2] I developed this idea in my article "Pouchkine et Mickiewicz", in *Revue de Littérature Comparée*, No. 65 (Paris, 1937); and in my book *Life and Culture of Poland* (New York, 1944), pp. 185–9.

in the light of the tribute he paid to him in *The House of the Dead*. Perhaps it was natural that the hysterical outbursts of the hero of the *Notes* should be replaced by the quiet development of this same theme in *Crime and Punishment*. This quiet development, when contrasted with the violence of the act of murder committed there, enhances the dynamism of Dostoevsky's idea. And the idea derives from Dostoevsky's personal feelings of insecurity. After reversing Pushkin's hierarchy of characters, Dostoevsky sets about rehabilitating the intelligent man, even in the *Notes*, but in this work his actions destroy any possible superiority he might have over the direct man. Here one meets the *credo quia absurdum*. In order to establish and affirm his superiority, the intelligent man resorts to acts intellectually and morally absurd. A strange effort to liberate man from the enslaving chains of intellectualism! In a way Stavrogin's paradoxical search for freedom, as well as for proofs of his power, is similar. In *The Possessed* it seems as though Dostoevsky returns to the hysteria of the *Notes*. But between the two works, in *Crime and Punishment*, the reasonings are calmer and more contemplative, despite the tortures to which Dostoevsky subjects the hero. In this novel the problem of rationalism versus irrationalism, of the intelligent and the direct man, receives a more precise expression: Dostoevsky openly voices his conception of the Superman and his absolute rights. It was his attempt to intellectualize his heroes of *The House of the Dead*. Merezhkovsky is right to wonder at the calmness with which the author lays before the reader, and with mathematical precision, his theory. Merezhkovsky writes:

> "A man speaks about human affairs as though he were not a man, but a being from another world, as a natural scientist might describe an ant-hill or a bee-hive. He investigates not that which ought to be, but that which is, not the desirable, but the actual, just as though there were no connection between the moral and the religious worlds, as though there were no relationship between the thought of goodness and the thought of God, or as though this very thought of God never existed in the heart and conscience of mankind."[1]

If we are to believe Raskolnikov's confession to Sonya, he committed his crime for his own sake, in order to prove his superiority to himself. This is closely related to the speculations of the hero in the *Notes* about free will. And in essence Kirillov's suicide is for the same purpose: to assert himself.

[1] D. S. Merežkovskij, *L. Tolstoj i Dostoevskij* (St. Petersburg-Moscow, 1912), Vol. VIII, p. 117.

If Kirillov's act has all the traits of a tragic absurdity, there are other manifestations in Dostoevsky's works, less tragic but not less absurd, of the same desperate need of self-affirmation. I have already alluded to *The Gambler*, more particularly to the episode of the gambler's ridiculous behaviour with respect to the Baron and Baroness Burmerhelm. In this case, as I have tried to show, we have an obvious example of the opposition of the Russian formlessness, revolutionary in its very essence, to the western-European form, of the Russian anarchic disrespect for convention to tradition which for centuries was the basic factor in the development of western-European civilization. The episode narrated by Dostoevsky in *The Gambler* is a variant *avant la lettre* of Stavrogin's extravagances, such as the biting of the governor's ear, as well as his wild and criminal acts, like the stealing of money and the raping of the child. All of these express the same desire for self-affirmation, self-assertion, and serve to check the hero's power, self-control and independence. For the same purpose, Dostoevsky's dialectic even utilizes "the dramatic lack of action"—the kind of "eloquent silence" —as is seen in Stavrogin's passive acceptance of Shatov's slap in the face.

If we examine all of Raskolnikov's intellectualizing, we find he is primarily concerned with the rights and privileges of the superior, exceptional man as opposed to the "trembling creature" (an expression, by the way, taken from Pushkin's *Imitations of the Koran*).[1] It occurs to me that *Crime and Punishment* might have as an epigraph Stendhal's sarcastic assertion in the short story *The Cenci*, to the effect that:

> "It was this religion (i.e., the Christian), doubtless, which taught the world that a poor slave, a gladiator, had a soul absolutely equal in capacity to that of Caesar himself; we have, therefore, to thank it for having produced a delicacy of feeling."[2]

And indeed, if compared with the *Notes*, *Crime and Punishment* contains a new element, that of élitarianism. Raskolnikov is still not an aristocrat by birth, though he is by attitude, but the next usurper-superman, Stavrogin, will be an aristocrat even by birth.

Unfortunately for them, all of Dostoevsky's supermen, strange children of two fathers—the hero from the *Notes from Underground* and

---

[1] Dostoevsky also paraphrased this expression in *The Gambler* as "all the rabble, trembling over a gulden . . ." (see chapter 2).

[2] H. M. Beyle (de Stendhal), *The Abbess of Castro and Other Tales* (translated by C. K. Scott Moncrieff) (New York: Boni & Liveright, 1926), p. 167.

the Orlovs from *The House of the Dead*—collapsed. Merezhkovsky and Shestov have revealed that Dostoevsky's main grievance against his hero was his weakness. This is related to the Napoleonic question, which has not been discussed in this essay in connection with Dostoevsky but which has been handled quite thoroughly by Merezhkovsky. It is worth while to note that Napoleon obsessed the Russian imagination for almost a whole century, and Russian literature insistently illustrates this obsession. In *The Uncle's Dream*, for instance, Marya Alexandrovna "used to be compared in some respects to Napoleon", and the uncle "resembled Napoleon". Our hero from the *Notes from Underground* dreams of how he will "defeat the obscurantists at Austerlitz". In his horrible conversation with his valet Apollo he stands "with folded arms *à la Napoleon*".[1] Even Chichikov passed as a Napoleon. Gogol's officials searched for apocalyptic numbers in the name of Napoleon, and Turgenev's Teglev was busy with some other numbers and calculations connected with the same name. So there is nothing astonishing in the fact that Raskolnikov measured himself to Napoleon's stature. This causes Porfiry to say to him: "Come now, who among us in Russia doesn't consider himself a Napoleon now?"[2]

Apart from Napoleon, an additional source of inspiration for Dostoevsky's meditations on the superman stems from Pushkin's *Imitations of the Koran*, where Mohammed impresses him as the aristocratic prophet. Pushkin was not a religious man and Christian motifs seldom appear in his poetry, but nevertheless he retained a kind and benevolent feeling about humanity. Dostoevsky, on the other hand, constantly appeals to the Orthodox Church, is always dragging in ikons, but this does not hide the terrible truth that Dostoevsky's prophet has a cross in one hand and a sword in the other. Raskolnikov's slogan—"*Vive la guerre éternelle* until a New Jerusalem!"—is not his alone.

The essential point is that despite the established reputation of Dostoevsky as a writer who probed the depths of the human heart and the widest horizons of universalistic thought, his main preoccupation was with man face to face with mankind, and not with man facing the universe. Dostoevsky is unlike the Polish Romantic poets, for whom the problem of the superior man is related to the nation. They, too, discuss issues of unjustified martyrdom, but they seek some superior justification, a religious sanction for the suffering in life. Theirs was a literature which searched for a theodicy, and therefore the victim, who appeared

---

[1] Cf. *White Nights and Other Stories by F. M. Dostoevsky*, translated by Constance Garnett (New York: Macmillan Co., 1918), p. 94.
[2] *Crime and Punishment*, Part III, chapter 5.

as a senseless sacrifice from the purely humanistic point of view, acquired a universal meaning. Human suffering enriches the spiritual content of the world, and, when confronted with this, the superior man is made equal to the inferior.

In a way, the non-religious Turgenev knew such élans of thought. (I have in mind Turgenev's Lukeria and Liza.) The same may be said of Pushkin. I doubt, however, whether it is possible to find any such essence in Dostoevsky's works. Pascal, the Romantics, and Tolstoy considered reason at best only a flimsy refuge, at worst a prison. In the face of all the storms of the world they were prepared to see in this prison a refuge, but all of them, Pascal included, believed that one should depart from this flimsy tent only with goodness as one's goal. Chernyshevsky, the progressive rationalist against whom Dostoevsky particularly fought in the *Notes*, trusted in the positive effects of the milieu on the individual. In Chernyshevsky's opinion evil deeds are committed because in some cases they are advantageous to the one who commits them. But this is so in an environment which creates possibilities for such calculations. Given a better environment in which good acts would become advantageous, the individual might become harmless and even useful and act in an honest and generous way. "Then the evil people might see that they cannot be evil; and they would become good, for they were evil only because it was harmful to them to be good."[1] This is what Dostoevsky read in Chernyshevsky's novel *What to Do?*, and he was infuriated with the idea of advantage. In the second period of his life Dostoevsky was opposed to the Chernyshevsky-Fourier "crystal palace", to their "ant-hill".

Mochulsky, in his penetrating analysis of the *Notes from Underground*, devoted particular attention to two themes which have been discussed above: the "enigma of conscience" and the "critique of pure reason". Mochulsky's comments are worth considering. "Without conscience man is an animal. But conscience arises only from conflict with reality, from a break with the world."

> "So, exclusiveness and solitude are indispensable conditions to the existence and activity of human conscience; on the other hand, it is always bound to the whole of humanity, it is oecumenic [*soborno*]. In this painful contradiction lies the tragedy of human personality. This personality defends its own rights and at the same time it is constantly attracted by men and it realizes its dependence on them. Conscience opposes itself to the world—it is alone— everything is against it."

---

[1] Cf. Močul'skij, *op. cit.*, p. 207.

From this very conflict of which Dostoevsky's hero is aware originate his outbursts of ambition, vanity, suspicion, and mistrustfulness. This explains all the vile acts committed by the underground man, who perpetually enjoys the masochistic satisfaction of self-humiliation. Mochulsky comes to the conclusion that here "the ethical plan is replaced by the aesthetic plan", and he sees in this a genuine psychological discovery by Dostoevsky. "Debasement is painful, but a piercing consciousness of debasement can become a voluptuous pleasure."

This is the essence of the item "the enigma of conscience". The second item presents, as was mentioned, a "critique of pure reason" for the sake of free will, for the sake of full personal independence of the human personality. Dostoevsky's hero fights against rationalism, against the "philosophy of necessity", to the acceptance of which "pure reason" leads. Mathematics and science prove that man cannot oppose himself to the laws of nature. Dostoevsky's hero tries to crush "the impossible" of "pure reason" by the I-do-not-want, I-do-not-like-it of the human free will. The acceptance of scientific laws means to Dostoevsky's hero acceptance of death. Against the "two-times-two-makes-four" he brings his "two-times-two-makes-five". Mochulsky tries to compose apologetics for Dostoevsky's "personalism". He explains that Dostoevsky, in his fight with Chernyshevsky's "debasing" idea of "advantage", presents his conception of vile disadvantageous acts committed by the individual precisely in order to prove to himself his free will and his independence of "pure reason".[1]

One may accept the theory of irrational acts, disadvantageous acts, the aim of which would be the establishment of human independence. But why should one accept the assertion that vile and criminal acts should be the only ones which could grant that freedom?

There is no doubt that Dostoevsky could not accept Chernyshevsky's progressive optimism, nor could he have ever accepted Pascal's "bet", or so it seems to me. Chernyshevsky's "advantages" were humiliating to Dostoevsky and he could not find any guarantees of freedom in such a system. And, of course, Dostoevsky would have denied Pascal's "advantage" of the acceptance of the existence of God. In Dostoevsky's world freedom from rationalism is acquired either through crime or through absurdity. Dostoevsky carries this even further. His hero from the underground does not see any limits to the assertion not only of his free will but to his insolent egotism:

"I say, gentlemen, hadn't we better kick over the whole show and scatter rationalism to the winds, simply to send these logarithms

[1] Cf. Močul'skij, *op. cit.*, pp. 203–10.

to the devil, enabling us to live once more at our own sweet foolish will!..."[1] "Because I only like playing with words, only dreaming, but, do you know, what I really want is that you should all go to hell. That is what I want. I want peace; yes, I'd sell the whole world for a farthing, straight off, so long as I was left in peace. Is the world to go to pot, or am I to go without my tea? I say that the world may go to pot for me so long as I always get my tea."[2] "I believe in it, I answer for it, for the whole work of man really seems to consist in nothing but proving to himself every minute that he is a man and not a piano-key! It may be at the cost of his skin, it may be by cannibalism!"[3]

These quotations are eloquent enough, I believe.

But were the heroes of the *Notes from Underground* and of *Crime and Punishment* aware of Pushkin's assertion that "villainy and genius are incompatible"? This we cannot know. Dostoevsky certainly remembered it well, and if his heroes were not convinced of it, it was not their fault.

One may object that it is difficult to deduce all of these speculations from the relationship between Pushkin's stories and the *Notes* and *Crime and Punishment*. But one thing is clear: Dostoevsky was the one who substituted a solo for Pushkin's duet, sounding thereby a "terrible melody" torn from the tortured souls of his heroes. He was the one who used the human soul as a battleground for the struggle between instinct and intelligence. Where Pushkin had innocent, genuinely virtuous admiration for the man of action, who in his stylization was a free creature of God, Dostoevsky perversely assumed that the man of action is essentially a violator of human and divine laws. True, one may state in answer to this that Pushkin held dualistic views on Peter the Great and Catherine the Second and that his attitude toward Poland showed that he sometimes accepted the principle of violence and even crime. But this was so in his politics. Contrary to Mickiewicz, who demanded the "evangelization" of politics, Pushkin, as I once said, paraphrasing Mickiewicz, was in politics and history a "man of the Old Testament", and he, like the majority of people of his generation, admitted two moralities, one in private life and another in politics. This held as long as politics did not touch his own existence. It suffices to mention again his relations with Nicholas the First and his letters to his wife, in which he expressed his

---

[1] Cf. *Notes from Underground*, Part I, chapter 7.
[2] *Ibid.*, Part II, chapter 9.
[3] *Ibid.*, Part I, chapter 8.

indignation over the union of the gentleman and the spying monarch in the person of the Emperor.[1]

Pushkin's theme of juxtaposing two separate and contrasting human types, after passing through Dostoevsky's morbid psychological analysis, acquired quite a special moral significance. The human personality was tormented by an interior conflict: it was not the moral instinct and religious faith that revolted against the demands of an outraged intelligence, but the opposite—intelligence rebelled against morality and religion. To Mozart's assertion (which later tortured his murderer, Salieri) that villainy and genius are incompatible, Raskolnikov might have answered that weakness and genius are incompatible.

When one examines the long tortuous road which Dostoevsky's heroes followed, one may conclude that it was a road which began with Pushkin's Salieri, who "checked harmony by algebraic rules", and led to Mozart, "the frivolous idler", and that on that road in order to attain the organic unity of a Mozart the calculating, impotent intellectual had apparently to acquire the powers of the "stupid man of action". On this road we find a procession of men who strive to change their very nature. The procession commences with Golyadkin and Prokharchin, is interrupted by the Orlovs and Petrovs, and resumes with the hero from underground and Raskolnikov. It concludes with the Raw Youth and Stavrogin. It is a procession of usurpers, all of whom are defeated. All their efforts to reach their goals are vain. Among them, like terrible shades from hell, move Valkovsky, Svidrigaylov and Ivan Karamazov.

The concentration or coalescing of two separate personalities, representing two different outlooks, into one human being in Dostoevsky's characterizations—it is this that attracts the imagination and curiosity of the ambivalent man of our times. The best evidence of this attraction is to be found in Gide's famous book on Dostoevsky, and it would be difficult to deny that Gide is a typical figure in the moral crisis, which characterized pre-war western-European culture.[2]

Henri Massis, in his studies on Gide, expressed the opinion that Gide used Dostoevsky as a mask behind which he hid himself. I should like to bring a slight correction to this statement. Gide used Dostoevsky in order to express, with his help, his own moral ambivalence and perversity. And for this purpose he could not find a better mask.

---

[1] Concerning this point, see my works: *Pouchkine et la Pologne*; my study on *The Bronze Horseman, Jeździec Miedziany*, etc.; and the article "Panslavism", in *European Ideologies* (New York: Philosophical Library, 1948).

[2] See Régis Michaud, *Modern Thought and Literature in France* (New York and London, 1934).

"Dostoevsky's ideas are important to me, the more so that I make them my own."[1]

But, after all, this is purely a question of phraseology. I entirely agree with Massis's perspicacious and courageous critique of Gide's book. One of the most striking episodes in the ideological friendship of Gide with Dostoevsky is Gide's fascination with what he calls the simultaneousness of the existence of evil and good in man, revealed by Dostoevsky. Gide praised Baudelaire's aphorism: "There is in every man, at every hour, two simultaneous postulations—one toward God, the other toward Satan." Massis noted that Gide underlined the word *simultaneous*, and this is what Gide particularly cherishes in Stavrogin's avowal (Stavrogin's letter to Dasha):

"I am still capable, as I always was, of desiring to do something good, and of feeling pleasure from it; at the same time I desire evil and feel pleasure from that too."

And Massis justly points out that Gide is not struck by the inconsequence, by the dualism of all this, but precisely by the simultaneousness.[2]

In one of his attacks against Gide, Massis brought to the fore Claudel's statement, "*le mal ne compose pas*", and, to support his moralistic criticism of Gide, he quoted a letter of Claudel in which the great French poet explained his statement:

"There is nothing obscure or original in this formula . . . this is an application of the old Greek myth of *eros* and *eris*. Evil, following the classic definition, is the erection of a particular goal, let us say, the immediate good of the individual, to the dignity of a goal in itself. And this is at once an error, a stupidity, a sin and a disorder. . . ." (Further on in the letter, Claudel also brings a Christian confirmation to his formula.) "The great works of art are those in which the principle is so rich and so general that it serves to aggregate in one harmonious and significant ensemble the greatest number of beings. All of them lead ultimately to an impression of grandeur and serenity. Some other works, dramatic and moving, possess a beauty which precisely results from the lack and from the heart-rending need of that order and that love. And finally, there are those gloomy, sardonic works, or those filled with discouragement, which delight in evil and try in vain to find a principle of organization in it."[3]

[1] André Gide, *Dostoïevsky* (Paris: Plon, 1923), p. 78.
[2] Henri Massis, *D'André Gide à Marcel Proust* (Lyon: Lardanchet, 1948), p. 100.
[3] *Ibid.*, pp. 129–30.

Yes, Massis is right:

". . . if contradictory *postulations simultaneously* co-exist in the conscience, if they do not succeed each other in as short a time as could be imagined and do not yield their place to each other, we can neither oppose, choose, nor fight them; there is no more contradiction, identity, nor sufficient reason. The rules are shattered. 'Then everything is allowed', as Ivan Karamazov says."[1]

"This co-existence of the two contradictory postulations *en acte* is conceived in a purely affective and palpable order and it is, indeed, toward these irrational regions of the ego that Gide turns; his object—and in this he is in accord with Bergson—is to tear out what the latter calls the 'cleverly woven web of our conventional ego', to show us 'under this apparent logic a fundamental absurdity'."[2]

And let us not forget that Gide is enchanted to see that in Dostoevsky's novels "intelligence always plays a demoniac rôle".[3]

Desperately following the road of an irreducible individualism which determined his acceptance of the simultaneousness of evil and good in the human soul, Gide, after having tried to identify himself with everything, was unable to identify himself with anything and finally lost his own identity. The only identity which might be found in him is his identity with Dostoevsky.

Who knows, this might be a sign of greatness—if we assume that Dostoevsky's art gives the essence of human condition.

* * * * *

In order to avoid any accusations of partiality, I will present a few quotations from a brilliant article of a Russian writer, G. Adamovich, which recently appeared and which deals, as it happens, with Chaadaev, Dostoevsky, Gide, and Tolstoy. I became acquainted with this article when all my studies on Dostoevsky were completed.

"There is no writer who could have expressed better or given fuller feeling to the absence of right in the world and to the existence of pain, at times still too acute to be considered with the calm of Buddha—a natural phenomenon. . . . Right is a vague word: what is

[1] *Ibid.*, p. 101.
[2] *Ibid.*, p. 267.
[3] A. Gide, *Dostoïevsky*, p. 147.

right, 'what is truth', what is justice? But a precise definition does not exist. Something is not quite as it should be in life, partly through the fault of men, partly independently of them, and this means that no one is responsible."

Adamovich emphasizes in his article how terrible an impression a young man must get about the world from Dostoevsky's novels. However, this terrible impression is derived not from any separate reasoning of the writer, but "from the general terrible misfortune of the world as it is represented by him". Adamovich believes that this first "incomparable impression" given by Dostoevsky is "beneficial and unavoidable if the young man has an active soul. Yes, yes, this is unquestionable. . . ."

"But . . .
But the person who later on fails to realize that in Dostoevsky himself, in his visions and creations, something is not quite as it should be, that there is something deeply arbitrary in his basic creative representation, this person might also awaken doubts . . . not as to his moral responsitivity but rather as to his intellectual requirements, to his capacity to distinguish the essential from the accidental, the real from the imagined."

Adamovich believes that in the moral chaos which characterized the last decades of our century:

"Dostoevsky must have become the 'master of thoughts', and if not of thoughts, of souls. Sometimes people say that literature influences life and not life literature: absurd! Dostoevsky perhaps influenced the spiritual countenance of our contemporaries, but only because time itself prepared the ground for this. Revolutions and wars were not caused by him, but revolutions and wars shook minds and nerves, filled human souls with revulsion for the established mode of existence and created those types of intellectuals, the anarchic dreamers, the irritated and somehow inverted aestheticians innumerable in our days."

Adamovich believes:

"that Dostoevsky was responsible for many modern literary and artistic moods, for the ostentatious uncontrolled anxiety which gushed through the fissure which he opened, for the imprudence in basic points of view . . . and for the certitude that it is possible to imagine and depict whatever one wants, as the world anyhow every year becomes more and more like a madhouse."

"In short, he is responsible for the fundamental ruthlessness of themes and situations, for the mad, metaphysical 'everything is allowed', which having once broken loose cannot be easily and quickly brought under control. . . . Dostoevsky will pay, probably, for his present influence and fame by a long, and for some time probably exaggerated, eclipse. . . ."[1]

---

[1] Cf. G. Adamovič, "Kommentarii", in *Opyty*, New York, 1953, Vol. I, pp. 96–9.

V

Dostoevsky and Belinsky

THOSE who have read Dostoevsky's letters, the memoirs of Dostoevsky's contemporaries like Annenkov or Grigorovich, or at least the books of Levinson, Grossman or Mochulsky, know the vicissitudes through which Dostoevsky's relations with Belinsky passed. Belinsky was the one who, after having read *Poor Folk* at Nekrasov's behest, sanctified Dostoevsky's genius by telling the author at the very beginning of his literary career that he "would become a great writer". Actually he confirmed Nekrasov's opinion that Dostoevsky was "a second Gogol". Naturally enough, Belinksy immediately became an object of adulation for Dostoevsky. This honeymoon did not last long. Belinsky's critical remarks about *The Double, Mister Prokharchin* and *The Landlady* did not please their author. Dostoevsky, after the extraordinary success of *Poor Folk*, felt offended by this criticism. In speaking about *The Double*, Belinsky admitted the mastery of its author and even saw some sparks of talent in *Mister Prokharchin*, despite the "terrible boredom" of the former and the "thick darkness" of the latter, which "hides from the reader its occasional bright sparks". *The Landlady* was, according to the critic, a kind of literary "monstrosity". In his private remarks Belinsky was even more outspoken. He wrote to Annenkov that

"this *Landlady* is terrible rubbish . . . in it he (Dostoevsky) attempted to reconcile Marlinsky with Hoffmann, having thickened the mixture with Gogol. We were duped by Dostoevsky the genius. I myself, the first of his critics, acted like an ignorant lout. Look: I have just read Rousseau's *Confessions*, and through this work I was seized by the greatest repugnance for this gentleman as he is so similar to Dostoevsky, who is profoundly convinced that the whole human race envies and persecutes him. Rousseau's life was vile and immoral!"[1]

[1] Cf. André Levinson, *La Vie pathétique de Dostoïevsky* (Paris, 1935), pp. 113-14.

Belinsky's critical verdicts were again decisive: Dostoevsky faced complete disaster. Needless to say, Dostoevsky was deeply affected by these judgments, especially as the whole crowd of *The Contemporary*—Nekrasov, the Panaevs, Turgenev, Annenkov and others—assumed a similar attitude. Such was the situation before Dostoevsky's exile to Siberia. In his official deposition of 1849, during the investigation of the Petrashevtsy, Dostoevsky explained his "quarrel" and his "break" with Belinsky by a difference of "ideas on literature and its goals".[1] No doubt this explanation was not entirely true—personal resentment cannot be underestimated. I do not agree with Grossman's opinion that the main cause for this break is to be found in the sphere of Dostoevsky's and Belinsky's religious outlooks.[2] Grossman alludes to the letters in which Dostoevsky attacks Belinsky for his anti-Christian tendencies. He quotes a letter to Strakhov in which Dostoevsky writes that "This man obscenely abused Christ in my presence . . ."[3] However, these testimonies belong to a much later period. The letter to Strakhov which Grossman quotes was written in 1871. We know that in the second part of his life Dostoevsky's former admiration for Belinsky changed into violent hatred, which certainly affected Dostoevsky's retrospective judgments concerning the Russian critic. The epithets which he uses in his letters whenever he mentions Belinsky are an eloquent proof of Dostoevsky's feelings; I would say that these outsized epithets degrade Dostoevsky much more than they did Belinsky.

Dostoevsky's hatred for the Russian critic found still another expression; one may believe Levinson and Grossman, who state that in the figure of Foma Opiskin (*Selo Stepanchikovo*, written in Siberia during Dostoevsky's exile), Dostoevsky created a parodistic portrait of Belinsky.[4]

---

[1] Cf. L. Grossman, *Put' Dostoevskogo* (Moscow, 1928), p. 63.
[2] Cf., *ibid.*, pp. 63–4.
[3] Cf. F. M. Dostoevskij, *Pis'ma*, Vol. II, p. 364; and Grossman, *op. cit.*, p. 64.
[4] Yu. N. Tynyanov, in his book *Arkhaisty i Novatory* (Leningrad, 1929), revealed the obvious ties between the speeches of Foma Opiskin and Gogol's *Selected Passages from a Correspondence with Friends* and came to the conclusion that Dostoevsky, in his figure of Opiskin, parodized Gogol. André Levinson, in his book *La Vie pathétique de Dostoïevsky* (Paris, 1935), launched a supposition that Dostoevsky had in mind not Gogol, but Belinsky. L. P. Grossman in his critical edition of *Selo Stepančikovo i ego obyvateli* (Moscow, 1935), strongly supported Levinson's suggestion, developed it and justified it with biographical facts and texts taken from Dostoevsky's letters. S. Mackiewicz, in his book *Dostoevsky* (London, 1947), independently from Levinson and Grossman, whom Mackiewicz had not read, came to the same conclusions. (Cf. also my article "Błok w Warszawie, Tajemniczy Polonofil i Prototyp Opiskina" —*Wiadomości*, Vol. VI, Nos. 35/36, 283/284, 9 September, 1951, London, p. 6.) Even before I became acquainted with Tynyanov's work, the ties between Opiskin and Gogol were obvious to me; but Grossman's arguments convinced me. However, I myself would try to reach a compromise. *Selo Stepanchikovo* was written while Dostoevsky was still in Siberia. As I mentioned above it might be easily supposed that Dostoevsky could have felt bitter not only toward Belinsky, but also toward

In the meantime there took place Dostoevsky's fatal reading at the Petrashevtsy meeting on 15 April, 1849, of Belinsky's famous "Letter to Gogol". This letter dealt with Gogol's *Selected Passages from a Correspondence with Friends*. The main accusation against Dostoevsky during the trial of the Petrashevtsy circle was concerned with his reading of Belinsky's "Letter". It would be easy to assume that Dostoevsky could have nurtured additional resentment against Belinsky as against the one who indirectly had caused his imprisonment and exile. Besides, as I stressed in the section on the *Notes from Underground*, Dostoevsky, during his Siberian period, went through an ideological crisis ending with an apostasy from his former faith and beliefs. His later violent attacks against Belinsky might be considered as proof and illustration of this ideological change in Dostoevsky's mind. This change resulted in Dostoevsky's politically reactionary views and in his propaganda of Russian nationalism, imperialism and orthodoxy. The letter to Strakhov which we have mentioned belongs to that very period.

Gogol's book *Selected Passages from a Correspondence with Friends*, as soon as it appeared, provoked general consternation not only among the circles of Russian Westerners, but even among Gogol's friends—the Slavophils. This book, written in a dogmatic, didactic and sermonizing style, is a kind of apology of the patriarchal conditions of contemporary Russian life and a rejection of any necessity for reform and foreign influences. It is an indirect defense of the institution of serfdom and of landlord privileges, and it eulogizes the existing political order in Russia based on autocracy. Gogol's sentimental admiration of Russian patriarchal country life in the empire of Nicholas I coloured all of his social, political and religious conceptions. The state is an estate, the head of which creates good, as does the head of the state, for both are instituted by God; this picture reflects a similar picture of heaven—also an estate with God as lord and master. The régime of Nicholas, so greatly admired by Gogol, is considered by him not as a temporary, transitory régime, but as an ideal one, whose example should be and eventually will be followed by Europe.[1]

Gogol, a bitterness directed against those whose combined efforts had brought him to the galley. And yet, Grossman is right, for nowhere do we find in Dostoevsky's writings any attacks against Gogol. On the contrary, his admiration for Gogol remained unshaken, whereas his hatred toward Belinsky, as I mentioned above, found its sharpest insinuative expression in Dostoevsky's correspondence. Besides, the present study shows the conformity of Dostoevsky's views with Gogol's outlook, expressed in his *Selected Passages*. But this does not change the fact that Dostoevsky used Gogol's phraseology in his portrayal of Foma Opiskin.

[1] Cf. N. Korobka, "N. V. Gogol", in *Istorija Russkoj Literatury XIX veka*, pod red. D. N. Ovsjaniko-Kulikovskago (Moscow, 1911), Vol. II, p. 327.

"A state without an all-powerful monarch is an automaton; it would be a great achievement if such a state would reach the level of the United States. And what is the United States? Carrion. Man in the United States is washed out to such a degree that he is not worth a straw. A state without an all-powerful monarch is just like an orchestra without a conductor. . . ."[1]

In the Russian Czar and autocracy Gogol saw an ideal on the highest level of political life; the general government, on a lower level, is another ideal which western Europe is very far from achieving. Western Europe, in Gogol's opinion, suffers because of numerous civil laws which invade foreign spheres like mores and the Church.

"In other words," writes Gogol, "the more one looks into the organism of the provincial administration the more one is amazed by the wisdom of its founders: one feels that God Himself was the invisible builder, using the hands of the monarchs. Everything is fullness and sufficiency; everything is just so arranged as to assist in good deeds. . . ."[2]

Gogol is no less apologetic when he speaks about the Russian Church and clergy:

"This church, which, like a vestal virgin, has remained the only one since the times of the apostles in its original immaculate purity, this church, which, with all its deep dogma and a minimum of exterior rights, as though taken directly from heaven for the Russian people, this church, which is alone able to settle all our doubts and problems, which is able to create an unheard of miracle in the face of all Europe . . . this church is unknown to us. . . ."

After this follows a passage in which Gogol describes the desperate condition of the Catholic Church.[3]

Parenthetically I may remark that Gogol himself could not but admit the fact that the Russian clergy was not granted the same social respect which the clergy enjoyed in countries of Catholic or Protestant traditions.[4] In the chapter on the Russian landlord, which is one of

[1] Cf. *Selected Passages from a Correspondence with Friends*, chapter 10.
[2] Cf. *Selected Passages from a Correspondence with Friends*, chapter 28.
[3] Cf. *ibid.*, chapter 19.
[4] Compare Pushkin's remarks about the Russian clergy in his letter to Chaadaev which I mentioned above. (Cf. the study *Russia and the West*; and see the draft of additional remarks of Pushkin to this letter: "Quant au clergé, il est en dehors de la société, puisqu'il est barbu. Nos souverains ont trouvé commode de le laisser là, où

the most curious in the book, Gogol feels the necessity to take the Russian priest under his protection:

> "If the priest is bad, the landlords themselves are to blame; they, instead of offering the priest the hospitality of their homes as a member of the family, to nourish in him the desire for conversations of a higher order which could educate him, abandon the young, inexperienced priest among the peasants, when he does not even know what a peasant is; the peasants put him in such a position that he is obliged to connive and to please them, instead of having from the very beginning a certain power over them. People cry that they have bad priests, that these priests have acquired peasant manners and that they are no different from the simple peasants. . . . And now this is what you should do. Arrange to have the priest dine with you every day. Read religious books with him. . . . Now the most important,—take the priest everywhere with you, wherever you are overseeing the work, so that in the beginning he would be with you in the capacity of an aide, and so that he would personally see all your affairs with the peasants. Here he will clearly learn what a landlord is and what a peasant is, and what their interrelations should be. And in the meanwhile the peasants will have

---

ils l'ont trouvé. Il n'est pas de la bonne société et ne veut pas être peuple. Comme les eunuques il n'a de passion que pour le pouvoir. . . . La religion est étrangère à nos pensées, à nos habitudes . . . mais il ne fallait pas le dire. . . ." (Cf. *Sočinenija Puškina*, izd. Imp. Ak. nauk; *Perepiska* (St. Petersburg, 1911); Vol. III, p. 389.)

A good example of how Russian landlords treated their priests is also provided by Turgenev in his story "Two Landed Proprietors" (in *Memoirs of a Sportsman*). Turgenev's "kind" landlord, Mardary Apollonych Stegunov, with his insidious and contemptuous hospitality, persecutes a young priest and obliges him against his will to drink vodka, saying, "What nonsense! How is it possible in your calling not to drink!" (Isabelle Hapgood omitted this last phrase in her translation, as she often does whenever she finds some passages difficult or undesirable.)

Cf. also the following remarks of Herzen: "Where does one see the good influence of the Eastern Church? Where is the nation, among those which have accepted its dogma, that it has civilized or emancipated since the fourth century up to the present time? Is it Armenia, Georgia, the tribes of Asia Minor, the poor inhabitants of Trebisond? Finally, is it Morea? We may be told that the Church could not do anything with these nations, spoiled, perverted, nations without a future. But the Slavs—a race healthy in body and soul—what did they gain? The Eastern Church penetrated Russia in the flowering, bright Kievan Period, at the time of the Grand Duke Vladimir. It brought Russia to the sorrowful and odious (*gnusny*) time described by Kotoshikhin, it blessed and sanctioned all measures taken against the freedom of the people. It taught the czars Byzantine despotism; it prescribed blind obedience under the yoke of slavery. Peter the Great paralyzed the influence of the clergy; this was one of his greatest deeds, and then, they would like now to restore this influence?" This text belongs to the article "Muscovite Panslavism and Russian Europeanism", which appeared for the first time in German in 1851.

See A. I. Gercen, *Izbrannye filosofskie proizvedenija* (Moscow: Ogiz, 1946), Vol. I, pp. 323-4.

more respect for the priest when they see that he is arm in arm with you."[1]

Despite these reservations, Gogol's general conclusion is "Thank God first of all that you are a Russian." He has no doubts that the Russian conditions of life are the best. "How can we put everything in its right place?" asks Gogol in another passage.

> "In Europe it is impossible to do this: she will shed blood in vain battles and will achieve no success. In Russia the possibility exists: here this can be worked out insensibly—not by any innovations, upheavals and reforms, and even not through conferences, committees, discussions, and not by journalistic talks and chatter. In Russia the initiative may be given by any general governor ... and how simple!—by nothing else than his own example, by the patriarchal tone of his life. . . ."[2]

Belinsky reacted to this amazing book in an article which he published in 1847 in *The Contemporary*. He did not spare Gogol in his article, and gave numerous edifying quotations from Gogol's book.

On the 20 June, 1847, Gogol sent a letter to Belinsky in which he expressed the pain Belinsky's article had caused him. Belinsky was at this time ill, and was staying with Annenkov in Salzbrunn where he was undergoing medical treatment.

> "When I started to read Gogol's letter to Belinsky," writes Annenkov in his memoirs, "he listened to it completely apathetically and distractedly, but having himself run through the lines addressed to him, Belinsky suddenly started and murmured:—'Ah, he does not understand why people are angry at him,—it is necessary to explain it to him.' "[3]

This explanation was Belinsky's famous "Letter to Gogol".

Grossman, in his book *The Road of Dostoevsky*, points out that Dostoevsky's meeting with Belinsky left a deep trace in the consciousness of the great Russian writer. Grossman maintains that in "The Legend of the Grand Inquisitor" Dostoevsky put in the mouth of his "fantastic hero" Belinsky's philosophical arguments which he had

---
[1] Cf. *Selected Passages*, chapter 22.
[2] Cf. *Selected Passages*, chapter 28.
[3] Cf. V. Veresaev, *Gogol' v žizni* (Moscow-Leningrad: Academia, 1933), p. 362.

heard from the critic during their discussions about Christ. And Grossman on one page cites some few quotations from the "Legend" which are intended to show this dependence of Dostoevsky on Belinsky.[1] Quite independently from Grossman, I myself came to the conclusion that "The Legend of the Grand Inquisitor" had some ties with Belinsky; however, not with those discussions about Christ, mentioned by Grossman, but with Belinsky's "Letter to Gogol" and its vehement criticism of the Orthodox Church and the Russian clergy. Of course, I cannot quote Belinsky's marvellous text in its entirety, but, inasmuch as its English translation has only recently appeared and is not well known in this country, I feel it necessary to give rather extensive quotations, which, however, I shall confine only to the items connected, in my opinion, with the "Legend".

Let us quote in full the most important passages for our purposes out of Belinsky's "Letter to Gogol", and then analyze them in more detail in regard to "The Legend of the Grand Inquisitor".

> "And you would expect me not to become indignant? . . . Why, if you had made an attempt on my life I could not have hated you more than I do for these disgraceful lines. . . . And after this, you expect people to believe the sincerity of your books' intent! No! Had you really been inspired by the truth of Christ and not by the teaching of the Devil you would certainly have written something entirely different in your new book. . . . Proponent of the knout, apostle of ignorance, champion of obscurantism and Stygian Darkness, panegyrist of Tartar morals—what are you about! Look beneath your feet—you are standing on the brink of an abyss! . . . That you base such teaching on the Orthodox Church I can understand: it has always served as the prop of the knout and the servant of despotism; but why have you mixed Christ up in this? What have you found in common between Him and any church, least of all the Orthodox Church? He was the first to bring to people the teaching of freedom, equality and brotherhood and set the seal of truth to that teaching by martyrdom. And this teaching was men's *Salvation* only until it became organized in the church and took the principle of Orthodoxy for its foundation. The church, on the other hand, was a hierarchy, consequently a champion of inequality, a flatterer of authority, an enemy and persecutor of brotherhood among men—and so it has remained until this day. But the meaning of Christ's message has been revealed by the philosophical movement of the preceding century. And that is why a man like Voltaire, who stamped out the fires of fanaticism and ignorance in Europe by

[1] Cf. Grossman, *op. cit.*, p. 65.

ridicule, is, of course, more the son of Christ, flesh of His flesh and bone of His bone, than all your priests, bishops, metropolitans, and patriarchs! Do you mean to say you do not know it! It is not even a novelty now to a schoolboy.... Hence, can it be that you, the author of *The Inspector General* and *Dead Souls*, have in all sincerity, from the bottom of your heart, sung a hymn to the nefarious Russian clergy, which you rank immeasurably higher than the Catholic clergy? Let us assume that you do not know that the latter had once been something, while the former had never been anything but a servant and slave of the secular powers; but do you really mean to say you do not know that our clergy is held in universal contempt by Russian society and the Russian people? Of whom do the Russian people relate obscene stories? Of the priest, the priest's wife, the priest's daughter and the priest's farmhand. Does not the priest in Russia represent for all Russians the embodiment of gluttony, avarice, servility and shamelessness? Do you mean to say you do not know all this? Strange! According to you the Russian people is the most religious in the world. That is a lie! The basis of religiousness is pietism, reverence, fear of God. Whereas the Russian man utters the name of the Lord while scratching himself somewhere. He says of the ikon: *If it isn't good for praying it's good for covering the pots.*

Take a closer look and you will see that it is by nature a profoundly atheistic people. It still retains a good deal of superstition, but not a trace of religiousness. Superstitition passes with the advances of civilization but religiousness often keeps company with them, too; we have a living example of this in France, where even today there are many sincere Catholics among enlightened and educated men, and where many people who have rejected Christianity still cling stubbornly to some sort of god. The Russian people is different; mystic exultation is not in its nature; it has too much common sense, a too lucid and positive mind, and therein, perhaps, lies the vast scope of its historic destinies of the future. Religiousness with it has not even taken root among the clergy, since a few isolated and exclusive personalities distinguished for such cold ascetic reflectiveness prove nothing. But the majority of our clergy has always been distinguished for their fat bellies, scholastic pedantry and savage ignorance. It is a shame to accuse it of religious intolerance and fanaticism; rather could it be praised for an exemplary indifference in matters of faith. Religiousness with us appeared only among the Schismatic sects who formed such a contrast in spirit to the mass of the people and were so insignificant before it numerically.

Belinsky in the thirties
Portrait by K. A. Gorbunov (1871)

... I would remark but this: when a European, especially a Catholic, is seized with a religious ardour he becomes a denouncer of iniquitous authority, similar to the Hebrew prophets who denounced the iniquities of the great ones of the earth. With us, on the contrary: no sooner is a person (even a respectable person) afflicted with the malady which is known to psychiatrists as *religiosa mania* than he begins to burn more incense to the earthly god than the heavenly one, and so overshoots the mark in doing so that the former would fain reward him for his slavish zeal did he not perceive that he would thereby be compromising himself in society's eyes. . . . What a rogue our fellow the Russian is. . . .

Another thing I remember you saying in your book, claiming it to be a great and incontrovertible truth: that literacy is not merely useless but positively harmful to the common people. What can I say to this? May your Byzantine God forgive you that Byzantine thought, unless, in committing it to paper, you knew not what you were saying. . . ."

Then, as if in answer to Gogol's assertion that, assuming that he had erred, his errors were sincere, Belinsky compares Gogol's works to the efforts of a current literary circle with tendencies similar to those of Gogol. He makes the reservation, however, that the works of this circle "have rendered full meed to the Byzantine God and left nothing for Satan, whereas you, wanting to light a taper to each of them, have fallen into contradiction. . . ."[1]

I think that the relationship between these pages and Dostoevsky's "Legend" is obvious. Belinsky's thought expressed in the following words,

"... That you base such teaching on the Orthodox Church I can understand: it has always served as the prop of the knout and the servant of despotism; but why have you mixed Christ up in this? What have you found in common between Him and any church, least of all the Orthodox Church? . . ."

became practically the main theme of the "Legend": the abyss between Christ and Church. True, Dostoevsky could have known various western-European poems written on the motif of the Returning Christ, a motif which I myself tied with the "Legend" in my

[1] Cf. V. G. Belinsky, *Selected Philosophical Works* (Moscow: Foreign Language Publishing House, 1948), pp. 505-8.

study "Christ et la Révolution dans la poésie russe et polonaise".[1] But I believe that it was Belinsky who stimulated Dostoevsky. There is no doubt that Dostoevsky the author of *The Brothers Karamazov* was bound to feel particularly offended for the Orthodox Church. With his usual adroitness he twisted Belinsky's arguments, attacking the Orthodox Church and comparing it unfavorably with the Catholic, into an aggression against the Catholic Church—and so, in his "Legend", he opposed Christ not to the Orthodox Church, but to the Catholic. Belinsky's second assertion is not less important:

"... He (Christ) was the first to bring to people the teaching of freedom, equality and brotherhood and set the seal of truth to that teaching by martyrdom. And this teaching was men's *Salvation* only until it became organized in the church and took the principle of Orthodoxy for its foundation. The church, on the other hand, was a hierarchy, consequently a champion of inequality, a flatterer of authority, an enemy and persecutor of brotherhood among men—and so it has remained until this day. ..."

This item has again been developed in the "Legend" as an accusation directed against the Catholic Church. Authority and hierarchy became the first two principles of the Catholic Church in Dostoevsky's interpretation of Catholicism. Belinsky's declaration that the Catholic clergy was much superior to the Russian clergy could only enrage Dostoevsky. Belinsky's emphasis on the rôle of superstition in Russian quasi-religious life found an answer in Dostoevsky's third organizational principle of the Catholic Church: miracle. Belinsky's sarcastic remarks about the lack of respect for the priest among the Russian people, and his statement that the Russian people were the least religious in the world, have been answered not in the "Legend" but in the chapters dealing with Zossima, with the institution of the *startsy* and the Russian monasteries. How inconsistent and fraudulent Dostoevsky is! The abuse of authority and power is supposed to be the main sin of the Catholic Church, but what do we find in the chapter about the *startsy*?

"An elder (*starets*) was one who took your soul, your will, into his soul and his will. When you choose an elder, you renounce your own will and yield it to him in complete submission, complete self-abnegation. This novitiate, this terrible school of abnegation, is

[1] Cf. *Mélanges, en l'honneur de Jules Legras,* Travaux publiés par L'Institut d'Études Slaves (Paris, 1938), Vol. XVII.

undertaken voluntarily, in the hope of self-conquest, of self-mastery, in order, after a life of obedience, to attain perfect freedom, that is, from self; to escape the lot of those who have lived their whole life without finding their true selves in themselves. This institution of elders is not founded on theory, but was established in the East from the practice of a thousand years. . . . In this way the elders are endowed in certain cases with unbounded and inexplicable authority. . . ."

In other words the Catholic Church acts through usurpation, while the Orthodox *starets* is selected through free will. And who obliges the Catholic faithful to join monasteries and holy orders? This is what Dostoevsky passes over in silence. The miracle is another "fraud" of the Catholic Church. But Alesha had the right to believe in the story of the coffin which was cast forth from the church. Dostoevsky emphasizes that:

". . . The question for our monastery was an important one, for it had not been distinguished by anything in particular till then: they had neither relics of saints, nor wonder-working ikons, . . ."

But this implies something which of course everyone knows: the existence of those relics and miraculous ikons in *other* Russian monasteries and certainly in churches. As if answering Belinsky's refutation concerning the lack of religiosity among the Russian people, the *starets* Zossima preaches:

". . . The salvation of Russia comes from the people. And the Russian monk has always been on the side of the people. We are isolated only if the people are isolated. The people believe as we do, and an unbelieving reformer will never do anything in Russia, even if he is sincere in heart and a genius. Remember that! The people will meet the atheist and overcome him, and Russia will be one and Orthodox. Take care of the peasant and guard his heart. Go on educating him quietly. That's your duty as monks, for the peasant has God in his heart."[1]

Whether Dostoevsky or Belinsky was right is not important here. I have only wished to show that Belinsky's passionate "Letter", which indirectly sent his former friend to Siberia, where Dostoevsky's ideas

[1] Cf. Fyodor Dostoevsky: *The Brothers Karamazov*, Garnett translation, Modern Library edition, pp. 27, 28, 377.

underwent a pathetic change, became a source of inspiration for Dostoevsky's dogmatic Orthodox anger.[1]

* * * * *

Whenever I think about Dostoevsky's "melancholic" Grand Inquisitor I see him together with the words *miracle, mystery, authority* in his mouth, and with bread in his hand. And I remember his last words to Christ: "For if anyone has ever deserved our fires, it is Thou. Tomorrow I will burn Thee...." Involuntarily another image rises in my memory. The third chapter of Słowacki's *Anhelli* (1838) contains the following lines:

"And when they had gone a little way they beheld a camp all of little children and striplings who had been driven to Siberia and they were resting by a fire.

And in the center of the throng on a Tartar horse sat a Russian priest, who had at his saddle two baskets of bread.

And he began to instruct those children according to the new Russian faith and according to the new catechism.

And he questioned the children on unworthy matters, and the striplings answered him, striving to please, for he had at his saddle baskets of bread and could feed them; and they were hungry.

Then, turning to Anhelli, the Shaman said: 'Tell me, hath not

[1] After I had written the present study (in the spring of 1951), Professor G. P. Struve attracted my attention to the article of A. Rammelmeyer, "Dostojevskijs Begegnung mit Belinskij (Zur Deutung der Gedankenwelt Ivan Karamazovs)", which appeared in *Zeitschrift für Slavische Philologie*, Band XXI. Heft I (Heidelberg, 1951), pp. 1–21. (The second part has not yet appeared.) Whether Mr. Rammelmeyer will utilize in his study Belinsky's letter to Gogol, I do not know. I wish to state that my comparative analysis of Dostoevsky's and Belinsky's texts is completely independent of this publication. Professor Struve also attracted my attention to a passage in Belinsky's letter to Botkin of 8 September, 1841, from which I quoted some other passages above in my study on Chaadaev. The passage which Professor Struve had in mind contains, indeed, striking, even in phraseology, similarities with Ivan's "rebellion". We do not know whether Dostoevsky had any knowledge of this letter, but the resemblances are certainly apparent. "What is it to me that life in general goes on, while the individual suffers? What is it to me that genius on earth lives in Heaven, while the populace grovels in the dirt? What is it to me that I understand the idea, that the world of ideas is open to me in art, in religion, in history, when I cannot share all this with those who should be my brothers in humanity and my fellow-men in Christ, but who are strangers and enemies to me through their ignorance? What is it to me that for the chosen there is blessedness, while the majority doesn't even suspect its possibility? Away, then, with blessedness if it is available to me alone among thousands! I do not want it if I cannot share it with my lesser brothers!... (See V. G. Belinskij, *Izbrannye sočinenija* (Moscow, Ogiz, 1947), p. 647). No less important is another letter of Belinsky to Botkin, dealing with Mickiewicz, which I quote below —see p. 343.

Słowacki in the late thirties
From a lithograph by Sommer based on a contemporary portrait of unknown authorship

this priest gone beyond bounds in sowing evil seed and in staining the purity of soul in these little ones?

'Lo, already they have forgotten to weep for their mothers, and here they fawn upon him for the sake of bread, like young whelps; they bark out evil things and those that are contrary to the faith;

'Saying that the czar is the head of the faith and that in him is God, and that he can counsel nothing contrary to the Holy Spirit, even when he commandeth things which are like crimes, for in him is the Holy Spirit.

'Therefore will I use against this priest fire from heaven to burn him up, and I will destroy him before the eyes of the children.'

As soon as the Shaman had pronounced the word of his malediction, that priest caught fire upon his horse and from his breast came flames which joined together in the air above his head."[1]

This is a good answer, *avant la lettre*, to Dostoevsky, as well as an excellent commentary to Belinsky's "Letter to Gogol". Słowacki symbolically presented the results of the subjugation of the Russian Church to the State. By implication he showed the flagrant contradiction which existed between the Russian "propaganda of faith", which served the needs of the State, and any Christian concept of religious freedom. Słowacki's Russian priest is indeed a perfect pendant to Dostoevsky's Grand Inquisitor.

---

[1] Cf. Juljusz Słowacki, *Anhelli*, translated from the Polish by D. P. Radin (London: Allen & Unwin, Ltd., 1930), pp. 30–1. *Anhelli* first appeared in Paris in 1838.

VI

Dostoevsky and Poland

1. DOSTOEVSKY AND THE POLES IN SIBERIA

THE arsenal used by Dostoevsky for the characterization of his figures and for the description of their behaviour is well known: venomous allusions, incriminations, gossip, blackmail—often *pathetic* "crocodile tears", artificial poses and gestures, paralogisms, hypocrisy, ideological surprises—"leaps and bounds", spiteful "small words", "half words", furious diminutives, "naïve" irony, hysterical outbursts, scandals, etc., etc. But there are some passages which escape the average reader of Dostoevsky. There are "small words", "slight insinuations", which Dostoevsky employs—let us say—*pro domo sua*. The function of these allusions is a speculative one: he intends them for himself, he enjoys in solitude the pleasure which they convey. They are so covert, so hidden, that the admiring reader is not able to recognize them. Thus he secretly unloads his hatred and experiences a clandestine happiness.

It is known that Dostoevsky hated the Poles. This hatred for Poland and the Poles was so vehement that it might be called pathological. In Poland and in the Polish character he singled out only the negative elements, forming from these shortcomings the notorious types of his "Polyachishki". The defects noticed by Dostoevsky were possibly true to the type of a Pole traditional in Russian literature, but their gigantic exaggeration was nothing but a fantastic falsehood. We are reminded of Stevenson's novel in which the secret elixir drowned all that was good in Dr. Jekyll, wherepon there appeared Mr. Hyde, a monstrous criminal. The Poles of Dostoevsky seem to have drunk this elixir. They are, as J. Stempowski said, in his study "Poles of Dostoevsky",[1] "specific psychological and moral constructions appearing under the names of Poles". They represent a combination of a feeling of honour and dignity, of patriotic sentiment and of formal affection for ceremonious aspects

---

[1] Cf. *Z piśmiennictwa rosyjskiego i ukraińskiego* pod red. dra Wacława Lednickiego (Cracow: Polskie Towarzystwo dla badań Europy wschodniej i Bliskiego Wschodu, 1934).

of life, mystical faith in their own value and importance, coupled with the shrewdness of gangsters, lack of scruples and of every real sense of honour. They are hypocritical, like *Tartuffe*, and at the same time *fanfarons*. Duality is the chief feature of their souls. Scandal is always the climate in which the essence of their personality appears, and in the light of scandal the truth of the personality is terrible, deeply repulsive.

His Poles are characterized by one more and very peculiar trait: there is no hope of salvation for them—they are firmly stabilized in their ignominy. Dostoevsky's method of procedure toward them is always the same—they are always found out. Full of high dignity and pride when they come on the stage, they are quickly unmasked, presented as liars, monsters, impostors, tricksters, thieves. Irrevocably, when the masks are taken off, they appear as "false counts" (*The Idiot*) or sharpers with marked cards and stolen money in their pockets (*The Brothers Karamazov*, *The Gambler*). That procedure of unmasking false dignity is very characteristic in the attitude of Dostoevsky toward Poles. There is only one group of Poles in his works whom Dostoevsky does not plunge into that phantastic moral degradation—his fellow convicts in Siberia, in *The House of the Dead*. But even in that case he could not sympathetically understand the essence of the unconsolable, constantly tortured dignity of those distinguished Poles. He quoted with a sort of sorrow the confession of one of them about the relations he had with the criminals in the galley: *Je hais ces brigands*.[1] And here is a striking fact. Dostoevsky gives, anyway he tries to give, an objective characterization of these Poles, who belonged to the nobility and had been put in the galley for their political patriotic activities:

> "There were several men belonging to the upper classes in the prison. To begin with there were five or six Poles. The convicts particularly disliked the Poles, even more than those who had been Russian gentlemen. The Poles (I am speaking only of the political prisoners) were elaborately, offensively polite and exceedingly uncommunicative with them. They never could conceal from the convicts their aversion for them, and the latter saw it very clearly and paid the Poles back in the same coin."[2]

In the fourth chapter Dostoevsky mentioned the Poles on another occasion:

> "Besides the Circassians there was a group of Poles in our room and they made a family apart, and had hardly anything to do with

[1] *The House of the Dead*, translated by Constance Garnett (New York, 1923), p. 264.
[2] *Ibid.*, p. 26.

the other convicts. I have mentioned already that their exclusiveness and their hatred of the Russian prisoners made them hated by everyone. They were men worn out with sufferings, depressed; there were six of them. Some of them were educated men. . . . During my later years in prison I used sometimes to get books from them. The first book I read made a great, strange and peculiar impression upon me. I will speak of these impressions more particularly later; they were most interesting to me, and I am sure that to many people they would be utterly unintelligible. Some things one cannot judge without experience. One thing I can say, that moral privation is harder to bear than any physical agonies. When a peasant goes to prison he finds there the company of his equals, perhaps even of his superiors. He has lost a great deal, of course—home, family, everything—but his environment is the same. The educated man condemned to the same punishment often loses infinitely more. He must overcome all his cravings, all his habits, live under conditions that are insufficient for him; must learn to breathe a different air. . . . He is a fish out of water . . . and often a punishment that is supposed to be equal in law is ten times as cruel for him. This is the truth, even if we consider only the material habits which have to be sacrificed."[1]

A little farther, Dostoevsky adds, as if *en passant*, a new trait which he will develop in another passage and which is quite significant:

"But the Poles formed a group apart. There were six of them and they kept together. The only other person they liked in our room was a Jew [Dostoevsky of course uses the derogatory term *zhid*] and him they liked simply because he amused them."[2]

In the eighth chapter of Part Two, *Comrades*, he says:

"Besides these three Russians there were eight others, Polish prisoners, of the upper class in the prison while I was there. Some of them I got to know pretty well and was glad of their friendship, but not all. The best of them were morbid, exclusive and intolerant to the last degree. In the end I gave up talking altogether with two of them. Only three of them were well educated."[3]

[1] Cf. *The House of the Dead*, chapter IV. I was obliged to correct Garnett's translation, as it is inadequate in parts.
[2] Cf. *The House of the Dead*, loc. cit.
[3] *Loc. cit.*, again with some corrections of Garnett's texts.

In the following passage Dostoevsky describes the good-natured tempers and the education of these people, the wonderful power of self-control, adding of M., whom he knew better than some others, that "this very excess of self-control was what I did not like; one somehow felt that he would never open his heart to anyone". He describes B. as "a very kind-hearted and even great-hearted man". He confesses that he "never ceased to love him". He tries to comprehend them:

". . . They were all morally sick, embittered, irritable and mistrustful. It was easy to understand, it was very hard for them, much worse than for us. They were far from their own country. Some of them were exiled for long periods, ten or twelve years, and what was worse, they regarded everyone around them with intense prejudice, saw in the convicts nothing but their brutality, could not discern any good quality, anything human in them, and had indeed no wish to do so. And, what was very easy to understand also, they were led to this unfortunate point of view by the force of circumstance, by fate."[1]

They did not regard "everyone around them with intense prejudice". And Dostoevsky has to admit this himself in the next line:

"To the Circassians, to the Tartars and to Isay Fomich (a Jew) they were cordial and friendly, but shunned the other convicts with abhorrence. Only the Starodubovsky, the Old Believer, won their entire respect."[2]

Dostoevsky has mentioned in a previous passage that the convicts hated the Poles. But in the same passage he says:

"It is remarkable, however, that all the while I was in prison none of the convicts ever taunted them with their nationality and religion or their ideas, as Russian peasants sometimes, though very rarely, do with foreigners, especially Germans."[3]

Dostoevsky cannot pass over in silence the respect with which the Poles were surrounded there. In Chapter II, "The Theatricals" (Part One of the book), he writes:

---

[1] Cf. *The House of the Dead*, loc. cit.
[2] *Loc. cit.*
[3] *Loc. cit.*

"Almost all the inmates of our ward went to the performance except the Old Believers and the Poles. It was only on the very last performance, on the fourth of January, that the Poles made up their minds to be present, and only then after many assurances that it was nice and amusing and that there was no risk about it. The disdain of the Poles did not irritate the convicts in the very least, and they were welcomed on the fourth of January quite politely, they were even shown into the best places."

For the attentive reader of Dostoevsky's *The House of the Dead* there is no doubt that it was the feeling of personal dignity which characterized the Poles that won for them this respect. There are episodes in the book which prove this; I have in mind the description of the flogging in the second part of the book, Chapter II ("The Hospital", continued). We read:

"M., for instance, described his punishment to me. He was not of the privileged class and received five hundred strokes. I heard of this from the others and asked him myself whether it were true, and how it happened. He answered with a certain brevity, as though with an inward pang; he seemed to avoid looking at me and his face flushed; half a minute later he did look at me; there was a gleam of hatred in his eyes, and his lips were quivering with indignation. I felt that he could never forget that page in his past. But our Russian people (I will not guarantee there were no exceptions) took quite a different view of it."! [*Sic*!]

Though M., the Pole, did not belong to the nobility, his feelings of personal dignity were not weak. It is a question of a different civilization, of a different historical past. No less eloquent is another episode of a Pole who had been flogged. The major insulted a group of convicts:

"He roared, 'They are tramps, brigands!' Z., who at that time knew very little Russian and who thought they were being asked who they were, tramps or brigands?—answered, 'We are not tramps, we are political prisoners.'
'Wha-aat? You are insolent! Insolent!' roared the major. 'To the guard-house! A hundred lashes, at once, this instant!'
The old man was flogged. He lay down under the lashes without a protest, bit his hand and endured the punishment without a cry, a moan, or a movement. Meanwhile B. and T. went into the prison where M., already waiting for them at the gate, fell on their necks though he had never seen them before. Agitated by the way

the major had received them, they told M. all about Z. I remember how M. told me about it.

'I was beside myself,' he said. 'I did not know what was happening to me and shivered as though I was in a fever. I waited for Z. at the gate. He would have to come straight from the guard-house where the flogging took place. Suddenly the gate opened: Z. came out with a pale face and trembling white lips, and without looking at anyone passed through the convicts who were assembled in the yard and who already knew that a "gentleman" was being flogged; he went into the prison ward, straight to his place, and without saying a word knelt down and began to pray. The convicts were impressed and even touched. When I saw that old grey-headed man,' said M., who had left a wife and children in his own country '—when I saw him on his knees praying, after a shameful punishment—I rushed behind the prison, and for two hours I did not know what I was doing; I was frantic. . . .'

The convicts had a great respect for Z. from that time forward, and they always treated him respectfully. What they particularly liked was that he had not cried out under punishment."[1]

I have no doubt that this kindness, comprehension, sympathy and even admiration which Dostoevsky shows here for his unfortunate Polish comrades derives from his friend Baron A. E. Wrangel. In his humane book *Reminiscences about T. M. Dostoevsky in Siberia*, Wrangel expressed his particular sympathy for the Poles in exile there. He quotes letters to his father in which he stresses the fact that he was particularly concerned with the unfortunate Polish political prisoners, with all these educated youths.[2] He also mentions the fact that Dostoevsky did not like them.[3] Wrangel had the position of Prosecutor in Semipalatinsk. It was here that Dostoevsky started to organize his notes for *The House of the Dead*, and I may assume that the respectable, just Wrangel calmed Dostoevsky's hatred. At any rate, *The House of the Dead* is an exceptional book for many reasons, among them Dostoevsky's attitude toward the Poles. In this book they are not at all evil.

"Dostoevsky gives here a very careful and precise analysis of their psychology and moral character. He shows what he dislikes in them—their exceptionality and self-control, their too lofty feeling of personal dignity. These are very European, very Polish features. For these traits, Dostoevsky disliked them. But here he is patient,

[1] Cf. *The House of the Dead*, pp. 257–8.
[2] A. E. Wrangel, *Vospominanija o F. M. Dostoevskom v Sibiri*, p. 115.
[3] *Ibid.*, p. 28.

tolerant, even kind. What did he do later? With the same elements, absolutely the same, he made the terrible creatures which he called 'Polyachishki' and which are the expression of his hatred. So those whom he found in the depths of the galley he finally put into the depths of human degradation."[1]

These were my conclusions made in complete fairness to Dostoevsky before I had investigated an important document bringing quite a special light on to this whole story. I relied upon Dostoevsky alone. The Poles whom he described spoke only through his pen. It happens, however, that we have a witness—a Pole, one of those whom Dostoevsky described in *The House of the Dead* and who published his memoirs, in which he told the true story of Dostoevsky's relations with him and other Polish political prisoners. So now *audiatur et altera pars*.

First, let us get a closer view of Szymon Tokarzewski, the author of *Seven Years of Penal Servitude*, which has been compared to Pellico's *Le mie prigioni*. This striking book presents horrifying details about Russia of the second part of the nineteenth century, about the ignominious, infernal conditions of prison camps in Siberia, about the persecution of Polish fighters for freedom, about floggings, sometimes to death, about the unspeakable insults imposed upon human dignity, about the rotten Russian administration and about human sufferings forgotten, ignored, and so often passed over in silence by historians who either do not dare or simply do not want to reveal the truth. Out of this book, written with the greatest simplicity and modesty, out of the described Gehenna of human torment, arises the natural, organic greatness of the soul of this Polish Pellico. This book, as well as Tokarzewski's biography, shows an unbreakable, invincible idealist who from his earliest days to his last remained faithful to his ideals of freedom and justice. A man of this kind cannot lie and cannot distort the reality of human relations. Their essence is always evident in this unsophisticated and genuinely sincere story.

Szymon Tokarzewski belonged to an old Polish noble family. His father was a wealthy landlord in the province of Lublin. This man, whose youth and life could have been comfortable and prosperous, exchanged all the advantages which were given to him by his birth and by a robust constitution for arrest, thirty years of prison, hard labour camps, exile, and finally tuberculosis. In 1839, when Tokarzewski was eighteen years old, he attended Mass at the cathedral of Zamość. The dean of the cathedral, Tokarzewski's uncle, Wojtasiewicz, was obliged to read a Russian governmental decree from the pulpit. It contained a

[1] See my article, "Mickiewicz, Dostoevsky and Blok" in *Slavic Studies* (New York: Cornell University Press, 1943), pp. 78–9.

list of Polish political prisoners who had been sent to the mines of Siberia, and a warning that in the event that any of them should escape, it was the duty of all subjects on meeting them to turn them over to the police dead or alive. The priest's voice broke and he left the pulpit in tears. He took his nephew into the sacristy, pushed him toward the crucifix, and obliged him to swear that he would follow in the path of all these prisoners. This oath was not forgotten. Soon afterwards Tokarzewski met the famous priest Ściegienny (the son of a simple Polish peasant), who had begun intense propaganda among the Polish peasants under the Russian and Austrian yoke. His main goal was the emancipation of these peasants and he believed that this could be achieved only in an independent Poland. In this way he combined social and patriotic aims. Tokarzewski joined Father Ściegienny's activities and became the priest's emissary. Wearing a peasant dress with a poor bag on his shoulders, he wandered from the province of Lublin to the provinces of Kielce and Kraków, spreading Ściegienny's ideas in the villages. In a few years their activities were denounced and Tokarzewski was arrested by the Austrian authorities in Lwów, sent to Lublin, then to Warsaw, and then to the fortress of Modlin. Father Ściegienny was sentenced to death. At the moment when the noose was placed around his neck a decree of grace was read: the sentence of death was replaced by hard labour for life in Siberia.[1] Tokarzewski's sentence included the loss of all privileges, the confiscation of his estate, two thousand lashes and ten years of hard labour in Siberia. The two thousand lashes were reduced, by mistake, Tokarzewski believes, to five hundred.

Dostoevsky, in his book *The House of the Dead*, reports on his talks with the Poles about flogging. He was curious to know whether it was very painful. He also emphasized that M. (the real name of this Pole was Mirecki) was not a nobleman and he stresses the fact that nobles were not supposed to be flogged. Indeed Tokarzewski gives many details about the particular sufferings of Mirecki in the Siberian prison. The

[1] It is well known how much Dostoevsky's biographers wrote about the circumstances surrounding his near-execution, how dramatically they emphasized the sadism of the Russian authorities who let Dostoevsky and his companions believe that the death sentence after the Petrashevtsy trial would be carried out and that the grace of the Emperor came almost at the moment when the soldiers were preparing to fire. These descriptions give the impression of a particularly malignant cruelty applied to Dostoevsky and his fellow-prisoners. Not only Dostoevsky's biographers laid stress on this terrible experience in the life of the great Russian writer, but Dostoevsky himself told this story in *The Idiot*, and he underlines the rarity of such a procedure: "There was one very strange circumstance about it—strange because such things rarely happen" (*The Idiot*, Constance Garnett translation, p. 56). Tokarzewski relates Father Ściegienny's story as a natural one—because Poles were accustomed to the most fantastic tortures applied to them by the persecuting Russian authorities.

infernal Major Krivtsov, known to every Russian through Dostoevsky's book, used to tell Mirecki, whom he especially enjoyed tormenting: "Thou art a peasant and it is allowed to beat thee." This is Tokarzewski's story, which we do not find in Dostoevsky's book but which I suppose Tokarzewski had the opportunity to relate to Dostoevsky:

"A nobleman cannot be physically punished. Therefore, before the execution of punishment, all of us who belonged to the 'privileged caste' were put in a line; the executioner approached, slapped us on both cheeks, then broke two wooden swords over our heads, after which the auditor announced: 'So-and-so, his Imperial Majesty has deigned to bestow on you the rank of muzhiks'.

After this horrible ceremony the execution began.

The sentenced, completely naked, was put on the square in such a position that he exposed his back to a line of soldiers. These soldiers passed by him and each one dealt him a blow with a stick; they continued rotating until the number of blows in the sentence had been dealt. The blows were weak or strong depending on whether the individual soldier had a human heart or the bloody instincts of a savage beast. Sometimes wealthy people bribed the soldiers through the sergeant so that they would not beat too hard. But this occurred very seldom, because, first, the sentences were generally read to the delinquents on the very day of execution, and besides at those times there reigned among us such a desire for martyrdom and the redemption of the Fatherland, such a heartfelt brotherly love united all of us that everyone, whether young or old, said, 'I do not want to suffer less than my fellow prison-mate. I do not want to suffer less.'

From my colleagues I know that not all executions took place in the same way. Some of the delinquents were attached to a post like Christ; some others were led in front of a line of soldiers. One circumstance, however, was always the same: the Earth, that beloved Earth of ours, while we were being flogged with sticks was abundantly flooded, not sprinkled, with our blood! No! no, flooded.

As I was the one to whom the greatest number of blows had been assigned, I went first as if by right of seniority. Karasiński followed immediately behind me.

I held close to my breast a medallion with the image of the Virgin of Częstochowa . . . I desired to pray, but I could not remember a single line of prayer; only after every blow by a soldier I repeated either 'It is to your glory, Queen of the Polish Kingdom' or 'It is for your redemption, dear Fatherland.'

Did I suffer during the flogging? . . . No! Did I see my executioner? No! The entire surroundings disappeared from my view.

Only before my eyes flashed some circles of light.

Perhaps in this bloody hour my soul had separated itself from my body and then remained in some super-earthly regions. . . . Is it possible? Let the physicians and psychologists answer.

I may firmly assert and state that a man during religious and patriotic ecstasy does not feel physical pain."

I think that this is the best answer to Dostoevsky's question "whether flogging was very painful", and it should have satisfied his curiosity.

Tokarzewski remained in his Siberian prison until 1857, when the amnesty of Alexander II secured to him the possibility of returning to Poland. Very soon Tokarzewski again started his patriotic, revolutionary activities which put him into contact with artisans and workers. In order to intensify these contacts, in order to unite himself entirely with the proletariat, he decided to become a shoemaker, following the example of Kiliński, the famous Warsaw hero of the 1794 uprising, who had taken up the same trade. Tokarzewski's modest house in Warsaw became a meeting place for outstanding Polish patriots, young students, artisans and workers. In 1863, after the Insurrection, he was deported to Ryazan, whence he was sent again to prison in Warsaw. In 1864 he was sent to the hard labour camp in Aleksandrovsk on the shores of the Amur. Then he remained in exile in Irkutsk and in the province of Kostroma. He finally returned to Poland in broken health, with tuberculosis, in 1883, after the coronation manifesto of Alexander III. He died on 3 July, 1890, in Warsaw. His memoirs (besides several other articles and stories) appeared first in 1907 in an edition terribly mutilated by Russian censorship. In 1918 appeared the second edition, which I am using here. These memoirs provide many details of the life in Dostoevsky's prison camp which were omitted by Dostoevsky. There are many such details which in connection with Wrangel's book give a truer and thus more terrible picture of the penal system and of the political persecutions of czarist Russia. But as these macabre details are outside the scope of my present publication I cannot present them here, although the temptation is strong enough. I must confine myself only to the problem of Dostoevsky's relations with the Poles. And here again Tokarzewski's book corrects many important characteristics in Dostoevsky's picture of these relations. The paragraphs already quoted from Tokarzewski's book as well as the short outline of his astonishing biography must bring one to the conclusion that Tokarzewski is a witness whom one can respect and trust. He does not show at all any national narrow-mindedness. He mentions in his memoirs some facts revealing the base and crude reactions of various Russian milieux toward the Polish insurrectionists while they were marching through Russia to their Siberian prison. But on the other hand he also describes some deeply attractive Russian personalities, especially several women who showed a sincere and touching sympathy for these Polish martyrs in the service of ideals, and an interest for the culture of their enslaved country. He described in his book the wonderful friendship (which, by the way, Dostoevsky was forced to admit in *The House of the Dead*) with the Circassians, with a Jewish convict and with one Old Believer. Dostoevsky pretends that quarrels took place among these Poles and that the quarrels sometimes degenerated into complete breaks of relations. Dostoevsky would like us to believe, for instance, that all of them, including Bogusławski and Tokarzewski, greatly disliked the old Professor Żochowski, the mathematician, who on his very arrival at the prison was so terribly insulted by Krivtsov and afterwards received three hundred blows. Dostoevsky calls Żochowski "stupid" and "disagreeable". He emphasizes, as I mentioned before, the hatred of the Poles for the criminals in the prison. The following passage from Tokarzewski's book will show the truth about Tokarzewski's relations with Żochowski and at the same time will explain that hatred for the criminals, which Tokarzewski does not at all deny:

"I return to the previous story about our fate. They led us to the gate of this infernal gulf in which I wasted seven years of my life, where my flowering youth passed, where my masculine forces and my health were lost, where I endured suffering above the level of human endurance, and from which I emerged able to say together with the poet, 'Like Dante I went alive through Hell.' They opened the doors of the barracks. In the doorway stood Olech Mirecki, who, although he had not known us before, threw himself with a sorrowful smile into our arms. Together with Olech a group of rascally convicts greeted us, they who were to become our comrades for seven years. . . . Oh my God, how monstrous these figures appeared to us. And these shapes of men or of the damned approached us and extended their hands, hands so many times covered with blood, so many times soiled by offense and crime. And we were obliged, though with horror and revulsion, to offer them our hands. I pulled away my hand and pushing everyone aside I entered the barracks

"Two Worlds"
By K. Górski

with my head held proudly aloft. This was a very undiplomatic action on my part. All these brigands became indignant; they called me 'Satan' and 'Devil'; they hated me, all of them, and any of them who had the will and desire offended me in their own way. There were some weeks when I could not go quietly through the yard because from every side curses and insults fell upon me like hail. There were moments during which if the earth had opened under my feet I would have jumped into the abyss without any meditation, in the hope that I would find there something better than that which surrounded me here. And there is no possibility to hide oneself, nowhere, not even for a single minute can one remain alone. . . . Everywhere moral filth—everywhere are they, they, they . . . criminals. Despair and madness entirely seized me. Once I ran into the yard with my heart heavy in my breast, with my head full of the wildest thoughts, and I started to walk in long strides the square which at that time was my whole world. I was in such pain, and in this pain so helpless, that I decided to commit suicide. . . . I was strong, I thought, and if I should strike my head against the wall, once, again, with my full strength, that would be an end to everything. I would certainly have realized this desperate decision, because suicide appeared to me as the only escape from suffering, insult and persecutions. My dear Professor Żochowski saved me from sin, cowardice, and from the loss of salvation for my soul. This was the twilight hour when the brigands had not yet returned from work, and we, having finished the 'portion' assigned to us, were already in the barracks. Żochowski went out for prayer. This old man, so terribly injured by Waśka [Tokarzewski refers to Major Krivtsov] on the day following his arrival at Omsk, when he had received three hundred strokes which the drunken Major had assigned to him—this old man, living in the same surroundings as I, was still so serene. . . . He did not imprecate his fate, he did not curse, but looked at everything, at everyone, with the calmness of a sage and the tolerance of a Christian. I felt so base in comparison with him, so faint-hearted, so simple, that I threw myself at his feet enchained by fetters and I pressed my aching head to his knees and in tears I whispered: 'Let us pray together, Father! Let us pray and then pray for me, oh, pray for me every day!'

And afterwards, whenever I recalled this moment of pagan despair, the blush of shame enflamed my cheeks. In that God-forsaken moment I had forgotten that God had endowed me with *will*, with that power before which everything must humble itself. . . . My will impelled me to suffer for the Fatherland, to suffer quietly, without explosions of despair, to suffer in silence."[1]

Tokarzewski, as I mentioned, met Dostoevsky. Dostoevsky described this meeting and the acquaintance with Tokarzewski and other Poles in *The House of the Dead*. In Tokarzewski's book this is what we find in the chapter on Dostoevsky:

"Theodor, the son of Michael Dostoevsky, this famous novelist, author of *Poor Folk*, this glory of the Northern capital, seemed to us as someone who had not grown to a stature equal with his fame. No doubt he had novelistic talent. But I shall not concern myself with his novels; rather shall I deal with his character. Through what means had this man become a conspirator? Through what means had he taken part in a democratic movement, he, proud above measure, proud of the fact that he belonged to the privileged caste? Through what means could this man have desired the emancipation of the peasants, he who recognized only one caste and only one opinion, that of the nobility, which had the exclusive right to national leadership?

'Nobility', 'noblemen', 'nobility', 'I am a nobleman', 'we, the nobility', he constantly repeated whenever he addressed us Poles. I always interrupted him: 'Excuse me, sir, I think that in this prison there is no gentry, there are only men deprived of rights, only convicts.' Then he would foam with anger: 'And you, sir, are evidently pleased that you are a convict,' he shouted with anger and irony. 'That I am just such a convict as I am, I am happy!'—I quietly answered.

So through what miracle had Dostoevsky become a conspirator? Probably he had involuntarily let himself be seized by the contemporary movement, considering the fact that he confessed to us his anguish that the waves of conspiracy had brought him to this penal servitude at Omsk. It was unfortunate that Dostoevsky hated the

---

[1] S. Tokarzewski, *Siedem lat Katorgi, Pamiętniki 1846–1857* (Warsaw, 1918), pp. 9–29, 150, 60–62, 146–149. Against Dostoevsky's emphatic assertions that, in general, the convicts disliked the Poles, the following passage from M. Janik's book, *The Poles in Siberia*, might be quoted. "The Polish community lived in solidarity, with the esteem of their fellow prisoners, and endowed (by the latter) with short sobriquets. Thus Żochowski was called *swiatoj* (the saintly one), Bogusławski *bolnoj* (the sick one), and Tokarzewski *chrabryj* (the courageous one). In 1851 they lost Żochowski. Having fallen more and more in spirit through misery, lack of comfort, and moral suffering, he died in the Omsk hospital at fifty years of age." M. Janik, *Dzieje Polaków na Syberji* (Cracow: Nakładem Krakowskiej spółki wydawniczej, 1928), p. 217. It is worth while to note that Józef Żochowski left behind several works, among them: *The Philosophy of the Heart or Practical Wisdom* (Warsaw, 1845); *Physics* (2 vols.) (Warsaw, 1841–42); *The Life of Jesus Christ* (Warsaw, 1847). See Janik, *op. cit.*, p. 218.

Poles, because judging by his traits and his name it was possible to recognize his Polish origin. He used to say that if he ever found out that a single drop of Polish blood flowed in his veins, he would immediately have himself purged of it. How painful it was to listen to this conspirator, this man sentenced to prison for the cause of freedom and progress, when he confessed that he would be happy only when all the nations would fall under Russian rule. He never admitted that the Ukraine, Volhynia, Podolia, Lithuania and finally the whole of Poland were countries seized by Russia, but affirmed that all these regions of the globe had forever been the property of Russia; that the divine hand of justice had put these provinces and countries under the sceptre of the Russian Czar because they would never have been able to exist independently and that for a long time they would have remained in a state of dark illiteracy, barbarism and abject poverty. The Baltic provinces, in Dostoevsky's opinion, belong to Russia proper; Siberia and the Caucasus he put in the same category. Listening to these arguments we acquired the conviction that Fyodor Mikhaylovich Dostoevsky in certain respects was affected by insanity. But for his part he repeated these absurdities with obvious enjoyment. He stated even that Constantinople should long ago have belonged to Russia, as well as the whole of European Turkey, which he thought would very soon become the flower of the Russian Empire. Once Dostoevsky recited to us his poem, an ode describing the inevitable entry of the victorious Russian army into Constantinople. The ode was indeed beautiful. However, none of us was earnest in his praise of it, and I asked him: 'And haven't you an ode for the return trip?'

He boiled with rage, and springing at my face he called me an ignoramus and a barbarian. He shouted so terribly that amongst all the prisoners there spread the rumor that 'the political prisoners are fighting'. In order to cut short this shameful scene we went out of the barracks into the yard.

According to Dostoevsky there existed only one great nation predestined for a magnificent mission—the Russian nation. 'The French,' he insisted, 'at least to some extent resemble men, but the English, Germans, Spaniards—they are simply caricatures.' The literatures of other nations in comparison with Russian literature are simple literary parodies. I remember that when I told him that in 1844 a subscription had been announced in Poland for the translation of *The Wandering Jew* he did not want to believe me at first, and finally accused me of lying. Finally Durov interfered [Tokarzewski also gives an interesting picture of this famous friend of

Dostoevsky] and convinced him of the truth of my assertion. In spite of this he was not quite persuaded, because, if I may say so, it lay in his very nature to deny everything that was great, beautiful and noble in the cultures of all nations, not to speak of the Poles, whom he especially hated. He would have liked to smash and annihilate everything foreign in order to prove paradoxically the superiority of the Russians over the other nations of the world. Dostoevsky often became unbearable in his discussions. Conceited and brutal, he forced us into such a position that we not only did not care to have any further discussions with him, but we really did not want to know him at all.

Perhaps this unevenness of character, this explosiveness of Dostoevsky's temper, was a sign of sickness, because, as I already mentioned, both these Petersburg gentlemen [he has in mind Durov] were quite nervous and sick.... Through what quirk of fate, then, had this pupil of the Cadet Corps, Fyodor Mikhaylovich Dostoevsky, found himself in penal servitude as a political prisoner? According to his own testimony he used to read very much; undoubtedly the pictures of the great French Revolution had inflamed his imagination, but this did not burn very hot; he probably had found in works of great thinkers exalted ideas which had penetrated into his brain and seized his heart, and he had allowed himself to be put on a road which he subsequently wished to leave as soon as possible. When these two men arrived in Omsk and settled with me under one roof it seemed to me that I saw two small lights shining in the gloomy Northern sky. The illusion disappeared almost immediately. I have already mentioned that we severed relations with Dostoevsky. After his release from the prison, he was sent for military service into a battalion stationed in Semipalatinsk. There, on the occasion of the Crimean war, he wrote a poem in which he placed Czar Nicholas over all the Olympian gods; he wanted this poem published in the newspapers. Perhaps by flattery he expected to obtain a reduction of his sentence and in return for the dithyramb possibly to receive a rich reward. These aforementioned facts justify the opinion which all of us Poles who were in the Omsk prison expressed of Dostoevsky: that he was a man of weak and low character. The fact that he hated the Poles might be pardoned. We bore and pardoned still greater hatreds, but we did not try to captivate Mr. Theodor Dostoevsky because 'a petted wolf and a friend whom one must captivate bring little advantage'. When the excitement arose around the affair in which Dostoevsky was implicated, I was already a prisoner on the way to Siberia—that is, outside the civilized world where opinions and views clash and where one is finally able to form a conclusion based on facts. What kind of people were the other participants in this movement? I do not know, but what is well known to me is the fact that among the small number of honest and educated Russians whom I met in Siberia this movement awakened neither sympathy nor interest. Very different was the case of the Decembrists!"[1]

Tokarzewski's revelations are most valuable. I wrote the following about *The House of the Dead* before I had read Tokarzewski's memoirs:

"The example of *The House of the Dead* is very important. It is a unique book among the works of Dostoevsky; in this book he gives a true, realistic story of his experiences and in it we do not find any of the 'artistic deformation', exaggeration, and Gogolian fantasticalness and grandiloquence which characterize the rest of his novels and stories. Here life goes on in its 'Euclidian' real tempo and measure; here every character is true, as this is a naïve, direct appreciation of the world in which we live. And Poles in this climate, in this 'ontology', are true, honorable human beings without those terrible moral abysses which appear in Poles belonging to his later works. . . ."[2]

In the light of Tokarzewski's revelations the "truth" also becomes ambivalent. In this case Dostoevsky's ideological gambling is especially subtle. His attitude toward the Poles in *The House of the Dead* is relatively more generous and fair when compared with the attitude he assumes in his novels. However, one small detail should be brought to light. At the present moment I have not in mind Dostoevsky's political quarrels with the Poles, his imperialistic inclination toward Constantinople, his Pan-Russianism covering almost the whole of historical Poland, the Baltic provinces and the Caucasus. What I wish to point out is the fact that Dostoevsky emphasized almost on every page which contained Poles their "typical exclusiveness", their "national and social aloofness"—thus creating a legend which has been repeated up to the present by every Russian, and not merely by those who have read Dostoevsky. Yet on the very same pages he stressed his comprehension and tolerance for this exclusiveness. He appears in his book as someone who was not in agreement with this stand, who could not approve of this attitude opposed to his Christian pity and humility, but still as

[1] Cf. Tokarzewski, *op. cit.*, pp. 165–73.
[2] Cf. *Slavic Studies*, as above, p. 79.

someone who was able to extend his goodwill to such a degree as to defend before the Russian reader those "poor Poles" whom suffering had made morbid, bitter, and unsociable.[1] Now when we have before our eyes the story of Dostoevsky's talks with the Poles about nobility, Dostoevsky's unfairness appears in all its strength, as subtle as it is. From Tokarzewski's book we see that Dostoevsky was the one who constantly shouted about his nobility and irritated Tokarzewski, who certainly had the right to feel this way since by his whole life he had proved his solidarity with the peasants, artisans, and workers.

I have often mentioned the "Polyachishki" who appear in *The Gambler*, *Crime and Punishment*, *The Brothers Karamazov*, and *The Idiot*; I should like to tarry now for a while with the first appearance of such a type in Dostoevsky's novels. The average reader, after reading *The House of the Dead* and becoming acquainted with Dostoevsky's seeming

---

[1] He indeed convinced Khranevich. Cf. V. Khranevič: "Dostoevskij po vospominaniju ssyl'nago poljaka" in *Russkaja Starina* (St. Petersburg, 1910), Vol. 141, pp. 367–76 and 605–621. Opposed to Khranevich's vulgar nationalism and rude approach to Tokarzewski's book is the objective review by S. Braylovsky. Cf. "F. M. Dostoevskij v omskoj katorge i poljaki" in *Istoričeskij Vestnik* (St. Petersburg, 1908), Vol. CXII, pp. 189–98. See also *F. M. Dostoevskij v omskoj katorge* in *Zven'ja* (Moscow-Leningrad: Academia, 1936), Vol. VI, pp. 495–512; this is a translation of another very interesting fragment of Tokarzewski's reminiscences about Dostoevsky. The story which Tokarzewski candidly gives in this fragment is without any bitterness toward Dostoevsky. It would be worth while to quote here Janik's comments on the subject of the relationship which existed between Dostoevsky and his Polish prison mates. One must admire the tolerant interpretation of this relationship which Janik based on Dostoevsky's *The House of the Dead* and Tokarzewski's memoirs: "The opinion of Dostoevsky about his fellow prisoners is incomparably more indulgent than their opinion of him, although coloured by the sorrow of disillusionment.... Reading today these mutual opinions, one gets the impression that between Dostoevsky and our exiles endured a constant misunderstanding, unavoidable between representatives of the ruling people and the defenders of the freedom of the subjugated people. Dostoevsky insufficiently, perhaps, remembered that in a political conversation as an enlightened man he should have avoided, even in the heat of argument, that which might injure the feelings or smother the hopes of Polish patriotism. True, he was a political prisoner, just as were our exiles, but even in this rôle he was a Russian; he was at home, while our people were in double captivity. Therefore, our exiles were affected, they wrote spitefully about that which was a personal misfortune of Dostoevsky, they expressed themselves rather more harshly about him than justice and the long friendly relations would permit. Who knows, even, if these long Omsk conversations didn't play a part in strengthening Dostoevsky's chauvinism, for he himself wrote that the prison impressions acted so strongly upon him that 'to tear myself from them is too painful, well-nigh impossible'. Both sides fell here as victims of a system of czarist government which wanted to achieve the greatness of Russia by the conquest of those who were weaker, and by this system it poisoned the souls of the rulers and the conquered. The rôle of our people, in any case, was defensive, therefore deserving, despite everything, a greater understanding." M. Janik, *op. cit.*, pp. 218–19. The reader has to remember and realize that Janik judged Dostoevsky's attitude only on the basis of *The House of the Dead*, a book in which, as I said myself, Dostoevsky appears to be exceptionally candid in the expression of his anti-Polish feelings. Janik did not investigate the literary and biographical materials concerning Dostoevsky which I brought to the fore in my studies.

tolerance and objective attitude toward the Poles, might be astonished by the violent anti-Polish thrusts in his other purely fictional works. Only in the light of Tokarzewski's book has the truth been revealed about Dostoevsky's Polish feelings. The first example of this attitude in his fictional works is found, as I mentioned, in *Uncle's Dream*, which, we must remember, preceded *The House of the Dead*. *Uncle's Dream* and another novel of the same kind, *Stepanchikovo*, were the first works which Dostoevsky wrote after he left the prison compound and the first which were published before his return to Russia. He himself called *Uncle's Dream* "a trifle of dove-like gentleness and remarkable innocence"—he was sure that the censor would not object to anything in these works. As we know, the censor, who at that time was Goncharov, found only one objectionable word in *Stepanchikovo*—we do not know what this word was. Grossman in his introduction to *Stepanchikovo*[1] convincingly proved that after all the debasing manifestations of loyalty, humility and avowed remorse which Dostoevsky expressed in numerous letters to Russian officials, after his patriotic poems which praised Russian orthodoxy and imperialism, after his expressed plans to serve the government with political pamphlets, after his glorification even of Nicholas I, *Stepanchikovo*, with its idyllic picture of a patriarchal Russian countryside and a kind retired Colonel who lives in perfect harmony with his peasants, was an eloquent illustration of the author's loyalty. In a way, *Uncle's Dream*, a joyful and even foolish vaudeville, is a product of the same inspiration, which alone prevents these two works from being quite innocent and dove-like. But, as we know, there are also some other elements of sadness in them. *Stepanchikovo* is a terrible, cruel parody of Belinsky.[2] This parody indicates not only a complete ideological break with Belinsky, but feelings of venomous hatred which later found their violent and frequent expression in many of Dostoevsky's letters. *Uncle's Dream* presents a satirical, allegorical picture, the first one from Dostoevsky's pen, of the superficial, vain, stupid Europeanization of Russia. The European names, ideas, historical facts mentioned there give the impression of a burlesque ideological masquerade. Besides, what is even more important, *Uncle's Dream* brings the first complete dethronement of the idealistic dreamer and of the "poor oppressed man" who was Dostoevsky's main hero before Siberia. In one of the grotesque dialogues between the prince and one of his fellow players the prince expresses his willingness to write again a vaudeville which he had at some time in his past written:

[1] Cf. F. M. Dostoevskij, *Selo Stepančikovo i ego obyvateli*, etc., redakcija L. P. Grossmana (Moscow: Gos. Izdat., 1935).
[2] Cf. another section of this volume, "Dostoevsky and Belinsky".

" 'Of course! I am ready to write it again, indeed ... though I have completely forgotten it. But I remember there were two or three puns such that ...' (and the prince kissed his finger-tips) 'and altogether when I was abro-ad I made a re-gu-lar fu-rore. I remember Lord Byron. We were on friendly terms. He danced the Cracoviana enchantingly at the Vienna Congress.'

'Lord Byron, uncle! Upon my word, uncle, what do you mean?' 'Oh, yes, Lord Byron. Though perhaps it wasn't Lord Byron, but someone else. Quite so; not Lord Byron, but a Pole, I remember perfectly now. And that Pole was ve-ry ori-gi-nal, he gave himself out for a count, and it afterwards turned out that he was some sort of head cook, but he did dance the Cracoviana most en-chant-ing-ly and at last he broke his leg. I wrote some verses on that occasion too: "Our dear little Pole/To dance was his rôle," and what came then, I can't remember.' "When he broke his limb/No more capers from him." ' "[1]

For what reason did Dostoevsky need this Polish "head cook", "false count" dancing the Cracoviana, a man whom the prince confused in his memory paralyzed by senility with Lord Byron? It could be a revenge on Byron, famous for flamboyant enthusiasm toward Poland, expressed in so many poems and followed by an equal anti-Russian sentiment. It could also be another trait of "dove-like" loyalty on Dostoevsky's part. I repeat, *Uncle's Dream* was written in Siberia. We know from *The House of the Dead* rather much about Dostoevsky's relations with Poles there. In this case Dostoevsky showed a different face. Now his attitude is no longer one of presumed tolerance and objectivity, although one may say that this is a simple, innocent joke. In any event, it is a superfluous episode. It is a kind of intrusion, artistically unmotivated. Naturally, Dostoevsky could justify this joke by the general chaos reigning in his hero's distorted mind—everything is superfluous in the prince's brain. However, where did Dostoevsky get the picture of this dancing Pole? Again, *The House of the Dead* might be of some help. It includes one Polish episode which, perhaps, could be connected with this "Cracoviana". In *The House of the Dead* (Part Two, chapter II, "The Hospital—continued") we read:

"That morning M. and B. introduced me to the overseer of the brickyard, a sergeant called Ostrozski. He was a Pole, a tall thin old man of sixty, of extremely dignified and even stately appearance. He had been in the army for many years, and though he was

[1] Cf. *An Honest Thief and Other Stories*, translated by Constance Garnett (New York: Macmillan Co., 1919), p. 39.

a peasant by birth, had come to Siberia as a simple soldier after 1830, yet M. and B. loved and respected him. He was always reading the Catholic Bible. I conversed with him and he talked with much friendliness and sense, described things interestingly, and looked good-natured and honest. I did not see him again for two years. I only heard that he had got into trouble about something; and suddenly he was brought into our ward as a lunatic. He came in shrieking and laughing and began dancing about the ward with most unseemly and indecent actions. The convicts were in ecstasies, but I felt very sad."

This is a painful and even macabre explanation, but against the background of previous examples the suggested explanation seems not too improbable.

Let us return again to *The House of the Dead*. The Pole M., whom he mentions so often in this book, absorbed his mind for a long time. He appears again in 1876 in *The Diary of the Writer*, in the famous story of *The Peasant Marey*, and again Dostoevsky mentions his exclamation: "*Je hais ces brigands!*" Mr. Mochulsky in his book on Dostoevsky,[1] like many other Russian admirers of the writer, contrasts Dostoevsky with the "exclusive" Poles:

"Dostoevsky did not become angry and was not crushed; he accomplished the greatest act of Christian humility: he recognized that the truth is on the side of the enemies, that they are 'an extraordinary people', that 'in them lies the soul of Russia'. In the pitch-dark hell of penal servitude the writer found that which he worshipped forever: the Russian people."[2]

I do not think that the Polish prisoners in Siberia had any reason to worship these people.

Even Dostoevsky himself tries to understand and to justify this Polish attitude. However, I have something else in mind. In his letter to Madame N. D. Fon-Vizin, written from Omsk in February, 1854, Dostoevsky wrote:

"It is almost five years that I have been under guard in a crowd of people, and not for one hour have I been alone. It is as normal a necessity to be alone as it is to eat and drink; otherwise in this enforced communism you become a misanthrope. The society of people becomes a poison and a plague, and this is the unbearable

[1] Cf. K. Močul'skij, *Dostoevskij, Žizn' i tvorčestvo* (Paris: Y.M.C.A. Press, 1947).
[2] *Ibid.*, p. 161.

suffering which has weighed on me most in these four years. There were moments when I hated everyone I met, the innocent and the guilty, and I regarded them as thieves who had stolen my life without being punished for it. The most intolerable misery occurs when you yourself become unjust, evil and hateful; you are aware of all this, you even reproach yourself—and you cannot leave. This has been my experience. I am sure that God has spared you the same trial. I think that as a woman you have greater powers of endurance and forgiveness."[1]

The reader remembers Tokarzewski's terrible confession. Thus— *Quod licet Jovi non licet bovi.*

There is no doubt that Dostoevsky's attitude toward Poland and the violent expressions of these feelings possess all the traits of a guilt complex. The Polish problem was a difficult one for the Russian conscience. A religious thinker, a writer, who constantly preached the cult of Christ, humility, pardoning, love-of-fellow-man, sympathy and pity for the insulted and injured, could not silently pass by the crime of the partitions of Poland. From this point of view Dostoevsky's anti-Polish vociferations may appear as an effort to still his own conscience. Every Polish episode is an attempt to show that Poland does not deserve anything but that which was meted out to her. These feelings could have been strengthened in Dostoevsky by the supposed Polish past of his family. True, there existed in the Polish Commonwealth a family of landlords bearing the same name, the representatives of which held high official positions, possessed estates and the Polish coat-of-arms *Radwan*. But I do not think that Dostoevsky the writer had any real connections with this family.[2] Nevertheless, among the members

[1] Cf. Dostoevskij, *Pis'ma*, pod red. A. S. Dolinina (Moscow-Leningrad: Gos. Izdat., 1928), Vol. I, p. 143.

[2] I think that Mackiewicz might be right in his rejection of the fantastic speculations of Dostoevsky's daughter about the author's noble Polish origin. Mackiewicz justly points out that Dostoevsky's father, the son of an Orthodox priest, was not a member of the class of nobles. He was elevated to the Russian nobility through his governmental service. Mackiewicz deals only with the naïve genealogical theories of Dostoevsky's daughter. However, scholars like M. V. Volotskoy and L. Grossman also deduce Dostoevsky's family from the Polish nobles of the same name. They affirm, though, that this Polish family, well known in historical documents, originated with a Russian fugitive, Danila Irtishch, who received Dostojewo through a decree of Fedor Yaroslavich, Prince of Pinsk; this right of possession was later confirmed by Polish kings. In the opinion of these scholars, the main branch of the family became Polonized and converted to Catholicism. But neither Vototskoy nor Grossman has any proofs of the ties between the family of the writer and the Polish Dostojewskis. In their genealogical reconstructions there is a wide gap between the Polish Dostojewskis and the family of the great writer. It could be that Dostoevsky's family indeed originated in White Ruthenia before they appeared in the Ukraine, but that they were peasants, who received their name from the place *Dostojewo* which

of the writer's family there took place talks about their origin. Whether Dostoevsky was of Polish origin or not is unimportant. He belongs to Russia. But the idea that he could have had some Polish ties probably disturbed him and could have strengthened anti-Polish feelings in a personality like his. (By the way, Nietzsche, in contrast to Dostoevsky, liked the idea of his possible Polish origin. He played with the legend of his ties with the Polish titled family of the Nieckis who had the same coat-of-arms as the Dostojewskis, and he saw in this fact an explanation of his congeniality with Dostoevsky.)[1]

I will not describe all the Polish episodes which appear in Dostoevsky's novels. There is one, though, which is particularly outstanding. Before I describe it I should like to stress one common trait, besides Dostoevsky's hatred for Poland, which appears in all these episodes. All of them are absolutely useless from the point of view of novelistic needs. The scandal at the Marmeladovs' in *Crime and Punishment* could have been described without the humiliation of the "Polyachishki". The performances of the grandmother in *The Gambler* did not need the disgusting Poles as an entourage. In *A Raw Youth*, two Poles, disgusting as usual, appear episodically only in order to give Dostoevsky the pleasure of correcting their bad French accent. They have no other rôle in the novel.[2] Grushenka's story in *The Brothers*

belonged to their Polish landlords. They could also have been Ruthenian Uniats. I do not deny the possibility that there existed an Orthodox branch of the Polish noble family Dostojewski. But still the origin of the priest Dostoevsky who was the writer's grandfather remains unexplained. (Cf. Mackiewicz, *op. cit.*, and Aimée Dostoevsky, *Fyodor Dostoevsky, a Study* (London: William Heinemann, 1921). Cf. also M. V. Volotskoj, *Khronika Roda Dostoevskogo* (Moscow: Koop. izdat., 1933); and L. Grossman, *Dostoevskij, Žizn' i trudy* (Moscow-Leningrad: Academia, 1935).

Another conjecture has been suggested to me by Mr. M. K. Pawlikowski, Associate in Slavic Languages at the University of California. According to Mr. Pawlikowski, cases are known of completely impoverished noble families in these former Polish Eastern provinces whose descendants found themselves intermingled with the peasantry, as they had either lost their documents or could not finance the customary procedure, established by the Russian Government, leading to the recognition of noble status. This could have been the case of the Russian branch of the Polish Dostojewskis. The speculation of Russian scholars and writers dealing with the legendary connections of Dostoevsky's family with the historically known Dostojewskis in White Ruthenia and Lithuania were recently brought to a *credo quia absurdum* by Henri Troyat in his book *Firebrand, The Life of Dostoevsky* (New York: Roy, 1946); see pp. 12–13. This book adds very little if anything to the brilliant biographies of Dostoevsky by A. Levinson and L. Grossman.

[1] Nietzsche indeed was very proud of his legendary Polish ancestry. In 1883 he wrote that "as a boy I was rather proud of my Polish descent". He mentions that "in all essentials I have remained a Pole", that his "appearance has always been characteristic of the Polish type". He adds: "a small album of mazurkas which I composed as a boy bore the inscription, 'In memory of our ancient forebears!' and I reflected them in many a judgment and many a prejudice." Cf. *The Life of Nietzsche* by Frau Förster-Nietzsche (New York, 1912), Vol. I, pp. 5–6.

[2] Cf. *A Raw Youth*, Part III, chapter 5, paragraph 3.

Karamazov could have been accomplished without the participation of Pan Musiałowicz and Pan Wróblewski. All these Poles appear to be insulted and injured, and they are all rascals. It is *The Brothers Karamazov* episode which is especially outstanding. Here are several salient details: first, the repulsive physical appearance of the two Poles in question; second, as stressed by Dostoevsky, their arrogant and insolent behaviour, which from the very beginning arouses the reader's feelings of antipathy. They constantly speak Polish. (By the way, Dostoevsky shows a perfect command of the Polish language. Here the wording of his Polish phrases is particularly correct.)[1] The atmosphere of unpleasantness which Dostoevsky creates around these Poles is strongly supported by the growing feelings of suspicion and contempt which the reader senses in Grushenka—and Grushenka is a character endowed with great moral prestige. This is why, when the other persons who take part in the conversation begin to tell insulting stories about Polish girls and ladies in Poland, the indignation expressed by the Poles is ridiculous. Mitya's behavior toward them in the beginning conforms to Mitya's generosity and frankness. However, from time to time he lets escape small signs of the mocking attitude, usual in Russia, toward the supposedly Polish characteristic of meticulous defense of personal dignity. Now comes the episode of the toasts to Poland and Russia at Mitya's suggestion and with his champagne. Mitya and the Poles drink to Poland. Then Mitya suggests a toast to Russia. Everyone tosses off his glass, including Grushenka, who doesn't drink to Poland, but who states that "to Russia even I shall drink"—everyone, that is, with the exception of the Poles. When Mitya insists that the Poles also drink, Pan Wróblewski exclaims: "to Russia within the frontiers of 1772". The other Pole agrees and they drink their toast. "You're fools, you *panowie*," bursts from Mitya's lips. The Poles show offense, but Grushenka calms them. Then, as the reader knows, occurs the episode of the cards, in which Dostoevsky reveals that his two Poles are cardsharpers. Mitya tries to buy them but finally throws them out and locks them in another room of the inn. Needless to say, during all these episodes, even before the revelation of their dishonest play, the behaviour of the Poles is mocked. What is the function of this episode? It is one of marvellous political propaganda. The year 1772 to which the Pole alluded is the date of the first partition of Poland. Everyone will agree

---

[1] Striking proof of Dostoevsky's excellent command of Polish may be found in the drafts and notes connected with *The Brothers Karamazov*. There are five pages completely filled with long dialogues in Polish, for which Dostoevsky uses a Russian phonetic transcription. Every phrase is not only correct, but even idiomatic. Dostoevsky faithfully adheres to the rules of Polish syntax and grammar, and in all these phrases he makes only two or three mistakes. Cf. *F. M. Dostoevskij, Materialy i Issledovanija*, pod red. Dolinina (Leningrad, 1935), pp. 199–203.

that it was quite legitimate for a Pole not to be willing to recognize the act of the partitions. This legitimate protest, however, has been put in the mouths of men whom the reader considers stupid, arrogant, insolent, and who later turn out to be card-sharpers. In this manner the protest itself becomes an object of derision. Mitya's exclamation, "You're fools, you *panowie*," emphasizes even something else, the unrealistic character of the Polish dreams of possible future independence. Dostoevsky's malignity goes even farther. I have mentioned the fact of the naturalness of the Poles' reactions. Dostoevsky also admits this when his Pole answers Mitya with the question: "Can one help loving one's own country?" Had Dostoevsky put this phrase in the mouth of Mitya or Grushenka the effect would have been completely different. One must not forget that in the beginning of the card episode the Poles told a story about a certain Podwysocki. This story reflects the high idea which the Poles have of honour. Mitya immediately expresses his doubts. And how eloquent is the unmasking of the Poles by Grushenka:

" 'Oh, go back where you came from! I'll tell them to turn you out and you'll be turned out,' cried Grushenka, furious. 'I've been a fool, a fool, to have been miserable these five years! And it wasn't for his sake, it was my anger made me miserable. And this isn't he at all! Was he like this? It might be his father! Where did you get your wig from? He was a falcon, but this is a gander. He used to laugh and sing to me. . . . And I've been crying for five years, damned fool, abject, shameless I was!' "[1]

And what can we say about the remainder of the Poles' story? Even though the Polish gentlemen have gravely insulted Grushenka, they have no scruples about asking her for money, first for two thousand roubles, then for gradually diminishing sums, and finally she receives their letter and request for one rouble! This letter includes a receipt signed by both Poles. When Grushenka visits them out of pity, she finds them in complete destitution, but instead of being grateful the Poles greet her "with arrogant dignity and self-assertion, with the greatest formality and pompous speeches". One may easily understand the fact that practically all these disgusting details of the character and behaviour of the two Poles were gathered in order to kill the year 1772. Dostoevsky is merciless and terribly adroit. Here the ideological gambler appears again. When the Poles were locked in the room by Mitya, when Mitya had become drunk, he suddenly came to the door and shouted: "Be

---

[1] Dostoevsky, *The Brothers Karamazov*, translated by Constance Garnett (New York: Random House, 1945), pp. 521–2.

quiet, my pretty boy, eat a sweetmeat." How dishonest Dostoevsky is here! He establishes an escape for himself by giving public opinion a sweetmeat. There is no doubt that the whole Polish episode in *The Brothers Karamazov*, whose central point is the discussion about the Polish historical frontiers and partitions, is an echo of Dostoevsky's arguments with Tokarzewski in Siberia. Tokarzewski's book again becomes a kind of searchlight which helps us to discover in the whole Karamazov episode another proof of Dostoevsky's malignity and unfairness. He presented the discussions he had had with Polish political prisoners in Siberia in the form of a talk between the generous Mitya and the Polish scoundrels. And again Dostoevsky tries to be "true to reality". The main Pole in *The Brothers Karamazov* "appeared to be an official of the twelfth class retired"; he had served in Siberia as a veterinarian, and his name was Pan Musiałowicz". This is the factual information which Dostoevsky gives concerning his Polish cardsharper. The average reader would not find anything here deserving special comment. But the feelings of even an average reader change when he learns that Dostoevsky did not invent the name of his hero. He knew this name from Siberia. Under what circumstances? Jan Musiałowicz was one of the four Polish political prisoners who in 1850 arrived at the same prison which held Tokarzewski and Dostoevsky. Thus even in this case Dostoevsky was overwhelmed by the mischievous desire to give a half-distortion of reality, and through it the complete degradation of a fellow prisoner, a political prisoner. But how are we to explain this parody of truth and these lapses of Dostoevsky's conscience?—especially as they could satisfy only Dostoevsky himself. This was a secret dagger-thrust which only now appears in its true light.

The Poles in *The Brothers Karamazov* and in other novels represent Dostoevsky's general idea about Poland; through these Poles he expresses his passionate faith that Poland is impossible in a true new world. In that sense Dostoevsky was the greatest enemy Poland ever had.

I mentioned above that I would not examine all the Polish episodes in Dostoevsky's novels, but there is one which for some time puzzled me. I have in mind the surprising finale of *The Idiot*. How are we to explain the fate of Aglaya Epanchina? She is certainly the most attractive, the most independent and morally strong, the most deeply Russian of all Dostoevsky's feminine figures. How can we explain the fact that Dostoevsky predestined for her a future which, in his own mind, was the worst of all possible degradations? She escaped the vile Ganya Ivolgin and could not be contained by the weak arms of the Idiot, and after all her sentimental adventures she found herself attached to an émigré, a Polish count, whom she married against the will of her parents.

> "The count was not even a count, and if he was really an exile it was owing to some dark and dubious incident in his past, but he fascinated Aglaya by the extraordinary nobility of his soul, which was torn with patriotic anguish. He fascinated her to such a degree that even before she married she became a member of a committee for the restoration of Poland and had, moreover, visited the confessional of a celebrated Catholic priest, who gained a complete ascendancy over her mind."[1]

Is this a phenomenon of masochism or a manifestation of the same guilt complex we shall discuss a little later? Aglaya is Dostoevsky's prettiest flower—and she is thrown into the "mud of the Polish world". Yes, *habent sua fata libelli*. This epilogue to *The Idiot* is interesting, particularly against the background of Dostoevsky's anti-Polish feelings, and in connection with the prestige with which he endowed Aglaya. But if we detached this episode from Dostoevsky's world of ideas and fiction, we would have a simple cliché. Turgenev, in a really fascinating short story, *A Quiet Backwater* (which, by the way, is, in my opinion, the literary birthplace of Chekhov), also gave one of his heroines in marriage to an unpleasant Pole "from the shores of the Vistula", Stelchinsky, who as soon as he left Russia became "Count de Stelchinsky". Turgenev presented several Polish types of this character —compare *First Love*. Stelchinsky

> "frequented gambling-houses, the Kursaals in the watering places. . . . At first he lost a great deal of money, then left off losing, and his face assumed the peculiar expression, half suspicious, half impudent, which is seen in a man liable to being suddenly involved in some unpleasant affray. . . . He rarely saw his wife. Nadyezhda Alexyevna was not dull in his absence, however. . . . She did not go alone. She was accompanied by several admirers."[2]

As a matter of fact, the epilogue to *The Idiot* is a kind of variant to Turgenev's novel *On the Eve*. Turgenev assigned as a companion to his attractive and noble heroine a heroic Bulgarian patriot; she not only followed him and joined him in political activities, but after his death continued these activities herself, having become entirely devoted to

---

[1] Cf. F. M. Dostoevsky, *The Idiot*, "Conclusion".
[2] Ivan Turgenev, *Novels* (*A Quiet Backwater*), translated by C. Garnett (New York: Macmillan, 1921), Vol. XVI, pp. 359–60.

the patriotic cause of her foreign husband. One of the main themes of the book is connected with the very fact that its strong and determined hero was not a Russian. This was a challenge to Turgenev's Russian readers. I should like to point out another important aspect of Turgenev's novel. He presented a Bulgarian patriot and made his heroine become deeply indignant because of all the national persecution which the Bulgarians were suffering under the Turks. Needless to say, it would have been much more natural for Turgenev to replace this Bulgarian story with another one, much closer to Russia: the subjugation of Poland by Russia. Having this consideration in mind, one feels an element of falsity and hypocrisy in Turgenev's novel. Whatever Insarov says about the sufferings of his compatriots and whatever Elena's reactions are, they would sound much more natural if Insarov were not a Bulgarian but a Pole. Whether Turgenev did not dare to bring in a Pole or whether he had no desire to do so—his feelings for Poland were never too warm—it would be difficult to say. At any rate, Dobrolyubov dared to challenge Turgenev, and he did so in a very witty manner. This is what he said in his famous article about the novel *On the Eve*, entitled "When Will the Real Day Come?":

> "It seems to us that indeed a Bulgarian could perhaps be replaced here by another nationality—a Serb, a Czech, an Italian, a Hungarian—but (only not a Pole) not a Russian. (Why not a Pole, of course there can be no doubt; and why not a Russian—in this is contained the entire question. . . .)"[1]

Now, my idea is that Dostoevsky accepted Dobrolyubov's challenge and replaced the Bulgarian by a Pole. But this sarcastic solution of the problem raised by Dobrolyubov was probably, as in many other instances, enjoyed by Dostoevsky alone.[2]

No less gloomy is the aspect of the Polish problem under Dostoevsky's

---

[1] Cf. N. A. Dobroljubov, *Izbrannye sočinenija* (Moscow-Leningrad: Ogiz, 1947), p. 231.

[2] André Levinson (cf. *La Vie pathétique de Dostoïevsky*, Paris, 1935, p. 182) and later Stanisław Mackiewicz (*Dostoevsky*, London, Orbis, 1947) both advanced the supposition that in Aglaya one may find a poetic portrait of Miss Anna Korwin-Krukowska, whose father, the general Korwin-Krukowski, was a rich landlord in White Ruthenia, who belonged to a Russianized Polish family. I need not explain the rôle of Anna Korwin-Krukowska in Dostoevsky's life. If the suppositions of Levinson and Mackiewicz are correct the ultimate fate of Aglaya represents another characteristic play of Dostoevsky with the facts. We know from the author's second wife that Anna married a Frenchman, a communard, who was sentenced to death, and that Anna's father paid a bribe of twenty thousand francs to some French officials so that his son-in-law and his daughter could escape from France. (Cf. *Vospominanija A. G. Dostoevskoj*.) Thus, the real French communard became in *The Idiot* the false Polish count.

pen when he writes to his friends. His letters from this point of view are particularly significant as in them he supposedly gave a completely free expression to his feelings and thoughts. The derogatory term "Polyachishki" is constantly used here just as in his novels. In his letter to A. N. Maykov on 18 February [1 March], 1868, from Geneva he writes: "Here I meet only wretched 'Polyachishki'—in the coffee-shops in enormous crowds—but I do not enter into any relations with them."[1] In his letter to the same A. N. Maykov from Vevey on 19 July [2 August], 1868, complaining about the censoring of his letters, he says:

"Should I not refer to some *personage*; should I not ask not to be suspected of treachery to my fatherland and of relations with the 'Polyachishki'; and that my letters be not seized? This is disgusting! But they should know that the nihilists, the liberals of the *Contemporary*, have for three years been throwing mud at me because I broke with them, because I hate the 'Polyachishki' and love my fatherland. Oh scoundrels!"[2]

In his letter to I. S. Turgenev on 17 June, 1863, from Petersburg, he explains what happened to his review *Vremya*. Because of N. N. Strakhov's article, "The Fatal Question", Dostoevsky's review was suspended.

"You know the trend of our review: it is for the most part Russian and even anti-Western. Is it possible to imagine that we would take the side of the Poles? Despite this, they accused us of anti-patriotic convictions, sympathy toward the Poles, and forbade the review for an article which to our minds showed the highest degree of patriotism. It is true that there were in the article several awkward expressions, omissions, which provided reason for its misinterpretation. These omissions, as we ourselves now see, were actually quite serious and we are guilty in this respect. But we based our hopes on the former trend of our review, well known in literature, and we thought that they would accept the article and not understand the omissions in a false sense;—in this respect we made our mistake. The sense of the article (it was written by Strakhov) was the following: that the Poles despise us as barbarians and they flaunt their European civilization to the extent that their moral (that is, the most lasting) reconciliation with us cannot be foreseen. But since they did not understand these expressions in the

---

[1] Cf. F. M. Dostoevskij, *Pis'ma*, Vol. II, p. 80.
[2] Cf. *ibid.*, p. 131.

article, they interpreted it in this way: that *we ourselves* believe that the Poles have a higher civilization than we do, that we are inferior to them, that naturally they are right and we are in the wrong. Several reviews (*Den'*, by the way, among them) seriously began to point out to us that the Polish civilization is only superficial, aristocratic and Jesuit, and consequently not at all higher than ours. And imagine: they point this out to us, and we ourselves had in mind the very same thing in our article; and this is not all: they point this out to us when we *textually* stated that this vaunted Polish civilization has carried, and still carries, death in its heart. This was textually stated in our article. It is a remarkable fact that many of the honest persons terribly indignant with us, by their own admission *have never read* our article. Well, enough of this; the affair is over, you can't go back."[1]

But one thing should be pointed out: Dostoevsky's hatred toward Poland was connected with the great importance he placed upon the Polish problem and Polish-Russian relations in the past, during his time, as well as for the future. A proof of this might be found in his description of the novel he conceived but did not write, and which later developed into *The Possessed—The Life of a Great Sinner*. Giving the outline of this novel, he includes the influence of a Polish Jesuit on the moral, religious and ideological development of his hero —all of which he expressed in his letter to Maykov from Florence of 11/23 December, 1868.[2] In another important letter to Maykov from Florence of 15/27 May, 1869, he states how he would describe Russian history in the form of *byliny*, historical songs and poems. After having characterized the chief early periods and events, this is what he says about the finale of this epic:

"I would reach Biron and Catherine, and then I would go up to the emancipation of the peasants and to the boyars, who spread out in Europe with their last miserable roubles, to the ladies, fornicating with the Borgheses, to the seminarists preaching atheism, those humane citizens of the world, the Russian counts writing critical articles and novels, etc., etc. The Poles should occupy very much space. Then I would finish with fantastic pictures of the future: of Russia in two centuries and along with her the faded, lacerated and bestialized Europe and her civilization."[3]

[1] *Ibid.*, Vol. I, pp. 317–18.
[2] Cf. *ibid.*, Vol. II, p. 150.
[3] Cf. *ibid.* As we know, Poles do not play any rôle in *The Possessed*. Dostoevsky introduced them into his novel *The Brothers Karamazov*, but here their rôle was changed—they became simple scoundrels. They have no influence in the formation

Does this not confirm Tokarzewski's reports of his political talks with Dostoevsky and his opinions of the great Russian writer? But if we put aside all emotional considerations, we must at least come to the conclusion that the Polish problem was and still is a great problem for the Russian political conscience, and Dostoevsky was aware of this as was his great predecessor in this field, Pushkin.[1]

2. DOSTOEVSKY AND SPASOWICZ (FETYUKOVICH)

When the prosecutor characterizes Fedor Pavlovich Karamazov, he says:

> "Look at our vice, our profligates. Fedor Pavlovich, the luckless victim in the present case, was almost an innocent babe compared with many of them. And yet we all knew him, *'he lived among us!'* "[2]

The reference, *"he lived among us"* (*on mezhdu nami zhil*) is, of course, the beginning of the charming poem of Pushkin addressed to Mickiewicz. To apply to Fedor Pavlovich Karamazov what Pushkin said to Mickiewicz ... the insinuation is clear enough. Dostoevsky, I repeat, enjoyed his malignity in solitude. The reference seems to have passed unnoticed until now, in spite of the quotation marks which Dostoevsky used. The editors of the latest Russian edition of Dostoevsky did not observe it, and I do not find this verse among the *Pushkiniana* listed in the Index of that edition. Even Professor Bem was unaware of the reference until I drew his attention to it when I was in Prague in 1937, and God knows how carefully he traced Pushkin in Dostoevsky.

---

of the Russian "accidental race". However, in the notes to *The Possessed* and to various smaller works from which originated *The Possessed* and later *The Brothers Karamazov* there are allusions to a "Polish Count" who apparently was to arrive from abroad with Liza Tushina and was supposed to play an unpleasant rôle in the tale about Captain Kartuzov. There also appears in these notes the figure of a Polish priest, to whom Dostoevsky alludes in a letter of 25 January/6 February, 1869, to S. A. Ivanova: "... the enthusiastic Catholic priest ... in the style of St. François Xavier". (Cf. Dostoevskij, *Pis'ma*, Vol. II, p. 161.) This figure, as the exiled Priest Słońcewski, is only episodically mentioned in *The Possessed* as a temporary member of the circle of S. T. Verkhovensky. (Cf. *Zapisnye tetradi F. M. Dostoevskogo* (Moscow-Leningrad: Academia, 1935); and *The Possessed*, Part I, chapter 1.

[1] See my book *Pouchkine et la Pologne*. In the light of Tokarzewski's original text, Henri Troyat's statements dealing with Dostoevsky's relations with his Polish prison mates are ridiculous, see Troyat, *op. cit.*, pp. 152–3 and p. 158.

[2] *The Brothers Karamazov*, translated by Constance Garnett, p. 875. The italics are the author's. Concerning Spasowicz, see also the statements of Ivan about the lawyers (ch. IV, in "Pro and Contra.").

As we are interested here in the malignity of Dostoevsky, let me quote another example. Very often his attacks were directed against his contemporaries with whom he was quarrelling; very often his insinuations were so malicious that only their direct victim was able to recognize the bad intention. It appears to be a sort of fair play, a sort of delicate discretion. In reality, it was just the contrary—a person attacked in such a manner felt himself absolutely defenseless. What could he do? It is a typical stab in the back—an anonymous attack.

It is known that Dostoevsky disliked Spasowicz, that he attacked him in his articles violently and mordaciously, that he finally tried to represent him in parody, in the person of the lawyer Fetyukovich in *The Brothers Karamazov*. All those who knew Spasowicz, who remembered his portrait by Repin, who had any idea about his method of pleading, the style of his very individual eloquence, could easily recognize him in the physical portrayal of Fetyukovich, the content of his speech, the method of his inquiry. The speech of Fetyukovich reproduces in several instances all the essential characteristics, of course parodized by Dostoevsky, of Spasowicz's court-room speeches. The best proof of this is offered by Dostoevsky himself in his article about Spasowicz's speech in the Kronenberg affair.[1] Even the etymology of the name—Fetyukovich ("Fetyuk—sombre man, hypochondriac, grumbler, growler; even worse than that—Fetyuk—it is an offensive word for a man")[2] proves a hostile intention. In one of the chapters which include Fetyukovich's speech he is called by Dostoevsky an "adulterer of thought". In his article on the Kronenberg case Dostoevsky uses the term "prostitution of talent". Some details of this case reappear in the stories which Ivan relates to Alesha. All these allusions were clear—but there was another one, a secret one, which only intimate friends of Spasowicz were able to discover.

During the trial of Mitya, a sharp discussion took place between the prosecutor and Fetyukovich. The prosecutor, in his second speech, attacked Fetyukovich's religious positivism and especially his "autonomous morality":

"And we will not from the tribune of truth and good sense correct the Gospel of our Lord, Whom the counsel for the defence deigns to call only 'the crucified lover of humanity', *in opposition to all orthodox Russia*, which calls to him 'For Thou art our God!' "[3]

[1] *Diary of a Writer*, pp. 210–38. See also Saltykov-Shchedrin's account of the Kronenberg case in *Nedokončennye besedy*.
[2] Cf. the sense that is given to this word by Nozdrev in *Dead Souls* of Gogol and in the *Story about Captain Kopeykin*. Cf. M. I. Mikhelson, *Russkaja Mysl' i Reč'*, Vol. II, p. 580.
[3] Cf. *The Brothers Karamazov*, p. 893. Italics are mine.

"At this the President intervened and checked the over-zealous speaker, begging him not to exaggerate, not to overstep the bounds, and so on, as presidents always do in such cases. The audience too was uneasy. The public was restless: there were even exclamations of indignation. Fetyukovich did not so much as reply; he only mounted the tribune to lay his hand on his heart and, with an offended voice, utter a few words full of dignity. He only touched again, lightly and ironically, on 'romancing' and 'psychology', and in an appropriate place quoted, 'Jupiter, you are angry, therefore you are wrong,' which provoked a burst of approving laughter in the audience, for Ippolit Kirillovich was by no means like Jupiter. Then *à propos* of the accusation that he was teaching the young generation to murder their fathers, Fetyukovich observed with great dignity that he would not even answer. As for the prosecutor's charge of uttering opinions opposed to the orthodox religion, Fetyukovich hinted that it was a personal insinuation and that he had expected in this court to be secure from accusations 'damaging to my reputation as a citizen and a loyal subject'. But at these words the President pulled him up, too, and Fetyukovich concluded his speech with a bow, amid a hum of approbation in the court. And Ippolit Kirillovich was, in the opinion of the ladies, 'crushed for good'."[1]

To be able to understand the sense of this "insinuation"—and the most striking fact is that Dostoevsky himself speaks about "insinuation"—one must know that Spasowicz, being the son of an Eastern Orthodox father and a Roman Catholic mother, should have belonged officially to the Eastern Orthodox Church. But he was a Pole brought up in a Roman Catholic tradition. Such an allusion towards his religious status was damaging, because of the drastic persecutions which at that time were borne by Poles, White Russians and Ukrainians who originated from mixed marriages and did not embrace the Eastern Orthodox religion or who belonged to the Uniate church established in Poland in the sixteenth century.

One must also observe with what artfulness Dostoevsky has hidden under the applause of the audience his own point of view in the affair!

The solidarity of the public with Fetyukovich appears as the culmination of Dostoevsky's malignity. And the stylization of Fetyukovich's reply! Especially his commentary about the "accusations"—"damaging to my reputation as a citizen and a loyal subject!" But all that is deeply hidden, secret—who, especially now, will see the point in which Spasowicz was bitten?

[1] Cf. *The Brothers Karamazov*, p. 943.

And when you realize who Spasowicz was, what a really great man he was, what a glorious and generous rôle he played in the development of Russian culture, literature, jurisprudence, criminology, if you realize that this great Pole represented a policy of Russian-Polish understanding and peace, you must agree that the hatred of Dostoevsky against Poland and Poles was really unlimited. Dostoevsky never said that Fetyukovich was a Pole, but he gave him all the features of malicious adroitness, of great moral elasticity, and of accentuated personal dignity with which he generally characterized Poles.

Worthy of consideration is the fact that Dostoevsky ends his last article on the Kronenberg suit with an harangue maintained exactly in the same tone of "official, national indignation" which characterizes the prosecutor's attack against Fetyukovich. In his article Dostoevsky addresses Spasowicz as would a Russian lecturing someone who obviously is a foreigner, as a Russian proud of the "sanctities" which "Russians love", "because they are, in fact, holy", and "in reality solid". "These are the sanctities of family" "in which we believe" and which "we defend", independently of the fact that order and the state "are solidly founded upon them".[1] How, by the way, may one reconcile this with the complaints about the "disorder", "chaos", "lack of tradition and form" in the Russian "accidental tribe" which Dostoevsky displayed in *A Raw Youth*? But the destruction of "the adulterer of thought" was a sufficiently important goal to justify the sacrifice of consistency of thought.

However, there is to be found in the same novel another episode, the main parts of which I have already utilized in my essay "Europe in Dostoevsky's Ideological Novel", which is indirectly connected with Spasowicz. The particular detail in this episode which I have in mind, as well as the parodistic portrait of Spasowicz given in *The Brothers Karamazov*, illustrates, furthermore, how closely Dostoevsky connected his novels with the actual social and political problems of Russian life discussed at the time. While Dostoevsky was writing his *Brothers Karamazov* a strong wave of anti-Semitism was sweeping over Russia. There is no doubt that the Russian government played a rôle in the instigation of these currents. It is worth while to note that Pobedonostsev's correspondence with Dostoevsky was filled with anti-Semitic declarations. In 1878 and in 1879 the Russian press was involved in a passionate discussion on the theme of ritual murders in connection with the Kutais affair, which was fomented by the Russian government. Despite all the evidence to the contrary nine Jews were accused of the ritual murder of a Georgian girl, who mysteriously disappeared on the eve of Jewish Easter. In *The Citizen*, in which

[1] *Diary of a Writer*, Vol. I, p. 237.

Dostoevsky himself published a feuilleton, appeared articles based on a report prepared by a high Russian official by the order of the Minister of Foreign Confessions for Nicholas I, for the heir to the throne, the Grand Dukes, and the members of the Council of State. Some other articles also appeared dealing with the "murders of Christians committed by Jews for the procurement of blood". This whole anti-Jewish propaganda developed in a series of articles. There were also protests. Among them was one from Spasowicz, who publicly declared that "in my deep opinion cases like the present one only show the excessive vitality of legends of old times, ridiculous as these legends are". *The Citizen*, with which Dostoevsky deeply sympathized, violently attacked Spasowicz, mocking his jurisprudential activity.[1]

The reader remembers the dialogue between Liza and Alesha. When Liza asks Alesha, "Is it true that Jews steal and slaughter children for Easter?" Dostoevsky's Alesha, his chosen messenger of the great Christian Resurrection of Russia, answers, "I don't know." Who, then, is more skeptical—Spasowicz the Positivist or Dostoevsky the Christian?

3. DOSTOEVSKY AND MICKIEWICZ

(a) PETERSBURG

Three times Mickiewicz appears openly under the pen of Dostoevsky. In the *Eternal Husband* Velchaninov sings a popular romance of Glinka composed to words of a famous poem of Mickiewicz, *My Darling*. Then indirectly but "openly" there is a reference to Mickiewicz in the quoted speech of the prosecutor in *The Brothers Karamazov*. And finally, Dostoevsky speaks about "new" Konrad Wallenrods in his article about *The New Conciliatory Efforts of Poland* (in 1877). It appears to me, however, that there were other reminiscences of the great Polish poet in the mind of Dostoevsky, but these were hidden or even unconscious.

Well known are the Petersburg motifs of Pushkin and Gogol which are so easy to discover in the Petersburg of Dostoevsky. *The Queen of Spades*, *The Bronze Horseman*, and the tales of Gogol produced their undoubted influence on the stylization of Petersburg and on the interpretation of its "soul" in the works of Dostoevsky. I think, however, that there was somebody else—perhaps unconsciously for Dostoevsky—who suggested to him some thoughts on the theme of

[1] Cf. L. Grossman, "Dostoevskij i pravitel'stvennye krugi 1870-x godov", in *Literaturnoe Nasledstvo*, Vol. XV, pp. 83–123.

Petersburg: it seems to me that this was Mickiewicz. In this sense the most striking is the following description of Petersburg by Dostoevsky:

"It was quite dusk when Arkady returned home. When he reached the Neva he stood still for a minute and turned a keen glance up the river into the smoky frozen thickness of the distance, which was suddenly flushed crimson with the last purple and blood-red glow of sunset, still smouldering on the misty horizon... Night lay over the city, and the wide plain of the Neva, swollen with frozen snow, was shining in the last gleams of the sun with myriads of sparks of gleaming hoar frost. There was a frost of twenty degrees. A cloud of frozen steam hung about the overdriven horses and the hurrying people. The condensed atmosphere quivered at the slightest sound and, from all the roofs on both sides of the river, columns of smoke rose up like giants and floated across the cold sky, intertwining and untwining as they went, so that it seemed new buildings were rising up above the old, a new town was taking shape in the air.... It seemed as if all that world, with all its inhabitants, strong and weak, with all their habitations, the refuges of the poor, or the gilded palaces for the comfort of the powerful of this world, was at that twilight hour like a fantastic vision of fairy-land, like a dream which in its turn would vanish and pass away like vapor into the dark blue sky."[1]

Is it too much to claim that the following passage from *The Suburbs of the Capital* of Mickiewicz may be considered as a possible source for Dostoevsky's description?

> Now all is silent here ... Snow is on the ground,
> The clocks have thundered twelve from near and far,
> And now the winter sun is westward bound.[2]
> The spacious heavens their vaulted depths unfold,
> Cloudless and silent, empty, pure and cold;
> Quite colorless, a pale, transparent sky,
> As lifeless as a frozen traveller's eye.
>
> Above that city which we now draw near
> Rise fairy castles gleaming in the sun;
> Pillars and walls and balconies appear
> Like hanging gardens reared in Babylon.

---

[1] *A Faint Heart*, in *The Novels of Fyodor Dostoevsky*, translated by Constance Garnett (New York, 1918), Vol. X, pp. 198–9.

[2] "In St. Petersburg during winter dusk begins about three o'clock." Mickiewicz. See Noyes, *op. cit.*, p. 469.

From out two hundred thousand chimney throats
Upward the smoke in straight dense columns floats;
These like Carrara marble gleam and shine,
Those glow like rubies with a rosy light.

Aloft the summits perish and unite,
And into balcony and arch entwine,
While roofs and walls of pearl ascend the skies,
Like those illusive cities that arise
From out the Great Sea's waters, calm and clear,
Or in the Lybian desert haze appear:
These from afar the weary travellers see.
They ever seem at hand and ever flee . . .[1]

As I mentioned in the section on Chaadaev, we have here not only a literal description of the city based on actual observation, but Mickiewicz also notes the mirage-like effect suggested by the ephemeral and fantastic aspects of Petersburg. As we know, this theme was developed by Dostoevsky in *A Raw Youth*:

"But I will remark, however, in passing, I consider a Petersburg morning—which might be thought the most prosaic on the terrestrial globe—almost the most fantastic in the world. That is my personal view, or rather impression, but I am prepared to defend it. On such a Petersburg morning, foul, damp and foggy, the bold dream of some Herman out of Pushkin's *Queen of Spades* (a colossal figure, an extraordinary and regular Petersburg type—the type of the Petersburg period!) would, I believe, be more like solid reality. A hundred times over, in such a fog, I have been haunted by a strange but persistent fancy: 'What if this fog should part and float away, would not all this rotten and slimy town go with it, rise up with the fog, and vanish like smoke, and the old Finnish marsh be left as before, and in the midst of it, perhaps, to complete the picture, a bronze horseman on a panting overdriven steed.' In fact, I cannot find words for my sensations, for all this is fantastic, after all, poetic, and therefore nonsensical; nevertheless, I have often been and often am haunted by an utterly senseless question: 'Here they are all flitting to and fro, but how can one tell, perhaps all this is someone's dream, and there is not one real person here, nor one real action. Someone who is dreaming all this will suddenly wake up—and everything will suddenly disappear.' "[2]

[1] Cf. Noyes, *op. cit.*, pp. 342–3.
[2] See also *A Raw Youth*, in *The Novels of Fyodor Dostoevsky*, Vol. VII, p. 132.

I think that all these "nonsensical" speculations are closely connected with Mickiewicz. We are reminded too of his poem *Oleszkiewicz*, especially its beginning and its end:

> When winter makes the sky glow cold and clear,
> It turns dark blue; black spots of frost appear.
> Like those that mark a dead man's frozen face,
> When near a stove is placed the stiffened clay,
> And drawing warmth, not life, to its embrace,
> It breathes forth only vapors of decay.
> Warm winds begin to blow . . . Those towers of smoke,
> That airy city of gigantic size,
> That vision of enchantment thinned and broke,
> And fell in ruins from the darkened skies.
> Smoke flowed in rivers through each street and square,
> Mixed with warm vapors in the close, damp air;
> Before night fell, the snow's relentless thaw
> Had buried pavements neath a Stygian flood.
> Sleighs fled away, and carriage and landau
> Cast off their runners; wheels splashed through the mud.
> But in the humid, smoke-filled murky night
> The carriages and cabs are lost to sight;
> Only their lanterns wander to and fro,
> Like flames that over marshlands dance and glow. . . .

And now the end. After devoting two stanzas to Alexander I, the poet, through the mystic painter Oleszkiewicz, develops his vision of a punishing storm which will devastate and annihilate the "city of crime and flesh":

> These wretched serfs who in their hovels cower,
> And not the Czar, will first meet punishment:
> For lightning, striking a dead element,
> Smites first the lofty mountain and the tower;
> But in the world of men this is reversed:
> It strikes the lowly and the guiltless first.
> 'Mid quarrels, lust and wine they fall asleep,
> Poor corpse-like skulls, to waken in the morn!
> Rest ye, dull hearts, in slumber sunken deep,
> Till the Lord's wrath awake you like the horn
> Of forest hunter, whose swift sword lays bare
> A path of slaughter to the world boar's lair!
> I hear . . . afar . . . the storm winds raise their heads
> Like polar monsters, from their icy beds:
> Already they have spread their cloudy wings;
> They mount upon the wave, its strength unchained.

> I hear! Now the deep ocean, unrestrained,
> Champs on its icy bit, strikes out, and springs.
> Now to the skies it arches its moist neck;
> Now! Still on chain, but one, holds it in check . . .
> Soon that will part! They strike it blow on blow . . .
> He spoke: Then sensing his lone auditor,
> Blew out his candle and was soon no more.
> Thus had he gleamed and gone, foreboding woe,
> Like an ill omen, smiting suddenly,
> Then passing by . . . an awesome mystery.[1]

All this is really amazing. I need not emphasise the similarity of the impressionistic pictures of Petersburg which we find in Mickiewicz and Dostoevsky. But one may say that in *A Faint Heart* we have also another motif besides the fantasticalness—a juxtaposition of "the refuges of the poor" and "gilded palaces for the comfort of the powerful", and in *A Raw Youth*, the other juxtaposition—of the prosaicness and fantasticalness of Petersburg. The motif of the poor and of Petersburg's prosaicness are both eloquently developed in Mickiewicz's satires, especially in the passage of the poem *Oleszkiewicz* which presages the apocalyptical destruction of Petersburg as God's punishment. On the other hand, the poem *Saint Petersburg* brings a sharp satirical—one might even say naturalistic—picture of the prosaicness of Petersburg. Mickiewicz mocks not only the chaotic cosmopolitanism of this "accidental city" when he describes the "Babel" of signs:

> . . . From every housefront here a signboard calls
> Amid so many tongues, such varied script,
> The eye and ear find Babel. 'There,' one tells,
> 'A Khan of the Kirghiz, a Senator,
> Head of the Polish Office, Achmet dwells.
> Here Monsieur Joco,' states another door,
> 'Gives lessons in Parisian French. He plays
> Bass viol in the band; he overlooks
> Distilleries and schools; he also cooks.'
> A signboard over yonder sounds the praise
> Of great Piacere Gioco, known to fame
> As sausage-maker for the maids of court,
> Who keeps a ladies' school of great report.
> That lengthy sign bears Pastor Diener's name,
> A knight of many orders of the czar.
> Today he preached a sermon on the theme
> That by God's grace the czar is pope, supreme
> As lord of faith and conscience' guiding star.

[1] Cf. Noyes, *op. cit.*, p. 366.

> He likewise calls the Anabaptist bands
> And the Socinians and Calvinists,
> That, as the Russian Emperor commands
> And his ally, the Prussian King, insists,
> They all accept a new religious rite
> And into one new faith and church unite.
> Here 'Ladies' Clothes'; 'Sheet Music' there we read,
> Or 'Children's Toys,' or 'Knouts,' or what you need.[1]

In this poem he also presents a Gogolian, Hogarthian parade of the banal Petersburg crowds:

> ... Beside the crowding common herd of folk
> Move two vast columns in slow promenade,
> Like church procession, or like floes along
> A river bank, by rushing waters tossed.
> And whither goes this slowly dragging throng,
> This herd of sables heedless of the frost?
> This is the fashionable walking hour;
> Who cares though wintry winds blow cold and keen?
> For after all here may the czar be seen.
> His empress and the mistresses in power.
> Officials, ladies, marshals make their way;
> First, second, fourth, in even sets they pass
> Like cards thrown from a gamester's hand in play,
> Kings, queens, and knaves, the mighty ruling class!
> Court cards and common cards, both black and red,
> Fall to this side and that. Alike they tread
> The splendid street, magnificent and long,
> The mighty bridges, granite-lined and strong...[2]

At this point I should like to add some special comments. Mr. Mochulsky, in his very interesting book on Dostoevsky,[3] brings to the fore Dostoevsky's famous article of 1861, *The Petersburg Dreams in Verse and Prose*, and he compares some passages of this article with Gogol's *Nevsky Prospekt*.[4] Mr. Mochulsky justly sees in these passages of Dostoevsky's article a literary confession which describes the ideological birth of Dostoevsky's first novel *Poor Folk*. Before I quote the respective passages from Dostoevsky and Gogol, I should like to call the reader's attention to the fact that Dostoevsky in his article textually repeated the beginning of the last paragraphs of *A Faint Heart*, which I have already quoted above. Though indeed the descriptive portion of these

---

[1] *Ibid.*, pp. 344–5.
[2] *Ibid.*, pp. 345–6.
[3] Cf. Močul'skij, *op. cit*, p. 27.
[4] *Ibid.*, pp. 27–8.

paragraphs is repeated by the author in his article, the conclusions are different. The inference of the passage from *A Faint Heart* is connected with the story of which it is a part, whereas the meditations and reflections contained in the article obviously refer to the *Poor Folk*. Since I have already quoted the first part of the passage in question, let us now look at the conclusions in the article, for they have some elements significant for our present subject:

". . . Suddenly a strange thought came to my head. I started, and my heart seemed at that instant flooded with a hot rush of blood suddenly kindled by a powerful overwhelming sensation I had never known before. In that instant I as though understood something which up to that time had only stirred in my mind without meaning; something shone through that was new, in quite a new sphere, something known to me through vague rumors, through some secret signs. I suppose that from this very minute my existence began . . . tell me sirs: Am I not a visionary, a mystic from my very childhood? . . .
And suddenly, being alone, I began to think about this. And I began to look around, and suddenly saw some strange persons. They were all strange, queer figures, completely prosaic, not at all Don Carloses and Poses but thorough titular secretaries, and at the same time as though fantastic titular secretaries. Someone hidden behind this whole fantastic crowd made a grimace before my eyes, tugged along threads and springs which moved little dolls, and he laughed, constantly laughed! And another incident appeared to me; in a dark corner, a titular heart, honest and pure, moral and devoted to authority, and together with him a girl, insulted and mournful, and their whole story deeply tore at my heart. And if this entire crowd of which I dreamed were collected it would compose a grand masquerade . . ."[1]

There is no doubt that the item of the small, protesting victim, of the petty official, might be connected with Gogol's *Overcoat*, and with Pushkin's *Postmaster* in Dostoevsky's acceptation of this short story. But there is also no doubt that Pushkin's *The Bronze Horseman* must be taken into consideration and *The Bronze Horseman*, as I have explained in my study on this poem,[2] cannot be understood without Mickiewicz's satires. The motif of punishment, of the unjust city, of the humble victim, of the poor—all this is contained in Mickiewicz's *Digression*, especially in the poem *Oleszkiewicz*.

[1] *Loc. cit.*
[2] Cf. *Jeździec Miedziany*, p. 124.

We have no biographical proof that Dostoevsky read and knew Mickiewicz, but he might have known the relationship between *The Bronze Horseman* and Mickiewicz's *Digression* from Pushkin's footnotes to *The Bronze Horseman*. In the same way the legend of Mickiewicz's stay in Russia, which never ceased to attract Russian minds, could have excited his curiosity enough for him to read Mickiewicz. And in this case again we have as if a kind of avowal so characteristic for Dostoevsky: "Something known to me through vague rumours, through some secret signs." Involuntarily there emerges from Dostoevsky's text the figure of the mystic painter Oleszkiewicz, appearing in the Petersburg darkness with his mysterious lantern, his prophecies, and his threats against those who "under Satan's heel continue their crimes".

But this is not all. In Dostoevsky's *Notebooks*, in connection with *The Possessed*, appears an extremely interesting passage dealing with Shatov. In the remark which I have in mind Dostoevsky opposes the Russian quivering and trembling attitude to the western-European firm, century-old tradition of effort, work, economy and confidence in one's own power "which is the essence of nationalism". This is what he says: "We do not have anything of this kind [i.e., solid tradition, firm hopes]. We have no faith in ourselves, for this is impossible, there is nothing to believe in." Then, obviously playing with the name of Shatov (*shatost*—"unsteadiness"), he continues: "There is a two-century-old unsteadiness in everything. Our whole reform beginning with Peter consisted only of this—that he took a stone which was lying flat and he managed to stand it up on one of its corners. We have remained in this position and are balancing—when the wind blows we shall fail."[1] The reader remembers the end of Mickiewicz's *The Monument of Peter the Great*:

> Thus it has galloped long, with tossing mane,
> Like a cascade, leaping into the void,
> That, fettered by the frost, hangs dizzily.
> But soon will shine the sun of liberty,
> And from the West a wind will warm this land.
> Will the cascade of tyranny then stand?[2]

Again the similarities are obvious. Dostoevsky's imagery and his metaphor are exactly the same as those of Mickiewicz.

I think that all these juxtapositions show similarities which are striking enough to be taken into consideration. It seems to me that

---

[1] Cf. *Zapisnye tetradi F. M. Dostoevskogo*, kommentarij I. I. Ignatovoj i E. N. Konšinoj (Moscow-Leningrad: Academia, 1935), p. 298.
[2] Cf. Noyes, *op. cit.*, p. 350.

they are even more striking than the resemblances between the "Petersburg lyrics" of Dostoevsky and Gogol which M. Mochulsky emphasizes: "In the *Nevsky Prospect*," says Mochulsky,

> "the mystery of Petersburg grows with the approach of night. 'Then, (in the dusk) comes the mysterious time when the street lamps throw a marvellous, alluring light upon everything . . . Everything is a cheat, everything is a dream, everything is other than it seems! . . . It deceives at all hours, the Nevsky Prospect does, but most of all when night falls with masses of shadow on it, throwing into relief the white and dun-coloured walls of the houses, when all the town is transformed into noise and brilliance, when myriads of carriages roll over bridges, postilions shout and jolt up and down on their horses, and when the demon himself lights the street lamps to show everything in false colours.' "[1]

I do not at all deny the powerful suggestiveness of Gogol's images in Dostoevsky's Petersburg tales. I think, however, that Mochulsky's quotation might be paralleled with a quotation from Mickiewicz's *Oleszkiewicz*:

> But in the humid, smoke-filled, murky night
> The carriages and cabs are lost to sight;
> Only their lanterns wander to and fro,
> Like flames that over marshlands dance and glow . . .[2]

The people of Poland, Lithuania, White Ruthenia and Russia know that the flames which "dance and glow over the marshlands" are deceiving flames and in the popular imagination are lighted by the devil. I still believe that Oleszkiewicz's mystical proclamation of reward for the sufferings of the poor and of the punishment for the powerful should not be overlooked in this connection. By the way, Gogol wrote his *Nevsky Prospect* in 1835, two years after the publication of Mickiewicz's *Forefathers' Eve*. I will not discuss the problem of whether or not he read Mickiewicz, as this is not my present task.

(b) Jankiel's "Polonaise of the Third of May" and Lyamshin's "Franco-Prussian War"

One of the most perfect popular and poetical episodes in Mickiewicz's *Pan Tadeusz* is the playing of Jankiel on the dulcimer in the

[1] Cf. Močul'skij, *op. cit.*, p. 28. Cf. *The Overcoat and Other Stories* by N. Gogol (New York: Knopf, 1923), pp. 84, 122, 123.
[2] Cf. Noyes, *op. cit.*, p. 363.

twelfth and last Book of the poem. How alive it is today, how full of pure, high poetical charm! No modern book of poetry is so near to Homer as this Polish book; none is so near to Poles now, in days of exile.

"Jankiel with half-closed eyes sat silent and held the hammers motionless in his fingers.

He lowered them, at first beating a triumphal measure; then he smote the strings more briskly, as with a torrent of rain; all were amazed, but that was only a test for he suddenly broke off and lifted both hammers aloft.

He played anew; now the strings trembled with motions as light as though the wings of a fly were sounding on the string, giving forth a gentle, hardly audible buzzing. The master fixed his gaze on the sky, awaiting inspiration; he looked down and surveyed the instrument with a haughty eye, he raised his hands and lowered them altogether, and smote with both hammers at once; the auditors were amazed.—

All at once from many strings there burst forth a sound as though a whole janissaries' band had become vocal with bells and cymbals and drums. *The Polonaise of the Third of May*[1] thundered forth! The rippling notes breathed of joy, they poured joy into one's ears; the girls wanted to dance and the boys could not stand still—but the notes carried the thoughts of the old men back into the past, to those happy years when the Senate and the House of Deputies, after that great day of the Third of May, celebrated in the assembly hall the reconciliation of King and Nation; when they danced and sang, 'Vivat our beloved King, vivat the Diet, vivat the people, vivat all classes!'

The master kept quickening the time and playing with greater power, but suddenly he struck a false chord like the hiss of a snake, like the grating of iron on glass—it sent a shudder through every one, and mingled with the general gaiety an ill-omened foreboding.

---

[1] "After the disaster of the first partition the patriotic party in Poland made efforts to save their country, which culminated in the Four Years' Diet (1788-92). The labors of this Diet, which again was convoked under the forms of a confederacy, culminated in the Constitution of 3 May, 1791. This measure, which was drawn up in secret and rushed through the Diet at a time when most of its probable opponents were absent, transformed Poland from an aristocratic republic into a constitutional hereditary monarchy, abolished the *liberum veto*, and secured religious toleration. Amid great enthusiasm the King took the oath to the new order of government." See Adam Mickiewicz, *Pan Tadeusz*, translated from the Polish by G. R. Noyes (London, 1917), pp. 333-4.

Mickiewicz
Daguerreotype c. 1840

Disturbed and alarmed, the hearers wondered whether the instrument might not be out of tune, or the musician be making a blunder. Such a master had not blundered! He purposely kept touching that traitorous string and breaking up the melody, striking louder and louder that angry chord, confederated against the harmony of the tones; at last the Warden understood the master, covered his face in his hands, and cried, 'I know, I know those notes; that is *Targowica!*'[1] And suddenly the ill-omened string broke with a hiss; the musician rushed to the treble notes, broke up and confused the measure, abandoned the treble notes, and hurried his hammers to the bass strings.

One could hear louder and louder a thousand noises, measured marching, war, an attack, a storm; one could hear the reports of guns, the groans of children, the weeping of mothers. So finely did the wonderful master render the horrors of a storm that the village girls trembled, calling to mind with tears of grief the Massacre of Praga, which they knew from song and story; they were glad when finally the master thundered with all the strings at once, and choked the outcries as though he had crushed them into the earth.

Hardly did the hearers have time to recover from their amazement, when once more the music changed; at first there were once more light and gentle hummings; a few thin strings complained together, like flies striving to free themselves from the spider's web. But more and more strings joined them; now the scattered tones were blended and legions of chords were united; now they advanced measuredly with harmonious notes, forming the mournful melody of that famous song of the wandering soldier who travels through woods and through forests, ofttimes fainting with woe and with hunger; at last he falls at the feet of his faithful steed, and the steed with his foot digs a grave for him. A poor old song, yet very dear to the Polish troops! The soldiers recognized it, and the privates crowded about the master; they hearkened, and they remembered that dreadful season when over the grave of their country they had sung this song and departed for the ends of the earth; they called to mind their long years of wandering, over lands and seas, over frosts and burning sands, amid foreign peoples, where often in

---

[1] "In the next year (1792) ... a group of upholders of the anarchic state of affairs, one of whose leaders was Ksawery Branicki, formed with the support of Russia a confederacy which was proclaimed at Targowica, a small town in the Ukraine, and the object of which was the undoing of the work of the Four Years' Diet. The Russian Armies entered the country and overcame the resistance of the Polish troops, two of the foremost leaders of which were Prince Joseph Poniatowski, the nephew of the King, and Kościuszko." See *ibid.*, p. 334.

camp they had been cheered and heartened by this folk song. So thinking, they sadly bowed their heads!

But they raised them straightway, for the master was playing stronger and higher notes; he changed his measure, and proclaimed something quite different from what had preceded. Once more he looked down and measured the strings with his eye; he joined his hands and smote with the two hammers in unison: the blow was so artistic, so powerful, that the strings ran like brazen trumpets, and from the trumpets a well-known song floated to the heavens, a triumphal march. 'Poland has not yet perished; march, Dąbrowski,[1] to Poland!'—And all clapped their hands, and all shouted in chorus, 'March, Dąbrowski!'

The musician seemed amazed at his own song; he dropped the hammers from his hands and raised his arms aloft."[2]

It is a supposition only, as almost everything in this study, but now take Dostoevsky's novel *The Possessed*, the chapter "On the Eve of the Fête", and read the following passage, in which Lyamshin, who has composed a new piece for the piano, has succeeded in persuading Yulia Mikhaylovna to hear it.

"The piece turned out to be really amusing, and bore the comic title of 'The Franco-Prussian War'. It began with the menacing strains of the 'Marseillaise':
Qu'un sang impur abreuve nos sillons.
There is heard the pompous challenge, the intoxication of future victories. But suddenly mingling with the masterly variations on the national hymn, somewhere from some corner quite close, on one side come the vulgar strains of 'Mein leiber Augustin'. The 'Marseillaise' goes on unconscious of them. The 'Marseillaise' is at the climax of its intoxication with its own grandeur; but Augustin gains strength; Augustin grows more and more insolent, and suddenly the melody of Augustin begins to blend with the melody of the 'Marseillaise'. The latter begins, as it were, to get angry; becoming aware of Augustin at last she tries to fling him off, to brush him aside like a tiresome insignificant fly. But 'Mein leiber Augustin' holds his ground firmly, he is cheerful and self-confident, he is gleeful and impudent, and the 'Marseillaise' seems suddenly to become terribly stupid. She can no longer conceal her anger

---

[1] "The leader of the Polish Legions who fought for France from 1797–1813. Their first field of activity was in Northern Italy—there arose in 1797 the famous song of the Legions 'Poland has not yet perished while we still live'." See *ibid.*, p. 334.

[2] Mickiewicz, *Pan Tadeusz*, pp. 323–6.

and mortification; it is a wail of indignation, tears and curses, with hands outstretched to Providence.

Pas un pouce de notre terrain; pas une de nos forteresses.

But she is forced to sing in time with 'Mein leiber Augustin'. Her melody passes in a sort of foolish way into Augustin; she yields and dies away. And only by snatches there is heard again:

'*Qu'un sang impur* . . .'

But at once it passes very offensively into the vulgar waltz. She submits altogether. It is Jules Favre sobbing on Bismarck's bosom and surrendering everything . . . But at this point Augustin too grows fierce; hoarse sounds are heard; there is a suggestion of countless gallons of beer, of a frenzy of self-glorification, demands for millions, for fine cigars, champagne and hostages. Augustin passes into a wild yell . . . 'The Franco-Prussian War' is over. Our circle applauded, Yulia Mikhaylovna smiled, and said, 'Now how is one to turn him out?' Peace was made."[1]

I think that Dostoevsky took the idea of the disturbance of a national hymn by a noisy "insolent" melody from the wonderful passage of Mickiewicz which I quoted above, but he made a parody of it. Dostoevsky could have openly parodied, but that would have been in bad taste. There were so many reasons to "parody" Jankiel's performance by a transposition into a *Marseillaise* and "Mein lieber Augustin". It was again a pleasure which he enjoyed in solitude! Dostoevsky says at the end of Lyamshin's playing: "The rascal [Lyamshin] really had talent. Stepan Trofimovich assured me on one occasion that the very highest artistic talents may exist in the most abominable blackguards, and the one thing does not interfere with the other." Is this not striking! And it is not all: "There was a rumor afterwards that Lyamshin had stolen this burlesque from a talented and modest young man of his acquaintance, whose name remained unknown."[2] For me, these words are a secret confession, a sort of admission. And why is there also this following detail? "This worthless fellow who had hung about Stepan Trofimovich for years, who used at his evening parties, when invited, to mimic Jews of various types, a deaf peasant woman making her confession, or the birth of a child . . . a pig, a thunderstorm."[3] Is not that a continuation of a parody and sarcastic deformation of Jankiel's "universal music"? Is not the sudden reference to "mimicking Jews", as well as the fact that Lyamshin him-

---
[1] Cf. Dostoevsky, *The Possessed*, pp. 301–2.
[2] Dostoevsky, *loc. cit.*
[3] *Ibid.*

self was a Jew, a proof that Jankiel the Jew, unconsciously perhaps, existed in the memory of Dostoevsky?[1]

(c) THE FELDJÄGER

Everybody remembers the terrible, cruel, painful dream of Raskolnikov about the beaten horse ... Dostoevsky later came back to this dream and related in connection with this a story of his own experience. I have in mind Chapter III in *The Diary of a Writer* for January, 1876.

> "Our children are educated and grow up meeting with abominable scenes. They see how a peasant, having put an excessive load on his cart, beats his horse which is stuck in the mud; he beats his bread-winner, striking it in the eyes with a whip ..."

After this picture, obviously connected with Raskolnikov's dream, Dostoevsky relates what he saw somewhere in the district of Tver, when in 1837 he was going with his brother from Moscow to Petersburg in order to enter the Engineering School.

> "One early evening we stopped at a roadside inn. I do not remember in which village, it seems to me it was in the district of Tver; the village was large and rich. We were to leave in half an hour and in the meantime I was looking through the window, and I saw the following thing. Opposite the inn there was the posthouse. Suddenly a courier's *troyka* flew up to the porch, and a *feldjäger* jumped out. He was in full uniform, in a large three-cornered hat with white, yellow and, it seems to me, green plumes ... The *feldjäger* was a tall, exceedingly robust and vigorous fellow with a florid face. He ran into the post-house and there must have 'knocked off' a glass of vodka ... Meantime another smart relay *troyka* drove up, and the coachman, a young fellow about twenty years old, in a red shirt and holding his home-spun overcoat in his hands, leaped

[1] In order to be pedantically cautious I may add that perhaps Nozdrev's hurdy-gurdy should not be neglected: "The hurdy-gurdy played not unpleasingly but apparently, something must have happened to its innards, inasmuch as a mazurka wound up with 'Malbrouk to the Wars Has Gone', while 'Malbrouk to the Wars Has Gone' was unexpectedly terminated by some long-familiar waltz. Nozdrev had long since quit grinding, but the hurdy-gurdy had one particularly lively reed that would not quiet down, and for a while thereafter it kept on tootling of its own accord." Cf. *Chichikov's Journeys or Home Life in Old Russia* by Nikolai Gogol (New York: Readers' Club Press, 1942), p. 63. But by including this in my article I myself am following Lyamshin's music.

up to the coach-box. Immediately the *feldjäger* ran out of the building and took his seat in the carriage. The coachman started off, but the carriage had hardly begun to move when the *feldjäger* rose and silently, without any words, lifted his impressive right fist and, from above, lowered it powerfully down on the coachman's head. The latter bent forward, lifted his whip and with all his strength flogged the middle horse. The horses sprang forward, but this did not appease the *feldjäger* at all. There was here a method, and not an irritation, there was something intentional and stabilized by long experience. The terrible fist swung again, and again struck. Then again and again—it went on thus till the *troyka* vanished out of sight. Of course the coachman, scarcely able to stand the blows, incessantly flogged the horses, like a madman, and finally he flogged them to such an extent that they flew frantically . . .

This abominable picture remained in my memory for ever. I never could forget the *feldjäger* and afterwards I unwillingly was inclined to explain many shameful and cruel traits of the Russian people in a very partial manner . . . This picture appears in my mind as, so to say, an emblem, as something which showed very objectively the connection between the cause and effect . . ."[1]

I am sure that Dostoevsky related here the truth, the very truth. But in *The Road to Russia* of Mickiewicz, I read what follows:

> Now the kibitka suddenly flies by:
> The ambulances, guns, and guards who ride,
> Rush madly from the road as it comes nigh;
> Even the leader's wagons draw aside.
> Still on and on it flies; the gendarme whacks
> The driver with his fist; the driver thwacks
> The soldiers with his whip; the throng gives way;
> The wheels crush any one who dares to stay.
> Whither? Who rides within?—No one will ask.
> The gendarme speeds on some important task:
> Surely he rides on orders from the Czar . . .

The poet added to this passage the following note:

"The common folk of Russia are fully convinced that the Czar is quite equal to carrying off any other monarch in a police kibitka. And in very truth it is hard to say what answer a *feldjäger* would receive in certain states if he came on such an errand . . ."[2]

[1] F. M. Dostoevskij, *Dnevnik Pisatelja za 1873 i 1876 gody*, pp. 168–70.
[2] Cf. Noyes, *op. cit.*, p. 340.

In another note Mickiewicz says:

"The *feldjägers* or field-shooters of the czar, are a sort of gendarmes; they are especially hunting persons who are suspected in the eyes of the government. They used to drive in kibitkas—that is in wooden carriages without springs and iron, narrow, flat and higher in the front than in the rear. Byron speaks about these carriages in his *Don Juan*. The *feldjäger* usually arrives in the night, he seizes the suspected person and never tells where he will take him. The kibitka has a post-bell. Unless one has been in Lithuania (Poland) one will with difficulty realize the fear which arises at every house at the doors of which the post-bell is sounding."[1]

The story of Dostoevsky is a pathetic one. The story of Mickiewicz is really "an emblem", an ironic and satiric emblem.[2]

(d) "Pro and Contra" and *Forefathers' Eve*, Part III

All the examples of similar images of Petersburg in their apocalyptical, fantastic stylization, the parallels between Jankiel's "Polonaise of the Third of May" and Lyamshin's "Franco-Prussian War" and the *Feldjäger* episodes are in my opinion so convincing that it is difficult to consider them accidental. However, as the reader knows, the results of comparative analysis are the only arguments at my disposal for the defense of my hypothesis concerning Dostoevsky's possible knowledge of Mickiewicz.

It happens that I made another small but very interesting discovery which, I must confess, excited me. In Dostoevsky's notes for *The Brothers Karamazov*, as I have already mentioned, there are several pages entirely filled with Polish phrases. Dostoevsky obviously listed these phrases to use them for the talks of the Poles in his novel. As

---

[1] Cf. *Pisma Adama Mickiewicza* (Leipzig: Brockhaus, 1885), Vol. III, pp. 249–50.

[2] In his charming tale, *The Lefthanded*, Leskov reproduced the same picture, but he reproduced it in an innocently comical style: "Platov used to drive hastily and with ceremony: he used himself to sit in the carriage and on the coach-box two cossacks with whips took their place on both sides of the coachman. They belaboured him without mercy in order to make him drive. If it happened that one of the cossacks began to doze, Platov would call him to order with a kick, and then they drove even more furiously. These measures of prompting were so efficient that it was quite impossible to stop the wild horses at any post-house—every time they galloped a hundred yards too far. In every such case the cossacks again belaboured the coachman and then the carriage would come back to the porch. . . ." (Cf. chapter VIII.)

I pointed out in my previous study,[1] this catalogue reveals Dostoevsky's surprisingly good knowledge of the Polish language—I repeat, his phrases are not only correct, but idiomatic. In passing I should like to stress the importance of these Polish phrases in Dostoevsky's *Notebooks*. One may assume that the Polish phrases which appear in various works of Dostoevsky, particularly in *The Brothers Karamazov*, could have been submitted for correction to someone with a perfect command of the Polish language. This was the case, for instance, of Tolstoy, who, having introduced several Polish sentences into his pro-Polish short story *What For?*, asked the famous contemporary Polish scholar in Petersburg, J. Baudouin de Courtenay, to correct these sentences. At Tolstoy's request the sentences were sent to Baudouin de Courtenay by Dr. Makovicky.[2] There is no doubt, on the other hand, that no one corrected Dostoevsky's notes; the author obviously wrote them for his own use, but still they show, as I have already stated, a genuine knowledge of the Polish language.

In the list of Polish phrases connected with *The Brothers Karamazov* there is one short phrase which particularly struck me since I immediately recognized it as a conceivable reproduction of the incantational refrain from *Part I* and *Part II* of *Forefathers' Eve*:

Ciemno wszędzie, głucho wszędzie,
Co to będzie, co to będzie?
(All is silent, all is dark;
What is coming? Listen! hark!)[3]

Dostoevsky writes: "Tsikho vshendze, bendze, Tso-to. Diyabli." ("All is silent, what is coming? Devils.")[4] The similarity is obvious. I must add that an element of mockery is also present. We have to assume that Dostoevsky read Mickiewicz, and this assumption is almost inevitable, as it is difficult to suppose that Dostoevsky could have become acquainted with this couplet in any other way. Dostoevsky's line shows that he did not remember the exact wording of Mickiewicz's couplet, but merely preserved in his memory the general impression of the incantation. The change of word order—"bendze, Tso-to"—instead of the correct Polish "Co to będzie" is either a simple slip of Dostoevsky's pen or an influence of the Russian syntax. The word "Diyabli" is not insignificant; this word brings in the element of mockery which I

---

[1] Cf. "Dostoevsky and the Poles in Siberia".
[2] Cf. W. Lednicki, *Quelques aspects du nationalisme et du christianisme chez Tolstoï*, p. 80.
[3] Translation in Noyes, *op. cit.*, p. 95.
[4] In these notes Dostoevsky used Russian phonetic transcription. Cf. *F. M. Dostoevskij, Materialy i Issledovanija*, p. r. A. S. Dolinina (Leningrad, 1935), p. 203.

mentioned above. It might also allude to the general character and tone of *Forefathers' Eve*, especially *Part II* in which the poet presents a folk rite (still preserved at Mickiewicz's time in Lithuania, Prussia and Courland) connected with the ancient belief in the possibility of communication with the souls of the dead.[1] As we know, the poet wished to reproduce the spirit of these folk ceremonies and tried to recreate their characteristic picturesqueness and historic exoticism. There appear in this ultra-romantic poem all kinds of mysterious phantoms, spirits, angels and devils, which exhibit a colourful mixture of Pagan and Christian traditions. For the sake of his romantic realism the poet stressed in the picture of the ritual gathering at the cemetery an atmosphere of tension brought about through the apprehension and expectations of the awe-inspired crowd; the incantations of the chorus are a kind of musical leitmotif of horror in this poetic symphony. Dostoevsky's word "Diyabli", if I am right, in general mocks Mickiewicz's poem, and in particular its rudimental folk style. Dostoevsky pokes fun at Mickiewicz's lines: "All is silent, what is coming? . . . Devils." All these elements, I believe, encourage further investigation.

It would be rather difficult to presume that Dostoevsky, who had always been so deeply absorbed by the Russian-Polish problem, would not have stretched his hand toward the writings of a poet who had formulated the philosophy of the Russian-Polish historical relations. *Forefathers' Eve, Part III* from this point of view is certainly the most important of Mickiewicz's works; and not only the *Digression*, in which Mickiewicz developed his "Historiosophy", but all of *Part III*, with its Preface in prose, its Dramatic Section, its famous "Improvisation", its "Dedicational Poem", and with all its symbolic force. In this poetic work, despite its Romantic fragmentariness, one may discover a unity of thought and structure. The poet framed the fate of two great nations with the vast idea of the fight between good and evil in the Lord's world. One nation is triumphant with its physical, material power, and the other nation is its victim. One is temporarily possessed by the Spirit of Evil, of which the main incarnation is autocracy which destroys the very concept of freedom, and the other nation, having established a historical tradition of freedom, tries to reach sanctity through suffering and to recover its lost freedom. Whole nations and individuals are involved in this battle, and their lives reflect the spiritual combat. This great fight proceeds before God, and from it arises the problem of the incompatibility of God and love: how can the all-loving God allow undeserved martyrdom and the sufferings of the innocent? Mickiewicz singles out one man to become the apostle of the suffering masses. This man reaches the highest degree of human

[1] Cf. the poet's Introduction to *Forefathers' Eve, Part II* in Noyes, *op. cit.*, p. 93.

spiritual power, and he challenges God for the sake of millions of men with whom he identifies himself. Never before in modern literature has the consciousness of actual, personal power found such a dynamic expression.

As tempting as this personal consciousness of power is, as justified as this protest is from a rationalistic point of view, the poet shows the sinful essence of his hero's pride. Still, Mickiewicz does not abandon his hero; his soul is saved by the intervention of a prayer emerging from a candid heart immersed in humility before the Lord: Father Peter's prayer exorcises the evil spirits. The poet split himself into these two figures of his drama; they are both intimately close to him.

Already in this moral, religious and psychological development one may find trends and concepts which should have attracted the creator of Stavrogin with his omnipotence, of Ivan Karamazov with his rationalistic challenge to God, and of Tikhon and Zossima with their patience and humility.

And there are some other reasons why Dostoevsky might have been attracted by Mickiewicz. Mickiewicz's poetry from beginning to end was a true story, following step by step the poet's life. It was a poetic hypostasis of this life; the poet locked the spiritual essence of his own existence in poetic symbols which acquired a general significance. And this life consisted of falls and ascensions. I once called Mickiewicz a poet of Heraclitean movement;[1] Wacław Borowy found another formula, calling Mickiewicz the "poet of transformation".[2] Movement and transformation, are the poet's favourite symbols. In them he enclosed the substance of his own spiritual development. These symbols of transformation, which often rise to the inspired heights of transfiguration, appear in *Grażyna, Konrad Wallenrod, Pan Tadeusz*, and particularly in *Forefathers' Eve, Part III*. The dynamic factor which created this movement was the ever-present desire for self-perfection.

Tolstoy has often been compared to Mickiewicz from this very point of view, and the comparison is a justified one. In both cases we have writers whose main inspiration comes from the inside, from the interior life. This gives an autobiographical character to their works. In addition, in both lives we see the same zeal for moulding of the personality and the intensification of the spiritual content of its life at any cost. This zeal finally leads both writers to reject their art for the sake of superior ethic values. And each of these men was endowed with

[1] Cf. my book *The Life and Culture of Poland*, pp. 167–70, 172–80, 206–11.
[2] Cf. *Adam Mickiewicz*, a symposium edited by M. Kridl (New York: Columbia University Press, 1951), pp. 35–57. As a matter of fact, quite independently of Borowy, I myself called Mickiewicz a poet of transfiguration. Cf. "Ex Oriente Lux", in *Semitic and Oriental Studies*, University of California Publications in Semitic Philology, Vol. XI, 1951. This study was written before Borowy's essay was published.

a powerful memory which served not only the artist, but also the moralist. In a study dealing with Pushkin and Mickiewicz, I stressed Mickiewicz's admiration for Pushkin's famous poem, "The Prophet", another poem of transfiguration. I even went so far as to connect with "The Prophet" the scene in *Forefathers' Eve, Part III* in which the poet, in order to emphasize the radical change in his hero's personality, made him write with charcoal, first on one side of the prison wall, "D. O. M. GUSTAVUS OBIIT M.D. CCC. XXIII. CALENDIS NOVEMBRIS"; and then on the other side, "HIC NATUS EST CONRADUS M.D. CCC. XXIII. CALENDIS NOVEMBRIS".[1] How characteristic that the single poem of Pushkin's which Mickiewicz translated was "Remembrance", a poem certainly connected with Mickiewicz's interpretation of "The Prophet". And how characteristic that "Remembrance" should be the favourite poem of Tolstoy.

Mickiewicz was aware of his faults and he was constantly raising himself from them, often with a supreme effort of will. This persistent combat immensely strengthened his personality and secured to it a superior prestige. One should remember also the passionate and sensual essence of Mickiewicz's nature; in this, again, Tolstoy was very close to him. Mickiewicz would not have become a poet of transformation without a profound knowledge of his own nature; this was an indispensable condition. And here we approach another trait of Mickiewicz's poetry which could have had a spiritual interest for Dostoevsky. I have in mind the rôle of the dream in Mickiewicz's poetry. True, the dream, the mystery of the night and occult sciences attracted the curiosity of all Romantics and of poets and writers of that period, whether or not they belonged to the Romantic school. Suffice it to mention the German and French Romantics with their interest in mystic writers of the Middle Ages and of the sixteenth, seventeenth and eighteenth centuries, like Boehme, Angelus Silesius, de St. Martin, Swedenborg, and finally Calderón, the author of *La vida es sueño*, so popular among the German and Polish Romantics. The Romantic period was a period of dream: Jean Paul Richter, Novalis, Tieck, Von Arnim, Brentano, E. T. A. Hoffmann, Nodier, Gérard de Nerval—all of them were tempted by the mysterious revelation of the dream, all of them were "priests of the night". Even Pushkin, with all his realism, common sense and rationalism, explored these tantalizing regions: in his poetry the dream appears with a special insistence; witness the dreams and visions of Tatyana, the Pretender, Mozart, Grinev, Herman and Eugene (in *The Bronze Horseman*). Mickiewicz, however, found a particular significance in this phenomenon of human psychology. In Mickiewicz's poetry the dream acquires an ethic sig-

---

[1] Cf. "Ex Oriente Lux", etc., pp. 255–6.

nificance. *Forefathers' Eve, Part III* is built almost entirely on dreams; all the heroes dream: Konrad, Father Peter, Novosiltsev and Eve. Each dream characterizes the dreamer; the dream becomes another battle-field for the powers of evil and good in their fight for the human soul. But this soul is not, even in the dream state, a passive object of this struggle. Kleiner justly said that in Mickiewicz one may find the "insomnia of the conscience".[1] And to the ethical value of the dream Mickiewicz adds a mystical significance; for him the mystery of the dream cannot be reduced to mere memory and imagination:

Prisoner. [*Awakens, wearied, and looks through the window. Dawn.*]
O silent night, thou fall'st, and who will ask
From whence thou art? We see thee at thy task
Of scattering star points as a sower seed,
Yet who therein thy future course will read!
"The sun has set!" So from the towers high
The gray astronomers boom gravely forth.
Why has it set? They make us no reply.
The shadows come and cover all the earth,
Men fall asleep and no one questions why;
They wake, unmarveling, when darkness lifts,
To see the daily marvel of the sun;
Shadow and splendor change like sentry-shifts—
But what great ruler thus commands the sky,
What captain orders his high bidding done?
   And sleep? Ah, that dim, deaf, and silent shore
Where spirits wake, why do men not explore
Its bounds, its times, and their signification?—
The sleeper, waking, mocks his own creation.
The wise men say, dreams are but memory!
   Curst be their chill decision!
Are then my recollection and my vision
All one? These prison walls I see,
   Are they but memory?

The joys and chastisements of sleep, they say,
   Are only fancy's play.
Dullards, whom fancy ever disregards,
   Prate of her to us bards!
I who have dwelt in her and measured her domain,
I know, beyond her farthest edge lies dream;
Sooner will day be night and pleasure pain
Than dreams and visions a remembered gleam.

---

[1] Cf. J. Kleiner, *Mickiewicz* (Lublin: Towarzystwo Naukowe Katolickiego Uniwersytetu Lubelskiego, 1948), Vol. II, p. 278.

> [*Lies down and rises again. Goes to the window.*]
> Sleep comes with visions now magnificent,
> Now terrible, but always leaves me spent.
>   [*He dozes*]
> . . .

Chorus of Night Spirits.
> God binds us by day, but at dark we ride free,
>   We are sluggards that fatten by night;
> The satans then teach us their minstrelsy,
>   License and passion and spite.
> At dawn of the sacrament man may partake,
>   Holy and thankful at heart,
> But night the blood-sucking, the venomous snake,
>   Awaits him with poisoning dart.
> Spirits of darkness, come flame through his head,
>   Sing him your feverish song;
> Wait on him, serve him, for soon he instead
>   Shall serve us—may his slumber be long!

Angel.
> Both heaven and earth have offered prayers for thee,
> And now the tyrants soon must set thee free.

Prisoner.   [*Wakes and meditates.*]
> O you who prison, scourge, and slay your own,
> Who night and day in careless revels spend,
> Do you recall one single dream at dawn,
> Or, recollecting, do you comprehend?
>   [*He slumbers.*][1]

And so it happens that Mickiewicz became a philosopher of the dream for its own sake. As I have said, the dream in his poetry acquires an ethical value.

"This ethical element in his theory," says Kleiner, "is the most significant. The enhancing of the rôle of psychic spheres from behind the consciousness often serves the tendency of reducing human responsibility. The strengthening of the power of the mysterious world, which makes impossible any choice between good and evil, often flows from the desire to justify oneself and to transfer the guilt to incalculable factors. With Mickiewicz the process is directly opposite: the inclusion of dreams in the organism of life as a whole means their acceptance into the sphere of ethics. And this means an immense broadening of the field of moral responsibility."[2]

[1] Noyes, *op. cit.*, pp. 251–3.
[2] Cf. Kleiner, *op. cit.*, p. 279.

E. T. A. Hoffmann's conception of the dream contains the same element; in his *Elixir of the Devil* he writes that "even crimes committed in a dream, even the simple intention of guilt requires a double chastisement".[1] As we may observe, the dream has the same function in Dostoevsky's works. Varied are the dreams of men in Mickiewicz's works; some of them reveal their own spiritual substance, some are sent like messengers of good and evil powers. Good powers may send bad dreams as a warning, but in general the dream uncovers the human personality. In this sense, the dreams of Novosiltsev and Eve are particularly eloquent. The truth is hidden in dream. This is why the dead mother will ask the guardian angel about her son's dreams.[2]

There is no need to stress the importance of dreams for Dostoevsky. All his heroes are obsessed by visions, hallucinations, and nightmares; dreams visit them day and night. They often find themselves in a state of catalepsy. Well-known examples of this are Raskolnikov, Svidrigaylov, Myshkin, Stavrogin, Versilov, the Raw Youth and Ivan Karamazov. Dostoevsky was even envious of Tolstoy's dreams, and with good reason—well known is the power and place which the dream acquired in Tolstoy's novels; *Anna Karenina* alone suffices as a convincing illustration. We find the following passage in *The Brothers Karamazov*, in which the Devil speaks to Ivan:

"*C'est du nouveau, n'est-ce pas?* This time I'll act honestly and explain to you. Listen, in dreams and especially in nightmares, from indigestion or anything, a man sees sometimes such artistic visions, such complex and real actuality, such events, even a whole world of events, woven into such a plot, with such unexpected details from the most exalted matters to the last button on a cuff, as I swear, Leo Tolstoy has never invented. Yet such dreams are sometimes seen not by writers, but by the most ordinary people, officials, journalists, priests... The subject is a complete enigma. A statesman confessed to me, indeed, that all his best ideas came to him when he was asleep. Well, that's how it is now, though I am your hallucination, yet just as in a nightmare, I say original things which have not entered your head before. So I don't repeat your ideas, yet I am only your nightmare, nothing more."[3]

Dostoevsky's own epilepsy inspired him and strengthened the feelings in the author for the aesthetic and psychological importance of the

[1] Quoted by Albert Béguin in *L'Ame romantique et le rêve* (Marseilles, 1937), Vol. II, p. 275.
[2] Cf. *Forefathers' Eve, Part III*, Prologue, in Noyes, *loc. cit.*
[3] Cf. *The Brothers Karamazov*, Garnett translation, Part IV (continued), Book XI, chapter 9, p. 777.

dream. Naturally, the German and French Romantics, Hoffman in particular, and certainly Pushkin and Tolstoy were Dostoevsky's guides and teachers in this. I do not mean to imply that Mickiewicz was another teacher; rather, I simply believe this element in Mickiewicz's poetry could have attracted Dostoevsky's attention. Mickiewicz seldom touches sensual themes in his poetic description of dreams. Only from time to time does passion in its sensual, impure expression invade the visions of his heroes. But there are only very slight allusions to this in Mickiewicz's poetry. The poet's main feelings of guilt are connected with the problem of national and patriotic responsibility. His falls are those of a man who cannot allow himself selfish enjoyment of life in the face of the suffering community. In this sense, the "Ode to Youth" became a self-command for Mickiewicz's whole life. The poet's main drama took place during the Insurrection of 1830–1831, when he found himself in a state of moral paralysis, and his vigilant conscience, seized by that "insomnia", could not pardon his indecision. Mickiewicz waited too long and searched for all kinds of pretexts and justifications in order not to join the fighting army. This was the time that his tired being was plunged in sensuality, in an "animal existence", which he mentioned in a letter to the Princess Zinaida Volkonsky. This "animal existence" tormented him, as he was still faithful to his idealistic attachment to Eve Ankwicz, whom he had met in Rome and whom he could not marry. This Roman love became crowned with the deep religious crisis through which Mickiewicz passed in Rome with Eve Ankwicz as his spiritual cicerone. Soon after the defeat of the Insurrection and just before the writing of *Forefathers' Eve, Part III*, on 23 March, 1832, Mickiewicz wrote a mysterious poem which we call "The Dream in Dresden", a spontaneous poetic reproduction of a dream Mickiewicz had had the preceding night. Rafał Blüth has given a penetrating analysis of this poem, using Freud's method of investigation.[1] He showed in his admirable reconstruction of all biographical details and texts from Mickiewicz's correspondence the subtle interweaving of themes of sentimental and patriotic guilts in Mickiewicz's poem. In *Forefathers' Eve, Part III* all these themes reappear distributed among the dreams of the heroes. Mickiewicz's dreams, then, could have attracted Dostoevsky.

There are still some other elements of possible attraction. To Konrad's pride and self-confidence, as I mentioned above, is opposed Father Peter's humility. The figure of Father Peter could easily be transplanted on Dostoevsky's world. The Priest, who in his past was a "sinner" himself, is endowed not only with humility but with merciful patience. Without anger or protest he accepts slaps on the face inflicted by Novosiltsev's order; his prayer saves Konrad's soul. He is the one to

[1] Cf. *Przegląd Współczesny*, June and July, 1925.

whom the poet granted the power of clairvoyance and prophecy. He predicts the punishment from heaven upon the heads of those who have insulted him, and these predictions are fulfilled. He is the one whom the poet elected for the vision of the future of Poland and Russia. The resemblance to similar features in Zossima is obvious.

These are only general remarks. Now I should like to approach some concrete items in the Dramatic Section of *Forefathers' Eve, Part III*, especially the "Improvisation", which might have some connections with "Pro and Contra" in Dostoevsky's *The Brothers Karamazov*.

First I should like to point out a certain structural resemblance between Dostoevsky's novel and Mickiewicz's drama. One might say that each of these works could be compared to a Gothic cathedral with its two towers emerging from the nave of the church. In *Forefathers' Eve, Part III* we may see two main spires: Konrad with his "Improvisation", and Father Peter with his vision. In *The Brothers Karamazov* we also have two "towers": Ivan's "Legend of the Grand Inquisitor", and the doctrine of Father Zossima. In both cases we have an obvious juxtaposition. In *Forefathers' Eve, Part III* we see not only the two towers of a medieval cathedral, but the vast nave with its façade adorned with sculpture symbolizing the universe. Here we find God, Heaven, Hell, Angels, Devils, Sinners and Saints. Novosiltsev and his crowd are possessed by the spirits of Hell, as in Dante's *Inferno*. Opposed to this sphere are the Angelic maidens, Eve and Marcelina. And in between, as if in Purgatory, are the suffering young prisoners. Let us not forget that *Forefathers' Eve, Part III* is a forum for the great historic Russian-Polish trial.

In Dostoevsky's *Summa Theologica, The Brothers Karamazov*, a novel which others have often compared to a cathedral, we have the same complexity of symbols and allegories. The characterizations of town and monastery, the constant terrible storms of desire and lustful passions, the revolts, fights, abuses, crimes, and murders, in which not only the central figures are involved, but the whole crowd of secondary characters, the combats between rationalism and irrationalism, the glories of resurrection, the problems of love for one's fellow man, of autonomous virtue, of faith, of the conflicts between church and state, of crime and punishment, of the relativism of human judgment and absolute truth—all these elements make of *The Brothers Karamazov* another *Divina Commedia*, with its Paradise, Purgatory and Inferno. Here too we have the eternally damned souls in Fedor Pavlovich Karamazov, Smerdyakov and the Polish "scoundrels", the heavenly spheres represented by Zossima and his monks, the tormented inhabitants of Purgatory, Dimitry, the fallen angel, Ivan, and the "silent prophet", Alesha. I should like to add one curious detail. On Dostoevsky's manuscripts usually appear designs of Gothic arches, windows and churches. Such is the case also of part of the manuscript of *The Brothers Karamazov*, namely the chapter "Pro and Contra".[1] And it is interesting to note that on the frontispiece of the Paris edition (1833) of *Forefathers' Eve*— the edition Dostoevsky most probably used—there is a rich Gothic design with motifs very similar to Dostoevsky's sketches framing the whole page.

Another detail worthy of mention is that Konrad's collapse after his improvisation contains all the marks of epilepsy—Mickiewicz *uses* the term *epilepsy*; Konrad bites his lips, foam appears on his mouth. Dostoevsky could not have overlooked this.

Although the action of Dostoevsky's novel does not take place either in Petersburg or in Moscow but in a provincial town, Skotoprogonievsk (Cattle Run), with its monastery, inns, court-house and its suburbs, this town symbolizes the whole of Russia: Dostoevsky used to say, "Russia should not follow Petersburg, but Petersburg Russia". And although the Poles play only an episodic rôle in the novel, and are present as if for the sole purpose of being unmasked as scoundrels, Mitya's discussion with them on Russia and Poland presents in essence the dilemma of Russian-Polish historical relations. In my study, "Dostoevsky and the Poles in Siberia", I showed the significance of the fact that the natural defense of Polish rights is put in the mouths of scoundrels. Could this not be a hidden answer to Mickiewicz? Mitya's exclamation, "You are fools, *panowie*," was addressed to the Polish scoundrels, but who was Dostoevsky's ultimate addressee?

Mickiewicz's romantic poem is a work in which are brought together lyricism, drama, satire, pathetic indignation, sarcasm, realism and metaphysics, journalism and passages of historical epic style, grotesque and sublime elements. And still the poet himself points out, in his Preface, "that he has portrayed conscientiously both the historic scenes and the characters of the persons acting in them".[2] Thus in his own belief, a real truth is at the bottom of his fantastic drama. The method of intensification of the presented situations and of the passions and thoughts of the characters involved in them is not a new procedure in Mickiewicz's art. *Part IV* of *Forefathers' Eve*, which was written and appeared before *Part III*,[3] and which deals with a purely personal, sentimental problem, presents a similar aesthetic procedure. This *Part IV* consists almost entirely of a long, infrequently interrupted monologue.

---

[1] Cf. *F. M. Dostoevskij, Materialy i Issledovanija*, p. 119. Cf. also *Iz arkhiva F. M. Dostoevskogo, Idiot, neizdannye materialy*, pod red. P. N. Sakulina i I. F. Bel'čikova (Moscow-Leningrad, 1931), pp. 45–9; and *Zapisnye tetradi* F. M. Dostoevskogo.

[2] Cf. Noyes, *op. cit.*, p. 249.

[3] Cf. My Preface for an explanation of the whole structure of *Forefathers' Eve*.

It is a confession of a Polish Werther, a broken-hearted, abandoned lover. In order to give a full, exhaustive expression of the agony of his hero, who is actually his alter-ego, Mickiewicz brings onto the stage an insane man, the ghost of a suicide. This suicide talks to a priest, who was formerly his teacher, and to children who are about. Now he talks to them, now to himself, as if completely forgetting their presence, then suddenly he again addresses this astonished and shocked audience. The disorder of reminiscences and emotions, the perpetual change of themes, followed by a change of metric forms and sequences, the unexpected alternations of moods, are justified by the fact of the hero's insanity. But this very condition grants the abnormal confession psychological truth. In a way Mickiewicz's method is in essence readily comparable to Victor Hugo's *Le Dernier jour d'un condamné*, which was so highly praised by Dostoevsky in the Foreword to his short story, *The Meek One*. In Victor Hugo's story Dostoevsky admired the fantastic device, which was to presume

> "that a man condemned to death would have been able (and would have had the time) to keep a diary not only on his last day but even in his last hour—and, literally, during his last minute. However, had he not resorted to this fantasy, the work itself would be non-existent—the most realistic and verisimilar of all his writings."[1]

It is known that in his story Dostoevsky explained the basic principles of what he called his "fantastic realism". There is no doubt that Gustaw's confession (this is the name of Mickiewicz's hero of *Part IV*) follows exactly the same device, even strengthened by the fact that his confession is made after, and not before his death. The monologue of the Meek One's husband is carried on exactly in the manner in which Mickiewicz proceeds. In his Foreword Dostoevsky unveils the secrets of his methods, and they are identical with Mickiewicz's techniques which I described above:

> "It stands to reason that the process of the narrative lasts several hours, with interruptions and interludes in a confused form: now he speaks to himself, now he addresses, as it were, an invisible listener —some kind of a judge. Thus it also takes place in real life. If a stenographer could have eavesdropped on him and transcribed everything after him, the sketch would have been rougher and less polished than it appears in my version; nevertheless, it seems to me that the psychological order would, perhaps, have been the same.

[1] Cf. F. M. Dostoievsky, *The Diary of a Writer*, translated and annotated by Boris Brasol (New York: Scribner's Sons, 1949), pp. 491–2.

x

Now, this supposition relative to the stenographer who had recorded everything (after whom I have edited this record) is what I denote as fantastic in this story."[1]

Is this not a perfect commentary on Mickiewicz's *Forefathers' Eve, Part IV*? In a way, the same basic principles preside in *Forefathers' Eve, Part III* and in *The Brothers Karamazov*.

At any rate, the main theme which I should like to single out for my analysis of Dostoevsky's hypothetical relationship with Mickiewicz is that of the rebellion against God. Rebellion takes place in both works, and in each case it has the same rationalistic character and the same motivation. The sequence of episodes which illustrate the process of rebellion is identical.

In *Forefathers' Eve, Part III* we are in the company of Mickiewicz's schoolmates, imprisoned by the Russian authorities for their activities in secret student societies, the goals of which were learning, morality, and the preservation of national culture. The "Philomaths" and "Philarets", as these societies were called, are innocent victims of the Russian persecution. The Russian satrap, Novosiltsev, hoped to unearth a plot and thereby enhance his career. The poet shows us a cell in which various students are gathered. They tell different stories about the excesses and abuses of the Russian persecutors, and about the sufferings of their victims. Mickiewicz emphasizes their youth; he even calls them "children", stressing the fact that not only University students, but little boys have been imprisoned and sent to Siberia. Among the students who are telling all these stories there is Konrad, the poet, who silently listens to the sad reports. All these themes and talks, dialogues and monologues are preparation for the outburst of the "Improvisation" with its religious rebellion as a *finale*.

Mickiewicz uses all his powers of expression to make the description of the martyrdom of Polish children as poignant as possible:

> ... From the square
> The captain of police came riding up—
> He looked a great man holding triumph here,
> The triumph of the czar o'er—little boys!
> A drum beat, and the jail doors opened wide.
> I saw them then. Behind each one walked guards
> With bayonets, behind these wasted lads,
> Sickly and small and all like new recruits
> With shaven heads and chains upon their legs.
> Poor boys! The youngest, only ten years old,
> Complained he couldn't lift his heavy chains

[1] *Loc. cit.*

And showed his foot all flecked with blood and bare.
  The captain then rode up to see to this—
  So kind and just, himself would test the chains!
  'Ten pounds, quite right; that is the weight prescribed.'[1]

The poet describes how all that mass of children were imprisoned, tortured, beaten and exiled in chains to Siberia. Some of them committed suicide. Others were strong enough to preserve their courage and determination, and they remained proud and uncomplaining. One of them died in the face of the silent crowd, another boy cried from his kibitka in which he was enchained, "Poland has not yet perished". The poet used the examples of the children's sufferings in order to make his plea particularly moving; the martyrdom of Polish children became a symbol of Poland's martyrdom. One of the monologues ends with the following words:

>   . . . Down the road
>   Like lightning flashes the kibitkas flew
>   In one we did not see the prisoner; but
>   His hand stretched deathlike toward us from the straw,
>   Shook in the jostling cart as in farewell.
>   They passed but, caught in a moment in the crowd
>   Before the whips had quite dispersed the throng,
>   The dead man stopped before the empty church.
>   I heard the bell and glanced inside and saw
>   The priest about to elevate the host,
>   And then I cried: Lord, who to save the world
>   Didst shed by Pilate's judgment guiltless blood,
>   Accept this sacrifice of children from
>   The judgment of the czar: 'tis not so great,
>   Not holy, but it is as innocent.'[2]

The episode of Pani Rollison, the mother of a tortured boy, deserves some special attention. She meets Novosiltsev, who is responsible for her son's life. I will not tarry with the emotional power of this scene. One detail is important. Pani Rollison is lulled by Novosiltsev and she is ready to pardon him; she is happy to believe that his reputation for cruelty is false, and that he is not the one to be blamed for her son's fate. It is the theme of the mother's right to pardon the martyrdom of her child which particularly interests me here. This same motif of the mother and the unpardonable suffering of the child reappears in another scene, during the ball. Now Pani Rollison knows the truth. She confronts Novosiltsev:

[1] Cf. Noyes, *op. cit.*, p. 261.
[2] *Ibid.*, p. 263.

> Pani Rollison. I'll find you out! I'll smash your
>   brutal head,
> As was my son's! Tyrant, my son is dead!
> They threw him from the window!—Have you groans?
> My son, down on the pavement, on the stones . . .
> Ha, you old drunkard, sprinkled with much blood!
> Where are you, crocodile of lies and mud?
> I'll tear you piecemeal, as my Jaś was torn—
> They threw him from the window, and I mourn
> My only child, sole source of life to me—
> Is there a God, that leaves such monsters free?
>   Father Peter. Blaspheme not, woman! For your son
>   breathes yet.
>   Pani Rollison. He is alive? Who speaks? Whom have
>   I met?
> Is that true, father? No, I had not proved him.
> "He fell," they shout! I ran. They had removed him.
> I did not see his corpse, lorn of my kind.
> I did not see my son's corpse. I am blind!
> But there I smelt blood. And by God I'm sure
> I smell it here, my son's blood; sprinkled, sir,
> On some one. Here's his executioner!
> [*She walks straight toward the* Senator. *The* Senator *gets out
>   of her way;* Pani Rollison *falls on the floor in a faint;* Father
>   Peter *and the* Starosta *go up to her.*
>   *A thunder clap is heard.*][1]

Even a Russian woman, the Councillor's wife, protests against the persecution of the children:

> Say what you
>   please, terror is terror still.
> I'll stay no longer in this house of ill;
> I told you: "Husband, why those boys abuse?"—
> Though I kept silence while you flogged poor Jews.
> But children![2]

This scene belongs to a section which comes after the "Improvisation", but the theme of this episode remains in the same order of ideas and arguments which led Konrad to this rebellion.

There is another passage in the section following the "Improvisation" which I should like to quote, the story of the Corporal:

[1] *Ibid.*, pp. 325–6.
[2] *Ibid.*, p. 327.

In Praga I have seen them hew down priests;
In Spain beheld men hurled alive from towers;
I have seen mothers with their breasts pierced through,
And children dying upon Cossack pikes,
Frenchmen upon the snow and Turks impaled;
I know the aspect dying martyrs wear,
And that of murderers, Turks, and Muscovites.[1]

I will not touch here those parts of the "Improvisation" which deal with the poet and his creative power, with poetic inspiration and imagination or with the theme of the Superman. I have in mind only one motif, that of rebellion against a God who tolerates the abuses displayed before Konrad. Having reached the culmination of his inspiration, at which point he feels the omnipotence of his poetic power and his complete union with the suffering nation, Konrad challenges God:

> My name is million, for I love as millions:
> Their pain and sufferings I feel;
> I gaze upon my country fallen on days
> Of torment, as a son would gaze
> Upon his father broken on the wheel.
> . . .
> Hear me if that be true which once I heard
> With filial faith, that thou dost love the earth
>   To which thou gavest birth;
>   Hear me, if once thy word
> Saved from the flood within the sheltering ark,
> With man and each original beast, the spark
> Of love: if love be no monstrosity,
> Whose nature is impermanence,
> That cannot ripen to maturity:
> If in thy rule love is not anarchy:
> If on the millions crying, "Save us, Lord!"
> Thou dost not gaze with an unmoved regard,
> As thou wouldst gaze on the confusion wrought
> By some false reckoning: if in creation,
> As thou hast planned and made it, love is aught
> But a wrong figure in thy calculation,
>   Then hear me, Lord![2]

Let us examine some other passages of the "Improvisation":

---
[1] *Ibid.*, p. 281.
[2] *Ibid.*, pp. 277–8.

> Now let me see and let me feel at last thy loftiness.
> Give me the power I seek, or tell me how
> To gain it, I have heard of prophets who
> Could reign o'er spirits, and so can I too.
> I would have power o'er souls no less
> Than thou in heaven dost possess,
> To rule them as dost thou.
>
> *[A long silence.]*
> *[With irony.]*
>
> Still thou art silent. I have fathomed thee.
> And read the secret of thy sovereignty:
> He lied who called thee love, thou art
> Wisdom alone . . . .
> . . .
> Thou givest all the fruits of earth
> To mind to leave the heart in dirth;
> On me, who have most power to feel,
> Thou dost bestow the shortest time of weal . . . .
> Now—and I challenge thee—come forth! Once more,
> Bearing my soul to thee as to a friend,
> I call upon thee solemnly, attend, attend!
> No answer?—Yet in person thou didst war
> With Satan. Spurn me not: Although alone
>   I challenge thee.
> I and a nation's mighty heart are one;
> The thrones, powers, armies follow in my train.
> If thou dost drive me on to blasphemy,
> A bloodier conflict thou shalt join
> Than ever Satan waged with thee;
> For Satan sought dominion for the mind,
> I battle for the heart of all mankind.[1]

Then comes the final outcry of rebellion:

> Silent, though I have opened all my heart!
> I conjure thee, give me the smallest part
> Of all the power that pride doth arrogate;
> From that least part what joy I would create!
> Silent! Then if thou doth despise the heart,
> Give up this power to the mind. Foremost
> Am I of men and of thine angel host,
> I know thee better than thy seraphs, part
> Of thy dominion I deserve. Then say

[1] *Ibid.*, pp. 275–7.

> If I am wrong. But I speak true, for thou
> Art silent still and trustest certainly
> In thy strong arm. But thou shalt know
> That love can burn what mind can never break.
>   My fire is love, and I
>   Will heap it up till it burn high.
>   Then, as with powder, I will fill
>   With it the cannon of my will.
> Voice.   Voice.
> Flame on through space!   Mercy, grace!
>
> Speak, or I thunder forth, and if I can
> Not shatter nature into shards, yet all thy plan
> Of wheeling world and planets, every star,
> Shall rock, as I proclaim to all creation
> From generation unto generation
> That thou art not the father— . . .
>   The voice of Satan whispers: "But the czar!"[1]

Here the rebellion reached its culmination, but the poet at this very moment dissociated himself from his hero: the last blasphemy is pronounced by the Devil. Konrad's soul is possessed by the spirits of Hell; truth is elsewhere. As we know, the knowledge of truth has been given to Father Peter. We also know that his prayers saved Konrad from eternal damnation. This is a grave but subtle detail. The poetic cascade of the "Improvisation" is so powerful that toward its end one scarcely can distinguish the voices. The word "czar" shouted by the Devil rhymes with a word which Konrad pronounced. This last accent does not destroy the development of emotions and ideas. The "Improvisation" expresses the revolt of human reason against Divinity, of which this reason cannot conceive. Konrad knows only one superior motive—love for mankind; he does not know Divine motives which cannot be embraced by human reason. Then, although the word "czar" was not pronounced by Konrad it harmonizes with his own rational interpretation of the world. Konrad's attitude is not one of agnosticism; he is a deist who opposes to the inhuman Creator the commands of the human, autonomous conscience. We may even find in his attitude an "anti-theistic agression", to use Professor T. Zieliński's formula.[2] In other words, we have here a juxtaposition of God and Man, of religion and ethics. Mickiewicz, the sinner, approved of this revolt, which could have meant a sort of self-liberation from his own feelings of guilt, a kind of escape towards the "incalculable factors". But let us not forget

---
[1] *Ibid.*, pp. 278–9.
[2] Cf. J. Kleiner, *Mickiewicz*, Vol. II, Part 1, pp. 345 and 348.

the "insomnia" of Mickiewicz's conscience. His conscience stopped the effusion of Konrad's words and made the Devil whisper: "But the czar!"

Is this an expression of ambivalence, or one of religious faith? As acceptable as was Konrad's revolt, Father Peter's humility was wiser in the poet's eyes.

I trust that the reader remembers the talk between Alesha and Ivan Karamazov which precedes Ivan's "improvisation"—"The Legend of the Grand Inquisitor".[1] Ivan tells Alesha several stories depicting human sadism. His main purpose is to prove that not God, but rather the Devil has been made after man's image, and that cruelty is the essence of human nature. His stories develop in a kind of *crescendo* of sadism. By these stories Ivan justifies his rebellion. His most important argument, as was that of Mickiewicz, is the suffering of the innocents, the children. The suffering of innocent children is not accepted by Ivan as a justifiable expiation of the sins of humanity. This becomes the philosophic foundation, the chief ethical motive for his refutation of the world established by God. Exactly like Konrad, Ivan does not deny the existence of God; he rejects God in the name of suffering humanity.

The stories he told Alesha are, as a matter of fact, almost identical with those which Konrad heard from his friends. Even the Corporal's story has its parallel in Ivan's reports about the cruelty of the Turks and Circassians, and about babies tossed in the air and caught on the points of bayonets. After Ivan's most terrible story about a child chased by hounds,[2] he asks Alesha what should be done with the Russian general who ordered this bestiality. Alesha exclaims, "To be shot!" And then comes Ivan's long monologue in which he explains that he used the example of children only in order to make his development more obvious:

> " 'Listen! I took the case of children only to make my case clearer. Of the other tears of humanity with which the earth is soaked from its crust to its center, I will say nothing. I have narrowed my subject on purpose'."[3]

[1] Dostoevsky himself considered the "Legend" the culminating point of his novel. Cf. Dostoevsky's letter to Lyubimov, 10 May, 1879, in *Byloe*, 1920, Book XV.

[2] I may add that the theme of cruelty and injustice, the rôle of which I analyzed in *Forefathers' Eve, Part III*, is also treated in *Part II* of the poem, though in a slightly different stylization—one with social implications. The poet presents examples of peasants tyrannized by the cruel lord: children chased by dogs, a destitute woman and her child who are refused aid and dragged into the snow where they freeze to death. (Cf. Noyes, *op. cit.*, pp. 102 and 103.) Some of these episodes have traits in common with Ivan's examples of maltreated children.

[3] Cf. *The Brothers Karamazov, op. cit.*, p. 289.

He does not accept these sufferings as "manure for future harmony"

" 'I don't want the mother to embrace the oppressor who threw her son to the dogs! She dare not forgive him! Let her forgive him for herself, if she will, let her forgive the torturer for the immeasurable suffering of her mother's heart. But the sufferings of her tortured child she has no right to forgive; she dare not forgive the torturer even if the child were to forgive him' !"[1]

Again, exactly as in *Forefathers' Eve, Part III*, comes Ivan's rebellion:

" 'I don't want harmony. For love for humanity I don't want it. I would rather be left with the unavenged suffering. I would rather remain with my unavenged suffering and unsatisfied indignation, *even if I were wrong.* Besides, too high a price is asked for harmony; it's beyond our means to pay so much to enter on it. And so I hasten to give back my entrance ticket, and if I am an honest man I am bound to give it back as soon as possible. And that I am doing. It's not God that I don't accept, Alesha, only I most respectfully return Him the ticket.'
'That's rebellion,' murmured Alesha, looking down."[2]

It seems to me that these two roads of thought, Mickiewicz's and Dostoevsky's, are quite similar. Of course, one might make some reservations, though they are not very essential. Mickiewicz illustrates the martyrdom of his nation by the sufferings of innocent children; he challenges God for such a monstrous injustice. The children symbolize Poland, they suffer for Poland. Ivan Karamazov gives his examples of human sadism and of innocent suffering from Russian life, and these examples are used in a general sense. His oppressors as well as his children are almost anonymous. He sometimes defines the oppressors as Russian landlords, Turks or Circassians, and their victims as Russian or Bulgarian children. He fights against God for mankind.[3] This is not a very important difference. First we must remember that *Forefathers' Eve, Part III* belongs to the period of Mickiewicz's Messianism. The poet's conception of Polish martyrdom had a universalistic scope. Poland was suffering for other nations and this suffering was justified

---

[1] Cf. *ibid.*, p. 291.
[2] Cf. *loc. cit.*
[3] My speculations about the possible relationship between *The Idiot* and Turgenev's *On the Eve* might also be taken into consideration in this case. Dobrolyubov, had he been alive, might very well have asked Dostoevsky whether the Bulgarian children could not have been replaced by Polish children in Ivan's stories.

by the advent of a new era—one of Christianization of politics. Even at the end of his Preface to *Forefathers' Eve, Part III* the poet says:

". . . and to the compassionate nations of Europe who have wept over Poland as the feeble women of Jerusalem over Christ, our nation will speak only with the words of the Saviour: 'Daughters of Jerusalem, weep not for me, but weep for yourselves'."[1]

A student of mine, I. N. Belousovich, to whom I once suggested the present subject as the theme of a paper, wrote in his report:

"Mickiewicz did not restrict the universality of the theme; quite the contrary, though remaining within the limits of the plot of *Forefathers' Eve, Part III*, he endowed it with increased depth and power by transforming one relatively insignificant episode first into a national tragedy and then into an example of Divine injustice which threatens to disrupt the entire structure of Christian philosophy."

Certainly the contents of the "Legend" and of the "Improvisation" are different. The "Legend", despite its general philosophic implication, is an attack against the Catholic Church. I will not tarry here with the old motif of the "Returning Christ", which Dostoevsky utilized in his "Legend".[2] As a matter of fact, one may find in the "Legend" trends present in Protestant literature, whose main goal was to show the abyss existing between the Catholic Church and the teachings of the Gospels and which was trying to bring Christians back to this unsoiled teaching. On the other hand, we do not find any items of this kind in the "Improvisation". But we may still find Mickiewicz expressing elsewhere a critical attitude towards the Catholic Church, similar to the leanings of the "Legend". Mickiewicz's lecture of 1844 on Slavic Literatures contains the following remarks about the church:

"These classes—the upper strata in the church—departed from the cross; they did not wish to suffer, they strove always to avoid suffering, and locked themselves in books, theology, and doctrines. Everyone knows that it costs less pain to write and to argue than to tell the truth sincerely and to suffer in its defense. Strength is born only of pain . . . If, then, he who wishes to be a creator in art or a

---

[1] Cf. The Preface to *Forefathers' Eve, Part III*, Noyes, *op. cit.*, p. 249.
[2] I have already remarked on this theme in my study "Christ et révolution dans la poésie russe et polonaise", in *Mélanges en l'honneur de Jules Legras*, Travaux publiés par l'Institut d'études slaves, XVII, Paris, 1939.

true leader in politics must of necessity enter into partnership with the spirit of the suffering masses yearning for the future, what should be the suffering of those who represent the church? It is pain beyond description, the agony which Saint-Martin called prophetic agony, quite different from artistic torment or the suffering of an individual; it is the pain one suffers for millions! He who is concerned only with his own salvation is incapable of feeling such pain . . ."[1]

When in 1848 Mickiewicz discussed with Pope Pius IX his project for a Polish Legion against Austria, in a moment of emotion and excitement he caught the arm of the Pope and cried out: "Do you know that the spirit of God is now in the smocks of the workers of Paris!"[2] These manifestations of social radicalism and revolutionary Catholicism became characteristic for Mickiewicz in the years preceding and immediately following the French Revolution of 1848 and the Italian revolutionary movements of the same period.

Dostoevsky could have read Mickiewicz's *Slavic Literature*, and of course he did not know of the episode with the Pope. However, Dostoevsky could have found in another section of *Forefathers' Eve, Part III*, in the temptation of Father Peter, some items which could have pleased him:

> Father Peter. Who art thou, come!
> Spirit. I am Lucretius and Leviathan.
> Voltaire, *der alte Fritz, Legio sum.*
> Father Peter. Tell me what thou hast seen.
> Spirit.   I saw a beast.
> Father Peter. And where?
> Spirit.   In Rome.
> Father Peter.   He doth not yet obey!
> I'll pray again. [*He prays.*]
> Spirit. But I will mind you, priest.
> Father Peter. Where was the prisoner?
> Spirit.   In Rome, I say.
> Father Peter. Thou liest.
> Spirit.   By my honor, by my bride,
> My coal-black love who ever sighs for me—
> You know her name that I thus swear by?—Pride!—
> How void you are of curiosity!
> Father Peter. [*To himself.*] The demons are perverse. I
>   will abase
> Myself before the Lord and seek his grace.

---

[1] This passage is taken from Mickiewicz's Lectures III and IV in 1844. Cf. my study "Mickiewicz at the Collège de France, 1840–1940", in *The Slavonic and East European Review*, 1941, Vol. XX, p. 169.

[2] *Ibid.*, p. 159.

> [*He prays.*]
> Spirit. What need of that?— Why, I am going, I
> Admit I crawled into this soul awry.
> Like a hedgehog's skin turned inside out, it cuts
> And sticks its quills into my very guts.
> > [*The priest prays.*]
> > But you're a master, though a simple brother.
> > Asses! They'd make you Pope if they did right.
> > But no, the Church doth honor fools, and smother
> > Your merits—luminary, star of light!
> > > Father Peter. Tyrant and flatterer, proud yet base, thou art,
> > > Who crawlest through the dust to stab the heart![1]

This interlude was certainly connected with the complacent attitude toward Russia of Pope Gregory XVI. Polish Romantic literature contains another even more drastic page illustrating the moral decadence of the Pope: the marvelous Vatican scene in Słowacki's *Kordian*. In my book, *Life and Culture of Poland*, I underlined the ideological similarities between this scene and "The Legend of the Grand Inquisitor". In his work Słowacki reveals the imprisonment of the Catholic Church by materialism and utilitarianism.[2] Of course, Dostoevsky's views in this matter were still quite different from those of the Polish poets, due to the fact that the indignation of the latter was stirred by the connivance between Pope Gregory XVI and Nicholas I.

We should remember once again that Konrad's revolt was not entirely his own. The spirit of evil participated in it. This was not a full participation, but the pride which Konrad shows from the very beginning of his challenge to God, even before its last blasphemous accent, has elements of Promethean pride. Konrad asks God to cede him His power in order to bring about the happiness of millions. He is sure that he will do this better than God did. He reveals at the same time contempt for the multitude. He will rule them as a despot:

> And so I come to seek in heaven the art
> > To make them yield to me,
> And with the power I have o'er nature, bind
> > The human mind.
> As I rule birds and planets with my nod,
> So will I rule my fellow man, my rod
> No sword—that calls forth sword; no song——
> For it must germinate too long;
> Not learning—it will soon decay;

---

[1] Cf. Noyes, *op. cit.*, pp. 283–4.
[2] Cf. *Life and Culture of Poland*, pp. 245–8.

Not miracles—too loud are they;
But I will rule men by the love in me,
As thou dost rule forever, secretly.
What I desire, at once let all
Divine, and joyously fulfill;
And if they shall oppose my will,
Let them suffer, let them fall.
. . .
Give me the rule of souls! This lifeless building
That common people call the world, and praise,
I so despise that I have never tested
Whether my word has not the power to raze
And ruin it . . ."[1]

But Konrad is a *sui generis* Prometheus. His first statement points out that his power is of the same kind as God's. In the manner of God, he did not "seek" his power. He is "a creator born". And at the same time he demands that God give him the power of miracle. In other words, he wants to achieve a miracle which God does not want to bring about and which God alone is able to achieve. As Kleiner has pointed out, this is illogical and irrational, but psychologically understandable.[2]

The "Legend" is also a product of a mind possessed by the spirits of evil. The comments which Dostoevsky makes in the chapter about Ivan's nightmare imply the Devil's participation. The Devil speculates on the same themes, and several times repeats the same thoughts which Ivan expressed in his talks with Alesha and in his "Legend". The Devil himself stresses this when he says "I say original things which have never entered your head before. So I don't repeat your ideas, yet I am only your nightmare, nothing more." Whether Dostoevsky conceived Ivan's Devil as an independent entity or whether he was simply thought of as an hallucination of a schizophrenic mind, whether we face here metaphysical or psychological considerations, it would of course be difficult to decide. Doubtless there remains one thing: in both cases the authors tried to reduce the responsibilities of their heroes. Still another conclusion is possible. Dostoevsky led to its ultimate end that which Mickiewicz only suggested. Konrad was saved from his religious apostasy, whereas Ivan's fate was more drastic. Ivan's "Legend" is from beginning to end anti-Christian. I believe that Romano Guardini is right when he says that even the figure of Christ in the "Legend" has nothing to do with the Christ of the Gospels. Guardini calls attention to the personality of Ivan, the creator of the "Legend":

---

[1] Cf. Noyes, *op. cit.*, pp. 274–5.
[2] Cf. Kleiner, *op. cit.*, Vol. II, Part I, p. 351.

"And then, truly, who is the one who forged such a Christ? A man who himself does not believe in the Redeemer, but who imposes as a norm to the humble and timid believers the product, entirely notional, of his disbelief! Or if he believes in God, he does not 'accept his creation'. Gloomy and dramatic is the state of this soul, woven by contradictions and completely filled with a denial more destructive than a simple negation of God; he is a man whose encounters with Satan are frequent and common and with whom he is in perfect agreement on all points. . . . The Grand Inquisitor is Ivan himself insofar as he repels the world and wants to wrest it from the hands of God, as God has formed it badly! And he does it with the pretension of arranging it differently and better than the first Author. . . ."[1]

Guardini also points out something else, another proof of the play between rationalism and irrationalism, in its essence very close to Konrad's case:

"And this is Ivan with his quivering nerves; he still loves this world and he would not like it to be different than it is, because it is only in this way that this world is able to give him what he is seeking; consequently, he wants to maintain it in this state in order to protest against it, and protesting, to continue to enjoy it."[2]

In both Mickiewicz's and Dostoevsky's texts appears the theme of self-deification; this is an old theme in western-European literature, connected with the displeasure with God's world, a theme common to such a degree that it even forms a medieval anecdote about Saint Peter, who says that he would have ruled the world better than God. The German poet Hans Sachs elaborated this anecdote. These items were known to Mickiewicz from Angelus Silesius, Eckhart, and of course Byron, as Polish scholars have shown.[3] The problem of equalizing the human creative personality with God has also been touched by Herder in his *Die älteste Urkunde des Menschengeschlechts* (*The Oldest Document of the Human Race*), in which he defines, in the following way, the rôle of man in the world: "Gottes Stelle zu vertreten, zu herrschen, zu walten mit Schöpferkraft und Allgüte wirksam, still und verborgen, ein Gott der Erde zu sein, Segen, Leben und Glückseligkeit zu verbreiten."[4]

[1] Cf. Romano Guardini, *L'Univers religieux de Dostoïevski* (Paris: Editions du Seuil, 1947), pp. 137, 139.
[2] Cf. Guardini, *op. cit.*, p. 139.
[3] Cf. Kleiner, *op. cit.*, Vol. II, Part I, pp. 348-9.
[4] Quoted by Kleiner, *ibid.*, p. 349.

Alfred de Vigny's *Le Mont des oliviers* contains many items common to those which I am discussing here. Dostoevsky could easily have read this poem, which appeared in *La Revue des deux mondes* in 1862. And this poem, I am convinced, and hope one day to prove, is closely connected with Mickiewicz's "Improvisation". So Mickiewicz still remains, if all my conjectures are valid, as an independent source of inspiration for Dostoevsky.

Finally, the stylization of the Devils in both works is similar— the use of foreign language, the grotesque elements, and most of all the emphasis on the base, petty character of the spirit of evil. And both Mickiewicz and Dostoevsky opposed to their heroes' attempts at self-deification on the thesis of Christian self-abnegation; let us not forget the equation Konrad: Peter—Ivan: Zossima.

It is evident that one of the main problems in *Forefathers' Eve* and *The Brothers Karamazov* is the religious problem. Mickiewicz himself emphasized this in his Preface:

> All writers who have mentioned the persecution in Lithuania during that period agree that in the case of the Wilno students there was something mystical and mysterious. The mystical, gentle, yet inflexible character of Tomasz Zan, the leader of the young men; the religious resignation, the brotherly love and harmony of the young prisoners; the divine punishment that visibly overtook their persecutors, made a deep impression on the minds of those who were witnesses of the events or who shared in them. The story of this episode seems to carry the reader back to ancient times—times of faith and of miracles.[1]

The religious character of *The Brothers Karamazov* has been shown and explored so often that any additional mention on my part would be superfluous. In these two books we have not only two parallel, different attitudes toward God, Konrad's and Father Peter's, Ivan's and Zossima's, but two different conceptions of God. In both books there takes place the eternal fight between rationalism and irrationalism, between reason and faith. This fight had a long story in Mickiewicz's life; and he early defended the rights of faith against reason. His romance "Romanticism", which expresses the credo of the young poet in his first public collection of poems—*Ballads and Romances*—is a strong apology of faith, an affirmation of the existence of the unknown world, closed to the "spectacles of the sage", but open to the "eyes of the soul". After having displayed Romantic ecstasy before the Creator and Nature in his *Crimean Sonnets*, even with some pantheistic accents, Mickiewicz,

[1] Cf. Preface to *Forefathers' Eve, Part III*, Noyes, *op. cit.*, p. 248.

on the road of genuine religious exaltation in Rome, reached an intimate familiarity with the Divinity, expressed in his "Evening Discourse".

God who appears in the "Improvisation" is a God of reason, a God of the rationalists and skeptics, a God of numbers, skiences, of thought and not of heart. Mickiewicz will develop the same items in his Paris lectures, when speaking about Derzhavin's "Ode to God":

"Of what kind of God is the poet singing? A God known in the eighteenth century was a God who belonged to no one; it was not the God of Israel, omnipresent, a God with a living voice; neither was it a God of the Christians. It was some abstract substance which was worshipped in prolix and heavy rhymes, filled with mathematical concepts. The poet, desiring to describe the Superior Being, acts like Spinoza: he begins to enumerate that which his Being is not, in order to give a conception of what it must be. He repeats a thousand times over that God has never had a beginning and will never have an end; he continues a similar list of negations, seeking an ideal of greatness; and with the speech of a geometer he presents the indefinableness of space and time. All such poems are just a denial of that which they presume to prove: they show the skepticism of their time."

Further on Mickiewicz opposes to the agnosticism of the century of enlightenment the genuine faith in God which characterizes the Middle Ages, during which time there were no odes to God produced, but in whose religious writings one could still feel the fragrance of God. Mickiewicz points out that the eighteenth century did not wish to mix God into everyday affairs: "They declared unto God their highest respect, but they politely pushed Him outside life's boundaries, and delivered Him into the region of abstract notions."[1]

As I previously mentioned, the story of Konrad is not simple. His conception of God re-echoes the rationalistic conceptions of the eighteenth century, but at the same time he underlines the dangers hidden in a God who is wisdom alone. If man may reach God only with his mind and not with his heart, this same man, "who delved in books alone,/In numbers, corpses, metals, stone, . . ." ". . . shall find poison,

[1] Cf. Lecture XII of the second year (Friday, 11 February, 1942).
I may again quote Guardini, who, in his critique of the "Legend", notes its "purely exceptional Christianism, detached from the average domain" and emphasizes the "importance of the Christian fact in the everyday life of each individual. . . ." "This Christ has none of the holy love relationship with the real world which purifies and renews it, but His is a simple compassion which implies the abandonment of the world." Cf. Guardini, *op. cit.*, p. 134.

"A Reading of *Pan Tadeusz* in the Mines" (1835)
By K. Górski

powder, ... steam, ... smoke, ... and empty laws". This is a prediction of the destructive potentialities of sciences, as well as of the consequences of a religious and ethic relativism. And it is paralleled by Ivan's "everything is allowed". This is not the end of all the philosophical complications of which the "Improvisation" consists. Konrad's criticism here follows the road of Mickiewicz's opposition toward rationalism. Nevertheless, the same Konrad asks God for the power of miracle by which he would rule mankind. I have already stressed the autocratic character of this ambition, which is very similar to that of the Grand Inquisitor. And still I have something more to add. Konrad's supreme goal is to secure happiness to mankind, as the God of wisdom is indifferent to it. In this Konrad again follows the rationalists of the eighteenth century—the English and French thinkers, and, as Kleiner states: "Their aim was the creation of an order which would grant to the greatest number of men conditions of a happy existence. This idea was promulgated by Bentham's utilitarianism and it was developed later, at the very same time that Mickiewicz was busy with *Forefathers' Eve, Part III*, by the Saint-Simonists, the most successful heirs of the enlightenment."[1]

As we know, Father Peter's God was a different one, and Father Peter with Christian humility accepted suffering, the significance and justification of which do not belong to human reason. One may say that Ivan's conception was exactly the same as Konrad's. His Grand Inquisitor was trying to convince Christ that the road of rationalism and rationalistic autocracy, granting mankind happiness at the expense of freedom, was the right road. This was the basis of his imposed bargain with Christ.

There remains another important detail which I should like to clarify: Konrad's blasphemy—"That thou are not the Father, but the czar!" I think that this item is connected with Mickiewicz's rejection of Hegel's philosophy. We know that Mickiewicz attended some of Hegel's lectures in 1829 in Berlin. We also know that these lectures did not awaken any enthusiasm in him:

"I attend Hegel's lectures from time to time. Two lectures were devoted to the difference between 'Vernunft' and 'Verstand'. I see that I belong to the older generation, and as a 'stationnaire' by no means shall I ever reach an understanding with the local metaphysicians."

He stresses in the same letter that "here philosophy confused the minds", and "I am afraid I might switch over to the side of Śniadecki,

[1] Cf. Kleiner, *op. cit.*, Vol. II, Part 1, pp. 332-3.

the Hegelians annoy me so much".[1] Of course, these comments in themselves are not very instructive. Fortunately, we have Mickiewicz's Paris lecture of Tuesday, 29 June, 1841, in which he discusses Hegel's philosophy and particularly his conception of God. It seems to me that these remarks, though they belong to a later period of Mickiewicz's life, throw a revealing light on the "Improvisation". This is what Mickiewicz says in his lecture:

> "According to Hegel, God, as a spirit, as a force, as Being and non-Being, the God of the Universe, is realized in man. This God, who grows like a herb, like an organic substance, like a child and like a man, finally acquires self-perception in the human mind. To put it more clearly, there is no other personal God besides man. Thought is realized in man, in him it acquires the knowledge of its own being. But the historical God, the collective God, not stopping at inhabiting the individual man who understands his own thoughts as a philosopher, is incarnate in the nation. According to Hegel, God was at one time incarnate in Oriental empires, in Babylonian and Persian kings, as for instance in Ninus. Later He moved on to Greece, where He was particularly busy with fine arts, and produced a brilliant epoch of art mastery. Then He travelled to Rome, where He appeared as a God of politics. Finally, transforming Himself once again, He became embodied in the German race. Hegel does not say which state He now chooses for His habitation, but from Hegel's political system it is very easy to guess that He is in Prussia. The historical God has become Prussian."

In the light of these ironic commentaries it becomes easier to discern the essence of Konrad's God. This whole framework of arguments enables me to accept Wacław Kubacki's interpretation of the "Improvisation", which almost entirely parallels mine. In his very interesting study, *Palmyra and Babylon* (in which, by the way, he carries on an offensive against my interpretation of Pushkin's *Bronze Horseman*) Kubacki says:

> "The older philological studies have already shown, and the more recent ideological analyses have confirmed the fact that the 'Great Improvisation' in its first draft did not belong to Konrad's

---

[1] Cf. Mickiewicz's letter to F. Malewski from Berlin, 12 June, 1829. The brothers Śniadecki were outstanding scientists at the University of Wilno while Mickiewicz was studying there; they represented the tradition of rationalism and classicism of the period of enlightenment.

patriotic drama, and that it was a part of another, more general creative conception. Indeed, this section, which one could call an expression of intellectual Titanism and Prometheanism of the century of enlightenment, does not match the history of Polish culture and thought. True, this motif comes forth only negatively, as something against which the poet fights in Konrad and against which Konrad fights in God, but it does come forth! Because the God of the 'Improvisation', the God with whom Konrad struggles in this national drama, is neither a national nor a Messianic God. . . . This God is One of the eighteenth century— the superior Intellect and the cold, relentless 'raison d'état' of the universe: ('If on the millions crying "Save us, Lord", Thou dost not gaze with an unmoved regard, as Thou wouldst gaze on the confusion wrought by some false reckoning . . .') A romantic and Messianic God will be the God of the exorciser and mystic, Father Peter. In Poland the God of the 'Improvisation' could, in the last instance, be only a God of a few exceptional people, of the Educational Commission, of Kołłątaj, of Staszic, of the brothers Śniadecki. Instead, He was a natural God of the mathematician, of the artisan, of the mechanic, of the builder, the inventor, legislator, promotor of civilization, the chief and statesman—the God of Peter the Great! This is why it was not difficult for the devil to whisper to Konrad the blasphemous thought that this God, to whom Konrad so loftily and proudly speaks, is the Czar!"[1]

Thus we see how the Western rationalists of the eighteenth century and Derzhavin, Hegel and the Czar, meet in Konrad's God.

All this meticulous dissection has little direct connection with the theme Mickiewicz-Dostoevsky. One may be sure that if Dostoevsky read *Forefathers' Eve*—which is my hypothesis—he could not have been aware of the complex ideological origins of Mickiewicz's philosophical and religious speculations. There is no doubt, however, that Dostoevsky could have grasped the religious dualism which characterizes Mickiewicz's poem, and which suited his own Manichean attitude.

Among Mickiewicz's religious poems, written or conceived in Rome, in which his religious meditations found their ultimate poetic expression, two poems are particularly important for my present analysis: "Reason and Faith" and "The Sages". "Reason and Faith" is an extremely valuable commentary on *Forefathers' Eve, Part III*. In this poem the rebellious Prometheus, the knight of reason, fighting for universal happiness, bows his head in the face of God: "Oh human

[1] Cf. W. Kubacki, *Palmira i Babilon* (Wrocław: Wydawnictwo Zakładu Narodowego Imienia Ossolińskich, 1951).

reason! Thou, so small before the Lord, a drop in His almighty palm!" Here the poet again fights the proud savants with their slogans of "necessity" and "accident", representing the cynical philosophy of relativism.

The other poem, "The Sages", "conceived in France and written in Dresden", as Mickiewicz noted on the manuscript, obviously resulted from meditations about French rationalism, Voltaireanism and skepticism. This particular poem is my last argument. If Dostoevsky indeed knew Mickiewicz and knew his works he could not have overlooked "The Sages". I shall allow myself to quote this poem in its entirety.

The Sages

In thought that brought no rest nor peace of heart
    The sages fell into uneasy doze——
When far below them in the crowded mart,
    "God comes among us!" loud the cry arose.
"He should be slain," they said, "who breaks our rest:
The crowd protects him now; by night 'twere best."

So when the night came and their lamps were lit,
    Even as whetstones books of weighty words
Used they to sharpen their hairsplitting wit
    Till it was keen and cold and swift as swords.
Blind pupils led they forth to capture God,
But to destruction led the path they trod.

"Is't thou?" they cry unto mild Mary's son.
    " 'Tis I," he answers, and the pupils fly
In dread; the sages fall before that One.
    "Is't thou?" They tremble. "Yea," he saith, " 'tis I."
But, seeing that God awes but does not strike,
They then became more cruel, more demonlike.

They stripped him of his robes of mystery,
    And with cold reasoning they pierced his side;
They flogged his body with their mockery
    And cast him in a grave digged by their pride:
Yet from their souls, dark as that grave, he came,
And offered them salvation in his name!

Thus did the sages fill their cup of pride,
    And terror for her Lord the world o'erwhelm:

Yet 'twas but in their souls that he had died——
He lives, and peace is in heavenly realm.[1]

The historical frame and the actual events are different from those in the "Legend", but the theme is the same: "the expulsion of God by atheistic rationalism", to quote Kleiner again.[2] This is obviously the main theme of the poem, but one may also discern in it allusions to a conflict between an organized church and the Redeemer, the killing of Christ in the human heart. The poem follows, though in a stylized form, the Gospels, but its symbolic sense is clear:

> They stripped him of his robes of mystery,
>   And with cold reasoning they pierced his side;
> They flogged his body with their mockery
>   And cast him in a grave digged by their pride:
> Yet from their souls, dark as that grave, he came,
> And offered them salvation in his name!

As I have mentioned, between *Forefathers' Eve* and "The Grand Inquisitor" there is another poem, Alfred de Vigny's *Le Mont des oliviers*, inspired by the same spirit of love for mankind as the one that Konrad feels and the one promulgated by Ivan, and led by a similar religious rationalism. Konrad did not obtain an answer. Konrad's God symbolized in Mickiewicz's poem the silence and indifference of the European conscience, imprisoned by a relativistic philosophy, in the face of the Polish tragedy. Vigny's Christ heard only silence. Vigny's God, modelled after the despotic Jahveh of the Old Testament and after the cruel Lord of Jansenius's doctrine of predestination, could not give an answer to Christ in His agony. Ivan's Christ silently kissed the Grand Inquisitor. The theatrical kiss of Ivan's Christ, placed on the lips of the Grand Inquisitor, implies even a deeper absence of divinity in the human world. This is the Son and not the Father who abandons mankind. Vigny did not commit any apostasy from his rationalism, and added to his poem the famous stanza "Silence", in which he opposed to the "eternal silence of divinity" the "cold silence of the just"; "disdain" to "absence". His solitary love of mankind and worship of human dignity found a refuge in a philosophy of stoicism. Mickiewicz, like Pascal, experienced the miracle of divine grace. His Father Peter and his poem "Evening Discourse" prove this.

Dostoevsky's philosophy is identical. My task is not to test Dostoevsky's sincerity of feelings and religious conceptions. In other

---
[1] Cf. Noyes, *op. cit.*, p. 243.
[2] Cf. Kleiner, *op. cit.*, p. 466.

studies I have tried to show the paradoxical coexistence of hatred with his Christian apologetics. There is no doubt that the entire political output of Mickiewicz, and *Forefathers' Eve* in particular, is filled with a deep love for his fellow man. Without mentioning Dostoevsky's political, social and religious intransigence, animosity and malice, even Ivan, who assumes the attitude of revolt against a God who allows the suffering of the innocent, confesses that love for one's fellow man is impossible and he presents the conception of a purely abstract love of mankind. My task has been simply to juxtapose two literary texts and to raise the question whether the similarities which characterize them are purely accidental.

This mosaic of details, of fragmentary juxtapositions and comparisons serves a purely speculative purpose. I need not stress again that everything here is hypothetical; we have no biographical facts, no avowals, no witnesses to confirm all these suppositions. The circumstance that Dostoevsky remained almost completely silent about Mickiewicz is perhaps not a strong argument against my "theory". On the contrary, if I am right, Dostoevsky had every reason to hide this source of his inspiration. Here and there some half-words, which I mentioned above—as in the case of Lyamshin—encourage suspicion. Mickiewicz, the poet of moral action, of freedom and of Christianization not only of politics, but even of the Church itself, the poet whose realism was, in a way, so close to Dostoevsky's "fantastic realism", and finally the legendary friend of Pushkin, could not be overlooked by Dostoevsky.

Lastly, one has to take into consideration the fact, mentioned above, that Pushkin's *Bronze Horseman*, in which Dostoevsky was so interested, contains in the poet's footnotes direct allusions to Mickiewicz's *Digression*. These footnotes alone could have excited Dostoevsky's curiosity, although he had no knowledge of the literary genealogy of *The Bronze Horseman* and its ideological relationship with Mickiewicz's *Digression*. Russian reviews which Dostoevsky used to read were still paying attention and tribute to Mickiewicz and his poetry. For instance, P. P. Dubrovsky in 1858 published a study in the *Notes of the Fatherland* consisting of four articles of some one hundred and forty pages. In 1868 appeared A. F. Hilferding's study on the views of the Western Slavs toward Russia (in the second volume of his *Collected Works*), in which he discusses Mickiewicz. In 1871 was published N. V. Gerbel's anthology, *The Poetry of the Slavs*, which contains over forty translations from Mickiewicz's works, including *Pan Tadeusz*. Also included is an article on Mickiewicz by A. Budilovich. In 1879 Katkov's review *The Russian Messenger* contained a study of V. V. Makushev on Towiański with several passages dedicated to Mickiewicz. None of these studies could directly mention *Forefathers' Eve, Part III*, a work forbidden by the Russian censors; but they obviously allude to it, most frequently in a derogatory manner, attacking Mickiewicz's "destroyed mind", "pathetic blindness", "exaggerations" and "unnaturalness"; but at the same time they praise the poetic beauties of Mickiewicz's works.[1] One may find a completely different reaction by Herzen toward Mickiewicz's *Forefathers' Eve, Part III*. This is what he writes in his *Diary* of 1843 (January):

". . . I am reading Mickiewicz. There is very much that is beautiful and highly artistic in this lamentation of the poet. Heavens, how beautiful is his picture of the Russian road in winter! An endless desert, white, cold, a sea with its breast closed to the wind which sweeps this desert from the Pole to the Black Sea. The roads which cut across this desert result not from trade, not from the needs of the people, but they are traced by the order of the Czar, etc., etc. Admirable, also, in this poem is the section about Peter's monument. Mickiewicz compares it (and puts this comparison in the mouth of a pilgrim) with the quiet pose of Marcus Aurelius in Rome. . . ."

Further, Herzen describes Mickiewicz's allegorical picture of Peter the Great. Of course, Herzen was abroad and was free to write whatever he wished in his *Diary*.[2] It is worth while to stress that with the exception of a few unfriendly statements, written in the period of his Hegelianism, and later rejected by himself with great remorse in his letter to V. P. Botkin of 10–11 December, 1840, Belinsky spoke about Mickiewicz with genuine admiration and enthusiasm. He generally placed Mickiewicz among the greatest poets of the period.[3] The passage on Mickiewicz in Belinsky's letter to Botkin deserves to be quoted:

"Two thoughts about the past torture me: first of all, that occasions for pleasure occurred to me and I let them pass, as a consequence of petty idealism and the shyness of my character; and secondly, my cowardly acceptance of base actuality. My God,

---

[1] Some of the works quoted here are not readily available, and therefore I have utilized the quite interesting study of S. S. Sovetov, "Tvorčeskij put' Adama Mickeviča". Cf. *Učënnye Zapiski Instituta Slavjanovedenija* (Moscow, 1950), Vol. II, pp. 119–37.
[2] Cf. *Sočinenija A.I. Gercena* (Genève-Bâle-Lyon, 1875), Vol. I, pp. 79–80.
[3] Cf. Belinsky's article on Griboedov's *Wit Works Woe* (1839).

how many repugnant, petty things have I uttered in print in all honesty, with all the fanaticism of wild conviction. More than ever, I am now saddened by having expressed sentiments against Mickiewicz in that sickening article about Menzel. By what right should one take from a great poet the sacred prerogative of lamenting the fall of that which is more dear to him than everything in the world and in eternity—the fall of his country, his fatherland; how can we take away his right to damn his executioners, and what sort of executioners?—Cossacks and Kalmucks who acquired devilish tortures in order to squeeze money out of their victims (they beat them with goose-feathers on their . . . , they placed girls of noble birth on small fires before the eyes of their fathers—these are facts of our European war with Poland, facts which I heard from eyewitnesses). And precisely that noble and great poet I called in print a 'shouter', a 'poet of rhymed pamphlets' !"[1]

Is this not a striking acceptance of Mickiewicz's *Forefathers' Eve, Part III*?

We know now many interesting details about Belinsky's ties with several Polish émigrés in the University of Moscow and with their literary society, particularly with T. Zabłocki, A. Bielecki, and several others, all men who deeply admired Mickiewicz. There is no doubt that Belinsky knew *Forefathers' Eve, Part III*. On 21 August, 1834, N. V. Stankevich wrote to V. I. Krasov: "First, ask Belinsky to hand over to you the three volumes of Mickiewicz and the two volumes of the Dictionary—it seems to me that I gave them to him." Obviously Stankevich referred to Mickiewicz's Parisian edition, which included *Forefathers' Eve, Part III*.[2]

Whether Dostoevsky knew of Belinsky's private statement is difficult to determine, but, if so, the parallelism between *Forefathers' Eve, Part III* and "Pro and Contra", which I am trying to prove, would acquire a particularly significant aspect. It would shed additional light on Dostoevsky's methods. But this is only a conjecture. In any case, Dostoevsky certainly read Belinsky's public statements and among them there are two especially interesting appraisals which could have impressed him. In his article of 1835 on the poems of Vladimir Benediktov, Belinsky opposed Mickiewicz's powerful art to the grandiloquent artificiality of Benediktov's descriptions:

---

[1] Cf. Belinsky's letter to V. P. Botkin, 10–11 December, 1840: V. G. Belinskij, *Izbrannye sočinenija* (Moscow: Ogiz, 1947), p. 636. The main passages of Belinsky's statement were censored before 1905.

[2] Cf. M. Poljakov, "Studenčeskie gody Belinskogo" in *Literaturnoe Nasledstvo* (Moscow, 1950), Vol. LVI, pp. 303–436.

"Mickiewicz, one of the greatest world poets, understood well the magnificence and hyperbolism of descriptions, and therefore in his *Crimean Sonnets* he very wisely assumed the speech of an orthodox Mohammedan; indeed, this hyperbolic expression of wonderment for Chatyr Dagh seems to be very natural in the mouth of a worshipper of Mohammed, in the mouth of a son of the East."

Belinsky's second statement deserves particular attention. In an article "About the Russian Tale and Tales of Gogol" (1835), in which he discussed "realistic and idealistic poetry", he reckoned among this latter group works like Goethe's *Faust*, Byron's *Manfred*, Mickiewicz's *Forefathers' Eve*, Thomas Moore's *Lalla Rookh*, the fantastic visions of Jean-Paul, and Goethe's *Iphigenia* and Schiller's *The Bride of Messina*. Belinsky's remarks on the essence of this "idealistic poetry" are extremely valuable for some items discussed in the present study, as they deal indirectly with Dostoevsky's views on his own "fantastic realism". I am even ready to believe that these reasonings of Belinsky laid the foundation for Dostoevsky's views. Belinsky writes:

"This modern *idealistic* poetry originates from ancient poetry; for it borrowed from the ancients its noble character, its majesty and its poetical lofty language, so different from the ordinary spoken language; it also borrowed its aloofness from everything petty and worldly. . . . However, there are points of contact in which these two types of poetry meet and fuse [Belinsky has in mind realistic and idealistic poetry]. At these points one should place first the poems of Byron, Pushkin, Mickiewicz. [Belinsky's letter to Botkin, although written much later, might be considered as additional proof that Belinsky refers, in this case, to *Forefathers' Eve, Part III*, even though he does not indicate which part of Mickiewicz's poem he has in mind, obviously because of the censorship.] These are poems in which human life is represented as much as it is possible to do so in truth, but only in its most solemn manifestations, in its most lyrical moments. . . ."

Belinsky's further argumentation, dealing with Dostoevsky's favorite drama of Schiller, *The Robbers*, very closely approaches, as it were, the aesthetic problems which Dostoevsky much later discussed in his essay on *The Meek One*, aesthetic devices which are so evidently used in *Forefathers' Eve, Part IV*:

"Such is Schiller's drama, *The Robbers*—this flaming, wild dithyramb, similar to lava bursting out of the depths of a young, energetic soul—in which the events, characters and situations are as if manufactured in order to express the ideas and feelings which had so strongly agitated the author; that for these feelings lyrical forms would have been too narrow. Some people seem to find in Schiller's early dramatic works much phraseology: for instance, they say that instead of the enormous monologue of Karl Moor, telling the robbers about his father, a man in a similar situation would have said perhaps two or three words. In my opinion he would not have said a single word, and would perhaps have merely indicated his father with his hand. And nevertheless, under Schiller's pen, Moor says a great deal; but still, in his words there is not a shadow of phraseology. The thing is that here the author speaks and not the character; that in this whole creation there is not the truth of life, but there is the truth of feeling; there is no reality, no drama, but there is an endless amount of poetry; the situations are false and unnatural, but the feelings are genuine, the thought is deep...."[1]

Belinsky developed all these views, as the reader may see, on the basis of Schiller's, Byron's, Pushkin's and Mickiewicz's poetry. This fact was of course clear to Dostoevsky. What was also clear to him, as I pointed out before, was that even if Belinsky had had the desire to devote more time and attention to Mickiewicz's *Forefathers' Eve, Part III*, these attempts would have been in vain, for the censor would not have passed them.

I have no more arguments at my disposal. This is the end. I hope that the reader understands my point of view. My purpose has not been at all to advance the presumption that without Mickiewicz, without *Forefathers' Eve, Part III*, Dostoevsky would not have been able to write *The Brothers Karamazov*. The ties between *Crime and Punishment* and Balzac's *Père Goriot* are well known. Grossman has demonstrated that the nucleus of *Crime and Punishment* is to be found in the talks between Rastignac and Bianchon and between Rastignac and Vautrin in Balzac's novel. We know about Dostoevsky's dependence on Pushkin, Gogol, Dickens, Victor Hugo, Stendhal, even on Eugène Sue; but Dostoevsky's literary indebtedness certainly does not diminish the achievements and the prestige of his art and the idea we have of his personal creative powers. The goal of all of us who are busy with comparative studies on Dostoevsky is to ascertain the various elements which gradually, consecutively and sometimes simultaneously contributed to the making of the thinker, the writer and the artist. In my

[1] These quotations are taken from *V. G. Belinskij, Stat'i i recenzii* (Moscow: Ogiz, 1948), in three volumes.

present studies I have tried to show the importance of the Polish factor in Dostoevsky's world, a factor which he himself so often indirectly indicated, and a factor which generally, especially in this country, has been neglected. Mickiewicz's rôle in this world of Dostoevsky—if it indeed existed—was more secret than the rôles of many others; but for this very reason its discovery is all the more tempting.

The reader remembers Dostoevsky's allusion in *The House of the Dead* to a book given him by his Polish prison-mates in Siberia, a book which made "a great, strange and peculiar impression" upon him. He pointed out that these impressions were "most interesting" to him, and that he was "sure that to many people they would be utterly unintelligible". As we know, he never disclosed this secret. Is it wishful thinking on my part to presume that this book was Mickiewicz's *Forefathers' Eve, Part III*?[1]

That Dostoevsky was acquainted with Mickiewicz's work is beyond doubt. O. Pochinkovsky, who worked for a whole year with Dostoevsky, points out that the great writer perpetually persecuted her because of her presumed Polish origin. "And this only because of the fact," we read in her article, "that having spent several years in our western

[1] One of my colleagues expressed some doubts as to the possibility of the Polish exiles in Siberia having Mickiewicz's works there, especially those which were forbidden in Russia. First, I should like to remark that in general, of course, copies of Mickiewicz's forbidden works could be found in Russia. We know, for instance, that S. Sobolevsky secretly brought the Parisian edition of Mickiewicz's works from abroad in 1833 and offered it to Pushkin. Pushkin used this copy while he was writing his *Bronze Horseman*. (See *Rukoju Puškina*, p.r. M. Cjavlovskogo *et al* (Moscow-Leningrad: Academia, 1935), p. 550.) Second, as far as the Polish exiles in Siberia are concerned, we have no direct proofs in this matter but there are some indirect testimonies. Antoni Pawsza, who was sentenced to hard labour in Siberia for his part in the Insurrection of 1830–1831, and whose father, by the way, also spent three years there for the Kościuszko Insurrection, left valuable notes on his stay in Siberia. "For the year 1840 he notes that there arrived in Tobolsk the sixteen-year-old Sikorska from Ołyka, exiled by Governor-general Bibikov for sending Mickiewicz's verses to her brother, who was in the 'Kantonist' school in Smolensk." M. Janik, *op. cit.*, p. 165. "In the realm of spiritual life, the common libraries were a means of self-help. They tried to found them in every place where there was a large number of exiles. Some of the best stocked libraries were those in Orenburg, Tobolsk, and Nerchinsk.... Thanks to these libraries and the newspapers which were sent to them the exiles remained in close contact with the intellectual life of the homeland, kept themselves informed of the literary and political news, sometimes with astonishing rapidity, and, what is more, maintained and developed their own intellectual life." *Ibid.*, p. 290. "Because the majority of the people (the exiles) were young and well educated, the women of the place studied Polish for the establishment and preservation of social contacts with them, and they read Mickiewicz and our novelists. There were even times when it became fashionable in Orenburg to wear grey coats, because the Polish soldiers wore them. Polish dances were learned, and the mazurka was executed no worse than in Warsaw." *Ibid.*, p. 246. Finally, the picture *"Pan Tadeusz* in the Mines", which I have reproduced in this book, might also be considered an indirect proof of the existence of copies of Mickiewicz's works among the Polish exiles in Siberia.

provinces, I once described to him with enthusiasm the picturesque surroundings of a Lithuanian town and the beauties of Mickiewicz's poems. 'And still,' he interrupted me—'your precious Mickiewicz sang the praises of Wallenrod, that is to say—a traitor and a liar. And a true poet should never glorify traitors or liars. *Never!*'—he repeated with bitter passion, squinting his eyes and sarcastically twisting his lips."[1]

---

[1] O. Počinkovskaja, "God raboty s znamenitym pisatelem", *Istoričeskij Vestnik*, February, 1904, pp. 488–542. I am indebted for this quotation to my student, Mr. Robert L. Jackson.

VII

Blok's "Polish Poem"

THE culminative point in the development of the ethico-historical theme of *Retribution*, Blok's most mature and most complete—even though unfinished—poem is the "retribution" in the tragically interwoven fate of Russia and Poland.

It is curious that the Russian commentators on this work have paid no attention to the fact that *Retribution* is, however it be interpreted, the great Russian poet's "Polish Poem". It has been mentioned, of course, that the poem is "biographically" connected with Blok's sojourn in Warsaw at his father's funeral, that it is obliquely connected through the *Iambi* with the poet's half-sister Angelina Alexandrovna Blok, whom the poet met for the first time in Warsaw after his father's death. . . . But no one has ever drawn attention to several quite significant acts: that Poland and her fate occupy the chief place in the ideational plane of the poem, that this fact is strikingly apparent in the remarkable Preface to the poem, that the "Polish theme" is developed pathetically in its third chapter, and that this third chapter, during a certain period of Blok's work on *Retribution* (in the first quarter of 1911), was called by the author "A Warsaw Poem"—at that time Blok conceived this third chapter as a separate poem.

For this there have been two reasons. One is of a particular, the other of a general order. No one ever suspected such a possibility in Blok. How is this poet of Russian symbolism, in spirit a nationalist, and moreover the singer of the Russian Revolution, the author of the *Verses on a Beautiful Lady*, *The Scythians*, and *The Twelve*, to occupy himself of a sudden with so "narrow" and alien a theme as that of Poland and her tragic fate? Would it not seem advisable to try to find the key to the riddle, or at least to try to "describe" this unusual phenomenon? But this has not hitherto been done. The Russian scholars remained silent. It may be that from the moment when Poland became an independent country it ceased to attract their interest. The turmoil of the Russian Revolution imposed new themes of a more vital and demanding character on literature and literary research. With the passage of time the historical reminiscences connected with Poland, especially with Polish revolutionary movements and sociological speculations on Polish "feudal culture", reappeared in Soviet publications, but Blok's ideological affiliation with Poland still remained unexplored. The Russian emigration was also absorbed by its own problems, and, I dare say, never lost a feeling of resentment caused by the fall of the Russian Empire and the territorial losses involved. As far as Poland is concerned these resentments were expressed by silence, at best. It would, indeed, be very difficult to find even in the most representative reviews —scholarly or literary—published by the Russian émigrés in Europe or in America any studies dealing with Poland or even with the problem of Russo-Polish relations. From time to time political polemics have found their way into these reviews, but any cultural interest in Poland has been missing. The pre-revolutionary situation was completely different.

Leaving out the question of Polish cultural influence in Muscovy during the sixteenth and seventeenth centuries, we find that beginning with the eighteenth century almost every Russian writer occupied himself with the Polish problem. Be it Lomonosov, Fonvizin, Derzhavin, Karamzin, Dmitriev, Glinka, Prince Vyazemsky, N. Turgenev, I. Kireevsky, Griboedov, Prince A. I. Odoevsky, Denis Davydov, Bestuzhev, Ryleev, Kozlov, Zhukovsky, Pushkin, Chaadaev, A. N. Wulf, A. Turgenev, Tyutchev, L. Pavlishchev, Countess Rostopchin, Gogol, Princess Z. Volkonsky, Belinsky, K. Pavlova, Shevyrev, Pogodin, the Polevoys, Aksakov, Khomyakov, Herzen, Bakunin, Katkov, Polonsky, Samarin, Nekrasov, Saltykov-Shchedrin, A. Tolstoy, Leontiev, Leskov, Pisemsky, Fet, Turgenev, Dostoevsky, Strakhov, Vladimir Soloviev, Chicherin, Pypin, V. Ivanov, Korolenko, Bunin, Kuprin, Balmont, Bryusov, Prince E. N. Trubetskoy, Khlebnikov— not to mention the Lazhechnikovs, Zagoskins, Ilovayskys, Krestovskys, Markeviches, Saliases and Klyushnikovs, who specialized in so-called "Polish intrigue"—all these writers, poets, thinkers, many of them representing the flower of Russian literature, in one way or another, negatively or positively, episodically or deliberately, touched on Poland, portrayed Polish types, talked about Poland, and often expressed a definite "programmatic" view of the Russo-Polish question. Not infrequently they show traces of a good knowledge of Poland. I am not even speaking of Mickiewicz's stay in Russia, to which I refer so often in this book. The theme of Pushkin-Mickiewicz of itself, especially after the thousands of pages and the labours of many scores of scholars and researchers who have written on it, is a theme for a whole monograph. More and more new literary facts are being discovered in recent times, all tending to show that this is a very important chapter of Pushkiniana[1]—perhaps one of the most important.

And Tolstoy? It was even possible to write a whole book on Tolstoy's relation to Poland, and in this book the lion's share is given to facts.[2] In his day, Pypin printed a sizable work, *The Polish Question in Russian Literature*, without at all touching Tolstoy, Dostoevsky, and the great majority of those whom I have mentioned here.

And translations? Almost everything in Polish that was of any significance was translated into Russian in the second half of the nineteenth century and the beginning of the twentieth: Kraszewski, Orzeszkowa, Prus, Sienkiewicz, Sieroszewski, Przybyszewski, Żeromski. Reymont, Żuławski, Tetmajer, Wyspiański, Berent—let alone the great Polish Romantics, Mickiewicz, Słowacki, and Krasiński. Also to be mentioned are the beautiful *History of Polish Literature*, written by Spasowicz for the *History of Slavic Literatures* by Pypin and Spasowicz (1881); a Russian translation of George Brandes' *The Romantic Literature of Poland* (1913); L. Kozłowski's "Polish Romanticism" in *The History of Western Literature (1800–1910)*, edited by Professor F. D. Batyushkov (Moscow, 1914); the brilliant outline of a *History of Polish Literature* (lectures) by Professor V. N. Shchepkin (Moscow, 1916); the two-volume *History of Modern Polish Literature* by A. N. Yatzimirsky; and also the two-volume monograph on Mickiewicz by Professor A. L. Pogodin; to say nothing of numerous articles on Polish literature in *The Messenger of Europe*, in *Russian Thought, Russian Riches, The Scales* and in *Apollon* (in this publication from 1909 to 1913 there appeared regular reports on Polish literary and artistic life, reports signed with the pseudonym Swastica) and even in other magazines like *Russian Antiquity, The Historical Messenger*, not to speak of the works of such Russian historians and literary historians as Kostomarov, Milyukov, Lyubavsky, Kareev, Kornilov, Peretz, Zhdanov, Sobolevsky, Frantsev, Sirotinin, Speransky, Tikhonravov, and many others.

Such was the state of affairs in the nineteenth century and the beginning of the present one. In our own time the picture has altered. In Soviet Russia, interest in Poland has taken on a definite hue, but all

---

[1] On this, see: W. Lednicki, *Przyjaciele Moskale*,—Travaux publiés par la Société Polonaise d'Études concernant l'Europe Orientale et le Proche Orient; Nr. XII (Cracovie, 1935), esp. pp. 156–7. Also: V. Lednicki: "Pouchkine et Mickiewicz," *Revue de Littérature Comparée*, Janvier-Mars, 1937 (fascicule spécial consacré à Pouchkine) (Paris, 1937), pp. 129–44. Cf. also G. Struve, "Mickiewicz in Russia" in the *Slavonic and East European Review*, Vol. XXVI, No. 66 (November, 1947); and the monumental monograph on Mickiewicz by Juliusz Kleiner, Vols. I–II (Parts I and II) (Lublin, 1948).

[2] Venceslas Lednicki, *Quelques aspects du Nationalisme et du Christianisme chez Tolstoï* (Les variations Tolstoïennes à l'égard de la Pologne). Travaux publiés par la Société Polonaise ... etc. (Cracovie, 1935).

the same it has somehow existed. Polish books have been translated, works on Mickiewicz and Pushkin have been appearing, a special study of Polish literature has been taken up by Professor Chernobaev, who visited Poland and maintained scientific relations with Polish scholars. The same might be said of a number of Russian linguists, then and now. Needless to say, at the present moment with changed political relations between Soviet Russia and her enslaved Polish neighbour, one may observe a considerable increase of Polish studies in Russia. These studies are, of course, maintained under strict political control and aim at political goals. However, several new translations from Mickiewicz and Słowacki have appeared, an edition of the works of Eliza Orzeszkowa, and many other translations from modern Polish poets and writers.

The Russian emigration, on the other hand, as I have already stressed, denied interest in Poland and maintained toward her an attitude of indifference usually crowned by ignorance of Polish history, literature, culture, and language.[1]

* * * * *

I shall not—I cannot—treat of *Retribution* in its entirety, as that would take too much space. I shall dwell *only* on its Polish motifs. I may say at once that here we have to do with much material and with important material. This falls, in the first place, into two divisions: that printed by the poet, which we can therefore accept—with certain reservations—as the established text of the poem, and that which represents and comprises rich variants, the rough copies and plans. The established text, in its turn, falls once again by external indication into that which is said in the preface in prose and that which is contained in the poetic text of the third—and last—chapter of the poem.

---

[1] There were and are exceptions: Portugalov, Artzybashev, Philosophov, N. S. Arseniev, S. Kulakovsky, V. Fisher (and several young poets and writers), who lived in Poland after her restoration and by force of circumstances participated vitally in her cultural and political life; beyond the borders of Poland—Merezhkovsky in connection with his enthusiasm for Piłsudski; Khodasevich, thanks to his Polish extraction; of course Milyukov; some other scholars like Professors Frantsev, Bitsilli, K. Taranovsky, G. Fedotov, G. Struve, M. Karpovich, R. Jakobson; the well-known novelist, Aldanov; friends of my father who wrote of him after his death—V. A. Maklakov, Prince P. D. Dolgorukov, P. N. Milyukov, N. V. Teslenko, A. V. Amphiteatrov, I. V. Hessen, and many others. I should particularly mention the articles on Poland of Mikhail Koryakov, a former Red Army officer, who did not return to Russia and who, after having spent some time in Poland, published articles in the New York publication *Novy Zhurnal*, articles expressing his admiration for Polish culture, literature, and for Polish devotion to freedom. Finally, I should mention P. B. Struve's *Rossiya i Slavyanstvo*, a review which appeared in Paris before the last war. In the most recent years Russian émigré reviews, such as the abovementioned *Novy Zhurnal*, *Vozrozhdenie*, and *Opyty*, to note only the most important, from time to time publish articles on Polish themes.

Blok *c.* 1807

Finally, we have two different aspects, two different motifs of the Polish theme: on the one hand, the fate of Poland and the theme of retribution connected therewith; on the other, concrete pictures of Warsaw. And both, naturally, are interwoven with each other, together depicting an extraordinarily eloquent and, as I have already said, pathetic development of the theme of Polish—or, if you wish, Russian—retribution. If to this is added the fact that *Retribution* is very deeply and intimately connected with the personal experiences of the poet, the significance of this Russian poetic *declaration* cannot but become especially bright and evident. Finally, it cannot be forgotten that *Retribution* is, in the artistic sense, Blok's most finished, most brilliant, and most mature production, as well as his most Pushkinian production. This is true not only from the point of view of the language, style and images, not only from the point of view of the Pushkinian realism which the poet here approaches. This poem is rooted in *Eugene Onegin* and in ... *The Bronze Horseman*. Reading this poem, one sometimes seems to be reading the best and most *important* of Pushkin's writings. This is especially noteworthy, for this circumstance precludes any possibility of admitting in this profoundly mature work the presence of anything accidental, of anything not thought out to the very end of poetic thought. Strange, is it not, that people like Petronik or Ivanov-Razumnik (and even Desnitsky), who have analyzed Blok's *The Scythians* in the greatest detail and compared it with, of all things, Pushkin's "To the Calumniators of Russia" (which Blok himself, not without a certain irony, recalls in his diary[1]), have not thought of appraising *Retribution*! Not less strange is the fact that P. Medvedev, who made a thorough analysis of Blok's dramas and larger poems, did not pay any greater attention to the obvious Polish character of *Retribution*, although he mentioned the fact that the poet added a subtitle "A Warsaw Poem" to its third chapter. Not so strange as amusing is Mr. Mochulsky, who considers the Polish theme an accidental and artificial element in the poem, but the same Mochulsky states that the poet needed a "universal resonance which strengthened the sound of

---

[1] *Dnevnik Al. Bloka*, pod red. P. N. Medvedeva (Leningrad, 1928), pp. 234–6. On the other hand, it is very characteristic that in the plan of the edition of a "little" Pushkin, in which there would be "everything needful", Blok includes the ode "To the Calumniators of Russia" (*Ib.*, pp. 110–12). There is, however, one small exception: about twenty years ago a little article on *Retribution* and the Polish motifs of the poem appeared in Warsaw, I believe in the weekly, *Wiadomości Literackie*, written by S. Kulakovsky, but I do not remember the details of the article. I should also mention two excellent studies of my late friend, K. V. Zawodziński, both of which emphasized the Polish elements in *Retribution*. Zawodziński particularly stressed the ties between Blok's poem and Mickiewicz's *Forefathers' Eve*. Cf. *Przegląd Warszawski*, Warsaw, November, 1923; and *Twórczość*, Cracow, November, 1946. The last article is a general study on Blok.

his voice". " 'The Polish theme' secures to his verse a superior tension."[1]

Let us begin at the beginning, with the Preface, in other words with the motif on the plane of *ideas*. In this preface the poet utters several extraordinarily important thoughts. First of all he speaks of his poem as of a production "full of revolutionary presentiments", then he underscores its connection with his own personal life, fixing dates: "The poem *Retribution* was conceived in the year 1910 and in main outline written in 1911." (Blok worked on it, however, down to the year 1921.) Then comes a description of the salient characteristics of these years, exceptional in scope and vividness. Here also is the most remarkable of Blok's formulae, so often repeated since by many others: "I recall the conversations by night out of which first grew the awareness of the *indivisibility and the immiscibility of art, life, and politics*." How meaningful this is, and how important the fact that this profound thought is uttered just here, in *Retribution*! He speaks further on of "the tragic awareness", "of the immiscibility and the indivisibility of everything—of contradictions irreconcilable and demanding reconciliation!"

At this point one would like to add that one of them is the Russo-Polish contradiction, "irreconcilable and demanding reconciliation!" And the thought comes to mind that this formula arose in the poet's head in connection with his profound thinking about Poland and about her Russian destiny.

Further on, the poet develops his "character" of the year 1910 and his presentiments of future catastrophe, and finally comes to the description of the intent of his poem, which took birth in his mind just at this pre-catastrophic time. The iambic meter was chosen as "the simplest expression of the rhythm of the time when the world, preparing itself for unheard-of events, was intensively and systematically flexing its physical, political, and military muscles. . . ."

"The basic idea and theme" of the poem, he says further, is as follows:

> "The theme consists in showing the development of the links of the unified chain of a generation. Separate offspring of every species develop to their appointed limit and then are swallowed up anew by the surrounding milieu; but in each offspring there ripens and recedes something new and something more fused together, at the cost of infinite losses, personal tragedies, failures in life, downfalls and so on; at the cost, finally, of the loss of those infinitely high qualities which in their time have shone as the brightest gems in

---

[1] Cf. P. Medvedev, *Dramy i poemy A. L. Bloka* (Leningrad, 1928), p. 208. Cf. also K. Močul'skij, *Aleksandr Blok* (Paris: YMCA Press, 1948), p. 298.

the crown of mankind (for example, the quality of humaneness, virtue, irreproachable honesty, high morality, and so on). In a word, the universal maelstrom is sucking up into its eddies almost all of man; of his personality there remains hardly a trace. . . .

A man there was—and then was not; there remains trashy, flabby flesh and a rotting little soul. But the seed is cast forth, and in the next youngling grows something new and more stubborn; and in the last youngling this new and stubborn thing begins finally to operate tangibly on the environment; and thus the generation, having undergone the retribution of history, of the milieu, of the age, begins in its turn to create retribution; the last youngling is already capable of snarling and giving forth leonine growls; he is ready to grasp with his little manlike hand at the wheel whereby the history of mankind moves forward. And perhaps he really will grasp it. . . ."

This part of the exposition of the theme already contains a Polish element: "the last youngling, ready to grasp with his little manlike hand at the wheel whereby the history of mankind moves forward . . ." is indeed the Polish youngling, however strange it may appear to the reader.

What else do we find? "I wished to embody such an idea in my Rougon-Macquarts on a small scale, in the brief fragment of the Russian race, living in the conditions of Russian life: Two or three links, and we can already see the legacy of dark antiquity . . ." declares the poet sadly. "Through catastrophes and downfalls," we read on, "my Rougon-Macquarts gradually free themselves from the *éducation sentimentale* of the Russian gentry" (this is a purely biographical notation, connected with the special attachment of the poet's father, Professor Blok, to Flaubert), "the coal is turned to diamond" (a very significant phrase which returns continually in Blok's revolutionary *Iambi* and also in *Retribution*), "Russia—into a new America; into a new, and not the old, America."

"The poem"—I am quoting further—"must consist of a prologue, three long chapters, and an epilogue. Each chapter is framed by the description of events of world-wide significance; they have comprised its background. . . ." Later on the poet gives the contents of the first chapter, in which against the background of the Russo-Turkish War is narrated the life of a "demon"—the poet's father, who, according to Dostoevsky (this has been preserved in family traditions), resembled Byron—appearing in an enlightened, liberal Russian family. This is the "first swallow" of "individualism" and, moreover, of the incipient *fin de siècle*.

The second chapter, says the poet, embraces the end of the nineteenth century and the beginning of the twentieth, and it "was to be devoted to this demon's son,"—"the heir to his rebellious passions and morbid depressions, the unsentimental child of our century". . . . Here is the beginning of the strictly Polish part of the poem, connected with intimate facts of Blok's personal life. "This also is but one of the links in a long series; of it, also, apparently nothing remains besides a spark of fire thrown into the world, besides a seed hurled on a passionate and sinful night into the bosom of some quiet and womanly daughter of a foreign people. . . ." Here Blok is giving the scheme of a personal love affair on the streets of Warsaw. But this is not only a scheme, it is an unexpected sublimation, the elevation of the subjective, accidental fact to events of a higher order, to events the outcome of which lies in the hands of the historic Nemesis and Muse.

In the third chapter is described how the father ended his life, what became of the formerly brilliant demon. . . . The action of the poem shifts from the Russian capital, where it had hitherto been developed, to Warsaw—which seems at first "the backyard of Russia", but later, apparently, is summoned to play a "certain Messianic rôle", connected with the destinies of *"God-forsaken and lacerated Poland* . . ." "Here, over the fresh grave of his father, ends the development and the mortal road of the son, who gives way to his own offspring, the third link of that same ever high-soaring and low-falling tribe."

"In the epilogue must be depicted the youngster, dandled and lullabied by his simple mother, lost somewhere in the broad cloverfield of Poland, unknown to anyone and herself knowing naught. But she lulls her son and feeds him at the breast, and the son grows; already he begins to play, he begins to repeat after his mother, syllable by syllable: 'And I shall go out to meet the soldiers . . . And I shall throw myself on their bayonets . . . And for thee, my freedom, I shall go up onto the black scaffold.' . . ."

This part of the introduction leaves us in no doubt whatever, it seems to me: Poland's future avenger, the fighter for her freedom, the knight of retribution, is the last youngling of the Russian stock! And this last offspring must be born "in the broad cloverfields of Poland", and the one to "lull him on her knees" and "feed him at her breast" will be his Polish mother.

The poet's idea is a peculiar and deeply ethical one: an idea with ethical pathos. Its pathos, of course, consists in the fact that the personification of the idea of retribution, of Polish retribution, must be the son of a Russian man, representing a long-standing Russian cultural tradition, and a Polish woman "unknown to anyone and herself knowing naught". Precisely in this lies the very idea of retribution—this *is* the *retribution*.

And are those not eloquent statements about Warsaw, "seemingly at first the backyard of Russia", "but later summoned to play a certain Messianic rôle"? And truly, all this is unexpected under the pen of Blok. And what is to be said of the words "God-forsaken and lacerated Poland"? I am convinced that never did any other Russian write *thus* about Poland, save perhaps the charming Countess Eudokiya Rostopchin[1] and—Lev Tolstoy.[2]

> "Here, obviously, is the circle of human life, shrunken to its utmost, the link of a long chain; that circle which will finally itself be distended and press against the environment, the periphery; here is the offspring of the species which perhaps will finally grasp with its little hand at the wheel that moves human history...."

In other words, only this last offspring of the Russian race—its Polish offspring—"will begin to press against the environment" and will finally "grasp with its little hand at the wheel that moves human history...."

There, the milieu has been "sucking up", and "of the personality there has remained almost no trace at all ... it has itself become unrecognizable, disfigured, mutilated". "A man there was—and then was not...." Where, indeed, and how has a man "finally" made his appearance, "stopped" "the wheel of history"? In Poland!

Herein is concealed the deeply touching, purificatory idea of the ethical justification of the rights of "God-forsaken and lacerated Poland". "Lacerated" by whom? *By Russia*. But let us go on.

> "The whole poem must be accompanied by a definite leitmotif of 'retribution'; this leitmotif is the *mazurka*, a dance which bore on its wings Marina [The poet alludes here to Maryna Mniszech, the Polish wife of Dimitry the Pretender, perhaps remembering Pushkin's stylization of her in *Boris Godunov*.], dreaming of a Russian throne, and Kościuszko with his right hand stretched forth to the skies, and Mickiewicz at Russian and Parisian balls. In the first chapter this dance is lightly wafted from the window of some Petersburg flat—the dull 'seventies; in the second chapter the dance booms out at the ball, mingled with the clang of the officers' spurs, like the foam of the Veuve Cliquot champagne of *fin-de-siècle* renown; still dull years—Gipsy, Apukhtin years; finally, in

[1] I refer to her deeply pro-Polish poem on Poland and Russia, "The Forced Marriage".
[2] Cf. Tolstoy's charming story *Za čto? (What For?)*

the third chapter, the *mazurka* rages, it peals out in the snowstorm borne over nocturnal Warsaw, over the snow-blanketed Polish cloverfields. In it already is distinctly heard the voice of *Retribution* . . . July, 1919."[1]

What a remarkable Russian retort to the anti-Polish poems of Derzhavin, Pushkin, Zhukovsky, Tyutchev and others! Here is he who a hundred years later "drank the health of Lelewel", "with the call— Poland has not perished" and "when the revolt of Warsaw fell . . . drooped and sobbed like a Jew over Jerusalem! . . ."[2] Marina—Pushkin's Marina—with her "dizzying pride", "Kościuszko with his right hand stretched forth to the skies", and Mickiewicz . . . Yes, all this is striking, amazing, and unexpected. . . . Who would have thought that this could be written by Blok in the year 1919!—and conceived in the years 1910– 1911! Whence and how did all this come to him? But first let us turn to the poetic text, to the third chapter of the poem; it is no less worthy of note.

*   *   *   *   *

I shall begin now with the pictures of Warsaw. He was not pleased by it. When Blok, in December of the year 1909—the gloomiest month in Warsaw—saw it, the city could not have been pleasing to him. And he does not conceal this. And this negative impression of his, in view of the ideal content of the poem, is all the more important: Blok was not taken with the external visage of Warsaw.

Of what sort is this first impression?

> The father lies in the 'Allée of Roses',[3]
> No longer quarrelling with his lassitude,
> And the son's train hurtles into the frost
> From the banks of his native sea . . .
> Policemen, rails, lamps,
> The jargon and the age-old *peyoth*,—
> And here, in the rays of a sick dawn,
> Are the Polish backyards of Russia . . .
> Here all that was, all that is,
> Is puffed up with a vengeful chimera;
> Copernicus himself cherishes vengeance,[4]

---

[1] A. Blok, *Sočinenija v odnom tome*, redakcija . . . V. Orlova (Moscow-Leningrad: Ogiz, 1946), p. 241.

[2] Draft of Pushkin. See more details on this in my study in this book on Chaadaev.

[3] The name of a street in Warsaw.

[4] The celebrated monument to Copernicus which stood before the "Palace of Staszic", destroyed by the Germans in 1939. In independent Poland the "Palace of Staszic" housed the Varsovian Society of Friends of Science and the Mianowski Foundation—also a scientific institution. In Blok's time this house, then made over on the Russian state style and model, was the site of a Russian high school.

Leaning over an empty globe . . .
'Revenge! Revenge!'—in cold iron
Rings like an echo over Warsaw:
Now Pan Frost on his wicked steed
Jangles his bloody spurs . . .
Now comes the thaw: more vividly shines
The edge of the sky with sluggish yellow,
And the eyes of the *Pannas*[1] more boldly blacken
Their caressing and flattering circle . . .
But everything in earth or Heaven
Is still as full of sorrows as before . . .
Only the rail to Europe, in the damp murk
Sparkles with honest steel . . .
The filthy station; at home,
They are given up craftily to the snow-storms;
The bridge across the Vistula, like a prison . . .[2]

The poet calls Warsaw "foreign" for his father, always returning to pictures of storm, fog, snow; he speaks about "unfamiliar squares", about "some endless enclosure—of the Saxon garden,[3] it must be . . ."

In the rough drafts and variants his references are even sharper: "amid thy sadness, O Warsaw!" "How boring, cold and sick", "full frenzy over the black Vistula", "then did dirty Warsaw place on my heart a new ulcer as my reward", "the curse, the blast-forge of the factory, and the raging Varsovian boredom", "The platform of the dirty station, the whistling of a snowless storm, The gray dream of the broad Vistula, All breathes . . . boredom . . ."[4]

We find the same depression in the poet's letters to his mother, written from Warsaw and in a notebook from the year 1909:

"December first, evening. I am riding up to Warsaw. . . . A candle is twinkling. My ticket has been taken away. . . . For a

[1] Polish word for girls.
[2] "Otec ležit v 'Allee Roz',/Uže s ustalost'ju ne sporja,/A syna poezd mčit v moroz/Ot beregov rodnogo morja . . ./Žandarmy, rel'sy, fonari,/Žargon i pejsy vekovye,—/I vot, v lučakh bol'noj zari/Zadvorki pol'skie Rossii . . ./Zdes' vsë, čto bylo, vsë čto est',/Naduto mstitel'noj khimeroj;/Kopernik sam leleet mest',/Sklonjajas' nad pustoju sferoj . . ./'Mest'! Mest'!'—v kholodnom čugune/Zvenit, kak èkho, nad Varšavoj:/To Pan-Moroz na zlom kone/Brjacaet šporoju krovavoj . . ./Vot ottepel': blesnet živej/Kraj neba želtliznoj lenivoj,/I oči pann čertjat smelej/Svoj krug laskatel'nyj i l'stivyj . . ./No vsë, čto v nebe, na zemle,/Poprežnemu polno pečal'ju . . ./Liš' rel's v Evropu v mokroj mgle/Pobleskivaet čestnoj stal'ju . . ./Vokzal zaplevannyj; doma,/Kovarno predannye v'jugam;/Most čerez Vislu, kak tjur'ma . . ."
Cf. A. Blok, *Sočinenija v odnom tome*, p. 252.
[3] Famous garden in Warsaw.
[4] See A. Blok, *Sobranie sočinenij* (Leningrad: Izd. pisatelej v Leningrade, 1911–1921), Vol. V, pp. 161–218.

quarter of an hour already we have been able to see the glow over Warsaw—that cursed companion of great cities...."

In a letter to his mother: "... Warsaw does not very much take my fancy..."[1]

The poet was in a low, sullen, sad mood. Nor is he any gayer in these drafts on Russia:

> ... Where devils cover the sky with murk,
> Where one hears the guffaw of the yellow press,
> The jargon of the newspapers and the shriek of the ads,
> Where under the mask of provocations
> Is hidden morbid cynicism,
> Where nihilism triumphs—
> Sexless fellow-traveller of "stylizations",
> Where the air reeks with the "New Times",
> Where caddishness grows worse year by year ...
> Where all-powerful and ever-present
> Are only officer, gendarme and Jew ...
> Where his wife tries to besmirch
> The eternal memory of Tolstoy ...[2]

Nor, naturally, does the poet's personal love affair look any brighter. It is also spoken of in a gloomy note in a notebook: "The first. Arrival. Death. Evening at the Belyaevs' ... 2. Services ... 3. Services ... 4. Burial rites. Dinner at the Belyaevs'." On 5 December the poet saw his sister Angelina, dining again at the Belyaevs'. Then: "6th, Sunday—In lodgings. Spekt.[orsky] and beadle." 'Got drunk.' 7th, Monday—In lodgings. 8th, Tuesday—Fin.[ancial] affairs. Drinking. 9th, Wednesday—Did not go to services at the cemetery because of drunkenness. Wandered around alone. 10th, Thursday—Fin.[ancial] affairs, at 1:30 to Mlle. Meding, to the school. The apartment. Evening and supper at the Belyaevs'. *At the Polish woman's place.* 11th, Fri. Apt., the Belyaevs. Deadly dejection. 12th, Saturday—Bel.[yaevs], apt. Drank at Aqu.(arium)."—[this was a "café-chantant" in Warsaw, well known at that time.—W. L.]—and so on.[3]

On the 14th Blok made another visit to the Aquarium and drank

---

[1] *Ibid.*, p. 164.

[2] "... Gde nebo krojut mgloju besy,/Gde slyšen khokhot želtoj pressy,/Žargon gazet i vizg reklam,/Gde pod licinoj provokacij/Skryvaetsja bol'noj cinizm,/Gde toržestvuet nigilizm—/Bespolyj sputnik 'stilizacij',/Gde 'Novym Vremenem' smerdit,/Gde khamstvo s každym godom—pušče,/Gde polnovlastny, vezdesušči/Liš' oficer, žandarm—i žid,/Gde pamjat' večnuju Tolstogo/Stremitsja omŕačit' žena ..." *Ibid.*, p. 174.

[3] *Ibid.*, p. 163. *Italics mine,* W. L.

champagne. 15 December—the note: "Delirium". On 18 December he went away to Petersburg.

The episode with the Polish woman is told fleetingly in the poem, but somewhat more precisely in the drafts and variants.

> ... Still bright, the cafés and bars,
> The "New World"[1] traffics in bodies,
> The shameless pavements are teeming,
> But in the alleyways is no life,
> There, darkness and the howl of the storm ...
> My dear and innocent hero,
> Hard on the burying of your father,
> You wander, wander endlessly
> In a diseased and lustful crowd ...
> No longer thoughts, no longer feelings,
> In the empty pupils, no gleam,
> As if the heart, from exile,
> Had aged by ten years ...
> Here the lamp sheds a shy light ...
> Like a woman from behind the corner
> Someone fawningly crawls up ...
> Here she has wheedled up, crawled up,
> And the heart is quickly squeezed
> By an inexpressible sadness,
> As if a heavy hand
> Had bent it down to the ground and crushed it ...
> And he no longer walks alone,
> But really together, with someone new ...
> Here swiftly he is led
> Up the mountain by "The Cracow Suburbs".[2]

And here, amid all this, and against the background of his gloomy Warsaw impressions, the description of the "meeting" with the dead father and the latter's funeral, amid this murk of personal sadness, uttered with the utmost poetic power, the "pathetic" ideal theme

[1] The name of a street in Warsaw.
[2] The name of a street in Warsaw.
"Ešče svetly kafē i bary,/Torguet telom 'Novyj Svet',/Kišat besstydnye trotuary,/No v pereulkakh—žizni net,/Tam t'ma i v'jugi zavyvan'e .../Geroj moj milyj i nevinnyj,/Edva pokhoroniv otca,/Ty brodiš', brodiš' bez konca/V tolpe bol'noj i pokhotlivoj .../Uže ni čuvstv, ni myslej net;/V pustykh zenicakh net sijan'ja,/Kak budto serdce ot skitan'ja/Sostarilos' na desjat' let .../Vot robkij svet fonar' ronjaet .../Kak ženščina iz za ugla/Vot kto-to l'stivo podpolzaet .../Vot—podol'-stilas', podpolzla,/I serdce toroplivo sžala/Nevyrazimaja toska,/Kak by tjaželaja ruka/K zemle prignula i prižala .../I on už ne odin idet/A točno s kem-to novym vmeste .../Vot bystro pod goru vedet/Ego 'Krakovskoe Predmest'e'." Cf. A. Blok, *Sobranie sočinenij*, Vol. V, pp. 98–101.

suddenly begins to sound. . . . its new and precisely *pathetic* variation. The words in which it sounds are inexpressibly beautiful and full of genuine inspiration:

> Country under the burden of insults
> Under the yoke of insolent violence—
> As an angel drops its wings—
> As a woman loses all shame.
> The national genius is speechless
> And remains silent,
> Lost in the fields, the people
> Is too weak to cast off the yoke of idleness.
> The mother but weeps senselessly all night
> Over the renegade son,
> And the father hurls a curse at the foe
> (The old have nothing to lose! . . .)
> But the son—he has betrayed the fatherland!
> He greedily drinks wine with the foe,
> And the wind lashes at the window,
> Calling out to conscience and to life . . .[1]

The poet's voice grows more and more furious and excited, the words fall scourging, biting, haughty, scornful:

> . . . Wast not thou also, Warsaw,
> The proud Poles' capital,
> Compelled to slumber by a gang
> Of warring Russian villains?
> Life is dully lidded over in the underground,
> Silent are the magnates' palaces,
> Only Pan Frost everywhither
> Hurtles about at will!
> His grey head
> Soars raging over you,
> Or his flapping, reversible sleeves[2]
> Are flung up over the houses by the storm,
> Or his horse falls to neighing—and, with sound of strings,
> The telegraph-wire answers,

---

[1] "Strana pod bremenem obid,/Pod igom naglogo nasil'ja—/Kak angel, opuskaet kryl'ja,/Kak ženščina, terjaet styd./Bezmolvstvuet narodnyj genij,/I golosa ne podaet,/Ne v silakh sbrosit' iga leni/V poljakh zaterjannyj narod./I liš' o syne, renegate,/Vsju noč' bezumno plačet mat',/Da šlet otec vragu prokljat'e/(Ved' starym nečego terjat'! . . .)/A syn—on izmenil otčizne!/On žadno p'et s vragom vino,/I veter lomitsja v okno,/Vzyvaja k sovesti i k žizni . . ." Cf. *ibid.*, pp. 97–8.

[2] The poet obviously refers to the Polish "kontusz"—the old nobleman's coat with open sleeves.

> Or the Pan, raving, jerks the halter,
> And the iron distinctly repeats
> The blows of the frozen hoof
> Against the desolate pavement . . .
> And once again, head drooping,
> Speechless, the Pan, crushed by longing . . .
> And, roaming on his wicked steed,
> Jangles his bloody spurs . . .
> Revenge! Revenge!—Thus the echo
> Rings in cold iron over Warsaw . . .[1]

In the rough drafts and variants are several important fragments worth adducing:

> Then met we, thou and I,
> I was ill, my soul rusty . . .
> Sister, destined by fate,
> The whole world seemed Warsaw to me! . . .
>
> . . . We dogged after the coffin
> From the city to an empty field
> Through unfamiliar places.
> The cemetery was called "Freedom".
> Yes, we hear songs about freedom
> When the gravedigger's shovel strikes
> Against the clods of yellowish clay . . .[2]
>
> Is it not with this that Warsaw is sullen,
> That in this capital of the Poles
> There rules an insolent gang
> Of warring Russian villains?
> That some sovereign thief
> Is building Russian cathedrals
> When the citizens' glances might be charmed

---

[1] ". . . Ne takže l' i tebja, Varšava,/Stolica gordykh poljakov,/Dremat' prinudila orava/Voennykh russkikh pošljakov?/Žizn' glukho kroetsja v podpol'i,/Molčat magnatskie dvorcy,/Liš' Pan-Moroz vo vse koncy/Svirepo ryščet na razdol'i!/Neistovo vzletit nad vami/Ego sedaja golova,/Il' odkidnye rukava/Vzmetutsja burej nad domami,/Il' kon' zaržet—i zvonom strun/Otvetit telegrafnyj provod,/Il' vzdernet Pan vzbešennyj povod,/I četko povtorit čugun/Udary merzlogo kopyta/Po opustelojmostovoj . . ./I vnov', poniknuv golovoj,/Bezmolven Pan, toskoj ubityj . . ./I, stranstvuja na zlom kone,/Brjacaet šporoju krovavoj . . ./Mest'! Mest'! Tak èkho nad Varšavoj/Zvenit v kholodnom čugune!" Cf. *ibid.*, p. 98.

[2] "Togda my vstretilis' s toboj./Ja byl bol'noj, s dušoju ržavoj . . ./Sestra, suždennaja sud'boj,/Ves' mir kazalsja mne Varšavoj! . . ." ". . . My šli za grobom po pjatam/Iz goroda v pustoe pole/Po neznakomym ploščadjam./Kladbišče nazyvalos': 'Volja'./Da, pesn' o vole slyšim my,—/Kogda mogil'ščik b'et lopatoj/Po glybam gliny želtovatoj . . ." Cf. *ibid.*, p. 172.

Only by a Catholic cathedral?
That all that the Governor will say
Is a grey opaque murk,
And the wrathful Pole
Gives him the bird? . . .

And the son looked, trying to glimpse
But a narrow window in the night,
But everything darted by, floating around
In a great grey blob.
(In those days there was anguish over Warsaw,
And no doubt something perished.)[1]

It is impossible not to acknowledge that in all these lines resounds a lyrical feeling, with rare force and beauty, of the suffering of a foreign, enslaved nation. This poetic Russian remorse, it seems to me, is unique. And the fact that it is written by a Russian, and written at such a time—first in 1910 and later in 1921, that is already after the Russo-Polish war of 1920—gives epic significance to this beautiful lyric. After *Retribution*, in my opinion, it is difficult to echo with heart and soul "To the Calumniators of Russia" and "On the Anniversary of Borodino", despite this or that quasi-conciliatory note that their defenders claim is contained in these odes, ringing with the clank of arms and noisy imperialism.

As has already been said, Blok did not finish *Retribution*, but there has been preserved a "Plan for a continuation" dated 1911:

"Infinitely right is he who becomes crestfallen, who rejects the superficial joys of life. The son dropped down to the Cracow Suburb in that very place in the ninth chapter: the man who drops his hands and gives up his right. Nothing to argue against that. Everything is so terrible that (every) personal ruin, (every) digging-in of one's own (individual) soul into the ground, is everybody's right. This is the retribution against the little knot of oligarchs who oppress the whole world. Thus also the 'country under the burden of insults' . . ."[2]

---

[1] "Ne tem li pasmurna Varšava,/Čto v sej stolice poljakov—/Carit nakhal'naja orava/Voennykh russkikh pošljakov?/Čto stroit russkie sobory/Kakoj nibud' deržavnyj vor/Tam, gde plenjal by graždan vzory/Liš' katoličeskij sobor?/Čto vse, čto gubernator skažet,/Est' seryj, neprogljadnyj mrak,/I kukiš iz karmana kažet/Emu ozloblennyj poljak?" "A syn gljadel, prozret' pytajas'/V noči khot' uzkoe okno,/No vse mel'kalo, rasplyvajas'/V bol'šoe seroe pjatno./(V te dni nad Pol'šej toskovalo,/I giblo, verno, čto nibud'.)" Cf. *ibid.*, pp. 207, 211.

[2] A. Blok, *Sočinenija v odnom tome*, p. 581.

That is the end that was to be put to this singular, wonderful, new *Bronze Horseman.*

*   *   *   *   *

I shall not recount the history of the genesis of the poem; it can be found in the latest editions of Blok—by the State Publishing House, edited by V. Orlov, or in Volume V of the edition of the Publishing House of Writers in Leningrad. I am interested in Blok's unexpected Polonophilia. Whence and how was this morally bewildered and indignant view of Russo-Polish relations elaborated in him? Where must the source of his inspiration be sought? Who were the people and what were the books which had such an effect on a poet whose intellectual and artistic interests were, all in all, oriented in what would seem to be a totally different direction? One should take into consideration not only these intellectual and artistic interests, but also the poet's family, its origins and traditions.

Let us not be deceived by Blok's non-Russian name. The poet's mother belonged to an essentially Russian family of rich landlords, the Beketovs. The poet's great-grandmother was a Yakushkin, a niece of the famous Decembrist. Blok's father was a descendant of Lutheran immigrants from Mecklenburg who became Russianized in the eighteenth century. Some of them were court-physicians and surgeons of the Russian Czars. The court-surgeon, Ivan Blok, was ennobled by Paul I. His son, Alexander, held various court positions at the time of Nicholas I and received several estates in the Petersburg province from the Czar. Alexander's son, Lev Blok, the grandfather of the poet, was a Kammerjunker and later became the Marshal of Nobility in the Gdov district of the Saint Petersburg province. He was married to the daughter of Cherkassov, the governor of Pskov.[1]

This short genealogical outline shows that from both sides of his family Blok belonged to an old Russian nobility, and was deeply rooted in the national past of his country. A. Lunacharsky justly considers Blok an expression of the Russian nobility: "He should be put in the same line with the ideologists of the nobility and, so to speak, at the end of this line. To a certain degree he might be called the last great artist of the Russian nobility."[2]

---

[1] Cf. M. A. Beketova, *Al. Blok, Biografičeskij očerk* (Moscow-Leningrad: Academia, 1930), pp. 11–15, and the poet's autobiography in Al. Blok, *Sobranieسočinenij* (Leningrad, 1911–1921), Vol. I, p. 83.

[2] *Ibid.*, p. 15.

The answer, then, to the question of Blok's mysterious Polonophilia is not very easy to find. The clues are meagre and the source materials very modest, but still I have been able to find something. I hasten to announce that probably a great deal more could be found in Poland, let alone in Russia. In America I lack some necessary sources of information, and therefore on many occasions conjectures and hypotheses will have to do.

Factually, *Retribution* is connected with Blok's stay in Warsaw in December (from 1 December on) of the year 1909, where he went after receiving the news of his father's mortal illness. As is well known, the poet's father, Alexander Lvovich Blok, was professor of public law at the University of Warsaw. After his divorce from Alexandra Andreevna Beketov, the elder Blok was married in Warsaw to Maria Timofeevna Belyaev. By this marriage he had a daughter Angelina, who died in February 1918. The poet dedicated to her memory his *Iambi*, verses of the years 1907–1914, closely connected with the poem *Retribution*. He rarely met his sister but maintained profoundly sympathetic relations with her. I know nothing of her, or of the family of the Belyaevs; it is possible that, bred in Warsaw, she could speak with her brother in the spirit of *Retribution*, and oblique testimony to this is furnished by the fact that it was to her memory that the poet dedicated his *Iambi* with the very significant motto from Juvenal's *Satires*: "Facit indignatio versum."[1]

The poet's father, as we know, was not distinguished by any Polish sympathies. The position he occupied in Warsaw was ultra-Russian-Statist, and the memories of him that have been preserved in Polish circles are not good. So it can only be supposed that Angelina Alexandrovna Blok held other views, and perhaps the very idea of *Retribution* is indirectly connected with possible discord between father and daughter on this subject.

In Blok's notebook for 1909, from which I have already quoted fragments, there is a note referring to Sunday, 13 December: "Dinner. To Mme. Wasilewska."[2] Who this evidently Polish Mrs. Wasilewska was, I do not know. It may be that she gave Blok certain suggestions of a literary character, relating to Poland; this is possible, but I am in no position to establish it here.

There still remains, so far as concerns the eighteen days spent by Blok in Warsaw in 1909, the "Polish woman", "the quiet and womanly daughter of a foreign nation", with whom "the son" spent "a passionate

---

[1] A. Blok, *Sočinenija v odnom tome*, p. 186. There were, however, rumours that Angelina Alexandrovna Blok was a Catholic, to which her name—Angelina—might testify.

[2] A. Blok, *Sobranie sočinenij* (Leningrad, 1911–1921), Vol. V, p. 163.

and sinful night". About her, of course, we know nothing besides what is said in the variants of 1921:

> From under the hooves already raised
> Over the doomed head,
> From under the horse's foaming bit,
> From the snowy storm cloud
> Rises the vision of a young maiden.
> All—all is tenderness, all—demand,
> And her voice is like the murmur of the strings.
>
> A simple maiden is before him . . .
>
> How are you called?—Maria.
> Where were you born?—In the Carpathians.

—I am tired of living.—I will not abandon you. You will die with me. You are lonely?—Yes lonely.—I will bury you where nobody will know, and I will set up a cross, and in the spring the clover will blossom over you.

> —Maria, dear Maria
> My life is dull and empty!
> Why do your young and tender lips
> Curl like serpents?
> With what thought . . .
> —Be gay, my sombre guest,
> Sorrow will pass without a trace.
> —Where are we?—We are far away, in the suburbs
> There are hardly any human habitations here.
> Tell me, were you thinking of your fiancée?
> —No, I have no fiancée.
> Tell me, are you longing for your wife?
> —No, no, Maria, not for her.
> With a smile she opens
> Her arms to him
> And all that was retreats
> And disappears (in oblivion).

And he dies in her arms. Everything—confused élans, unbodied thoughts, the will to the heroic act that has (never) been achieved—everything dissolves on the breast of this woman.

> Maria, dear Maria
> My life is empty, I am tired of life!

I have not accomplished that...
That, which I ought to have accomplished....[1]

And, finally, there is Warsaw itself; but I have already spoken of this.

Blok's mother, Alexandra Andreevna Beketov, the daughter of the famous Russian botanist and president of the University of Petersburg, Andrey Nikolaevich Beketov, was married a second time to Franz, in Polish Franciszek, (Felixovich) Kublicki-Piottuch, then a lieutenant in the guards of the Grenadiers' regiment. Several years before this, probably at the very beginning of the 'eighties, the brother of F. Kublicki-Piottuch, Adam, was married to the poet's mother's sister, Sophia Andreevna Beketov. Here I may remark that the product of this marriage, Felix—known in the family under the name of Ferol (a diminutive that the poet had thought up in childhood)—and Andrey (in Polish–Andrzej)—Andryusha—were the first companions of Blok's childhood; one of them was his junior by three years, the other by five. Andrey was, by the way, a deaf-mute from birth. Later he was taught to speak and lip-read.[2] They were united by a very great and warm friendship,[3] but in 1900 Sophia Andreevna, her husband, and their sons went away to Barnaul, where her husband Adam (Felixovich) had been appointed director of the District of Altay.[4] Later, however, Blok's cousins appeared often in his life, when all three were grown men; we see them for example in a photograph taken in 1909 "under the lindens in the Shakhmatovsky garden" (the Beketovs' estate, in the

---

[1] "Iz-pod kopyt, už zanesennykh/Nad obrečennoj golovoj,/Iz-pod udil konja, vspenennykh,/Iz snežnoj tuči burevoj/Vstaet viden'e devy junoj,/Vsë—vsë—nežnost', vsë—prizyv,/I golos, točno rokot strunnyj./Prostaja devuška pred nim . . ./Kak nazyvat' tebja?—Marija./Otkuda rodom ty?—S Karpat.
—Mne žit' nadoelo.—Ja tebja ne ostavlju. Ty umreš' so mnoj. Ty odinok?—Da, odinok.—Ja zaroju tebja tam, gde nikto ne uznaet, i postavlju krest, i vesnoj nad toboj rascvetet klever.
—Marija, nežnaja Marija,/Mne žizn' postyla i pusta!/Začem zmejatsja molodye/ I nežnye tvoi usta?/Kakoju . . . dumoj . . ./—Bud' veselyj, moj gost' ugrjumyj,/Toska minuet bez sleda./—Gde my?—My daleko, v predmest'i,/Zdes' net počti žilykh domov,/Skaži, ty dumal o neveste?/—Net, u menja nevesty net./Skaži, ty o žene skučaeš'?/—Net, net, Marija, ne o nej./Ona s ulybkoj otkryvaet/Emu ob'jatija svoi/I vsë, čto bylo, otstupaet/I isčezaet (v zabyt'i)./
I on umiraet v eë ob'jatijakh. Vse nejasnye poryvy, nevoploščennye mysli, volja k podvigu, (nikogda) ne soveršennomu, rastvorjaetsja na grudi ètoj ženščiny.
Marija, nežnaja Marija,/Mne pusto, mne postylo žit'!/Ja ne sveršil togo . . ./Togo, čto dolžen byl sveršit'." *Ibid*, pp. 106–8.
[2] Cf. M. A. Beketova, *op. cit.*, p. 42.
[3] Later, however, they apparently grew apart, as witness Blok's *Diary*, the note of 28 July, 1917 (*Dnevnik Al. Bloka*, Vol. II, p. 58).
[4] Cf. *Pis'ma Aleksandra Bloka k rodnym* (Leningrad: Academia, 1927), p. 314.

Klinsky district of the province of Moscow, bought by A. N. Beketov in the 'seventies) together with I. D. Mendeleev, Blok, his wife Lyubov Dmitrievna (née Mendeleev), the poet's mother, S. A. Kublicka(ya)-Piottuch, and M. A. Beketov(a)—the poet's aunt, who has written a number of books about him and about his mother.[1]

The family of the Kublicki-Piottuchs was an old member of the Polish nobility. The particular generation of the poet's stepfather, however, had evidently become Russified and apparently had lost touch with Polish life and culture. That this Russification took place just in that generation is testified to on the one hand by the names, Adys' (in Polish, strictly, Adaś), Lucian, and Felicia their sister, by her first and apparently Polish marriage the wife of Leon (Leonid) (Yakovlevich) Łoziński, also finally Russified. By her second marriage she was wedded to a Russian, Brazhnikov. All these Russian, Orthodox marriages (at that time, to be sure, there was no "freedom of worship" in Russia) are another testimony to the Russification of just this generation of this line of the Kublicki-Piottuchs. I note that F. F. Łozińska(ya)-Brazhnikov(a) was still called in the family by a Polish diminutive, Fela. There are also other Polish relatives of the poet's stepfather who appear from time to time: the family of Wiktor (Konradovich) Niedźwiecki (the father, K. Niedźwiecki, a Pole and a lawyer). The Niedźwieckis were not Russified—at least the father, Konrad Niedźwiecki, was not.

What did these surroundings of Polish origin which the poet had felt from earliest childhood give him in the way of Polish culture? Very little, I think. I shall not speak about all the possible sources of influence. I shall confine myself to a few words about the poet's stepfather, using the books of M. A. Beketov and the autobiography of the poet. First of all, the stepfather from the start acted completely "indifferently" toward his stepson and "did not enter into his life".[2] Beketov even says that this attitude of the man toward the child estranged him greatly from Alexandra Andreevna.[3] In short, even if Franz Felixovich did live in an inwardly Polish manner, he could share none of it with Blok because of their mutual relations. "Sasha lived somehow beyond this indifference of his stepfather toward him," says M. A. Beketov.[4] And, indeed, in F. F. Kublicki-Piottuch there hardly existed any of this secret —much less overt—Polish content. Some traces or other of some predispositions toward Poland exist, but very superficial ones. His batmen,

---

[1] M. A. Beketova, *Al. Blok i ego mat'* (Moscow-Leningrad: "Petrograd", 1925), pp. 56–7.
[2] Cf. M. A. Beketova, *Al. Blok, Biografičeskij očerk*, p. 46.
[3] Cf. M. A. Beketova, *Al. Blok i ego mat'*, pp. 128–9.
[4] Cf. M. A. Beketova, *Al. Blok, Biografičeskij očerk*, p. 46.

for example, happened to be Poles—I know of two, Władysław and Bronisław. In not one word does the poet betray the "Polishness" of his new family in his autobiography, and not once did he make any mention of it in his letters.[1] He only says in his autobiography that his aunt M. A. Beketov used to translate Polish authors, among others Sienkiewicz. And even M. A. Beketov herself nowhere said a word anent the "Polishness" of this family.

The lieutenant, later colonel and general in the guards of the Grenadiers' regiment, Franz Felixovich Kublicki-Piottuch, was "an inarticulate, rather shy man"; he had "neither good looks, nor daring, nor military chic, nor a strong temperament", says M. A. Beketov.

"He was a modest drudge in a bourgeois fashion, *entirely devoted to his duty in the service*,[2] serious and far from stupid, stout-hearted, capable of deep attachment, but completely devoid of imagination and poetry. . . . He possessed qualities that were rare in a military man: not the least fanfaronade, no contempt for 'shtryuki' (civilians) —he never pronounced the word—great respect for science, for which incidentally he had a serious bent, respect for literature, of which he was utterly ignorant. He treated his family handsomely, was distinguished by unusual simplicity, an absence of false modesty and superfluous self-love, and was very kind in an intimate circle when he felt around him a benevolent atmosphere. I add to this that he was far from a run-of-the-mill officer—honest and well-versed in his work, he regarded his obligations with unusual conscientiousness, *everything that concerned the service, regulations, military information, he studied to perfection*,[3] was very good to soldiers, extraordinarily solicitous and serious; true, he was not averse to handing out a cuff or two, but that after all was in the tradition of the military at that time, and anyway he was rapidly broken of this habit by his wife, who in general had a good influence on him. Soldiers loved and respected him, and in general he was a man wholly worthy of respect, although uninteresting. . . ."[4]

Well do I remember this type—this sympathetic type—of Pole; but these are people who were "sucked up" by the environment, drawn in by the goodheartedness of the Russian way of living, so familiar to those who knew the real Russia; these were people who submitted to the

[1] In any case the family took no part in any of the Polish organizations in Petersburg.
[2] Italics mine.—W. L.
[3] Italics mine.—W. L.
[4] M. A. Beketova, *Al. Blok i ego mat'*, pp. 126–9.

attractive force of Russian culture, which in such cases naturally denationalized the Poles in Russia far more efficaciously than could Russian police in Poland. But all the same, however sympathetic these people could be in everyday practical life, they were weak people—not to mention the arrant opportunists for whom personal gain was higher than any moral obligation toward their enslaved fatherland. Often the only thing these people still had of Poland was "Polish goodbreeding". It is sufficient to look at the photograph I referred to above: both young Kublickis at once produce the impression of their obvious physical Polish birth and breeding. This family, as I have already said, is an old and well-known one; they had places not far from Kovno and in the Ukraine, and one of the representatives of that family, a woman who thirty years ago was married to a Polish landowner of the Province of Mogilev, is a relative of mine.

Evidently all these Kublickis, Łozińskis, and even Niedźwieckis, gave Blok nothing in the way of Polish influences. All the next generation—Blok's coevals—had already definitely lost all connection with Poland. The children lived in a completely ultra-Russian, state atmosphere. To cite an example, in childhood Blok and his cousins put out a children's magazine, *The Messenger*. In the first year of "publication", in November, there appeared an "extra" supplement to the magazine *The Messenger* for the year 1894, on the occasion of the death of Alexander III. "On the cover," relates M. A. Beketov, "was his portrait, and in the appended text was a little article about the death of 'his late Majesty Emperor Alexander Alexandrovich', put together à la *New Times*,[1] by the editor Alex. Blok and the reporter of the magazine F. Kublicki."[2]

No, from this Polish circle Blok could take nothing for his *Retribution*, except possibly the stimulus for the striking verses:

> ... The mother but weeps senselessly all night
> Over the renegade son,
> And the father hurls a curse at the foe
> (The old have nothing to lose!)
> But the son ... he has betrayed the fatherland!
> He greedily drinks wine with the foe ...

These verses perhaps came to him as a result of his reflections on all these dear, fine, but weak, irresponsible people. ... But we must search elsewhere.

*   *   *   *   *

[1] A famous reactionary newspaper in Petersburg.
[2] *Ibid.*, p. 42.

As we know, Blok spent the greater part of July, all of August and part of September, 1911, with his wife in Brittany and Normandy, and also in Belgium and Germany. As always he wrote to his mother often, constantly and circumstantially. These letters of his are very interesting and significant; in them he forebodes war and catastrophe, often expressing himself very sharply about "the monstrous absurdity that civilization has come to".[1] One of these letters contains a remarkable passage, undoubtedly connected with *Retribution*. Speaking about Europe, about strikes in England, about the situation in France, about the fact that Wilhelm "seeks war and, apparently, will fight . . .", the poet suddenly passes to different themes, although they are connected with his "revolutionary" and "catastrophic" feelings.

". . . In all this there is another interesting thing, that in Europe everyone is at home. The newspapers are interested not only in the 'great powers', but do not neglect Italy and Spain; all parts of the world are always on everyone's lips. They all have colonies in Africa—money in America. Asia is mentioned more seldom, Europe is rather cold to Asia for some reason; but positively least of all do they think and talk about Russia, or, better, about things Slavic in general. The Slavic has never gone into their civilization, and, what is most important of all, it has like some alien astral body flown through Catholic *culture*. This is especially interesting to me. I hope to observe this secret invasion of Slavic pathos *by its offshoot, the most essential for me now*;[2] in one corner of Paris, back of Notre Dame, behind the morgue, is a little island where Baudelaire and Théophile Gautier lived; now, there in the old house, is a Polish library, and right by it a little museum of Mickiewicz (who lectured in Paris in the 'forties). To put it in another way, on this islet, little-frequented and quiet though in the centre of Paris, *it is as if a sign were set up*;[3] this is *one of the ferments of the future*—a magic mirror, in which can be seen the souls of Byron, Mickiewicz, the French and Slavic revolution, etc., etc. Well, I am tired of writing. God be with you, Sasha."[4]

At one time I wrote and published a French work, *Christ et révolution dans la poésie russe et polonaise*, in which I linked Blok's *The Twelve* with Krasiński's *Undivine Comedy*.[5] I already tried at that time to find traces

[1] *Pis'ma Aleksandra Bloka k rodnym*, Vol. II, p. 166.
[2] Italics mine.—W. L.
[3] Italics mine.—W. L.
[4] *Pis'ma Aleksandra Bloka k rodnym*, Vol. II, pp. 167–8.
[5] *Mélanges en l'honneur de Jules Legras*, Travaux publiés par l'Institute d'études slaves, XVII, Paris, 1939. Comp. also my study "Mickiewicz, Dostoevski and Blok" in *Slavic Studies*, Cornell University Press, 1943.

of Polish influences in Blok's poetry—the connection of *The Twelve* with Krasiński seems very likely to me, and in my researches I chanced upon the fragment of Blok's letter to his mother, just adduced. In Mickiewicz's library was a book in which the visitors to the museum had been signing their names since quite long ago. I checked this book many times myself and with the help of the employees of the library, but found no signature of Blok for the year 1911. He had, however, evidently been in the museum. He knew not a little about Mickiewicz, as witness not only his remark about lectures, but his comparison with Byron: to all who have worked on Mickiewicz it is well known to what degree the connection of Mickiewicz with Byron was close and significant. But the chief thing is not in this—the chief thing is this very fact, the poet's prevailing interest in Poland which he himself underlines: "a sign has been set up".

* * * * *

However, as Blok's *Retribution* remained unfinished, it is still the Preface which shows especially well Blok's knowledge of Polish Romantic literature. Particularly illustrative is the striking image of the mother singing lullabies to the son who is awaited by the struggle for freedom, by bayonets and "the black scaffold", and who must from his very infancy be prepared for such a destiny. This image was undoubtedly suggested by the stirring verse of Mickiewicz, "Do Matki Polki" ("To A Polish Mother"). This work requires special comments. It is a deeply touching poem which depicts the unsolvable tragedy of the enslaved. When Herzen quoted this poem in his *Diary* of 1843 (January) he said: "How many calamities lie behind this lullaby!"[1] This poem did not escape Blok's attention; his own "Polish mother" is extremely close to Mickiewicz's "Polish mother". I have already quoted Blok's picture of a mother "lost somewhere in the broad cloverfields of Poland" who teaches her son by syllables: "And I shall go out to meet the soldiers ... And I shall throw myself on their bayonets ... And for thee, my freedom, I shall go up onto the black scaffold ..."[2] This is Mickiewicz's poem "To A Polish Mother":

> O Polish mother, if the radiant eyes
>   Of genius kindle in thy darling's face,
> If even in his childish aspect rise
>   The pride and honour of his ancient race;

[1] Cf. *Sočinenija A. S. Gercena* (Genève—Bâle—Lyon, 1875), Vol. I, pp. 80-1.
[2] Cf. A. Blok, *Sočinenija v odnom tome*, p. 241.

If, turning from his playmates' joyous throng,
   He runs to find the bard and hear his lays,
If with bowed head he listens to the song
   Of ancient glory and departed days:

O Polish mother, ill must be his part!
   Before the Mother of Our Sorrows kneel,
Gaze on the sword that cleaves her living heart—
   Such is the craven blow thy breast shall feel!

Though peoples, powers, and schisms a truce declare,
   And though the whole wide world in peace may bloom,
In battle—without glory—must he share;
   In martyrdom—with an eternal tomb.

Soon bid him seek a solitary cave
   And ponder there—on rushes lay his head,
Breathe the foul vapors of a hidden grave,
   And with the envenomed serpent share his bed.

There will he learn to hide his wrath from reach,
   To sink his thought as in the abyss profound,
Slyly to poison with miasmic speech,
   And humbly, like the serpent, kiss the ground.

A child in Nazareth, our Savior mild
   Fondled the cross whereon he saved mankind:
O Polish mother, I would have thy child
   Thus early learn what playthings he will find.

His young arms load with chains, his body frail
   Full soon have harnessed to a barrow, so
Before the headsman's axe he shall not pale,
   Nor at the swinging halter crimson grow.

Not his to venture like a plumèd knight
   And plant the holy cross on pagan soil,
Nor like a soldier of new faith to fight
   In Freedom's cause, and for her sake to toil.

One day an unknown spy will challenge him,
   A perjured court his adversary be,
The jousting-field, a secret dungeon grim;
   A powerful foe the verdict will decree.

> And for the vanquished man as monument
> The gallows tree will rear its sullen height;
> For glory—but a woman's tears, soon spent,
> And fellow patriots' whispered words by night.[1]

I believe that the poignancy of Blok's lines becomes particularly striking against the background of Mickiewicz's poem, in which the Polish poet stressed especially one consequence of enslavement—the necessity of stratagem, subterfuge and duplicity. Blok simply expressed the whole Polish tragedy. But there is no doubt that Mickiewicz's Polish despair, connected with the consciousness of the moral degradation of human dignity to which enslavement fatally brings the enslaved, could have only strengthened in Blok feelings of compassion and indignation.

The theme of subterfuge and stratagem appeared in Mickiewicz's writings even before the poem "To A Polish Mother"—in *Konrad Wallenrod*, to which *Retribution* is also very close, as the very idea of retribution is an integral one in *Konrad Wallenrod*. The following lines from *Konrad Wallenrod* could be used as a motto for *Retribution*:

> ... where I do not go
> My song will penetrate on tireless wings;
> The minstrel to the knights at war will sing,
> The mother to her children croon it low—
> The mother to her children. From that song
> Shall rise up an avenger of our bones.[2]

Konrad Wallenrod is one of the most representative poems of Mickiewicz. In the form of a Byronic historical narrative poem the poet presented the story of a young Lithuanian who devoted his entire life, his personal happiness, his love and even his honour, to the task of avenging the sufferings of his nation. His main goal was the liberation of Lithuania

---

[1] Cf. *Poems by Adam Mickiewicz*, edited by G. R. Noyes (New York, 1924), pp. 237–38. The same theme was developed by the poet in his talk with Miss Henryka Ewa Ankwicz: "A long enslavement, a heavy foreign yoke imposed upon a nation are not only a terribly great misfortune, which is expressed by the word *enslavement*, but even more terrible are their consequences when they endure for a long time,—they debase the whole nation, they take away from it its traits of nobility, they make it spiteful, dirty, avid, materialistic, envious. And only in the influence of this enslavement should one try to find the shameful stigma of passions which became as if the second nature of the Jews, Greeks, and even to a certain extent of the Italians. Let us pity them, but let us not condemn them, because who knows whether we will not become similar to them if the merciful Lord does not free us." Cf. Adam Mickiewicz, *Dzieła wszystkie* (Warsaw, 1933), Vol. XVI, p. 97.

[2] Cf. *Konrad Wallenrod*, "The Farewell" in *Poems by Adam Mickiewicz, op. cit.*, pp. 226–7.

from the yoke of the Teutonic Knights. In order to reach this goal, he acted with stratagem and subterfuge; he pentrated the Order, became its Commander and led the Order to complete destruction in battle against the Lithuanians. The poem has cryptic political implications. The poet, who placed his story in Lithuania of the Middle Ages, hid the poem's real political sense, which was connected with the enslavement of Poland by Russia. With this hidden meaning the poem has played a rôle of a stimulant for patriotic feelings and activities in the life of the Polish nation. It shows the necessity of limitless sacrifices for the nation, and at the same time reveals the moral disasters brought about through enslavement. It certainly became a powerful spiritual factor at the time of the Polish Insurrection of 1830–1831. The poem contains another important trait. Konrad was fired up in his patriotic activities by Halban—the Wajdelota, a bard, a minstrel. So poetry became here a double source of inspiration. With *Konrad Wallenrod* begins the Polish Romantic poetry of the "national bards" and "prophets" who took into their hands the spiritual fate of their nation. As we know, Blok often mentions the Polish Messianism in his notes. *Konrad Wallenrod*, in the strictest sense of the word, was not yet a Messianic poem—Mickiewicz's Messianism started later; nevertheless, the whole atmosphere of the poem, its main ideological trends, the very concept of revenge—all this remains in close ties with Blok's *Retribution*. *Konrad Wallenrod* has had a rich life in Russia. It was and has remained one of the most popular poems of Mickiewicz in that country, despite its anti-Russian implications.

The same item of revenge appears in *Forefathers' Eve, Part III*, especially in Konrad's "Song" before the "Improvisation" (as well as in the *Digression* in the poem *Oleszkiewicz*). No less important is the detail that the future avenger would be the son of a Polish father and a foreign mother. This is found in the "Song" of one of the prisoners (Felix Kulakowski):

> I shall wed a Tatar maiden
> In that wilderness afar:
> For among my offspring I may
> Breed a Pahlen for the czar.[1]

This theme reappears in Father Peter's vision, in the famous enigmatic lines:

> But see—a child escapes, grows up—he is our savior,
> The restorer of our land!

[1] *Ibid.*, p. 267.

Born of a foreign mother, in his veins
The blood of ancient warriors—and his name
Shall be forty and four.[1]

One has also to remember that in Blok's conception the mother will be Polish but the father will be a Russian. The ties between *Retribution* and Mickiewicz are obvious, but the idea of *Retribution* is still closer to Krasiński's *Iridion*, a tragic poem of revenge, retribution and ultimate Christian forgiveness. The theme of the avenger appears also in Słowacki's *Lilla Weneda*.

Krasiński's poem, allegorically of course, much in the same way as Mickiewicz's *Konrad Wallenrod*, under the guise of Greece and Rome speaks about Poland and her enslavers, and is connected with the Insurrection of 1830–1831. The poet placed the action of his tragedy in Rome during the reign of Heliogabalus, at the time when Rome was about to fall—it was the centre of the world and also the centre of the world's sins. The tradition of ancient republican Rome has irretrievably perished, and the diadem of the Caesars adorns the head of a foreign, alien upstart lacking both force and power. The son of Caracalla, he knows only the gory voluptuousness of the rites of Mitra; he is a child with the instincts of an old man. He has neither passion nor will; in him lives only the fire of voluptuous corruption. He is surrounded by a court of just such debauchees, and the few honest people, preserving the legacy of their noble antiquity, are powerless and deprived of the possibility to do anything. All faith and ideals are in ruins. The end of the old world approaches. Nowhere is there any hope of salvation. And against the background of this general moral collapse there looms the figure of the Greek, the personification of living love for one's country, patriotic suffering, thirst for vengeance and destruction. This Greek—the legendary Greek—is created to the measure of the heroes of ancient tragedy. He is moved by his idea, but his idea also rends his soul. In the Greek statue is lodged a Polish soul.

The poet gave his hero a complex genealogy. He is a descendant of Philipomenes, "next to the last of the people who fought against the city". After him there was no longer any fighting, there was only the chain of hatred. This heritage did not cease—the idea of vengeance secretly continues to live up to the moment when the hour of retribution approaches: Amphilochus, Iridion's father, appears. He understands that the city is travelling toward suicide, and he wants to help the city in this. But retribution and vengeance have come from two different sources—the spirit of retribution united in itself two elements:

[1] *Ibid.*, p. 292.

the soft and skeptical Greek soul, weakening and internally disintegrating Rome, on one side, and on the other—invasion. Iridion, the personification of revenge, united the two elements; he is indeed a product of them, being the son of the Greek Amphilochus and the inspired priestess of Odin, in whose bosom lives the soul and the future of the northern peoples. Thus he represents the union of the ancient Greek pagan world and elements of new barbarian peoples, preordained for Christian civilization. Long and terrible is the road of his torments, struggle and sacrifices—the most horrible including the necessity of giving up his beautiful sister Elsinoe to the lustful passion of Heliogabalus. The moment of Rome's ruin draws near. The struggle has broken out fiercely. The city must fall. It is saved by Christianity, by the fact Rome is to become its home. Thus all the sacrifices are in vain—even Elsinoe, perished in vain! Iridion is unhappy and shattered. He—the worthy descendant of the Themistocles—seeks death in suicide. Then a mysterious old man, the demoniac, omniscient Massinissa, promises him that a day will yet come when Iridion will sate his heart with vengeance. He lulls him to sleep until the promised day. In the epilogue comes the awakening. But Iridion has awakened a reborn man. Love for his fatherland, patriotic suffering, have rejected the spirit of revenge. This love in him now is peace of mind, and in answer to arrogance and insults his soul puts faith now in the name of the Lord, "for they will pass, but thou and my word remain". With this legacy of faith and forgiveness, with the legacy of voluntary sacrifice, Iridion goes away "to the earth of graves and thrones". Love for his fatherland—"the country under the burden of insults"—now awaits a new ordeal: the desired goal, freedom of his country, may be attained not on the path of vengeance but that of holiness.[1]

Iridion was twice translated into Russian at the start of the twentieth century—by Umansky in 1904 and by Khodasevich in 1906. I might add that in 1906 there appeared the second edition of A. Kursinsky's translation of the *Undivine Comedy* (after the translations of Gerbel, Mikhaylov, Berg, and Lebedev, in 1871 and 1874). Blok knew Khodasevich and Kursinsky personally. Finally, in his *Diary* of 1921, in a note referring to 20 June, Blok wrote *inter alia*: ". . . Translations. Krasiński: Sleep thou . . . Angel of night. . . ."[2]

In 1906 (the June issue) the famous review *Vesy* published a beautiful portrait of Zygmunt Krasiński by Cyprian Norwid, one of the greatest Polish poets, who was also an outstanding artist. The same issue was adorned by vignettes of modern Polish painters. *Vesy* in 1905 (September–October) published an article "The Drama of Will" by

[1] Cf. S. Tarnowski, *Zygmunt Krasiński* (Cracow, 1893), pp. 189–97.
[2] *Dnevnik Al. Bloka*, Vol. II, p. 247.

Wacław Makowski (especially translated into Russian for the review) which discussed Wyspiański, Słowacki and Krasiński, as well as Przybyszewski. In October of 1909 *The Messenger of Europe* printed an article by Tadeusz Nalepiński—"The Soul of Poland"—discussing the tragic essence of the Polish outlook. Between the years 1909 and 1913 in the review *Apollon* appeared articles on Chopin, on Polish modern painting by Stefan Wierzbicki, an article by M. Voloshin about a modern Polish sculptor, Edward Wittig, and those excellent reports on Polish literary life which I mentioned above. In one of them (May–June, 1910) Blok could have read a statement which was certainly appealing to him: "The secret and eternal substance which is laid in the soul of Poland cannot be discovered in the frivolous cabaret life which Warsaw leads." The article, dealing mostly with Słowacki and Wyspiański, implies that this substance can be found in Polish poetry. In the review *Russian Thought* (September, 1911) Blok could have found an article by E. Zagorsky (probably the Polish journalist E. Zahorski, whose wife was a poetess known under the pseudonym Savitri) discussing recent Polish novels (Berent, Reymont and others) and ending with the statement that it is "more difficult to be a Pole than a citizen of the world". Zagorsky emphasizes the moral value and the ethical significance of Polish patriotism. Particular attention should be given to Władysław Berent's novel, *Winter Field*, which appeared in 1911 both in Polish and in a Russian translation. It is a novel in which the highly talented Polish author juxtaposed the proletarian classes—the "winter crops"—and the fatigued, demoralized Polish bourgeoisie and intelligentsia, lost for the nation, unable to materialize their patriotic ideals. The novel is a story of a ball in Warsaw. Erotically exhausted couples, members of the aristocracy, University professors, artists and bankers move across the stage between dances. The mazurka resounds. The scene is dominated by the figure of a Russian Colonel, a strong personality and a friend of the Poles. He tries to convince a young Polish idealist to leave the decrepit world to which he belongs and to join the Russian army. During the ball, news arrives about the outbreak of the Russo-Japanese War. There is no doubt that the whole atmosphere of this novel, the author's critical attitude towards the decadent *fin-de-siècle* bourgeoisie, the mazurka, all fits very well into the climate of Blok's Preface to *Retribution*. We must remember that on 21 February, 1911, Blok wrote to his mother as follows:

"I feel that in my thirty-first year I can finally sense an important crisis within me which colours my poem and my feelings about the world. I think that the last shadow of 'decadence' has passed. I definitely wish to live and I see before me many simple, good and attractive possibilities—even in things which I did not notice formerly. . . . I am able to read articles on the peasant problem with enthusiasm and . . . the most banal novels of Breshkovsky, who is closer to Dante than . . . Valery Bryusov. . . ."[1]

Finally, I should like to mention that between 1905 and 1917 my father, Aleksander Lednicki, delivered several lectures on Polish culture and literature—on Konopnicka, Mickiewicz, Matejko and Chopin. Some of these lectures appeared in various reviews like *Russian Thought*, and in the publications of the Society of Slavic Culture in Moscow.

As concerns the theme of pardoning insults, Blok could have found, besides Krasiński's *Iridion* and Mickiewicz's *Konrad Wallenrod*, the Third Part of Mickiewicz's *Forefathers' Eve*, in which is given a similar Christian lesson of love and humility, and another Polish variant in Słowacki's *Kordian*—a plan in which is developed the moving, dialectic (*à la* Raskolnikov *avant la lettre*) justification of murder for a purpose of a higher order, the murder of a tyrant in the name of a patriotic purpose. And this dialectic, cogent in its logical strength and political expediency, the truth of the ethical indignation of a "country under the burden of insults", is crushed by the Christian heart's natural incapacity for murder. For the prime matter of the human soul is, for the poet, goodness.[2] Need I mention Słowacki's *Anhelli*!

In those years Słowacki was being translated by Balmont and other writers—for example, *Lilla Weneda* and *Salome's Silver Dream* by Balmont; *Anhelli* by Vinogradov in 1913; *Maria Stuart* by Yanchuk in 1914; and in 1915 there appeared several translations of the poet, among them those of K. Viskovatov. I am not mentioning many translations which appeared even much earlier, in the 'eighties and 'nineties of the nineteenth century. I rather think that Polish romanticism, deeply Christian and full of knightly dignity, which elevated so high the moral and ethical freedom of the human personality, must have intensified to the utmost in Blok's sensitive and noble soul a feeling of wrath and indignation for the "country under the burden of insults", for "God-forsaken and lacerated Poland". Not in vain does the poet cry, sick at heart: "He dreams he sees the dawn, Thy dawn, O God who hast forsaken Poland!"[3]

*   *   *   *   *

[1] Cf. *Pis'ma Aleksandra Bloka k rodnym*, Vol. II, pp. 124–5.
[2] Cf. V. Lednicki, "Jules Słowacki," *Revue de l'Université de Bruxelles*, No. 1, Octobre–Novembre, 1927.
[3] A. Blok, *Sočinenija v odnom tome*, p. 252.

It is not difficult to feel in the *Retribution* the rhythm of the iambus of *The Bronze Horseman*. Anyone who knows Pushkin's poem closely cannot help catching the interecho of *Retribution* and *The Bronze Horseman*, cannot help noticing that many designs for the pictures in *Retribution* mount up just like hoarfrost on the clean pane of Pushkin's poem. Sometimes Blok, clearly with intention, reproduces Pushkin's "style" and even uses his rhymes.

I cannot adduce examples—there are too many. But I must add that the picture of Warsaw under the falling snow in the gale of the tempest, bathed in the "faint" light of the street lamp, with the "hero" —"dear and innocent", who "quietly leaned over" toward the "endless enclosure" of "what must be the Saxon garden"—is obviously sustained in the quality of a pendant to the image of Petersburg in *The Bronze Horseman*.

What is important for me here, however, is something else. The likeness, or more truly the link, between *Retribution* and *The Bronze Horseman* and the meaning of this link are far more deeply hidden. This is not only a likeness but a singular kind of discussion, of polemic. It is a secret conversation of poet with poet.

In *The Bronze Horseman*—a dualistic and antinomic poem—the gist of the matter consists in the contraposition of the element of personality to the element of the state. And, however we interpret the poet's final conclusion, the poem is deeply imbued with the protest made by the enslaved, wounded, lost, oppressed personality. Behind the brilliant façade of Petersburg—the triumphant capital of Empire—is heard the piercing voice of indignant, protesting personality. In *The Bronze Horseman* is set up the sign of tragedy. That tragic voice was not drowned out by the "parade" of the "Introduction". Who, however, "set up" this "sign"? Mickiewicz. I have mentioned above that *The Bronze Horseman* was Pushkin's answer to Mickiewicz, an answer to Mickiewicz's "Petersburg Satires". Blok of course knew about this. He could not but know it. We should recall that in 1906 Blok graduated from the Historico-Philological Faculty of the St. Petersburg University, at which he had been a student of the Slavic-Russian Section. Therefore, already at that time he was certainly acquainted with Polish literature in general, and in particular with Mickiewicz and his relations with Pushkin. The work of a Polish scholar, Professor József Tretiak, who was the first to discover the mysterious connection between *The Bronze Horseman* and Mickiewicz's *Forefathers' Eve*, was analyzed in detail by Braylovsky, who wrote an extensive review in 1908 in *Pushkin and His Contemporaries*. It was also treated in Bryusov's famous Preface to *The Bronze Horseman* in Vengerov's edition of Pushkin, in which Blok himself took part by contributing commentaries to several of Pushkin's lyrical poems. Blok of course did not know all that we know about the relations of Mickiewicz and Pushkin, but he could not help knowing that the tragic element in *The Bronze Horseman*, the element that stirred the world of *The Bronze Horseman*, flowed into Pushkin's poem from *Mickiewicz's*.

And, just as the "Bronze Horseman" "leaps" along the pavements of Petersburg, "Pan Frost" "rushes about" "the desolate pavements" of Warsaw. Only "Pan Frost" stands opposite the "Bronze Horseman". This *genius loci* is the genius of wrath and retribution. And who knows what the meeting of these two "horsemen" might be and how it might end, if a poet made them meet! It is possible, I believe, to regard *Retribution* as an unique development of Pushkin's and Mickiewicz's theme, as an unique Finale of that polemic. Blok felt the "invasion" of the element of Mickiewicz into the world of Pushkin's poem; he divined the mysterious, occult meaning of its presence in that world. So the poet breathed life into Eugene, he took his "dear and innocent" hero into "the country under the burden of insults", to Warsaw, making him there "cast" his Russian seed of revenge and retribution "on the bosom of some quiet and womanly daughter of a foreign people. . . ."

I should like to stress the fact that the first two chapters of *Retribution* are also connected with Pushkin. They often re-echo Pushkin's *Eugene Onegin*, and they also contain not only a kind of parallelism with *The Bronze Horseman*, discernible in the Third Chapter, but they give a direct answer to Pushkin's glorification of Petersburg and of its founder. Further, they oppose the optimism of Pushkin's "Introduction" which, by the way, was itself the most explicit answer to Mickiewicz's *Digression*. This is how Pushkin refuted Mickiewicz's ominous prophecy:

> Now, city of Peter, stand thou fast,
> Foursquare, like Russia; vaunt thy splendor!
> The very element shall surrender
> And make her peace with thee at last.
> Their ancient bondage and their rancors
> The Finnish waves shall bury deep
> Nor vex with idle spite that cankers
> Our Peter's everlasting sleep![1]

Blok's answer to Pushkin practically follows Mickiewicz's path:

---

[1] *The Works of Alexander Pushkin*, edited by A. Yarmolinsky (New York: Random House, 1936), p. 97.

> O my unembraceable city,
> Why did you rise above the abyss . . .
> In vain the winged angel
> Erects a cross over the fortress . . .
> Flee these shaky regions,
> Flee this square
> Bewitched and made transparent by the dawn . . .
>
> . . . . .
>
> In those dead and mute years
> It seemed, somehow,
> That Petersburg was the lord of Russia . . .
> But Fate already was making a sign of warning.[1]

And then the poet describes a dream which comes with alarming sounds as if from the sea. In this dream he sees a fleet with Peter the Great on one of the ships:

> Czar! Do you rise again from the grave,
> To cut a new window?
> It is awful: in the white night
> Both—the corpse and the city are as one.
> O Russia, what kind of dreams,
> What kind of storms await you?[2]

There are several other passages in the poem which, in a way, reproduce Mickiewicz's stylization:

> Work hums in Europe
> And here—the gloomy dawn
> Looks into the mud as before . . .[3]
>
> And autocracy hastens
> To transform as quickly as possible
> All those who ceased to be pawns
> Into castles and knights.[4]

This corresponds very closely to Mickiewicz's card game and to the chess game of Custine.[5]

* * * * *

[1] A. Blok, *Sobranie sočinenij* (Leningrad: 1911–1921), Vol. V, p. 76.
[2] *Ibid.*, p. 79.
[3] *Ibid.*, p. 42.
[4] *Ibid.*, p. 47.
[5] See above, p. 53.

There are a few more Polonica[1] in Blok's texts besides those I have adduced above. In July of 1909 Blok wrote the following piece of verse: "Morning in Moscow."

> Delightful it is to rise at an early hour,
> To glimpse the light trace on the sand.
> Delightful it is to recall thee,
> That thou art with me, my charm.
>
> I love thee, my *panna*,
> My carefree youth,
> And the limpid tenderness of the Kremlin
> On this morning is like thy charm . . .[2]

The line "To glimpse the light trace on the sand" might be a reminiscence of a charming passage in *Pan Tadeusz*. I quote only one line: ". . . near the gate could be seen on the sand the trace of a small foot . . . the trace was clear but light". The Russian: "Legky sled na peske uvidat'" corresponds exactly to the Polish: "Ślad widać nóżki na piasku . . . Ślad wyraźny lecz lekki." Blok's use of the Polish word "panna", which means in Polish "girl", confirms, in a way, my conjecture.[3]

In his *Notebook XIV* (end of August–end of October, 1906) we find a note in which Blok mentions the "almost hysterical devotion" of Polish literature to the idea of freedom. Poland is an "eternal stimulant

---

[1] In the *Diary* (March, 1918) there is a characteristic note: ". . . Yes, I do have treasures which I can 'share' with the people. Last night and today. Pososhkov (a rabid reformer, coming from the people) through A. Grigoriev.
"Chaadaev—to go on even through this temptation. *Polish messianism*. The revolution—that is I—not alone, but we. Reaction—solitude, lack of talent, kneading clay." (*Dnevnik Al. Bloka*, p. 110.) Italics are mine.—W. L.
Generally speaking, there are far more of these Polonica, that is, they are extant in great quantity in *Materials and Notes*, connected with *Retribution*. Not only are detailed and exact notes devoted to the Polish agitation of 1861, the insurrection of 1863, the activity of Marquis Wielopolski, but a goodly number of ironic exclamation points can be found on the subject of different "well-meant" declarations which Blok cites in connection with Polish events of the time. Cf. A. Blok, *Sobranie sočinenij* (Leningrad, 1911–1921), Vol. V, pp. 149, 152, 153 *et al*. Here are many details touching the Polish theme of *Retribution*, details of the three "variations"—the three "mazurkas", texts, for example, such as: "And the air is redolent of clover from the banks of the Niemen. What sort of marvel is this? I freeze to death and hear sounds of paradise in my sleep . . ." "In vain did the outraged Copernicus glorify his people." . . . (Cf. pp. 158–215.)

[2] "Upoitel'no vstat' v rannij čas,/Legkij sled na peske uvidat'./Upoitel'no vspomnit' tebja,/Čto so mnoju ty, prelest' moja./Ja ljublju tebja, panna moja,/Bezzabotnaja junost' moja,/I prozračnaja nežnost' Kremlja/V èto utro, kak prelest' tvoja." Cf. A. Blok, *Sočinenija v odnom tome*, p. 211. Italics are mine.—W. L.

[3] Cf. *Pan Tadeusz*, Book I, 95–107.

Krasiński in 1850
Engraving by J. M. St. Eve after portrait by Ary Scheffer

of Europe like the Jews" "from Goszczyński (*The Castle of Kaniów*)—all of them are mystics (*Forefathers' Eve*)—Krasiński—Przybyszewski". He mentions Soloviev's statements about the missions of the Polish and the Jewish nations. He also mentions K. Balmont's article, "The Flutes of Human Bones".[1] Blok had in mind Soloviev's famous study *On the National Problem*, in which the author stressed the Western character of Polish civilization and the fact that these cultural ties with the West are stronger than the racial ties with Russia. I think it is worth while to quote Balmont here:

> "From childhood days insinuating sounds of the Polish language reached Russian ears; they died out, grew weak, came again, quickly arose insinuatingly and powerfully, insinuatingly, but powerfully. Brother and sister have long been separated. They should unite. The separation gives rise to false thoughts, false feelings, false longitudes of space and fantasy. All of this will be destroyed by a flash of light. The brother and sister are rushing toward one another in the first moment of freedom.
>
> The Polish language is the energy of a stream which tears mountains asunder. The Russian language is the overflowing of the steppes, the distribution of unconstrained equals. The proud bronze music of the consonants—the humid drawn-out melody of the vowels—two languages, Polish and Russian—two great streams of the Slavic tongue.
>
> When afar there sounds the Polish language, the Russian ear avidly harkens:—'Is that my native tongue? Are they speaking Russian? No, wait. There is something else. I understand and yet I do not understand. Something secret is mixed into a simple thing. Did not I myself speak in that manner some time long, long ago. We were together—then I left.' O, in that meeting there is a strange charm—the sad melody of parting and reunion. The Polish language teaches strength to the Russian tongue: it is energy. In the places where they coincide they have the same strength, or they rival with eternal victories and without conquest, being equally beautiful. In the places where they separated one may hear in the drawn-out tones of the Russian language the softness of silver; in the compressed bursts of the Polish language one may hear the shrieks of steel and bronze. The Russian will say: 'Veter' (wind), the Pole answers: 'Wiatr'. The Russian says: 'Nichego' (nothing), the Pole answers: 'Nic'. The Russian shouts: 'K oruzhiyu' (To arms), the Pole answers: 'do broni'.

[1] Cf. *Zapisnye knižki Al. Bloka*, redakcija P. N. Medvedeva (Leningrad: Priboj, 1930), p. 61.

We Russians need the Polish language for it teaches us vengeance. It teaches strength, speed.

The Russians need the Polish soul. . . ." ("White Lightning", 1908, pp. 182–3).[1]

In *Notebook XXXII* (January–July, 1911) we find a long note connected with Polish legends—the legendary Polish King Popiel and Queen Wanda, Polish historical songs of the fourteenth century, and the dynasty of the Piasts. He emphasizes the "gloomy and tragic character" of Polish legends and songs. There is a note dealing with a different theme—the Polish and Hungarian Kings and Queens, the first election of a monarch in Poland, Queen Jadwiga at the close of the fourteenth century, the union of Lithuania and Poland, the Christianization of Lithuania and the defeat of the Teutonic Knights. The poet expresses satisfaction with the fact that the useless missionaries disappeared. He quotes Polish expressions.[2]

In the year 1918, on the 14th (1st) of February, Blok noted in his *Diary*:

"Yesterday (31st January). E. F. Knipovich. Black agate. Neck. Perfume. There is also what there is in the contemporary youth, but suffered from that and—a struggle. To listen quietly. Strindberg, Ibsen, Grigoriev. A woman, perhaps, can travel the way of Faust. Honesty of life. To sit by a stove and read Dostoevsky. 'I feel good.' Reads all the time. Can't go out evenings. Difficult, as always in a family where they all love one another very much. Polish and German blood. . . ."[3]

Reflection on this theme, we see then, did not leave him. Finally, there are other important notes in the *Diary*.

One dates from the 12th of July, 1917, and therefore comes after the well-known Proclamation of the Provisional Government announcing the independence of Poland:

"The separation of Finland and the Ukraine today suddenly frightened me. I begin to fear for 'Great Russia' . . . If Russia crumbles? Will all the 'old world' crumble, and will the historical process be closed up, to give way to a new one (or a different one); or will Russia be 'the handmaid' of strong state organisms? . . ."[4]

The silence in respect to Poland is significant.

And the other: 20 October, 1920, after the Russo-Polish War:

---

[1] *Zapisnye knižki Al. Bloka*, pp. 218–219.
[2] *Ibid.*, pp. 145–6.
[3] *Ibid.*, p. 44.
[4] *Dnevnik A. Bloka, 1917–21* (Leningrad, 1928), p. 44.

"When the Russians (Reds) were approaching Warsaw, Lloyd George was for war with Russia. The trade unions came out authoritatively against war; but not at all against war with Russia; they would have come out just the same if it had been proposed to them to fight against the Kaffirs, the Negroes—Europe in general has had enough of war. . . ."[1]

This is characteristic. It is worth remarking, finally, that the very fact that Blok was busy with *Retribution* in 1919, 1920, and 1921 is also striking. It means that the war of the Bolsheviks with Poland in no way changed his position. He published *Retribution* in 1921, declaring in the Preface that the poem had been conceived in 1910 and sketched in 1911, but under the Preface he put the date of the year 1919. I think that this dating was perhaps prompted by considerations of censorship; after the war of 1920 it was safer to put the dates 1909, 1910, and 1919. But even with such dates, I should think, it needed great bravery to put *Retribution* into print in Soviet Russia after the defeat at Warsaw.

* * * * *

And still I have not yet answered the question of where we must seek the source of at least Blok's information about Poland, if not his Polonophilia—which I explain partly by his familiarity with Polish literature. I think that the person who played the significant informational rôle in the life of the young Blok was a Pole, his friend Count Aleksander Rozwadowski.

Unfortunately I do not command any abundant sources of information about this man: I know nothing about him other than the fact that he was spoken of by Blok, Bely, and S. M. Soloviev in their letters and by Beketov in her biography of Blok, besides one letter of his to Blok which Blok copied word for word to transmit to his friend Soloviev. From this meagre material the following can be established: Count Aleksander Rozwadowski[2] was at the very beginning of the nineteen-hundreds a student in the physico-mathematical department at the University of Petersburg. Blok evidently made his acquaintance through the Mendeleevs; in favour of this supposition there is the fact that Rozwadowski was best man at Blok's wedding. The fullest description of him is given by S. M. Soloviev—apart from one very valuable statement by Blok himself and several (but as always hardly

[1] *Ibid.*, p. 174.
[2] The title of this line of the Rozwadowskis was confirmed in Russia in 1872. Cf. Jerzy Hr. Dunin-Borkowski, *Almanach Błękitny*—Genealogja żyjących rodów polskich (Lwów, 1908), p. 809.

serious) "speculations" by Bely. Describing Blok's wedding in his *Recollections*, S. M. Soloviev says as follows:

". . . I sat not far off from the great chemist (D. I. Mendeleev). . . . Next to me sat an attendant, the young Polish Count Rozwadowski whom Blok called 'the Petersburg mystic' [Soloviev incorrectly writes Razwadowski, and this mistake is repeated in many editions—Razwadowski is phonetically strange to the Polish ear; this surname, noble and, with most of its bearers untitled, comes from Rozwadów Wielki, in the province of Lublin], I got along with him at once. We were both extremely orthodox in inclination, and hostile to the new religious movement then headed by Rozanov and Merezhkovsky. The Count was a vegetarian. D. I. Mendeleev began to criticize vegetarianism. 'Impossible to eat of a living thing!' he said ironically; 'well, and rye is a living thing, is it not?' Then he began to laugh at metaphysics. His sight was bad, and his son read aloud to him from the history of ancient philosophy. D. I. learned for the first time about the systems of Pythagoras and Plato, and it all seemed proper nonsense to him. Rozwadowski kept silence. At times he objected, quietly and with restraint. 'The chief thing is humility,' he said to me under his breath. 'One must not stand out, must be unnoticeable, blend in with the environment.' . . ." "At the wedding-table, set with mayonnaises,[1] I was again next to Count Rozwadowski. Never shall I forget him. Small, white, lean and neurasthenic, but obstinate and strong in his weakness. We soon were drinking on thee-and-thou terms. He told me that the climate of Petersburg was harmful to him and that he was going south. The talk settled on Poland, Catholicism, and the Holy Virgin. The Count was preparing himself for the monastic vows. In autumn of that year, with his enigmatic way of expressing himself, Blok wrote to Bely about Rozwadowski: 'Now one of us, "true to the Spanish star", perhaps already is going toward Cracow in black cassock. . . .' "[2]

As a matter of fact, Blok wrote a bit differently to Bely on the 13th of October, 1903:

"Autumn has gilded and gone. At this moment while I am writing belated answers to you, perhaps one of 'us' (not you and me, but these few of us 'devoted to the Spanish Star') is going along the Austrian border in a priest's cassock. I have no data to confirm

[1] Soloviev here indicates all kinds of cold dishes garnished with mayonnaises.
[2] *Pis'ma Aleksandra Bloka* (Leningrad: "Kolos", 1925), pp. 18–20.

this, and if I had, I should not be justified in communicating it even to you. But now, losing myself in the realm of conjectures, I wish to *inform you* of them *without fail*. You may have heard of this strange man from Sergey Soloviev. Between me personally and him, somehow (and at some moment, although I do not even know when) something was interwoven—large and bluish, and later lost in 'the azure-unworldly firmament'. There were brief glances, watch-cries, someone tendered us invisible hands when we went over a precipice. I should like this man's praises, though they be anonymous, to trickle down to *you* too. . . ."[1]

M. A. Beketov, telling about Rozwadowski, confirms the fact that Blok made his acquaintance through the Mendeleevs and gives us to understand that Rozwadowski was especially attached to L. D. Mendeleev—and this does indeed appear, by means of distant hints, in the letter from Blok to Bely that I have cited:

". . . There were several attendants. One of them, Rozwadowski, is mentioned by Andrey Bely in his jottings.[2] He was a young, high-born Catholic Pole, the comrade of one of Lyuba's brothers,

---

[1] *Aleksandr Blok i Andrej Belyj, Perepiska* 'redakcija V. Orlova (Moscow: Izd. gos. lit. muzeja, 1940), pp. 51–2.

[2] A. A. Bely has added nothing essential or interesting to the history of the friendship of Blok and S. Soloviev with Rozwadowski. He has added to already known facts only one more of his conversations with Blok, which took place in the spring of 1921, about Rozwadowski, and as usual he has not refrained from his own nonsensical commentaries: ". . . characteristically: the name of Count Rozwadowski [Bely, of course, writes Razwadowski, incorrectly] has burst out only once into outward conversation with A. A., namely in the last conversations when in the spring of this year, before his departure to Moscow, A. A. was at my house with R. V. Ivanov and S. M. Alyanski. A. A. and I, as if somehow accidentally, passed over in the conversation from criticism of the Struevsky magazine (published in Sofia) to the Russians in Yugoslavia, to Slavic and Polish questions: and here A. A. informed me of some sort of Polish bishop, very reactionary in inclination and operating in Poland, recalling that his secular name was Count Rozwadowski. Here A. A. smiled at me and said, 'You know, this is probably the same Rozwadowski.' From the smile which appeared on his face I understood him to be alluding to that distant epoch when A. A.'s attendants, present at his wedding, included one who was awaiting the accession of a new, theocratic period, of a world-wide revolution nearly at that very wedding of A. A., whereas another went straight from the wedding on his search for the 'star', and this star brought him perhaps only to the reactionary episcopal tiara." A. Belyj, "Vospominanija ob A. A. Bloka" in *Zapiski mečtatelej*, No. 6, 1922, pp. 33–4.

In my opinion Bely, according to his custom, said what he did about the "reactionary episcopal tiara" for the witticism of the thing. I think that Blok told him about the metropolitan, Count Szeptycki, of whom he makes mention incidentally in his *Diary* (*op. cit.*, p. 44). Blok mentions Metropolitan Szeptycki in his *Diary* in connection with his Ukrainian activity and "Austrian orientation". At best, Bely was always muddling things up—for the witticism of the thing.

Ivan Dmitrievich, who was best man. This wedding was for him an event which influenced his whole life. After the marriage he went away to Poland and entered a monastery...."[1]

Clear and romantic. Possibly it was that way. I dimly recall now that my mother's cousin, Michal Odlanicki-Poczobutt, who was at the Mendeleevs and also in love with L. D. Mendeleev, used to tell me something about this Rozwadowski. But this uncle of mine was a very ordinary man and never related anything interesting in his life. At any rate, Rozwadowski represents an important moment in Blok's life at that time. The best proof of this is the fact that he continually returns to him in his letters of that time and later.[2] Thus, on 30 August, 1903, he writes to his mother:

"... I am awfully glad of Serezha's (Soloviev) rapprochement with Rozwadowski. Rozwadowski possesses great 'immobility' and is strongly inviolable. You must expect good of him. He is greatly, hearteningly ponderous. He *will bring into* the blood of *our priestly-*German mysticism a *large* share of Polish-politico-religious breeding and a share of religious liberalism. For the synthesis (!!!) it is important...."[3]

This statement of Blok, as I have already said above, is extraordinarily noteworthy and important—why, I shall explain further. After Rozwadowski's departure from Petersburg, Blok writes to S. Soloviev on 8 October, 1903, "... No news about Rozwadowski...."[4] Finally, on 29 January, 1904, he writes to Soloviev:

"When I arrived in Petersburg I found on the table *a letter from the count*, which I transmit to you in full. Here it is: 'Address: Autriche, Dalmatie, Raguza, poste restante. 23/1/1904. My dear A. A. ... L'homme propose, Dieu dispose. Unfortunately we have not chanced to see each other. Events turned out such that I abandoned Petersburg, and probably forever. I do not like Petersburg and do not regret it. There is too much cold in it, too much egoism. What I always looked for in people was a heart. However, I have preserved some pleasant recollections also. You and I became acquainted very recently, nevertheless it is with the

---

[1] M. A. Beketova, *Al. Blok, Biografičeskij očerk*, p. 83.
[2] *Pis'ma Aleksandra Bloka k rodnym* and *Pis'ma Aleksandra Bloka* (Leningrad: "Kolos", 1925).
[3] *Pis'ma Aleksandra Bloka k rodnym*, Vol. I, pp. 92–3.
[4] *Pis'ma Aleksandra Bloka*, p. 57.

greatest pleasure that I now recall our long conversations and strolls in the bright May evenings. And I am writing you now so that our relations may not be broken off. Of myself I have nothing to communicate except perhaps that the West is much more after my heart than the East is. My health was rather bad, so I was taken south. My mother and sister and I are now in Raguza. What a charming spot. In a month we are going to Rome. Here I do nothing; I rest, bask in the sun for hours and enjoy myself. Of myself there is nothing more to tell. But I shall await news of you with the greatest impatience; I am vitally interested in everything that goes on in Petersburg, especially in a certain direction. And so what is the *New Way* doing, and Merezhkovsky and Rozanov, and their followers? Is the power of darkness spreading?

'Tell me, pray, is Serezha Soloviev in Petersburg? I believe he was planning to come. Give him my regards, my memories of him are of the very best. Please write about everything, everything interests me, and what in particular, you know better than I! Is it true that a certain mystic attraction to the West is being disclosed in Petersburg? That interests me greatly. Goodbye, dear A. A., how is Lyubov Dmitrievna? God grant her and you happiness, I wish it for you with all my soul. A. Rozwadowski.' I have copied word for word. I still have not answered. May this help you get over your scarlet fever. . . . Yours, Al. Blok."[1]

This letter—keeping in mind Rozwadowski's special situation with respect to Blok—is of the utmost value, and it cannot but have been a very important factor in the great rôle that this man played in general, or so I believe, in Blok's *Weltanschauung* and especially in the matter of the establishment of Blok's attitude toward Poland. But, independently of this purely personal element, it contains thoughts that are also very essential for Blok, not to mention several valuable factual points. We learn therefrom that "long conversations and strolls" took place as early as May, 1903, that the connection between Rozwadowski and Blok must not cease. Remarkable also is this emphasizing of the "attraction to the West", "the West is far more after my own heart than the East is", "search for heart", Petersburg's "cold and egoism". If all this is connected with what Soloviev quoted about the necessity of "humility", there is no doubt that we can, without any special straining of the facts, infer that it was just this Rozwadowski who became the source of Blok's more intimate penetrating acquaintance with Polish Romanticism and Polish Catholic mysticism. Also characteristic is Blok's remark in his letter to his mother about Rozwadowski's

[1] *Pis'ma Aleksandra Bloka*, pp. 67–8.

"great *immobility*" and "inviolability", "encouraging ponderosity" and "Polish-religious good-breeding", "religious liberalism". Tie all this in with *Forefathers' Eve*, with *Iridion*, with *Kordian*, and the result is a well-knit system of a whole poetic and also practical doctrine of the free human and national personality, which in staunch suffering realizes true holiness and confers true, genuine freedom.

And Rozwadowski—just as Polish Romanticism—was connected with the West, with the Western, Catholic conception of personality. Those two elements—the West and the Catholic theodicy, justification of the human personality, were very close to Blok; they were "after his own heart". Testimony to this is furnished by the period of his mysticism, his cult of Western medievalism, his interest in western-European civilization; from this grows the beautiful bloom of his Polonophilia.

Retribution is after all a poem concerning not only *race* but *personality*, which finally finds a possibility of "swelling out" and "palpably acting on the environment", "snarling and giving forth leonine growls" and "grasping . . . at the whole whereby the history of mankind moves". That this "activism" of personality finds a negative expression in Blok, that it effluxes into "revenge" and becomes the personification of "retribution", whereas the thesis of Mickiewicz, Krasiński, and Słowacki, and even of the poet's personal friend, Rozwadowski, was "humility", is not to be wondered at. Blok represented the opposite side, the enemy; he was a noble "Russian bard" voicing a new song "in the camp of the Russian warriors", and it was not up to him to speak about "humility" and summon thereto "a country under the burden of insults", to invoke humility on a people enslaved! Just here lies the striking, unique pathos of the poem. And I am inclined to be of the opinion that the one who could have set the poet on that road was none other than Rozwadowski—by dint, perhaps, not even of his mystical theories, from which Blok himself later, as we know, digressed, but through those special sentimental circumstances and conditions in which fate had placed him and from which he evidently found a most worthy existence. I think it befell Blok on this plan of personal life to encounter the fact of personal "practical humility", which gave wings in an especially poetic way to his profoundly moving thoughts on Poland and her tragic fate.

* * * * *

It is necessary only to add one thing more in confirmation of what has been written above. I wish to quote one letter that is very important from my point of view. It was written by Blok to his friend Vladimir Alexeevich Pyast (Pestovsky). On 6 June, 1911, Blok wrote him:

"Dear Vladimir Alexeevich; first of all—mend your ways. I was wandering through woods and fields and felt fit to give you one piece of advice and one little warning. *The advice:* You have a great quantity of publicistic duties (not at all the 'tramway' or the 'acting state councillors'). As your will, temperament, and interests call you to the study of sociology and to publicistic activity, you owe it to yourself to learn to know the Russian *country life*, be it only separate places; first, those places without which it is impossible to know Russia (i.e., Great Russia); second, those amid which your own stock lived and was formed; from it you inherited *demonism* [italics mine, W. L.] and *will* constructed on the European model. *This is Western Russia.* You know this, I think, but you do not conceive with sufficient clarity what knowledge of the country life can give you, to what degree it can alter your innate demonism (which we talked about, remember, before I set out for Reinhardt's spectacle); alter, in two directions: either kill it, that is, destroy all will, make a man Russian in the Chekhovian sense (or the Rudinian sense, say); or—multiply it tenfold, that is, sharpen the will, tune it perhaps in supra-European harmony."[1]

This is very clear and indicative. No less notable is the Preface to *Retribution* and those passages in the poem in which Blok speaks of western-European individualism, of "demonism", of Byron, and, finally, of his own father as of "the first swallow of individualism".

There is a note in Blok's *Diary* of 1911, which, in my opinion, casts an ultimate light on the problem of the inclusion of the Polish theme in *Retribution*. This note is also connected with *The Scythians* and proves that the Mongolian topic which plays such an important rôle in *The Scythians* preoccupied the poet before 1918.

"Whence all these 'astrakhans' and jewels on all these ladies of the Nevsky Prospekt?" we read in the *Diary* of 1911. "In every 'astrakhan'—a bribe. In the holy times of Alexander III they used to say—'look how smartly she is dressed, what airs she gives herself!' Now everyone is smartly dressed. But the

---

[1] V. Pjast, *Vospominanija o Bloke* (Petersburg: "Atheny", 1923), p. 93. (Italics mine.—W. L.) R. O. Jakobson asserts that Pyast considered himself a Pole and even linked himself by means of "romantic" genealogical constructions with the Polish dynasty of the Piasts! This circumstance naturally gives still more significance to the above-mentioned letter of Blok's. The same R. O. Jakobson thinks that Blok's "Polonism" was fortified by his rapture over Vrubel, who was of Polish extraction. Finally, in Jakobson's opinion, Blok's Catholic tendencies could be somewhat dependent on the fact that Angelina Alexandrovna Blok was Catholic (which may be true), and also under the influence of the Catholic sympathies of Vyacheslav Ivanov, who is known to have gone over finally to Catholicism.

eyes are dull, double chins have been acquired, there is no enthusiasm, neither for shops nor for adultery. The pretty mug of any lady—is a share, a coupon, a bribe. Everything is going to pieces, the threads are rapidly rotting from the inside ('they are decomposing'), while the external appearance still holds. But if one should tug slightly—then all the astrakhans will fall apart, disclosing the filthy face of a tormented, bloodless, violated body.

We, too: yawning in the face of the yellow threat, while China is already in our midst.

Irrepressibly and impetuously the purple blood of the Aryans is becoming yellow. The human mugs in the streetcars, Menshikov's carefree laughter (Judas, Judas), a woman's naked body under the rotting astrakhans on the Nevsky—testify to this and only to this.

There remains a small last act: the actual seizure of Europe. This will take place quietly and delightfully and openly. The adroit little puppet, the Japanese, will place his friendly strong little hand on the shoulder of the Aryan and with his lively, black, curious little eyes will look into the heavy and dull eyes of the former Aryan. Stolypin, not long before his death, jumped out of his bed one night because he dreamed about a revolutionary battleship approaching Kronstadt. Of this they do still dream, but of 'greater horrors' they do not yet dream.

This is when it will become necessary to reveal all the secret regenerations of the New World (Poe) and of the Slavic world. (Pushkin, Russian history, Polish 'Messianism', Mickiewicz's little island in Paris, Ravenna, to awake Galla.) One must find in the Aryan culture a glance which would be capable of looking unwaveringly and quietly (majestically) into 'the curious, black, steady, and bold gaze of 1) the old man in the streetcar, 2) the author of that letter to a female provocateur, which once Sologub read aloud in the former Café de France, 3) of Menshikov selling us to the Japanese, 4) of Rozanov, propagating intercourse with sisters and animals, 5) of the beaten Suvorin, 6) of the lady on the Nevsky, 7) of the German-Russian pederast . . . impossible to enumerate everything. The meaning of tragedy lies in the hopelessness of fight; here there is no room for despair, apathy, giving up. A superior consecration is needed."[1]

This striking note is a key, in my opinion, to the understanding of the amalgamation of the Third Chapter with the First and Second Chapters of Blok's *Retribution*.

[1] *Dnevnik Bloka*, pp. 39–41.

In the first two chapters Blok expresses the idea and the feeling of the end of a great period in Russian history and even of the end of Russia and Europe. This idea and these feelings obsessed him before the First World War and the Russian Revolution. The note quoted above is one of the many proofs of this. It is extremely significant that in this note in which he describes the moral deterioration of Russian society he mentions Polish Messianism and "Mickiewicz's little island in Paris". The words "a superior consecration is needed" explain his thought. Obviously the poet found in the Polish Romantic doctrine that spiritual and moral energy with which he bound his hopes for salvation and the absence of which he felt in his own society. In order to be entirely faithful to the poet's text, I feel obliged to attract the reader's attention also to the words "Ravenna" and "to awaken Galla". The poet alludes here to one of his famous *Italian Poems*— "Ravenna"—in which he evokes the shade of Dante and calls the Roman Empress Galla Placida Augusta, the "blessed Galla", obviously following the apologetic tradition of Catholic writers who glorified this passionate and ambitious woman because of her religiosity. Extremely important are the poet's comments to this poem in which he stresses the personal character of his thoughts about Galla, who "from the shameful chariot of a barbarian was thrown by tumultuous fate onto the throne of the Western Roman Empire, the heart of which, in those days, was the sumptuous Ravenna". The poet describes Galla's features as "now virginal and tender and now firm and cruel, almost like the face of a legionnaire". He also alludes to the Basilica containing the ashes of the holy martyr Apollinarius. He ends his commentary in the following way: "Sanguis martyris—semen fidei tuae, Ravenna."[1] So "the blood of a martyr is the seed of faith".

These commentaries explain why the poet listed together his "Polish Messianism", "Mickiewicz's little island in Paris", and "Ravenna". The name of Pushkin is probably a sign of Blok's longing for the brilliant Russian past. Now we may also understand why the poet combined the first and the second chapters of his poem with the third one, which is so deeply Polish in the depiction of the Polish martyrdom. Blok's understanding and interpretation of Polish Messianism was certainly exceptional. He perceived the very essence of it, its *ethical pathos*. Noteworthy is the fact that even Tolstoy, who was such a powerful and intransigent opponent of patriotism, when writing about the Polish Messianism qualified "this movement born of patriotism" as a "strictly Christian and a profoundly moving one by its elevation and sincerity".[2]

[1] A. Blok, *Sočinenija v odnom tome*, pp. 608–9.
[2] Cf. V. Lednicki, *Quelques aspects du nationalisme et du christianisme chez Tolstoï*, p. 83.

Blok's ethical approach to life and even to poetry is an undeniable feature of the great poet. Polish Messianism was not the only goal of the poet's dreams and efforts to find a stable idea which would show the road to salvation. Tolstoy was another example and factor. This is what Blok wrote on the 12th of December, 1908, in his *Notebooks*:

"Tolstoy lives among us. It is difficult for us to evaluate and understand this as we should. Often we realize too late that the miraculous was close to us. We should remember that the very existence of a genius is a constant source of light for his contemporaries. This light protects even the near-sighted from the most dangerous regions. We do not understand that despite our terrible deviations from the road of truth, we luckily avoid the most terrible abysses; that we owe this good fortune, which constantly repeats that it is not too late, perhaps only to the vigilant and never setting sun, Tolstoy. The intelligentsia must hasten to understand Tolstoy from early youth, before the inherited disease of phantasmal activities and idle irony weaken spiritual and physical forces."[1]

Against this literary and political background the "Polish line" in Blok is by no means accidental and casual. On the contrary, Blok was certainly quite aware of the great moral significance of his literary act. His *Notebooks* and his letters show that he started to meditate on the Polish problem several years before he wrote his *Retribution*. I think that Blok was helped in his analysis of the Polish question and its Christian meaning for Russia by Vladimir Soloviev with his remarkable studies, *The National Question*, and articles about Mickiewicz, Pushkin, and others. Possibly Professor B. Chicherin also did not pass by without leaving a trace in Blok. Also important were, of course, Blok's Polish readings. In any case, Blok did not indulge in the confusion of love and hatred so characteristic of Dostoevsky and he did not appease his conscience with the help of great but empty words about the "impossibility of building personal happiness on the sufferings of one's fellow men". Blok was much more honest, much more manly. In this consists his great merit. His way was clear, he refused to deceive himself; and he made an unambiguous choice between what in his letters to Pyast he called the "Chekhovian" Russian and the Russian with a "sharpened will" following a "supra-European model".[2]

---

[1] A. Blok, *Zapisnye knižki*, pp. 88–9. Cf. also Blok's famous article on Tolstoy, "Sun over Russia".

[2] I might recall that even Dostoevsky took up arms against the use of the word "Byronism" as a "swear-word"; cf. *The Diary of a Writer*.

In this sense, on the plane removed from the purely literary, technical dependences and reverberations, on the ideological, ethical plane, *Retribution* is in its highest symbolic significance a singular retort not only to Pushkin's anti-Polish odes and *The Bronze Horseman*, but also to Dostoevsky. It can be understood in this way not only in regard to the question of human personality but also as regards the national question, to which Blok, as we can see, attributed an ethical and religious significance.[1] Dostoevsky, as I showed in my preceding studies, provided an explanation for his hatred of the Poles and Poland in *The House of the Dead*. To Dostoevsky's revolt against Polish "exclusive individualism", Blok opposed the "inviolable" and "immovable" (as Blok said of Rozwadowski) personal element, the uncompromising feeling of one's dignity.

And when one thinks about *Retribution*, so closely linked with just this Polish individualism, nurtured in the Polish people by centuries of aristocratic liberal culture, taking birth in the ancient republican traditions and currents of the Renaissance and the Reformation, with

---

[1] He mentions Dostoevsky in the first chapter of *Retribution* in regard to his father: "A certain young scholar ... made himself at home in the Vrevsky's salon. ... Once (he was passing through the drawing-room) Dostoevsky noticed him ... 'Who is this fine fellow?' he asked ... Softly bending toward Vrevskaya: 'he resembles Byron' ..." (*Sobranie sočinenij* (Leningrad, 1911–1921), Vol. V, p. 60.) It is characteristic that in his *Diary* he responds as follows to the *Diary of a Writer*: "We already know what it means to be outside of politics: it means to shut one's eyes bashfully to Gogol's *Correspondence with Friends*, to Dostoevsky's *Diary of a Writer*. ..." Note of 28 March, 1919, p. 154.

He writes to his mother on 18 May, 1917, concerning a commission of inquiry: "... And I have 'big days' all the time, i.e., I continue to bury myself in the history of this infinite tribe of Russian Rougon-Macquarts, of Karamazovs, eh? The absorbing novel, with its thousand actors and fantastic combinations, the novel most in the spirit of Dostoevsky (whom Merezhkovsky so unexpectedly truly called 'the prophet of the Russian revolution'), is called the story of Russian autocracy. ..." (*Pis'ma Aleksandra Bloka k rodnym*, Vol. II, p. 364.)

I may note in passing that in the copious *materials for the poem*, printed in the Edition of the "Writers' Publishing-House", are still other notes on Dostoevsky. Among other things Blok speaks of "Hatred for Dostoevsky" in a note on his funeral, about the fact that "Grandmother hates Dostoevsky". A. N. Beketov, meeting him, "because of her gentle disposition, cannot hate ..." (*Sobranie sočinenij* (Leningrad, 1911–1921), Vol. V, p. 146.)

In *Notes to Retribution*, in the plan of the first part: "Dostoevsky—obscurantist" (*ibid.*, p. 160). These materials and notes (years 1911–1913) testify to a very meditative attitude on the part of the poet toward his broad historical theme and to his great preparatory work and systematic historical reading. We have here detailed conspectuses and chronological outlines, lists of the main historical events, beginning during the last years of the reign of Alexander II. There are detailed analyses here of the historical works and recollections of S. S. Tatishchev, Shchedrin, Herzen, L. F. Panteleev, A. Tun, S. G. Svatikov, M. Lemke, Shchegolev, *The Past*, *The Messenger of Europe*, *The Bell*, and the like, and the "Political Processes" of Mikhaylov—Pisarev, Chernyshevsky, through unpublished documents. Here, too, as I said before, is a great deal about the Polish events of the years 1861–1862.

the Polish principles of Christian personality, humble but defending its rights to liberty, all of which was personified by Polish romantic poetry, the thought involuntarily arises that Blok—with all that he said in his letter to Pyast and in his Preface to *Retribution* about "demonism" and "sharpened personality"—Blok, the author of *Retribution*, showed himself closer to the Polish notion of Christianity and to the national idea in its Polish style than to the Christianity and "universalism" of Dostoevsky—"the obscurantist"—to quote Blok.

Tolstoy, who wrote his charming "Polish" story under the title "*What For?*", wrote it in order to give once and for all a proof of the entire annihilation of his former anti-Polish inclinations.[1] He was also nearer to the Christian truth, with his "narrow rationalism", "ethical individualism", and "moral utilitarianism"—for he fought down even the slightest instincts of malice in himself and destroyed the pettiest and most casual weed in his heart if there ever was one there. And I think that the world lost nothing by that fact, however cleverly L. Shestov may have reasoned on the subject that Tolstoy acted that way for personal perfection and personal salvation, setting for himself and indicating to others a personal, not an universalistic goal. In this sense Tolstoy did not show himself to be in discord with western-European Christianity, he did not show himself to be in discord even with the Russian notion of good and evil, in spite of the fact that he never drew anything from Dostoevsky's teachings. I repeat again, the pathos of Russo-Polish relations is an essentially and deeply religious pathos. It is a unique criterion of the evaluation of Christianity in the life of these two nations and the persons belonging to them. No dialectics can help here, any more than they could help the Slavophils or Dostoevsky, or any more than they can help their modern epigones. Nor will an indifferent refusal of responsibility help: it is hard to live by such a refusal in private life and it is hard to live with it in history; it is hard for the Russians and Poles to live with the "domestic quarrel of Slavs among themselves" unsolved in their hearts.

The greatest national geniuses of Poland understood this—Mickiewicz, Krasiński, Słowacki, and that is just why they strove for a Christianization of politics and international relations, why Mickiewicz taught his unhappy compatriots—

"Verily I say unto you: do not seek what will be the government in Poland; it is enough that ye know that it will be better than any ye know; and do not inquire about its boundaries, for they will be greater than ever. And each of you in his soul preserves the seed of future laws and the measure of future boundaries. The

[1] Cf. V. Lednicki, *Quelques aspects*, etc., pp. 51–100.

more ye broaden and better your souls, the better will be your laws and the wider will be your boundaries."[1]

In Russia, the very same thing was understood and taught not by Dostoevsky—but by the greatest of all Russians, the old man of Yasnaya Polyana, and after him by the greatest and most youthful Russian poet of modern times—Blok, in his "Polish poem". And it seems to me that one ought to harken to this voice of great and pure poetry, for in it, when it is truly great and truly pure, resounds the soul and conscience of the nations, unfeigned and untemptable by any kind of craftiness. And it is beautiful!

> Life is without beginning or end.
> The chance event lies in wait for us all,
> Over us is unlifting dusk
> Or else the brightness of the face of God.
> But thou, O Artist: believe firmly
> In beginnings and in ends. Know thou
> Where Hell and Heaven await us.
> To thee it has been given to measure all
> That thou seest with passionless gauge.
> Let thy glance be hard and clear.
> Wipe away the accidental lines
> And thou wilt see: the world is beautiful.
> Learn where is the light,—thou wilt understand,
> Where is the darkness . . .[2]

---

[1] See *Books of the Polish Nation and the Polish Pilgrimage* in Noyes, p. 409.
[2] The beginning of *Retribution*.
"Žizn'—bez načala i konca./Nas vsekh podsteregaet slučaj./Nad nami sumrak neminučij,/Il' jasnost' bož'ego lica./No ty, khudožnik, tverdo veruj/V načala i koncy. Ty znaj,/Gde steregut nas ad i raj./Tebe dano besstrastnoj meroj/Izmerit' vsë, čto vidiš' ty./Tvoj vzgljad—da budet tverd i jasen./Sotri slučajnye čerty—/I ty uvidiš': mir prekrasen./Poznaj, gde svet,—pojmeš', gde t'ma." Cf. A. Blok, *Sočinenija v odnom tome*, p. 241.

VIII

Conclusion

THESE studies, which deal with the problem of Russia's relations to the West in the nineteenth century and the beginning of the twentieth, as well as with the rôle of Poland in these relations, and particularly with that part played by Mickiewicz, of necessity could not include some very important political events and literary facts which determined the development of the ideas and attitudes herein analyzed and discussed.

Around these main themes with which my book is concerned have emerged several other problems, such as the rôle of autocracy in Russian social, political, and cultural life, the problem of the Europeanization of Russia, the problem of patriotism in its broadest sense. To these should be added the problem of the literary interrelations of the Russian writers and poets with whom I have dealt in this book, and also their reactions to Mickiewicz's interpretation of Russia.

One must realize that behind Chaadaev's nostalgia for the West, behind Pushkin's poem addressed to the "mysterious Russian Polonophil", behind the Polish and French evaluations of the catastrophe of the December Revolution, behind Dostoevsky's anti-Europeanism and hatred of Poland, behind Belinsky's sharp criticism of Gogol, and finally behind Blok's *Retribution* are to be found two essential factors: Russian autocracy and the westernization of Russia.

One may share to a large degree Pushkin's opinion that for the thousand years of Russian historical development the most creative— Pushkin said "the only"—power was Russian autocracy. I should like again to modify Pushkin's view by applying it exclusively to the political development of Russia. Particularly important, in my opinion, is the undeniable fact that during her thousand years of life Russia never succeeded in establishing any institution which was able to defend the rights of the individual or of the community against the overwhelming power of autocracy. And this is what Mickiewicz, Ancelot, Vigny, Custine felt and expressed in their writings. As the

Tolstoy in 1908

reader may have observed, the views of Chaadaev, Pushkin, Lermontov, Belinsky, Herzen, and Blok were not very different. And all of them emphasized how deeply this political structure affected Russian society.

The problem of Russia's westernization also contains tragic elements. Without entering into any detailed analysis of the rôle and extent of the Western influences which are discernible in pre-Petrine Russia, let us anyhow consider Peter as a symbol of the Europeanization of Russia. Peter's reforms were an act of Russia's autocracy, which had very concrete and special goals: the adoption of European achievements of material culture. The monarchy neither impelled its subjects to follow the European course nor did it embark upon such a course itself, but the two hundred years of cultural coexistence with Europe on the part of the Russian élite—and this was the only Europeanized class in Russia—fatally deepened the influence of European culture in Russia. The Russian élite absorbed European political, social, and cultural conceptions and in consequence found itself in lonely opposition to the autocracy, as the extent of this Europeanization surpassed the limits which Russian autocracy was ready to accept. Even more deeply was the élite separated from the masses, as the latter remained untouched by Europe's culture. To quote Blok: "From both the will of the czar and the will of the people, they frequently experienced pain."

From this situation developed the revolutionary trends so characteristic of the Russian intelligentsia of the nineteenth and twentieth centuries aiming at political and social reforms: politically they tended toward the abolition of autocracy, and socially, in the beginning, toward the abolition of serfdom and later toward the establishment of a closer spiritual understanding between the intelligentsia and the peasants. This philanthropic approach to the peasantry is extremely characteristic for the whole of Russian literature, beginning with Radishchev and ending with Dostoevsky and Tolstoy. And let us not forget that it was the Russian élite which was responsible for the great Russian cultural achievements, particularly the literary ones so deeply admired by the whole world.

The westernization of Russia carried with it other ideological complications. As I mentioned in my preface, Russian territorial expansion, in other words Russian imperialism, met on its road obstacles of a moral character. From this point of view perhaps the most fateful events, as far as Russia's annexations are concerned, were the partitions of Poland and later the Polish insurrections, especially the Insurrection of 1830–1831 and that of 1863, which created violent fermentation, not only in western Europe, but, what is more important for the sake of the ideas which I am defending in my book, in Russia itself. The Anglo-Saxon reader would certainly be amazed if he should read, for instance, the fascinating correspondence between the Grand Duke Constantine and his brother, Emperor Nicholas I, in which the Grand Duke gives the most powerful and passionate critique, from the legal, political, and moral points of view, of the act of partitioning. There is no doubt that views similar to those expressed by the Grand Duke Constantine tormented many Russian consciences during the whole of the pre-revolutionary era, although few of them read this correspondence. However, one great literary event became crucial as far as the problem of the Europeanization of Russia was involved, from the point of view of its moral significance. This event was the appearance of Pushkin's anti-Polish and anti-European odes, published by the poet after the defeat of the Polish Insurrection of 1830-1831. The intransigent and even ferocious attitude which Pushkin took in this case determined the attitude of many generations of Russians toward Poland and Europe. It would be difficult to mention here, as I was able to do in my book *Pouchkine et la Pologne* and in my study "Panslavism", all the writers and poets who followed Pushkin in this respect. These odes became a canon, a national catechism, an ideological citadel erected by the powerful hand of the great Russian poet, in which he imprisoned the thought of many Russian politicians, writers, and poets. It would be difficult to evaluate the enormity of the moral disaster achieved by Pushkin. One may believe that had Pushkin taken a different attitude the fate of Russian-Polish relations, and therefore partly of Russian-European relations, would also have been different. We cannot underestimate Pushkin's prestige. But what is, in addition to these considerations, especially sad for me—and the developments with which my book deals explain this feeling—is the fact that the abyss created on the ideological level between Russia and Poland and Russia and Europe was the achievement of a man who was the outstanding and captivating symbol of Russian Europeanism—a Russian who indeed might be considered the Peter the Great of Russia in the field of her spiritual culture. I have mentioned in my book at least a few of Pushkin's friends who sharply criticized the poet on the occasion of the publication of his odes. Some of them were in real despair. The best proof that this despair of the "Russian-Europeans" was justified might be found in the innumerable expressions, during the Polish Insurrection and after its defeat, of indignation and sorrow on the part of Spanish, English, Italian, French, German, and American poets, writers, and journalists. These pro-Polish and anti-Russian manifestations continued a tradition established in European poetry by Byron. Byron's rôle should not be overlooked in this case. In 1833 Ballanche was perhaps the one who made the most explicit statement as far as the Polish catastrophe was concerned. This is what he wrote in the review *Le Polonais—Journal des intérêts de la Pologne*:

> "The destinies of Europe are being reorganized in the shelter of this living tomb (Poland) which continues to protect us. . . . The anathema which rises from the bloody mines of Poland excludes Russia forever from the European confraternity. I recommend to the Editor of this present issue to entitle it from now on, *Journal des intérêts d'Europe*."

The reader may see that the ideas which fill Mickiewicz's *Forefathers' Eve, Part III*, the *Digression*, and his *Books of the Polish Nation and of the Polish Pilgrimage* were exactly the same. Needless to say, the fact that Mickiewicz was a Pole and a great poet who acquired an exceptional prestige among the élite of Russian society during his stay in Moscow and Petersburg, the fact that Pushkin and many other outstanding Russian poets became intimate friends of the Polish poet, all this added a particular significance to Mickiewicz's views on Russia and on Russian-Polish relations. It suffices to say that Pushkin copied by hand entire passages from Mickiewicz's *Digression* while he was preparing his beautiful poetic answer to Mickiewicz, *The Bronze Horseman*. But what must not be ignored is the fact that *The Bronze Horseman*, though an answer to Mickiewicz, undeniably absorbed some very essential ideas of the Polish poet, and I do not need to emphasize the rôle which Pushkin's *Bronze Horseman* played in Russian literature and Russian thought. The problem of the State and of the individual, which emerges from this highly symbolic poem, absorbed Russian consciences for many decades. Despite the brilliance of the apology of Petersburg and of the Russian Empire which is displayed in Pushkin's "Introduction" to *The Bronze Horseman*, the content of the poem is a tragic one; undoubtedly Mickiewicz's interpretation of Petersburg and Russian autocracy contributed to the tragic atmosphere which characterizes Pushkin's poem. Mickiewicz acted directly on those Russians who read him, but also acted indirectly, and this latter latent action was even more important, through the medium of Pushkin's poem. Against this background the implications of Chaadaev's *Philosophical Letters*, as well as all of the personal and social details involved in that great ideological adventure, acquire quite a special significance. Is it necessary to emphasize the fact that all these themes, almost without exception, reappear in Dostoevsky's writings, and that Dostoevsky's dialectic was directed not only against Chaadaev, but, if my hypotheses are correct, against Mickiewicz as well?

Returning to the problem of Russian imperialism, which was so passionately discussed by Mickiewicz in connection with the Polish tragedy, I should like to focus the reader's attention on Pushkin and Dostoevsky. Pushkin, in his odes, was mainly concerned with one great political issue: leadership in the Slavic world. Who was to be the leader, Russia or Poland? But when, in his other writings, he discussed the rôle of Russian imperialism in different areas, as for instance in the Caucasus, he raised the question of Russia's civilizing mission, and he criticized the inefficiency and idleness of the Russian Orthodox Church in this region. There is no doubt that Pushkin was aware of the essentially different conditions which Russian imperialism faced in the West and in the East. Dostoevsky, however, refused to comprehend the necessity of this distinction, although he did, it is true, emphasize Russia's rôle in Asia in his last writings. But he discussed the problem in a rather vulgar manner: "In Europe we were hangers-on and slaves, whereas we shall go to Asia as masters."

In my preface I briefly alluded, without any specific references, to the possible justifications which an historian might be able to present for the growth of an empire. But I insisted on the respect due to the spiritual personality of every nation, large or small. Now there remains one particular detail which especially in our days has been often neglected by the modern defenders of Russian imperialism. Their general tendency is to compare Russian imperialism to that of European nations and of the United States. The most recent statements are perhaps the most exemplary. Professor N. S. Timasheff, in his article "Russian Imperialism or Communist Aggression?" in his polemics with K. Marx, F. Engels, and J. Byrnes, says:

> "Yes, Russia advanced 700 miles toward Berlin: but, from the day the United States gained independence to the end of the Mexican war, in other words, in 65 years, the United States advanced toward the Pacific by 1,500 miles. Yes, Russia acquired a large area between 1853 and 1914. But, between the same years, Great Britain, France, Germany, Italy, and Belgium partitioned among themselves the continent of Africa which, in 1853, belonged to the Europeans only in its periphery. Only a few would know that the Belgian share of Africa, the so-called Belgian Congo, is approximately as large as the totality of the Russian acquisitions between 1853 and 1914 which have so frightened Secretary of State Byrnes, and that the share of France, 3.5 million sq. mi., was approximately four times larger."[1]

[1] *Soviet Imperialism, Its Origins and Tactics* (Notre Dame, Indiana: University of Notre Dame Press, 1953), p. 25.

Is this the statement of an historian, of a humanist, or that of a civil engineer? Although I think that even a civil engineer could see the difference between the African jungles, the American prairies, and European areas of thousand-year-old civilization. We know the industrial achievements of the Belgians in the Congo and we also know the accomplishments of the United States in its annexed or purchased territories. The rôle of Russia in Poland, however, was described with sufficient eloquence by Blok—I will refrain from quoting the great Russian poet's exact terminology. Fortunately the tradition of Chaadaev's thought has not perished. Let me answer Professor Timasheff by quoting an outstanding modern Russian historian, J. Fedotov, whom his compatriots like to call "the Chaadaev of our times":

> "We love the Caucasus, but we look upon its subjugation through the romantic poems of Pushkin and Lermontov. But even Pushkin dropped the cruel word about Tsitsianov, who 'destroyed, exterminated tribes'. From childhood we have learned about the peaceful annexation of Georgia, but there are few who know with what treachery and with what debasement for Georgia Russia repaid her for her voluntary union. Few know even that after the surrender of Shamil up to half a million Circassians emigrated to Turkey. And these are matters of recent days. The Caucasus was never completely pacified. One should remember that the same applies to Turkestan. Subjugated with extraordinary cruelty, it rebelled during the first war, and it rebelled also under the Bolsheviks. Until the revolution the Russian cultural influence in general was weak in Central Asia. After the revolution it was of such a character that it succeeded in making the name of Russia hateful.
>
> Finally, there remains Poland, that open (even today) wound in the body of Russia. In the end all of the Russian intelligentsia —including even the nationalistic intelligentsia—became reconciled to its separation. But the intelligentsia never was conscious either of the depth of the historical sin committed—for a whole century—against the soul of the Polish nation or of the naturalness of that indignation with which the West looked upon the Russian domination of Poland. It is precisely to Poland that the Russian Empire is indebted for its fame as 'the prison of nations'.
>
> Was this reputation deserved? In the same measure as it was deserved by other European empires. They carried the seeds of a higher culture to the savage or barbaric world at the price of exploitation and oppression. These processes will be mocked only

by the person who excludes himself from the heritage of the Hellenic world. For Russia the problem is complicated by the cultural diversity of her western and eastern borderlands. Along the western border the Russian administration dealt with more civilized nations than the dominating nation. Therefore, despite the mildness of her régime in Finland and the Baltic regions this régime was felt as an oppression. The Russian culture-bearers had nothing to accomplish there. For Poland Russia was really a prison, for the Jews a ghetto. The Empire bore with its whole weight upon these two nations. But in the East, despite all the crudity of the Russian administration, the cultural mission of Russia is unquestionable."[1]

In any case it would be very difficult for a stranger to accept the idea of the Russian Empire: one may admire Russian literature, music, love the Russian people and fall under the charm of the beautiful Russian language, but one would have to violate one's conscience to be able to find any superior justification for that *castrum doloris* which the Russian Empire has always been for people and nations.

When, fifteen years ago, I utilized Custine's book on Russia, I was not aware of the fame which this book was to acquire in America in connection with the new English translation prefaced by the American Ambassador to Soviet Russia, General Walter B. Smith. The fact that Ambassador Smith found in Stalin's régime traits of the historical Russian autocracy caused violent reactions in the circles of the Russian emigration in Europe and in America. As a matter of fact the Polish historian Jan Kucharzewski was the first to emphasize in his monumental work, *From White Czardom to Red*,[2] this continuity of the Russian autocratic system. I am not concerned here with any current political problems, but I should like to defend Custine's interpretation of Russia, which has also been vehemently criticized. The reader might be interested in knowing that whereas in 1937 the outstanding Soviet historian, E. Tarle, stated in *Literaturnoe Nasledstvo*: "The shameful ugliness of the régime of Nicholas I was revealed in this book in no way fully and decisively,"[3] V. Nechaeva, in the same *Literaturnoe Nasledstvo* in 1952, qualifies Custine's book as "a shameless lie and obvious ignorance".[4] *Habent sua fata libelli.*

The deduction from Custine's book of any implications applicable to the present time was not my purpose. I simply wished to demonstrate

---

[1] Cf. G. P. Fedotov, *Novyj grad* (New York: Izd. imeni Čekhova, 1952), pp. 189–90.
[2] An English version of this work appeared in America in 1948 under the title, *The Origins of Modern Russia.*
[3] *Literaturnoe Nasledstvo*, Vols. 31–2, p. 604.
[4] *Literaturnoe Nasledstvo*, Vol. 58, p. 322.

that Custine's views on Russia were based on his talks with Mickiewicz before departing for Russia, on his talks with Prince Kozlovsky and Chaadaev, as well as on his reading of Pushkin and Lermontov. But while on the subject, I may put forth a gratuitous defense of Custine and Ambassador Smith by citing Blok's last speech, delivered in 1921 in Petersburg, commemorating Pushkin:

"Pushkin was killed not only by d'Anthès, it was the lack of air which killed him. And his epoch died with him."

Quoting Pushkin, Blok says:

" 'Here on earth there is no happiness, but there is peace and freedom.' *Peace! Freedom!* These are indispensable for every poet, but here peace and freedom are taken away from us; not our petty quiet life, but the peace of the soul necessary to creativeness. Not the freedom to talk, to pronounce words, but freedom to create, the secret freedom. And so the poet dies, because he can't breathe any more: life has lost its meaning for him."[1]

The study on Blok's Polish poem showed to the reader the connections which obviously exist between *Retribution* and Pushkin's *Bronze Horseman*. This study also showed the great attention which Blok paid not only to Poland but to Polish Romantic poetry, particularly to Mickiewicz and Krasiński. As my purpose was to demonstrate first of all the Polish element in Blok's poem, which appears in the third chapter, I did not analyze the first two chapters. However, I should like to stress that these first two chapters are certainly no less important and significant than the third one.

Blok's *Retribution* in a way emphasizes the dualism which characterizes Pushkin's *Bronze Horseman*. Indeed, on the one hand as a glorification, or even as a defense, of Petersburg and Peter the Great, *The Bronze Horseman* ends a long series of panegyrics of the eighteenth and the beginning of the nineteenth centuries which sing of the splendours and beauties of the Russian capital as well as of the prestige of its emperor. On the other hand, the element of disaggregation introduced into the poem by the reading of Mickiewicz, along with Gogol's impressionistic vision of Petersburg, inaugurates in Russian letters a new attitude toward this city. Certain authors turn away from the capital of Peter the Great and go to seek their inspiration in the provinces and in Moscow; others do continue, it is true, to situate their works in the

[1] A. Blok, *Sobranie sočinenij*, Vol. 3, pp. 144–5.

frame of Petersburg, but they are primarily haunted by the extraordinary, fantastic side, by the city's tragic essence as evoked by Pushkin and Gogol. But, as this book shows, Mickiewicz has to be taken into consideration here, and not only in connection with *The Bronze Horseman* and with *Retribution* but with the stylization of Petersburg which we find in Dostoevsky.

Blok's poem is foreboding in its very essence. It deals with Russia's past and with Russia's future. The poet expresses in it the awareness of the end of a great period and is frightened by the feeling he has of the future which awaits Russia and the whole of Europe. And I again must stress the significance of the fact that Blok had no doubts as to whether the inclusion of his Polish chapter in this poem was appropriate and acceptable. I tried to explain the motives which guided the poet in this seemingly "accidental" amalgamation of the Russian and Polish themes.

The poem brings many gloomy descriptions of Russian life, of Petersburg, and of the Russian landscape. Those who know Blok's *Diary*, his *Notebooks*, and his correspondence must remember his remarks about Russia "flying blindly in her adorned troyka toward the abyss of time" [in 1908], about "the divine and swinish face of my country", about "the mud, the stunted bushes", about "the solitary mounted policeman in the fields", about "my unhappy Russia, covered with the spit of her officials", and about "my dirty homeland, slobbery and stupid . . ."[1] There is no doubt that in all these passages and in so many others one may find a confirmation of the essential topics familiar to the reader from my quotations from Chaadaev, Custine, and Mickiewicz, to mention only the most important authors herein discussed.

Dostoevsky has a large place in this book. I must confess that in my investigations of him I was not concerned with purely formal literary problems. When I traced in Dostoevsky's works the fate of various themes, characters, and motifs suggested by Pushkin and the fate of some of the characters suggested by Turgenev and Tolstoy, when I advanced and developed my hypothesis of the possible reverberation of Mickiewicz's poetry in Dostoevsky's novels, I was mostly interested in Dostoevsky's ideology, and, I freely admit, in Dostoevsky's personality. My goal—I dare to say so—was didactic. I tried to fight against this genius of moral confusion. Here and there I have opposed to him the honest mind of Tolstoy.

I have quoted Blok's formula on "the indivisibility and immiscibility of art, life, and politics". The reader of course realizes that politics are an intrinsic part of the discussions presented here; further,

[1] Cf. N. Berberova, *Alexandre Blok et son temps* (Paris: du Chêne, 1947), p. 127.

he should realize that to the question of politics is indivisibly linked that of patriotism. Chaadaev, Pushkin, Lermontov, Mickiewicz, Dostoevsky, and Blok represented and depicted various aspects of this human attribute. Patriotism is nourished from many sources, and in order to arrive at an understanding of the essence of patriotism one should perhaps study it among the peoples of subjugated nations and among the exiled, for in their lives it acquires a special power and Chaadaev's "sobs", Pushkin's "contempt for my country", Lermontov's "Meditation", Belinsky's "indignation", Blok's passionate revulsion against the reality of Russian life, derived from a deep attachment to their country. All this was an expression of that ideal conception cherished by them of what their country should be. There are many examples of a similar sharp criticism of Poland in the writings of Mickiewicz, Słowacki, Krasiński, Prus, Żeromski, and Wyspiański. These *sui generis* "interor émigrés" can be found in various countries, as I have stated in my studies. This last attitude reveals some of the most salient traits of patriotism—its idealism, its disinterestedness and impracticality.

Indeed, in some cases, none of those elementary physical or empiric factors to which I have alluded before have any decisive and active power in the formation of patriotic feelings. One may love one's country without having been born in it, without having been happy in it—even when one has been happy and fortunate in another country. What lies then at the bottom of patriotism in such cases? Simply the attachment to the idea of one's country. This idea embraces the notion of the historical past of the country and the conception of its cultural rôle. And the cherishing of this idea does not necessarily depend on personal experiences, fortunate or unfortunate. Montalembert once gave an explicit definition of this purely idealistic, disinterested and impractical character of patriotism: "I owe them (the Poles) one of the greatest boons of life; the honour of knowing and understanding the grandeur and beauty of lost causes." Cultivated patriotic feelings demand personal sacrifices, and this is what makes one immune to philistinism and opportunism. They impose an ethical approach to life and affirm personal dignity and self-respect. Let us not, however, forget Sienkiewicz's definition of patriotism:

> "One has to love his motherland more than anything else, and one has first of all to think about his motherland's happiness. However, the first duty of a real patriot is to take care that the idea of his motherland not only does not work against the happiness of humanity, but, on the contrary, that this idea becomes one of the foundations of the universal happiness. Only thus may the existence

and the development of the motherland become a cause in which the whole of mankind would be interested. In other words, the motto must be 'Through Motherland to Humanity' and not 'For Motherland against Humanity'."[1]

Some of these considerations might be less familiar to the Anglo-Saxon and, in particular, to the American reader. All happy nations are alike, all unhappy ones are unhappy in their own ways, to paraphrase the beginning of *Anna Karenina*.

---

[1] Wacław Lednicki, *Henryk Sienkiewicz (1846–1946)* (New York: Polish Institute of Arts and Sciences in America Series, 1948), pp. 8–9.

INDEX

Russian names in this index are spelled according to the method of transcription used in the main text of the work.

The names of translators which appear in the footnotes in connection with English translations of foreign works are not included in the index. Names of editors appearing in the footnotes in connection with bibliographical information are indexed only with respect to the first reference.

ADAMOVICH, G. V., 246–8
Aksakov, I. S., 137, 350
Aldanov, M. A., 352
Alexander the Great, 217
Alexander I, Emperor of Russia, 27, 74, 78, 112, 214–18, 298
Alexander II, Emperor of Russia, 271, 397
Alexander III, Emperor of Russia, 271, 371, 393
Alyansky, S. M., 389
Amphiteatrov, A. V., 352
Ancelot, J. A. F. P., 36, 37, 109, 110, 116–19, 124–6, 131, 400
Ankwicz, H. E., 318, 375
Annenkov, P. V., 249, 250, 254
Anthès, Baron G. C. d', 83, 407
Aristotle, 16, 79
Arminius, 174
Arnim, L. J. von, 314
Aronson, M. I., 124
Arseniev, N. S., 352
Artsybashev, M. P., 194, 195, 352
Asmus, V., 28, 41
Avvakum, 58

BACON, F., 48
Bakhtin, M. M., 133, 134
Bakunin, M. A., 66, 350
Ballanche, P. S., 48, 83, 402
Balmont, K. D., 350, 380, 385
Balukhaty, S. D., 110
Balzac, H. de, 159, 206, 227, 346
Barante, Baron E. de, 65, 66
Barbier, A., 59
Barclay de Tollay, General M. B., 217
Barry, Countess J. B. du, 135
Bartenev, P. I., 72, 73

Batyushkov, F. D., 351
Baudelaire, C., 245, 372
Baudouin de Courtenay, J., 311
Béguin, A., 317
Beketov, A. A., 359, 360, 365–7, 369, 372, 373, 379, 390, 391, 397
Beketov, A. N., 368, 369, 397
Beketov, M. A., 365, 368–71, 387, 389, 390
Beketov, S. A., 368
Belchikov, I. F., 320
Belinsky, V. G., 18, 59, 61, 71, 249–51, 254–61, 279, 343–6, 350, 400, 401, 409
Bellay, J. du, 76
Belousovich, I. N., 330
Bely, A. A. (B. N. Bugaev), 387–9
Belyaev, M. T., 360, 366
Bem, A. L., 181, 222, 227, 291
Benckendorff, Count A. C., 73, 85, 94, 120
Benediktov, V. G., 344
Bentham, J., 337
Berberova, N. N., 49, 408
Berdyaev, N. A., 146, 147
Berent, W., 351, 379
Berg, N. V., 378
Bergson, H., 15, 231–4, 246
Bernstein, D., 219
Bestuzhev, A. A., 24, 87, 249, 350
Bibikov, D. G., 347
Bielecki, A., 344
Biron (Biren), J. E., Duke of Courland, 290
Bismarck, Prince O. E. von, 174–6, 307
Bitsilli, P. M., 130, 352
Blagoy, D. D., 131
Blok, Alexander A., 18, 49, 206, 250, 268, 349, 350, 353–69, 371–3, 375–99, 400–1, 405, 407–9

INDEX

Blok, Angelina A., 349, 360, 366, 393
Blok, A. I., 365
Blok, A. L., 355, 359, 365, 366, 393
Blok, I. L., 365
Blok, L. A., 365
Blok, L. D. (*see* L. D. Mendeleev)
Blüth, R., 131, 318
Bogoslovsky, N. V., 79
Bogusławski, I., 272, 274
Böhme, J., 314
Bonald, L. G. A. de, 27, 48
Boratynsky, E. A., 119
Borowy, W., 313
Botkin, V. P., 71, 260, 343–5
Brandes, G., 351
Branicki, Count A., 64–6
Branicki, Count K. (Member of Targowica Confederacy), 305
Branicki, Count K. (author of *Les Nationalités slaves*), 64–7
Brasol, B., 148, 321
Braylovsky, S. N., 278, 381
Brentano, C., 314
Breshkovsky (Breshko-Breshkovsky), N. N., 380
Brodsky, N. L., 65
Bryusov, V. Ya., 350, 380, 381
Buddha, 246
Budilovich, A. S., 342
Buhle, J. G., 26
Bułharyn, T., 118, 122
Bunin, I. A., 350
Byrnes, J., 404
Byron, Lord G. G., 22, 39, 64, 81, 82, 180, 216, 217, 234, 280, 310, 334, 345, 346, 355, 372, 373, 375, 393, 396, 397, 402

CAESAR, Caius Julius, 216, 239
Calderón de la Barca, P., 314
Carlyle, T., 15
Catherine II, Empress of Russia, 78, 112, 243, 290
Celle, H. de la, 112
Chaadaev, P. Ya., 17, 21, 26–31, 33–6, 38–50, 56–62, 64, 67, 72–88, 94–8, 100, 101, 143, 246, 252, 260, 297, 350, 358, 384, 400, 401, 403, 407–9
Chateaubriand, Viscount F. A. de, 27, 48

Chekhov, A. P., 194, 195, 287, 393, 396
Cherkassov, A. L., 365
Chernobaev, V. G., 352
Chernyshevsky, N. G., 241, 242, 397
Chicherin, B. N., 350, 396
Chopin, F., 379, 380
Chrzanowski, I., 39
Chulkov, G. I., 131, 135
Claudel, P., 245
Coleridge, S. T., 56
Conrad, J., 14
Considérant, P. V., 159
Constantine, Grand Duke, 402
Copernicus, N., 358, 384
Corneille, P., 133, 159
Custine, Marquis A. L. L. de, 17, 21, 28, 35, 36, 51–9, 61–3, 67, 73, 97, 125, 131, 383, 400, 406–8

DĄBROWSKI, General H., 306
Danilevsky, N. Ya., 167
Dante Alighieri, 79, 82, 83, 148, 272, 319, 380, 395
Davydov, D. V., 83–6, 350
Delvig, Baron A. I., 120
Derzhavin, G. R., 336, 339, 350, 358
Descartes, R., 27, 48
Desnitsky, V. A., 146, 353
Dickens, C., 159, 195, 196, 206, 211, 346
Diderot, D., 206
Dimitry the False, 218, 357
Diogenes, 217
Dmitriev, I. I., 91, 350
Dobrolyubov, N. A., 135, 288, 329
Dolgorukov, Prince P. D., 352
Dolgoruky (Dolgorukov), Prince A. N., 66
Dolgoruky (Dolgorukov), Prince S. V., 66
Dolinin, A. S. (Iskoz), 138, 219, 221
Dostoevsky, A. (L. F.), 282, 283
Dostoevsky, A. G., 157, 158, 288
Dostoevsky, F. M., 15, 18, 19, 38, 42, 51, 58, 67, 70, 71, 74, 82, 96, 97, 133–79, 180–4, 187–94, 197, 199–214, 220, 222–31, 234–48, 249–51, 254, 255, 257–61, 262–72, 274–97, 299–303, 306–14, 317–22, 328–36, 339–42, 344–8, 350, 351, 355, 372, 386, 396–9, 400, 401, 403, 404, 408, 409

INDEX

Dostoevsky, M. A., 274, 282
Dubrovsky, P. P., 342
Dumas, A., 159
Dunin-Borkowski, Count J., 387
Dupuy, E., 15
Durov, S. F., 275, 276

ECKART (Eckhart, Meister), 334
Eckstein, Baron F. d', 27
Eichenbaum, B. M., 66, 211, 212, 233
Engelhardt, B. M., 133, 134
Engels, F., 404

FALCONET, E. M., 58
Favre, J., 307
Fedor Yaroslavich, Prince of Pinsk, 282
Fedotov, G. P., 352, 405, 406
Fet, A. A. (Shenshin), 211, 350
Fichte, J. G., 26
Fisher, V. M., 63, 352
Flaubert, G., 355
Fock, M. Ya von, 120, 121, 124
Fonvizin, D. I., 42, 69, 350
Fon-Vizin, N. D., 151, 281
Förster-Nietzsche, E., 283
Fourier, F. M. C., 159, 241
France, A., 137
François Xavier, St., 291
Frantsev, V. A., 351, 352
Frédricks (Fredericks), Baron D. P., 66
Freud, S., 138, 149, 150, 218, 230

GAGARIN, Prince G. G., 66
Gagarin, Prince I. S., 33, 65
Galla Placida Augusta, 394, 395
Garnett, C., 264
Gautier, T., 372
Gerbel, N. V., 342, 378
Gershenzon, M. O., 28, 40, 79, 80
Gershtein, E. G., 65, 66
Gervais, N. A., 66
Gide, A., 138, 157, 244-6
Glinka, F. N., 350
Glinka, M. I., 295
Glinka, S. N., 49
Godunov, B., Czar of Muscovy, 41, 214, 216, 218, 219

Goethe, J. W. von, 345
Gogol, N. V., 94, 180, 200, 206, 207, 211, 240, 249-57, 260, 261, 292, 295, 300, 301, 303, 308, 345, 346, 350, 397, 400, 407, 408
Golitsyn, Prince D. V., 73
Goncharov, I. A., 134, 200, 208, 209, 279
Goncourt, E. de, 193
Goszczyński, S., 385
Granovsky, T. N., 61
Grech, N. I., 121, 122
Gregory XVI, Pope, 332
Griboedov, A. S., 26, 38, 343, 350
Grigoriev, A. A., 384, 386
Grigorovich, D. V., 249
Grossman, L. P., 128, 133, 137, 152, 158, 173, 176, 196, 249-51, 254, 255, 279, 282, 283, 295, 346
Grydzewski, M., 65
Guardini, R., 333, 334, 336
Guizot, F. P. G., 27, 48, 83

HAPGOOD, I., 253
Heeckeren, Baron L. van, 83
Hegel, G. W. F., 27, 337-9, 343
Heine, H., 39, 135, 148, 156
Heliogabalus, 377
Helvetius, C. A., 234
Herder, J. G. von, 334
Herzen, A. I., 27, 28, 36, 61, 65, 66, 95, 96, 112, 132, 193, 253, 343, 350, 373, 397, 401
Hessen, I. V., 352
Hilferding, A. F., 342
Hoffmann, E. T. A., 249, 314, 317, 318
Hogarth, W., 300
Homer, 22, 304
Hugo, V., 159, 206, 321, 346
Hus, J., 128

IBSEN, H., 386
Ignatov, N. I., 302
Ilovaysky, D. I., 350
Irtishch, D., 282
Isaev, M. D., 150, 153
Iskoz (*see* Dolinin)
Istrin, V. M., 86, 88

INDEX

Ivan III, Czar of Muscovy, 78, 167
Ivan IV, Czar of Muscovy, 78, 149
Ivanov (Ivanov-Razumnik), R. V., 353, 389
Ivanov, S. A., 291
Ivanov, V. I., 133, 350, 393
Izmaylov, A. E., 121

JACKSON, R., 348
Jadwiga of Anjou, Queen of Poland, 386
Jakobson, R. O., 130, 352, 393
James, H., 15
Janik, M., 274, 278, 347
Juvenal, D. J., 366

KACHENOVSKY, M. T., 26, 49
Kakhovsky, P. G., 111
Kallenbach, J., 47
Kamenev, L. B., 66
Kant, I., 26, 27, 48, 234
Kantemir, A. D., 42
Karamzin, E. A., 121
Karamzin, N. M., 122, 188, 215, 216, 350
Kareev, N. I., 351
Karpovich, M. M., 352
Kasprowicz, J., 71
Katkov, M. N., 158, 165, 342, 350
Kaun, A. S., 206
Kepler, J., 222
Khitrovo, E. M., 90, 91
Khlebnikov, V. V., 350
Khodasevich, V. F., 63, 352, 378
Khomyakov, A. S., 33, 81, 88, 350
Khranevich, V. I., 278
Kiliński, J., 271
Kireevsky, I. V., 123, 124, 350
Kleiner, J., 315, 316, 327, 333, 334, 337, 341, 351
Klyushnikov, V. P., 350
Knipovich, E. F., 386
Kock, C. P. de, 159
Kołłątaj, H., 339
Konopnicka, M., 380
Konshin, E. N., 302
Kornilov, A. A., 351
Korobka, N. I., 251

Korolenko, V. G., 350
Korwin-Krukowska, A. V., 288
Korwin-Krukowski, General V. V., 288
Koryakov, M. A., 352
Kościuszko, T., 90, 305, 347, 357, 358
Koshelev, A. I., 123, 124
Kostomarov, N. I., 351
Kotoshikhin, G., 253
Kovalevsky, S. V., 155
Kozlov, I. I., 350
Kozlovsky, Prince P. B., 97–101, 104, 407
Kozłowski, L., 351
Krasiński, Z., 16, 18, 233–5, 351, 372, 373, 377–80, 385, 392, 398, 407, 409
Krasov, V. I., 344
Kraszewski, J. I., 351
Krestovsky, V. V., 350
Kridl, M., 19, 313
Krzyżanowski, J., 19
Kubacki, W., 338, 339
Kublicki-Piottuch, Adam, 368
Kublicki-Piottuch, Andrey, 368
Kublicki-Piottuch, Felix, 368
Kublicki-Piottuch, Franciszek, 368–71
Kublicki-Piottuch, S. A., 369
Kucharzewski, J., 33, 74, 406
Kukolnik, N. V., 75
Kulakovsky, S. Yu., 352, 353
Kuprin, A. A., 194, 350
Kursinsky, A. A., 378

LALOU, R., 15
Lamennais, F. R. de, 27, 39, 48, 83, 159
Langlois, C. V., 112
Lauzun, Duke A. de, 135
Lazhechnikov, I. I., 350
Lebedev, P. (translator of Krasiński's *The Undivine Comedy*), 378
Lednicki, A., 352, 380
Leger, L., 15
Legras, J., 258
Leibniz, G. W. von, 50
Lelewel, J., 39, 72, 93, 94, 98–104, 358
Lemke, M. K., 56, 73, 85–7, 94, 397
Leontiev, K. N., 350
Leparski, S., 114
Lermontov, M. Yu., 17, 21, 59–67, 76, 94, 96, 182, 188, 194–6, 200, 211, 401, 405, 407, 409

Lerner, N. O., 103
Leroy-Beaulieu, A., 15
Leskov, N. S., 310, 350
Levinson, A., 249, 250, 283, 288
Lloyd George, D., 387
Lomonosov, M. V., 350
Łoziński, L. Ya., 369
Łoziński-Brazhnikov, F. F., 369
Lunacharsky, A. V., 365
Luther, M., 174
Lycurgus, 222
Lyubavsky, M. K., 351
Lyubimov, N. A., 328

MACKIEWICZ, S., 250, 282, 283, 288
Madaule, J., 227
Maistre, Count J. de, 48
Maklakov, V. A., 352
Makovicky, D., 311
Makowski, W., 379
Makushev, U. V., 342
Malewski, F., 124, 338
Marcilli, G. de, 112
Marcus Aurelius, 343
Markevich, B. M., 350
Marlinsky (*see* A. A. Bestuzhev)
Marx, K., 159, 404
Masaryk, T. G., 33
Massis, H., 15, 244–6
Matejko, J., 380
Mauriac, F., 135
Maykov, A. N., 158, 164–7, 172, 191, 289, 290
Medvedev, P. N., 353, 354
Melgunov, S. P., 87
Mendeleev, D. I., 388
Mendeleev, I. D., 369
Mendeleev, L. D. (wife of A. A. Blok), 369, 372, 389, 390, 391
Menshikov, M. O., 394
Menzel, W., 344
Merezhkovsky, D. S., 136, 149, 181, 234, 238, 240, 352, 388, 391, 397
Mérimée, P., 15
Merzlyakov, A. F., 26
Mézières, A., 223
Mianowski, J., 358
Michaud, R., 244
Michelangelo Buonarroti, 22
Michelet, J., 21, 22

Mickiewicz, A., 16–29, 32–9, 41, 43, 45–56, 58–61, 64, 65, 67, 76, 96–8, 105–8, 114, 115, 117–19, 122–7, 130, 131, 206, 218, 220, 233, 234, 237, 243, 260, 268, 291, 295–307, 309–48, 350–3, 357, 358, 372–7, 380–3, 392, 394–6, 398, 400, 403, 404, 407–9
Mickiewicz, W., 21, 22
Mikhaylov, M. I., 397
Mikhaylov, M. L. (translator of Krasiński's *The Undivine Comedy*), 378
Mikhaylovsky, N. K., 59, 61, 149
Mikhelson, M. I., 292
Milyukov, P. N., 94, 351, 352
Mirecki, O., 269, 270, 272
Mniszech, M., 357
Mochulsky, K. V., 133, 148, 155, 188, 189, 207, 241, 242, 249, 281, 300, 303, 353, 354
Modzalevsky, B. L., 34, 103
Mohammed, 222, 240, 345
Mohammed II, 166
Molière (J. B. Poquelin), 133, 159
Montaigne, M. de, 17
Montalembert, Count C. de, 409
Moore, T., 345
Muraviev, A. G. (Countess Chernyshev), 114
Muraviev, N. M., 114
Muraviev-Apostol, I. M., 123
Musiałowicz, J., 286
Myasoedov, G. G., 25, 33, 34

NADEZHDIN, N. I., 27, 83, 84, 86
Nalepiński, T., 379
Napoleon I, 161, 214, 216–18, 222, 227, 237, 240
Napoleon III, 66
Nashchokin, P. V., 192
Nechaev, S. G., 122
Nechaeva, V., 406
Nekrasov, N. A., 249, 250, 350
Nerval, G. de, 314
Newton, Sir I., 222
Nicholas I, Emperor of Russia, 27, 59, 66, 72, 73, 81, 103, 108–10, 112–14, 117, 119, 120–2, 124, 127, 197, 243, 251, 276, 279, 295, 332, 365, 402, 406
Niedźwiecki, K., 369
Niedźwiecki, W., 369

INDEX

Nietzsche, F. W., 15, 178, 283
Nikolsky, Yu. A., 157
Nodier, C., 314
Norwid, C., 378
Novalis (F. von Hardenberg), 314
Noyes, G. R., 19

OBLEUKHOV, D. A., 26
Odlanicki-Poczobutt, M., 390
Odoevsky, Prince A. I., 350
Odoevsky, Prince V. F., 123, 124
Odyniec, E., 122
Oleg, Prince, 77
Oleszkiewicz, J., 24, 39, 47, 48, 107, 298, 302, 303
Olizar, Count G., 114–16, 131
Orlov, M. F., 94
Orlov, V. N., 358, 365
Orzeszkowa, E., 351, 352

PANAEV, I. I., 250
Panov, E. D., 27, 86, 87, 100, 101
Panteleev, L. F., 397
Pascal, B., 58, 241, 242, 341
Paskevich, Prince I. F., 92
Paul I, Emperor of Russia, 365
Pavlishchev, L. N., 350
Pavlova, K. (Jaenisch), 350
Pawlikowski, M. K., 283
Pawsza, A., 347
Pellico, S., 268
Peretz, V. N., 351
Pereverzev, V. F., 146
Pericles, 34
Peter the Great, 30, 32, 38, 49, 52, 70, 78, 81, 82, 88, 108, 109, 120, 122, 125, 161, 165, 166, 170, 243, 253, 302, 339, 343, 401, 402, 407
Peter III, Emperor of Russia, 112
Petronik (P. N. Savitsky), 353
Phelps, W. L., 15
Philosophov, D. V., 352
Pigarev, K. V., 130
Pigoń, S., 39
Piksanov, N. K., 110, 111, 113, 114, 120–2, 124, 128
Piłsudski, J., 352
Pisarev, D. I., 136, 397

Pisemsky, A. F., 350
Pius IX, Pope, 331
Plato, 48, 388
Pobedonostvev, K. P., 137, 138, 158, 294
Pochinkovsky, O., 348
Poe, E. A., 394
Pogodin, A. L., 351
Pogodin, M. P., 33, 34, 124, 131, 350
Pokrovsky, M. N., 109, 219
Polevoy, K. A., 350
Polevoy, N. A., 350
Polonsky, Ya. P., 350
Polyakov, M. Ya., 344
Poniatowski, Prince J., 305
Portugalev, V. V., 352
Pososhkov, I., 384
Prévost d'Exiles, A. F. (Abbé Prévost), 206
Proust, M., 245
Prus, B. (A. Głowacki), 351, 409
Przybyszewski, S., 351, 379, 385
Pułaski, F., 101
Pushkin, A. S., 17, 18, 21, 24–6, 29, 33–6, 42, 49, 50, 53, 59, 61–104, 105, 108, 110, 117–24, 126, 127, 130, 143, 164, 166, 170, 172, 173, 176, 180–7, 190, 192, 194–200, 206, 207, 209, 211–23, 225–8, 237–41, 243, 244, 252, 253, 291, 295, 297, 301, 302, 314, 318, 338, 342, 345–7, 350, 352, 353, 357, 358, 381, 382, 394–7, 400–5, 407–9
Pyast, V. A. (Pestovsky), 392, 393, 396, 397
Pypin, A. N., 350, 351
Pythagoras, 388

QUÉNET, C., 33, 34, 36, 40, 48, 49, 50
Quinet, E., 21

RACINE, J. B., 133, 159
Radishchev, A. N., 99, 104, 401
Raevsky, M. N. (Princess Volkonsky), 114
Rambaud, A. N., 15
Rammelmeyer, A., 260
Raphael Sanzio, 154
Reeve, H., 234

INDEX

Repin, I. E., 292
Reymont, W. S., 351, 379
Richter, J. P., 314, 345
Rostopchin, Countess E. P., 350, 357
Roth, L. O., 123
Rousseau, J. J., 152, 156, 157, 159, 249
Rozanov, V. V., 388, 391, 394
Rozhalin, N. M., 123, 124
Rozwadowski, Count A., 387–92, 397
Ryleev, K. F., 24, 111, 113, 119, 120, 350

SACHS, H., 334
Saint-Martin, L. C. de, 314, 331
Saint-Simon, Count C. H. de, 337
Saitov, V. I., 50
Sakulin, P. N., 320
Salias de Tournemir, E. V. (E. Tur), 350
Saltykov-Shchedrin, M. E., 292, 350, 397
Samarin, Yu. F., 350
Sand, G. (A. L. A. Dudevant), 159
Savitri (A. Zahorska), 379
Scheler, M., 15
Schelling, F. W. J. von, 26, 27, 34, 48
Schelting, A. von, 33
Schiller, J. C. F. von, 133, 135, 159, 206, 234, 345, 346
Schlegel, F. von, 27
Schloezer, C. von, 26
Schopenhauer, A., 15, 233
Ściegienny, P., 269
Ségur, Count L. F. de, 103
Sękowski, J., 122
Seneca, 17
Serbinovich, K. S., 120
Shakespeare, W., 133, 135, 149, 159, 216, 223
Shakhovskoy, Prince D. I., 28, 29, 31, 41, 48, 79, 80
Shalikov, Prince P. S., 122
Shchedrin (see Saltykov-Shchedrin)
Shchegolev, P. E., 65, 66, 397
Shchepkin, V. N., 351
Shcherbatov, Prince D. M., 26
Shcherbatov, Prince I. D., 26
Shestov, L., 136, 149, 226, 228, 234, 240, 398
Shevyrev, S. P., 33, 123, 124, 350

Shimanov, N. A., 110
Shuvalov, Count A. P., 66
Shuysky, Prince V. I., Czar of Muscovy, 41
Sienkiewicz, H., 351, 370, 409, 410
Sieroszewski, W., 351
Silesius, A., 314, 334
Simmons, E. J., 206
Sirotinin, A. N., 351
Sismondi, J. C. L. de, 79
Skobelev, M. D., 177
Słowacki, J., 16, 18, 71, 115, 234, 260, 261, 332, 351, 352, 377, 379, 380, 392, 398, 409
Smith, General W. B., 406, 407
Śniadecki, brothers (J. and J.), 337–9
Sobolevsky, A. I., 351
Sobolevsky, S. A., 33, 34, 36, 124, 347
Sologub, F. K. (Teternikov), 394
Solon, 222
Soloviev, S. M., 387–91
Soloviev, V. S., 16, 28, 350, 385, 396
Somov, O. M., 120
Sophia Paleolog (wife of Ivan III), 167
Soulié, F., 159, 206
Sovetov, S. S., 343
Spasowicz, W., 64, 291–5, 351
Speransky, M. N., 102, 351
Spinoza, B., 27, 48, 336
Stalin, J. V., 406
Stankevich, N. V., 344
Staszic, S., 339, 358
Stempowski, J., 262
Stendhal (M. H. Beyle), 159, 171, 239, 346
Stevenson, R. L., 262
Stirner, M., 159
Stolypin (Mongo), A. A., 66
Stolypin, P. A., 394
Strakhov, N. N., 138, 149, 151, 155, 157, 158, 161, 162, 250, 251, 289, 350
Strémooukhoff, D., 131
Strindberg, J. A., 386
Stroganov, Count S. G., 83, 84, 95, 101, 102, 103
Struve, G. P., 96–101, 104, 260, 351, 352
Struve, P. B., 352
Sue, E., 159, 206, 346
Suslov, A. P., 139
Suvorin, A. S., 394
Suvorov, Count A. V., Marshal, 90
Svatikov, S. G., 397

Sviniin, P. P., 119
Svyatoslav, Prince, 77
Swedenborg, E., 314
Szeptycki, Count A., Metropolitan, 389

Taranovsky, K. F., 352
Tarle, E. V., 406
Tarnowski, Count S., 378
Tasso, T., 44
Tatishchev, S. S., 397
Teslenko, N. V., 352
Tetmajer-Przerwa, K., 351
Thackeray, W. M., 211
Theofan Prokopovich, 77
Thomas à Kempis, 39
Tieck, L., 314
Tikhonravov, N. S., 351
Timasheff, N. S., 404, 405
Timkovsky, R. F., 26
Titov, V. P., 123
Tokarzewski, S., 268–79, 282, 286, 291
Tolstoy, Count A. K., 350
Tolstoy, Count L. N., 15–18, 22, 58, 75, 96, 134–6, 139, 157, 188, 198, 211–14, 231, 233–8, 246, 311, 313, 314, 317, 318, 351, 357, 360, 395, 398, 399, 401, 408
Tolstoy, Count Ya. N., 119
Towiański, A., 342
Tretiak, J., 381
Troyat, H., 283, 291
Trubetskoy, Prince E. N., 350
Trubetskoy, Prince S. P., 114
Trubetskoy, Princess K. I., 114, 115
Truzson, F. I., 211
Tsinsky, L. M., 87, 95, 100
Tsitsianov, Prince P. D., 405
Tsyavlovsky, M. A., 347
Tumansky, V. I., 24
Tun (Thun), A., 397
Turgenev, A. I., 72, 74, 75, 83–9, 93, 350
Turgenev, I. S., 15, 71, 96, 97, 134, 149, 151, 157, 159, 161, 165, 182–7, 191, 193–5, 200–3, 205, 206, 209, 213, 240, 241, 250, 253, 287–9, 329, 350, 408
Turgenev, N. I., 26, 86, 87, 88, 350
Tuwim, J., 50

Tynyanov, Yu. N., 250
Tyutchev, F. I., 105, 128–31, 159, 350, 358

Umansky, A. (translator of Krasiński's *Iridion*), 378
Urusov, Prince S. S., 233

Valéry, P., 95
Valmiki, 81
Valuev, Count P. A., 66
Venevitinov, D. V., 33, 123, 124
Vengerov, S. A., 68, 219, 221, 381
Veresaev, V. V. (Śmidowicz), 149, 231, 234, 236, 237, 254
Veselovsky, A. N., 59, 61
Vigny, Count A. de, 39, 105, 113, 115, 131, 198, 222, 335, 341, 400
Villiers-le-Duc, A. de, 112
Vinogradov, A. (translator of Słowacki's *Anhelli*), 380
Viskovatov, K. (translator of Słowacki), 380
Viskovatov, P. A., 158
Viskovatov, S. I., 122
Vladimir, Prince, 253
Vogüé, Viscount E. M. M. de, 15
Volkonsky, Prince S. G., 108, 114
Volkonsky, Princess Z. A., 25, 33, 318, 350
Voloshin, M. A., 379
Volotskoy, M. V., 282, 283
Voltaire, de (F. M. Arouet), 159, 255, 331, 340
Vrubel, M. A., 393
Vyazemsky, Prince P. A., 33, 34, 49, 72, 83–6, 88–94, 97, 118, 119, 122, 123, 215, 216, 350

Wagner, R., 15
Wielopolski, Marquis A., 384
Wierzbicki, S., 379
Wittig, E., 379
Worcell, Count S., 101
Wrangel, Baron A. E., 139, 150, 151, 153, 267, 271

Wulf, A. N., 350
Wyspiański, S., 15, 71, 351, 379, 409

YAKUSHKIN, I. D., 26, 365
Yanchuk (translator of Słowacki), 380
Yarmolinsky, A., 67
Yatzimirsky, A. N., 351

ZABŁOCKI, T., 344
Zagoskin, M. N., 350
Zahorski, E., 379

Zaleska, J. (Mrs. B. Zaleska), 117–19
Zan, T., 335
Zawodziński, K. W., 353
Zdziechowski, M., 112
Żeromski, S., 71, 135, 351, 409
Zgorzelski, C., 62
Zhdanov, I. N., 351
Zhikharev, N. I., 73
Zhukovsky, V. A., 72, 81, 85, 88, 89, 91, 93, 119, 123, 196, 197, 215, 350, 358
Zieliński, T., 327
Żochowski, J., 272–4
Żuławski, J., 351
Zweig, S., 138